DICTIONARY OF FURNITURE

SECOND EDITION

DICTIONARY OF FURNITURE

SECOND EDITION

CHARLES BOYCE

A ROUNDTABLE PRESS BOOK

Checkmark Books®
An imprint of Facts On File, Inc.

Dictionary of Furniture, Second Edition
A Roundtable Press Book

Checkmark Books
An imprint of Facts On File, Inc.
11 Penn Plaza
New York, NY 10001

Library of Congress Cataloging-in-Publication Data
Dictionary of furniture / Charles Boyce.—2nd ed.
     p. cm.
"A Roundtable Press book."
Includes bibliographical references.
ISBN 0-8160-4229-2 (hardcover: alk. paper)—
ISBN 0-8160-4158-X (pbk.: alk. paper)
1. Furniture—Dictionaries. I. Boyce, Charles.
NK2205.D5 2000
749'.03—dc21   00-035334

Checkmark Books are available at special discounts when purchased in bulk quantities
for businesses, associations, institutions or sales promotions. Please call our Special
Sales Department in New York at (212) 967-8800 or (800) 322-8755.

You can find Facts On File on the World Wide Web at http://www.factsonfile.com

Cover and text design by Joan M. Toro
Illustrations by Norman Nuding and Ed Lam
Consultant: Joseph T. Butler

Printed in the United States of America

VB Hermitage 10 9 8 7 6 5 4 3 2 1
       (pbk) 10 9 8 7 6 5 4 3 2 1

This book is printed on acid-free paper.

For Marya, without whom nothing

CONTENTS

Foreword
ix

Introduction
xi

A to Z entries
1

A Guide to Buying Furniture
335

Places to Visit
340

Bibliography
355

Index
367

FOREWORD

In the 15 years since the *Dictionary of Furniture* was first published a great deal of furniture has been created, and although no earthshaking stylistic revolutions have come about, there are nonetheless any number of new designers and ideas to be recorded. While inclusiveness in this matter is impossible within the constraints of space imposed by a revision of a book of this scope, I have included those new furniture makers who have particularly impressed me.

My own awareness of the world's furniture making has increased during those 15 years, and I have been able to improve the range of the book's coverage, most especially with respect to modern Australian design and the traditional furniture of Africa. Also, a wider acquaintance with the timber used in wood furniture around the world—notably in China—has produced a crop of new entries.

Perhaps most important, additional material has been added to the front and the back of the book that I hope will be of practical use to the reader. The introduction is a general history of world furniture making, and it offers a broad perspective for the entries that follow. At the back of the book, an essay on the ins and outs of buying furniture, especially antiques, is meant to provide a primer on fine points to be considered, and two large un-fine points that I cannot resist repeating here, so important are they: (1) buy from a reputable dealer, and (2) educate yourself.

Also at the back of the book are two new features that will permit further exploration of the world of furniture by the reader: a bibliography and a gazetteer of excellent public collections of fine furniture. Both are necessarily imperfect— whole books would be entirely appropriate for either—but I think they offer very sound approaches for reader and traveler. And so, in either case, bon voyage.

INTRODUCTION

There's furniture everywhere, though most of us don't notice it until we mash a knee on a desk leg. Yet we use these elementary household objects—"movable articles in a room . . . that render it fit for living or working," as *The American Heritage Dictionary* puts it—in every aspect of our lives, in homes, offices, and public places. Furniture has a small number of basic uses—for storage; for sitting or reclining; and to provide flat surfaces on which to dine, write, or perform other tasks. But this belies the tremendous variety which fertile imaginations have brought to its design. Just as the fine arts do, furniture gives expression to our always-changing sense of how things should be. But the ubiquity of furniture makes this easy to forget. This book is meant to open our eyes and reawaken our minds to a remarkable area of human practical and artistic endeavor.

***

Splendid anecdotes illustrate the linkage between furniture and the larger world. For instance, Louis XIV of France (1638–1715), the Sun King, made a decorative style a key part of his domestic policy. In an effort to control the wealth of the nobility, he required French aristocrats to imitate in their homes the extravagantly luxurious architecture and furnishing of Versailles, which were meant to impress all Europe with the country's wealth. So opulent a standard—including a roomful of solid silver furniture—was set by Louis' designer, Charles Le Brun, that in following it the nobles impoverished themselves (at least by their own standards) and could not afford to, say, raise a private army. And yet they could not afford to just ignore this fashion, either, for those who did lost the king's favor and in doing so were likely to lose valued perquisites and sources of income as well. French aristocrats of the 17th century were truly "slaves of fashion." Noblemen therefore competed to commission the newest, most richly adorned furniture Parisian *ébénistes,* makers of the grandest furniture, could devise. And thus was created Louis XIV–style furniture.

But even as that opulent style arose, royal policy prepared the ground for its replacement. As Louis declined—he had been bedridden for many years before his death in 1715—the French economy was as moribund as he was, due to a long series of debilitating wars. The king's pursuit of glory had proved disastrous. In these final years, Louis was no longer able to police the nobility, and leading aristocrats began to abandon Versailles for the delights of Paris, building town houses and calculatedly creating a new style that demonstrated their release. Furniture and interior decoration was pointedly lighter in feeling, and motifs were derived from the beauties of nature and anecdotes of love rather than from implements of war and the grandeur of ancient Rome.

Thus, the rococo was born.

***

Similar dynamic relations between social and aesthetic development are found everywhere in the history of furniture. In the European decorative arts tradition in particular, the alternation of periods between the classical—symmetrical, grave, and grand, with an emphasis on balance and rigor—and the romantic—exuberant, often frivolous, with an emphasis on movement and playfulness—is often in tune with political and social trends. The change from baroque to rococo is but one example. Contrariwise, in Chinese and Japanese furniture, the profoundly conservative nature of these cultures yielded styles that changed little over centuries, excepting the punctuation of occasional introductions of form or motif from India and Persia, or, in recent years, from Europe and America.

Changes in the technical capabilities of furniture makers are significant in all cultures, especially with the modern development of radically new techniques, most notably factory production, the molding of materials by steaming or vacuum-forming, and the use of power tools. New materials—steel, plywood, and plastics, among others—have also added to furniture designers' options. Analogous developments occurred in olden times as well. For example, the ancient invention of the lathe introduced turned wood to furniture design. Economic developments often play an important role, such as when the growth of cities and their wealthy elites in medieval Europe generated a sharp rise in demand for furniture in many new forms. And trade and communications between cultures frequently have as great an impact on furniture design as they do in other ways. The development of furniture thus both mimics and is formed by human development on larger scales.

***

Furniture did not exist for most of humanity's time on earth. The hunters and gatherers who wandered the prehistoric world made do without it. The very few hunting and gathering cultures that have survived into modern times demonstrate this, for none of the known primitive tribes have designed or made furniture. The earliest known furniture is stone platforms that served as couches or beds in neolithic dwellings that can be dated to about ten thousand years ago. There was surely other furniture, made of more perishable materials, that has not survived. But ancient farmers can have had little time to build any but the crudest furniture. With the slow development of surplus wealth, and the growth of villages and towns, came the division of society into specialized occupations, including political, religious, and military elites and the craft workers who provided them with, among other things, furniture.

The earliest producers were the ancient Egyptian and Mesopotamian cultures, though furniture was a luxury in both, rare even in palaces. Portable tables and beds appeared early, but thrones were the most important early pieces, as nascent societies confirmed their hierarchical organization with symbolic trappings.

In Egypt, large pieces of wood were scarce, so craftsmen combined small pieces and in doing so devised basic techniques still used today, such as mortise-and-tenon joints and dowels. By about 1500 B.C., nails and hinges were in use. The principal furniture forms made were chests, beds, and stools, with some light tables and chairs. Beds, originally simple frames from which were slung hammock-like arrangements of hide or cords, evolved through ever higher models to large pieces requiring a mounting block. Egyptian furniture spread to ancient Greece, over an expanding web of trade routes.

In Mesopotamia, the earliest culture was the Sumerian (c. 3000 B.C.), which both influenced and was influenced by Egypt. During the later Assyrian and Babylonian Empires (c. 1350–539 B.C.), quite heavy furniture was made, elaborately decorated with precious materials such as gold and ivory, using motifs from Egypt as well as a local repertoire that included the characteristically Assyrian winged bull. Most importantly, the lathe was invented in Mesopotamia and was transmitted to Greece, and thus Europe, via the Persian Empire.

***

Greek furniture was largely inspired by Egypt, except that the *kline,* or dining couch, came from Mesopotamia. The Greeks devised a number of new forms, including the *klismos* chair and the first round tables. Also, in the Hellenistic era (conventionally 336-31 B.C.—from Alexander the Great's coronation to the final establishment of Roman dominance in the eastern Mediterranean, at the Battle of Actium), late in Greece's period of cultural ascendancy, the cupboard first appears. As in so many other areas, Greece formulated a tradition for the West from the practices of their predecessors.

Following the flow of history, Greek taste was diffused around the ancient world, first by the colonies that Greek city-states established throughout the Mediterranean basin from the 8th century B.C. on; then east to the fringes of India by Alexander the Great's empire, beginning c. 330 B.C.; and finally by the Romans, whose adaptations of Greek tastes overran Europe and North Africa with its armies and government.

Roman design built on the Greek tradition but displayed a penchant for practical innovation. This was perhaps most significantly demonstrated in the evolution of the *kline,* to which Roman designers added first the *fulcrum,* or headboard, and, later, a back, making the first couch, the *lectus.* Romans took wicker furniture from the Etruscans and devised a form that was popular for centuries, a wicker chair whose back extended into a hood above the user.

The Romans combined their innovations with a fondness for lush ornamentation, using precious metals, ivory, jewels, and rare woods. This taste was doubtless stimulated by the mighty Roman Empire's great wealth and its access to materials from throughout the known world. (This odd conjunction of practicality and opulence is similar to the combination of Yankee ingenuity and consumerist excess that has coexisted in American taste in this century.) A wide repertoire of decoration evolved, incorporating motifs from around the Roman world. Roman images have recurred again and again in Western decorative art and are still in use.

When the empire fell to the great barbarian invasions of the fifth and sixth centuries, its design traditions deteriorated badly but never failed altogether. During the period of intense upheaval in Europe, medieval furniture developed very slowly and emerged in the Romanesque style. In the east, the Roman tradition was more fully retained, while undergoing a powerful transformation into Byzantine furniture.

***

In the early medieval period (c. A.D. 450–750), Western Europe's furniture was informed by the economic and cultural deprivation following the collapse of the empire. Only the richest and most powerful nobles possessed anything but the crudest domestic furniture, and even that was simple and sparse. They traveled constantly among various residences throughout their domains, for no one tract of land could support for long the immense retinues of soldiers and courtiers that maintained and demonstrated their power. Consequently, household goods consisted largely of easily transportable items, with little bulky furniture. A house's rooms were not yet associated with particular uses; furniture such as dining tables or beds could be, and were, set up in any room. Such forms as the folding stool and the *couchette,* a wheeled bed, were widely used. Moreover, the aesthetics of furniture was relatively unimportant, for the pieces of any consequence would most likely be swathed in fine fabrics or tapestries. For all these reasons, the range of furniture forms was severely limited.

The church was the great user of furniture at this period. In church buildings, furniture tended to be built into the architectural scheme, but in monasteries and libraries, specialized forms were used, such as the lectern and cupboards designed to hold books. The decoration and style of these pieces derived from church architecture; in fact, furniture tended to look like buildings, with such details as arcading and pilasters, and even, occasionally, buttresses.

Only one great stylistic change occurred during the long medieval period. Until the 12th century, furniture makers strove to evoke the Roman imperial past by employing what remained of the classical repertoire of forms and decoration, in what we now call the Romanesque style. But around 1100 A.D., a "modern" style, now known as Gothic, arose. It employed a greater naturalism in decoration and emphasized verticality in structure. During the Gothic period, especially in the ports of the North Sea and the city-states of northern Italy, an emerging business class had a comfortable and settled way of life that generated the range of domestic furniture we are familiar with today.

***

In contrast to the medieval West, the Byzantine Empire (A.D. 476–1453), successor to the Eastern Roman Empire, remained fairly stable, though its enemies gradually ate away at its territory. Classical traditions and techniques of craft endured; in particular, a range of metal X-frame stools and chairs, successors to the Roman *sella curulis,* were quite common, as were benches, small tables, and stools with legs, stretchers, and rails of finely turned woods. Grand Byzantine furniture was massive, rigid, and severely formal, often covered with jewel-studded ivory panels bearing the stylized religious imagery for which Byzantine art is best known. The extravagance of furniture in the Byzantine capital, Constantinople, is exemplified by a literary reference to a solid gold dining table that seated 36.

Books were a valued component of Byzantine culture, and lecterns, bookcases, desks, and pieces combining them, were popular. Carved or painted decoration included semi-abstract decoration from Middle Eastern traditions, including designs from Persia and, later, Islam. From the 10th century on, motifs originating as far away as China were used, demonstrating the reach of Byzantine trade.

After the fall of Constantinople in 1453, the influence of Byzantine furniture and decorative art continued to be felt for centuries throughout the Balkans and Russia, domains of Eastern Orthodox Christianity.

***

Outside Europe, people were making furniture also, of course, but the dynamic of its development was very different. For reasons unknown, furniture seems to have been little used in the East's early civilizations—from the ancient cities of the Indus River valley (c. 2500–c. 1500 B.C.) to Shang dynasty China (c. 1600–1027 B.C.)—and a very limited range of forms was pursued. These cultures thus began making furniture somewhat later than their western counterparts in Mesopotamia and Egypt, though it is not known whether the earlier initiative influenced the later one. Somewhat later, by Roman times in the West, a clear but slight influence on the East is evident, either directly, through knowledge of Western furniture, or through intermediary cultures. But at any rate, as Europe approached the Renaissance, furniture traditions in Asia were progressing much more slowly.

India was the first of the eastern cultures to receive any influence from the West. Thrones, the earliest known Indian furniture, appear in carvings of the third century B.C., and may have been informed by Mesopotamian designs. Low, flat platforms, either polygonal or lotus-shaped, they had short legs carved as animal feet. Beds, similar to Egyptian and Mesopotamian models, were low rectangular frames. A larger bed, sometimes featuring a headboard, arrived with the beginnings of Moslem rule around A.D. 1000, but beds have never been very popular in India; bedding on the floor has always been the usual sleeping arrangement. Chairs and stools were introduced from Bactria, the easternmost of the Hellenistic kingdoms that survived the brief empire of Alexander, and were later retransmitted to China. Caning, prominent before the second century A.D., is India's one great original contribution to the furniture of other cultures. Because insect damage is a major problem in India, furniture was usually made of stone, ivory, or silver, and was always very expensive. Until colonial times, furniture was scarce, even among the elites.

***

Because China has undergone repeated periods of war and social unrest, very little furniture has survived, and almost none from older periods. Nevertheless, much can be learned from art and literature. It is known that the Chinese began making furniture in very ancient times, and that Chinese furniture has always depended on highly sophisticated joinery, in which nails and screws are eschewed entirely, and glue or dowels are employed only rarely. This practice responded to wood's repeated expansion and contraction in China's extremes of weather. Elaborate joints—especially an amazing array of different mortice-and-tenon joints—had been developed by medieval times. The lathe and turnery were unknown.

Before the Shang dynasty and the creation of the Chinese Empire (that is, before the second millennium B.C.), a screen *(ping)*, an armrest *(ji)*, a variety of low tables, and a low platform (ancestor of the *kang*), were made. These forms served sitters on mats, placed on the floor, the ground, or the platforms. Other early forms included a framework of open shelves, the predecessor to the grand wardrobes of later tradition. Lacquer was already used, providing protection against insects, as big a problem as in India, especially in southern China, the early cultural leader.

Little Chinese furniture is known in detail until the rise of the medieval Tang (T'ang) dynasty (A.D. 618–907), which followed a long troubled period of political and social collapse after the fall of the mighty Han dynasty, the chronological and developmental equivalent to the Roman Empire (Note: Chinese dynastic names are given first in the recently adopted Pinyin transliteration, followed by the older Wade-Giles transliteration, unless the two are identical.) The Tang is considered a "golden age" of Chinese decorative arts, but its furniture is known only from paintings and manuscripts. A very large revolving bookcase, the *shuan lun jing chang,* was used in Buddhist monasteries. The massive *chuang*—a platform with railings—emulated the thrones of Indian tradition and served as a chair of estate, a prestige item reserved for the highest-ranking member of a household. Small tables and the *ji* were still made, to be used on the *kang.* The screen underwent a portentous change, incorporating for the first time painted panels. These have remained a principal vehicle for fine painting to this day, in both China and Japan.

In the Song (Sung) dynasty (960–1279), seating furniture was brought by merchants over the Silk Road from India and the West, and the X-frame chair, in both fixed and folding forms, was made in a variety of styles. The *san cai tu hui,* or "chair of the old man who has been drinking" was popular for centuries. The Ming dynasty (1368–1644) brought another "golden age," thought by many to be the greatest. A group of chairs featured a cubical frame below the seat, consisting of the legs and four low stretchers. The upper parts took different forms, colorfully named for fancied resemblances to the shape of the arms and back, among them the "scholar's cap" chair and the "chair like a hanging lantern shaped like a chair."

A similarly wide variety of tables arose, including the "altar table," the showpiece of a Ming household, and a number of specialized pieces intended for such uses as formal presentations, painting, and gaming. These designs frequently incorporated distinctively Chinese foot and leg forms that survive today, notably the "horse-hoof foot" and the "elephant-trunk leg." Ming case furniture was grand and massive, with cupboards taller than a man. The most commonly made was a tall two-door wardrobe surmounted by a quite substantial "hat cupboard," with matching doors, each featuring modest hardware of brass or *paktung,* a Chinese alloy of copper, zinc, and nickel. Another large form was a massive closed bookcase whose base was wider than its top.

Materials included a widening range of exotic hardwoods, many from Southeast Asia, which an expanding China dominated militarily. Lacquer was applied to less splendid surfaces, and furniture entirely of lacquer was also made. Root furniture, fashioned from the gnarled roots of trees, was brought to a state of great sophistication. Porcelain was also employed in molded, barrel-shaped forms called *dun,* which were used as stools, generally outdoors. This is still a prominent piece of Chinese furniture, even in the West. Porcelain plaques also decorated especially ornate chairs and tables. Ming designers created the Chinese furniture forms most familiar today, and Ming designs continued in use through the next, and last, imperial dynasty, the Qing (Ch'ing) (1644–1911).

China resisted the imposition of political and cultural Western influence, as was the case for East Asia in general (Japan was a late and lone exception), but unavailingly. Weakened by Western demands and its own inadequacy, the empire fell to revolution in 1911. An almost constant state of turmoil has reigned in China throughout the 20th century, and there has probably been little energy available to effect changes in furniture styles, though there is very little information on which to judge. Nevertheless, the historical conservatism of Chinese design probably means that the forms and methods of traditional furniture making will survive.

***

In Japan, furniture has traditionally existed only in a very limited range of forms, the most important being screens—the familiar, multipaneled *byobu,* decorated with fine paintings, and the wide, low, single-paneled *tsuitate,* akin to the modern room divider—and *tansu,* a range of storage chests in a variety of sizes and configurations. Accustomed to sitting on the floor (a practice that was transmitted to Japan from China with the great waves of immigrants, obscure in origin but probably from southern Korea, who overwhelmed the aboriginal hunters and gatherers of the Japanese islands around the third century A.D.), the Japanese made no other furniture at all, except a few light, portable tools: small reading stands, writing desks (less than a foot high), a wooden headrest, an armrest, and various boxes. Kimono racks were also made, but the only piece of furniture not easily portable was the *butsudan,* the family shrine. Unless lacquered, this furniture was largely undecorated, apart from metal hardware at the corners of the case pieces. This austere regime came originally from the conservative world of ancient China, and Japanese furniture was, until modern times, even less apt to change than that of the Chinese. But beginning in the 19th century, Japan opened itself to Western influences and itself influenced the West.

Korean furniture, like Japanese, has been strikingly conservative and has thus displayed little dramatic development over time. Since at least the last few centuries B.C., Korean furniture has emulated that of northern China in its forms and techniques. In the 20th century, however, Korean makers have made a specialty of case furniture modeled on the Japanese *tansu.*

***

The history of post-medieval European and, later, American furniture, is very complex. Many different styles have evolved in a pattern of linked influences that often doubles back on itself. What follows is a cursory survey of the high points.

The Middle Ages came to an end with the flowering of philosophy and art that we know as the Renaissance. Beginning in the 14th century in northern Italy, scholars and artists sought to revive the cultural and intellectual world of ancient Greece and Rome. In the decorative arts, this meant the adaptation of ancient architectural and ornamental devices. In furniture, this reformulation was superficial at first: the unspecialized forms of medieval furniture were made with ancient Roman decorative motifs. These included putti, urns, and mythological beasts such as the sphinx and the chimera. Human figuration was also popular, especially in the miniature busts known as Romayne work. More elaborate carving favored the use of gesso and *pastiglia,* soft and workable materials. And walnut, easily worked, became the material of choice over the traditional oak, which is a much harder wood. Also, pictorial images promoted the development of elaborate inlay techniques, including *intarsia* and *pietra dure.*

The first new form was the *cassone,* which is basically the traditional chest decorated with paintings on panels. However, particular rooms—and particular types of furniture—began to be associated with particular uses, and a wider array of forms evolved. The *cassone* became the *cassapanca,* a couch. A light side chair, the *scabella,* emerged, as did the *credenza,* a sideboard that became a standard piece of furniture. Many sorts of cupboard were devised, including the armoire.

Originally Italian, the Renaissance style seduced the rest of Europe, especially after King François I of France invaded Italy in 1494 and, impressed by the arts and architecture he encountered, brought Italian craftsmen and artists (including the likes of Leonardo da Vinci and Rosso Fiorentino) back to France. The result was the François I style, a distinctive amalgam of northern Gothic and Renaissance decorative arts that was powerfully influential throughout northern Europe.

***

By the second half of the 16th century, Renaissance decorative styles had evolved into the phase we distinguish as mannerism. Astounded by ancient Rome's painted interiors, recently discovered, designers throughout Europe began adorning furniture with a phantasmagoria of extravagant and bizarre images, united by fields of arabesques and strapwork. The motifs included strangely rendered human heads, fantastic creatures such as griffins and winged beasts, and multitudes of naturalistically rendered vines, flowers, and birds. Known as "grotesque ornament," this mode continued to be used throughout the baroque and rococo periods.

François's successor gave his name to the Henri II style, French mannerism in the decorative arts. In furniture, this mode involved denser and more complicated carving, particularly of the human figure, in such elements as caryatids, atlantes, and terms. Furniture forms grew ever more elaborate. Various subtypes of cupboard evolved. The draw-leaf was applied to all sorts of table forms, from simple, light pieces to the largest, the grand display piece known as the *table à l'Italienne.* Tables and cabinets often bore complex marquetry and pietra dure work. Pendant finials were applied to each corner of many tables. In short, mannerist furniture was, to the taste of our age, overdecorated.

As the 16th century ended, Paris, not Rome, was the artistic capital of Europe. But in France, the Wars of Religion (1562–98) stalled the country's cultural development, and mannerism thus lingered as the major European style until the development of the baroque Louis XIV style in the second half of the 17th century. Today, the term *baroque* suggests decoration that is too greatly elaborated and too grandiose, but the baroque style emerged as a simplifying reaction against the excesses of mannerism.

***

The baroque style stressed grandeur, opulence, and a symmetry organized around sweeping S-curves, a compositional device developed in early 17th-century Italian painters. It had first been used in ecclesiastical architecture, as part of the Catholic Church's Counter-Reformation aesthetic program, meant to demonstrate the continuing power and wealth of the church despite its loss of Protestant northern Europe. The baroque effects its drama with a strong unity that is very different from the crowds of vignettes that characterize mannerism. Architectural motifs continued to flourish, but baroque designers employed highly theatrical broken or curved pediments and created dramatic contrasts of light and shadow with deep moldings and carving. Exaggerated fullness of scale and proportion lent grandeur to these pieces, and opulent materials—marbles, gilt bronze, and exotic woods—brought an aura of magnificence to the rooms they embellished. The baroque sense of drama also embraced the exotic, and Europe's first wave of enthusiasm for Chinoiserie was one consequence.

Early in the period, the influence of Rome was still powerful, especially in Spain, where the Italian baroque was emulated in the exuberant style of Churrigueresque furniture. To the north, in France, the baroque came to full flower at midcentury, and Louis XIV found its glorious and often absurdly expensive expression well-suited to his purposes, as we have seen. When Louis revoked France's famous guarantee of religious toleration, the Edict of Nantes in 1685, thousands of Protestant craftsmen and their families fled to other countries, especially the Netherlands and England, thereby spreading the baroque style throughout northern Europe, where it dominated taste for almost a century.

***

In England, on an island off Europe, artistic revolutions arrived late. The Renaissance did not appear until well into the 16th century, when mannerism was already established on the continent. The result was Tudor furniture, an unsophisticated use of Renaissance motifs on medieval furniture. However, a few distinctively English forms were developed, most notably the Nonsuch chest and the farthingale chair. Jacobean furniture arose as the baroque was gaining strength abroad but added little to this repertoire. Named for King James I, who ruled from 1603 to 1625, the Jacobean style continued in use through the reign of James's son, Charles I, until the outbreak of the English Civil Wars in 1642. The success of the Puritan revolutionaries in this conflict mandated the very austere and conservative Commonwealth furniture.

In 1660, the English monarchy was restored, in the person of King Charles II. Charles, who had spent his years of exile in Holland and France, was quite responsive to the arts, and he had acquired a taste for the baroque. He recruited many continental cabinetmakers and sculptors to work in England. The Great Fire of 1666 destroyed most of London, creating a market for furniture to fill the new buildings that rose thereafter. This furniture was made in an enthusiastic version of the continental baroque known as Restoration furniture.

King Charles indulged in extreme opulence, going so far as to commission suites of furniture veneered in silver. However, such excess was not wholly in tune with the national character. Though the baroque continued to dominate English design for several generations, a reaction against the Restoration aesthetic produced less grandiose versions—the William and Mary and Queen Anne styles. These in turn were succeeded by the idiosyncratic Palladian style, in the second quarter of the 18th century.

***

Even further from the centers of style, the British colonies in America followed London styles, but they took them up later and retained them longer. Thus, the American baroque only began in the William and Mary style, which did not arrive until near the end of the century and did not give way to the Queen Anne style until after that monarch's death in 1714.

Other colonial styles evolved around this time, such as Spanish Colonial furniture, another American development. The Spanish Empire in the New World was fabulously rich in gold and silver, and fine furniture was soon being produced there. Generally European in form, its decoration was influenced by indigenous traditions. In Mexico, elements of Mayan art were carved in furniture; in what is now the southwestern United States, makers borrowed the geometrical motifs of the local Indians; and Incan motifs were used in Peru.

In India, from the 17th century on, European empire builders introduced Western furniture, and they provided a market in the West for Indian craftsmen producing furniture in a variety of styles, such as Indo-Portuguese and Burmese furniture, employing indigenous materials and decorative techniques. British influence dominated, and most Indian furniture of the 19th and 20th centuries has followed British styles.

***

In Europe, national traditions were quick to respond to the rococo of Paris, once the Sun King died. Rococo began as the Régence style, named for the period of Louis XV's minority, when France was ruled by a regent (1715–23). Régence lasted somewhat longer, but it was a transitional style, and rococo furniture reached its maturity in the Louis XV style, around 1730. Lighter and more playful than baroque, yet clearly a grand style, rococo featured asymmetrical ornamentation and picturesque motifs that have charmed people ever since.

In Italy, Austria, and the Catholic countries of southern Germany, where the Counter-Reformation had encouraged the most grandiose of baroque styles, the rococo was similarly exaggerated; in northern Germany, rococo decoration tended to be applied to older, more stately baroque forms, a manner adopted in Scandinavia. British rococo was milder and less extravagant than the French prototype. Its curves were smoother and simpler, its asymmetries less pronounced, its motifs less fantastic. And comfort was deemed more important.

Pattern books were important in this period, and in England one of the most influential pattern-book makers, Thomas Chippendale (1718–79), gave his name to several varieties of British rococo furniture: American Chippendale (for the varieties made across the Atlantic), Chinese Chippendale, and Chippendale Gothic. The first of these characteristically trailed London by half a generation and lasted well into the 19th century, especially as so-called Country Chippendale. Chinese Chippendale, as the name suggests, employed Chinoiserie motifs. Like it, Chippendale Gothic, which emulated the decorative stonework of medieval cathedrals, grew out of the period's taste for the exotic.

***

Rococo was succeeded by the neoclassical style, a reversion to the sterner, architechtonic ideas of classical antiquity. Among the historical styles of Europe, the neoclassical is most closely associated with a great social movement outside the arts. As Enlightenment philosophers and writers formulated and popularized the notion that the legitimacy of governments should reside in the consent of the governed—the most important of the ideas that eventually led to the French Revolution—they looked to the Roman republic for historical precedent. Artists and designers, spurred by the contemporary reaction against the rococo, were further inspired by the fortuitous discovery of a trove of new classical motifs in the ruins of Herculaneum and Pompeii, first excavated in 1738. The furniture to which such images were applied was severely angular by comparison to its predecessors; the *bombé* shape and the serpentine front were discarded, and cabriole legs were supplanted by square or cylindrical ones. Marquetry became increasingly simpler and less copious until, by the 1780s, plain wooden panels were the norm.

In Paris, a reaction against the ever more whimsical extravagances of rococo set in during the 1760s, yielding first the Transition style and then the fully neoclassical Louis XVI style, whose considerable opulence and formal solemnity was meant to suggest grandeur, hearkening back to the Sun King. This period has been called the "golden age of French cabinetmaking," when Paris harbored many great cabinet makers, often from other countries.

At about the same time, the architect and designer Robert Adam (1728–92) led a similar alteration in taste in Britain. The Adam style, whose influence was chiefly confined to America and northern Europe, was by comparison less stern. Its emphasis on light-colored materials and painted decoration—often floral motifs derived from ancient Greek vase painting—made for a sense of gaiety and pleasure rather than grandeur and pride. If rather more understated than its French cohorts, Adam's furniture was nevertheless opulent and very expensive. Two furniture designers, George Hepplewhite in the 1780s and Thomas Sheraton in the '90s, presented a neoclassical style more suitable to bourgeois tastes, being both less rich in materials and more austere in character. Their pattern books were the principal sources for makers of American Federal furniture.

Europe, too, had followed neoclassical Paris and London. By the 1790s, as the French Revolution changed virtually all aspects of European life, rococo furniture was gone except in a few corners of the region, chiefly Venice, Spain, and parts of Catholic Germany.

***

The period of the French Revolution and Napoleonic Wars (1789–1815) altered the Western world in many realms, including that of the decorative arts. At first, furniture design remained fairly stable. Elements of the Louis XVI style persisted during the Revolution in the Directoire and Consular styles. In Napoleonic Europe, the Empire style was a grandiose reworking of that mode. It was expressly intended, like the Louis XIV style, to aggrandize the new monarch, Napoleon. Self-consciously majestic, it was massive and formal. Its decorative schemes involved, along with the usual range of classical motifs, a specially devised iconography featuring the letter N, often within a laurel wreath; the bee, Bonaparte's heraldic symbol; eagles, the Roman (and Napoleonic) military emblem; and the swan, a device introduced by the Empress Josephine.

Despite the French Revolution and the Napoleonic Wars, Paris remained the art capital of Europe, and the Empire style influenced furniture makers throughout the continent. In Britain, its monumentality influenced the highly eclectic Regency style, among whose practitioners was Thomas Sheraton, who added French ideas to his later pattern books. These in their turn helped stimulate the Directory style in America. France had been an American ally since the Revolutionary War, so French styles were already popular in America, and Directory furniture quickly evolved into the American Empire style.

The French neoclassical model persisted beyond the Napoleonic Wars, which completed the cycle of the French Revolution with the restoration of the French monarchy and others. Such styles as Restauration, Louis XVIII, and Charles X incorporated elements of the neoclassical with references to the *ancien régime*. Even the Biedermeier style, a simplifying mode that was developed in Germany and Austria and was associated with the newly dominant bourgeoisie, was clearly in the continuum of post-Renaissance high style that had begun in the 17th century. But the dam was about to break.

***

The remarkable flowering of modern and contemporary furniture, in a remarkably diverse range of styles, some entirely novel and others nostalgic revivals, can be bewildering. This is perhaps fitting, given the complexities and confusions of modern life. Speaking generally, its roots are perhaps best seen as comprising two linked strands: the 19th-century growth of industrial techniques and the concomitant nostalgia for "the world we have lost," an imagined golden age before the onslaught of the machine age and its social dislocations.

Ironically, the modern begins with historical revivals, in the eclectic Revival styles that arose around 1840, shaking off the long dominance of the neoclassical. The newly powerful middle classes did not want to associate themselves with the grandeur of monarchy and its echoes of imperial Rome; nor could they afford it. At the same time, they sought the reassurance of familiarity, and so designers turned to earlier periods for inspiration.

Two trends initially arose, the Neo-Gothic and Rococo Revival styles, and each quickly developed distinct national and regional variants. Neo-Gothic was much more popular in Britain, America, and northern Europe, while the rococo was more prominent elsewhere. Around 1850, the Renaissance Revival style joined the mix, and it provoked even greater variation—Italy followed Italian Renaissance models, German-speaking countries followed German Renaissance models, and so on. Moreover, the Renaissance revival, based as it was on the classicizing Renaissance, reintroduced classical elements. This led to neoclassical revivals including the French Louis XVI Revival style (which was promoted by Napoleon III, ruler of France's Second Empire, in the manner of his uncle and namesake) and Britain's inaccurately named Queen Anne Revival style.

Significantly, the rise of these various styles coincided with the early 19th-century emergence of factory-produced furniture. Mass manufacturers produced vast quantities of mediocre furniture in the revival styles—or in pastiches of more than one. As early as the 1850s, beginning in Britain, designers and artists rebelled against this influx, focusing on craftsmanship and materials, and developed new modes, most notably those of the Arts and Crafts movement and Art Nouveau. They employed new designs, distancing themselves from the Revival styles. These artists and designers often drew on the spare aesthetics of Japan (and thus, ultimately, China), thereby furthering the ongoing mingling of Eastern and Western traditions. Both the Arts and Crafts movement and Art Nouveau were highly influential on early 20th-century design throughout the Western world. Their offspring ranged from the Prairie School and Mission furniture in the United States to Art Deco in France (and elsewhere) to Scandinavian modern.

But the industrialization of furniture making also offered opportunities. Fine furniture could now be made available to the great mass of the public who could not afford the carefully crafted handmade furniture of the reformers. Such groups as the Art Furniture Movement in Britain, the German Deutsche Werkstätten and Deutscher Werkbund, and the Roycroft Community in the United States, were among the first designers to attempt combining the notions of fine design and mass manufacture. Especially in Germany, where the Bauhaus style emerged from these endeavors, they laid the groundwork for the International Style of the mid-20th century, centered on the ideas of functionalism: the importance of utility and designs that emphasize the industrial process and its modern materials.

***

Since the Second World War, furniture design has blossomed in a myriad of directions. In America, partly influenced by the presence of European refugees, furniture makers revived the International Style pieces of Marcel Breuer, Le Corbusier, and others. Charles Eames and Eero Saarinen led a revolution in materials; their new methods of molding plywood and plastic and joining them to steel elements were influential throughout the world, especially on Britain's Contemporary Style and in Scandinavian modern furniture. Eames was also a pioneer of ergonomic design, intended to create furniture whose shapes and sizes were attuned to the configuration of the human body, particularly in those pieces intended for work ("ergonomic" is from the Greek *ergon,* meaning "work"). Plastic, in particular—inexpensive, easy to work with, and extremely versatile—lent itself to the flowing lines and informal character of postwar furniture and has been prominent in all styles since.

In the 1960s, the sensible, smooth "good taste" that came to dominate furniture under the influence of Eames and Saarinen triggered the inevitable reaction. Pop furniture, inspired by Pop Art and the general sense of irreverence that permeated the decade, used vivid colors and purposefully vulgar imagery to both parody and exploit consumerist culture. Well-known pieces included inflatable armchairs and a baseball-glove-shaped chair by the Italian firm De Pas, D'Urbino, Lomazzi; and Allen Jones' pornographically sculptural work. This furniture's tone of satire and oddity reflected the social and political upheaval of the times.

In the 1980s, a more purely formal variant of anti-, or non-International Style furniture, arose, sometimes known as "Memphis style," after the firm of Italian designer Ettore Sottsass. Milan, home of Memphis style and of an influential annual furniture show, is the epicenter for designs in which whimsy is as prominent as in Pop designs but is abstract, featuring forms in odd shapes and unexpected arrangements of elements, often with plastic veneers in several different colors and patterns within a single piece.

It should be emphasized that Functionalism and International Style furniture have not disappeared; they continue to coexist with newer styles among leading trends in contemporary decorative art.

Within all these stylistic developments, a highly significant factor in 20th-century furniture design and manufacture has been the close involvement of many architects. Since at least the early 18th century, some architects in many periods have designed furniture for their own buildings—note, for instance, François Cuvillies, William Kent, Benjamin Latrobe, and A. W. N. Pugin—but only in modern times have architects made a practice of designing furniture for the general market. In addition to Breuer, Le Corbusier, Eames, Saarinen, and Sottsass, mentioned above, important architect-designers of the period include Alvar Aalto, Frank Gehry, Walter Gropius, and Ludwig Mies van der Rohe.

The eclecticism of contemporary furniture design encompasses a return to the most ancient modes of making furniture in the work of various makers who collectively represent the Handicraft Revival. Emerging in the 1970s, such makers as Wharton Esherick, George Nakashima, Wendell Castle, and John Makepeace place a great emphasis on craftsmanship in wood, rather than mass production in new, synthetic materials.

***

The history of furniture, then, proceeds from beginnings in isolated parts of the neolithic world as humans first became settled dwellers in houses, through a progressively more complex linkage of one local sort of design to another, and arrives at—or rather, continues on from—the linked strands of progress and nostalgia that give rise to the amazing eclecticism of contemporary design. The contents of this book present the steps on the way, offering brief glimpses of a myriad of furniture makers, designers and schools—and their products, the furniture itself. Collectively, they display the manifold roots of furniture design as well as its potential for the future. The reader will not only be dazzled by an astonishing range of creativity, but may also, perhaps, detect the shape of furniture design to come.

NOTE

Chinese entry titles are given first in the Pinyin transcription, followed in parentheses by the older, more familiar Wade-Giles transcription, unless the two are identical.

Entries are filed word-by-word; for example, *cabinet stand* precedes *cabinetmaker*.

A

AALTO, HUGO ALVAR HENRIK (1899–1976)

Finnish architect and designer; a leader in SCANDINAVIAN MODERN design. Though primarily an architect, Alvar Aalto designed much furniture that has been immensely influential both in Finland and in the United States. In Helsinki, as a young man, he studied the work of Josef HOFFMAN and the WIENER WERKSTÄTTE, and he worked for a time for Eliel SAARINEN. After the First World War, Aalto practiced architecture in what was later known as the INTERNATIONAL STYLE, and when he began to design furniture in the 1920s, he followed that style. However, he always used wood, to the exclusion of metal, and his style was less rigidly functionalistic than characteristic BAUHAUS designs. Following the example of THONET's bentwood chairs, and continuing in the International style, Aalto designed in the 1930s the laminated beechwood chairs for which he is best known. He was the first designer employing the cantilever principle in chair design (*see* Mart STAM) with wood instead of tubular steel. Aalto also designed fabrics, glassware and lighting fixtures; in 1935 he established a company to manufacture and sell these products. This firm, Artek, is still extant, and many of Alto's designs are still in production.

AARNIO, EERO (b. 1932)

Contemporary Finnish furniture designer. Aarnio is best known for two chair designs of the 1960s, the "Globe" or "Ball" chair (1966) and the "Gyro" or "Pastilli" chair (1968). The latter is made of reinforced fiberglass molded into a flattened sphere, with a hollow carved into the top and one side to make a seat. All curves, it rocks on the floor without legs or pedestal; it thus wittily and completely ignores the traditional character of a chair. The "Globe" chair is an ovoid fiberglass shell, higher than it is wide and with a large, circular opening. It revolves on a cast aluminum base, and both base and chair are painted in a primary color. The user sits in the opening, which is completely upholstered and sometimes equipped with stereo speakers. Evocative of space travel, this chair has a fantasy element to it, as does contemporary POP ART FURNITURE but its sculptural elegance and ingenuity place it in the line of development stemming from Charles EAMES and continuing through SCANDINAVIAN MODERN design, as in the work of Arne JACOBSEN.

ABACUS

In the classical ORDERS OF ARCHITECTURE, the topmost member of the CAPITAL of a column; slab on which the ARCHITRAVE rests.

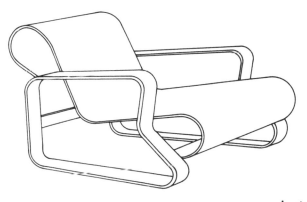

laminated chair by Aalto

1

acanthus

**pedestal design by
Robert Adam**

ABILDGAARD, NIKOLAI ABRAHAM (1743–1809)

Danish painter and NEOCLASSICAL STYLE interior designer. Best known as a neoclassical painter, Abildgaard also designed a small amount of furniture in about 1800, first for his own use and then for the Danish royal family. Like French painter Jacques-Louis DAVID, he attempted to replicate ancient GREEK FURNITURE, as seen in ancient pottery painting.

ABURA

Nigerian HARDWOOD; plain, pale yellow-brown in color. Abura's uniform texture and susceptibility to stain make it useful for furniture, especially moldings.

ACACIA

Any of several hundred species of HARDWOOD tree, distributed worldwide, several of which are valuable to furniture makers. Some have been in use since very early times (*see*, for example, EGYPTIAN FURNITURE). Hard and very durable woods, the acacias range in color from pale green to a variety of browns, sometimes with streaks of a contrasting color, in generally straight grains.

ACANTHUS

Ornamental motif consisting of a conventionalized leaf of *Acanthus spinosus,* a Mediterranean plant with large, prickly leaves. Originally used in ancient Greek architecture to decorate column capitals of the CORINTHIAN ORDER, the acanthus has been used on furniture in most European styles since the Renaissance, excluding the modern styles that repudiate historical references. In British and American furniture, it was particularly notable as the ornamentation on the knees of cabriole legs in the QUEEN ANNE STYLE and in ROCOCO FURNITURE, and it was also very widely used in the REGENCY STYLE.

ACROTER

Plinth or pedestal for a statue or other ornament, placed at the apex or lower corners of a PEDIMENT. More loosely, the term often refers to the ornament itself. A decorative device of classical architecture, the acroter was com-monly used on European case furniture in all of the NEOCLASSICAL STYLE, especially in the 18th century. Also called *acrotere, acroterion* and *acroterium.*

ADAM, ROBERT (1728–92)

British NEOCLASSICAL STYLE architect and designer. The ADAM STYLE, the British neoclassical decorative mode of the 1760s–1780s, is named after him. He was born in Edinburgh, son of the well-known Scottish architect William Adam. In 1754 Robert Adam began four years of study in Rome under the French neoclassical designer J.-L. Clerisseau. There he associated with French and Italian artists and met the Italian engraver G. B. PIRANESI, whose creative response to classical architecture influenced him deeply. Adam studied the architectural ornamentation of ancient buildings and developed a vast repertoire of classical motifs, with which he would create a new style of decoration. He launched his career in London in 1759, and his success was immediate and lasting. For the rest of his life, in partnership with his brother James (1730–94), he always had several architectural commissions in progress. He employed many designers and furniture makers, including Thomas CHIPPENDALE Jr. and Michelangelo PERGOLESI. Adam felt that an architect should design not only the exterior but also all the details of an interior, in order to maintain a coherent decorative scheme. He rigorously followed this doctrine, designing furniture, carpets, even keyhole plates and fireplace gratings for his rooms. A striking innovation in dining-room furniture is usually attributed to Adam—the use of a SIDEBOARD flanked by PEDESTALS. The Adam style, a reaction against the whimsical fancies of the preceding rococo (*see* ROCOCO FURNITURE), revolutionized British interior decoration and furniture design, and Robert Adam has always been best known for the style's light and airy grace. He was so famous in his own time that he was buried in Westminster Abbey.

ADAM STYLE

British NEOCLASSICAL STYLE in furniture and interior decoration of about 1760–90, named for its creator and principal exponent, Robert ADAM, the leading architect and designer of the period. The Adam style in furniture was characterized by the liberal use of classical motifs in painted or inlaid decoration on rectilinear forms with slender, elegant proportions. The use of light-colored woods and paint created an effect of charm and grace. Conceived to counter the frivolity and asymmetrical whimsy of the ROCOCO FURNITURE of the 1750s, the Adam style nonetheless had a prettiness and gaiety that the more solemn LOUIS XVI STYLE, the contemporary neoclassical mode of France, lacked.

While its straight lines and inlays contrasted with the curves and carved motifs of the rococo, the Adam style was marked chiefly by its repertoire of ornamentation, motifs from the ordered, rational world of classical architecture. Fluted COLUMNs, FESTOONs, SWAGs, PALMETTEs, ram's heads, SPHINXes and CHIMERAs were all featured on furniture. Cornices, aprons and moldings were decorated with PATERAE and ANTHEMIONs, the Greek KEY PATTERN and the VITRUVIAN SCROLL. These motifs were evocative of the classical world so admired during the Enlightenment.

Adam believed that an architect should pursue a coherent expression of this theme in his buildings, so he designed every detail of his interiors, including furniture, carpets and even keyhole plates and doorknobs. Furniture was thus regarded as part of an overall decorative scheme. Adam's furniture was often painted in pastel colors with gilt and other painted ornamentation. Angelica KAUFFMANN and Antonio ZUCCHI were frequently commissioned to paint mythological figures in idealized settings in framed panels of furniture as well as on walls and ceilings. One scheme of painted decoration that Adam devised was based on ancient Greek pottery painting and came to be known as the ETRUSCAN STYLE. Whether painted or inlaid, the furniture of Robert Adam was often further ornamented with gilding of either wood or bronze mounts. He also favored rare and exotic woods, and he frequently used marble or SCAGLIOLA panels for further enrichment.

This elegantly extravagant work could be afforded only by the rich, and Adam worked principally for the aristocracy. Other designers, most notably George HEPPLEWHITE and Thomas SHEARER, modified the style to suit a more middleclass clientele. Hepplewhite's less angular furniture, simple and elegant, typified by the SHIELD-BACK CHAIR, represented the Adam style in the 1780s. And in the 1790s Thomas SHERATON's pattern books continued to translate Adam designs to a practical and popular level. However, more archeologically oriented pieces appeared in Sheraton's designs, along with the first hints of the French influence that characterized the REGENCY STYLE.

Beginning in the same decade, the archeologizing tendencies of the Regency style led to the rejection of the Adam style as frivolous and overly decorative. However, its influence had already been enormous, not only in Britain, where it was dominant for 30 years, but in northern Europe, Russia and the United States, where the designs of Hepplewhite and Sheraton were very important to FEDERAL PERIOD furniture makers.

ADAMS, NATHANIEL (active before 1652, d. 1675)

Furniture maker from Boston, Massachusetts. Adams, who served his apprenticeship under the London-trained turner Thomas EDSALL, made AMERICAN JACOBEAN FURNITURE using elements of the English Jacobean style (*see* JACOBEAN FURNITURE) current in 17th-century America.

ADAMS, NEHEMIAM (c. 1769–1840)

FEDERAL PERIOD furniture maker of Salem, Massachusetts.

ADIRONDACK FURNITURE

Rustic style of American furniture manufactured from about 1898 to the early 1940s. Named because of its popularity among the owners and furnishers of camps, resorts and summer residences in the Adirondack Mountains in upstate New York, Adirondack furniture was marketed throughout the United States. It was produced chiefly in Indiana—first by the Old Hickory Chair Company, which was founded in 1898. This furniture, distinctively woodsy, was composed of round, unmilled HICKORY sticks, often with the bark left on, arranged in simple designs derived from country models. Unsawn lengths of sapling poles were bent to form most parts, except for the rockers of rocking chairs, which were sawn; chair seats and backs, which were woven of hickory bark; and tabletops, generally made of oak. Gustav STICKLEY's *Craftsman* magazine praised these pieces as an example of ARTS AND CRAFTS MOVEMENT furniture, but it seems clear that its manufac-

Adirondack rocker

turers were simply astute businessmen, not design reformers. Chairs and sofas made up the majority of Adirondack pieces, though tables, hatracks and various other items were produced in this style as well. In the 1930s and 1940s, influenced by the popularity of more modern styles, Adirondack designs became quasi-streamlined, and nylon webbing and other materials sometimes replaced woven bark.

ADNET, JACQUES (1900–84)

French furniture designer of the 1930s through the early 1950s. In the 1930s Adnet designed ART DECO furniture, which was somewhat out of style by then, and kept alive the conservative manner of Emile-Jacques RUHLMANN. After the war he was best known for furniture that was extensively, often almost completely, covered in fine leather—a fashion of the late 1940s and early 1950s.

AEGRICANES

Decorative motif; head of a goat or ram. A device taken from ancient Greek religious iconography, the *aegricanes* was used on furniture by NEOCLASSICAL STYLE designers of the late 18th and early 19th centuries.

AESTHETIC MOVEMENT

See GODWIN, William.

AFARA (also *limba*)

West African HARDWOOD, varying in color from yellow to dark brown, used in furniture both as solid wood and as veneer.

AFFLECK, THOMAS (1740–95)

Principal maker of PHILADELPHIA CHIPPENDALE FURNITURE. Born in Aberdeen, Scotland, and trained in Edinburgh and London, Affleck arrived in Philadelphia in 1763, having been hired by the new colonial governor of Pennsylvania, John Penn, as the "resident cabinetmaker" to the city. There he became a leading practitioner of the rococo style (*see* ROCOCO FURNITURE), as transmitted through Thomas CHIPPENDALE. Affleck (who was a close friend of Benjamin Franklin) made furniture in a more restrained style

than that of his contemporaries Benjamin RANDOLPH and Jonathan GOSTELOWE. He is known to have owned a copy of Chippendale's *The Gentleman and Cabinet-maker's Director;* he sometimes took furniture parts line-for-line from the book. He also used "Chinese Chippendale" fretwork occasionally. After the American Revolution Affleck continued to make Chippendale furniture into the FEDERAL PERIOD. However, he was also capable of working in the NEOCLASSICAL STYLE, as shown by the sturdy, severe chairs he made between 1791 and 1793 for the houses of Congress, which were then located in Philadelphia.

AFRICAN FURNITURE

Traditional furniture of the tribal societies of sub-Saharan Africa; chiefly BEDs and HEAD-RESTs for sleeping, and seating furniture. Though traditionally classed among the primitive cultures of the world, Africa's precolonial tribal peoples ranged from truly primitive hunters and gatherers of the southern deserts and the deepest jungle, to the culturally complex empires of West Africa. Still, the traditional African household featured the simple and scant range of PRIMITIVE FURNITURE typical of hunting and gathering societies around the world, though in consequence of European colonization it is better known and more widely collected in the West. Although modern Africa is increasingly similar to the West in its furnishings and architecture, the traditional mode, still in place in many parts of the continent, is dealt with here.

Traditional African housing differs greatly from that which is typical of the Western world. The home is not simply a building, or rooms within a building; it is a complex sprawling space, housing an extended family and often its numerous livestock. The centers of activity are outdoors, in compounds containing various buildings, each usually having but a single room, that are chiefly used for storage or shelter from bad weather and the dangers of night.

Accordingly, in the traditional African household, there is very little furniture. The chief components of the indigenous African furniture of centuries ago are beds, headrests, and stools, though chairs, which derive from European furniture but have developed distinctively African forms, have long been a fixture in the traditional repertoire. There is no CASE FURNITURE; household storage space is in baskets or ceramic vessels.

Bedding is often simply a woven mat or animal skin on the ground or floor (mats are also commonly used on ground or floor for sitting on and dining from; once, they also functioned as units of currency). However, wooden beds are also common, especially in the mixed grass- and woodlands of Central and West Africa, between the rain forest and the coastal lowlands, where substantial timbers are available.

Wooden beds are of two types. The simplest consists of a crudely fashioned panel of interwoven saplings, light branches or palm leaf ribs supported at either end by a light cross-pole, itself supported on small forked posts set in the ground. This sort of bed is used chiefly in the Sahel region, the scrub lands to the south of the Sahara Desert. Where mosquitoes are a serious problem, especially in the equatorial coastal regions of West Africa, similar beds are made on very tall legs, raising the users up to 10 feet off the ground, above the densest concentrations of the pests. Also, throughout the continent, African beds are often surrounded by "walls" of tightly woven mats or fabric hung on uprights, to protect against insects. Such beds can be quite wide, sometimes up to six or eight feet square, where the platform is constructed of heavier branches and covered with mats.

A more substantial wooden bed, often a prestigious possession indicating high social status, is composed of a solid wood platform supported about a foot off the ground by four thick legs, or by panels running lengthwise below the long edge of the platform and heavily decorated with carved symbols of good fortune. Such beds are often carved, platform and supports together, from a single block of wood. These beds are necessarily limited in width to that of the tree from which the wood was taken and seldom accommodate more than two people. Larger beds, usually the privilege of high-ranking men whose several wives may share the bed, are built like the platform beds described above.

A third sort of African bed is made of shaped and dried mud or clay. At its simplest, a mud bed is a low, solid platform, about a foot high and six feet long. More elaborate versions are higher and are hollowed out

below, to create a space for storage, or in which a fire might be built on chilly nights, or in which chickens or goats might be housed.

Beds of all sorts are usually accompanied by small stool-like wooden headrests (sometimes called *pillows*). These are sometimes built into the bed (especially in beds of solid wood), but more generally they are portable and are regarded as part of one's personal articles, not to be used by others.

One type of headrest is a simple plank with legs, usually three in number. Another, essentially a slightly altered form of the commonest sort of African stool (they can be distinguished from stools by their shorter and narrower tops), consists of two horizontal planks separated by a vertical column. The upper surface is shaped to receive a sleeper's neck and head. The pillar-like element in these headrests, as in the similar stools, is usually decorated with carving, often quite elaborate. Among the African stools most sought after by Western collectors is the so-called CARYATID STOOL of southeastern Congo (formerly Zaire).

These columnar headrests and stools, whose earliest known examples date to the ninth century A.D., are probably related to cognate pieces in ancient EGYPTIAN FURNITURE, though the direction of any influences between their cultures cannot be established using present-day archeological evidence.

African stools most commonly take this columnar, pillar-like form, but there are also many variations on the footed plank familiar in the west, with the number of legs varying from two (even, occasionally, one, in a device known as a sitting stick) to six or more. Sometimes the legs are set on a platform and the piece resembles the pillar-like variety; sometimes the "pillar" is sufficiently broad relative to the base and seat that the stool resembles a box. There are also stools, mostly in the Ashanti region of West Africa, that actually *are* boxes, being blocks of wood with a hollowed-out bottom in which magical packets can be stored for good luck. Another form, sometimes considered a chair, is low and has an upward extension on one side, usually in the form of a single stick of wood, against which a user can rest his or her back, while sitting almost on the ground. Indeed, some of these backrests, as they are usually called, actually lack seats, and are simply shaped or carved planks or sticks that are held at an angle to the ground by a supporting stick, and against which a user reclines.

As early as the 15th century, Europeans began introducing the chair to Africa, and many variations on the form have been made since. Chiefs and important traders were presented with examples of elaborate armchairs, often upholstered, and these became highly prestigious objects and were much imitated. Many African chairs and stools are decorated with leather and with brass studs (the latter often arrayed in dense fields), in imitation of RENAISSANCE FURNITURE forms imported from Portugal and Spain in the 15th and 16th centuries. Another popular form, the AKONKROMFI chair, derived from the folding chairs that many Europeans brought to Africa for their own use.

All of these seating forms have in common decorations that indicate, in the degree of their complexity and elaboration, the prestige and wealth of their owners. Often very intricately carved and further ornamented— with painting, shells, hair fiber, and, especially in mineral-rich West Africa, embossed sheets of bronze, silver, and, occasionally, gold—stools and chairs at their richest serve as THRONEs.

African stools and headrests present another aspect of traditional African furniture that varies greatly from Western cognates. These pieces are not intended for use by anyone but their owners. Like personal toiletry items in the West, such furniture is light and conveniently taken from place to place, and is used wherever the owner goes. (Accordingly, African households traditionally contained no furniture for the use of visitors.) An African would be startled and dismayed should someone else in his family, let alone a stranger, venture to sit on his or her stool. Among some peoples, notably the Ashanti, stools are regarded (or were in older times) as actually containing the souls of their owners. The stools of chiefs were thus accorded great spiritual importance, since their owners were felt to embody in themselves the collective soul of their tribe; upon the death of such a figure, their stool was often placed in a shrine and accorded supernatural status. The Ashanti of the 19th century set aside a Golden Stool that represented the soul of the entire people, and no one, of even the highest royal rank, was permitted to sit on it. In Mali, tradition speaks of similarly important stools made of

fired ceramics in the period before European penetration, and there are medieval references to a huge nugget of gold that was part of such a throne.

As such, chairs are usually the exclusive perquisite of male elders, although there are many exceptions. For instance, among the We people of Liberia, when a young woman is inaugurated into the young women's society of her tribe, she will dance with the stool or chair of her grandfather, the furniture symbolizing her connection to her ancestors.

Thus, while the traditional African furniture of the centuries before European contact was materially much less elaborate than contemporary furniture in East Asia and the West, it probably had much greater emotional, even spiritual, impact on its users. It is unsurprising that in the context of the Western museum, where most readers of this book will have encountered it, African furniture seems of a piece with the ritual objects and masks with which it is displayed.

AFRICAN MAHOGANY

African HARDWOOD related to and resembling American MAHOGANY and used, from the late 19th century onward, as that wood's supply diminished, as an alternative to it. Somewhat less red in color than its American relative, African mahogany is nonetheless used widely in reproduction furniture as well as in the mass manufacture of office furniture and as plywood.

AFRICAN WALNUT

West African HARDWOOD; plain brown wood used in furniture making for structural elements and usually covered with a more interestingly figured veneer. Although it resembles European WALNUT in color, African walnut is not actually a walnut, botanically speaking; rather, it is related to MAHOGANY.

AFRORMOSIA

West African HARDWOOD, yellow to brown in color and widely used in furniture making for both structural members and veneering. Afrormosia resembles TEAK and has tended to replace it in furniture and in shipbuilding since it entered Western markets after the Second World War.

AFZELIA
HARDWOOD of tropical Africa; reddish wood resembling mahogany. Quite dense, and therefore hard to work but very durable, afzelia is most commonly used in furniture making for tabletops. It is also known as *apa* and *doussié.*

AITKEN, JOHN (active 1790s)
FEDERAL PERIOD furniture maker of Philadelphia. Aitken worked in the manner of Thomas SHERATON and is probably best known for commissions he filled for George Washington, who lived in Philadelphia (then the nation's capital) for much of his presidency. His furniture made specifically for Mount Vernon can still be seen there.

AKONKROMFI CHAIR
AFRICAN FURNITURE form; a chair built to imitate the form of travelers' folding chairs used by Europeans from the earliest days of European exploration and colonization, though surviving examples of the African imitations are no older than the late 19th century. Akonkromfi chairs, whose name means "praying mantis," do not fold; they are generally carved from a single block of wood. Regarded as highly prestigious objects, they are heavily decorated and are often considered to be a sort of THRONE, used only on ceremonial occasions.

ALBERS, JOSEF (1888–1976)
German-American painter, sculptor and designer. Best known as a painter, Albers also taught furniture design and other courses at the BAUHAUS from 1923 to 1933. He designed tables and shelving units in the sculptural manner of Gerrit RIETVELD and chairs, both of bentwood and of metal, in the cleaner, simpler style associated with Marcel BREUER. The chairs could be dismantled for storage or transport. When Hitler closed the Bauhaus in 1933, Albers went to the United States and became an important force in American painting and design. He taught at Black Mountain College for 16 years and at Yale University from 1950 until his death.

ALBERTOLLI, GIOCONDO (1742–1839)
Italian NEOCLASSICAL STYLE ornamental designer and interior decorator. Albertolli, under the influence of G. B. PIRANESI, designed elaborate ornamentation using classical motifs. His designs were published between 1782 and 1805, and they had a wide influence on Italian furniture makers, notably Giuseppe MAGGIOLINI.

ALBINI, FRANCO (1905–77)
Modern Italian architect and designer. Best known for his museum interiors and exhibition designs, Albini also began to design furniture in the INTERNATIONAL STYLE in the 1940s. His designs bear the stamp of FUNCTIONALISM, in that the structure and the process of manufacture are highlighted. He also designed urban plans, interiors, exhibitions and various household goods.

chair by Albini

ALBRIZZI, ALEXANDER (b. 1934)
Contemporary Italian interior decorator and furniture designer based in London. Albrizzi, who studied law in Italy and was a journalist in Paris before he turned to design, is best known for a series of clear acrylic tables, with stylish geometrical lines, made in the late 1960s.

ALCOVE BED (also *lit à la Polonaise*)
French furniture form of the 18th and early 19th centuries. Designed to fit in an alcove, alcove beds were much more highly decorated on their exposed side than on the sides that faced the walls.

ALDEGREVER, HEINRICH (1501–61)
German engraver and designer of RENAISSANCE FURNITURE ornamentation. Aldegrever, of Soest, in Westphalia, produced numerous engravings that introduced Renaissance ideas and motifs from Italy into Germany in the first half of the 16th century.

ALDEN, JOHN (c. 1599–1687)
American furniture maker of the 17th century, best known as the abashed swain who is adjured to "Speak for yourself, John Alden," in Henry Wadsworth Longfellow's poem "The Courtship of Miles Standish." A cooper by trade when he arrived in Massachusetts in 1620, Alden is known to have made furniture in this country and is said to have been America's first furniture maker.

ALDER
European and American HARDWOOD; pale brown wood aging to a darker golden brown. European alder is usually used in plywood, while American red alder, the commonest commercial hardwood of the North American West Coast, is frequently used as a solid wood in furniture making.

ALIX, CHARLOTTE
See SOGNOT, Louis.

ALLISON, MICHAEL (active 1800–1855)
New York City furniture maker of the early 19th century, associated with the FEDERAL PERIOD and the AMERICAN EMPIRE STYLE. Early in his career, Allison was an exponent of the NEOCLASSICAL STYLE popularized by George HEPPLEWHITE and Thomas SHERATON. Like his contemporaries Duncan PHYFE and Charles-Honoré LANNUIER, Allison followed the influences of the French EMPIRE STYLE and produced some of the best of the grand pieces for which New York cabinetmaking of the period is renowned.

ALMA-TADEMA, LAWRENCE (1836–1912)
British painter and designer of the late 19th century. He was one of the most renowned British painters of his day and worked in a grand, academic, neoclassical manner. Alma-Tadema also designed furniture, employing an eclectic revivalist style with ornamental motifs from many earlier cultures, especially classical and ancient Egyptian. While his pieces were elaborately decorated with rich carving and inlay work, their forms were more ordinary, deriving from earlier neoclassical models.

ALTAR TABLE
English name for JI TAI SHI AN, CHINESE FURNITURE form, referring to its use in domestic religious celebrations.

ALUMINUM
Silvery white metal, any of several alloys; hard, light, corrosion-resistant material used in furniture since the Second World War.

AMARANTH
Another name for PURPLEHEART.

American Chippendale chair

AMBASZ, EMILIO
See PIRETTI, Giancarlo.

AMBOYNA WOOD (also *Amboina*)
Asian HARDWOOD; a PADAUK, light red to golden brown in color, very popular in 18th- and 19th-century European furniture. Occasionally used in ancient ROMAN FURNITURE, Amboyna wood did not reappear in Europe until the 18th century, when it was particularly popular in French ROCOCO FURNITURE. Later, British REGENCY STYLE cabinetmakers used it prominently. Its curly grain and light color contrasted handsomely with plainer, darker woods such as MAHOGANY. Amboyna wood is found from India to the Moluccas (it is named for the Moluccan island Amboina) but is most commonly exported from Burma.

AMBRY
See AUMBRY.

AMERICAN CHIPPENDALE FURNITURE
American ROCOCO FURNITURE made during the second half of the 18th century. All three editions of Thomas CHIPPENDALE's book *The Gentleman and Cabinetmaker's Director*, first published in England in 1754, had a tremendous impact on Colonial American furniture makers. (Until the late 19th century, however, American Chippendale furniture was known as the "New French" style.) Other British pattern books—such as those of Robert MANWARING, Thomas JOHNSON and Batty LANGLEY—were also used by American cabinetmakers, and established local tastes and variations also helped considerably to generate design features. Generally speaking, American Chippendale furniture was less elaborate and more conservative than the models in the *Director*. QUEEN ANNE STYLE forms continued to be used, now with rococo ornamentation applied to them. A taste for the architectural motifs of the PALLADIAN STYLE remained, and the ball-and-claw foot, out of date in Britain and thus not used by Chippendale, was extremely popular in the colonies. Mahogany, while commonly used, was often replaced by local woods. The major Colonial cities developed distinctive local styles (*see* BOSTON CHIPPENDALE FURNITURE; NEWPORT CHIPPENDALE FURNITURE; NEW

York Chippendale furniture; Philadel-phia Chippendale furniture), while smaller cities tended to adhere to Chippendale's published examples more strictly (*see* Thomas Elfe). In towns and rural areas, a number of simpler variants evolved somewhat later and continued to dominate their territories into the first years of the 19th century (*see* Country Chippendale furniture). In much of America, however, the Chippendale style was superseded by the neoclassical style of the Federal period by about 1790.

American Empire style

Neoclassical style current in American furniture from about 1810 to the 1830s. Based on elements from the French Empire style and the British Regency style, the American Empire style was characterized by massive and bold furniture with rounded corners and other curvilinear components with an emphasis on expanses of figured veneer, most often of mahogany.

The neoclassical style in furniture had become well established in the United States in the earlier Federal period, immediately after the American Revolution, when workers followed British Adam style design. Such motifs as the urn, the kylix, husks, paterae and foliate festoons were adopted then and remained popular in later work. In the first decade of the 19th century, the Directory style, an American rendering of the British Regency manner, had introduced some adopted French ideas, including archeologically inspired forms that were also favored in the American Empire mode—most notably chairs based on the ancient Greek klismos and the Roman sella curulis. The American Empire style presented a greater elaboration of ideas already present in the Directory style. In the following decades, the late work of Thomas Sheraton, the chief source for Directory style makers, continued to influence American makers. Two other Regency designers, Thomas Hope and George Smith, published pattern books (1807 and 1808, respectively) that were also important to the development of this style. Reeding, paw feet (*see* Paw foot, *under* Foot) and the water leaf were popular American Empire motifs that were taken from these British sources. Regency design also introduced Égyptiennerie elements, taken from French designers.

The French influence on American Empire style design was also felt more directly as a result of the publications of Pierre de La Mésangère, the presence of numerous *émigré* cabinetmakers from France, especially in New York, and the example of imported French furniture, which steadily increased in quantity. In addition to the winged sphinxes and chimeras of ancient Egypt, French-inspired American Empire motifs included caryatids, monumental carved supports in the form of animal legs, carved swans and heavy, foliage-decorated scrolls. The French taste also promoted the more widespread use of gilt mounts. Imported from France, these ornaments were nevertheless not as common in the United States as they were at home.

The American Empire style reached its height in the work of two New York makers, C.-H. Lannuier, a French-trained immigrant, and Duncan Phyfe, the leading American cabinetmaker of his generation. Another notable exponent of the style, Anthony Quervelle, worked in Philadelphia. After 1830 the style was modified by the French Restauration style, producing the American amalgam sometimes called the "American Restoration" style but more often known as the Pillar and Scroll style, after its dominant motifs. This mode admitted the use of some non-classical ornamentation, such as Gothic motifs. It thus presaged the immediate future, for during the 1830s, the American Empire style was superseded by the new revival styles.

American Empire table

American Jacobean furniture

Furniture of English North American colonies during most of the 17th century, characterized by solid, rectilinear work, based on English Jacobean furniture. Most existing 17th-century American furniture comes from New England, and thus the inaccurate term *Pilgrim furniture* is sometimes applied to this work. This foursquare furniture was sturdy and simple. Oak was the usual material used, and only a narrow range of forms was made; among settlers who were learning how to live on the edge of a wilderness, furniture limited to mere necessities.

Decoration was similarly restrained, restricted to the use of a few techniques that were economical in terms of time and materials. It was in the somewhat Mannerist style of English work of the first half of the century,

American Jacobean Brewster chair

consisting of shallowly carved, sometimes painted, ARABESQUES and ornamental TURNERY, including applied split SPINDLES. Supports were turned posts, often with bulbous shapes, and bun feet (*see* BUN FOOT, *under* FOOT) were common. Chests, the most common American Jacobean furniture form (*see* CONNECTICUT SUNFLOWER CHEST; GUILFORD CHEST; HADLEY CHEST), and the WAINSCOT CHAIR provided the flat surfaces appropriate for this sort of ornamentation.

Gradual elaboration of the chest led to the COURT CUPBOARD (2), PRESS CUPBOARD and CHEST OF DRAWERS. The BREWSTER and CARVER CHAIRS, made of turned posts and spindles, the LADDER-BACK CHAIR and the TRESTLE TABLE were plainer forms. The DROP-LEAF TABLE, a space saver, was popular, and an American variant, the BUTTERFLY TABLE, was developed toward the end of the period. Convertible beds, such as the TRUNDLE BED and the PRESS BED, were also popular. Like all 17th-century American beds, they were undecorated and extremely simple in construction, often merely a frame to hold a mattress. A few elaborately carved oak bedsteads and canopies were imported from England, but such pieces were not made in America.

Several makers of American Jacobean furniture are known, including Thomas DENNIS, Nicholas DISBROWE and William SEARLE. By 1680 the American seaboard cities had a merchant class that sought the fashionable styles of England, and elements of BAROQUE FURNITURE were adopted in the AMERICAN WILLIAM AND MARY STYLE. Though Jacobean furniture was no longer dominant, its forms and ornamentation persisted on the western frontier until well into the 18th century.

AMERICAN MODERNE

Style of furniture design and decoration popular in the United States in the 1930s. It is characterized by sleek, shiny surfaces, bold shapes with curving elements contrasting with straight lines (often in asymmetrical arrangements) and a fondness for the look of polished metal contrasted with the color black. American Moderne is derived from the two principal European developments of the 1920s, ART DECO and the INTERNATIONAL STYLE. Like Art Deco designers, those of American Moderne favored gloss and shine and tended to use geometrical and botanical

motifs in decoration that was limited to small areas of a given piece. The International style sparked interest in the new materials and processes of modern manufacture and helped promote the use of rectilinear forms, generally modified with curving elements. An element of technological fantasy is often present in American Moderne furniture, as in the use of streamlined effects, taken from industrial design, that suggest the glamor of long-distance travel. Another element of technological fantasy is in the "skyscraper" furniture of Paul FRANKL, which evokes the architectural marvels of the day. Other important furniture designers in the style are Donald DESKEY, Norman Bel GEDDES and Russel WRIGHT. In addition, American furniture designers in the International style are often associated with the term *American Moderne*. Among these designers may be noted William LESCAZE and Gilbert ROHDE.

AMERICAN QUEEN ANNE STYLE

Style of American BAROQUE FURNITURE, based on the English QUEEN ANNE STYLE and dominant in the second quarter of the 18th century. Due to the time it took for fashions from Britain to reach the distant Colonies, Queen Anne style furniture did not begin to be made in North America until the 1720s, some time after the death of Queen Anne, in 1714. Moreover, the American Queen Anne style had a longer life span than its British counterpart, continuing to influence American furniture long after 1750.

Following the British Queen Anne style, American makers favored sparsely ornamented WALNUT furniture; in America solid walnut, as opposed to veneered pieces, was more popular, due in part to the greater availability of the wood and in part to the less developed Colonial veneering techniques. As in Britain, the design esthetic of the American Queen Anne style was based on the curving line, best exemplified by the CABRIOLE LEG (*see under* LEG). The Baroque love for ensembles of dramatic curves was expressed in the typical chairs of the period, in which the bold double curve of the leg was echoed in rounded, or yoke, backs (*see* YOKE-BACK CHAIR); SERPENTINE arms; and FIDDLE-BACK SPLATS. Similarly, the skirts of tables and scrolling bonnet tops of high case pieces created effects of continuing movement. In America the

American Queen Anne side chair

British BALL-AND-CLAW FOOT (*see under* FOOT) did not become fashionable until later in the century, with the American Queen Anne style foot typically being a PAD FOOT or a PAD-AND-DISK FOOT (*see under* FOOT). American chairs and tables in the Queen Anne style tended to have lighter parts and more delicate proportions than their British prototypes, and the austere restriction of ornamentation practiced in Britain was less rigorously followed in the Colonies. Simple INLAYS in different-colored woods were quite common, with carved ornamentation used relatively freely. In Philadelphia, then the most cosmopolitan American city, the contemporary British PALLADIAN STYLE was felt to some degree, and the local carving style was especially elaborate. There the principal motifs of the Queen Anne style, the ACANTHUS leaf and the COQUILLAGE, or scallop shell, were carved with striking realism, in contrast to more stylized renderings elsewhere. There were other regional variations as well. In New England an attenuated verticality was favored and the use of stretchers was retained, while elsewhere the British example was followed and they were dispensed with. New York furniture also tended to have slender proportions, while in Philadelphia and more southern centers, ampler pieces were made. As in Britain, the early 18th century was a period of prosperity in America, and a growing variety of specialized furniture forms reflected this new wealth and leisure. The DRESSING TABLE, the CARD TABLE (1) and a variety of TEA TABLES adorned the houses of merchants and landowners. The SECRETARY was widely made as well. A distinctively American combination of forms arose, the matching HIGHBOY and LOWBOY.

In the 1750s the style of American furniture changed. Responding to British ROCOCO FURNITURE, Colonial makers began to produce AMERICAN CHIPPENDALE FURNITURE, and for the first time, many distinctly individual American craftsmen rose to prominence. But the American Queen Anne style continued to influence these later makers, and its reliance on graceful, curving lines was an influence even after the American Revolution, in the NEOCLASSICAL STYLE of the FEDERAL PERIOD.

AMERICAN REGENCY STYLE
Another name for DIRECTORY STYLE.

AMERICAN RESTORATION STYLE
Another name for PILLAR AND SCROLL STYLE.

AMERICAN WHITEWOOD
British name TULIP POPLAR.

AMERICAN WILLIAM AND MARY STYLE
Style of American BAROQUE FURNITURE, dominant in the last years of the 17th century and the first quarter of the 18th; provincial variant of the English WILLIAM AND MARY STYLE. Sometimes, for convenience, the period is said to have begun as early as 1675, thus including the occasional American use of RESTORATION FURNITURE features in what was essentially still the style of AMERICAN JACOBEAN FURNITURE.

In British North America the early 18th century was a time of rapid expansion, both geographically and economically. A merchant class that could afford fine furniture emerged in the burgeoning cities of the Atlantic seaboard, and similarly, a class of wealthy landowners arose in more rural areas. Not only was furniture imported from England, but native makers followed the more cosmopolitan styles of London, though distance and the conservatism of provincial taste naturally resulted in a time lag in the adoption of new fashions.

In the American William and Mary style, the straightforward rectilinearity of 17th-century furniture was replaced by the curves and color of the Baroque. Curving profiles of table aprons and seat rails were echoed by scrolled stretchers. The SPANISH, or PORTUGUESE, FOOT (*see under* FOOT), known in America as the "paintbrush foot," was popular, especially on chair legs. Carved ornamentation incorporated curvilinear foliate designs in deep, dramatic relief on elaborate front stretchers and high, crested chair backs. JAPANNING came into fashion, particularly in Boston. Plain OAK was replaced in fashionable furniture by more highly figured woods, especially WALNUT and maple (*see* BIRD'S-EYE MAPLE).

A number of new furniture forms appeared, including the SECRETARY, the SLANT-TOP DESK, the HIGHBOY and the LOWBOY, all of which became staple forms throughout the rest of the century. The GATE-LEG TABLE remained very common, and a new variety, the BUTTERFLY TABLE, evolved in

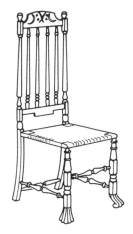

American William and Mary chair

Connecticut. An increasing use of upholstery testified to a greater concern for comfort in furniture.

The American William and Mary style constituted a transition from the still-medieval tastes of American Jacobean furniture toward the esthetic worldliness of European fashion. This increasing sophistication was more fully embraced in the subsequent AMERICAN QUEEN ANNE STYLE.

AMORINI
Another name for *putti* (*see* PUTTO).

ANDAMAN ROSEWOOD (also *Andaman redwood*)
Another name for the variety of PADAUK from the Andaman Islands.

ANDREWS, GORDON (b. 1914)
AUSTRALIAN FURNITURE designer. Australia's best-known modern industrial designer, Andrews has worked in a number of areas (in 1965, he designed Australia's new currency), but he is renowned for his furniture. He was an early proponent of the INTERNATIONAL STYLE introduced into the country by his close associate, Marion Hall BEST. His "Rondo" chair is probably Australia's most familiar piece of modern furniture—an upholstered, sinuously molded single-piece seat and back atop a metal leg and foot consisting of a spindle rising from an asterisk-like, six-stem base.

ANEGRÉ
Another name for ANINGERIA.

ANGEL BED
Eighteenth-century English name for French LIT À LA DUCHESSE or similar BED, especially one whose CANOPY hung from a TESTER that was attached by chains to the ceiling.

ANGLO-JAPANESE STYLE
See GODWIN, William.

ANIMAL'S-BALL-AND-CLAW FOOT
See under FOOT.

ANINGERIA (also *anegré*)
African HARDWOOD, pinkish yellow in color and used for veneer. A plain wood of uniform texture, aningeria is frequently printed with simulations of other, more expensive woods. It is sometimes erroneously called Tanzanian walnut.

ANTEFIX
Upright ornament placed at the corners of the rooflike tops of case furniture in 18th- and 19th-century NEOCLASSICAL STYLE furniture. The antefix commonly took the form of an ANTHEMION, an animal head or some other classical motif. Its use derived from its appearance on ancient sarcophagi, where it took the form of a specialized roof tile, designed to conceal the joints between rows of tiles.

ANTHEMION
Decorative motif consisting of a radiating cluster of stylized honeysuckle flowers and leaves. Originating in ancient Greek art and architecture, the *anthemion* was popular in European NEOCLASSICAL STYLE furniture of the late 18th and early 19th centuries.

ANTHEMION-BACK CHAIR
Eighteenth-century NEOCLASSICAL STYLE chair in which the back is composed of a large, openwork ANTHEMION motif.

ANTIQUE, LE STYLE
See STYLE ANTIQUE, LE.

ANTIQUES
Pieces of furniture that have special value because of their age. The question of what is or is not an antique has been answered in several ways. When antiques first began to be collected extensively, in the second half of the 19th century, the furniture of the 18th century was particularly highly regarded, and it was generally opined that 19th-century furniture—beginning with work in such late NEOCLASSICAL STYLES as the EMPIRE, REGENCY and DIRECTORY STYLES—was debased, compared to its illustrious predecessors and thus of little value or interest to the collector. This view was widely accepted until well into the 20th century and was reinforced by a 1930 U.S. government rul-

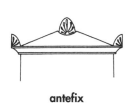

antefix

anthemion

anthemion-back chair

ing that stated that only objects made more than 100 years earlier could be regarded as antiques for customs purposes and admitted into the country duty-free. This regulation was thus generally construed to indicate that an antique was an item made before 1830. A 1966 ruling reiterated this formula, specifying an age of 100 years prior to date of entry.

Such a definition, though, has the disadvantage of referring to nothing but chronology. It may thus exclude work that either is more highly valued as artistry or craft or is essentially no different from that which it includes. Therefore, an alternate approach is widely taken, at least tacitly: an antique may be seen as a piece of furniture that was made in a historical style—one that no longer has currency—and was made while that style was in fashion. It reflects the social values and tastes of a different epoch from our own, for a changing world has left it behind. Age is not abandoned as a criterion, which would degrade the term *antique* to a simple token of valued status, but it becomes a matter of relation to current taste rather than of years.

Some antique furniture was occasionally included in the great collections of art, curiosities and "objects of virtue" assembled by wealthy connoisseurs of the 17th and 18th centuries, but the systematic collecting of furniture for its own sake began only in the mid-19th century. Like the REVIVAL STYLES in newly made furniture of that period, the craze for antiques reflected a search for cultural values by the new middle classes that had risen to wealth and power following the collapse of the privileged *anciens régimes* of Europe. Ransacking style history, these new elites appropriated the fine objects of the past, as if to assert their equal claim to perquisites of status to which they would once have been denied access.

In its early development, antique collecting was associated with the nationalistic fervor of the times. Thus, British collectors focused on 18th-century British work, especially ROCOCO FURNITURE and ADAM STYLE pieces. In the United States, similarly, furniture of the FEDERAL PERIOD and earlier, known collectively as "Colonial furniture," was valued, and in France there was a vogue for the LOUIS XIV, XV and XVI STYLES. In Germany, where French fashions had dominated in the 18th century, RENAISSANCE FURNITURE was resurrected, and relatively recent BIEDERMEIER STYLE furniture was collected as

well. With the growing interest in antiques, a parallel phenomenon arose—that of REPRODUCTION FURNITURE, which began as an effort to provide replicas of specific pieces and quickly became favored by buyers who could not afford the real thing. By 1884 an American magazine could report, "the making of antiques has become a modern industry."

By the 1920s collectors were both more numerous and more knowledgeable, thanks to the educational influence of museums and specialized publications. This trend continues; public and private collections have amassed, with increasing comprehensiveness, the furniture of all historical epochs, including those of non-Western cultures. The great commercial success of both antiques and reproduction furniture testifies further to the prevalent awareness of antique furniture and its cultural values among today's educated public.

ANTIQUE VERT
Decorative device, paint on wood simulating the dark green patina of ancient bronze. *Antique vert* is darker than VERDIGRIS, which it resembles.

ANTWERP CABINET
See KUNSTSCHRANK.

APA
Another name for AFZELIA.

APPLIQUÉ
Decorative detail or ornament that is shaped or worked and then attached to a surface of a piece of furniture.

APRON (also *skirt*)
Horizontal support placed below the SEAT RAIL of a chair, a tabletop or the bottom framing of a piece of case furniture. Often the apron is carved in a decorative profile, pierced or otherwise ornamented.

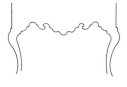

apron

ARABESQUE
Flat, ornamental pattern used to decorate panels or other flat surfaces. The arabesque is composed of flowing lines representing

arabesque pattern

foliage, abstract scrolls, geometrical forms and so on, often enclosing depictions of human or animal figures. Deriving from Spanish-Islamic decoration, and related to MUDÉJAR STYLE work of the Middle Ages, the arabesque spread throughout Europe in the 16th century, especially to the Netherlands and Italy, where the Spanish ruled.

ARBUS, ANDRÉ (1903–69)

French furniture designer of the 1930s. After the vogue for ART DECO ended, he carried on that style in the tradition of Émile-Jacques RUHLMANN. Arbus produced furniture characterized by fine materials and craftsmanship and by decoration in a neoclassical mode.

ARCADING

Decorative motif first appearing in MEDIEVAL FURNITURE. Derived from the classical architectural arcade, arcading is a horizontal element composed of a series of arches on COLUMNS or PILASTERS. It may be painted, inlaid, or carved, in RELIEF or PIERCED.

ARCH

Architectural device; curved or pointed structure forming the upper edge of an opening, as in a doorway or window, or joining two supports. In furniture the arch has been used mostly in ornamentation. It has been featured in all of the European furniture styles that have referred to architecture, from ROMANESQUE FURNITURE, through RENAISSANCE FURNITURE, to the 19th century's REVIVAL STYLES and the contemporary POST-MODERN FURNITURE.

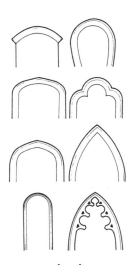

1 segmental arch
2 horseshoe arch
3 depressed or basket arch
4 round trefoil arch
5 four-centered Tudor arch
6 equilateral arch
7 round arch
8 lancet arch

ARCHED STRETCHER
See under STRETCHER.

ARCHITRAVE

Lowest horizontal element on an ENTABLATURE, which also includes FRIEZE and CORNICE. The architrave rests directly on the CAPITAL of each supporting COLUMN and is usually undecorated. Entablatures, including architraves, are often used to decorate case furniture, especially in variants of the European NEOCLASSICAL STYLE of furniture.

ARCHIZOOM

Italian architecture and industrial design firm, in operation from 1966 to 1974. Founded in Florence by six architects and designers, including Paolo DEGANELLO, Archizoom produced designs for buildings, interiors, exhibitions, furniture and other items. Reflecting the vehement social protests of the period, Archizoom's furniture designs were deliberately bizarre, in defiance of a conventional world that was seen as meaningless. However, Archizoom's evident concern with function and the intelligent use of material reveals the group's development from the INTERNATIONAL STYLE and the principles of FUNCTIONALISM. One of its best known designs (1970) was a chair consisting of a rubber sheet topped by a small upholstered pillow, hung from stretchers joining two triangular frames of metal chrome. It is called the "Mies" chair, in ironic homage to Ludwig MIES VAN DER ROHE, the famed radical designer of simplified furniture. This chair and other extraordinary pieces were offered as examples of "counterdesign"; yet they stand in the mainstream of the freewheeling design world of modern Italy.

ARK

In MEDIEVAL FURNITURE another term for COFFER; CHEST intended for transport and thus equipped with a domed or hipped lid designed to facilitate runoff of rain. The term is still used to describe chests with a detachable, hipped lid.

ARM BOW
See under WINDSOR CHAIR.

ARM STUMP

Support for chair arm; vertical member rising from the SEAT RAIL to the forward termination of the arm or to a point just behind it.

ARMADIO

Italian word for *cupboard;* also, 16th-century Italian RENAISSANCE FURNITURE form. Originally a CASSONE with doors instead of a lid, the armadio became a small, two-tiered piece similar to the later English PRESS CUPBOARD. It had massive architectural decoration, generally including pilasters supporting monumental cornices.

ARMOIRE

French WARDROBE form. The armoire is a large, upright CUPBOARD, either shelved or unshelved, sometimes having drawers or pigeonholes, that is completely enclosed by a door or doors across the front. Massive in size and proportions and generally decorated with architectural motifs, the armoire differs from other wardrobe forms in that it has no drawers below the cupboard and often no feet. The earliest armoires—wide, stolid variants of the medieval PRESS—were painted inside and out, but by the end of the 14th century, the form was elaborately carved. During the Renaissance the piece became lighter, taller and narrower. It has retained this shape, though its ornamentation has changed through subsequent centuries. Usually, armoires are still made so that they can be dismantled for moving.

ARMOIRE À DEUX CORPS

French RENAISSANCE FURNITURE form; two-tiered CUPBOARD. The upper section was recessed from the front of the lower section and not as wide from side to side. Each section had two paneled doors that were generally decorated with copiously carved relief. The *armoire à deux corps* was architectural in appearance, intended to resemble the classical buildings that had such influence on all of the Renaissance arts. Each element bore a cornice supported by pilasters or columns, commonly caryatids, and the top was often crowned with a pediment.

ARNDT, ALFRED (1896–1976)

German furniture maker and teacher, who headed the BAUHAUS workshop until 1931. He stressed the goal of creating inexpensive, functional furniture that could be mass-produced and assembled from standardized parts (*see* FUNCTIONALISM). In addition, he furthered the work of Walter GROPIUS in developing UNIT FURNITURE.

ARROW-BACK WINDSOR CHAIR

See under WINDSOR CHAIR.

ART CABINET

VICTORIAN PERIOD furniture form; CABINET enclosed with glass and composed of numerous open shelves or small compartments, sometimes with mirrored walls. Intended to display ornamental objects, the art cabinet satisfied a taste of the times that called for decoration with a multitude of small things to look at. An art cabinet might be supported by legs or a stand, or it could be hung on a wall.

ART DECO

French decorative style of the 1920s; known in its own day as "Art Moderne" or "Jazz Moderne." It is characterized by the restrained, stylized use of ornament, simple furniture shapes, an emphasis on fine craftsmaship and an opulent use of precious and exotic materials. The term was coined in the 1960s and derives from the title of the 1925 Paris World's Fair, *L'Exposition Internationale des Arts Décoratifs et Industriels Modernes.* Interiors and rooms in the Art Deco style were prominent at the fair. Art Deco began before the First World War as a reaction against the stylistic excesses of its predecessor, ART NOUVEAU. A number of the creators of the new style had practiced in the old (*see* Maurice DUFRÊNE; Paul FOLLOT; Paul IRIBE; A.-A. RATEAU). Designers within the Art Nouveau movement helped develop a taste for the simple forms and classical lines that characterize Art Deco. The WIENER WERKSTÄTTE and the DEUTSCHER WERKBUND, German Art Nouveau design groups, devised plain, geometrical forms that influenced French designers. Frank Lloyd WRIGHT's designs, introduced around 1910, also contributed to the desire for clean, classical lines.

The antiornamental design creed developed by some of these predecessors, notably Adolf LOOS, did not influence the development of Art Deco, though it led to such other design movements of the 1920s as DE STIJL, FUNCTIONALISM and the esthetics of the BAUHAUS. Other influences operated on Art Deco development. Diaghilev's Ballet Russe, which opened in 1910, blazoned color and exoticism, as did a growing vogue for African art throughout the period, and the effervescent postwar society of the 1920s added to the new taste for drama and color. Art Deco designers did not adopt austerity as a goal. On the contrary, the style emphasized extrava-

armoire

armoire-à-deux-corps

Art Deco bedside table by Ruhlmann

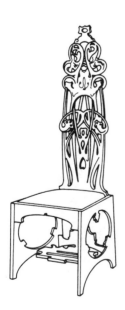

Art Nouveau chair

gance, in the form of fine handicraft, expensive materials and designs that showed off these elements. While decorative ornaments were restrained and classical in form—featuring modest geometrical border patterns and framed floral motifs—they were brandished in complicated inlays of precious materials set in contrasting veneers of equally rare and expensive woods. The high degree of craftsmanship involved is especially well demonstrated in the work of Émile-Jacques RUHLMANN. Generally regarded as the leading exemplar of the Art Deco style, he is often equated with the great *ébénistes* of the 18th century.

Ruhlmann and others, conscious of their French design heritage, often modified traditional forms in their work and employed variations of 18th- and 19th-century neoclassical decorative motifs. This conservative group of Art Deco designers—including, among others, Ruhlmann, Follot, Jules LELOU and the partnerships known as DOMINIQUE and SÜE ET MARE—may be compared with another group thought of as the avant-garde, who devised novel forms and whose work showed the influences of African art and Cubism. Among these designers are Pierre LEGRAIN, J.-M. FRANK, Eileen GRAY and Marcel COARD.

Both groups indulged in the most prominent characteristic of Art Deco: the employment of expensive and exotic materials. Lacquer, rare woods of all colors and ivory were commonplace, with gold leaf, tortoiseshell, snakeskin, shagreen, vellum and tooled leather frequently used. Clément ROUSSEAU was particularly noted for his opulent pieces, and some designers were acclaimed for their specialities: André GROULT for shagreen, Clément MÈRE for elaborately tooled leather, Eileen GRAY and Jean DUNAND for lacquer. Wrought iron was a popular material, and there were several Art Deco metalworkers, such as Edgar BRANDT, Paul KISS and Raymond SUBES, who made furniture as well.

The financial collapse of 1929 and the rise of a modern functionalist esthetic—manifested in France as the INTERNATIONAL STYLE—spelled the end of Art Deco. Some designers—notably Gray, Frank and Francis JOURDAIN—effected a transition, but most did not. The pronounced extravagance of Art Deco left it an anachronism.

ART FURNITURE MOVEMENT
British furniture design movement of the 1860s and 1870s. The term *art furniture* was coined by Charles Locke EASTLAKE in his *Hints on Household Taste* (1868). The Art Furniture Company was established at about the same time by William GODWIN to manufacture furniture in the Anglo-Japanese style. Eastlake and Godwin, the two most important figures of the movement, advocated furniture designed with simple, rectilinear forms, sparingly decorated with low-relief ornamentation. Though both design movements reacted against the florid revivalist furniture of the day, the Art Furniture movement differed from the ARTS AND CRAFTS MOVEMENT in not rejecting the industrialization of furniture manufacture. Rather, Eastlake and Godwin wanted to see fine design incorporated into the unavoidable process of mass production. Art Furniture design, especially through the works of Godwin and Eastlake, has had a deep influence on modern design. Other designers associated with the Art Furniture movement are T. E. COLLCUTT, Bruce TALBERT, Christopher DRESSER and Thomas JECKYLL.

ART MODERNE
See ART DECO.

ART NOUVEAU
European design reform movement of the 1890s and early 20th century and the elaborate curvilinear design style that developed from it. The term comes from the name of a Paris shop established in 1895, but the Art Nouveau movement was not simply a Parisian trend. Rather, it was the collective European phenomenon of several movements, each aiming to develop a new style of design that would not be derivative of historical styles and that would lend itself to the creation of living spaces unified in theme. Consequently, abstract and organic motifs were the basic ingredients of the new style, but separate influences and developments produced radically different results in various European countries.

The earlier British reform movements (*see* ARTS AND CRAFTS MOVEMENT; ART FURNITURE MOVEMENT), which emphasized honest design and craftsmanship, had a strong impact on the development of Art Nouveau.

Another widely felt influence was that of Japanese design (*see* JAPONISME): light, open and asymmetrical. Other influences were more local in impact and contributed to the considerable variety within the movement. For instance 18th-century ROCOCO FURNITURE traditions influenced the designers of Nancy, France (*see* School of NANCY). Charles Rennie MACKINTOSH and his circle (*see* GLASGOW SCHOOL) drew on ancient Celtic calligraphy. In Norway the Dragonesque stylists (*see* Gerhard MUNTHE) employed Viking motifs. Dutch designers may have been influenced by the 17th-century metalworking tradition known as the auricular style.

In France two centers, Paris and Nancy, generated the decorative wing of Art Nouveau, a style dominated by imagery drawn from nature, open, curvilinear schemes and a characteristic use of extreme asymmetry. In Paris, centered around the shop of Samuel BING (*L'Art Nouveau*), were such furniture designers as Edward COLONNA, Georges DE FEURE and Eugene GAILLARD. In the small city of Nancy, designers led by Émile GALLÉ, including Louis MAJORELLE and Eugene VALLIN, employed a distinctive marquetry, and their use of decorative motifs from nature is most pronounced, with birds, flowers, insects, fish, even landscapes represented.

Art Nouveau found its greatest expression in Belgium. Belgian architects and furniture designers of particular note in the 1890s were Victor HORTA, Gustave SERRURIER-BOVY and Henri VAN DE VELDE. Their style was ornate and curvilinear, with organic motifs such as plants and insects; thus, it was closely related to the French style. The Belgian tendency toward abstraction allied their Art Nouveau style with that of Germany and Austria as well. Belgian designers also developed the WHIPLASH CURVE, the motif most associated with Art Nouveau.

Germany and Austria yielded an Art Nouveau style different from that of France. Under the influence of the Scottish Glasgow School and the British Arts and Crafts designer C. R. ASHBEE, Vienna and Munich—the principal centers—developed a version of Art Nouveau known as *Jugendstil* (after the magazine *Der Jugend*, first published in 1896). *Jugendstil* and French styles of Art Nouveau are similar in their emphasis on thematic unity of decoration and use of organic and abstract motifs to attain unity, but German and Austrian furniture looks very different from French pieces. *Jugendstil* furniture, in general, has simple, less curvilinear forms, which are designed for mass production, and has abstract, geometrical motifs more often than organic motifs. In Austria and Germany, Art Nouveau designers often formed communal groups, such as the WIENER WERKSTÄTTE, the DEUTSCHE WERKSTÄTTEN movement and the DEUTSCHER WERKBUND. In Vienna the most important Art Nouveau designers were Josef HOFFMANN and Kolo MOSER. In Munich the leaders were Richard RIEMERSCHMID, August ENDELL, Hermann OBRIST, Joseph Maria OLBRICH and Peter BEHRENS.

The British Arts and Crafts movement sparked the development in Glasgow, Scotland, of a design style that was very influential in the Art Nouveau movement. Led by Charles Rennie Mackintosh, the Glasgow School developed a decorative geometry that, through publications and exhibitions, had a marked impact on *Jugendstil* furniture.

In Holland, where Art Nouveau was known as *Nieuwe Kunst*, furniture design was influenced by the functional mode of *Jugendstil* as well as by the more effervescent style of French and Belgian work. The principal designers were Gerrit DIJSSELHOF, Theodore NIEUWENHUIS and C. A. LION-CACHET.

Art Nouveau was called *Stile Liberty* in Italy, after Liberty & Co., the British store that sold many products in the new style (*see* Arthur Lazenby LIBERTY). *Stile Liberty*, however, never gained much popularity in Italy, where a fondness for historical styles predominated. The leading Italian *Stile Liberty* designers were Pietro FENOGLIO, Giacomo COMETTI, Eugenio QUARTI and Carlo BUGATTI.

In Spain, Art Nouveau was known as *Moderno*. The only important practitioner there was the architect Antonio GAUDI, who designed furniture for his own buildings.

In Britain and the United States, Art Nouveau sparked little interest, though a few designers should be noted: E. G. PUNNETT of England and the Glaswegian George WALTON designed furniture for Liberty's; in America, Charles ROHLFS designed furniture that was popular in Europe.

The Art Nouveau movement influenced furniture design by presenting novel ideas at a time when factory production on a large scale was just about to begin. The movement peaked in popularity shortly after 1900, and its furniture style subsequently became relatively simpler, more functional and less ornamental as it yielded to the modern emphasis on utility.

ARTICULATE

To attach by means of a joint; to join two or more separate elements of a piece of furniture.

**Arts and Crafts chair
by Voysey**

ARTS AND CRAFTS MOVEMENT

Reform style in British applied arts of the late Victorian period. Based on the ideas of John RUSKIN and William MORRIS, the Arts and Crafts movement was a response to what Morris termed a "state of complete degradation" in the decorative arts. In Morris's view this state of affairs was produced by the Industrial Revolution and manifested in the shoddy objects of everyday use, put forth in debased revivalist styles by mass manufacturers. Morris proposed that artists return to preindustrial modes of production; that is, to handicraft, in communal organizations similar to the medieval craft guilds. In this manner the dissociation of artist and object, of art and use, would be overcome and the virtues of the preindustrial age reinstated. As ideology—and they were intended as ideology—these notions have been considered naive or retrogressive; yet by emphasizing craftsmanship and clean, simple design, and by offering strenuous opposition to revivalism, the Arts and Crafts movement advanced the decorative arts of the day in a revolutionary manner. Most subsequent furniture design, up to and beyond the First World War, bears its imprint.

In terms of style, the Arts and Crafts movement emphasized simple, utilitarian design; a reduction of excessive decoration; the use of unpretentious, traditional materials; and the employment of "honest" craftsmanship. Honest craftsmanship implied exposed joinery and the adaptation of rustic, utilitarian designs. In practice, the designers associated with the movement generally employed elements and motifs taken from GOTHIC FURNITURE of the Middle Ages, the "golden age" of crafts. Of course, individual ideology varied tremendously within the movement. Probably the purest Arts and Crafts furniture was made in the United States, where MISSION FURNITURE exemplifies its ideals. Amid the stylistic turmoil of late Victorian England, austerity of design as an ideal was often compromised by followers of the movement, and rich materials were not at all uncommon. Moreover, with time some designers came to accept the necessity of collaboration with the machine, while many abandoned the Gothic character of the style for the lighter QUEEN ANNE REVIVAL STYLE or the nascent ART NOUVEAU, or both.

The Arts and Crafts movement may be said to have begun when Morris and others started a manufacturing company to produce fine furniture and other household objects (1861). Eventually, several craftsmen's organizations were founded as manufacturing workshops, in pursuit of Morris's vision of the medieval guild. Among them were A. H. MACKMURDO's Century Guild (1882) and the Guild of Handicraft, established by C. R. ASHBEE (1888). These groups joined to form the Arts and Crafts Exhibition Society in 1888, to provide a venue for exhibitions and the exchange of ideas. The COTSWOLD SCHOOL and others migrated from London to rural areas to practice some version of Morris's romantic socialism and produced fine crafted furniture.

The Arts and Crafts movement had many of the same ideals as the ART FURNITURE MOVEMENT. The two trends shared an aversion to mass-produced revivals of French and other furniture styles, and they both favored clean, light lines in functional designs. Also, both groups displayed a taste for the medieval, inspired by Ruskin's anti-industrial sentiments and by the NEO-GOTHIC STYLE initiated by A. W. N. PUGIN. This taste for the medieval may also have been furthered by the intense British nationalism of the period, which encouraged—in addition to empire on a new scale—a fond, nostalgic view of days gone by. Unlike the Arts and Crafts movement, however, the Art Furniture movement was directed toward INDUSTRIAL DESIGN, not the rejection of the machine.

The British Arts and Crafts movement was widely influential. Continental Art Nouveau owes its antirevivalist stance and its concern with fine craftsmanship to British designers Mackmurdo and M. H. BAILLIE SCOTT and also to the GLASGOW SCHOOL, a Scottish branch of the movement. SCANDINAVIAN MODERN furniture adopted much of the movement's ideas and styles, filtered through Dutch and German sources. In the United

States the Arts and Crafts principles, as realized in the Mission style, influenced such early 20th-century masters as GREENE & GREENE and Frank Lloyd WRIGHT. The whole modern movement, as exemplified in the BAUHAUS esthetic—with its rejection of revivalism; its emphasis on simplicity, honest construction and utility; and its interest in the relationship between craft and society—owes much to the initial introduction of these concerns by the Arts and Crafts movement.

Other artists and designers associated with the Arts and Crafts movement are Edward BURNE-JONES, Ernest GIMSON, William Holman HUNT, George JACK, C. F. A. VOYSEY, Philip WEBB and, in the United States, John La Farge, Arthur and Lucia MATHEWS and H. H. RICHARDSON.

ASH

Pale HARDWOOD found throughout the Northern Hemisphere; white to pale yellow in color, sometimes with brown or black markings. A strong, flexible wood, ash has long been used to make inexpensive country furniture. Today it is mostly used for framing, especially as BENTWOOD.

ASH, GILBERT (1717–85)

American furniture maker; early exponent of NEW YORK CHIPPENDALE FURNITURE. A specialist in chairs, Ash may have been the principal formulator of a complicated pierced splat pattern, centered on a diamond shape, that was widely used in New York chairs of the day. His son Thomas ASH also made chairs.

ASH, THOMAS (active after 1774, d. 1815)

New York chair maker. The son of Gilbert ASH, Thomas Ash was an established maker of WINDSOR CHAIRS before the American Revolution. In the FEDERAL PERIOD, he became a specialist in the production of "FANCY" FURNITURE chairs based on Thomas SHERATON's designs.

ASHBEE, CHARLES ROBERT (1863–1942)

British architect and designer; major figure of the ARTS AND CRAFTS MOVEMENT. Trained as an architect and in practice primarily a silversmith, Ashbee designed furniture in the simple Arts and Crafts style but tended to use more decoration on his work than did other designers of the movement. He employed such devices as banding in contrasting woods, paint and gilt decoration, and inset enamel plaques. His greatest importance is his role as an organizer and proselytizer of the Arts and Crafts movement. Under William MORRIS's influence, Ashbee founded the Guild of Handicraft (1888), modeled on the medieval craft guild and dedicated to the restoration of handicraft techniques and simple rustic designs. He carried Morris's utopian, antiindustrial notions further and founded the School of Arts and Crafts (1904), a rural establishment that emphasized both handicraft and husbandry.

ASPLUND, GUNNAR (1885–1940)

Swedish architect and designer; an early proponent of SCANDINAVIAN MODERN furniture. One of the most important Swedish architects of the first half of the 20th century. Asplund, with Alvar AALTO, helped establish the popularity of FUNCTIONALISM in Sweden. His furniture elegantly combines modern simplicity and clarity with very little decoration and an emphasis on fine craftsmanship. In the 1920s, he was a pathbreaking modernist, in both architecture and furniture design; since about 1930, his designs have incorporated subtle evocations of traditional styles.

ASTRAGAL (1)

See ASTRAGAL MOLDING, *under* MOLDING.

ASTRAGAL (2)

Another name for GLAZING BAR, especially of wood. Although strictly incorrect (*see* ASTRAGAL MOLDING, *under* MOLDING), this usage is common.

ATHÉNIENNE

Late 18th-century French WASHSTAND, composed of a lidded basin, usually in the shape of an URN, atop a classically inspired tripod support. It was also used as a JARDINIÈRE, a CANDLESTAND or even an incense burner. The Athénienne was invented in 1793 by J. H. Eberts and was popular into the early 19th

Gunnar Asplund chair

century, during the NEOCLASSICAL STYLE vogue for furniture derived from classical archeology.

ATLAS (pl. *atlantes*)

Rare variant of a CARYATID, representing a male figure instead of a female one.

AUGER FLAME

Term for corkscrew-shaped FINIAL often placed on American Chippendale case furniture (*see* AMERICAN CHIPPENDALE FURNITURE). The name derives from the ornament's resemblance to the carpenter's auger, a large drill bit.

AUGSBURG CABINET

See KUNSTSCHRANK.

auger flame finial

AULENTI, GAE (b. 1927)

Contemporary Italian architect and furniture designer. Best known for her furniture and other objects, especially lamps, Aulenti has also designed buildings, taught architecture and design, and worked as an urban planner and a theatrical designer. She first gained notoriety for her advocacy of the neo-Liberty style of the late 1950s, a revival style based on ART NOUVEAU, which was a harbinger of the current post-modernist rebellion against FUNCTIONALISM and the BAUHAUS designers (*see* POST-MODERN FURNITURE). Aulenti has continued to take strong, controversial positions on design issues, and some of her designs reflect the recent Italian tendency toward iconoclasm. She made occasional use of the INTERNATIONAL STYLE's mannered descendent, high-tech, or Industrial style (*see* HIGH-TECH STYLE). Generally, however, her furniture has been a modest variant of mainstream modern design. It features smooth-lined chromium or stainless-steel frames that support glass tabletops or leather- or fabric-upholstered seating. Aulenti designs for Knoll and other manufacturers (*see* Florence Schust KNOLL).

AUMBRY (also *ambry*)

Medieval term with three related meanings: a wall niche enclosed by doors; a large, free-

standing furniture storage form with doors (such as the PRESS); and a small compartment with doors, sometimes built into the open medieval cupboard. This last element preceeded the later COURT CUPBOARD (2), whose compartment is also called an aumbry. The term *aumbry,* meaning "storage furniture," was replaced first by the term *press* and, in the 17th century, by *cupboard* in the modern sense.

AURICULAR STYLE

Late version of MANNERIST STYLE ornamentation developed in 17th-century Holland and Germany. Originally devised by the Dutch silversmith Paulus Van Vianen (c. 1568–1613), auricular style decoration was stimulated in part by the infant science of anatomy. It emphasized strange, curving forms resembling the interior of the human ear (hence, the name of the style and its synonym, "lobate style") or other parts of the body; the German term for the style, *Knorpelwerk,* means "cartilage work." These and other such exotic motifs as grinning masks, sea monsters and erotic figures merged with each other in sinuously complex arrays of fantastic imagery. The best-known furniture designer in the auricular style was the German Friedrich UNTEUTSCH, whose influence lasted throughout the 17th century.

AUSTRALIAN BLACKWOOD

HARDWOOD grown mostly on plantations in Tasmania and South Africa and used as a decorative veneer. It is a lustrous golden brown with dark brown markings.

AUSTRALIAN FURNITURE

The furniture of Australia; especially that of the second half of the 20th century. Soon after Australia's settlement by the British in the last years of the 18th century, local furniture making began, but the products were simply imitations of English furniture. At the end of the 19th century, the influence of such modern European styles as ART NOUVEAU reached the country, and by the mid-20th century, Australian designers such as Gordon ANDREWS, George KORODY, and Clement MEADMORE were combining aspects of the INTERNATIONAL STYLE and SCANDINAVIAN MODERN furniture. Entrepreneur Marion Hall BEST had much to do with the introduction of these styles to Australia.

In the last decades of the 20th century, Australian designers and makers have been remarkably syncretic, making furniture in distinctive styles combining the features of several of the modern trends common to European and American work. For instance, the furniture of Helmut LUECKENHAUSEN offers blended strains of avant-garde POP ART FURNITURE and the work of "Memphis" style followers of Ettore SOTTSASS. On the other hand, continuing respect for the clean lines of the International Style and Scandinavian modern furniture colors the work of such different designers as David EMERY, Marc NEWSON, and Leslie John WRIGHT. Craig WATSON produces architecturally influenced POST-MODERN furniture, and the HANDICRAFT REVIVAL of the 1970s, especially as presented by John MAKEPEACE, informs the work of George INGHAM and Leon SADUBIN.

AUSTRALIAN SILKY OAK
See SILKY OAK.

AUVERA, JOHANN WOLFGANG VAN DER (1708–56)
German sculptor and designer of ROCOCO FURNITURE and interiors. Auvera, who was noted for console tables with extremely elaborate carving, also made large figural sculptures.

bachelor's chest

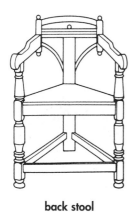

back stool

BA XIAN ZHUO (PA HSIEN CHO) (also *table of the Eight Immortals*)
CHINESE FURNITURE form of Ming (1368–1644) and Qing (1644–1911) dynasties; square table of normal height, intended to be placed in front of taller, narrow TANG HUA AN. Traditionally, art objects stood on the two tables, and a prized painting hung on the wall above. This arrangement was a basic component of a respectable Chinese home. A smaller square table similar to the *ba xian zhuo* was sometimes called a *table of the Six Immortals*, or LIU XIAN ZHUO. Both were named for figures in Taoist mythology.

BACCETTI, ANDREA (active 1860s and 1870s)
Italian maker of RENAISSANCE REVIVAL STYLE furniture. Bacetti, a Florentine, made particularly ornamental, heavy furniture with copious references to the styles of 15th- and 16th-century Italy as well as some pieces in a modest version of the MOORISH STYLE.

BACHELOR'S CHEST
Small 18th-century CHEST OF DRAWERS. Its top had a hinged LEAF that folded closed. When open and supported on slides or LOP-ERS, it doubled the area of the top and provided a writing surface. Appearing early in the 18th century, this chest was popular for about a hundred years. In modern usage, the term sometimes refers to any small chest of drawers.

BACK BOW
See BOW-BACK WINDSOR CHAIR, *under* WINDSOR CHAIR.

BACK POST
Another name for chair's STILE.

BACK SPLAT
See SPLAT.

BACK STAY
Another name for CROSS RAIL.

BACK STOOL
MEDIEVAL FURNITURE form; three-legged stool with one leg extending upward to constitute a crude back and generally bearing a crosspiece at shoulder level. The back stool usually had a triangular seat. Later, the term was also used to refer to a simple four-legged chair without arms, such as the FARTHINGALE CHAIR, or stools with backs, which were common in English TUDOR FURNITURE and JACOBEAN FURNITURE and AMERICAN JACOBEAN furniture. The Italian SGABELLO was another example of a back stool in this later sense. The term passed out of use in the early 18th century.

BADLAM, STEPHEN (1751–1815)
American FEDERAL PERIOD cabinetmaker of Dorchester, Massachusetts. Badlam became a cabinetmaker after the American Revolution, in which he was an officer and an adviser to Alexander Hamilton. He made NEOCLASSICAL STYLE furniture, following British pattern books and examples.

BAHUT
In MEDIEVAL FURNITURE, French term referring either to the covering of a COFFER or

ARK, to protect against the weather, or to a small box, usually with a rounded top, attached to the top of a larger chest and used for carrying articles that might be wanted during a journey. Later, the term came to denote any chest with a rounded top.

BAI YAN (PAI YEN)

CHINESE FURNITURE form of Ming (1368–1644) and Qing (1644–1911) dynasties; tall pharmacist's cupboard with many small drawers, which are referred to in its name, literally meaning "a hundred eyes." Intended to store pharmaceutical ingredients, mostly herbs, each drawer was subdivided into smaller compartments. The whole array stood behind two large doors that met at a central upright, where they were secured by fittings of brass or paktong. Below this main compartment were two or three larger drawers placed side by side.

BAIL HANDLE

Type of furniture HARDWARE. It is a drawer handle composed of a cast or molded metal loop, usually of brass, hung between two small knobs, each of which is the head of a bolt that pierces the drawer front and fastens the handle to the surface. In a century of development, the bail handle took three characteristic forms. It first appeared in about 1690, when it incorporated a metal plate behind it to protect the veneer from the swinging loop, or bail. This plate, sometimes called an ESCUTCHEON, was usually shaped as an elaborate Baroque CARTOUCHE. As the rococo style developed by the mid-18th century (*see* ROCOCO FURNITURE), these plates became even more complex and were frequently pierced. Then, in midcentury, the *swanneck handle* arose. Instead of a plate, this variant simply had a small metal rosette behind each bolt head. After about 1780 NEOCLASSICAL STYLE bail handles again used back plates. Made of brass, they were oval, round or almond-shaped and were stamped with ornaments, usually moldings around the edge. In variants of one or another of these styles, the bail handle has remained in use until the present. A RING PULL is also sometimes classed as a bail handle.

BAILLIE SCOTT, MACKAY HUGH (1865–1945)

British architect and furniture designer; a major figure in the ARTS AND CRAFTS MOVEMENT. Principally a domestic architect, Baillie Scott designed furniture in the interest of creating unified interiors. Both his design goal and his rustic style of furniture design reflect the influences of A. H. MACKMURDO and C. F. A. VOYSEY. Baillie Scott's early work shows his tendency to design sparsely decorated oak pieces, though he later came to use bold color and geometrical and botanical motifs. His best-known work is the large body of furniture he designed in 1898 for the Grand Duke of Hesse's palace in Darmstadt. Through this work and other commissions, his Arts and Crafts furniture was widely influential in Germany, while his decorative work had an impact on the youthful ART NOUVEAU style. Similarly, through widespread commissions, Baillie Scott's work was known in Scandinavia and the United States.

BALL FOOT
See under FOOT.

BALL TURNING
See under TURNERY.

BALL-AND-CLAW BRACKET FOOT
See under FOOT.

BALL-AND-CLAW FOOT
See under FOOT.

BALL-AND-RING TURNING
See under TURNERY.

BALLOON-BACK CHAIR

Nineteenth-century ROCOCO REVIVAL STYLE furniture form; SIDE CHAIR with a round, open-frame back composed of curved elements—namely, CREST RAIL, STILES and, usually, CROSS RAIL. This framework resembled in outline an aeronautical balloon. Based on an oval-backed LOUIS XV–STYLE side chair of the 18th century, the balloon-back chair did not usually have its predecessor's upholstered back panel and was thus lighter, with more obvious

bail handle

balloon-back chair

flowing lines. It developed in Britain in about 1850 and was very popular, especially there and in America, through the rest of the century.

BALLOON-BACK WINDSOR CHAIR
See under WINDSOR CHAIR.

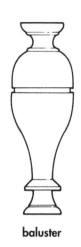

baluster

BALUSTER
Turned or carved upright post or pillar, commonly curved in outline, incorporating a vase or pear shape. It may appear in a chair back below the crest rail or in a column supporting a CORNICE on a cupboard. A group of balusters supporting a rail form a balustrade. The term *baluster* is also used for a stout turned member of any shape (*see* BALUSTER TURNING, *under* TURNERY). A split baluster may be used as an applied ornament. To make split balusters, a turned baluster is not actually cut in two. Rather, two pieces of wood are glued together temporarily and turned together on a lathe (*see* TURNERY). When separated, they are two split balusters.

BALUSTER TURNING
See under TURNERY.

BAMBOO
Construction material; hollow, woody stems of various large, mostly tropical, grasses, hard-walled and with ringed joints along their length. Although not very durable, bamboo has been used in furniture wherever these grasses are common. Elaborate thronelike chairs were made of the material in ancient INDIAN FURNITURE. In CHINESE FURNITURE bamboo work was traditionally intended for outdoor use, appearing chiefly in warm southern China. This furniture was produced using specially developed techniques of JOINERY. Bent pieces were sometimes formed by growing the plant in a prepared sheath. Colors of Chinese bamboo ranged from yellow to black; speckled or pied pieces were particularly prized. Bamboo furniture was highly valued, and wood was sometimes carved and painted to resemble it. In traditional JAPANESE FURNITURE, bamboo was only occasionally used, again for outdoor pieces.

In the West the 18th-century vogue for CHINOISERIE spurred the use of carved imitation bamboo in ROCOCO FURNITURE (*see*

banister-back chair

CHINESE CHIPPENDALE FURNITURE). In NEOCLASSICAL STYLE furniture, later in the same century, this *faux*-bamboo motif, sometimes painted to resemble the plant, remained popular—especially in informal pieces, when it might be painted a bright, nonbotanical, but cheerful color. The late 19th-century enthusiasm for JAPONISME generated another craze for bamboo furniture, especially in Britain and America. The real material was often imported by furniture makers—notably the Brooklyn, New York, firm NIMURA & SATO. Bamboo and wooden imitations are still employed for light, informal pieces of furniture, especially for outdoor use.

BAMBOO TURNING
See under TURNERY.

BANDING
Decorative device; narrow strip of inlaid wood whose color contrasts with that of the surrounding VENEER. In *straight banding*, the grain of the inlaid wood follows the strip, while in *cross banding*, the grain runs across the band. *Herringbone* or *feather banding* is composed of two strips of inlay whose grains lie at an acute angle to each other, creating a pattern that resembles a feather or the skeleton of a fish.

BANDY LEG
See under LEG.

BANISTER
Synonym for BALUSTER.

BANISTER-BACK CHAIR
Chair with a back composed of a row of turned uprights, or BALUSTERS, placed between the CREST RAIL and either the seat or a cross rail placed a few inches above the seat.

BANKER
Long, rectangular cushion used on a SETTLE.

BANTAM WORK
Eighteenth-century type of JAPANNING, using incised CHINOISERIE decoration in imitation

of COROMANDEL LACQUER. Bantam work is named for a village in Java where Britain had a trading post that shipped Coromandel lacquer.

BARBEDIENNE, FERDINAND (1810–92)

French foundryman and furniture maker; prominent during the Second Empire. Barbedienne designed and built furniture in a variety of the REVIVAL STYLES—in particular, the LOUIS XVI REVIVAL style—as well as producing pieces reflecting the Japanese taste (*see* JAPONISME) and excellent reproductions (*see* REPRODUCTION FURNITURE) of 18th-century pieces. He was also a leading bronze founder, casting works for Antoine-Louis Barye and other noted sculptors.

BARLEY-SUGAR TURNING

See under TURNERY.

BARNSLEY, ERNEST AND SIDNEY

See COTSWOLD SCHOOL.

BAROQUE FURNITURE

European furniture of 17th and early 18th centuries. Baroque furniture was originally based on the rich and bold ecclesiastical architecture of the Italian Counter-Reformation, which was intended to dramatize the continuing wealth and power of the Catholic Church in the face of its loss of Protestant northern Europe. Organized around the sweeping S-curve as both a compositional and an ornamental device, the baroque effected its drama with a purposeful unity of conception, replacing the assembled vignettes of the MANNERIST STYLE, in which a decorative scheme had been a series of individual motifs. Like baroque building façades, baroque furniture consisted of bold, solid compositions characterized by dynamic movement, and dramatic, sculptural elements were symmetrically arranged. An exaggerated fullness of scale and proportion lent grandeur to these pieces, as did a theatrical contrast of light and dark through use of deep moldings and carving and through striking juxtapositions of color. Rich materials such as marble, gilded bronze and rare woods contributed to the overall aura of magnificence. Although the resemblance of case pieces to buildings was no longer emphasized, as it had been in RENAISSANCE FURNITURE, the repertoire of motifs from classical architecture was retained. However, the baroque handled these devices in an unorthodox manner, incorporating pediments with curving and broken silhouettes, twisted columns with ornate capitals and profuse sculpture everywhere. Baroque furniture also used other ornamental motifs that had originated in classical times but only newly regained prominence—the CARTOUCHE and the CONSOLE, for example. The baroque sense of drama encouraged a fondness for the exotic, and new contacts with the Orient generated a vogue for CHINOISERIE that swept Europe during this period. Also, a high regard for Oriental LACQUER stimulated attempts to imitate it (*see* JAPANNING). New woods from the East and from America became popular, both as stimulating visual elements and as novelties.

Italian baroque furniture was especially figural in its decoration, and a number of noteworthy sculptors made furniture, including Filippo and Domenico PARODI in Genoa and Andrea BRUSTOLON in Venice, where this manner was most highly developed. At the beginning of the period, Italian influence was dominant everywhere in Europe, as it had been since the Renaissance, and the Italian baroque was thus adopted in other countries. In Spain, where both the Counter-Reformation and Italian design influence were felt early in the 17th century, exuberant CHURRIGUERESQUE FURNITURE replaced the austere DESORNAMENTADO STYLE in a country where Mannerism had never taken hold. Farther north, the baroque was beginning to displace Mannerism by mid-century. In France the state subsidized the development of the LOUIS XIV STYLE in the decorative arts. This opulent though less ornate variant of the baroque would hold sway over northern European design by the end of the century, especially after Louis's revocation of the Edict of Nantes in 1685 caused French Protestants, including many talented craftsmen, to flee to other countries. As a result of religious repression, therefore, French design began its reign over Western taste, which lasted for more than a century.

In the Low Countries the early Italian influence was transmuted into another variation, one that emphasized MARQUETRY and veneering (*see* VENEER), along with boldly profiled moldings and paneling. The Dutch in

baroque table

particular applied these techniques to the exotic new woods, especially ebony, that were arriving from their growing overseas trading empire. The furniture of the newly rich Dutch was suitably magnificent, with these decorative features being rendered in a striking array of rich and colorful materials by such specialists as Jan van MEKEREN and Dirk van RIJSWIJK. Dutch marquetry was also accompanied by carved ornamentation, especially later, when the influence of the Louis XIV style became strong.

German baroque furniture was severely rectilinear in form, varied only by heavy moldings and cornices on case pieces. However, the use of rare and expensive materials, such as ivory and precious stones, was avidly pursued, especially once the luxuriant French example was felt at the end of the century.

England did not receive the baroque impulse until the 1660s. RESTORATION FURNITURE—influenced by the taste of King Charles II, who had lived in France and Holland while in exile during the revolutionary Commonwealth—was the first to reflect the Continental style. Later, when Dutch magnate William of Orange became King William III of England, in 1689, he brought with him Dutch designers and craftsmen, most notably Daniel MAROT, who practiced a Dutch version of the Louis XIV style. A second phase of the English baroque, the WILLIAM AND MARY STYLE, thus arose. Subsequent British furniture was generally more independent of French influence than was work elsewhere, and in the QUEEN ANNE STYLE of the early 18th century, a truly national style was created. The final phase of British baroque furniture, the PALLADIAN STYLE, led by the architect and designer William KENT, turned for inspiration to the sculptural work of the 17th-century Italian baroque. This rich furniture sounded a florid coda to the evolution of the style in Britain. In the British Colonies of North America, however, baroque furniture, in the AMERICAN WILLIAM AND MARY and the AMERICAN QUEEN ANNE STYLES, appeared decades later than the British work that inspired it.

Meanwhile, in the first years of the 18th century, a new style began to develop in France—a lighter, less formal treatment of the baroque's curves and richness. This manner was to become known as the RÉGENCE STYLE—named after the regency that followed the death of Louis XIV in 1715. The Régence style marked the beginnings of ROCOCO FURNITURE, first in France and then elsewhere, in which freedom and playfulness in design replaced the grandeur and high drama of the baroque.

BARREL CHAIR
Modern chair with concave back extending below the seat, resembling a longitudinal segment of a barrel. Also, another name for the 18th-century GONDOLA CHAIR.

BARRY, CHARLES (1795–1860)
British architect and designer associated with the RENAISSANCE REVIVAL STYLE. Principally an architect, Barry also designed furniture for many of his domestic commissions. Not an innovative designer, he generally applied ornamentation of a vaguely Renaissance character to REGENCY STYLE furniture forms. He is best known as the architect of the British Houses of Parliament (for which A. W. N. PUGIN designed the furniture).

BARRY, JOSEPH B. (1757–1839)
AMERICAN EMPIRE STYLE cabinetmaker. Born in Dublin and trained in London, Joseph Barry had arrived in Philadelphia by the early 1790s. There he became a prominent maker of NEOCLASSICAL STYLE furniture, applying French-influenced ideas to the patterns of Thomas SHERATON. He also participated in the rise of the REVIVAL STYLES, using both ÉGYPTIENNERIE and NEO-GOTHIC STYLE motifs. His business prospered, and he opened a branch in Baltimore that became one of the noted practitioners of a Baltimore specialty—furniture with ÉGLOMISÉ panels.

BAS ARMOIRE
French EMPIRE STYLE furniture form; rectilinear COMMODE with two doors enclosing a stack of drawers.

BASILE, ERNESTO (1857–1932)
Sicilian architect and furniture designer associated with the ART NOUVEAU movement. Although Basile added Art Nouveau elements

to his decorative style, his furniture forms were essentially provincial and historically derivative in design. His design style—with its traditional, massive forms, elaborately carved detail and references to historical styles as far back as the Etruscans—can be seen as a forerunner of the pretentious, grandiose taste associated with Mussolini's reign in the 1920s and 1930s.

BASIN STAND
Eighteenth-century term for WASHSTAND.

BASKET CHAIR
WICKER chair, generally hooded, named for its tightly woven construction. Known to the ancient world, the basket chair has been a simple vernacular form for centuries. Today, though, the basket chair is often designed to hang from a ceiling.

BASSWOOD
American name for LIMEWOOD.

BAST SEAT
SPLINT SEAT made from bast, a fibrous material obtained from the stems of certain plants, such as flax and hemp, or from the inner bark of certain trees, such as lime and linden.

BAUDOUINE, CHARLES A. (1808–95)
American furniture maker in the ROCOCO REVIVAL STYLE. Baudouine, a New Yorker of French descent, had a furniture shop in that city by 1830. He made furniture of bent laminates of rosewood similar to the work of John Henry BELTER, whose patented methods he is sometimes said to have "pirated." His shop was virtually a small factory, which produced large quantities of furniture, and Baudouine also imported and sold French furniture and upholstery.

BAUHAUS
German design school, located in Weimar from 1919 to 1928, then in Dessau (1928–32) and in Berlin (1932–33); esthetic catalyst of the INTERNATIONAL STYLE of design and the theories of FUNCTIONALISM.

In 1919 Walter GROPIUS was appointed to succeed Henri VAN DE VELDE as director of Weimar's state-run School of Arts and Crafts. The school, with the DEUTSCHE WERK-STÄTTEN movement and the DEUTSCHER WERKBUND, was already in the vanguard of modern design. Gropius reorganized the institution as the Bauhaus (literally, "build house") and propounded its ultimate goal to be the creation of a "collective work of art—the Building—in which no barriers exist between the structural and decorative arts."

Besides employing the ideas of functionalism, the Bauhaus program addressed the problems of designing for mass manufacture. Bauhaus furniture designers employed chromium-plated metal tubes and favored polished surfaces, with variations of texture serving as decoration. These elements produced an intentionally machinelike appearance. This practice of creating machine-like pieces was adopted by designers of the International style, which developed from the Bauhaus esthetic and was prominent in Europe and the United States for decades. The Bauhaus emphasis on the collective nature of design and production—a process involving many people—and on the belief that designers had a responsibility to the people who would buy and use their work seemed to reflect a leftist political ideology. This, combined with anti-modernism, influenced the Nazis to close the school in 1933.

A number of important furniture designers were associated with the Bauhaus, notably Josef ALBERS, Marcel BREUER, Ludwig MIES VAN DER ROHE (director, 1930–1933) and, of course, Gropius. When the school closed, most of the designers went to the United States. As a group, their influence on design in the 1940s and 1950s was great; they popularized the simple lines and ingenious elegance of the modern, functionalist esthetic.

BAYWOOD
An older name for the Honduran variety of American MAHOGANY, referring to its export from the Bay of Honduras.

BEAD-AND-BUTT
Decorative device; arrangement of ASTRAGAL MOLDING (see under MOLDING) with framed paneling. The molding runs vertically, along

basin stand

Bauhaus table

the border of panel and STILES, but not horizontally.

BEAD-AND-REEL MOLDING
See under MOLDING.

BEAD-AND-REEL MOTIF
Decorative device; border or ornamental band composed of alternating round and oblong forms, which may be carved, inlaid or painted.

BEAD MOLDING
Another name for either ASTRAGAL MOLDING or BEADED MOLDING (*see each under* MOLDING).

BEADED DRAWER
Drawer whose front is bordered with COCK-BEAD MOLDING (*see under* MOLDING).

BEADED MOLDING
See under MOLDING.

BEAR'S-CLAW FOOT
See under FOOT.

BEAU BRUMMEL
Late 18th-century British and American furniture form; elaborate DRESSING TABLE with complicated fittings. Intended for men, the Beau Brummel was equipped for washing and shaving. The piece—which had multiple brackets and compartments and, often, more

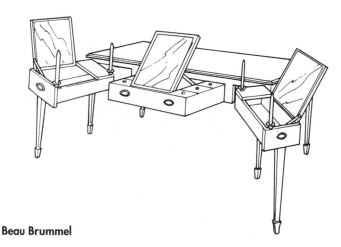

Beau Brummel

than one adjustable mirror—was a function of the period's craze for dandyism, and it was later named for the most famous dandy of them all. However, the 19th-century term is somewhat misleading, for the furniture form was most popular around the time Brummel, born in 1778, was still a child.

BECCHI, ALLESSANDRO (b. 1946)
Contemporary Italian furniture designer. Becchi is noted for a series of convertible sofa-beds without rigid structure, designed in the 1970s. The upholstered pad of polyurethane foam can be folded to make a couch or rolled for storage; it is held in either position by straps.

BED
Furniture form on which user may sleep or recline. It is usually composed of a flat, horizontal surface, supported by four vertical legs. Often the surface is a mattress or bedding borne by cross bars, straps or springs suspended within a frame, but it may also be a solid plane; sometimes it is supported by low walls rather than legs.

Until the late Middle Ages, beds tended to be a perquisite of wealth; most people slept on loose bedding or on the ground. Accordingly, beds have often served as symbols of rank (*see* BED OF ESTATE), built massively and bearing elaborate canopies (*see* CANOPY). On the other hand, portability has often been stressed, as in the TRUNDLE BED or FIELD BED. Since the 18th century, beds have tended to be increasingly simple in construction and decoration.

Many varieties of bed have been given specific names. (*See* ALCOVE BED; ANGEL BED; BED STEPS; BRASS BED; CHAIR-BED; COUCHETTE; CRADLE; CRIB; CUPBOARD-BED; DAYBED; DUCHESS; FOURPOSTER; JIA ZI CHUANG; KANG; KLINE; LECTUS; LIT À COLONNES; LIT À LA DUCHESSE; LIT À LA POLONAISE; LIT DE REPOS; LIT DROIT; LIT EN BATEAU; MURPHY BED; PATENT FURNITURE; PRESS BED; SLEIGH BED; SOFA-BED; TRESTLE BED; TRUSSING BED; TUSCAN BED; TWIN BED; WATERBED.)

BED OF ESTATE
In MEDIEVAL and RENAISSANCE FURNITURE, bed with elaborate accouterments, especially a CANOPY, intended for the ranking individual

in a household, like the CHAIR OF ESTATE. Among royal and other especially high-ranking individuals, the bed of estate might be used exclusively while receiving official visitors, a less elaborate bed serving for sleeping. CRADLES were occasionally treated similarly.

BED STEPS
Short sets of two or three steps, usually enclosed in panels, designed to provide access to very high beds. Developed in the late 17th century, they were most common in 18th-century British and American furniture.

BEDSTEAD
Frame of a bed, as opposed to its mattress and covers or its CANOPY.

BEECH
Very light brown HARDWOOD; with OAK, the commonest hardwood used in European furniture and also prominent in America and Japan. Beech turns well and is easily worked; it is commonly used as BENTWOOD and, being very light in weight, is often used in drawers. Since it takes most sorts of finish well, it is frequently used to make furniture that is to be painted, gilded or lacquered.

BEELDENKAST
Seventeenth-century Dutch furniture form; two-tiered CUPBOARD. The *beeldenkast* was distinguished by elaborate carved figures that appeared on its door panels and, often, as caryatids supporting cornices of both upper and lower sections. Similar to and derived from the French ARMOIRE À DEUX CORPS, its extensive carving made the beeldenkast a luxury item.

BEHRENS, PETER (1868–1940)
German architect and designer; a pioneer of modern design. Originally a painter, Behrens designed furniture and other objects in the austere German ART NOUVEAU style. He was a member of the DEUTSCHE WERKSTÄTTEN movement and went on to become one of the most important modern industrial designers and architects. He designed little, if any, furniture after 1901. Three great modern architects and furniture designers trained under Behrens: LE CORBUSIER, Walter GROPIUS and Ludwig MIES VAN DER ROHE.

BEL GEDDES, NORMAN
See GEDDES, Norman Bel.

BÉLANGER, FRANÇOIS-JOSEPH (1774–1818)
French architect and furniture designer in LOUIS XVI, DIRECTOIRE and EMPIRE STYLES. Bélanger was particularly noted for his use of ETRUSCAN STYLE decoration.

BELL-AND-BALUSTER TURNING
See under TURNERY.

BELLANGÉ, ALEXANDRE-LOUIS (1799–1863)
French furniture maker, son of Pierre-Antoine BELLANGÉ. Taking over the business on his well-known father's retirement in 1827, A.-L. Bellangé continued to make furniture in his father's manner for another generation. He also became an early maker of reproductions (*see* REPRODUCTION FURNITURE) in the LOUIS XV STYLE.

BELLANGÉ, PIERRE-ANTOINE (1758–1837)
French furniture maker associated with the EMPIRE and RESTAURATION STYLES. Bellangé became a *maître ébéniste* in 1788, on the eve of the French Revolution. Under Napoleon he received some imperial patronage, and after the restoration of the monarchy in 1815, he became *ébéniste* to Louis XVIII and then Charles X. His work reflected the stylistic evolutions of the day, ranging from Empire to the Gothic TROUBADOUR STYLE. He retired in 1827, when his business was taken over by his son, Alexandre-Louis BELLANGÉ.

BELLFLOWER
American FEDERAL PERIOD decorative motif consisting of a vertical arrangement of bell-shaped flowers in diminishing sizes, with the smallest at the bottom. Each flower had three or five petals, sometimes with a small circle below the central one. A variant of the contemporary British and Continental HUSK ornament, the bellflower derived ultimately from ancient Greek and Roman decoration.

bed steps

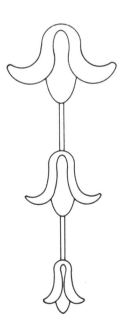

bellflower

BELLINI, MARIO (b. 1935)

Contemporary Italian architect and furniture designer. Best known as an industrial designer, Bellini has devised noted computer, calculator and typewriter designs for Olivetti; auto body stylings for Renault; lamps; electrical appliances; and other products. He has also designed a good deal of furniture for CASSINA and other companies. His furniture is ingenious and elegant, often modular and flexible, and its strong, simple forms reveal the influence upon Bellini's style of the mainstream modernism of earlier years (*see* INTERNATIONAL STYLE; FUNCTIONALISM). Particularly well known are the modular "Chair 932" (1967) and the "Cab" chair (1977), a simple, steel side chair sheathed in a zip-on leather cover. The "Colonnato" table (also 1977) calls for a glass or marble top to rest on, without joining, legs of wide marble columns that can be rearranged at will. Other recent tables consist of glass tops supported by irregular tripods of rectilinear wooden beams, arrangements that are abstract sculptures in themselves. Bellini is also noted for office systems he designed for Cassina in the 1970s. He is also a leading proponent of ERGONOMIC DESIGN.

BELTER, JOHN HENRY (1804–63)

chair by Belter

New York furniture maker; the leading American practitioner of the ROCOCO REVIVAL STYLE. Born Johann Heinrich in Germany and trained there as a cabinetmaker, Belter came to New York in about 1840 and quickly established himself as an independent furniture maker. He developed several mechanical processes that enabled him to produce highly innovative furniture. Making plywood sheets in laminated layers, he devised techniques of bending them in sweeping curves. By bending them twice, along two different axes, he produced three-dimensional components that he referred to as "dished" shapes. These elements were then carved with the elaborate naturalistic motifs characteristic of the American rococo Revival. For this work Belter also invented a mechanical saw that could carve complicated arabesques in these carved surfaces. These curved and carved sheets of wood were strong and simple, doing away with some of the joinery that had traditionally connected certain furniture parts and also permitting a more elaborate use of deeply modeled ornamentation, which had

not previously been possible. Furthermore, some of Belter's pieces incorporated areas of very high relief that were devised by gluing pieces of wood to the shaped forms. This furniture was widely imitated, and the term *Belter furniture* has been used to denote not only the work of Belter himself but all American rococo Revival pieces.

BEMBÉ, ANTON (active 1840s–1860s)

German furniture maker. Working in Mainz, Bembé was a leading maker in the mid-19th century REVIVAL STYLES. He was especially notable for pioneering the ROCOCO REVIVAL STYLE in the German-speaking countries.

BENDED-BACK CHAIR

Another name for the SPOON-BACK CHAIR of the QUEEN ANNE STYLE.

BENEMAN, GUILLAUME (active 1784–1811)

German-born French NEOCLASSICAL STYLE cabinetmaker. Beneman arrived in Paris in 1784 and became King Louis XVI's ÉBÉNISTE in the same year; he produced less opulent, more self-consciously austere furniture than did his predecessor, J.-H. REISENER. Following the Revolution, Beneman became a leading designer in the DIRECTOIRE and EMPIRE STYLES.

BENNETT, WARD (b. 1917)

Contemporary American furniture designer. Since the 1950s, Bennett has been noted for simple, functional wooden furniture whose structure is especially emphasized, in keeping with the canons of the INTERNATIONAL STYLE and FUNCTIONALISM. His use of flowing lines, however, is a departure from that style's angularity.

BENTWOOD

Steam-treated wood bent into shape for use as a furniture part. The technique was probably derived from the methods of such folk artisans as boat builders and wheelwrights. The use of bentwood goes back at least to the WINDSOR CHAIRS of 18th-century Britain. Early in the 19th century, Samuel GRAGG, an American, patented a bentwood chair, and German designers working in the BIEDERMEIER STYLE used bentwood parts. In the middle of the 19th century, one of these German designers, Michael THONET, began the practice of using bentwood rods to construct the frames of chairs and other furniture. Thonet is unquestionably the great master of this framing technique. At the same time, in the United States, John Henry BELTER bent and carved sheet plywood. In the 20th century, bentwood has been employed to good effect by, among others, Alvar AALTO and Marcel BREUER.

BÉRAIN, JEAN (1638–1711)

Important designer of LOUIS XIV–STYLE furniture and precursor of the RÉGENCE STYLE. Bérain worked under Charles LE BRUN at the GOBELINS workshops and became director there in 1683. He was also a major designer of theatrical scenery, costumes and fireworks for the frequent royal festivities. His furniture was most noted for its decoration, though he participated in the trend toward the use of curved legs and stretchers that made the later pieces in the Louis XIV style lighter. Bérain also made designs for the MARQUETRY of André-Charles BOULLE.

Bérain's style of decoration was lighter and more whimsical than Le Brun's or Jean LE PAUTRE's. While retaining the basic symmetry and classical order of earlier designs, he injected a strong element of idiosyncratic fantasy into his ARABESQUES, incorporating vignettes depicting bands of monkeys, in imitation of the characters of the commedia dell' arte, and whimsical canopies supported by fantastic CARYATIDS. This lightness of spirit anticipated the rococo style (see ROCOCO FURNITURE), and through both his position and an important PATTERN BOOK published in the year of his death, Bérain's influence on the next generation of designers was profound.

BERGÈRE

Eighteenth-century French furniture form; EASY CHAIR that was upholstered below the arms, usually with a large, loose cushion in its wide seat. The BERGÈRE sometimes took the form of a WING CHAIR; sometimes it had a low back that merged fluidly into the arms. First made in the LOUIS XV STYLE, in about 1725, it probably evolved from the CONFES-

SIONAL. By the late 18th century, it was also made in other countries, and it remains popular, both in REPRODUCTION FURNITURE and in newly designed pieces.

BERGÈRE-BOW WINDSOR CHAIR
See under WINDSOR CHAIR.

BERLAGE, HENDRIKUS PETRUS (1856–1934)

Dutch architect and furniture designer; early modernist. Berlage was a principal figure in the movement away from ART NOUVEAU, which took place in the early 20th century. He advocated a simpler style, like that of the British ARTS AND CRAFTS MOVEMENT. Berlage's furniture had bold but simple lines and rectilinear construction, with flat, restrained decoration composed largely of abstract motifs. As a writer and publicist, he helped introduce the American architect Frank Lloyd WRIGHT to Europe. Berlage's designs and ideas influenced such important modernists as his student Ludwig MIES VAN DER ROHE, Gerrit RIETVELD and the DE STIJL school.

BERMUDA FURNITURE

Furniture made in Bermuda in the 17th and 18th centuries, in simplified variants of English and Colonial American styles. Bermuda furniture makers were principally shipbuilders, and sturdy simplicity was their specialty. From JACOBEAN FURNITURE through the manner of Thomas CHIPPENDALE, they produced furniture distinctive for its intricate decorative DOVETAIL JOINTS (*see under* JOINERY), thought to be the signatures of otherwise anonymous craftsmen; idiosyncratic skirting profiles in tables and case furniture; and the predominant use of the island cedar, *Juniperus bermudiana*.

BERTOIA, HARRY (1915–78)

American furniture designer and sculptor. Born in Italy, Bertoia came to the United States in 1930. In 1937 he entered Cranbrook Academy (*see* Eliel SAARINEN) as a student, then became an instructor there in 1939. Among his teachers and colleagues at Cranbrook were Charles EAMES, Florence KNOLL and Eero SAARINEN. During the

bergère

chair by Bertoia

Second World War, Bertoia worked with Eames in California developing plywood molding techniques. After the war he worked for Florence Knoll; it was for Knoll Associates that he designed the furniture for which he is best known—a series of chromium-plated chairs whose seats consist of a welded lattice-work of light steel rods, molded in curves defining seat and back. Most famous of these chairs is the "Diamond" chair (1952), whose seat, arms and back are one multicurved, basket-shaped lattice, suspended within a boxy, legged substructure of steel rods. Two separate mountings make it possible for the sitter to adjust the angle of the seat to one of two positions by shifting his or her weight. The physical and visual lightness of these chairs, along with their elegance of design, have made them modern classics, and they have been produced in great numbers. After the mid-1950s Bertoia concentrated on sculpture and no longer designed furniture.

BEST, MARION HALL (b. 1905)

Australian interior decorator and entrepreneur. Through her importation and display of the works of such major 20th-century designers as Eero SAARINEN, Isamu NOGUCHI, Charles EAMES, and Florence KNOLL, Best was a dominant influence on AUSTRALIAN FURNITURE design from the 1950s through the 1970s.

BEURDELEY, LOUIS-AUGUSTE-ALFRED (1808–82)

French furniture maker, prominent in the Second Empire. Beurdeley was a specialist in 18th-century REPRODUCTION FURNITURE and designs in the LOUIS XVI REVIVAL style. He inherited his father's furniture business, and his own son, Alfred-Emmanuel-Louis Beurdeley, succeeded him, focusing entirely on reproductions until he sold the firm in 1895.

BEVEL

See under MOLDING.

BIBLE BOX

Seventeenth-century form associated with JACOBEAN AMERICAN FURNITURE; small

Bible box

chest with sloping top designed to support a book. Usually made of oak, the Bible box was intended to stand on a table. It is from such placement that the slant-top desk evolved.

BIEDERMEIER STYLE

Furniture style popular in northern Europe from about 1815 through the 1850s. Simplicity of form, restraint in decoration and a comfortable-looking appearance characterize the Biedermeier style, a bourgeois-inspired reaction against the magnificence of the French EMPIRE STYLE, which had dominated Europe prior to the fall of Napoleon. NEOCLASSICAL STYLE furniture forms were used—taken from Empire and, especially, British models and from the example of such German architects as Karl Friedrich SCHINKEL and Leo von KLENZE—though these forms were generally modified toward simpler, more purely geometrical shapes. Light-colored woods—such as ash, cherry, pear and maple—were used in plain expanses of veneer, so that the grain of the wood was often the chief decorative effect. Some ornament was used, but it was modest and secondary, though ebony was often applied, providing a striking contrast to the lighter veneers. Such ornament came from the neoclassical repertoire, most often architectural motifs such as columns and pilasters, but also decorative lyres or palmettes. Many motifs came from British sources, especially from the pattern books of Thomas SHERATON. Upholstery was common, in accordance with the comfort of the style.

Vienna was a principal center of production of Biedermeier furniture, with Josef DANHAUSER the leading maker there. In the north the dominance of Schinkel informed the design of the period. His most important follower among cabinetmakers was K. G. WANSCHAFF of Berlin. The Biedermeier style was popular throughout northern and eastern Europe, influencing the furniture of Scandinavia and Russia in particular. The simplicity of the style was associated with a post-Napoleonic relaxation of the hierarchical constraints and rigid mores of the *ancien régime,* but the rise of political reaction after the revolution of 1830, combined with the growing comfort and wealth of the middle class, began to alter that simplicity. In the 1830s the REVIVAL STYLES, especially the ROCOCO REVIVAL style, began to predominate, and after the revolutionary period of 1848–49 and the subsequent reaction, the Biedermeier style had become unfashionable.

In the late 19th century, a Biedermeier revival arose, lasting into the 1920s. An enthusiasm of the upper middle class, it was associated with German nationalism. Biedermeier ANTIQUES and REPRODUCTION FURNITURE became popular. It was not until this time that the term *Biedermeier* was used, by those who saw the style as old-fashioned and a symbol of reactionary values. *Biedermeier* was the mocking surname popularly given to designate the stereotype of a smug, bourgeois gentleman without culture. The term's origin is uncertain, though its literal meaning is clear: *bieder* means "plain" or "simple," and *Meier* is simply a common German surname.

BIENNAIS, MARTIN-GUILLAUME (1764–1843)

French EMPIRE STYLE metalworker and furniture maker. Goldsmith to Napoleon, Biennais is best known for his metalwork, but he also made furniture, mostly small pieces, often to designs by PERCIER AND FONTAINE and Baron DENON.

BILL, MAX (1908–94)

Swiss artist, architect, designer and writer. Originally trained as a silversmith, Bill studied at the BAUHAUS in the late 1920s and settled in Zurich in 1929 to paint and sculpt. In 1944 he began his career in industrial design, designing products, including some furniture, in a plain, geometrical manner concerned with function, economy and suitability of materials. In 1950 he cofounded the Hochschule für Gestaltung, in Ulm, West Germany. He served as director and taught architecture and design there until 1957, perpetuating the ideals of the Bauhaus, espousing FUNCTIONALISM and a mathematically oriented esthetic. Through this institution and his work, Bill influenced much postwar German design. In 1957 he returned to Zurich, where he concentrated on painting and sculpture.

BING, SAMUEL (1838–1919)

German entrepreneur associated with the ART NOUVEAU movement. Bing, an art dealer originally from Hamburg, Germany, visited the Far East in the 1870s, then established himself in Paris as a dealer in Japanese and other Oriental objects. By 1893 he was regarded as an arbiter of taste by the French government, which sent him to the United States to report on new design trends. There he was particularly impressed with the works of H. H. RICHARDSON and Louis Sullivan (*see* PRAIRIE SCHOOL). Bing knew that a number of European artists and designers were attempting to develop a new style of decoration and a contemporary design that would not be a revival of historical styles. In 1895 he opened a shop in Paris to market the works of this group. The shop was named *L'Art Nouveau,* and the new style, especially in its French manifestation, became known as Art Nouveau. The furniture designers promoted most actively through the shop were Georges DE FEURE, Edward COLONNA and Eugene GAILLARD, though Bing represented many other important designers in the style, both French and foreign.

Biedermeier sofa

BIRCH

Pale yellow HARDWOOD used in furniture both as plywood and in solid pieces. It is particularly prominent in SCANDINAVIAN MODERN furniture, having been especially favored by Finnish designer Alvar AALTO. Birch takes stain very well and is therefore often used to imitate more expensive woods, such as MAHOGANY or WALNUT.

BIRD'S-BALL-AND-CLAW FOOT

See under FOOT.

BIRD'S-EYE MAPLE

American HARDWOOD, figured form of sugar maple wood; pale brownish yellow in color with a random pattern of tiny, darker brown circles. Bird's-eye maple has been very popular as a decorative veneer since the late 18th century.

BIRDCAGE SUPPORT

Eighteenth-century hinging device used on some TILT-TOP TABLES to connect tabletop to pedestal base so that the top may revolve horizontally or tilt to a vertical position when not in use. With tiny spindles comprising each of its four sides, the device resembled a small cage.

birdcage support

BLACK BEAN
Australian HARDWOOD, brown with pale blond streaks, sometimes strikingly figured. A handsome wood, black bean is a very popular material for furniture in Australia, especially for veneering and inlay work. It is rarely available elsewhere, however.

BLACKAMOOR
Ornamental device; sculpted figure of an exotically clad black African, used to support a table, bed or GUÉRIDON in RENAISSANCE, BAROQUE and ROCOCO FURNITURE, especially in Italy.

BLACKWOOD
Another name for ZI TAN.

BLANKET CHEST
Any deep CHEST with hinged lid; more specifically, a MULE CHEST.

BLAU, LUIGI (b. 1945)
Contemporary Austrian architect and furniture designer. Blau's furniture, much of it designed for his architectural commissions, has become noteworthy because of its elegant, functional simplicity. His numerous designs of modular and collapsible furniture reflect the increasing demand, in the post-Second World War period, for mobile, versatile furniture. While clearly in the spirit of BAUHAUS design ideals, Blau's work is less formal and austere, and he favors the use of wood over metal or other industrial materials.

BLIN, PETER (active c. 1675–1725)
Maker of AMERICAN JACOBEAN furniture. Blin, who lived in Wethersfield, Connecticut, made CONNECTICUT SUNFLOWER CHESTS.

BLOCK-AND-VASE TURNING
See under TURNERY.

BLOCKFRONT
Case furniture feature of 18th-century New England, especially Newport, Rhode Island. The front of a blockfront piece is divided into three shallowly curved vertical sections of equal width, the outer two convex, the center one concave. The blockfront was first developed in a rudimentary form by the French cabinetmaker André-Charles BOULLE in about 1700 and subsequently became popular in northern Europe, though not in England. It first appeared in Boston as early as 1738 (*see* Job COIT Jr.). In Newport, where the blockfront was much more common than in Boston, Salem or Connecticut, the arched top of each section was commonly carved with a shell motif. This form of the blockfront was fully developed by John GODDARD and Job TOWNSEND and was a distinctive characteristic of their NEWPORT CHIPPENDALE FURNITURE. The blockfront was also occasionally used by New York makers.

BO
In JAPANESE FURNITURE, vertical metal bar that can be locked across a stack of drawers in a TANSU.

BOARD CHAIR
Simple vernacular chair consisting of a slab seat, four stick legs and a plank back inserted into a slot in the seat. Dating back at least as far as MEDIEVAL FURNITURE, the board chair was found throughout Europe in many variants, including the BACK STOOL, the SGABELLO and the German *brettstuhl.*

BOARD CHEST (also *boarded chest*)
Simple form of chest, each of whose six sides consists of a single board. Also called a *six-board chest.*

BOBBIN TURNING
See under TURNERY.

BOBTAIL
See under WINDSOR CHAIR.

BOG OAK
Blackish wood, similar to EBONY, from oak trees long submerged in a peat bog and thus dyed. In RENAISSANCE FURNITURE bog oak was sometimes used as a substitute for ebony in fine inlay work.

blockfront secretary

BOHLIN, JONAS (b. 1953)

Swedish designer of idiosyncratic variants on SCANDINAVIAN MODERN furniture. Bohlin's distinctive furniture, lighting, glass, and textiles have made him a leading figure in contemporary Swedish design.

BOIS CLAIR

Name for light woods, especially FRUITWOODS and maple (*see* BIRD'S-EYE MAPLE), popular in the RESTAURATION STYLE of early 19th-century France.

BOIS DE BOUT

French term for OYSTER VENEER.

BOIS DE ROSE

French term for TULIPWOOD.

BOIS DE SPA

Decorative technique of 17th and 18th centuries; style of JAPANNING used on furniture and other objects. *Bois de Spa* consisted of CHINOISERIE motifs depicted in gold on a black ground. It was named for the japanning workshops at Spa, in what is now Belgium, where it was a speciality.

BOLECTION MOLDING

See under MOLDING.

BOLSTER TOP

Decorative device; chair CREST RAIL whose central portion is carved to resemble a long cushion or pillow, one no wider than the rail itself (as distinguished from the similar PILLOW TOP). The bolster top appeared most often on the "fancy" chairs of American FEDERAL PERIOD furniture (*see* "FANCY" FURNITURE), especially those of Lambert HITCHCOCK.

BOMBÉ

Curved or swelling in shape; said especially of a COMMODE (1) or other case piece.

BONETTO, RODOLFO (1929–91)

Contemporary Italian industrial and furniture designer. Best known for his wide range of industrial designs, Bonetto also designed furniture in a less angular version of the INTERNATIONAL STYLE, using the newest synthetic materials and following the tenets of FUNCTIONALISM. His "Quattroquarti" table (1969) is well known, consisting of quarter-circle modules that can be rearranged into various formations. In the early 1960s he taught at Max BILL's Hochschule für Gestaltung.

BONGEN, ANDRIES (active 1770s)

Dutch maker of NEOCLASSICAL STYLE and ROCOCO FURNITURE. Bongen, who worked in Amsterdam, produced furniture with MARQUETRY decoration modeled on French examples, first of the LOUIS XV STYLE and later of the neoclassical LOUIS XVI STYLE.

BONHEUR DU JOUR

Late 18th-century French furniture form. It was a small, flat-topped DESK with compartmented drawers in the frieze and, at the rear of the top, a superstructure housing many small drawers and compartments behind a TAMBOUR slide.

BONNETIÈRE

FRENCH PROVINCIAL FURNITURE form; tall, narrow CUPBOARD intended to store the elaborate high bonnets worn by women in Normandy and Brittany. Developed in the late 17th century, the *bonnetière* was produced in those regions through the 19th century.

BONNET SCROLL

Eighteenth-century American term for SCROLL PEDIMENT (*see under* PEDIMENT).

BONNET TOP

Ornamental device on AMERICAN CHIPPENDALE FURNITURE. A covered pediment that extended over the top of a tall piece of case furniture, the bonnet top was a variation on the SCROLL PEDIMENT (*see under* PEDIMENT). It sometimes consisted of a scroll pediment and, behind it, slanted panels that covered the top of the piece. It could also be a shaped, solid piece of wood.

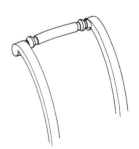

bolster top

bonnet top

borne

boss

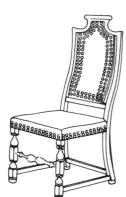

Boston chair

BONZANIGO, GIUSEPPE MARIA (1745–1820)

Italian NEOCLASSICAL STYLE sculptor, woodcarver and furniture maker. Bonzanigo was born in Asti, settled in Turin in 1773 and there worked for the Sardinian royal family for several decades, making sculptures, wall paneling and lavishly carved furniture based on the French LOUIS XVI STYLE. His virtuoso carving technique featured delicate, deeply cut images of fragile SWAGS and FESTOONS of flowers and foliage, often on a very small scale. When the armies of Napoleon occupied northern Italy, Bonzanigo altered his iconography to include Napoleonic motifs, but he clung to the outmoded pre-Revolutionary French style. In 1815, when the House of Savoy was restored to the throne of Sardinia, he resumed his position at court but focused primarily on portrait busts.

BOOKCASE

Case furniture form for storing books, consisting of tiers of shelves that are either open or enclosed by doors. Free-standing bookcases appeared in late BYZANTINE FURNITURE. In the West, however, the form was generally unknown until the 17th century, except as an architectural feature—either a shelved closet or a feature of wall paneling. Early books were very expensive and could only be owned in quantity by very wealthy people or by educational or ecclesiastical institutions. When the detached bookcase did become at all common, it usually was a very large form that closely resembled architectural shelving. In the 18th century the scale of bookcases gradually diminished, first in France and somewhat later in Britain, though they continued to be architectural in character, usually being decorated with such carved motifs as PILASTERS and PEDIMENTS. Smaller and simpler bookcases such as we know today began to appear in the early 19th century.

BOOTJACK FOOT

See under FOOT.

BORNE

Nineteenth-century furniture form, a circular OTTOMAN with a central backrest shaped like a truncated cone. Its name, meaning "milestone" in French, suggests both the importance and the massive size of this design, which was usually used in large rooms, often in public areas such as hotel lobbies. Sometimes the central cone was topped with flowers, a statue or even a fountain. The borne was a particularly extravagant example of the use of coil-spring, deep-buttoned UPHOLSTERY, which was developed in about 1830.

BOSS

Applied ornamental device, circular or oval in outline, usually attached to a veneer and often contrasting with its background. Deriving from a Gothic architectural device placed at the crossing points of ceiling ribs, the boss in furniture often appears where moldings intersect.

BOSTON CHAIR

Eighteenth-century American chair type; an early SPOON-BACK CHAIR. It was exported from Boston to the other Colonial centers in great quantity and was characterized by a back having a broad splat; overall, the chair curved slightly to the rear and then upward again. The splat and seat were usually upholstered in leather. Turned front legs and stretchers revealed the chair's origins in the WILLIAM AND MARY STYLE of the first years of the century; later examples had cabriole legs. The Boston chair remained popular until the time of the American Revolution.

BOSTON CHIPPENDALE FURNITURE

AMERICAN CHIPPENDALE FURNITURE produced in the Boston area between about 1755 and 1790. The furniture is characterized by very restrained ROCOCO FURNITURE designs, derived largely from the pattern book of Thomas CHIPPENDALE. Boston Chippendale furniture is distinctively sober, even simpler in character than nearby NEWPORT CHIPPENDALE FURNITURE, with restricted areas of carving and a corresponding emphasis on figured veneers. The most striking feature of the Boston style was the frequent appearance of the *bombé* shape in chests. Often tall case pieces were given bonnet tops, the pediment framing and flanked by corkscrew finials. As in Newport, BLOCKFRONT furniture was produced, but the blocking in Boston was generally shallower and less expansive over the front of the piece. Cabriole legs on chairs and tables were distinctively slender and delicate. Among the notable makers of Boston Chippendale furniture were John COGSWELL and Benjamin FROTHINGHAM.

BOSTON ROCKER

Nineteenth-century American ROCKING CHAIR, made in New England. The chair is characterized by a wood seat that curved down at the front and up at the rear. Derived from the WINDSOR CHAIR early in the 19th century, the standard Boston rocker form had been developed by about 1840. It was usually made of maple with pine seats, whose curves were produced by adding separate pieces of wood to the flat central part of the seat. It also had arms that followed the curve of the seat, a back of six to nine spindles (occasionally slats) and a large crest rail. It was generally decorated with painted or stenciled designs of flowers, fruit or a landscape. The design of the chair is sometimes attributed to Lambert HITCHCOCK, who manufactured Boston rockers. However many other, unidentified, New England furniture markers produced these chairs as well, so the origin of the design remains unknown. An armless version was called a "little Boston rocker," and another variant with a low back was known as a "Salem rocker."

BOUCHER, JUSTE-FRANÇOIS (1736–81)

French LOUIS XVI–STYLE furniture designer. Boucher, son of the famous rococo painter François Boucher, was noted for a long series of engraved designs for furniture, sculpture and architectural elements, published beginning in 1765. His furniture, influenced by the work of J.-F. NEUFFORGE, was in a heavy, rectilinear style that he called *à la moderne*.

BOULARD, JEAN-BAPTISTE (c. 1725–89)

French LOUIS XVI–STYLE chair maker. Boulard, who sometimes collaborated with J.-B. SENÉ, worked in an austere, restrained manner. His son carried on the family business, making EMPIRE STYLE pieces until 1832.

BOULLE, ANDRÉ-CHARLES (1642–1732)

Principal ÉBÉNISTE of the LOUIS XIV STYLE. Best known for his masterful MARQUETRY,

Boulle specialized in the brass and tortoise-shell veneering that became known as BOULLE MARQUETRY, but he also used many other materials. A superior worker in bronze, he modeled the elaborate mounts placed on his pieces. In addition, he was responsible for much of the parquet flooring and wall paneling at Versailles. After 1672 Boulle was employed by Louis XIV's GOBELINS workshops, but he also accepted many private commissions. After the royal shops were closed in 1694, he maintained his own shop, where he continued to design and make successful furniture in the RÉGENCE and LOUIS XV STYLES. After his death, his sons continued to make furniture based on his designs, employing as young men such later masters as Jean-François OEBEN and Étienne LEVASSEUR.

Boston rocker

BOULLE MARQUETRY

Popular INLAY technique of 17th and 18th centuries. Although first developed in medieval Italy, it is principally associated with its most accomplished practitioner, the French LOUIS XIV–STYLE *ébéniste*, André-Charles BOULLE. In Boulle marquetry, thin sheets of brass and tortoise-shell were glued together and cut with a FRETSAW in complicated designs, usually arrangements of ARABESQUE and GROTESQUE ORNAMENT. The brass and tortoiseshell were then separated, so the craftsman had identical images of figure and ground in each material. The pieces could thus be combined to produce a brass figure inlaid in a ground of shell or vice versa. The former, brass in shell, is known as *première-partie* marquetry; the latter, shell in brass, as *contre-partie*, or *contra-boulle*. In Boulle's time, these panels were generally set in ebony, though other materials, most notably rosewood, have also been used. Matching pairs of commodes or other pieces were often decorated so that one had *première-partie* panels; the other, *contre-partie*. Sometimes the two patterns were placed at opposite ends of a symmetrical piece or on the outside and inside of a cabinet door.

The technique was widespread in northern Europe by the early 17th century; Boulle's older contemporary Pierre GOLLE used brass and pewter in this way. In Boulle's time, and in part because of his example, brass and tortoiseshell marquetry was very popular in Germany, where J. D. SOMMER was a leading maker, and in England, where Gerreit JENSEN made it fashionable. Later makers in Britain and France, where it remained in vogue through most of the 19th century, tended to increase its striking effect by placing it over tinted metal foil, whose color was visible through the tortoiseshell, or by adding inlays of pewter, mother-of-pearl or horn, which was sometimes stained a bright color.

bracket

BOUVIER, MICHAEL (active 1819–59, d. 1874)

French-born Philadelphia furniture maker in the AMERICAN EMPIRE STYLE. After serving in Napoleon's army, Bouvier immigrated to the United States in 1815. By 1819 he was in the furniture business in Philadelphia, manufacturing pieces in the American Empire manner of Anthony QUERVELLE, the leading Philadelphia cabinetmaker of the day. Bouvier also ran a sawmill and imported exotic woods, marbles and other materials.

BOW-BACK WINDSOR CHAIR
See under WINDSOR CHAIR.

BOWFRONT

Eighteenth-century design feature in case furniture. The front of a bowfront piece described a continuous convex curve. The forms that most commonly featured a bowfront were probably the CHEST OF DRAWERS and the SIDEBOARD, but it was used widely in many ways. The term is sometimes used to denote a SERPENTINE front as well.

BOX-BED
See CUPBOARD-BED.

BOX STRETCHER
See under STRETCHER.

BOXWOOD

A HARDWOOD from any of several species of shrubs and small trees; most frequently the European box, which grows from Great Britain to Iran. The box tree is small, often shrublike, and its wood is accordingly only available in small pieces. Distinctively yellow

and very workable, box is particularly prized for its decorative qualities and is chiefly used in small features, such as BANDING, fine TURNERY, and carved ornaments.

A very similar wood, *Maracaibo boxwood* (not botanically a true box), is similarly used but offers the advantage of being available for larger items, and it is sometimes used for VENEER. It is found in northern South America.

BRACING STICKS
See under WINDSOR CHAIR.

BRACKET

L-shaped structure, one arm of which is fixed to a vertical surface, while the other projects at a right angle to support a horizontal element. Brackets are commonly used to brace a leg to the SEAT RAIL of a chair or to a tabletop. The term also refers to a small ornamental shelf so supported or to any lighting fixture attached to a wall.

BRACKET FOOT
See under FOOT.

BRADLEY, WILL H. (1868–1962)

American graphic artist; one-time designer of ART NOUVEAU furniture. In 1901 Bradley designed some Art Nouveau style furniture, which received wide attention and appeared in *The Ladies' Home Journal* in 1902. Although Bradley influenced American Art Nouveau designers, his furniture was apparently never manufactured.

BRANDT, EDGAR (1880–1960)

Most prominent of the French ART DECO metalworkers. Brandt designed and built a great deal of furnishings—including screens, console tables, pedestals, occasional tables, radiator cases and lamps—in wrought iron and other metals. He is particularly well known for his standard lamps, in which the upright is shaped like a long serpent.

BRANGWYN, FRANK (1867–1956)

English painter and designer associated with the ARTS AND CRAFTS MOVEMENT and ART

NOUVEAU. In the 1880s Brangwyn was an assistant to William Morris and a follower of A. H. MACKMURDO. In the 1890s he adopted an Art Nouveau style and worked for Samuel BING, designing furniture, textiles and carpets.

BRASS

Gold-colored alloy of copper and zinc. A very workable material that takes a high polish, brass has been used as furniture HARDWARE since the 17th century, especially for door or drawer handles (*see* BAIL HANDLE; DROP HANDLE; RING PULL) and keyhole ESCUTCHEONS. It has also been popular in INLAY work, notably in BOULLE MARQUETRY of the late 17th and early 18th centuries, and as STRINGING on early 19th-century NEOCLASSICAL STYLE furniture. Also, in about 1860 the BRASS BED was introduced.

BRASS BED

Bed with BRASS headboard and footboard. In the late 19th century, brass replaced iron in metal bedsteads (*see* CAST-IRON FURNITURE), being easier to work and more ornamental in appearance. Originally a RENAISSANCE REVIVAL STYLE form, the brass bed first appeared in about 1860, when it was heavily ornamented with sculptural castings, plaques of mother-of-pearl INLAY work and so on. As design reform movements (*see* ARTS AND CRAFTS MOVEMENT) influenced tastes, brass bed designs became simpler. The form remains popular today, and its ornamentation is very subdued, generally resembling simply turned wood.

BRASSES

Type of furniture HARDWARE; door or drawer handles (*see* BAIL HANDLE; DROP HANDLE; RING PULL) and keyhole ESCUTCHEONS.

BRATTISHING

Ornament used in RENAISSANCE FURNITURE; cresting of pierced carved work at the top of a screen or piece of case furniture.

BRAUWERS, JOSEPH (active 1800–1820)

Paris-trained AMERICAN EMPIRE STYLE cabinetmaker. Brauwers worked in New York in a French-inspired manner similar to that of C.-H. LANNUIER.

BRAZILWOOD

Orange to dark red HARDWOOD from Brazil, popular in early 19th-century European furniture for decorative veneering and inlay work. Today it is used principally for violin bows. Brazilwood is not named for the country; rather, the country is named for the wood. In the 16th century the word *brazil* denoted any botanical dye yielding a brassy red color. Such a dye may be extracted from brazilwood, and this product stimulated the first colonial exploitation of the region.

BREAKFAST TABLE

Variant of the PEMBROKE TABLE popular in Britain and America in the 18th century. The table was characterized by its light weight and mobility. It usually included a drawer, shelf or cupboard below its leaved top. Difficult to distinguish from any other Pembroke table, the breakfast table is simply the smallest, most elaborate form; the SOFA TABLE stands at the other end of the scale.

BREAKFRONT

Shape of late 18th-century case pieces with slightly projecting center section. The term is usually used as an adjective modifying the name of a form, as in *breakfront commode* or *breakfront bookcase*. Popular in late Chippendale style furniture (*see* Thomas CHIPPENDALE) in Britain and America, and in LOUIS XVI–STYLE furniture in France, the breakfront shape tended to replace the less austere and severe SERPENTINE front.

BRETTSTUHL

German variety of BOARD CHAIR.

BREUER, MARCEL LAJOS (1902–81)

Hungarian-born architect and designer; one of the most important 20th-century furniture designers. Breuer was born in Hungary and trained at the BAUHAUS from 1920 to 1925. He taught there until the school was closed and left Germany in 1935. Most of his important furniture designs were created in Europe; in America he worked chiefly as an architect.

In his youth Breuer followed the style of Gerrit RIETVELD and the complicated, formal esthetics of DE STIJL. Early in his career he

bellflower brattishing

chair by Breuer

produced the famous "Wassily" chair of tubular steel and leather, made for and named after painter Wassily Kandinsky. Breuer moved beyond the influence of De Stijl and displayed his characteristic combination of practicality and simple elegance with his version (1928) of the CANTILEVERED CHAIR invented by Mart STAM. The chair frame was made of a single curved length of tubular steel and fastened to the back and seat of the chair, which were made of wood and cane. His chair became an extremely influential piece of furniture and is still made and sold today. In Britain, during the late 1930s, Breuer designed furniture made of aluminum or laminated plywood, most notably a series of lounge chairs.

Breuer has influenced all furniture designers since the 1930s, in part through his use of such materials as tubular steel, fabric and laminated plywood, but mainly through his ingenious design style, which combined function with elegance and simplicity.

Brewster chair

BREWSTER CHAIR

Seventeenth-century AMERICAN JACOBEAN FURNITURE chair type. The chair was constructed of turned wood, except for a plank or rush seat, with decorative turned spindles in the back, below each arm and below the seat. It is named after William Brewster (d. 1644), an elder of Plymouth Colony who owned an early example of the chair.

BREYTSPRAAK, CAREL (active 1795, d. 1810)

Dutch cabinetmaker in the French EMPIRE STYLE. Working chiefly for Napoleon's brother Louis Bonaparte, king of Holland, Breytspraak followed French models, though, like most Dutch designers of the day, he was influenced by the relatively simple designs of Pierre de LA MÉSANGÈRE at least as much as by the more grandly imperial work of PERCIER AND FONTAINE. He favored smooth expanses of highly figured mahogany veneer, framed by simple rectangular moldings and sparsely ornamented with elegant gilt-bronze mounts.

BRIDGEN, ROBERT (active 1830s)

British furniture designer associated with the ELIZABETHAN REVIVAL STYLE. In 1838

Bridgen published a pattern book *Furniture with Candelabra and Interior Decoration,* which influenced many makers of so-called Elizabethan furniture.

BRIGHT, GEORGE (1727–1805)

Boston cabinetmaker, associated with AMERICAN CHIPPENDALE FURNITURE and with the NEOCLASSICAL STYLE of the FEDERAL PERIOD. One of the leading Boston craftsmen of his day, Bright was descended from several generations of furniture makers.

broken pediment

See under PEDIMENT.

BROKEN-SCROLL PEDIMENT

See under PEDIMENT.

BRONZE

Alloy of copper and tin used in furniture chiefly as HARDWARE (*see also* GILDING) rather than whole pieces, due to its considerable expense. However, bronze furniture has periodically been popular with the rich and powerful, especially in ancient ROMAN FURNITURE, where TABLES, STOOLS, and occasionally beds (see LECTUS) were cast in bronze.

BROOKS, THOMAS (1811–87)

Brooklyn, New York, furniture maker, associated with the RENAISSANCE REVIVAL STYLE. Active in a number of styles from at least 1841, Brooks is best known for his highly eclectic, richly ornamented Renaissance Revival work of the 1850s–1870s.

BRUNETTI, GAETANO (active c. 1736)

Italian ROCOCO FURNITURE designer who worked in Britain. In 1736 Brunetti published a PATTERN BOOK, *Sixty Different Sorts of Ornament,* that contained some of the earliest rococo design to be seen in Britain.

BRUSTOLON, ANDREA (1662–1732)

Venetian sculptor and maker of BAROQUE FURNITURE. Brustolon was the leading Italian furniture maker of his time, as well as a highly successful sculptor. His exuberant furniture designs featured such conceits as chair arms in the form of tree branches, supports in the form of exotically clad humans and deities, swarms of *putti* and elaborate festoons. These were all arranged in pieces whose effect was enhanced by Brustolon's sophisticated carving technique.

BRUYÈRE, ANDRÉ (b. 1912)
Contemporary French architect and furniture designer. Bruyère's curvilinear forms represent a modest reaction against the angularity of INTERNATIONAL STYLE designs. He employs restrained but unusual forms, occasionally approaching the bizarre—for example, a coffee table with a gently undulating geomorphic top.

BUBINGA
West African HARDWOOD resembling ROSEWOOD; used chiefly for inlay work and as a decorative veneer.

BUCKLE-BACK WINDSOR CHAIR
See under WINDSOR CHAIR.

BUCRANIUM (pl. *bucrania*)
Decorative motif; skull of an ox. A device taken from ancient Greek religious iconography, the *bucranium* was used on furniture by NEOCLASSICAL STYLE designers of the late 18th and early 19th centuries.

BUFFET
Loosely, any of various serving tables or cupboards, used for serving meals. Originally, in MEDIEVAL FURNITURE, the term applied particularly to a tiered arrangement of shelves intended to display plates, as opposed to the more utilitarian DRESSER (1). The most important medieval furniture form in terms of its symbolic ability to demonstrate the owner's social status, the buffet could have as many as six shelves; the number varied with the owner's social position. A five- or six-tiered buffet, for instance, was reserved for royalty. The buffet was invariably draped with fine fabrics, favored over cabinetry as a means to exhibit wealth, and was generally simply, even crudely, constructed. Supplementing this piece was a smaller, more practical arrangement of shelves

actually used for serving meals, an early form of CUPBOARD. This piece was sometimes decorated with fine carving or wrought iron work, and it was also called a buffet.

BUGATTI, CARLO (1855–1940)
Italian furniture designer associated with ART NOUVEAU. Trained as a painter and architect, Bugatti showed his first furniture—pieces in an eccentric style that combined freely interpreted elements of Islamic and Japanese design—in 1888. Operating a workshop in Milan, he developed his idiosyncratic style as a variant of the emerging Art Nouveau movement. He employed such stylistic devices as parchment panels; inlay work of ivory, wood and wrought metal; and painted decorations adapted from exotic, mainly Middle Eastern, design traditions. His furniture forms were sometimes conventional, sometimes bizarrely curvilinear. His "Snail Room" furniture, shown at the Turin Exposition of 1902, gained particular notoriety. The lines of his "Snail Room" pieces were sweeping, unbroken arcs and curves; the wooden frameworks of the pieces were completely covered with a stretched vellum that had been painted with geometrical, Islamic style decorations. After 1907 Bugatti stopped making furniture and moved to France, where he designed silverware and painted. His son Ettore designed the Bugatti automobiles.

BUHL
Old name for BOULLE MARQUETRY.

BULB TURNING
See under TURNERY.

BUN FOOT
See under FOOT.

BUREAU
Broad term with several definitions, covering several varieties of case furniture, all but two of them DESKS, or pieces designed for writing. In France the term includes all such forms, from the WRITING BOX through the BUREAU PLAT and the SECRÉTAIRE, to modern WRITING TABLES and PEDESTAL DESKS. In Britain,

on the other hand, it is reserved for forms with SLANT TOPS and compartments, such as the writing box and the SECRETARY, and including a nondesk, the LECTERN, a READING STAND, when it has storage space for books. In this sense, the term excludes flat-topped pieces like the pedestal desk and the LIBRARY TABLE. In American usage the term *bureau* refers to another nondesk form, a CHEST OF DRAWERS, especially when used in a bedroom.

BUREAU À CYLINDRE

French name for either CYLINDER-FRONT DESK or ROLL-TOP DESK.

BUREAU À GRADIN

Eighteenth-century French furniture form; flat-topped desk or BUREAU PLAT with a superstructure at one side of the top housing a set of small drawers or compartments.

BUREAU BOOKCASE

Eighteenth-century name for SECRETARY.

BUREAU DRESSING TABLE

Eighteenth-century term for LOWBOY.

BUREAU EN PENTE

Another name for SECRÉTAIRE EN PENTE.

BUREAU MAZARIN

Term used in the 19th century for 17th-century French furniture form; early KNEEHOLE DESK with four short legs at each end. Each set of legs was joined by an X-stretcher and supported a pedestal with drawers. The shallow kneehole space was backed by two drawers or a cupboard; above it a drawer was set in the frieze. The *bureau Mazarin* was generally made in the LOUIS XIV STYLE and was often veneered in BOULLE MARQUETRY. It was used as both a writing desk and a DRESSING TABLE.

bureau Mazarin

BUREAU PLAT

French furniture form; large rectangular WRITING TABLE with three wide drawers in the frieze and, usually, a leather top. Developed in the 17th century, the *bureau plat* has been very popular in France ever since.

BUREAU-TABLE

Late 17th-century British furniture form; DESK with drawers, above which was a wide, shallow compartment whose top—also the top of the piece itself—was a lid hinged at the back. This compartment had a FALL FRONT, so the piece could both house papers and provide a writing surface. In 18th-century American usage, the term referred to a DRESSING TABLE with drawers, short legs and a KNEEHOLE space (*see* KNEEHOLE DESK).

BURGAT, CLAUDE-LOUIS (b. 1717, active to 1782)

French furniture maker in LOUIS XV and LOUIS XVI STYLES, chiefly the former.

BURGES, WILLIAM (1827–81)

British architect and designer in the NEO-GOTHIC STYLE. Principally an architect, Burges also designed furniture for himself and for his clients. All of his furniture is elaborately decorative, inspired by the motifs of Gothic architecture and made of rich, varied materials. His designs were idiosyncratic, and he occupied an ambiguous position in the changing design world of his time. Burges shared many concerns with the ART FURNITURE MOVEMENT: the taste for simple, rectilinear forms; an antipathy toward the shoddily manufactured ROCOCO REVIVAL STYLE furniture of that period; the desire that fine design be employed in mass manufacture; and a taste for the medieval. However, his extravagant ornamentation and complex decorative schemes ally him more closely with A. W. N. PUGIN than with such younger figures of the Art Furniture movement as Bruce TALBERT and Charles EASTLAKE.

Burges is credited with reviving the use of painted decoration (c. 1856). His own furniture is often very heavily painted, either with images on panels or abstract patterns that emphasize the lines of the form. His pieces were painted by such notable artists of the day as E. J. Poynter and Edward BURNE-JONES; thus, his work bears an obvious, if superficial, similarity to some painted work of the ARTS AND CRAFTS MOVEMENT. Burges shared none of William MORRIS's esthetics, however, and his elaborate pieces are very different from the simpler works of such an Arts and Crafts designer as Philip WEBB. With William GODWIN and Talbert, Burges was an early appreciator of Japanese art, and he employed Japanese motifs in his work. Burges's style, on the other hand, has little in common with the simple, spare esthetics later associated with JAPONISME. He also designed neo-Gothic wallpaper and metalwork.

BURGOMASTER CHAIR
Another name for ROUNDABOUT CHAIR (1).

BURL (also *burr*)
Tumorlike growth on a tree trunk. A burl, when cut, usually has striking FIGURING, composed of intricately distorted grain, sometimes resembling tortoiseshell. Burl wood is valued for its decorative character. Available only in small quantities, it is generally sliced thinly and used as VENEER, but if large enough, as when it comes from AMERICAN REDWOOD, a burl may provide planks that can be used as tabletops. WALNUT, ELM and YEW commonly provide interesting burl wood.

BURL VENEER
Wood VENEER taken from a BURL, prized for its extraordinary appearance.

BURLING, THOMAS (active before 1772, d. 1800)
New York FEDERAL PERIOD cabinetmaker. Burling apprenticed under Samuel PRINCE and became a noted maker of NEOCLASSICAL STYLE furniture in the post-Revolutionary years. George Washington commissioned him to provide furniture for the first official presidential residence.

BURMESE FURNITURE
TEAK furniture made in Burma in 19th and early 20th centuries for export to the West. European furniture forms, mostly small tables and chairs, were covered with intricately carved decoration featuring dragons and other indigenous motifs. Another favored decorative device was the inclusion of small pieces of mirror or colored glass. Because Burma was a province of British India, most Burmese furniture was shipped to Britain.

BURNE-JONES, EDWARD (1833–98)
British painter and designer; close associate of William MORRIS. Burne-Jones, best known as a member of the Pre-Raphaelite group of painters, joined Morris, Philip WEBB and others in a movement to reform the applied arts through a reversion to preindustrial modes of production. Together they founded a manufacturing company, Morris & Co., which can be said to have marked the birth of the ARTS AND CRAFTS MOVEMENT. Burne-Jones's representational paintings decorated many pieces of furniture manufactured by Morris & Co. He also designed some furniture himself, in a simple NEO-GOTHIC STYLE.

BURNHAM, BENJAMIN (1729–99)
Cabinetmaker of Norwich, Connecticut, associated with COUNTRY CHIPPENDALE FURNITURE. Burnham was particularly noted for fine-quality BLOCKFRONT pieces that resembled those of Newport (*see* NEWPORT CHIPPENDALE FURNITURE) but were simpler in detail and were generally made of cherry rather than mahogany.

BURR
Another name for BURL.

BURTON, SCOTT (1939–89)
Contemporary American sculptor and furniture designer. Burton conceived of his work as sculpture but it always fulfills its function as furniture, through thoughtful design. His early pieces included bronze replicas of historical furniture—for example, a QUEEN ANNE–STYLE chair. These works have some of the fey wit of POP ART FURNITURE, but they are also intended more seriously as conceptual art and draw the attention of the user to the nature of the work as both art *and* furniture. His best-known works, made largely of stone, are hard-edged geometrical pieces, such as granite tables that are upside-down cones, or chairs that are formed by a smooth-angled cut in a rough stone block. These arise from the minimalist esthetic of the 1960s and are gen-

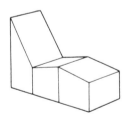

chaise by Burton

erally acclaimed as successful abstract sculptures. However, they are also comfortable, and their forms seem calculated to serve the furniture user, in the tradition of FUNCTIONALISM and ERGONOMIC DESIGN. Burton died of AIDS in 1989.

BUTLER'S TABLE (also *butler's tray*)
British furniture form of 18th and 19th centuries; portable table consisting of a wood or metal tray atop a folding stand. The tray generally had a solid wooden GALLERY with slots for carrying at each end; sometimes an oval tray had hinged edges that folded up to make a rectangular tray with a gallery. The stand was composed of two X-FRAMES joined at the top by canvas strips. Developed in the last half of the 18th century, the butler's table was very popular for over a hundred years.

BUTSUDAN
Traditional JAPANESE FURNITURE form; household shrine, either Buddhist or Shinto. It is a large, cupboardlike form with high, open shelves for statuary and offerings of food and drink.

BUTT JOINT
See under JOINERY.

BUTTERFLY HINGE
See under HINGE.

butterfly table

BUTTERFLY TABLE
American variant of the GATE-LEG TABLE developed in AMERICAN JACOBEAN FURNITURE and most prominent in the AMERICAN WILLIAM AND MARY STYLE in the early 18th century. This distinctively American DROP-LEAF TABLE, which probably was developed in Connecticut, is characterized by a SWING LEG (*see under* LEG), in place of the gate of a gate-leg table, that can be placed under each leaf; there were generally two wide leaves on either side of a narrow tabletop. The shapely curve of the outer edge of this support gave the table its name. The table also had splayed legs, which, in combination with the wings, gave it an air of vigor and movement in keeping with

the baroque character of the William and Mary style.

BUTTERNUT (also *white walnut*)
American HARDWOOD; member of the WALNUT family but pale—white to light brown in color—though darkening with age. Easily worked and taking a stain readily, butternut was a fairly popular furniture wood in 18th-century America. However, it was never a common wood, and it is now in very short supply. It has rarely been used in furniture since the mid-19th century.

BUTTONING
See UPHOLSTERY.

B.V.R.B.
See VAN RISENBURGH, Bernard.

BYOBU
JAPANESE FURNITURE form; a folding SCREEN. The *byobu* consists of wooden panels or frames, usually two to six in number, hinged to each other and covered on both sides with sturdy paper. A decorative wood frame surrounds each panel. It is usually lacquered and ornamented with wrought metal mounts, especially at the corners, where they provide an element of rigidity. A band of patterned brocade is attached where the paper meets the wood frame, and the paper thus bordered is painted with a landscape or other scene. Sometimes each panel has a separate picture, but normally a continuous representation covers the whole screen. An undecorated utilitarian variant is the FUROSAKI BYOBU.

BYZANTINE FURNITURE
Furniture of the Byzantine Empire (A.D. 476–1453) in the lands of the eastern Mediterranean. The Byzantine Empire included Italy until the fifth century A.D. Then, beginning in the seventh, the expansion of Islam limited the empire's domain to an ever-smaller territory in Asia Minor, the Aegean and the Balkans. Byzantine furniture was contemporary with MEDIEVAL FURNITURE in western Europe, where the collapse of the Roman Empire left an impoverished culture

and an accordingly primitive world of design. By contrast, Constantinople, which had become the eastern capital of the Roman Empire in 395 A.D., remained stable, and classical traditions and techniques of fine craftsmanship (*see* ROMAN FURNITURE) could endure. Though only one important piece of Byzantine furniture, the throne of Maximian, has survived, many others are known through such art forms as manuscript painting, mosaics and carved ivory panels.

Not surprisingly, Eastern art and design influenced Byzantine furniture. A stiff, hieratic stylization and a fondness for luxuriant but formal abstract or semiabstract ornamentation derived from Persia and, later, Islam. Beginning in the 10th century, Byzantine decorative motifs came from as far away as China.

The throne of Maximian, made in Constantinople in about 550 A.D., exemplifies the formal and opulent manner of grand Byzantine furniture. It is massive, rigidly foursquare and covered with ivory panels—some depicting religious figures in hieratic poses, others boasting bands of luxuriant ornamentation dominated by floral and animal motifs. However, many lighter forms of seating furniture were also used. Probably most common were simple framed wooden stools and benches, with turned uprights, stretchers and rails; elaborate turnings were a prominent feature of all Byzantine furniture. X-FRAME chairs and stools from the classical tradition (*see* SELLA CURULIS) appeared, usually made of metal, often with carved beast's heads topping supports whose bases were claw or paw feet. Some of these seats folded; others did not. Although Byzantine furniture retained much from the classical tradition, the Greek KLISMOS was lost, replaced by heavier forms. Footstools of all sizes and types accompanied Byzantine chairs.

The Byzantine ruling class valued learning and scholarship highly, and an important furniture form was the LECTERN, or book stand. Though sometimes freestanding, this piece was more typically combined with a desk or writing table that also often incorporated a cabinet or cabinets for storing books. Many lecterns were hinged, permitting the book to rest at various angles. Most lecterns were decorated—some with carved crocketing or other ornamentation, some with painted, semiabstract decoration in the Eastern manner.

The frequent extravagance of Byzantine furniture is indicated in a reference to a solid gold table that was large enough to accommodate 36 diners reclining on couches. This table was doubtless exceptional; Byzantine dining tables were usually made of less extravagant metal or stone. But they were large, reflecting a change from the Roman practice of serving diners on individual small tables. They also tended to be round or semicircular, and the users' couches, derived from the Greek KLINE, were arranged around it like spokes of a wheel. Often these tables were used to display fine craft, with elaborate cupboards fitted beneath the tabletop.

Small tables were also made. These were usually square, with slender legs joined by X-stretchers. Sometimes similar tables were obviously intended as writing desks, having a drawer in the frieze and stretchers on three sides.

Beds varied altogether from classical predecessors (Byzantine dining couches were not used for sleeping). The Roman LECTUS disappeared, and beds without headpieces were made, generally surrounded by a CANOPY supported by four columns. These columns, and often the bed's legs, were elaborately turned or otherwise decorated, sometimes reflecting architectural styles.

Cupboards were often similarly grand, with pilasters and pediments. A wide range of what we would now call presses or cupboards were made. These included bookcases, both open and closed. Chests of drawers were not yet produced, however, for the basic chest remained the most widely used piece of case furniture, as in earlier epochs. Chests ranged from very small jewelry caskets to large coffers, which doubled as benches or beds. All of these chests tended to be highly decorated with paintings, wood inlays or carved ivory panels, reflecting the Byzantine love of formal display.

The influence of Byzantine design survived the fall of Constantinople in 1453. A number of elements—especially such Eastern characteristics as interlacing decorative bands, rigid animal and foliage forms, and a severe formality—would be transmitted, via the Orthodox Church, to the furniture and decorative arts of southeastern Europe and Russia in later centuries.

Byzantine chair

C

CABINET

Form of CASE FURNITURE consisting of a CUPBOARD-like repository, usually fronted by door(s) and containing numerous small drawers or open compartments, intended to store and display small objects. Originating in Italy in the 16th century, the cabinet quickly spread throughout Europe. Three northern cities—Augsburg, Nuremberg and Antwerp—were particularly noted for their cabinets (*see* KUNSTSCHRANK). The cabinet was commonly designed in imitation of classical architecture. Throughout the 17th and early 18th centuries. It was the most important and elaborate piece of furniture made, and the word *cabinetmaker* came to mean a maker of particularly fine furniture.

CABINET STAND (also *casket stand*)

Low table, often with a raised rim around its edge, intended to support a CABINET, CHEST or other piece of case furniture. Intended to stand against a wall, a cabinet stand was ordinarily undecorated on one side. In the late 18th and 19th centuries, a common variety of cabinet stand was the KANG JI, a small table imported from China.

CABINETMAKER

A skilled maker of fine furniture. Originally the term referred strictly to the maker of CASE FURNITURE, the manufacture of which was regarded as a separate trade from the making of other FORMS. In modern usage, when both industrial producers and craftsmen produce a range of forms, the term is being replaced by (and is synonymous with) the more inclusive term, "furniture maker."

CABLE FLUTING

Another name for STOPPED FLUTING.

CABLE MOLDING

Another name for ROPE MOLDING (*see under* MOLDING).

CABOCHON

Decorative device; raised oval shape resembling a polished, unfaceted gem. Also, a similarly convex and smoothly rounded asymmetrical shape, resembling in form a cashew nut, sometimes used as a decorative element of a rococo style (*see* ROCOCO FURNITURE) finial.

CABRIOLE CHAIR or SOFA (also *chaise en cabriolet*)

Eighteenth-century name for an upholstered chair or sofa whose back curved into the arms in a smooth line. Such a piece might or might not

cabriole sofa

have CABRIOLE LEGS (*see under* LEG); the term referred to a sort of carriage, the cabriolet (from which our word *cab* comes), that had such seats.

CABRIOLE LEG
See under LEG.

CAFFIERI, JACQUES (1673–1755)
French FONDEUR-CISELEUR who made bronze mounts for ROCOCO FURNITURE. The leading metalsmith of his day, he collaborated with many prominent cabinetmakers, notably Antoine-Robert GAUDREAU.

CAMEL-BACK SOFA
Eighteenth-century British and American furniture form; SOFA whose serpentine top, from an upward curve in the center, swept smoothly downward on either side and back up slightly at each end. This form was featured in the designs of George HEPPLEWHITE.

CAMEL FOOT
See under FOOT.

CAMPAIGN FURNITURE
Portable, collapsible furniture, made in British India from the late 18th through the 19th centuries. Campaign furniture, also called *colonial furniture,* included such pieces as chairs, settees, chests, desks and beds. It was generally made of teak, rosewood or both, and its designs were variations on the principal British furniture styles of the day.

CAMPHORWOOD (also *zhang mu*)
Aromatic HARDWOOD of China and Japan, used for storage furniture because it is believed that its odor repels moths. Yellow with reddish streaks, camphorwood is also used as veneering, especially in MARQUETRY.

CANAPÉ
French term for upholstered SETTEE or SOFA. Although the term had referred to a DAYBED in the late 17th century, the first true *canapé* arose in the early 18th century as a high-backed, somewhat formal piece—a laterally

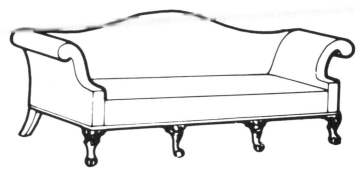

camel-back sofa

extended FAUTEUIL À LA REINE. During the century variations of the form developed. The MARQUISE was designed for two people. The CANAPÉ À CONFIDANTE had an extra seat facing outward, beyond the arm at each end. And the CAUSEUSE curved forward to allow two sitters to face each other. Gradually, the *canapé* became an informal piece; the 19th-century MÉRIDIENNE and OTTOMAN were thickly upholstered and intended for lounging. The term remains in use, denoting any comfortable sofa.

CANAPÉ À CONFIDANTE (also *confidante*)
Eighteenth-century French furniture form; wide sofa incorporating two small seats that faced outward, beyond the arms at each end.

CANAPÉ DE L'AMITIÉ (also *confidante*)
Type of 19th-century French SETTEE. It had an upholstered seat and an upholstered chair back at each end. These two backs were connected by an open wooden back composed of spindles. The *canapé de l'amitié* was a novelty item, reflecting the Second Empire's taste for coil-spring, deep-buttoned upholstery.

CANDLESTAND (also *torchère*)
Portable STAND intended to support a candle or lamp. Made in various styles from the Middle Ages onward, candlestands generally took the form of a very small platform, resting on either four legs or a central column. They ceased to be made in the 19th century, when improvements in lighting rendered them unnecessary.

CANE
See CANING.

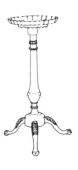

candlestand

CANEPHORUS

Decorative device; sculpted human figure, usually female, carrying a basket of fruit and flowers on her head. Derived from classical architecture, where it was used as a column, like a CARYATID, the canephorus was a popular motif for giltbronze mounts on LOUIS XVI STYLE furniture in 18th-century France.

CANING

The practice of weaving long, narrow strips of RATTAN bark or similar material to construct seats and backs of seating furniture. Caning originated in INDIAN FURNITURE, being light, cool, clean and fairly resistant to insect attack, always a concern for Indian cabinetmakers. At first popular chiefly in Britain and Holland, cane chairs spread gradually to other European countries in the course of the 18th century, but their use did not become widespread until the wholesale importation of Malayan rattan began in the 19th century.

canterbury

CANNELLATED

Decorated with FLUTING.

CANOPY

Covering or fabrics suspended above a throne or bed. Initially, in BYZANTINE and MEDIEVAL FURNITURE, the canopy served as an emblem and privilege of rank. Although curtains that were hung below a canopy to surround a bed might also provide privacy, warmth and protection from dust and insects, their primary importance was nevertheless symbolic. In any household only the ranking member's bed received a full canopy; the use of lesser, partial canopies, the half-tester and demicelure (*see* TESTER; CELURE), by other members supported further the hierarchical character of this furniture feature.

Gradually, in the era of RENAISSANCE FURNITURE, used of the canopy became less exclusive. The wooden or metal framework, or tester, was highly ornate and might be supported from the ceiling (in which case the canopy was called a SPARVER), from the wall or on corner posts with fanciful carved forms. Due to the love of opulence that characterized the period of BAROQUE FURNITURE, rich and abundant fabrics became popular in bed canopies. These were often topped with elabo-

rately upholstered valances and finials. In 18th-century France several different types of canopy developed, and thus beds received different names. (*see* LIT À COLONNES; LIT À LA DUCHESSE; LIT À LA POLONAISE). With the rise of the NEOCLASSICAL STYLE in the early 19th century, beds became simpler; the American FOURPOSTER often omitted draperies altogether. Gradually, the canopy passed out of use, except in reproductions or imitations of earlier beds.

CANTERBURY (1)

British furniture form; open-topped rack with slatted partitions for music books and sheet music. Introduced in the 1780s and still popular, the canterbury is generally called a magazine rack today. Sometimes with one or two small drawers below the rack, the canterbury usually had four short legs that were generally on castors. It is said to have first been purchased by an archbishop of Canterbury.

CANTERBURY (2)

British furniture form; serving stand of the late 18th century. A specialized TRIPOD TABLE, the canterbury stood on castors and was placed beside a dining table. Its top was an open container about 6 inches deep. One end was semicircular; here, plates were stacked next to an opening in the container's wall. The other, squared end was partitioned for silverware and cutlery. Like the betterknown music stand of the same name (*see* CANTERBURY [1]), it is associated with an archbishop of Canterbury.

CANTILEVERED CHAIR

Tubular steel chair that stands on only two front legs. Each leg has a rearward extension, or foot, that rests on the floor, thus supporting the weight of the sitter. The cantilevered chair was invented in 1924 by the Dutch designer Mart STAM and further developed by Marcel BREUER and others. Its resiliency and light weight are achieved very simply, in a design exemplifying the values of FUNCTIONALISM, the chief tenet of early modern design theory.

CANTON ENAMEL

See YANG CI.

CAPITAL
The head or topmost part of a COLUMN, consisting of a decoration surmounted by an ABACUS. As derived from the classical ORDERS OF ARCHITECTURE and from medieval Gothic architecture, columns with capitals have been prominent in most European furniture styles since the Renaissance, except those modern styles that have repudiated historical references.

CAPTAIN'S CHAIR
See under WINDSOR CHAIR.

CAPUCINE, CHAISE À LA
See CHAISE À LA CAPUCINE.

CAPUCIN, SECRÉTAIRE À (also *table à Capucin; bureau à Capucin*)
See SECRÉTAIRE À CAPUCIN.

CAQUETOIRE
French RENAISSANCE FURNITURE form; light, low chair with a tall, narrow back, a seat much wider at the front than at the back and curved arms. The chair was designed to accommodate the wide skirts popular in the late 16th century.

CARABIN, FRANÇOIS-RUPERT (1862–1932)
Alsatian sculptor and furniture maker associated with the ART NOUVEAU movement. Originally trained as a gem engraver, Rupert Carabin was inspired by the works of the French Symbolists to design furniture. His works were made of rich, dark woods, especially mahogany, that were carved with images of highly erotic nudes surrounded by decorative elements, such as grotesque masks and foliage. He worked in Paris and was associated with Samuel BING.

CARCASE
Framework or body of a piece of furniture, to which VENEER or some other surface is attached.

CARD TABLE (1)
Eighteenth-century British furniture form; square table whose top folded in half onto itself, thus saving space when not in use. Sometimes the legs folded in with the top; sometimes a SWING LEG (*see under* LEG) or GRASSHOPPER LEGS supported the folding half when open. The KNEES of the table's CABRIOLE LEGS (*see under* LEG) were usually decorated with a motif frequently repeated on the apron, but since it was placed against a wall when not in use, a card table was almost always undecorated on one side. Its top often had DISHED CORNERs to hold money or chips. Developed in the late 17th century, the card table was made in great numbers in Britain and America in the 18th. Late in the 18th century and early in the 19th, the popularity of the card table spread to Continental Europe, and it was made in France and Italy in the NEOCLASSICAL STYLES.

CARD TABLE (2)
Modern form of COLLAPSIBLE FURNITURE; table whose four legs fold up beneath the tabletop for storage.

CARL LEISTLER
Nineteenth-century Viennese furniture manufacturer. Probably best remembered now as first the employer and subsequently an early partner of Michael THONET, this firm was very fashionable in the 1840s–1850s. It made furniture in several REVIVAL STYLES. Though noted particularly for its NEO-GOTHIC STYLE work, it also produced ROCOCO REVIVAL STYLE furniture and early pieces in the RENAISSANCE REVIVAL STYLE.

CARLIN, MARTIN (c. 1730–85)
German-born French cabinetmaker; a leading ÉBÉNISTE of LOUIS XVI STYLE. Carlin was in Paris by the 1750s, and there he probably first worked for J.-F. OEBEN, whose sister he married; he formally became a master *ébéniste* in 1766. While he made a wide range of case furniture, including COMMODES (1) and SECRÉTAIRES, he specialized in small tables and desks, such as the BONHEUR DU JOUR. His pieces were commonly decorated with porcelain plaques set against a ground of ebonized wood. He used ORMOLU mounts in the form of swags of tasseled material, a personal hallmark.

caquetoire

card table

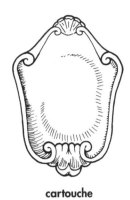

cartouche

Carver chair

CARLTON HOUSE TABLE (also *Carlton House desk*)
Late 18th-century British writing table with superstructure at back and sides housing small drawers and compartments. Usually several wide, shallow drawers were built in the frieze. Devised in the 1790s, this form was popular through the early years of the next century. It was presumably named for such a piece in Carlton House, then the home of the Prince of Wales.

CAROLEAN CHAIR
Another name for CHARLES II CHAIR.

CAROLEAN FURNITURE
Another name for English RESTORATION FURNITURE, referring to King Charles II.

CARRIER-BELLEUSE, ALBERT-ERNST (1824–87)
French sculptor and furniture maker during the Second Empire. Chiefly a highly fashionable academic portraitist and sculptor of decorative sensual female nudes, Carrier-Belleuse also designed elaborate RENAISSANCE REVIVAL STYLE furniture that often incorporated precious metals.

CARTON-PIERRE
French term for COMPO.

CARTONNIER
French term for filing cabinet; more specifically, 18th-century form for holding papers. It usually had two drawers or a small cupboard in its base and shelves or pigeonholes above, sometimes surmounted by a clock. It was sometimes a freestanding piece, sometimes mounted on one end of a BUREAU PLAT.

CARTOUCHE
Decorative motif used on RENAISSANCE, BAROQUE and ROCOCO FURNITURE. The cartouche derived from ancient Roman ornamentation excavated in Italy beginning in the 15th century and was a representation of a sheet of paper with scrolled ends or a shield, oval or abstract form with curled edges. It first appeared on furniture during the Renaissance and was especially popular in the 17th and 18th centuries.

CARVER CHAIR
Seventeenth-century AMERICAN JACOBEAN FURNITURE form. The Carver chair was constructed entirely of turned wood, except for a plank or rush seat. It was thus similar to the BREWSTER CHAIR, but it had decorative spindles only in the back. It is named after John Carver (d. 1621), the first governor of Plymouth Colony, who owned an early example of the chair. Carver died a mere four months after reaching the New World, so the original Carver chair may have come from England. Nevertheless, it was a model for many 17th-century Colonial furniture makers.

CARYATID
Decorative device; sculpted support in the form of a female figure. Derived from ancient Greek architecture, the caryatid appeared in RENAISSANCE FURNITURE and remained popular in the various NEO-CLASSICAL STYLES, especially in the DIRECTOIRE, EMPIRE and REGENCY STYLES. A rare variant using a male figure is called an *atlas* (pl. *atlantes*).

CARYATID STOOL
AFRICAN FURNITURE form made chiefly in southeastern Congo (formerly Zaire); a cylindrical STOOL whose pillar-like central element consists of carved figures, usually abstract female figures, whose backs are toward the center and whose upstretched arms support the seat. Similar configurations are made elsewhere in Africa as well. The name derives from the Western decorative device used in ancient Greek architecture.

CASE FURNITURE
Furniture built like a box and intended to contain something. The basic forms of case furniture are the CHEST and the CUPBOARD. Many other forms have been developed; prominent among them are the CABINET, the CHEST OF DRAWERS, the WARDROBE and the SECRETARY.

CASKET STAND
Another name for CABINET STAND.

CASSAPANCA

Italian RENAISSANCE FURNITURE form; a combined chest and seat. A CASSONE with a paneled back and arms, the massive *cassapanca* (literally *cassone* plus BANCA, meaning "bench") was most popular in 16th-century Florence, where it was a prominent household item. It was equipped with a mattress and cushions and often functioned as a CHAIR OF ESTATE.

CASSINA

Contemporary Italian furniture company, based in Milan. Cassina is noted for modern furniture in an innovative but simple, sober vein. Characteristically, the firm uses luxurious materials, which are often arranged to emphasize contrasts between, say, marble and glass, or fine wood and high-quality leather. Among the important Italian designers who have designed furniture for the firm are Mario BELLINI, Vico MAGISTRETTI, and Tobia and Afra SCARPA. Cassina is also noted for office furniture and systems, especially those designed by Bellini.

CASSONE

Italian RENAISSANCE FURNITURE form; CHEST usually intended as DOWER FURNITURE. Of paneled construction, *cassones* were often elaborately painted, on the front panel or the top, with mythological or religious scenes. Often these paintings were of such quality that chests were later dismantled, and their panels were framed and hung. Sometimes, though, the *cassone*'s decoration was carved in relief or inlaid. A specialized form was the CASSONE NUZIALE.

CASSONE NUZIALE

CASSONE with specialized ornamentation; dower chest whose decoration prominently featured the coats of arms of two families united by marriage.

CASTELLI FERRIERI, ANNA (b. 1920)

Contemporary Italian architect, urban planner and designer of a wide range of industrial products. Castelli Ferrieri's furniture relies heavily on the use of plastics, especially in storage and shelving systems, and emphasizes modular tables and chairs. Much of her furniture has been produced and sold by KARTELL, with whom she has been associated since 1966.

CASTIGLIONI, ACHILLE (1918–68)

Contemporary Italian architect and designer. Particularly known for his ingenious and striking lighting designs, Castiglioni also designed furniture for KARTELL and other manufacturers. One of his well-known pieces, designed in collaboration with his brother Piergiacomo Castiglioni, is the "Mezzadro" chair—more accurately a stool—which consists of an enameled metal seat, sculpted and pierced with circular holes, in imitation of a tractor seat, and cantilevered on a chromed steel strip that angles to the rear from a wooden front foot. Castiglioni also designed radios, televisions, other appliances, ceramics, glassware and flatware.

CAST-IRON FURNITURE

Nineteenth century innovation, intended chiefly for use outdoors or in such hard-wearing settings as cafés and public buildings. As smelting and casting techniques were improved early in the 19th century, iron furniture began to be manufactured—first in Britain in the 1840s, and somewhat later on the Continent and in America. Generally, the REVIVAL STYLES provided the inspiration for designers of cast-iron furniture, and the curving elements and naturalistic motifs of the ROCOCO REVIVAL STYLE were particularly suited to the fluid shaping that casting made possible. The BENTWOOD furniture of Michael THONET also influenced designs for iron pieces.

Chairs and settees were most frequently made, along with small tables, umbrella stands, fireplace fenders and tools, decorative

cassone

urns and JARDINIÈRES. Iron beds were also briefly favored, due to a then-common conviction that metal beds are more hygienic than wooden ones; however, by 1870 the BRASS BED had succeeded its iron counterpart in popularity. The demand for cast-iron furniture declined as its novelty wore off, late in the century. Its durability further discouraged sales, and foundries increasingly abandoned its manufacture, until, by the beginning of the 20th century, it was no longer made in any quantity. However, it rose to popularity again in the 1940s and continues to be made today.

laminated wood seating by Castle

CASTLE, WENDELL (b. 1932)

Contemporary American furniture maker; principal American exponent of the 1970s HANDICRAFT REVIVAL. Castle, who studied both industrial design and sculpture at the University of Kansas, is particularly well known for furniture that literally *is* sculpture. Organic forms—carved by hand from built-up blocks of laminated wood and free of decoration—take the shapes of tables, chairs and sofas without sacrificing abstract curvilinear shapes that are clearly esthetic, not functional, features. This work, produced in the 1960s and early 1970s, recalls the botanical forms and decoration of ART NOUVEAU furniture, to which Castle has always been drawn; but his more extravagant shapes reflect a conceptual freedom not felt 30 years ago, unless perhaps by GAUDI and BUGATTI. Castle's more recent work is no less idiosyncratic—for example, a long, triangular table with two carved legs at each corner. However, these pieces are less fluid in outline and more traditional in form. They are also decorated with exotic woods of striking pattern or color, in geometrical border patterns suggestive of ART DECO decoration, though without its prominent floral motifs. In all of Castle's work, the level of craft is notably high, and both his work and the teaching workshop he has run since 1970 have greatly influenced the character of the American revival of fine handcrafted furniture.

Wendell Castle seat

CASTOR

Small wheel and swivel, attached to each foot or corner of the bottom of a piece of furniture to make it easy to move without lifting. Invented in the 16th century, castors reached a peak of popularity in Victorian times and are still widely used.

CATHÉDRALE, LE STYLE

Nineteenth-century French term for the NEO-GOTHIC STYLE.

CAUSEUSE (also *confidante; tête-à-tête*)

Eighteenth-century French furniture form; upholstered SETTEE or SOFA whose ends curved forward so that two people sitting in it would nearly face each other.

CAUVET, GILLES-PAUL (1731–88)

French architect, designer and metalworker in LOUIS XVI STYLE. Best known for his work in silver, Cauvet also designed ornamentation for wall paneling, furniture and other objects. His pattern book of neoclassical designs, published in 1777, remained influential into the early 19th century.

CAVETTO MOLDING

See under MOLDING.

CEDAR

Any of a number of fragrant woods traditionally used to make chests. The three true cedars are the Atlas cedar of North Africa; the cedar of Lebanon, of biblical fame; and the deodar tree of India. All three are SOFTWOODS, pale brown in color and quite fragrant; their scent has long been thought to repel moths and other insects. This feature, combined with extreme durability, has traditionally made these woods attractive to makers of chests and other case furniture intended to store clothing. In the eastern United States, the Virginia juniper, also called the eastern red cedar, serves the same function; an African tree, the pencil cedar, is very similar. In the American West several woods—the incense cedar, the Port Orford cedar and the yellow cedar—are similarly fragrant and are used to make storage chests. In addition, several HARDWOODS of Central and South America are called cedars, because of their scent, and they, too, are used to make furniture. They are not exported in quantity, however, and outside Latin America they are principally known as the material from which cigar boxes are made.

CELLARETTE
Small CHEST, usually of wood. It is either lined inside with metal and filled with ice as a wine cooler or, unlined, compartmented and used to store wine and liquor bottles. The term is also used to denote a deep drawer or compartment intended to store bottles in a SIDEBOARD. The cellarette was in use as a separate piece of furniture prior to 1700, but the late 18th and early 19th centuries saw its greatest popularity, when it was made in the various NEOCLASSICAL STYLES, especially in Britain and America. In the southern United States, its widespread use continued until the late 19th century.

CELOUR
See CELURE.

CELURE (also *colour*)
Medieval term for a CANOPY over a bed. Sometimes the term referred to the vertical board behind the bed, from which a TESTER was erected. And sometimes it denoted the whole unit consisting of vertical board, tester, canopy and any other curtains or hangings. A demicelure, also called a half-tester, was a canopy that did not extend all the way to the foot of the bed. It was intended, in a medieval household, for the use of persons of less than the highest rank.

CENTENNIAL PERIOD REPRODUCTION FURNITURE
Copy or imitation of American antique furniture made in the last quarter of the 19th century, beginning around 1876, in connection with the first centennial of the Declaration of Independence, which was widely celebrated in the United States. The works most often reproduced were FEDERAL PERIOD furniture, especially from Baltimore; AMERICAN EMPIRE style pieces, most notably New York work; and Philadelphia CHIPPENDALE furniture. Now more than a century old, the finest Centennial reproductions can be difficult to tell from genuine period antiques. The best indicators are the frequent combination of elements from different areas—such as New York–style legs

on an otherwise Philadelphia style chair—and the presence of machine-made ornamentation. Further clues are signs of power tools elsewhere, as in machined DOVETAIL JOINTS and bandsaw or rotary saw blade marks on planks, all of which are fairly easily discerned with practice. Also, reproduction furniture frequently uses the cheaper and easier doweled joint where an early maker would have used a mortise-and-tenon joint (*see* JOINERY).

Though not very accurate, these reproductions were superior in design to the VICTORIAN PERIOD furniture that was then stylish, simply because the originals on which they were based were better. (The Centennial period is sometimes referred to as the *second period*.) Centennial period reproductions were immediately very popular and established a market in COLONIAL REVIVAL furniture that thrived for three-quarters of a century. They also helped trigger the first great boom of interest in antiques in America.

cellarette

CERTOSINA WORK
Type of INTARSIA or MARQUETRY using very small pieces of wood, bone, metal and mother-of-pearl to make complex geometrical patterns to cover the surface of a CASSONE or other chest or casket. It was popular in Lombardy and Venetia in the 14th–16th centuries. Certosina work was named after the Carthusian order of monks, whose proverbial patience the craftsman creating such a pattern would need.

CÉSAR (1921–98)
French sculptor and sometime furniture designer associated with POP ART FURNITURE. His best-known sculptures are pieces that consist of compressed automobile bodies. Born César Baldaccini, César has created a number of deliberately humorous pieces of furniture. One chair, for example, highlights a seat of soft foam, molded to present a seemingly sharp ridge to the sitter. In 1976 he designed the statuette awarded for excellence in French moviemaking—the equivalent of the U.S. Oscar—and the French awards are accordingly known as "Césars."

CEYLON SATINWOOD
Yellow to golden HARDWOOD from Sri Lanka, used principally for inlay and veneering. It is

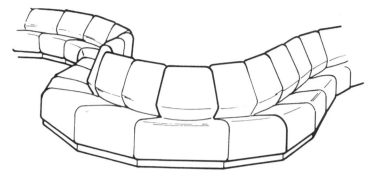

sofa by Chadwick

similar and related to WEST INDIAN SATIN-WOOD, but it is more highly figured. It has been used in European and American furniture since the early 19th century and is the principal commercial satinwood today.

CHADWICK, DON (b. 1936)

Contemporary American furniture and industrial designer. Chadwick, based in California, is best known for an ingenious set of modular seating units he designed, manufactured by the HERMAN MILLER FURNITURE CO. These units are made of polyurethane foam, which is molded to form platform, seat and back, then upholstered. There are three basic modules: one is rectangular; one is a truncated wedge, narrower in the front; and the third is the same wedge, but narrower at the back. These basic units may be connected side to side to form different layouts—straight lines, full arcs or various curves and meanders.

CHAIR

Seating form for one person, composed of horizontal surface, or seat, supported on legs and with a vertical element, or back, rising from its rear edge. Chairs were first made in ancient EGYPTIAN and MESOPOTAMIAN furniture, almost always as a grandiose piece intended as a THRONE. In fact, the chair has often since served as a symbol of rank and authority (*see* SELLA CURULIS; CHAIR OF ESTATE).

More ordinary chairs began to be made in abundance in GREEK furniture, from which the form passed on through ROMAN, BYZANTINE and MEDIEVAL furniture to the modern West and through INDIAN furniture to China (*see* HU CHUANG). The chair did not figure in PRIMITIVE or traditional JAPANESE FURNITURE.

Many types of chair have been given specific names. (*See* ANTHEMION-BACK CHAIR; BACK STOOL; BALLOON-BACK CHAIR; BANISTER-BACK CHAIR; BARREL CHAIR; BASKET CHAIR; BERGÈRE; BOARD CHAIR; BORNE; BOSTON CHAIR; BOSTON ROCKER; BREWSTER CHAIR; CABRIOLE CHAIR; CANTILEVERED CHAIR; CAQUETOIRE; CARVER CHAIR; CAST-IRON FURNITURE; CHAIR-BED; CHAIRTABLE; CHAISE À LA CAPUCINE; CHAISE À LA REINE; CHAISE À L'OFFICIER; CHAISE COURANTE; CHAISE MEUBLANTE; CHAISE VOLANTE; CHAMBER CHAIR; CHAMBER HORSE; CHARLES II CHAIR; CHAUFFEUSE; CHIAVARI CHAIR; CHUANG; COIFFEUSE (1); CORNER CHAIR; CRAPAUD; CROWN CHAIR; CROMWELLIAN CHAIR; CURULE CHAIR; DANTE CHAIR; DECK CHAIR; DENG GUA SHI YI; DIRECTOR'S CHAIR; EASY CHAIR; ELBOW CHAIR; FARTHINGALE CHAIR; FAUTEUIL; FAUTEUIL À LA REINE; GLASTONBURY CHAIR; GONDOLA CHAIR; GUAN MAO SHI; HIGH CHAIR; HIP-JOINT CHAIR; JIAO CHUANG; KLISMOS; LADDER-BACK CHAIR; LOHAN CHAIR; LUTHER CHAIR; MARTHA WASHINGTON CHAIR; MARYLAND CHIPPENDALE CHAIR; MEI GUI SHI; MISERICORD; MORRIS CHAIR; PEDESTAL CHAIR; PLASTIC FURNITURE; PLATFORM ROCKER; PRETZELBACK CHAIR; REVOLVING CHAIR; RIBBANDBACK CHAIR; ROCKING CHAIR; ROOT FURNITURE; ROUNDABOUT CHAIR (1; 2); SAN CAI TU HUI; SAVONAROLA CHAIR; SGABELLO; SHEAF-BACK CHAIR; SHIELD-BACK CHAIR; SIDE CHAIR; SILLÓN DE CADERA; SILLÓN DE FRAILEROS; SLAT-BACK CHAIR; SLIPPER CHAIR; SPINDLE-BACK CHAIR; SPOON-BACK CHAIR; SQUARE-BACK CHAIR; TABLET-ARM CHAIR; TURNED CHAIR; UPHOLSTERY; VOLTAIRE CHAIR; VOYEUSE; WAINSCOT CHAIR; WHEEL-BACK CHAIR; WICKER; WINDSOR CHAIR; WING CHAIR; YOKE-BACK CHAIR; ZANZIBAR CHAIR; ZUI WENG YI.)

CHAIR-BACK SETTEE

Late 17th- and 18th-century furniture form; SETTEE with back composed of two or three, occasionally more, linked OPENWORK chair backs of whatever style, rococo or neoclassical (*see* ROCOCO FURNITURE; NEOCLASSICAL STYLE), was current.

CHAIR-BED

Eighteenth-century furniture form; chair that unfolded to become a bed.

CHAIR OF ESTATE

In MEDIEVAL FURNITURE, chair reserved for use by the highest-ranking person in a household; in effect, a domestic THRONE. At the lowest levels of society, the chair of estate, perhaps a very crude one, was the only chair present; lesser ranking people either stood or sat on stools or benches. Among higher social strata, chairs of estate were usually ornamented to indicate their symbolic character. They were often carved with architectural motifs, such as ARCADING and PILASTERS, or had turned wood members imitating stone columns. Furthermore, they were generally painted in brilliant hues on a gilded or colored ground. Gradually, in RENAISSANCE FURNITURE, the distinction between this chair and all others diminished, but the use of chairs of estate lives on in the word *chairman*.

CHAIR-TABLE

MEDIEVAL FURNITURE form; armchair with large, round, oval or rectangular back attached by hinges to the backs of the arms. The back could be pulled down to rest on the arms, converting the piece into a table. The chair-table was made in Europe from late medieval times through the 17th century and, in America, well into the 18th century.

CHAISE À LA CAPUCINE

Rustic chair of 17th-century France, popular in the elegant world of the late LOUIS XIV STYLE. A straw-seated chair composed of turned elements, the *chaise à la Capucine* satisfied a desire for novelty in a society that was used to elaborate and expensive furniture.

CHAISE À L'OFFICIER

EMPIRE STYLE furniture form; chair with arm supports at front corners but no arms, intended for use by a man wearing a sword.

CHAISE À LA REINE

Eighteenth-century French term for an upholstered chair with flat back, as opposed to the more comfortable CHAISE EN CABRIOLET.

CHAISE COURANTE

Old French term for light, portable chair, as opposed to the relatively immobile CHAISE MEUBLANTE.

CHAISE D'AFFAIRES

French term for either CLOSE STOOL or CHAMBER CHAIR.

CHAISE EN CABRIOLET

Eighteenth-century French term for CABRIOLE CHAIR.

CHAISE LONGUE

French term (literally, "long chair") denoting a form of DAYBED, an armchair with elongated seat that can accommodate the sitter's outstretched legs. Originally developed from the daybed in the 17th century, the chaise longue first achieved great popularity in the late 18th century. Variant forms developed in France at that time: the DUCHESSE, with a rounded back; the DUCHESSE EN BATEAU, with a similarly rounded foot; and the DUCHESSE BRISÉE (the English "duchess"), composed of a seat and stool.

CHAISE MEUBLANTE

Old French term for very heavy chair, with undecorated rear, intended to be kept in one place against a wall, as opposed to the portable CHAISE COURANTE.

chair-table

CHAISE PERCÉE

French term for either CLOSE STOOL or CHAMBER CHAIR.

CHAISE VOLANTE

Nineteenth-century French term for very light, easily movable side chair, such as the CHIAVARI CHAIR or the BALLOON-BACK CHAIR.

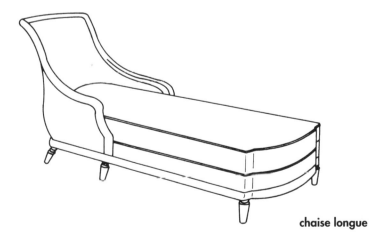
chaise longue

CHAMBER BOX
Another name for CLOSE STOOL.

CHAMBER CHAIR (also *commode chair; necessary chair; close stool chair*)
Eighteenth-century furniture form; portable toilet, successor to the CLOSE STOOL. The chamber chair appeared to be an ordinary chair in a fashionable style, but it had a hinged seat over an oval hole in a padded sub-seat and a deep apron concealing a shelf with a chamber pot.

CHAMBER HORSE
Late 18th-century exercise device incorporated into a low chair. A slender post rose above each of the front legs to the height of the chair back. A leather-upholstered seat contained a number of wooden planks, stacked one above the other and separated by sets of coiled springs. This accordionlike arrangement was compressed vertically when sat upon. The sitter grasped the two front posts and, pulling with his arms and pushing against the floor with his legs, got up and sat down repeatedly.

chamber horse

CHAMBERS, WILLIAM (1726–96)
British NEOCLASSICAL STYLE architect and designer. Principally known as one of the most important architects of late 18th-century Britain, Chambers also produced an eclectic range of furniture using neoclassical ornamental details and architectural forms. After journeys to China with the Swedish East India Co. in his youth, Chambers published *Designs for Chinese Buildings* (1757), which included furniture designs. This work had no impact on contemporary design, perhaps because it was more authentic than the whimsical CHINOISERIE of the day. Following subsequent architectural training in Paris and Rome, Chambers disclaimed any interest in Oriental design, calling it "inferior to the antique."

CHAMBERT, ERIK (1902–88)
Swedish artist and designer of SCANDINAVIAN MODERN furniture. In the 1920s and 1930s, Chambert was a prominent designer in Sweden, working also in America, France, and Germany. In the 1950s, he was a successful abstract painter in Paris.

Erik Chambert chair

CHAMFER (also *champfer*)
Narrow, oblique surface formed when a corner edge where two surfaces meet is planed or cut away.

CHANNON, JOHN (active 1733–83)
British ROCOCO FURNITURE maker. Channon specialized in furniture with marquetry incorporating brass inlays and with elaborate ormolu mounts, in the manner of French LOUIS XV STYLE work.

CHAPIN, AARON (1753–1838)
Connecticut FEDERAL PERIOD cabinetmaker. Son of Eliphalet CHAPIN, Aaron Chapin worked with his father in East Windsor until 1783, when he moved to Hartford and began to work in the NEOCLASSICAL STYLE, primarily following the patterns of George HEPPLEWHITE. His son Laertes succeeded him in business and died in 1847.

CHAPIN, ELIPHALET (1741–1807)
Connecticut COUNTRY CHIPPENDALE FURNITURE maker. Born in Somers, Connecticut, Chapin was trained in Philadelphia and began his career there. In 1771 he returned to Connecticut and settled in East Windsor. There he made furniture distinctive for such cosmopolitan elaborations as elegant pad feet and fancy carved finials, yet much sparer and simpler than corresponding Philadelphia work (*see* PHILADELPHIA CHIPPENDALE FURNITURE) in overall proportion and feeling, in keeping with the demands of Chapin's rural market. His son Aaron CHAPIN was his partner before he moved to Hartford in 1783.

CHAREAU, PIERRE (1883–1950)
French furniture designer and architect associated with the INTERNATIONAL STYLE. Originally a designer of furniture in the ART DECO style, Chareau was influenced during the 1920s and 1930s by BAUHAUS designers and LE CORBUSIER and gravitated toward the International style. His later furniture was simple and rectilinear in form and bore no ornament. Chareau was a member of the UNION DES ARTISTES MODERNES, the Paris organization that promoted the International style. He is particularly well known for a series

of designs, begun in 1924, for iron desks with trays that pivoted to provide extra working surfaces and for a tubular steel chair of 1930.

CHARLES II CHAIR (also *Restoration chair*)

English RESTORATION furniture form that also appeared in the AMERICAN WILLIAM AND MARY STYLE; high-backed chair with crest rail and front stretchers elaborately carved with baroque scrolls and floral motifs (*see* BAROQUE FURNITURE). Its other stretchers are turned, as are the legs and uprights, and it may or may not have arms. Caned, sometimes upholstered, panels comprise the seat and back. Frequently, a crown appears in the carving of the crest rail.

CHARLES X STYLE

French NEOCLASSICAL STYLE current during the reign of King Charles X (1824–30); a variation of RESTAURATION STYLE. Charles X–style furniture tends to be somewhat less massive than that of the earlier LOUIS XVIII STYLE, with less prominent bronzes, and with a greater emphasis on light-colored woods.

CHARPENTIER, ALEXANDRE (1856–1909)

French ART NOUVEAU furniture designer and medalist. Principally a metal worker, Charpentier made a number of finely crafted pieces of furniture in a decorative Parisian Art Nouveau style for Samuel BING. Some of these pieces had inlaid bronze panels (also of his design), which often depicted sinuous female nudes.

CHASING

Technique of decorating a metal surface. Designs or figures are engraved or embossed by using a chasing CHISEL—a chisel with a rounded rather than sharp edge—or a chasing hammer, a hammer with a rounded head.

CHATOL

Early 19th-century Danish furniture form; principal domestic piece made in the DANISH EMPIRE STYLE. A cylinder-front desk, the *chatol* was topped by cupboards containing fitted compartments for cutlery and glassware, reflecting the form's use in a chamber that served as both dining room and drawing room or study.

CHAUFFEUSE

French furniture form originating in the 17th century; chair with very low seat, intended for sitting close to a fire.

CHEESEBOX SEAT

Nineteenth-century American RUSH SEAT with a round shape like that of a COMPASS SEAT.

CHÉNAVARD, CLAUDE AIMÉ (1798–1838)

French furniture maker and decorator, associated with the NEO-GOTHIC STYLE. Best known for his neo-Gothic work, Aimé Chénavard also produced fashionable furniture and interiors in the other REVIVAL STYLES of the day.

CHERMAYEFF, SERGIUS IVAN (1900–96)

Russian-born British INTERNATIONAL STYLE designer of the 1930s. In 1928 Serge Chermayeff, educated in Britain and trained in art in Paris, married into the family that owned Waring & GILLOWS, a long-established, conservative firm of decorators and furniture makers. Through the firm, Chermayeff presented new furniture designs in the International style, including his own tubular steel stacking chairs. Thus, he was partly responsible for the successful introduction of functionalistic modern design. This new design style influenced, among others, the work of Wells COATES, Oliver HILL, Raymond McGRATH and E. M. FRY, all architects and designers; and Gordon RUSSELL, designer and furniture maker. Wells Coates and Chermayeff, in fact, visited the BAUHAUS in 1931 as part of their study of innovative design. In 1933 Chermayeff moved to the United States, where he practiced and taught architecture.

CHERRY

Smooth, long-grained HARDWOOD; handsome, easily worked and used in fine furniture. Cherry is a pale brown wood that darkens with age to a deep red-brown. The European cherry is somewhat rare, and its use is accordingly limited. The American black cherry has been widely used as a commercial

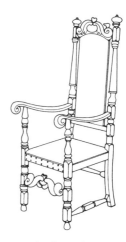

Charles II chair

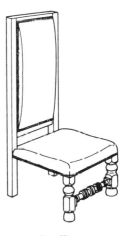

chauffeuse

timber in the southeastern United States for furniture and paneling since Colonial times.

CHERRY MAHOGANY
Another name for MAKORÉ.

chest-on-chest
Townsend-Goddard

CHEST
Very ancient furniture form; large lidded box intended for storage. First appearing in EGYPTIAN and MESOPOTAMIAN FURNITURE, the chest was the most important piece of domestic furniture until the CUPBOARD and the more elaborate CABINET overtook it when forms diversified during the period of RENAISSANCE FURNITURE. At that time, the chest gave rise, through the intermediary MULE CHEST, to the CHEST OF DRAWERS. However, the simple chest remained a popular piece of furniture through the 18th century, and it is still used today, though chiefly for transport or as a purposefully archaic form.

CHEST OF DRAWERS
Case piece; CHEST housing a stack of DRAWERS. The chest of drawers evolved in the 15th century from the most important case piece in MEDIEVAL FURNITURE, the chest. At first, small boxes were placed in chests as removable compartments, to avoid disturbing all of the contents of the chest in order to remove one item. Then it was realized that it would be simpler to remove the boxes on the bottom through the side of the chest, rather than unloading those above to get at them. At this time, chests were pierced below their main compartment, which opened from the top, and boxes were placed in these lateral openings. The development of

drawers, with slides and grooves to facilitate their operation, next produced the MULE CHEST. Eventually, during the 16th century, the top-loading chest compartment was simply eliminated, and the chest of drawers was born. This useful piece immediately underwent further development. In the 17th century the CHEST-ON-STAND and the CHEST-ON-CHEST arose in England to raise the drawers to a convenient height. The former form foreshadowed the American HIGHBOY, while the latter became known as the TALLBOY. In France a similar evolution occurred: the COMMODE was a raised chest of drawers; the CHIFFONNIÈRE, a tall one. The chest of drawers is now a staple item in Western furniture; most older varieties are reproduced (*see* REPRODUCTION FURNITURE), and new designs continue to be created.

CHEST-ON-CHEST
Seventeenth-century English furniture form; case piece composed of one CHEST OF DRAWERS on top of another, slightly wider one. The form developed in the late 17th century and evolved into the 18th-century TALLBOY, to which the term CHEST-ON-CHEST continued to apply, especially in America. In American usage the term can also refer to the HIGHBOY.

CHEST-ON-FRAME
Eighteenth-century name for HIGHBOY.

CHEST-ON-STAND
Seventeenth-century English furniture form; case piece composed of a CHEST OF DRAWERS on a tablelike framework with a flat top. The form first appeared in RESTORATION FURNITURE with a low stand whose thick legs were connected by ARCADING. By the end of the 17th century, though, the stand was high and had elegant turned or carved legs joined by stretchers. Drawers were often added to this frame, a shallow central one flanked by deeper ones. Early in the 18th century, the chest-on-stand was generally supplanted in England by the TALLBOY, a type of CHEST-ON-CHEST, though in America, as the HIGHBOY, it remained fashionable throughout the century.

CHESTERFIELD
Heavily upholstered SOFA with no exposed woodwork and whose back and arms usually

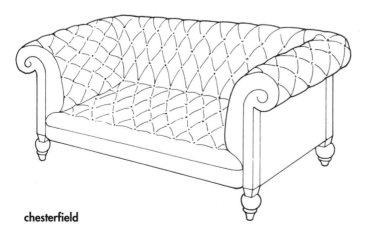

chesterfield

form a single curve. Associated with the VICTORIAN PERIOD In England, the chesterfield is a luxurious example of the use of coilspring, deep-buttoned UPHOLSTERY, which was developed in about 1830. The origin of the name is a matter of dispute.

CHESTNUT

Pale brown HARDWOOD used occasionally as veneering or inlay in furniture. It is easily stained and has an attractive grain, but it is not a strong wood. Highly resistant to rot, however, it finds its commonest application today in fencing. It was particularly popular for furniture in the early 18th century. Japanese chestnut is known as KURI.

CHEVAL GLASS (also *horse dressing-glass*)

Portable full-length mirror mounted within a rectangular structure or between two uprights. In either case, the mounting rests on TRESTLE supports, usually wheeled. This arrangement of legs gives the piece its names. The framed mirror was mounted on pins attached halfway up the sides so that it could be tilted. Developed in the late 18th century, the cheval glass was a prominent NEOCLASSICAL STYLE form early in the next century. It became especially popular in the EMPIRE STYLE in France, where it was known as a *Psyche*.

CHEVAL SCREEN

Low SCREEN composed of a single panel with low transverse feet, often with slides at each side so that the panel can be raised and lowered. Developed in the Middle Ages, the cheval screen has been used as a FIRE SCREEN, when its raised panel shields those nearby while permitting the circulation of heated air from below. It has also served, in its lowered or fixed position, as a simple room divider and protection against heat or drafts.

CHEVRON

Decorative motif resembling the letter *V*, either erect or upside down.

CHIAVARI CHAIR

Any of several light Italian side chairs, composed of simple, slender elements, that were

first made in the early 19th century and are still popular today. A *chiavari* chair has straight legs, usually turned, a BOX STRETCHER (*see under* STRETCHER), a RUSH SEAT and a simple back consisting of a CREST RAIL and a CROSS RAIL between turned STILES. Named for the town near Genoa where it was developed in about 1810, the *chiavari* chair was made throughout the 19th century in ornamented versions reflecting the various REVIVAL STYLES. Beginning in the 1930s, the original austere simplicity of the form was brought back by modern Italian designers—notably Gio PONTI.

CHIFFONIER (1)

Anglicized term for CHIFFONNIÈRE; light CHEST OF DRAWERS. In American usage, specifically a tall *chiffonnière*.

CHIFFONIER (2)

Nineteenth-century British furniture form; small table or cupboard taking any of various forms. A chiffonier might have a galleried top (*see* GALLERY) or a top surmounted by another shelf on decorative supports. Some had drawers, others shelves, still others one shelf between their legs. It was usually used as a small side table for serving food or drinks. Its name derives from the French TABLE EN CHIFFONNIÈRE.

cheval glass

CHIFFONNIÈRE

Eighteenth-century French furniture form; CHEST OF DRAWERS with somewhat shallow drawers, designed to store cloth, sewing materials and small items of apparel. Less roomy than a typical COMMODE (1), a *chiffonnière* did not extend as far from the wall it was placed against. A *chiffonnière* might be tall or short; the tall version, with many drawers, is referred to in the American usage of the Anglicized term CHIFFONIER (1).

After about 1800 the term *chiffonnière* became attached to the TABLE EN CHIFFONNIÈRE, originally a table used when sewing. This generated another English use of the term (*see* CHIFFONIER [2]).

CHIMERA

Decorative motif; image of fabulous winged animal, usually with head, body and front legs of a lion or goat, attached to the tail of a serpent. Originating in ancient Greek architectural ornamentation, the chimera, in various forms, was popular in RENAISSANCE FURNITURE, especially in the MANNERIST STYLE.

CHINA CABINET (also *china closet*)
Eighteenth-century furniture form; piece of case furniture with shelves, usually enclosed by glass doors, intended to store and display fine ceramics. The 18th-century fashion for collecting Oriental porcelain made this form an important item of domestic furniture.

CHINA CLOSET
Another name for CHINA CABINET.

CHINA STAND
Furniture form of 17th and 18th centuries; low table or tall platform intended to display a piece of porcelain. The form, Oriental in inspiration, arose in the late 17th century, when overseas commerce stimulated the vogue for collecting Oriental ceramics. It remained popular through much of the 18th century.

CHINA TABLE
Eighteenth-century name for TEA TABLE.

CHINESE CHIPPENDALE FURNITURE
Modern name for British CHINOISERIE furniture of the 1750s, named for examples in Thomas CHIPPENDALE's book *The Gentleman and Cabinet-maker's Director*. A uniquely British form of ROCOCO FURNITURE, Chinese Chippendale work was a manifestation of the period's enthusiasm for the novel and exotic. It was characterized by geometric FRETWORK in backs and sides of chairs and in friezes and galleries of small tables, as well as by pagoda-like superstructures atop case furniture and beds. The most popular forms in this style were chairs, settees, tables and small cabinets, where fretwork could dominate. Very little additional ornamentation was used; when it was, it was always angular in outline, matching the fretwork. This furniture was not invented by Chippendale; in fact, it was made prior to the publication of the *Director* in 1754. Other designers who created such

Chinese chair

Chinese furniture Tang dynasty table

pieces included Henry COPLAND, Matthias DARLY, INCE & MAYHEW, Matthias LOCK and Robert MANWARING. Chinese Chippendale furniture was popular only during the 1750s. It ceased to be fashionable with the rise of the ADAM STYLE, though it was briefly reprised early in the 19th century.

CHINESE FURNITURE
The history of Chinese furniture stretches back several thousand years, but it is difficult to reconstruct, even for fairly recent epochs, for two main reasons. First, China has undergone frequent periods of extraordinary upheaval scarcely paralleled in the West, generally accompanied by widespread destruction and pillage. As a result, very little furniture has survived from many periods whose Western counterparts are well represented. Second, Chinese taste, in furniture perhaps even more than in the other arts, has always been extremely conservative, and similar pieces have been made for centuries, often with only slight changes. This tendency was reinforced, beginning at least as long ago as the Ming dynasty (1369–1644), when the imperial government closely regulated the domestic furnishings of the various ranks of society; these rules varied very little for centuries. Thus, it has proved difficult to establish a developmental history of Chinese furniture by style and period, and most assignments of date are questionable.

Traditional Chinese furniture has been distinguished from remotest antiquity by its reliance on crafted JOINERY in construction, to the complete exclusion of nails and screws and with only rare use of glue and DOWELS. This joinery allowed for the repeated expansion and contraction of wood caused by the extreme changes of temperature that are typical of the weather in most of China. Many different MORTISE-AND-TENON JOINTS, plus the MITER and, to a somewhat lesser extent, the DOVETAIL JOINT (*see under* JOINERY), constituted the Chinese furniture maker's repertoire. TURNERY was unknown, and all furniture elements were carved, for the LATHE was never invented in or imported to China.

Until the late second century A.D., the Chinese sat on mats on the floor or ground and had no raised furniture, as developed in the West. (This manner of living was transmitted to Japan, and traditional JAPANESE FURNITURE still reflects it.) Nevertheless,

Chinese furniture making developed early. Typical Chinese joinery was practiced as early as 400 B.C. The most frequently made pieces at this early date were the PING, or SCREEN; the JI, an armrest; and various small tables. The most grandiose piece was a low platform on legs or paneled walls, the ancestor of the KANG. An open cupboard with shelves anticipated later wardrobe forms. LACQUER was already used on many pieces; it was developed to provide protection against insects—a great problem, especially in southern China, where most early development occurred.

China was first unified under the Qin (Ch'in) dynasty (249–207 B.C.), which was quickly succeeded by the long-lasting Han (206 B.C.–A.D. 220). During the Han, both the *kang* and the *ping* evolved more fully, as did several WICKER and wooden CHESTS. The major development during this dynasty came near its end, in about A.D. 200: raised and portable seating, in the form of stools and chairs, was introduced, probably from India. These forms were collectively called HU CHUANG, or "barbarian seating."

After the Han, a long, troubled period ensued, followed by the Tang (T'ang) dynasty (618–907), generally considered the first great "Golden Age" of Chinese art and crafts. Unfortunately, little furniture of the period has survived, though something is known of it from paintings and manuscripts. A huge revolving bookcase, the ZHUAN LUN JING CHANG, was used in Buddhist monasteries. The CHUANG, a CHAIR OF ESTATE related to the massive thrones of INDIAN FURNITURE, was an important piece. Small tables and the *ji* were still made. Furniture was ornamented with elaborate foliate SCROLLS incorporating images of flowers, birds and animals—a decorative repertoire influenced by the arts of Sassanian Persia.

The *ping* underwent a very significant change, incorporating for the first time painted panels; leading artists began to decorate these screens. Another Tang innovation was also to be long-lived—a standard arrangement including the TANG HUA AN, a long, narrow table, with a painting on the wall above it, and a smaller, square table, the table of the Eight Immortals, or BA XIAN ZHUO, in front of it. This combination was to be a basic component of domestic furnishings for a thousand years, into recent times. Such developments continued under the Song (Sung) dynasty (960–1279), when an important new form— the JIAO CHUANG, or X-FRAME chair—was added, in both folding and fixed pieces. One example was the SAN CAI TU HUI, or "chair of the old man who has been drinking," which was to be a favorite for the next five centuries.

Under the short Yuan (Yüan) dynasty (1280–1367), China was ruled by the Mongols, and a secure, ordered and flourishing society paved the way for the dynasty whose furniture is most familiar in the West— the Ming (1368–1644), which was an apex in the history of Chinese art. In furniture HARD- WOOD forms reached their peak of development. Numerous woods were popular: notably HUANG HUA LI, a ROSEWOOD; the strikingly figured "chicken-wing wood," or JI CHI MU; and two PADAUKS—ZI TAN, also known as "purple sandalwood," and HONG MU, a dark red wood. NAN MU, a yellowish wood, and CAMPHORWOOD were also used. XIANG SHA MU, a fragrant pine, was one of the few SOFT- WOODS employed. *Hua mu,* or BURL VENEER, was prized in any wood.

A variety of chairs were made in the Ming; they all featured a cubical frame below the seat, composed of the legs and a low BOX STRETCHER (*see under* STRETCHER) whose front element served as a footrest. Their upper parts varied, and the different designs bore striking names. The DENG GUA SHI YI, the "chair like a hanging lantern shaped like a chair," had arisen in the Song and would not outlast the Ming, but others were made through the subsequent Qing (Ch'ing) dynasty (1644– 1911), into recent times. These included the GUAN MAO SHI, or "scholar's-cap" chair; the LUO QUAN YI, or *lohan* chair; and the MEI GUI SHI, which had a low back. The X-frame *san cai tu hui* continued to be made, and at the end of the Ming, a similar chair arose—the ZUI WENG YI, or "drunken lord's chair." By the Ming two variants of the *kang* had evolved—the TA CHUANG, a spacious SETTEE, and the JIA ZI CHUANG, a TESTER bed. The KANG JI and KANG CUPBOARD were small pieces, intended for use on the platforms of the larger pieces, and they reached their fullest development in the Ming.

This period also produced elegant STOOLS—the DENG and the barrel-shaped DUN. A stool sometimes served as a small side table, or JIA JI, and various other forms fell into that category as well, including the *lute table,* or QIN ZHUO, and a number of GAM-

ING TABLES. A DRAW-LEAF TABLE, the YAN JI, was used to present food and drink on special occasions. The large, square HUA ZHUO provided a surface for painting or writing. The chief showpiece of a Ming dynasty house was the *altar table,* or *ji tai shi an,* intended for the practice of religious ritual. Tables most frequently had square legs with horse-hoof feet (*see* HORSE-HOOF FOOT, *under* FOOT), but other designs were also used—for example, the ELEPHANT-TRUNK LEG (*see under* LEG).

Ming case furniture was grandly massive, featuring a tall two-door wardrobe surmounted by the DING GUI, or hat cupboard, and the SHU GUI, a closed bookcase whose base was wider than its top. Another large form was the BAI YAN, or "hundred eyes," a pharmaceutical cupboard with many small drawers. A flat chest, the TANG XIANG, was designed for fur-lined clothing. For dining, a small but massively scaled CELLARETTE was often used. Case pieces, when in hardwood, bore very little ornamentation, featuring only modest HARDWARE of brass or PAKTONG, a Chinese nickel silver alloy.

Lacquered pieces, however, were decorated over every inch, and several lacquering techniques were perfected: DIAO TIAN, or "leather lacquer"; HUA QI, painted lacquer; TI HONG, red work known in the West as "Peking lacquer"; and two methods of inlaying other materials in lacquer—XIANG QIAN and YIN PING TUO. Screens of *ke hui,* known in the West as COROMANDEL LACQUER, were first made during the Ming period.

ROOT FURNITURE, fashioned from the roots of trees, was made with great sophistication in the Ming and Qing, although the practice had arisen somewhat earlier. PORCELAIN was also used in Ming furniture, sometimes in plaques set in the backs of especially ornate chairs, but more often as *dun,* or barrel-shaped stools, used outdoors. In the Qing another decorative technique was introduced to Chinese furniture makers: YANG CI, known in the West as *Canton enamel,* was the Chinese version of the European device of painting with enamels on metal plaques. Chinese craftsmen learned this technique in response to an imperial edict.

In the Qing dynasty, the final imperial epoch, furniture styles became more ornate, but basic forms did not change in most work. In the 18th and 19th centuries, however, a flourishing export trade arose, and Chinese furniture makers adopted European forms and ornamentation for their foreign customers. These pieces tended to be confused in decoration and shape, compared to work made for the domestic market. In the 20th century, China has been in a state of almost constant turmoil, and little is known of developments in furniture style; however, Western influence has become stronger in every field, and mass-production techniques are becoming increasingly common. Nevertheless, the esthetic conservatism of the Chinese will probably help to keep alive the ideas and methods of traditional furniture making.

CHINOISERIE

European decorative style using motifs from the ornamental and pictorial repertoire of Asian decorative art, chiefly China's but also including Japan's and India's. The first great fashion for Chinoiserie occurred in the second half of the 17th century. Scenes imitating Chinese and Japanese art were commonly applied to furniture and other objects. Monkeys, Oriental pheasants and exotic landscapes with Chinese figures were frequently presented, though in traditionally Western compositions. The enthusiasm for these motifs gave rise to the use of imported LACQUER and to the attempt to approximate it by JAPANNING, the greatest refinement of which was the development, by 1730, of VERNIS MARTIN. Imported screens of COROMANDEL LACQUER were taken apart and used as VENEER. In the ROCOCO FURNITURE of the 18th century, the fondness for Chinoiserie did not abate. In addition to the continued use of Oriental motifs, Chinese furniture was more directly imitated. For example, its FRETWORK inspired adaptations such as the "Chinese" pieces of English designer Thomas CHIPPENDALE (*see* CHINESE CHIPPENDALE FURNITURE). In the eclectic REGENCY STYLE of early 19th-century Britain, furniture incorporating "Chinese" fretwork, *à la* Chippendale, was briefly fashionable, appearing in the work of George SMITH and Thomas TATHAM, among others. Since that time, few Western furniture designers, with the notable exception of GREEN & GREENE, have shown much interest in Chinese design, although the early modern enthusiasm for JAPONISME (*see* ART FURNITURE MOVEMENT; William GODWIN) resulted in the use of many decorative motifs from Oriental art, some of them ultimately Chinese. However, in furniture history, the term *Chinoiserie* is generally reserved for the phenomenon of the 17th and 18th centuries.

CHIP CARVING
Carved decoration used on wooden MEDIEVAL FURNITURE and later forms throughout northern Europe. Shallow geometrical designs, commonly within ROUNDELS, were gouged and chiseled, especially on the panels of chests.

CHIPPENDALE, THOMAS (1718–79)
British ROCOCO FURNITURE maker and designer; publisher of first British PATTERN BOOK devoted entirely to furniture design, *The Gentleman and Cabinet-maker's Director* (1754, with new editions in 1755 and 1762). This book, familiarly known as the *Director,* presented all types of domestic furniture in the rococo manner adapted from the French LOUIS XV STYLE. While Chippendale's designs were not strikingly original—they were variations, sometimes quite close ones, of already published British and French work—they represented the maturity of British rococo furniture, sometimes called *Chippendale style* because the effect of the *Director* was so great (*see also* IRISH CHIPPENDALE FURNITURE). In the United States the term AMERICAN CHIPPENDALE FURNITURE is applied for the same reason.

A carpenter's son from Yorkshire, Chippendale had his own workshop in London by 1749. With the publication of the *Director,* he became famous, and his business flourished. He employed many cabinetmakers and designers—including Henry COPLAND, Matthias DARLY and Matthias LOCK—in one of the largest furniture-making establishments in London. His furniture emphasized carved ornamentation, in delicately decorated CABRIOLE LEGS (*see under* LEG) and chair backs (as in the hallmark RIBBAND-BACK CHAIR) and in applied motifs on secretaries (*see* SECRETARY) and other case furniture. He also shared the period's taste for the novel and exotic, and he popularized two uniquely British variants of rococo design, now called CHIPPENDALE GOTHIC FURNITURE and CHINESE CHIPPENDALE FURNITURE.

After about 1765 Chippendale made much furniture in the ADAM STYLE and in an Anglicized version of the LOUIS XVI STYLE, although these NEOCLASSICAL STYLE designs may have been created by his son Thomas CHIPPENDALE Jr. Following Chippendale's death from consumption, his son continued to run the business.

CHIPPENDALE, THOMAS, JR. (1749–1822)
British NEOCLASSICAL STYLE cabinetmaker and furniture designer. Son of Thomas CHIPPENDALE, the outstanding ROCOCO FURNITURE maker and designer, Chippendale the Younger, as he is sometimes known, may have designed the ADAM STYLE furniture produced by his father's workshops in the 1760s and 1770s. He carried on the business after his father's death in 1779, producing richly ornamented neoclassical style furniture based on the French LOUIS XVI STYLE. Also in 1779 he published a pattern book of neoclassical designs, *Sketches for Ornament,* markedly French in inspiration. He continued to follow French trends, as he became, in the 19th century, a leading REGENCY STYLE maker.

CHIPPENDALE GOTHIC FURNITURE
Modern name for British NEO-GOTHIC STYLE furniture of the 1750s, characterized by application of motifs from medieval ecclesiastic architecture to 18th-century furniture forms. Named after examples in Thomas CHIPPENDALE's book *The Gentleman and Cabinet-maker's Director* (1754), Chippendale Gothic furniture derived nothing from true GOTHIC FURNITURE, which was largely unknown at that time. Chair and table legs took the form of clustered columns; pointed arches and Gothic window TRACERY appeared on cupboard doors, chair backs and the paneled sides of case pieces. CROCKETS clung to vertical elements, and turrets and pinnacles topped secretaries (*see* SECRETARY) and bedposts. Occasionally, Gothic elements were even joined with the CHINOISERIE devices of CHINESE CHIPPENDALE FURNITURE. Chippendale Gothic furniture was also made by other designers, notably Batty LANGLEY and Sanderson MILLER.

CHIPPENDALE STYLE
Another name for British ROCOCO FURNITURE.

chip carving

Chippendale Gothic chair

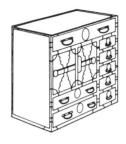

cho-dansu

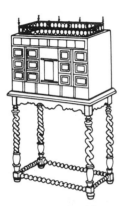

Churrigueresque
vargueño

CHO-DANSU

Traditional JAPANESE FURNITURE form; type of TANSU used in a shop to store a merchant's account books, writing materials and so on. It may have any of various combinations of drawers and compartments with sliding doors, but it generally includes a wide drawer across the top and a stack of small drawers at the right.

CHRISTIAN VIII STYLE

See DANISH EMPIRE STYLE.

CHRISTIANSEN, HANS (1866–1945)

German designer in the SEZESSION style. Christiansen studied painting and design in Hamburg and Munich; in 1890 he founded a company in Munich that dealt in paintings and interior furnishings. Christiansen visited the United States in 1893 and was so impressed by the work of Louis Comfort TIFFANY that he resumed studying design, under J. M. OLBRICH and others, on his return to Germany. Believing that the artist should practice all, or many, of the arts, he continued to paint; he wrote philosophy; and he designed furniture, jewelry, clothes, glass and ceramics. Christiansen's furniture was in the style of the Vienna Sezession: austerely rectilinear, with bold geometric decoration, dramatically contrasting colors and a frequent use of metal sabots.

CHUANG (CH'UANG)

Chinese term for any piece of raised furniture intended for sitting or reclining. It encompasses such prominent CHINESE FURNITURE forms as the HU CHUANG, JIAO CHUANG, TA CHUANG and JIA ZI CHUANG. The term may refer more particularly to the CHAIR OF ESTATE, popular in China from the late Han (c. A.D. 200) through the Tang (618–907) dynasties, based on the massive thrones of INDIAN FURNITURE.

CHUGLAM

Pale, yellow HARDWOOD of India, used in furniture, especially as decorative VENEER. A rare greyish variant, known as SILVER-GREY WOOD, was used in the 19th century, when it was more common.

CHURCHILL, LEMUEL (active 1805–28)

Boston DIRECTORY STYLE cabinetmaker. A follower of the English REGENCY STYLE, as exemplified by the patterns of Thomas SHERATON, Churchill was well known for furniture in an austere but elegant NEO-CLASSICAL STYLE.

CHURRIGUERESQUE FURNITURE

Spanish BAROQUE FURNITURE, characterized by extravagant use of inlaid and carved decoration. Seventeenth-century Spanish architecture and furniture takes its name from the Churriguera brothers, principal designers of the lavishly ornamented buildings of the time, contrasting sharply with the austere DESORNAMENTADO STYLE of the late 16th century. During the 17th century, under the influence of the Counter-Reformation, Spanish furniture makers first followed the example of Italy, applying dramatic carving and bold colors to traditional architectonic forms. Exuberant decoration in rich materials made evident the flow of wealth from Spain's American empire. Later in the century the French LOUIS XIV STYLE influenced the Churrigueresque; new forms and more gilding and upholstery were introduced, tending to mute the extraordinarily abundant carving of earlier work. The chief purely Spanish feature that remained was a trace of the Moorish MUDÉJAR STYLE, in elaborately geometrical INLAY work on cabinet fronts and tabletops.

The VARGUEÑO, an indigenous form, continued to be the dominant furniture form throughout this period. Previously an emblem of the greatest wealth and highest social status, it was now much more widespread among the middle class. It bore elaborate and colorful decoration derived from architecture and influenced by the German KUNSTSCHRANK, known through trade with the Spanish Netherlands. The PIE DE PUENTE, the traditional stand for a *vargueño,* generally stood on spiral-turned legs, a characteristic of baroque styling throughout Europe. The CHEST began to disappear in fashionable households and was replaced by the CUPBOARD, usually with heavy moldings in geometrical patterns on its doors. Late Churrigueresque cupboards often bore elaborate ACANTHUS leaf motifs.

The traditional Spanish tables, a long medieval table with box stretchers and the Renaissance form called a GUARDROOM TABLE, were still made, but with significant variations. Drawers appeared in the frieze, usually separated from one another by applied CONSOLES and bearing carved foliage or heavy geometrical moldings. Legs were complexly turned or carved, and TRESTLE legs were frequently hinged to the tabletop to permit folding. The SILLÓN DE FRAILEROS continued to be made, often with very wide, flat arms that served as small tables for the sitter. Late in the 17th century, the French upholstered FAUTEUIL, with its shaped back and elaborate stretchers, was imitated, though the upholstery was usually of Spanish leather, as opposed to the fine damasks and silks popular in France. However, by the end of the century, the Churrigueresque merged completely with French taste, which then dominated Spanish furniture for centuries. Churrigueresque furniture was a continuing influence on Latin American SPANISH COLONIAL FURNITURE through the late 19th century.

CIMA, GIUSEPPE (active c. 1840)

Italian designer and writer. Cima's book, *L'Addobatore Moderno,* published in Milan in about 1840, contained many furniture designs in several of the REVIVAL STYLES. It influenced Italian furniture makers for several decades.

CINNAMON WOOD

Another name for CAMPHORWOOD, referring to its scent.

CINQUEFOIL

Ornamental motif in GOTHIC FURNITURE; radially symmetrical five-lobed formalized leaf form, usually enclosed in a circle. Commonly used in Gothic TRACERY, the cinquefoil was also popular in the NEO-GOTHIC STYLE of the 18th and 19th centuries.

CISTA (pl. *cistae*)

ETRUSCAN FURNITURE form; small circular or oval CHEST of wood or bronze. The *cista* probably originated among the Italic tribes of central Italy. The Etruscans, during the fifth century B.C., began to make it their own, producing bronze *cistae* in large numbers. The *cista* stood on low feet, generally shaped like lion's paws. Standing up to several feet in height, its body was decorated with engraved renderings of lively figural scenes and was sometimes further adorned with garlands of light chains. It had a lid boasting figural sculptures, which served as handles.

CLAW-AND-BALL FOOT

See under FOOT.

CLAW FOOT

See under FOOT.

CLAW TABLE

Eighteenth-century name for PEDESTAL TABLE.

CLAWSON, JOHN (active 1646–60)

Dutch furniture maker who produced AMERICAN JACOBEAN FURNITURE in Providence, Rhode Island, where he lived from 1646 to 1660. Clawson used ornamental motifs and techniques current in Holland, though he produced pieces that resembled other American work, which was more expressly in the English Jacobean style.

CLOSE STOOL (also *night stool*)

RENAISSANCE FURNITURE form developed in the 15th century; portable toilet in the form of a box or chest whose hinged lid covered an oval hole in a padded or wooden seat above a chamber pot. The seat could be lifted in order to remove the pot. In time, arms and a back came to be attached to the box, leading to the CHAMBER CHAIR, which superseded the close stool in the 18th century. A parallel evolution into a cupboard form yielded another 18th-century piece, the NIGHT TABLE, sometimes called a close stool itself.

CLOSE STOOL CHAIR

Another name for CHAMBER CHAIR.

CLOSET-BED

Another name for CUPBOARD BED.

CLOTHES PRESS

Eighteenth-century British case furniture form. Designed for storing clothes, the clothes press

cinquefoil

consisted of a short CHEST OF DRAWERS topped by a CUPBOARD that contained, behind two doors, shelves, removable trays or small drawers; sometimes it also had a tall space where clothes could be hung on pegs mounted to the wall. From the medieval PRESS, more elaborate clothes cupboards evolved in the late 16th century. Popularized by the published designs of Androuet DU CERCEAU and Hans VREDEMAN DE VRIES, these pieces, including the Dutch KAST and the German SCHRANK, flourished in northern Europe during the next century. The British clothes press, particularly influenced by the *kast,* was developed and made popular in the early 18th century and was the immediate ancestor of the modern WARDROBE.

CLOVEN FOOT
See under FOOT.

CLUB CHAIR
Twentieth-century name for WING CHAIR.

CLUB FOOT
See under FOOT.

COAL FURNITURE
Furniture, chiefly tables, made from coal; briefly popular in Britain in the 1850s.

COARD, MARCEL (active 1920s)
French ART DECO furniture maker. Coard's bold designs reflect the 1920s vogue for primitive art and exotic materials. Thus, he is associated with Pierre LEGRAIN in the avant-garde wing of Art Deco designers, as opposed to such comparatively conservative designers as RUHLMANN or SÜE ET MARE. Coard was one of the furniture makers patronized by Jacques DOUCET.

COATES, WELLS (1895–1958)
English INTERNATIONAL STYLE industrial and furniture designer. Best known for built-in furniture and equipment, Coates also designed simple, economical furniture for several commercial manufacturers. He was influenced chiefly by the BAUHAUS designers and Sergius CHERMAYEFF.

COBB, JOHN (c. 1710–78)
British ROCOCO FURNITURE maker, best known for furniture produced in partnership with William VILE in 1755–65. The firm Vile & Cobb was extremely successful, enjoying royal patronage. It produced massive mahogany pieces with carved rococo ornamentation. After Vile retired in 1765, Cobb continued to produce furniture, often in a more flamboyant vein, incorporating elaborate metal mounts and richly inlaid ADAM STYLE decoration on rococo forms.

COCK-BEAD MOLDING
See under MOLDING.

COCK'S-HEAD HINGE
See under HINGE.

COFFEE TABLE
Twentieth-century furniture form; low table designed to be used in conjunction with the low chairs and sofas favored in modern times.

COFFER
Medieval type of CHEST. In MEDIEVAL FURNITURE a coffer, or ark, was a chest especially intended for transport. It had a domed or hipped lid designed to allow rain to run off, and it generally had no feet.

COFFRET
In MEDIEVAL FURNITURE, miniature CHEST (diminutive of COFFER). Designed to hold valuables, coffrets were heavily secured with iron bands and locks; they were sometimes bolted to the floor.

COGSWELL, JOHN (1738–1818)
American cabinetmaker; a principal maker of BOSTON CHIPPENDALE FURNITURE. Cogswell was best known for large case pieces, frequently using the *bombé* shape. Although his Chippendale work tended to be more elaborately ornamented than was usual in Boston, he became, in the FEDERAL PERIOD, a successful practitioner in the neoclassical modes of the day. In partnership with his son, John Jr., he produced sideboards and desks from the

patterns of George HEPPLEWHITE and Thomas SHERATON. These pieces often featured tambour doors and painted interiors, in the manner of John and Thomas SEYMOUR.

COIFFEUSE (1)

Eighteenth-century French ROCOCO FURNITURE form; open chair whose crest rail curved markedly downward in the center. This curvature allowed a woman's hair to be dressed while she sat in the chair—hence, its name—but it was used as an ordinary armchair as well.

COIFFEUSE (2)

Nineteenth-century French name for DRESSING TABLE.

COIL-SPRING

See UPHOLSTERY.

COIT, JOB, JR. (1692–1741)

Boston cabinetmaker associated with BOSTON CHIPPENDALE FURNITURE. In 1738 Coit made a secretary in the Chippendale manner, retaining elements of the earlier QUEEN ANNE STYLE. This piece is the earliest datable instance of the use of the BLOCKFRONT in American furniture.

COLE, HENRY (1808–82)

British designer and writer. In 1847, in response to the shoddy furniture that industry was mass-producing at the time, Cole founded Summerly's Art Manufacturers. Summerly's commissioned artists to design everyday objects and then sold the designs to commercial manufacturers. Among those that Cole commissioned were such artists and designers as painter John Linnell, architect M. D. Wyatt (who trained William BURGES) and designer Owen JONES. Cole's concern that fine design be employed in mass manufacture was later a principal influence on the ART FURNITURE MOVEMENT. Cole's views were publicized through his magazine, the *Journal of Design and Manufacture,* which he began in 1849. In 1857 Cole founded and curated a museum for the display of fine factory products, the Museum of Applied Art, which later became the Victoria and Albert Museum.

COLLCUTT, THOMAS EDWARD (1840–1924)

British architect and furniture designer associated with the ART FURNITURE MOVEMENT. Principally an architect, T. E. Collcutt also designed furniture, primarily for the firm COLLINSON & LOCK. He is most famous for an elaborate cabinet, built in 1871, that set a style standard for the Art Furniture movement, a dominant trend in British furniture manufacture until the 1890s. The cabinet's design was fiercely eclectic, reflecting the influence of JAPONISME and the various European REVIVAL STYLES of the day, and it displayed very flat decoration—painted, pierced and in low relief. The cabinet was later installed at the Victoria and Albert Museum.

coiffeuse

COLLINSON & LOCK

London furniture manufacturer of the 19th century. This firm made and sold furniture in all styles but was particularly noted for its production, in the 1860s and 1870s, of ART FURNITURE MOVEMENT pieces. T. E. COLLCUTT was a principal designer for the firm, and Collinson & Lock also employed designs by Bruce TALBERT and William GODWIN, among others. Besides Art Furniture, Collinson & Lock was also noted for its RENAISSANCE REVIVAL and QUEEN ANNE REVIVAL style furniture. In 1883 the firm began manufacturing A. H. MACKMURDO's famous, prototypical ART NOUVEAU chair. In 1897 Collinson & Lock was absorbed by its rival, GILLOWS.

COLOMBO, JOE CESARE (1930–71)

Leading Italian furniture designer of the 1960s. Joe C. Colombo's early death ended a career that was distinguished by highly innovative design. He enlarged the vocabulary of furniture design with furniture pieces that were idiosyncratic yet severely functionalistic (*see* FUNCTIONALISM). These works fulfilled the demands of the day for flexibility of use within open-plan architecture. Also, they were created in new styles intended to be independent of any room they might be placed in. Originally trained as a painter, Colombo began a career as an architect in 1953. In 1961 he opened his own design office in Milan, concentrating on furniture. He designed several elegant stacking chairs of molded plastic or plywood for KARTELL; these have since achieved recogni-

Joe Colombo stacking design

tion as classic designs. He is probably best known for his "Addition" seating system (1968), which consisted of movable groups of narrow polyurethane foam cushions of graduated heights, upholstered in stretch fabrics. These cushions could be inserted in any order into a low, almost hidden aluminum base; they formed different sorts of seating surfaces—chair, settee, chaise—depending on their arrangement.

COLONETTE
Decorative device; miniature column or longitudinal segment of a column, used as carved or applied ornamentation on furniture since Renaissance times.

COLONIAL FURNITURE
See CAMPAIGN FURNITURE.

COLONIAL REVIVAL FURNITURE
Collective name for the large body of reproductions of American antique furniture made from the late 19th century—beginning with CENTENNIAL PERIOD REPRODUCTION FURNITURE—through the first half of the 20th century. Such work, at all levels of craftsmanship and authenticity, dominated the American furniture market until the post–World War II era.

commode

COLONNA, EDWARD (1862–1948)
German ART NOUVEAU designer associated with the Paris style of the late 19th and early 20th centuries. Sometimes miscalled Eugene, Colonna was born in Germany and immigrated to America at the age of 20. He was briefly employed by Louis C. TIFFANY's Associated Artists and later designed interiors for railroad cars. When he returned to Europe, Colonna was employed in Paris by Samuel BING. From 1898 to 1903 he designed furniture, jewelry and other objects for Bing's shop, *L'Art Nouveau,* and was a principal exponent of the exuberant, botanical Parisian mode of Art Nouveau.

COLUMN
Cylindrical post used as a support in architecture, usually consisting of a plinth-like base, shaft and CAPITAL. In European furniture the column is largely a decorative feature, usually ornamented in accordance with the classical ORDERS OF ARCHITECTURE.

COMB
See COMB-BACK WINDSOR CHAIR, *under* WINDSOR CHAIR.

COMB-BACK WINDSOR CHAIR
See under WINDSOR CHAIR.

COMETTI, GIACOMO (1863–1938)
Italian ART NOUVEAU furniture designer. In Turin, Cometti designed rectilinear pieces, which show the influence of Eugenio QUARTI, the WIENER WERKSTÄTTE and Henri VAN DE VELDE upon his work. Later in his career he adopted the ART DECO style. He also designed fabrics and silverware.

COMMODE (1)
French furniture form; CHEST OF DRAWERS on legs. Developed in the late 17th century, the commode became a prominent piece of ROCOCO FURNITURE in the 18th. The term came to be used in English to refer to any chest of drawers similar to those of French design, especially if it were elaborately ornate. The first variant of this form to appear was the COMMODE-TOMBEAU, whose invention, in the late 17th century, is sometimes attributed to the great *ébéniste* André-Charles BOULLE. This somewhat awkward eight-legged form was succeeded in the early 18th century by the COMMODE À LA RÉGENCE, which developed late in the reign of Louis XIV but was made, in the RÉGENCE STYLE, throughout the regency following his death. The term *commode,* signifying convenience and accommodation, was first applied to this piece, a heavy-bodied chest with three or more tiers of drawers set on four short legs. In the subsequent LOUIS XV STYLE, the most prominent commode was the COMMODE CRESSENT, a lighter piece, with two tiers of drawers on tall CABRIOLE LEGS (*see under* LEG). In the classically oriented LOUIS XVI STYLE, heavier commodes with three or more tiers of drawers reappeared, often with a BREAKFRONT. A characteristic form of this period was the COMMODE À VANTAUX, whose drawers lay behind a pair of doors. Other distinctive 18th-century com-

modes were the COMMODE À ENCOIGNURES, the COMMODE EN CONSOLE and the DEMILUNE COMMODE. The obvious utility of the form and its well-established role as a vehicle for fine craftsmanship have ensured its continued production to the present day.

COMMODE (2) (also *bedroom commode; night commode*)

Euphemistic substitute for either NIGHT TABLE or POT CUPBOARD, 18th- and 19th-century toilet housings.

COMMODE À VANTAUX

Late 18th-century French CHEST OF DRAWERS whose tiers of drawers were concealed behind two doors. This COMMODE (1) of the LOUIS XVI STYLE first appeared in about the mid-18th century.

COMMODE À ENCOIGNURES

Eighteenth-century French CHEST OF DRAWERS; COMMODE (1), supported on short legs, with shelves or cupboards flanking one or two tiers of wide drawers.

COMMODE À LA RÉGENCE

Early 18th-century French CHEST OF DRAWERS, on short legs, with three or more tiers of drawers. This heavy-bodied COMMODE (1) was made throughout the period of the RÉGENCE STYLE.

COMMODE CHAIR

Another name for CHAMBER CHAIR.

COMMODE CRESSENT

Eighteenth-century French CHEST OF DRAWERS with two drawers, one above the other, a serpentine front and a decorative shaped apron, all supported by tall CABRIOLE LEGS (*see under* LEG). This most prominent COMMODE (1) of the LOUIS XV STYLE was named for its principal developer, *ébéniste* Charles CRESSENT.

COMMODE EN CONSOLE

Eighteenth-century French furniture form; case piece with single drawer and long legs.

This COMMODE (1) was developed in about the mid 18th century and was made principally in the LOUIS XV STYLE. It was named for its resemblance to a CONSOLE TABLE.

COMMODE-TOMBEAU

Seventeenth-century LOUIS XV STYLE French CHEST OF DRAWERS, consisting of BOMBÉ chest with two tiers of drawers, resting on eight legs, two at each corner. The piece's upper tier of drawers was supported by four long legs that curved outward around the convex lower tier. Four more legs, short and straight, one at each corner of the lower tier, gave additional support. Each of these was joined to its corresponding longer leg just above the foot. This early COMMODE (1), which did not wholly solve the problem of elegantly lifting a chest of drawers, is sometimes said to have been invented by André-Charles BOULLE. It is named for the resemblance of its shaped chest to similarly curved late classical sarcophagi.

COMMONWEALTH FURNITURE (also *Cromwellian furniture*)

Austere English furniture made during the Commonwealth, the revolutionary Puritan regime (1649–60) established by Oliver Cromwell. Essentially JACOBEAN FURNITURE with little decoration, Commonwealth furniture represents a hiatus in the evolution of English 17th-century design brought about by the Civil Wars (1642–49) and the assertively Spartan regime of the victors. The chief ornamentation on furniture consisted of simple turnings on stretches and legs and of some TURKEY WORK, as on the CROMWELLIAN CHAIR. With the collapse of the revolutionary government and the restoration of the monar-

commode Cressent

chy, in 1660, the influence of the European Baroque reached England, resulting in the development of RESTORATION FURNITURE.

COMPANION CHAIR (also *roundabout chair*)
Nineteenth-century British furniture form composed of three wide seats joined at a central point, each facing the next one's back. It was similar to the French INDISCRET, but it had very wide seats, each accommodating two people.

COMPASS SEAT
Chair seat of AMERICAN QUEEN ANNE STYLE, in the second quarter of the 18th century. A compass seat was very round in front, as though its curve had been created by a compass. Sometimes, its sides continued the curve to the rear, giving the seat a horseshoe shape. The compass seat was used in rural America for the rest of the 18th century, in the styles of AMERICAN CHIPPENDALE FURNITURE and the FEDERAL PERIOD, and into the 19th century. A common later variant, sometimes called a *cheesebox seat,* was a RUSH SEAT.

COMPO
Resinous mixture, similar to GESSO, used in the 18th and 19th centuries to make delicate molded decorations to be applied to furniture. Also called *composition.*

COMPOSITE ORDER
One of the ancient Roman ORDERS OF ARCHITECTURE. The Composite order combined elements from the IONIC and CORINTHIAN ORDERS. On a Composite column, Ionic VOLUTES were inserted onto a Corinthian CAPITAL, above the decorative ACANTHUS leaves and below the ABACUS. This striking arrangement demonstrated a pronounced Roman fondness for extravagant decoration and is sometimes called the Roman order.

COMPOSITION
See COMPO.

CONCRETE
An artificial STONE consisting of pebbles and/or chips of stone in a matrix of cement; commonly used in the 20th century for outdoor furniture. An inexpensive material, concrete is also extremely durable and weather-resistant. Additionally, it is easily worked, for it is simply cast in molds to a designer's specifications. Concrete furniture commonly incorporates wood or METALS, especially on surfaces that come in contact with the user.

CONFESSIONAL
French upholstered armchair popular in 17th-century LOUIS XIV STYLE. Its flat back was adorned with flat wooden panels, or "wings," projecting forward from the top half of the stiles. These wings could hide the face of the sitter, giving rise to the piece's name. In that it partially surrounded the sitter, the confessional foreshadowed an 18th-century development, the BERGÈRE.

CONFIDANTE
French term for any of several CANAPÉS. The term most frequently denotes one of four forms—two from the 18th century, the CAUSEUSE and the CANAPÉ À CONFIDANTE, and two from the 19th, the CANAPÉ DE L'AMITIÉ and the TÊTE-À-TÊTE. In all cases, the term refers to the ease with which two users could sit close together.

CONFORTABLE
Nineteenth-century term for LOUNGE CHAIR, especially as developed in France.

CONNECTICUT SUNFLOWER CHEST
Late 17th-century AMERICAN JACOBEAN FURNITURE form. The Connecticut sunflower chest, usually of oak or pine, stood on four short legs, had one or two drawers and was distinctively decorated. Originally gaily painted and ornamented with split BALUSTERS and carved panels, the chest generally displayed three panels; the central one bore a plant motif with three circular flowers. Nicholas DISBROWE and Peter BLIN were noted makers of this chest.

CONNELLY, HENRY (1770–1826)
Philadelphia FEDERAL PERIOD cabinetmaker. In the 1790s Connelly worked in a NEOCLAS-

confessional

SICAL STYLE based on the work of Thomas SHERATON. He followed that designer's late work in the early 19th century, making DIRECTORY STYLE pieces.

CONRAN, TERENCE (b. 1931)

British furniture and textile designer in the 1950s; entrepreneur associated with the CONTEMPORARY STYLE. Conran established the European chain of Habitat shops in 1964. These outlets, which market his own work and that of others, sell furniture, fabrics, kitchen equipment and other household goods in a range of postwar design styles aimed at a wide public. American branches of the Habitat chain are called *Conran's*.

CONSOLE

Ornamental BRACKET fixed upright against a vertical surface, either singly or in series, to support a horizontal element of a building or piece of furniture, especially a cornice (*see* MODILLION) or tabletop (*see* CONSOLE TABLE; occasionally, the term *console* simply designates the table). A console is usually shaped like an ogee curve in profile, often terminating in a volute at top and bottom. It has been used in most European furniture styles since the Renaissance.

CONSOLE DESSERT

LOUIS XVI STYLE furniture form; table with one undecorated side, intended to be placed against a wall, and one or two galleried shelves between its legs. A *console dessert* was used in the dining room as a SIDEBOARD. Its ends usually curved inward, with its front legs closer together than the rear ones.

CONSOLE TABLE

Table fixed to a wall and supported only by its front legs, which were usually in the form of an architectural CONSOLE, with an OGEE curve in profile, and a VOLUTE at top and bottom. It was developed in the late 17th century and was very popular throughout the 18th, especially as a PIER TABLE. Less specifically, the term may refer to any table intended to be placed against a wall and thus have one side left undecorated. In this sense, the console table appeared in ROMAN FURNITURE and in later European furniture from the Middle Ages onward.

CONSULATE STYLE

French furniture style of the first years of the 19th century. It was named for Napoleon's first government, the Consulate, which was created by coup d'état in 1799 and lasted until the declaration of the Empire in 1804. The Consulate style was a transitional mode. Like its immediate predecessor, the DIRECTOIRE STYLE, it still reflected, in an austere vein, the furniture of the pre-Revolutionary LOUIS XVI STYLE. However, it anticipated the grandly sumptuous manner of the EMPIRE STYLE and began to reflect the increasing confidence of republican France. Though difficult to distinguish in its general appearance from Directoire style furniture, Consulate style furniture tended to greater rectilinearity and formality, and its decoration more fully revealed the martial themes that would become prominent under the Empire. Also, ÉGYPTIENNERIE motifs became popular, following Napoleon's campaign in Egypt. Several new forms arose, including the tremendously popular LIT EN BATEAU, the LIT DROIT and a small, cylindrical GUÉRIDON, which was sometimes decorated to resemble a drum. The leading designers of the day were PERCIER AND FONTAINE, and Georges JACOB and his sons (*see* JACOB-DESMALTER) were the most prominent furniture makers. These two partnerships frequently collaborated, most notably, beginning in 1799, on the decoration and furnishings of the Château de Malmaison, the grand residence of Napoleon's wife, Josephine Beauharnais. This project profoundly influenced the evolution of the Empire style.

CONTEMPORARY STYLE

British furniture style of the 1950s. The Contemporary style was characterized by light, elegant pieces with long, low profiles; in case furniture blocky masses stood atop slender legs. The style's austere, unornamented appearance continued the 20th-century taste for FUNCTIONALISM, and the Contemporary style was essentially a descendant of the INTERNATIONAL STYLE of the 1930s. The progressive young designers of post-Second World War Britain—a group that included Robin DAY, Clive LATIMER, Ernest RACE and Dennis YOUNG—

console bracket

followed the informal lead of Gordon RUSSELL, an International style designer who had supervised the design of UTILITY FURNITURE during the war. These designers also responded to the two key International style offshoots of the postwar period, SCANDINAVIAN MODERN and the ERGONOMIC DESIGN work of such Americans as Charles EAMES.

The postwar world demanded new ways of living, with an emphasis on mobility and economy. The Contemporary style responded with light, versatile furniture and new forms, such as freestanding cabinets that functioned as room dividers, as well as storage units designed to house nontraditional products such as phonographs and records. New materials, principally metals and plastics, continued to be important, though the period also saw a revival in the popularity of wood—especially teak, reflecting the Danish influence.

In America the term *Contemporary style* has been used more loosely to describe all the smooth-lined postwar furniture that suggest simplicity, lightness and elegance of design, from the work of Eames to that of Don CHADWICK.

Hans Coray chair

CONTINUOUS-ARM WINDSOR CHAIR
See under WINDSOR CHAIR.

CONTRE-PARTIE
See BOULLE MARQUETRY.

CONVERSATION CHAIR
British name for VOYEUSE.

CONVERSATIONAL SOFA
See INDISCRET.

CONVERTIBLE FURNITURE
Furniture that can be adjusted to perform different functions by manipulating its parts. The SOFA-BED is the most familiar modern instance, but historical examples range from the medieval CHAIR-TABLE to 19th-century PATENT FURNITURE.

COPLAND, HENRY (active 1738–68)
British engraver and ROCOCO FURNITURE designer. Copland published engravings of his own designs as well as those of others. A book of his own designs appeared in 1746, and he subsequently collaborated with Matthias LOCK, Robert MANWARING and, most important, Thomas CHIPPENDALE.

COQUILLAGE
Decorative motif representing a scallop shell. The coquillage was especially popular on ROCOCO FURNITURE.

CORAY, HANS (1906–91)
Swiss artist and INTERNATIONAL STYLE furniture designer. Originally a painter, Coray turned to furniture design in the 1930s. Best known for the Spartina chair, his aluminum stacking chair which was made for the Swiss national design exhibition of 1938 and is still being made; he designed furniture through the 1950s, after which he returned to painting.

CORBUSIER, LE
See LE CORBUSIER.

CORINTHIAN ORDER
Last of the three ancient Greek ORDERS OF ARCHITECTURE to be developed; later adapted by the Romans. The Corinthian order was characterized by a plain base and column, similar to those of the IONIC ORDER, but with a much taller, bell-shaped CAPITAL composed of overlapping carved ACANTHUS leaves. From between the leaves, smaller stalks of carved foliage protruded, supporting a projecting ABACUS. The ENTABLATURE was undecorated, as in the Ionic. The Romans, who were particularly fond of ornamentation, used the Corinthian order more than its originators did, and they elaborated it somewhat. The Roman Corinthian order differed from the Greek chiefly in the entablature; the ARCHITRAVE bore three horizontal bands of narrow MOLDING, and MODILLIONS appeared below the CORNICE. Sometimes the FRIEZE was also ornamented.

CORNER BLOCK
Structural member of the frame of a piece of seating furniture; block or other shape fastened into a corner of the framing. The corner block joins two sides that meet at a corner with each

other and with a leg below them. It also forms, if necessary, the support for a SLIP SEAT.

CORNER CABINET

British furniture form of 18th and 19th centuries; case piece intended to display small objects on shelves and designed to fit in a corner. It had a diagonal or curved front and either stood on three feet or hung on a wall. The corner cabinet differed from the CORNER CUPBOARD in that it had glass doors.

CORNER CHAIR (also *roundabout chair; writing chair*)

Eighteenth-century furniture form; armchair with square seat placed diagonally. That is, one corner faced front, and the chair's back rose above the other three. The crest rail, whose top was shaped in a serpentine curve, was supported by three turned or carved posts, one at each corner, and, usually, two splats, one above each side. The legs, below each corner, varied from region to region, for corner chairs were made widely throughout Europe, Britain and America. Sometimes the rear leg was markedly less decorative than the other three; sometimes, however, the front leg bore more ornamentation than the others.

CORNER CUPBOARD

British and American furniture form of 18th and 19th centuries; case piece intended for storage and designed to fit in a corner. It had a diagonal or curved front and either stood on three feet or hung on a wall.

CORNICE

Horizontal molding or series of moldings; uppermost part of an ENTABLATURE, a device from classical architecture often used in case furniture.

CORNUCOPIA

Decorative motif; horn of plenty. A carved, inlaid or painted image of an animal horn overflowing with flowers and fruits, it symbolizes abundance and prosperity. Popular in many furniture styles, from RENAISSANCE FURNITURE to ART DECO, the cornucopia was particularly prominent in American "FANCY" FURNITURE of the FEDERAL period.

COROMANDEL LACQUER (also *ke hui*)

Chinese LACQUER screens decorated pictorially in several colors, with gilding and incised carving. They were used in Europe as screens and were also cut up in small pieces as decorative VENEER applied to Western furniture. These screens were made for export beginning in the 17th century. In England they were named for the Coromandel coast of India; the panels were often shipped to Europe from trading posts there.

COROMANDEL WOOD

HARDWOOD from the East Indies; a non-black EBONY. A mottled grey or grey-brown in color, Coromandel wood is used as a decorative veneer or in inlay work. It was particularly popular in 19th-century Britain, when it was named for its apparent source, the east, or Coromandel, coast of India. It is also known as *marblewood*.

COTSWOLD SCHOOL

Small group of craftsmen and designers within the ARTS AND CRAFTS MOVEMENT. The principal members of the Cotswold School, Ernest GIMSON and the brothers Ernest and Sidney Barnsley, were influenced by the ideas of William MORRIS and the styles designed for production by Morris & Co. The three craftsmen helped found a similar firm, Kenton & Co., in London, but the company collapsed financially. In 1895 Gimson and the Barnsley brothers left London and moved to the rural Cotswold Hills near Gloucester, where they established a workshop with the intention of producing finely crafted furniture of clean, simple design. They used mostly oak and walnut—both local woods—and they frequently chamfered the edges of their furniture, a practice that became a hallmark of the school. The ideals and style of the Cotswold School were carried on well into the 20th century by many local craftsmen, including Sidney Barnsley's son Edward.

COTTAGE FURNITURE

Inexpensive, mass-produced American furniture made in the latter half of the 19th century. This furniture was painted decoratively in light, bright colors, usually with motifs of fruits and flowers or abstract curvilinear designs deriving from the ROCOCO REVIVAL STYLE.

corner chair

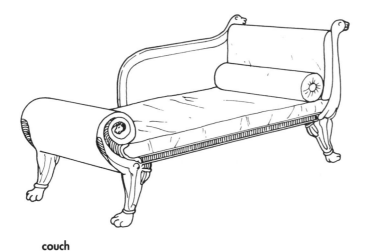

couch

COUCH

DAYBED in the general sense; furniture form on which one can either sit or recline. More specifically, the term refers to an 18th- and 19th-century form, a long upholstered bench with a back extending from a high headrest at one end about halfway toward the foot. The earliest couch form appeared in GREEK FURNITURE as the KLINE, an adaptation of the Egyptian bed that was intended for dining. The *kline* in turn evolved to become a ROMAN FURNITURE form, the LECTUS, which was not intended for reclining and was not a couch.

The independently evolved modern couch had similar origins—as its name, from the French verb *coucher,* meaning "to go to bed," reveals. It developed in the 17th century as a relatively modest substitute for the BED OF ESTATE; it was a sort of bench with slanted boards for reclining at either end. Sometimes these boards were hinged and adjustable to be either vertical or angled. This piece could be placed beneath a CANOPY, but it was a less elaborate, more portable item than a bed, and its use reflects an increasingly casual domestic world. Even less formal than this piece was the contemporary daybed, which had a reclining board at only one end; the term *couch* applied to either version. In the late 18th century, the term came to refer to a type of upholstered bench with a headrest and a half-back, as distinguished from the SOFA and the backless daybed. It was often, though inaccurately, called a "Grecian couch."

COUCHETTE

MEDIEVAL FURNITURE form. The couchette was a bed intended for a person of no rank and was thus quite simple. It lacked a canopy and could be folded up for transport. The couchette was often mounted on wheels so that it could be moved from one room to another.

COUNTER-TABLE

Flat-topped table or cupboard whose top surface is marked for measuring or counting; used for conducting business. The counter-table, which originated in the Netherlands in the 15th century, evolved into the modern display counter, found in retail stores.

COUNTRY CHIPPENDALE FURNITURE

AMERICAN CHIPPENDALE FURNITURE made in small towns and rural areas of eastern America in the late 18th century. Working in areas that were poorer than major Colonial centers, country craftsmen had to make furniture in a manner that would use both materials and production time sparingly. Thus, they altered the extravagant ROCOCO FURNITURE of the day. Abstraction of motif was their general rule: the rococo shell was rendered as a fan or a pinwheel; regular lattice patterns replaced more complicated foliate fretwork; corkscrew-turned finials were used instead of carved representations of flames. Similarly, rope-twisted turnings substituted for carved moldings, and the cabriole leg was either simplified or omitted. Also, mortise-and-tenon became a more common type of joinery than dovetailing. The country furniture makers served their clientele, who neither aspired to nor could afford the height of fashion, but who wished to be somewhat up to date.

In general, local woods such as walnut, cherry and maple were used instead of imported mahogany. The different regions used different secondary woods: ash and oak in New England, white pine in New York and Pennsylvania, and yellow pine in the South. Other regional variations were readily discernible. In the South an extreme reduction of ornamentation prevailed, permitting only a minimum of decoration in the simplest patterns. In Virginia, Chippendale-inspired pediment tops and bracket feet were used on case pieces that otherwise derived from the QUEEN ANNE STYLE. From Pennsylvania to the Carolina backcountry, the presence of a German immigrant population contributed to the use of decoration that was flat and simple and that reflected the traditional taste of the European peasantry. From New Jersey northward a conservative inclination produced a peculiar hybrid chair that was popular over a wide area. It had a round-shouldered Queen Anne style back, a Chippendale pierced splat, WILLIAM AND MARY STYLE turned legs and the timeless rush seat.

In New England, country Chippendale furniture was generally more sophisticated. In rural Connecticut ornamentation was used fairly extensively, though it was abstracted into less complicated motifs than those that prevailed in the cities. The names of a number of Connecticut craftsmen have survived, including Benjamin BURNHAM, of Norwich, known for excellent BLOCKFRONT desks, and Eliphalet CHAPIN, of East Windsor, who had trained in Philadelphia. In New Hampshire, where the use of striking ornamentation was most in vogue among country makers, the family of John Dunlap (see DUNLAP FAMILY) was especially prominent.

Being particularly remote from London, the source of the American rococo style, rural craftsmen adopted the style somewhat later than did those of the seaboard cities—in the 1760s at the earliest. But the style remained popular in the countryside long after the Revolution—even into the early years of the 19th century—when the NEOCLASSICAL STYLE of the FEDERAL PERIOD was dominant in the cities.

COUR, DE LA (active 1740S)

French ROCOCO FURNITURE designer who worked in Britain. Between 1741 and 1746 de la Cour, whose first name is not known, published a series of chair designs in which backs were composed of bands interlaced in loops. This feature was often used by later British designers, including Matthias DARLY, Henry COPLAND, INCE & MAYHEW and Robert MANWARING.

COURT CUPBOARD (1)

Medieval and Renaissance furniture form. The court cupboard was an open oak structure no more than four feet high (court means "short" in French)—a CUPBOARD in the original sense of the term. Generally having three levels, the piece was principally intended for the display

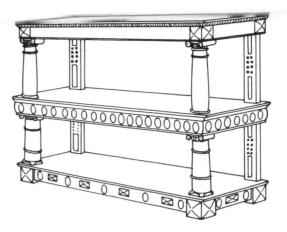

court cupboard

of fine plate, and it was often elaborately decorated with carved ornamentation. Popular from the Middle Ages through the 17th century, it survived into the 18th. The development of the AUMBRY resulted in another furniture form of the same name (see COURT CUPBOARD [2]).

COURT CUPBOARD (2)

Seventeenth-century English and American furniture form; a short, two-tiered CUPBOARD with a storage space above, enclosed by a door or doors, and an open shelf below, intended for both storage and display. It was known in its day as a CREDENCE. Generally produced in oak in the Jacobean style (see JACOBEAN FURNITURE), this piece was transitional between the more traditional form of short, open cupboard (see COURT CUPBOARD [1]) and the contemporary PRESS CUPBOARD.

COURTENAY, HERCULES (c. 1744–84)

Philadelphia woodcarver and gilder. Courtenay was employed by Benjamin RANDOLPH, a leading maker of PHILADELPHIA CHIPPENDALE FURNITURE. An immigrant from London, Courtenay, with John POLLARD, was responsible for producing much of Randolph's most elaborate ornamentation. Courtenay also worked in Baltimore.

COVE MOLDING

See under MOLDING.

COW-HORN STRETCHER

See under STRETCHER.

credenza

COWPERTHWAITE, JOHN (active 1818–25)
New York City chair maker. He produced "FANCY" FURNITURE, mostly to designs published by Thomas SHERATON.

CRADLE
Child's bed capable of rocking. It is a box either mounted on a rocker at each end or slung from a frame. The traditional cradle, on rockers, was developed in medieval times. It changed very little in structure until the 18th century, when it was first suspended from a footed frame, thus raising it high off the floor. Today, the cradle has largely been superseded by the CRIB.

CRAFTSMAN FURNITURE
See STICKLEY, Gustav.

CRANBROOK ACADEMY
See SAARINEN, Eliel.

CRAPAUD
Low, wide, heavily upholstered armchair. Introduced in the mid-19th century, the crapaud is an instance of the enthusiasm for deep-buttoned, coil-spring UPHOLSTERY, then newly developed. It takes its name, literally meaning "toad," from its squat shape.

CREDENCE
Obsolete term for a COURT CUPBOARD (2). In the 16th and 17th centuries, the term had a broader application, referring to any small side table or serving table used during meals. In modern usage it refers to a piece of church furniture—a table near the altar on which the eucharistic vessels are placed before use in a service.

CREDENZA
Italian RENAISSANCE FURNITURE form; serving table with a CUPBOARD below its surface. It was generally wider than it was high, with canted corners emphasized by PILASTERS that supported a bold CORNICE above two or three doors. The credenza evolved in the 15th century and became one of the most common pieces of furniture in Renaissance Italy, along with the CASSONE. In the 16th century, an upper, recessed tier was added, creating a form equivalent to the English PRESS CUPBOARD.

CRESCENT STRETCHER
See under STRETCHER.

CRESSENT, CHARLES (1685–1763)
French cabinetmaker of RÉGENCE and LOUIS XV STYLES. In his youth Cressent was apprenticed to both his father, a sculptor, and his grandfather, an *ébéniste*. His career later turned to furniture making, but his background in sculpture continued to influence his work. His furniture featured copious curves and was veneered in plain woods that contrasted with elaborate bronze mounts—his speciality—which he modeled, cast and gilded, all in his own shop. He was prosecuted for this violation of guild regulations, which insisted on specialization (*see* ÉBÉNISTE), but he was protected by the regent, who admired his work. His graceful style exemplified the opulent informality of the Régence period. He developed a type of COMMODE (1) with tall CABRIOLE LEGS (*see under* LEG) that became very popular in the Louis XV style and was known as the COMMODE CRESSENT. After about 1750 he abandoned decoration with extensive mounts in favor of floral MARQUETRY.

CRESSON, LOUIS (1706–61)
French MENUISIER; prominent chair maker in the LOUIS XV STYLE.

CREST RAIL (also *cresting rail*)
Top RAIL of the back of a chair or other piece of seating furniture, mounted atop the STILES.

crest rail

CRIAERD, MATHIEU (1689–1776)

French ÉBÉNISTE; prominent furniture maker in LOUIS XV STYLE. Criaerd, originally from Flanders, made furniture with both floral and geometrical MARQUETRY and also specialized in VENEERS of LACQUER or JAPANNING.

CRIB

High child's bed with adjustable sides that can slide below the level of the mattress to provide access and can be raised high enough to prevent the user from falling out.

CRINOLINE STRETCHER

See under STRETCHER.

CROCKET

Decorative device used in BYZANTINE and GOTHIC FURNITURE. A crocket consisted of carved flowers or foliage placed on an outer edge of a vertical element, such as a chair back, or at intervals on a vertical molding. It originated in masonry architecture, and the term derives from the French *croc,* meaning "hook," because the most common shape used was that of a curling leaf or uncoiling bud. Other images, including figures of animals and humans, were occasionally used. The device was also popular in the 18th- and 19th-century NEO-GOTHIC STYLE.

CROFT

British furniture form of late 18th and early 19th centuries; short filing cabinet. The croft had many shallow drawers, and drop leaves could expand its flat top into a writing surface. An alternative version had a FALL FRONT in the top drawer. The piece is named for the Rev. Sir Herbert Croft, a well-known lexicographer who commissioned the first such piece.

CROMWELLIAN CHAIR

Seventeenth-century English and American furniture form; simple square-framed armless chair with turned legs and upholstered panels of TURKEY WORK or leather for seat and back. This form represented the austerity of design in the period of COMMONWEALTH FURNI-TURE. In the English colonies of North America, it was made until late in the 17th century.

CROMWELLIAN FURNITURE

Another name for COMMONWEALTH FURNITURE.

CROSS BANDING

See BANDING.

CROSS-LAPPED JOINT

See under JOINERY.

CROSS RAIL

Horizontal member of a chair back, below the CREST RAIL. It is either a framing member at the bottom of the back below a panel, spindle or splat or, when broad and centered between crest and seat, a place for ornamentation.

CROSS-STRETCHER

See under STRETCHER.

CROTCH VENEER

Another name for CURL VENEER.

CROWN CHAIR

Eighteenth-century American furniture form; BANISTER-BACK CHAIR with high, pediment-like CREST RAIL that was often pierced with a heart-shaped hole.

CROW'S NEST

Another name for BIRDCAGE SUPPORT.

CRYPTOMERIA

Western term for the Japanese wood SUGI.

C-SCROLL

Decorative device, commonly used on ROCO-CO FURNITURE, that took the form of a letter *C,* with an inwardly curving spiral at each end. A C-scroll might be an element in a two-dimensional decorative scheme or a large

crocket

C-scroll

carved member of a piece of furniture, such as a leg or a support for a cornice.

CUCCI, DOMENICO (c. 1635–1705)

Italian ÉBÉNISTE who worked in France in LOUIS XIV STYLE. Cucci, who was employed by Charles LE BRUN at the royal GOBELINS workshops, specialized in large ebony cabinets that were ostentatiously decorated with extravagant materials, such as semiprecious stones, elaborate scenic panels of PIETRE DURE work and lavish gilt-bronze mounts. His work contributed significantly to the aura of regal splendor that the French decorative arts purposefully engendered under the Sun King.

CUP TURNING
See under TURNERY.

CUP-AND-COVER TURNING
See under TURNERY.

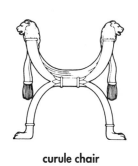

curule chair

CUPBOARD

Case furniture type that contains shelving housed within a case of panels, enclosed on the front by a door or doors and usually used to store household goods. Cupboards did not exist in the most ancient bodies of furniture (*see* EGYPTIAN FURNITURE); chests filled their function. Only in Hellenistic times, toward the end of the period of GREEK FURNITURE, did cupboards appear. They were more prominent in ROMAN FURNITURE but were still of secondary importance. The same was true in the early Middle Ages (*see* ROMANESQUE FURNITURE), when the cupboard, known as the PRESS, was often vividly painted to disguise its generally crude joinery. GOTHIC FURNITURE first began to feature a wider variety of presses, and more attention was paid to the form's construction and decoration. The press then began to evolve, yielding its modern descendants—the ARMOIRE, the CLOTHES PRESS and the WARDROBE—all of them cupboards.

The term *cupboard* began to be used in the Gothic era. Originally, as the name implies, it referred to an assemblage of shelves, or boards, for the display of cups, goblets, glassware or plates—a BUFFET, in the medieval meaning of the term. A late elaboration of this open form was the COURT CUPBOARD (1).

Part of the structure was sometimes enclosed with doors, producing a compartment called an AUMBRY. Such compartments were further developed in transitional forms such as the COURT CUPBOARD (2), or CREDENCE, and the PRESS CUPBOARD. Gradually, the whole piece became enclosed, and the term assumed its modern meaning.

CUPBOARD-BED (also *closet-bed*)

Seventeenth-century Dutch furniture form; bed built into the corner of a room. The paneled sides of the bed matched the paneling on the walls. Also called a boxbed.

CUPPED LEG
See under LEG.

CURL VENEER (also *crotch veneer*)

Wood VENEER with plumelike, curling FIGURING. The wood is taken from a part of a log where a branch diverges from the trunk.

CURULE CHAIR

X-FRAME chair with two sets of curved legs, usually at front and rear, popular in NEOCLASSICAL STYLE furniture. Derived by RENAISSANCE FURNITURE makers from medieval thrones and CHAIRS OF ESTATE, the curule chair had its ultimate origins in the ancient Roman form, the SELLA CURULIS. In the early 19th century, American furniture maker Duncan PHYFE designed an innovative curule chair whose X-frames were at either side, topped by arms. This popular variant influenced subsequent designs.

CUSHION CAPITAL

Architectural device often appearing in ROMANESQUE FURNITURE atop the COLUMNS of ARCADING. The cushion CAPITAL is a cube whose lower corners are rounded and tapered to join the column shaft.

CUSHION FRIEZE

Decorative device; an unornamented FRIEZE; plain band of wood, convex from top to bottom, running below the CORNICE of a piece of case furniture. The device, mimicking a similar one in wall paneling, was used on late 17th-and early 18th century English and American furniture, usually in conjunction with the similarly simple and sculptural FIELDED PANEL.

CUSHIONED-PAD FOOT
See under FOOT.

CUSPING
Decorative device in GOTHIC FURNITURE and architecture. The meeting point of two curves, as in TRACERY or at the top of a pointed arch, is highlighted by a small, carved ornament, usually taking the form of a projecting point, a trefoil motif or an abstract form resembling a flower bud.

CUTWORK
Another name for FRETWORK.

CUVILLIÉS, FRANÇOIS (1695–1768)
Leading German architect and designer of ROCOCO FURNITURE. Born in Flanders, young Cuvilliés became a court dwarf to the Elector of Bavaria. Realizing the youth's abilities, the elector sent him to Paris to study architecture in 1720–24. He subsequently had an extremely successful career as court architect for several successive electors, designing numerous buildings and interiors, including many of the chief monuments of the German rococo. His furniture followed the designs of the French LOUIS XV STYLE in a light, sparkling manner even more delicate and fantastic than that of his models. Beginning in 1738, he published a long series of engraved designs that had a tremendous influence on German interior designers and furniture makers throughout the century.

CYLINDER-FRONT DESK
Eighteenth-century furniture form; desk with solid wood lid in the form of a segment of a hollow cylinder. To open the desk, the cylinder is rolled up in the top interior. The term sometimes also refers to the ROLL-TOP DESK, where the cylinder is a TAMBOUR.

CYMA
S-shaped curve that may be part of a decorative design or the outline of a structural element, especially of an OGEE MOLDING (*see under* MOLDING).

CYMA RECTA
Curve or MOLDING whose upper part is concave and lower part convex.

CYMA REVERSA
Curve or MOLDING whose upper part is convex and lower concave.

CYPHER SPLAT
Chair SPLAT popular in 17th-century England and America. It was ornamented with carved initials, which were interwoven amid decorative SCROLLWORK.

CYPRESS
Aromatic SOFTWOOD found in temperate regions; today grown commercially in Southern Hemisphere and East Africa. Having a scent like CEDAR's, cypress has traditionally been used for interior work in storage furniture. (*See also* SOUTHERN CYPRESS, an unrelated species native to the southeastern United States.)

cyma curve

D

DADO JOINT
See under JOINERY.

DAGLY, GERHARD (active 1680s–1714)
Leading japanner (*see* JAPANNING) of
BAROQUE FURNITURE. A native of Spa, in
what is now Belgium, where japanning was an
important local industry (*see* BOIS DE SPA),
Dagly was the best-known practitioner of his
craft during his lifetime. He decorated wall
paneling and furniture with CHINOISERIE
motifs, both in the traditional black and gold
of Spa and in innovative schemes using bright
primary colors on a white ground.

DANHAUSER, JOSEF (1780–1829)
Austrian furniture maker; leading exponent of
the BIEDERMEIER STYLE. Born in Germany,
Danhauser trained as a sculptor and arrived in
Vienna by about 1800. There he at first made
ornaments to be applied to furniture. In 1804
he opened a furniture factory that became one
of the largest in Europe; he designed for it and
ran it successfully until his death. He produced some furniture in an aristocratic EMPIRE
STYLE, but most of his output was in the simpler mode later known as Biedermeier, which
he helped develop and which was made for
the rapidly expanding middle-class market.

DANISH EMPIRE STYLE
Early 19th-century furniture style in Denmark,
Norway and southern Sweden; a compound
of late 18th-century British NEOCLASSICAL
STYLE influence with that of French EMPIRE
STYLE, as received through imported German
work. The Danish Empire style featured
MAHOGANY veneers with geometrical MAR-
QUETRY in light-colored woods. Lunettes and
other arched details were favored, especially
on case furniture. Metal mounts were generally not used. A case piece, the CHATOL, was the
most characteristic Danish Empire form. The
leading Danish neoclassicist, Gustav Friedrich
HETSCH, stimulated the survival of the
Empire mode in Denmark until about the
mid-19th century. This late version featured
carved appliqués as ornamentation and was
known as the "Christian VIII style," after the
Danish king who reigned in 1839–48.

DANKO, PETER (b. 1949)
Contemporary American furniture maker.
Danko is best known for the "Danko" chair
(1976), an ingenious design in which a whole
armchair consists of a single sheet of plywood
that is pierced and bent to produce a handsome and comfortable piece of furniture. Now
manufactured by Thonet Brothers (*see* Michael
THONET), this chair represents a continuation
of earlier experiments by Alvar AALTO, Gerald
SUMMERS and others.

DANTE CHAIR (also *Dantesca chair*)
Nineteenth-century name for an Italian
MEDIEVAL and RENAISSANCE FURNITURE
form, an X-FRAME chair. Simpler than the
contemporary SAVONAROLA CHAIR, this form
had only two X-frames, one each at front and
rear. It was generally decorated with classical
motifs, in inlay or low relief. Dante Alighieri
(1265–1321), the great Italian poet who wrote
The Divine Comedy, used a chair of this sort
that has been preserved.

DARLY, MATTHIAS (or Matthew) (active 1741–80)

British engraver and ROCOCO FURNITURE designer. In 1751 and 1754 Darly published PATTERN BOOKS that helped to spread a taste for CHINOISERIE in Britain. He engraved many of the plates in Thomas CHIPPENDALE's *Director* (1754).

DAVENPORT (1)

Small British DESK with a slanting, lift-up top resting on a case, with drawers and cupboards opening on both sides rather than the front. First made in the late 18th century by the London firm GILLOWS, the desk is named for the otherwise unknown Captain Davenport who commissioned it. Especially popular in the 19th century, the davenport is still made and sold.

DAVENPORT (2)

Boxy, upholstered American SOFA type. Named after a sofa designed in about 1900 by the Boston furniture-manufacturing firm Irving & Casson & Davenport, the term *davenport* can also refer to a SOFA-BED.

DAVID, JACQUES-LOUIS (1748–1825)

Foremost French neoclassical painter. David also designed a small amount of furniture in the late 1780s, attempting to reproduce exactly the forms of ancient GREEK and ROMAN FURNITURE, which had been made known through the excavations at Pompeii and through Greek vase painting. He designed KLINE forms, SELLA CURULIS and KLISMOS chairs, and tripod STANDS, all in the black and red color scheme of Greek pottery and the ETRUSCAN STYLE. His designs were executed, for his own use and perhaps that of a patron, the Count of Artois, the king's brother, by Georges JACOB.

DAVIS, ALEXANDER JACKSON (1803–92)

American architect and leading American furniture designer in the NEO-GOTHIC STYLE. One of the most prominent architects of his day, Davis was noted for Greek Revival and neo-Gothic buildings. He also designed neo-Gothic oak furniture, both for his residential commissions and for a commercial manufac-

turer. His pieces followed the designs of A. W. N. PUGIN but adhered less strenuously to medieval models.

DAVIS, ROBERT (d. 1793)

Boston furniture maker and japanner (*see* JAPANNING). Davis was the son-in-law and successor in business of William RANDALL. He kept Randall's loosely organized compositional style alive, though it was overtaken in popularity in his own time by the Boston manner exemplified by Thomas JOHNSTON.

DAY, ROBIN (b. 1915)

British furniture designer associated with the CONTEMPORARY STYLE of the 1950s. Day was one of the young designers influenced by Gordon RUSSELL in the period immediately following the Second World War. He achieved his first recognition when storage units he designed in collaboration with Clive LATIMER won a prize at the New York Museum of Modern Art's "Low Cost Furniture Design" competition (1948). Day became the chief British proponent of the Contemporary style's long, low look in furniture, in which masses are placed above slender legs, often steel rods. Day has acknowledged Charles EAMES's role in directing him to a concern for FUNCTIONALISM, achieved through advanced production techniques. For instance, Day's "Polyprop" chair (1963) was one of the first furniture designs in a new material, molded polypropylene, and it is recognizably Eames-influenced. In the austere and formal simplicity of his work, Day's furniture reveals the continuing importance of functionalism and the INTERNATIONAL STYLE.

DAY, THOMAS (c. 1800–1861)

Nineteenth-century American furniture maker. A free black, Day was among the prominent building contractors and furniture makers of antebellum North Carolina. He employed a number of other cabinetmakers, both black and white, and produced furniture in various styles of the early VICTORIAN PERIOD.

DAYBED

In a general sense, any COUCH, CHAISE LONGUE, LOUNGE or other furniture form

davenport

Thomas Day chair

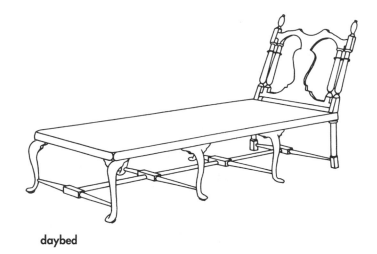

daybed

blow chair by De Pas

intended for daytime repose. More specifically, the term has been applied to a succession of forms, all designed for the same purpose. In MEDIEVAL FURNITURE the daybed was simply a pallet or mattress supported on a legged frame with a slanted section at one end to provide a headrest. In the 17th century the headrest came to resemble a sloping chair back more closely. It and the long seat were usually caned and equipped with upholstered cushions or were upholstered themselves. The frame was often supported by six or eight legs, with the piece being heavily ornamented in the MANNERIST STYLE of the day. In the late 18th century, this form of daybed was outmoded by the couch, and the term *daybed* began to take on its more general sense. In 18th- and 19th-century America, the term referred to a true bed that had a headboard and footboard of the same height and was placed lengthwise against a wall. Like the French ALCOVE BED, from which the American form had developed, this daybed was much more highly decorated on one side than on the other; ornamentation was usually in the NEOCLASSICAL STYLE. In modern times the term *daybed* may also denote the convertible SOFA-BED.

DE FOREST, LOCKWOOD (1850–1932)

American entrepreneur, painter and designer. Through his association with Louis C. TIFFANY, de Forest made his enthusiasm for the Middle East and India felt on American design of the late 19th century. De Forest imported furniture from the Far East, India and the Middle East. He even established his own workshop in Ahmedabad, India, to pro-

duce exotic furniture for the New York market and to make carvings and inlaid panels for use by American factories such as Tiffany's.

DE PAS, D'URBINO, LOMAZZI

Italian architecture and design firm established in Milan in 1966; associated with POP ART FURNITURE. This firm—headed by Jonathan De Pas, Donato D'Urbino and Paolo Lomazzi, all born in the 1930s—is primarily known for two striking chair designs, the "Blow" chair (1967) and the "Joe" chair (1970). The former is an inflatable chair of transparent or brightly colored polyvinyl chloride (PVC). The latter, named for former baseball star Joe DiMaggio, is a chair in the shape of a huge baseball glove, made of molded polyurethane foam and covered in leather.

DE PAS, JONATHAN

See DE PAS, D'URBINO, LOMAZZI.

DE PASSE, CRISPIN (1564–1637)

French furniture designer in the MANNERIST STYLE. In 1621 De Passe published a PATTERN BOOK that influenced a generation of furniture makers in northern Europe, especially in the Netherlands.

DE STIJL

Group of Dutch Modernist artists and designers prominent in the 1920s. De Stijl (literally, "The Style") took its name from the magazine of that title published by Theo VAN DOESBURG between 1917 and 1931. The group, influenced in part by the theories of H. P. BERLAGE, found beauty in austerity, and they purged design of all but what were seen as its basic constituents: primary colors and right angles. Through this esthetic of purity and reductionism, De Stijl attempted to express the spiritual nature of humankind. The paintings of Piet Mondrian and the architecture and furniture of Gerrit RIETVELD are considered to be the most representative works of the style. Other members of the group who also designed furniture were the painter and writer Van Doesburg and the architects J. J. P. OUD and Mart STAM. A secondary concern of De Stijl designers was the development of clarity and purity in architecture and industrial design; since the designers had no interest in FUNCTIONALISM, however, this concern remained secondary. In consequence, De Stijl furniture, especially that of Rietveld, is generally not considered good furniture in practical use, but is more important for the strength with which it demonstrates an esthetic program. It is through their contribution as the purist wing of Modernism that the De Stijl designers had their greatest impact on subsequent furniture design.

DEAL

British term for any of the SOFTWOODS, especially yellow PINE; term excludes American woods. Traditionally a common material in vernacular furniture, deal has also been used, since the 17th century, for the CARCASE in pieces of fine furniture veneered in more expensive decorative woods.

DECK CHAIR

Collapsible chair intended for outdoor use, especially on shipboard.

DEEP-BUTTONING

See UPHOLSTERY.

DEGANELLO, PAOLO (b. 1940)

Contemporary Italian architect and furniture designer. A founder of ARCHIZOOM, Deganello has designed daring, innovative furniture and has championed, through his work and as a teacher, the strain of pronounced individualism that has been prominent in recent Italian design. Important elements of his own work are, in his words, "subjectivity and the imaginary." Accordingly, his furniture is odd; he uses radically unfamiliar shapes and may combine various colors and decorative patterns in one given piece. But his work is also functional, designed for human use and comfort.

DELAFOSSE, JEAN-CHARLES (1734–91)

French NEOCLASSICAL STYLE architect and ornamental designer. He is best known for his published designs for furniture, metalwork and interior ornamentation; published between 1768 and 1785, these were influential on LOUIS XVI STYLE furniture makers. Himself

influenced by J.-F NEUFFORGE, Delafosse, a prolific worker, used a self-consciously dignified style, favoring thick FESTOONS of laurel leaves and Greek KEY PATTERNS on heavy, architectural forms that sometimes retained features of ROCOCO FURNITURE, such as scroll feet (*see* SCROLL FOOT, *under* FOOT).

DELANOIS, LOUIS (1731–92)

French MENUISIER noted for chairs in LOUIS XV and LOUIS XVI STYLES.

DEMICELURE (*demicelour*)

See CELURE.

DEMILUNE

Shaped like a half-disc when seen from above; usually said of a piece of case furniture, such as a COMMODE (1) or CONSOLE (*see* DEMILUNE COMMODE).

DEMILUNE COMMODE

Eighteenth-century French CHEST OF DRAWERS whose front curved like an arc of a circle. It had convex drawers in the center, flanked by small, convex compartments with shelves, either open or behind doors. This type of COMMODE (1) became popular in the LOUIS XVI STYLE of the second half of the 18th century.

DENG (TENG)

CHINESE FURNITURE form of Ming (1368–1644) and Qing (1644–1911) dynasties; STOOL with straight sides, as opposed to the barrel-shaped DUN. Various legged stools had been known in China since raised seating was adopted at the end of the Han dynasty (c. A.D. 200; *see* HU CHUANG). The *deng*, which usually had a square or polygonal seat—less frequently a round one—was distinguished by its very low BOX STRETCHER (*see under* STRETCHER). The stool commonly had an open framework; that is, the stretcher lay on the floor. Beginning in the 18th century, the *deng* was frequently enriched with elaborate carved or inlaid ornamentation, and its shape, as seen from above, became more complex; it was arranged in curvilinear lobes to represent floral or other motifs. A *deng* was often used as a small side table, or JIA JI.

deng

DENG GUA SHI YI (TENG KUA SHIH YI)
CHINESE FURNITURE form made from Song (960–1279) until early Ming (1368–1644) dynasties; chair with broad central SPLAT rising higher than STILES. The name means "chair shaped like a hanging lantern shaped like a chair with a high back."

DENNIS, THOMAS (c. 1638–1706)
Maker of AMERICAN JACOBEAN FURNITURE. One of the most important American furniture makers of his day, Dennis specialized in wainscot chairs, cupboards and chests, which were heavily ornamented with carved decoration. Originally from Devonshire, England, he had arrived in Portsmouth, New Hampshire, by 1663; in 1688 he moved to Ipswich, Massachusetts. He married the widow of William SEARLE.

desk on frame

DENON, DOMINIQUE VIVANT, BARON (1747–1825)
French archaeologist, engraver and EMPIRE STYLE designer of furniture and interiors. Denon, an archaeologist by training, accompanied Napoleon's military expedition to Egypt in 1799. He recorded the architecture and decoration of ancient Egypt in engravings that were published as a book, *Voyage dans la basse et haut Égypte,* in 1802 in Paris and London. This book sparked a tremendous enthusiasm for ÉGYPTIENNERIE motifs in both Britain and France and had an immense influence on designers and furniture makers in both the Empire style and the REGENCY STYLE. Denon became the supervisor of design for Napoleon's imperial court, and he also designed furniture that was executed by leading craftsmen, notably M.-G. BIENNAIS and JACOB-DESMALTER.

DENTICULATION
Decorative motif; series of small, tooth-like rectangular blocks, usually arranged along the lower edge of a cornice in case furniture. The device originated in ancient Greek architecture and became a feature of NEOCLASSICAL STYLE ornamentation.

DEODAR
See CEDAR.

DESK
Any piece of furniture intended for writing, including forms with SLANT TOPS, such as the British and American SECRETARY and the French SECRÉTAIRE, and flat-topped forms, such as the WRITING TABLE and the PEDESTAL DESK.

DESK-AND-BOOKCASE
Eighteenth-century name for SECRETARY.

DESK-ON-FRAME
Seventeenth- and early 18th-century English and American WILLIAM AND MARY or QUEEN ANNE STYLE furniture form; a desk consisting of a SLANT-TOP box set in a table frame that lacked a top. The desk could be as small and simple as a BIBLE BOX or medieval WRITING BOX, or rather larger, sometimes with a drawer below the space covered by the slanted lid. The drawer tended to make such desks too tall for use with an ordinary chair, and the simpler desks had little storage. Probably for these reasons, the desk-on-frame was not very popular, to judge by the small number of them that have survived, but it constituted a decisive step in the development of the SLANT-TOP DESK.

DESKEY, DONALD (1894–1989)
AMERICAN MODERNE decorator and furniture designer of the 1930s. Deskey is best known for the interiors and furnishings he designed for New York's Radio City Music Hall. His furniture illustrates how the American Moderne style is derived from both French ART DECO and the INTERNATIONAL STYLE. The asceticism of the International style is represented in Deskey's use of steel and synthetic fabrics, while his choice of rich materials and his decorative style was derived from Art Deco.

DESORNAMENTADO STYLE (also *Herrera style*)
Late 16th-century Spanish style in architecture and furniture. This austere reaction against the richness of the Italian Renaissance was created largely by architect Juan de Herrera (c. 1530–97). The *desornamentado* style insisted on a minimum of ornamentation and, indeed, a minimum of furniture. Some

decorative effect was permitted in the form of fielded panels, deep though plain mouldings and turned legs. While the exuberant CHURRIGUERESQUE STYLE of the 17th century promptly replaced Herrera's austerities in fashionable circles, the *desornamentado* style persisted in provincial Spain, and especially Mexico, for two centuries.

DEUTSCHER WERKBUND

Predominantly German group of reformist architects and designers. The group—based, in part, on the example of the DEUTSCHE WERKSTÄTTEN groups—was founded at Dresden in 1907 and dedicated to design reform and factory production of furniture and other household goods. Led by the writer and architect Hermann MUTHESIUS, who had studied and published on the British ARTS AND CRAFTS MOVEMENT, the Deutscher Werkbund promoted the ideas and work of its members through publications and exhibitions. Among the members were the Germans Richard RIEMERSCHMID, Bruno PAUL, Bernhard PANKOK and Walter GROPIUS; the Belgian Henri VAN DE VELDE; and the Austrians Josef HOFFMANN and Otto WAGNER. The Deutscher Werkbund advocated the application of art to industry and adopted an austere, functionalistic design style (*see* FUNCTIONALISM), which was derived from the German and Austrian wings of the ART NOUVEAU movement. The Deutscher Werkbund contributed to the foundations of modern design, both ideologically and stylistically. It inspired the creation of similar organizations in other countries and continued to play a prominent role in modern design through the 1920s, after which it was dissolved by the Nazi government.

DEUTSCHE WERKSTÄTTEN

German design reform movement composed of several different groups of designers organized to encourage design reform, beginning in the late 1890s. The first group, the Vereinigte Werstätten fur Kunst im Handwerk, was founded in Munich in 1897. Among the founding members were Hermann OBRIST, Bernhard PANKOK, Bruno PAUL, Peter BEHRENS and Richard RIEMERSCHMID. The group's ideas were influenced by the design reform movements of Britain (*see* ARTS AND CRAFTS MOVEMENT; ART FURNITURE MOVEMENT). Their intention was to develop and promote well-designed, machinemade furniture and other objects that, through mass production, could be made widely available and inexpensive. The same goal inspired the *Dresdener Werkstätten fur Handwerkkunst,* which was founded in Dresden in 1898 by furniture maker Karl SCHMIDT. A successor to the Munich group merged with the Dresden Organization in 1907, and this united organization, led by Riemerschmid, adopted the formal name *Deutsche Werkstätten,* though the term is also used to refer to the movement as a whole. The movement's success became evident in 1906, when its first wholly machinemade furniture was produced, from designs by Riemerschmid, Paul and Schmidt. The DEUTSCHER WERKBUND, a design reform group contemporary with the Werkstätten, had similar goals, but it focused more on architecture and industrial design than furniture.

DEVIL-TAIL HINGE

See under HINGE.

DIAO TIAN (TIAO T'IEN) (also *leather lacquer*)

Decorative LACQUER used on CHINESE FURNITURE of the Ming (1386–1644) and Qing (1644–1911) dynasties, bearing incised decoration in several colors. Lacquer of a distinctive burnished orange color was built up in several layers, in which pictorial scenes and motifs, set against various patterned backgrounds, were incised. The incised lines were filled with different-colored lacquers, and prominent outlines were gilded. The colors used were limited to greens, browns and black, with occasional reds or ochers. The effect produced was that of tooled leather—hence, the name by which the work is often known in the West.

DIAPERING

Ornamental pattern consisting of many small squares or diamond shapes, usually the latter, repeated in a checkered arrangement. Other motifs may appear within some or all of these geometrical shapes. The device originated in MEDIEVAL FURNITURE and architecture, and it is believed to have been derived from the characteristic weave of a type of cloth made in the

Belgian town of Ypres. It was thus *d'Ypres,* meaning "of Ypres"; hence, its name.

DIETTERLIN, WENDEL (1550–99)

German architect and engraver of MANNERIST STYLE ornamentation. In 1593 Dietterlin published a PATTERN BOOK, *Architectura und Austheilung,* composed of bizarre, sometimes erotic, designs, with much intricate STRAPWORK. His work was influential in Germany, the Netherlands and England.

DIFFRIENT, NIELS (b. 1931)

American furniture designer and authority on ERGONOMIC DESIGN. After studying architecture at Eliel SAARINEN's Cranbrook Academy, Diffrient worked briefly for Saarinen and then spent 25 years as an industrial designer. He formed his own company to specialize in furniture design and created ergonomically designed seating for KNOLL and others. Diffrient is also coauthor of *Humanscale* (1980–82), a three-volume technical guide to ergonomic design.

Niels Diffrient armchair

DIJSSELHOF, GERRIT (1866–1924)

Dutch designer and architect associated with the ARTS AND CRAFTS MOVEMENT and ART NOUVEAU. Influenced by the British design reform movements—especially the work of C. F. A. VOYSEY—Dijsselhof, with Theodore NIEUWENHUIS and C. A. LION-CACHET, founded Het Binnenhuis, a furniture-making atelier dedicated to design reform. Dijsselhof's own furniture was strongly in the Arts and Crafts tradition, with simple lines, exposed joinery and little decoration. He employed the abstract, organic motifs of Art Nouveau in his interior design, though in a restrained manner.

DING GUI (TING KUEI) (also *mao gui*)

Chinese furniture form of Ming (1368–1644) and Qing (1644–1911) dynasties; short, wide, chestlike box with doors on its front, placed atop a high wardrobe and intended for storage of headgear. Its name literally means "top cupboard," and the form is sometimes called a *mao gui,* meaning "hat cupboard."

DIPHROS

Ancient GREEK FURNITURE form; four-legged stool. Adapted from ancient Egypt, where sim-

ilar stools were in use in predynastic times (*see* EGYPTIAN FURNITURE), the *diphros* was a very light and portable piece. Its short, straight legs, either turned or rectangular in shape, were sometimes supported by STRETCHERS.

DIPHROS OKLADIAS

Ancient GREEK FURNITURE form; folding stool. Adapted from ancient Egypt, where similar stools appeared in about 2000 B.C. (*see* EGYPTIAN FURNITURE), the *diphros okladias* consisted to two X-FRAMES, in a collapsible arrangement with a metal bolt at each crossing point; the two were joined by a flexible seat of leather or fabric. The feet were often in the shape of animal paws, and stretchers no longer connected the feet, unlike in the Egyptian version. Sometimes it had fixed legs and a rigid seat. The *diphros okladias* continued to be made in Roman times and was the prototype for the SELLA CURULIS and medieval folding stools.

DIRECTOIRE STYLE

French furniture style of the French Revolution. The style is named for the Revolutionary government that succeeded the Reign of Terror in 1794, but it had actually begun to evolve even before the Revolution, in the ETRUSCAN STYLE decoration of late LOUIS XVI–STYLE furniture. The Directory government ended with Napoleon's coup d'état of 1799, and furniture produced thereafter belongs to the CONSULATE STYLE, which immediately preceded the EMPIRE STYLE. Though the two periods were very similar, Directoire style furniture exemplified the effect of the Revolution on the Louis XVI style, while Consulate style work began to take on the stiffer, more martial character of the Empire style. The Directoire style was thus a transitional mode between the final stages of the Louis XVI style and the beginnings of the Empire Style.

During the Revolution furniture was made in a severely simplified version of earlier Louis XVI–style work—smaller in scale, using less costly materials and decorated with minimal ornamentation, usually simple inlays of wood or brass. This style was first known as *le style républicaine,* and its austerity was in part necessitated by the weak French economy, which had been disrupted by revolution and war, but it also reflected a politically inspired reaction against the sumptuousness of the *ancien régime*. The limited decoration of this style included variations on the classically inspired ornamentation of prior decades, especially the painted figural scenes, stylized foliage and subdued color scheme of the Etruscan style. Other popular motifs were such Revolutionary symbols as the fasces and the Phrygian or Liberty cap (both derived from ancient Rome).

PERCIER AND FONTAINE, the leading designers of the Empire style, first worked in the Directoire manner, in which they found the basic repertoire of forms and ideas that they would present more grandly under Napoleon. The other most important designers and makers of the Directoire period included F.-J. BÉLANGER, Guillaume BENEMAN, J.-D. DUGOURC, Georges JACOB and Bernard MOLITOR. All of these men had worked for the king before the Revolution, and all except Dugourc went on to work for Napoleon in the Empire style.

DIRECTOR'S CHAIR

Modern folding chair composed of two X-FRAMES, at front and rear, each surmounted by an arm and a stile; canvas strips between them form seat and back. The director's chair, so called because its use is associated with filmmakers, is descended from portable chairs used by European armies since the 18th century.

DIRECTORY STYLE (also *American Regency style*)

American version of early REGENCY STYLE of Great Britain; transitional mode of the first years of the 19th century, linking the early FEDERAL PERIOD's delicately angular furniture with the heavier, more curvilinear AMERICAN EMPIRE STYLE. The Directory style takes its name from the contemporary term used to denote its British model, indicating the influence of the French DIRECTOIRE STYLE on such British designers as Thomas SHERATON. The American style was primarily based on Sheraton's late work and reflected British and French enthusiasm for classical and ancient Egyptian artifacts. The Greek KLISMOS chair appeared, and the chief items of decoration, aside from the Federal eagle, were paw feet (*see* PAW FOOT, *under* FOOT) of carved wood or cast brass, and classical FLUTING or its inverse, REEDING. The chief

Directory style furniture maker was Duncan PHYFE, of New York. Others included Lemuel CHURCHILL, of Boston; Henry CONNELLY and Ephraim HAINES, of Philadelphia; and Joseph BARRY, of Philadelphia and Baltimore.

DISBROWE, NICHOLAS (1612–83)

Maker of AMERICAN JACOBEAN furniture. Disbrowe, the son of a joiner, was originally from Essex, England. At 27, though, he was counted among the early settlers of Hartford, Connecticut. Disbrowe contributed to the development of the HADLEY CHEST and the CONNECTICUT SUNFLOWER CHEST.

DISHED CORNER (also *tray corner*)

Carved, shallow depression in each corner of a tabletop, intended to hold money or chips. The dished corner first appeared in 18th-century CARD TABLES (1).

DISHED SEAT

Concave seat with a depression slightly lower than the seat rail, intended to hold a cushion.

DISHED TOP

Tabletop, especially a circular one, with carved or molded rim, such as on a PIE-CRUST TABLE; or tabletop with DISHED CORNERS or other such carved, shallow depressions around its edge.

Directory chair

DISK FOOT

See under FOOT.

DISTRESSING

Treatment of wood so as to make it appear older than it is. The appearance of age is created by abrading the surface of the wood to imitate the wear of use. Burnishing with a piece of smooth metal further alters the color and visual texture. Given the market value of age, distressing is held in disrepute, except on a piece that is an acknowledged reproduction or on parts for repair.

DITZEL, HANNA (b. 1923)

Danish furniture designer. Also well-known for textile and jewelry designs, Hanna Ditzel

Hanna Ditzel chair

has been a leading figure in SCANDINAVIAN MODERN furniture design since the 1950s. Her work is functionalistic in character (*see* FUNCTIONALISM), with an emphasis on materials whose texture provides visual interest. Particularly noted are a group of cane chairs and stools from the 1960s. Since 1970 she has lived in England.

DIVAN
Furniture form of 19th century; upholstered platform on legs that has been defined as a couch without arms or back or as a bed without headboard or footboard. The divan was developed in France after 1830, when the invention of coil-spring UPHOLSTERY spurred an interest in luxuriant seating. It takes its name from a Turkish architectural feature, a dais set aside for persons of rank and furnished solely with an opulent array of cushions and fine fabrics (*see* MOORISH STYLE).

DOCUMENT DRAWER
Small, vertical box fitting a tall slot or compartment in 18th-century BUREAU or SECRETARY. It was designed to house papers on edge, as in a file.

DOG FOOT
See under FOOT.

DOG'S-PAW FOOT
See under FOOT.

DOGU-BAKO
Traditional JAPANESE FURNITURE form; tall TANSU or chest used by barbers, with drawers and compartments for combs, razors and so on.

DOLPHIN
Decorative motif; mythological fishlike sea creature. Derived from ancient Greek and Roman art, the dolphin appears in RENAISSANCE FURNITURE, especially that of Venice. It has been used in ornate pieces in most styles, having been particularly popular in 18th-century France and in the British REGENCY STYLE.

dolphin

DOLPHIN FOOT
See under FOOT.

DOMINIQUE
French firm that made ART DECO furniture in the 1920s. Dominique began in 1922 as a partnership between two designers, Andre Domin and Marcel Genevriere, and its furniture was of the restrained, finely crafted sort exemplified by the work of Émile-Jacques RUHLMANN.

DOREUR
French craftsman who specialized in gilding furniture and bronze mounts for furniture. Organized as a separate group under the Parisian guild system that dominated French furniture making in the 17th and 18th centuries, the *doreurs* were merged with the FONDEUR-CISELEURS in 1776, not long before the French Revolution abolished the guild system.

DORIC ORDER
Oldest and simplest of the three ancient Greek ORDERS OF ARCHITECTURE; developed before 500 B.C. and later adapted by the Romans. The Doric order was characterized by a simple, fluted COLUMN without a base. This column, whose height was between 4 and $6\frac{1}{2}$ times its diameter, was stockier than those of later orders. Its simple CAPITAL consisted of a flat slab, the ABACUS, above an encircling MOLDING, the *echinus*. The ENTABLATURE was similarly bold and simple, featuring a FRIEZE composed of alternating METOPEs and TRIGYLPHs, both very plain devices. The Roman Doric order was different in two ways: the column was slenderer and stood on a base; and the capital was more decorative, usually with ornamentation on the upper edge of the abacus.

DORSER (also *dosser*)
In MEDIEVAL FURNITURE, fabric hanging that covered the back of a throne or the backboard, or CELURE, of a bed.

DOSSER
Variant of DORSER.

DOUBLE COW-HORN STRETCHER
See COW-HORN STRETCHER, *under* STRETCHER.

DOUBLE H-STRETCHER
See H-STRETCHER, *under* STRETCHER.

DOUBLE-LYRE STRETCHER
See under STRETCHER.

DOUBLE OPEN-TWIST TURNING
See under TURNERY.

DOUBLE WINDSOR CHAIR
Another name for WINDSOR SETTEE.

DOUCET, JACQUES (1853–1929)
French couturier; prominent patron of ART DECO furniture makers. In the 1920s Doucet commissioned designs for furniture and decorative schemes for his Paris apartment, and in so doing promoted the Art Deco style. Among the designers who worked for him were Marcel COARD, Pierre LEGRAIN, Clément ROUSSEAU, André GROULT and Eileen GRAY.

DOUSSIÉ
Another name for AFZELIA.

DOVETAIL
Wedge-shaped element in a DOVETAIL JOINT (*see under* JOINERY) or a joint itself. Also, a symmetrical, butterfly-shaped appendage on one board that is inserted into a wedge-shaped cutout in another board, used to join the two boards edge to edge.

DOWEL
Small, usually cylindrical piece of wood used to join other pieces in a DOWELED JOINT, whether BUTT JOINT, SPLINED JOINT, MITER or MORTISE-AND-TENON JOINT. (*See each under* JOINERY.)

DOWER FURNITURE
Case pieces, especially chests, intended to store clothing, linens and other domestic goods accumulated by a young woman in anticipation of her marriage. These pieces were typically decorated with flowers, ARABESQUES and, most distinctively, the initials or names of the wedded couple. Common in Western furniture since late medieval times, dower furniture is represented by, among other forms, the CASSONE, the SCHRANK, the painted dower chest of American PENNSYLVANIA GERMAN FURNITURE and the HADLEY CHEST.

dower chest

DRAGONESQUE STYLE
See MUNTHE, Gerhard.

DRAKE FOOT
See under FOOT.

DRAW-LEAF TABLE
Also called a *draw table* or *draw-top table;* table with one or two leaves (*see* LEAF) that rest beneath the tabletop on sliding lengths of wood. These can be drawn out at each end to enlarge the top surface. Invented in the 16th century, the draw-leaf table was very popular for 150 years in northern Europe, especially in Britain, France and the Netherlands. Its popularity diminished with the development of the DROP-LEAF TABLE, but it is still in use today.

DRAWER
Small, open-topped box housed in a piece of case furniture or beneath a table-top so that it can be removed by being drawn out horizontally on slides or along grooves. In ancient EGYPTIAN FURNITURE tiny drawers were used in miniature tables and chests to store jewelry, cosmetics and game pieces. Oddly, the device was subsequently lost, and it had to be independently reinvented in Europe, in about the

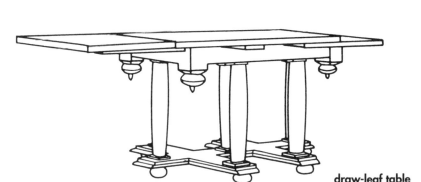

draw-leaf table

15th century. The drawer appeared in CHINESE FURNITURE at about the same time, perhaps through early Western contacts or a parallel invention. In Europe the drawer evolved from small boxes that were used as compartments in a CHEST to avoid disturbing all of the chest's contents in order to retrieve one item. It was then realized that it would be easier to remove the bottom boxes through the side of the chest rather than from the top, and the MULE CHEST, predecessor of the CHEST OF DRAWERS, developed. In RENAISSANCE and BAROQUE FURNITURE, the elaborate CABINET, with many drawers, became a showpiece of the decorative arts. Drawer handles have also proved to be a focus of attention for devisers of ornamentation (*see* BAIL HANDLE; DROP HANDLE; RING PULL). Eventually, the drawer became ubiquitous in case furniture, and specialized varieties evolved, such as the DOCUMENT DRAWER and the SECRETARY DRAWER.

DRAWER STOP

Small block or tongue of wood or metal, set, usually in pairs, in the front rail of a drawer opening. A drawer stop blocks the inward movement of the drawer front and thereby keeps the closing drawer from hitting the back of the piece and damaging it. (In many pieces, the drawer front overlaps the front rail of the opening and is stopped by it; in this case, no drawer stops are necessary.)

DRESSER (1)

Form of GOTHIC FURNITURE; utilitarian variant of the BUFFET, with a tablelike base topped by an arrangement of shelves. The dresser was used in the kitchen to prepare, or dress, food.

DRESSER (2)

Modern American term for a low CHEST OF DRAWERS, often topped with a mirror.

DRESSER, CHRISTOPHER (1834–1904)

English designer and writer associated with the ART FURNITURE MOVEMENT. Dresser began his career as a botanical artist, and later established himself as a botanist. He then turned to the decorative arts and followed Owen JONES and other proponents of exotic revivalism.

Dresser became attracted to Japanese art in the 1860s (*see* JAPONISME) and designed a vast amount of all sorts of household objects for mass manufacture, including furniture influenced by William GODWIN's Anglo-Japanese style and Charles EASTLAKE's Modern Gothic. He wrote extensively on design, and his written work was influential, though overshadowed by Eastlake's, whose proposals were similar. Dresser also designed pottery and silver.

DRESSING TABLE

Any table intended for use while dressing or applying makeup, usually equipped with a mirror and several small drawers or compartments to hold brushes, cosmetics and so on. Like the corresponding French term, *toilette,* the name denotes function rather than any particular form, though certain types of dressing table, such as the BEAU BRUMMEL and the TOILETTE EN PAPILLON, have received specific designations. Dressing tables were first used in the late 17th century, though these early forms often served other functions as well. For instance, the BUREAU MAZARIN, a well-known DESK, was also used as a dressing table. By 1750 specifically designed fittings, such as adjustable mirrors and bottle wells, were attached to tall, flat-topped tables; such fittings might also be part of another form—for example, a CHEST OF DRAWERS or a KNEEHOLE DESK. This practice was common in America, where the popular LOWBOY could function as a dessing table. Late in the 18th century, the complicated fittings of the Beau Brummel, a product of the fad for dandyism, brought the dressing table to its fullest elaboration. After this century of development, the dressing table had become a well-established form, and it is still popular.

DRESSOIR

Medieval term for DRESSER (1).

DROP

Decorative motif popular in late 18th century; any arrangement of small images in a pendant cluster, but especially the HUSK motif and its American variant, the BELLFLOWER.

DROP-FRONT DESK

Desk equipped with FALL FRONT for a writing surface.

DROP HANDLE
Type of furniture HARDWARE; door or drawer handle composed of a pendant brass ornament, usually pear-, tear- or ball-shaped. This ornament hangs from a bolt, which passes through a small, circular plate to attach the handle to the surface. The drop handle, introduced in RENAISSANCE FURNITURE, was most popular in the late 17th and 18th centuries, but it is still in use.

DROP-IN SEAT
Another name for SLIP SEAT.

DROP-LEAF TABLE
Generic term for a table type having leaves (*see* LEAF) hinged to the tabletop that hang vertically when not in use. The leaves, when raised and supported in any of several ways, enlarge the usable surface of the tabletop. (*See* BUTTERFLY TABLE; BREAKFAST TABLE; GATE-LEG TABLE; HANDKERCHIEF TABLE; PEMBROKE TABLE; SOFA-TABLE; SWING-LEG TABLE.)

DRUM TABLE
British NEOCLASSICAL STYLE furniture form of late 18th and early 19th centuries; PEDESTAL TABLE with circular or polygonal top and drawers around the frieze. Either the drawers were wedge-shaped, or every other one was a dummy. The top usually rotated on the pedestal. The RENT TABLE was a specialized version.

DUBELL, HEINRICH (active c. 1850s)
Viennese ROCOCO REVIVAL STYLE furniture maker.

DUBOIS, JACQUES (c. 1693–1763)
French furniture maker; ébéniste who specialized in LACQUER and VERNIS MARTIN veneers in LOUIS XV STYLE. His son was the better-known maker René DUBOIS.

DUBOIS, RENÉ (1737–99)
French furniture maker in TRANSITION and LOUIS XVI STYLES. Dubois, who inherited his father's successful furniture business (*see* Jacques DUBOIS), was an early maker of Louis XVI–style pieces, beginning in about 1765.

He favored VERNIS MARTIN veneering decorated with CHINOISERIE motifs. His work was very fashionable and was especially popular with Queen Marie-Antoinette. After 1779 he stopped making furniture to become a dealer, and he retired altogether in 1788.

DU CERCEAU, JACQUES ANDROUET, the Elder (c. 1520–84)
French architect and designer of MANNERIST STYLE decoration. Du Cerceau published one of the earliest PATTERN BOOKS of RENAISSANCE FURNITURE, in about 1550. He was a leading exponent of the HENRI II STYLE, and his many designs for furniture and buildings, most of them bizarrely Mannerist and filled with GROTESQUE ORNAMENT and complicated STRAPWORK, were highly influential in France and elsewhere in northern Europe through most of the 17th century. His most important book, *Les plus excellents bastiments de France,* was published in two volumes in 1576 and 1579.

DUCHESS
See DUCHESSE BRISÉE.

DUCHESS BED
See DUCHESSE BRISÉE.

DUCHESSE
Eighteenth-century French upholstered CHAISE LONGUE, with distinctively rounded back.

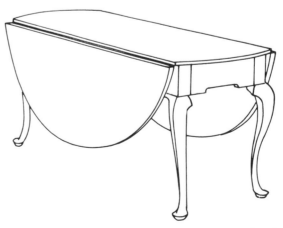

drop-leaf table

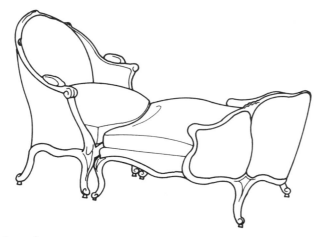

duchesse brisée

DUCHESSE BRISÉE (also *duchess*)
Eighteenth-century French upholstered CHAISE LONGUE. It consisted of either a round-backed armchair with a matching but separate footstool or of two such chairs that faced each other with the footstool between them. The separate elements could be attached to one another, but each could also be used alone. The *duchesse brisée* was very popular in Britain, where it was known as a *duchess* and assumed several forms, including Thomas SHERATON's duchess bed.

DUCHESSE EN BATEAU
Eighteenth-century French CHAISE LONGUE; DUCHESSE whose upholstered foot was enclosed by a low, curving wall of wood, matching the curve of the back.

DUFRÊNE, MAURICE (1876–1955)
French ART DECO designer. Early in the 20th century, Dufrêne designed in a Parisian ART

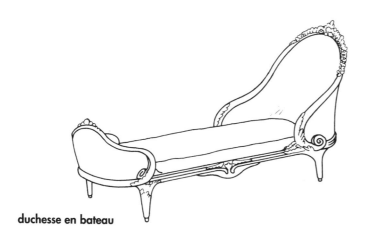

duchesse en bateau

NOUVEAU style. After following Henri VAN DE VELDE, however, he reacted against the style and became one of the initiators of Art Deco. Using traditional forms and restrained decorative motifs in his work, he designed interiors, furniture, textiles, metalwork and glass. Dufrêne had a great influence on French design before and after the First World War, through his widely known writings, his work and his professorship in Paris.

DUGOURC, JEAN-DÉMOSTHÈNE (1749–1825)
French architect and furniture designer in LOUIS XVI and DIRECTOIRE STYLES. As a young man, Dugourc studied classical architecture and design in Rome. When he returned to Paris, he became the assistant and later the brother-in-law of F.-J. BÉLANGER. Together they were largely responsible for making the ETRUSCAN STYLE of decoration popular in France. Dugourc's furniture designs emphasized the adaptation of archeologically correct classical forms and ornamentation and were used by J. B. BOULARD, Martin CARLIN, J.-B. SENÉ and others. In 1799 Dugourc moved to Madrid, where he practiced architecture. He returned to France in 1814 and pursued a successful career designing many things, especially fabric patterns, in the RESTAURATION STYLE.

DUMBWAITER
Eighteenth-century British furniture form; STAND of two or more (usually three) circular tiers with central post support on three or four short legs. The dumbwaiter was used as a serving table in the dining room. It first appeared in about 1740 and was popular throughout the century. In the early 19th century, it was superseded by the BUTLER'S TABLE.

DUN (TUN)
CHINESE FURNITURE form of Ming (1368–1644) and Qing (1644–1911) dynasties; barrel-shaped STOOL. Basically a framework supporting a circular seat, a *dun* could consist of simple members—convex, curving verticals joining a circular frame at the bottom and a disk at the top—or it might have decorative OPENWORK sides, as in the XIU DUN. Often the seat was a round marble plaque. An important piece of

outdoor furniture was the PORCELAIN *dun*, whose sides were frequently solid.

DUNAND, JEAN (1877–1942)

French ART DECO designer of metalwork and lacquer furniture. Born in Switzerland, Dunand was originally a sculptor but turned to the decorative arts after 1902, working chiefly in metal and lacquer, especially the latter. Before the First World War, he employed ART NOUVEAU's naturalistic forms, then adopted, in the 1920s, the restrained geometrical style now known as Art Deco. After the war Dunand established a furniture-manufacturing firm and produced simple furniture designed to provide surfaces for his lacquerwork. His decorative schemes generally combined large, smooth, undecorated areas with his flawless sheets of lacquer. Dunand sometimes collaborated with other designers, including Émile-Jacques RUHLMANN. He produced screens, cabinets, tables, chairs and other items, all veneered with as many as 20 coats of lacquer. Often these pieces were further decorated with geometrical designs in precious metals or inlaid eggshells, a Japanese technique that Dunand made a specialty.

DUNLAP, JOHN
See DUNLAP FAMILY.

DUNLAP, SAMUEL
See DUNLAP FAMILY.

DUNLAP FAMILY

New Hampshire family of cabinetmakers associated with COUNTRY CHIPPENDALE FURNITURE. John Dunlap (1746–92) was the leading member of the family, which dominated New Hampshire furniture making in the late 18th and early 19th centuries. His brother Samuel (1752–1820) and Samuel's four sons all made furniture that combined basic rectilinear forms with very busy carved decoration. Their chairs were tall and thin, in the manner of the WILLIAM AND MARY STYLE, but were made more fashionable by the application of rococo style carving (*see* ROCOCO FURNITURE). The Dunlaps used an idiosyncratic variety of Chippendale-inspired ornamentation, including distinctively carved shells, S-scrolled borders for the skirts of case pieces, fretted cornices and unusual moldings.

D'URBINO, DONATO
See DE PAS, D'URBINO, LOMAZZI.

D'URSO, JOSEPH PAUL (b. 1943)
American interior designer; leading exponent of "Industrial style" (*see* HIGHTECH STYLE).

DUSTBOARD
Horizontal panel placed between two drawers to prevent the passage of dust from one to the other.

DUTCH ANGULAR FOOT
See under FOOT.

DUTCH ELONGATED FOOT
See under FOOT.

DUTCH FOOT
See under FOOT.

DUTCH GROOVED FOOT
See under FOOT.

E

Eames chair

EAMES, CHARLES (1907–78)

American architect and furniture designer, one of the most important furniture designers in the post–Second World War period. Eames's experiments in molded materials and his creation of curvilinear, organic-looking forms for his extraordinary series of chairs altered the character of modern furniture design. He eschewed the angular, geometrical designs associated with the BAUHAUS for freer, though no more ornamental, pieces that suited the exuberant and increasingly informal postwar world. But this implies no lack of rigor; Eames was among the early and most thoroughgoing practitioners of ERGONOMIC DESIGN.

Eames was trained in architecture in St. Louis, and he opened his own design practice there in 1930. In 1936 he accepted a fellowship at Eliel SAARINEN's Cranbrook Academy. A year later he was appointed director of its department of experimental design, a post he held through 1939. At Cranbrook his colleagues and students included Harry BERTOIA, Florence KNOLL and Eero SAARINEN, Eliel's son, all of whom would become major furniture designers during the postwar period. At Cranbrook, Eames and Eero Saarinen began experiments with molded plywood that culminated in their chair designs of 1940. The two men gained their first renown when these designs won first prize in the New York Museum of Modern Art's "Organic Design in Home Furnishings" competition (1940).

These designs carried molding beyond the one-directional curves that Alvar AALTO and Marcel BREUER, among others, had used. Eames and Saarinen introduced complex, multidirectional curves, manipulating a single sheet of wood to form the seat, the back and the arms in a sculptural manner that strikingly anticipated subsequent work in molded plastics. The molded seat unit was mounted atop slender legs, which at first were wood, later steel rods. This clear differentiation of upper and lower structural elements characterized Eames's furniture throughout his career. This quality of Eames's work, along with his concern for new manufacturing techniques, is in accordance with the basic tenets of FUNCTIONALISM. Thus, the revolution in design that Eames sparked did not arise solely from his personal inspiration but is a logical development of the INTERNATIONAL STYLE of the 1930s as well.

In 1941, newly married to a Cranbrook colleague, painter and designer Ray Kaiser, Eames moved to Venice, California, where he worked on the development of new plywood-molding techniques for the U.S. Navy. This effort led him, after the war, to produce the chair now known as the "Eames" chair—two molded wooden elements, seat and back, attached by shock-absorbing rubber pads to a light metal frame that connects the two and also forms legs. In 1946, when the "Eames" chair entered production, the New York Museum of Modern Art gave him a one-man show, a unique honor for a furniture designer at the time. In the same year, Eames's furniture began to be manufactured and sold by the HERMAN MILLER FURNITURE CO. Many of Eames's chairs are still being produced today.

Eames's impact was by then international. His ideas and work influenced SCANDINAVIAN MODERN designers, especially Finn JUHL and Arne JACOBSEN, and postwar British designers were affected by his work when they developed the CONTEMPORARY STYLE. Indeed, most progressive furniture designed in the following quarter-century reflected Eames's innovations in form and materials. He himself went on to design other well-known pieces. These included the 1948 bucket-shaped one-piece plastic chair on rods (the result of work done on a Museum of Modern Art grant) and the famous 1956 lounge chair and ottoman of molded rosewood and leather on bases of cast aluminum. In addition to chairs, Eames designed sofas, chaises, tables, storage units in small modules that fit onto a low tablelike base, radio cabinets and other household objects. He also made films on design and designed buildings, interiors, machinery, fabrics and toys.

EAR

Decorative element; extension of the CREST RAIL of a chair beyond the STILE on either side. The ear is a common feature of 18th-century chairs in the style of Thomas CHIPPENDALE, of COMB-BACK WINDSOR CHAIRS (*see under* WINDSOR CHAIR) and of the Chinese GUAN MAO SHI.

EAST AFRICAN OLIVE
See OLIVEWOOD.

EASTLAKE, CHARLES LOCKE (1836–1906)
British writer on art, architecture and furniture design. A nonpracticing architect, Eastlake wrote widely on all aspects of design. As a theorist, he is associated with the ART FURNITURE MOVEMENT (he coined the term) and with the widespread desire for reform of the applied arts—a 19th-century reaction against the new phenomenon of mass manufacture. Thus, he shared concerns with such different figures as A. W. N. PUGIN and William MORRIS.

With Bruce TALBERT, Eastlake developed the Modern Gothic style, a less florid form of the NEO-GOTHIC STYLE, and Eastlake wrote an influential book promoting it. The book, *Hints on Household Taste* (published in 1868), advocated the use of simple, rectilinear forms with correspondingly modest decoration, consisting of low-relief carving combined with inlaid, incised or pierced motifs. Chamfered edges, ebonized or dark woods, and elaborate metalwork (especially hinges) were also recommended, and Eastlake specified that all decorative motifs should be stylized or geometrical,

not naturalistic. A characteristic feature of Modern Gothic furniture was the use of rows of spindles on chair backs and table aprons or skirts, by way of promoting lightness and some measure of additional decoration. Eastlake's intent was to counter the overly elaborate and fussy revivalist styles of the early Victorian period. While Modern Gothic can seem rather fussy to a modern eye, it was in its time revolutionary. Eastlake himself designed very little, if any, furniture, and it is believed that no instance of his work survives.

In Britain, Eastlake was only one of many reforming figures of the day, but in America his book made him a preeminent arbiter of taste in design. *Hints on Household Taste* was reprinted in Boston in 1872 and promptly went through seven American editions. Furniture denominated "Eastlake style" was manufactured for all markets. Much of this furniture was second- or third-rate work that did not reflect Eastlake's values, and the published designs of Bruce Talbert tended to influence even the better makers to produce more highly decorated work than Eastlake envisioned. Eastlake explicitly dissociated himself from most of the American work. Nonetheless, fine American pieces in the true Eastlake style were made, especially by the New York firms HERTER BROTHERS and KIMBEL & CABUS and by Daniel PABST of Philadelphia. The Eastlake style dominated progressive American furniture design in the 1870s and 1880s, but it was no longer popular by about 1895. In his demand for relative simplicity and honest craftsmanship, Eastlake prepared the way for American ARTS AND CRAFTS MOVEMENT designers, such as Gustav STICKLEY and GREENE & GREENE.

EASY CHAIR
Any large, heavily upholstered chair intended for comfortable lounging. In the 18th century, the term more specifically referred to the British WING CHAIR. Another well-known easy chair is the French BERGÈRE. Striking modern easy chairs include Eero AARNIO's "Globe" chair of 1966 and Charles EAMES's lounge chair of 1956.

ÉBÉNISTE
French cabinetmaker; specialist in veneered case furniture, as opposed to a MENUISIER, a

ear

chest of drawers in Eastlake style

joiner who made chairs and tables of plain wood decorated with carving. Under the Parisian guild system that dominated French furniture making in the 17th and 18th centuries, only a master craftsman could practice both disciplines, and this was rarely done. Metal mounts for furniture had to be prepared by a FONDEUR-CISELEUR, and any gilding, of mount or wood, was performed by a DOREUR. The term *ébéniste* arose because ebony was the principal material used for veneering when that craft was introduced into France in 1620 by Jean MACÉ. The guild system—and with it the enforced categories of production—were abolished in 1791 by the French revolutionary government. The term has since been used to refer to a furniture maker particularly distinguished for fine veneering, such as the ART DECO master Émile-Jacques RUHLMANN.

EBERTS, J.-H. (active 1793)
French inventor of the ATHÉNIENNE.

EBONIZED
Term describing wood stained black to resemble EBONY. Since the early 19th century, this practice has been used in wood furniture of many styles to evoke the exotic splendor of ebony, which has become rarer and more expensive.

EBONY
Any of several HARDWOODS native to an area ranging from India to tropical Africa, the most familiar of which are a dense black in color. Black ebony, although difficult to work, has long been valued for its color and smooth texture; it was used in ancient EGYPTIAN and MESOPOTAMIAN FURNITURE. From the 17th century on, European cabinetmakers used it, especially in decorative inlay work. Ebony was occasionally used in traditional CHINESE FURNITURE (*see* WU MU). In America it was used only in the late 19th century. There are a number of nonblack ebonies, some of which appear in furniture (*see* MACASSAR EBONY; COROMANDEL WOOD).

egg-and-dart

ECHINUS
OVOLO MOLDING (*see under* MOLDING) below the ABACUS in a CAPITAL of the DORIC ORDER and, by extension, the EGG-AND-DART motif with which this molding was often decorated.

ECKMANN, OTTO (1865–1902)
German painter and designer associated with the ART NOUVEAU movement. Principally a painter and book illustrator, Eckmann designed furniture for Samuel BING that was simple and rectilinear in form, within the ARTS AND CRAFTS MOVEMENT tradition, and decorated with stylized botanical designs in a conservative Art Nouveau mode.

EDIS, ROBERT WILLIAM (1839–1927)
British architect and furniture designer; practitioner of the "Free Renaissance" style (*see* RENAISSANCE REVIVAL STYLE). In 1881 Edis published an influential book, *Decoration and Furniture of Town Houses,* which helped establish the popularity of his eclectic style.

EDSALL, THOMAS (1588–1676)
Boston turner and maker of AMERICAN JACOBEAN FURNITURE. Born and trained in London, Edsall immigrated to Boston, where he was one of the three dominant furniture makers in the mid-17th century, along with Henry MESSINGER and Ralph MASON, for whom he often made turned ornaments.

EGERTON, MATTHEW, SR. (1739–1802)
Principal FEDERAL PERIOD cabinetmaker of New Brunswick, New Jersey. The leading member of a family of craftsmen who made furniture in New Brunswick until well into the 19th century, Matthew Egerton Sr. was noted for the production of the KAS, a regional specialty. He and his son Matthew Jr. also made other furniture in styles ranging from late Chippendale (*see* COUNTRY CHIPPENDALE FURNITURE) to the NEOCLASSICAL STYLE, especially as propounded by George HEPPLEWHITE.

EGG-AND-DART (also *egg-and-anchor; egg-and-tongue*)
Decorative motif, most commonly used on OVOLO MOLDING (*see under* MOLDING), consisting of repeating band of ovals alternating with darts or arrowheads. Differing treatments of the dart are reflected in the alternate names.

ÉGLOMISÉ

Decorative technique popular in case furniture of 18th and 19th centuries; painting or gilding—principally in gold, white and blue—of the reverse side of a glass panel applied to or used as a door. This technique has been used in glassware since ancient Roman times and was first applied to furniture in France at the height of the LOUIS XVI STYLE, when it was made fashionable by a maker of mirrors and picture frames, Jean-Baptiste Glomy, after whom it is named. *Églomisé* was used outside France by NEOCLASSICAL STYLE designers, especially by the cabinetmakers of Baltimore, Maryland, where the technique became a hallmark of locally produced FEDERAL PERIOD furniture. A Baltimore maker particularly noted for his *églomisé* work was Joseph BARRY.

EGYPTIAN FURNITURE

Furniture of the ancient civilization of the Nile valley, during the dynastic period (c. 3000–1000 B.C.). The contents and decoration of ancient Egyptian tombs reveal much information about the furniture of the period. Especially well known is furniture from the New Kingdom, beginning in about 1575 B.C., a period spectacularly represented by the treasures from the tomb of the pharaoh Tutankhamen. Surviving examples from earlier times are scantier and represent much less sophisticated work. In Egypt, as in the ancient world generally, furniture was used very little. It was affordable only by the wealthy and was rare even in palaces. The basic forms of Western furniture were created in ancient Egypt, however, and this culture directly influenced later antiquity (*see* GREEK FURNITURE; ROMAN FURNITURE).

Large pieces of wood were scarce in Egypt, so small pieces were joined together by lacing or, more important, by techniques still employed—such as MORTISE-AND-TENON JOINTS (*see under* JOINERY) and the use of DOWELS. By the time of the New Kingdom, furniture hardware, in the form of metal hinges and metal nails and pins, was used. The basic furniture forms were chests, stools, beds, light tables and some chairs.

Boxes and chests, in use from earliest times, usually had short feet and flat or domed lids that were initially lifted off the carcase, later hinged. Laminated panels were used in the construction of sarcophagi. Gradually, the interiors of these chests began to be partitioned into sections, and lids were made with various profiles, often gabled, often sloped back from a short curve upward near the front. By the New Kingdom elaborate decoration had developed and was displayed principally on chests. Geometrical, animal and floral motifs were applied in a variety of ways. Gesso underlay gold leaf and painted decoration, the latter often imitative of fine woods. Inlays of sheet gold and silver, faïence, mother-of-pearl and ivory were glued to panels or attached with pegs. The exposed pegs or nails often provided ornamental patterns.

Stools were known in predynastic times, made of wickerwork or framed of light woods or papyrus stems, with wicker or hide seats. During the Old Kingdom (c. 2700–2200 B.C.), backs and arms appeared, especially in thrones, though the arms were awkwardly high at first.

In about 2000 B.C., during the Middle Kingdom, the folding stool first appeared. It consisted of two X-FRAMES, each collapsible around a metal bolt at its crossing point. The two frames were joined by rails and a skin or leather seat. The legs, the elements of the Xs, generally terminated in duck's heads or, less often, in lion's paws. Sloping backs and better-proportioned arms made chairs more comfortable.

By the New Kingdom the most common seat was a light four-legged stool, usually painted white. Stool and chair feet now frequently took the form of lion's paws, and seats and backs were often curved for comfort. Cushions and pads were used, and padded footstools resembling the modern OTTOMAN appeared. Some vernacular stools, which were made for the common people, have survived. These include a crude three-legged model with a board seat and a four-legged wooden frame with rails, around which woven cord formed a seat.

Beds were at first low, rectangular frames from which hide or cord slings were suspended. They had short feet that were sometimes shaped like the hooves of a bull. In the Middle Kingdom the height of the frame increased, and lion's paws replaced the bull's hooves. Such carved feet, on beds and on other forms, were placed on small columns that actually terminated the legs to protect the carving from damage. Sometimes longer legs were placed at the head of a bed, creating a slope to

Egyptian chair

the foot, where a FOOTBOARD was often placed. In the New Kingdom, beds were built very high, often making a mounting block necessary. Though the sloping form disappeared, footboards without HEADBOARDS remained the norm. The user's head rested on a separate HEADREST, placed on the bed frame. Bedding was often of linen.

Tables were very small and slight and were intended simply as stands for light objects. They were built like stools but had longer legs, either three or four in number. Gaming boards, some with a drawer beneath them, were built similarly, forming the first gaming tables. Single drawers also adorned toiletry boxes, but no chests of drawers or cupboards were made; case furniture was represented only by simple boxes and chests.

Ancient Egyptian furniture was generally made from any of several local woods—chiefly fig, acacia and tamarisk—and from cedar, cypress and juniper imported from Syria. Also used were an ebonylike wood imported from the south and, occasionally, precious metals, ivory or other luxury materials. Papyrus and other reeds and rushes were used for seating and bedding, as were cotton and linen. Some ceremonial furniture was made of STONE, most commonly alabaster.

EGYPTIAN REVIVAL STYLE
See ÉGYPTIENNERIE.

ÉGYPTIENNERIE
European decorative style of 18th and 19th centuries that used motifs taken from ancient EGYPTIAN FURNITURE and art. Principally associated with the French EMPIRE and British REGENCY STYLES of the early 19th century, *Égyptiennerie* decoration incorporated SPHINXes, LOTUS blossoms, winged disks, obelisks, CARYATIDS in Egyptian dress and Pharaonic heads. Egyptian ideas and art had been familiar in ancient Rome, so 18th-century European NEOCLASSICAL STYLE designers became exposed to them as classical archeology developed, beginning in the 1740s. J.-F. NEUFFORGE published furniture designs using *Égyptiennerie* motifs as early as 1765, and they were also used by the Italian artist G. B. PIRANESI. However, *Égyptiennerie* became prominent only in the early 19th century, when Dominique Vivant, Baron DENON, published his highly influen-

tial book, *Voyage dans la basse et haute Égypte* (1802), which recorded ancient architecture, decoration and furniture that he had seen while in Egypt with Napoleon's military expedition in 1799. Denon himself became supervisor of design for Napoleon's court, and his book was very important to such British designers as Thomas SHERATON, Thomas HOPE and George SMITH. Because of its connection with the career of Napoleon, *Égyptiennerie* lost popularity precipitously when the emperor fell from power. In the 1860s and 1870s, though, a vogue for exotic ornamentation led to a reprise of Egyptian imagery in RENAISSANCE FURNITURE, especially in the American NEO-GREC STYLE.

EIGHT IMMORTALS, TABLE OF THE
See BA XIAN ZHUO.

ELBOW CHAIR
Eighteenth-century American armchair with a banister back (*see* BANISTER-BACK CHAIR). John GAINES was a well-known maker of elbow chairs, which were produced in New Hampshire, Massachusetts, Connecticut and New York.

ELEPHANT-TRUNK LEG
See under LEG.

ELFE, THOMAS (c. 1719–75)
London-born AMERICAN CHIPPENDALE FURNITURE maker and the principal cabinetmaker of Charleston, South Carolina. Elfe, whose staff of trained craftsmen were slaves, produced much furniture. He followed CHIPPENDALE's patterns closely and thus made more elaborate and ornamental work than was common in the Colonies. He is particularly well known for the use of complicated and delicate applied fretwork.

ELIAERS, AUGUSTE (active in Boston 1849–60)
French-born Boston furniture maker of the 1850s. Trained in France as a cabinetmaker and woodcarver, Eliaers came to Boston in 1849 and returned to France in 1860. During his brief career in America, he made furniture

in a combination of the ROCOCO REVIVAL and RENAISSANCE REVIVAL STYLES, producing massive, heavily carved pieces. He was recognized as one of the leading furniture makers of the day, though now he is best remembered for his patented convertible LIBRARY STEPS, an armchair that folded forward, hinged at the front of the seat, to become a five-step set of library steps. He patented other pieces (*see* PATENT FURNITURE), including a barber's chair and an invalid chair, and was also noted for the design and installation of vast, elaborate staircases.

ELIZABETHAN REVIVAL STYLE

British style of architecture and furniture design that arose in the 1820s. Known simply as "Elizabethan" in its day, the style actually derived more from RESTORATION FURNITURE, of the 17th century, than from the style current in Elizabeth's reign, in the late 16th century. Massive, heavily carved pieces, usually with bobbin- or corkscrew-turned uprights and stretchers, constituted the furniture of this style. The major furniture designers in this mode were architects Anthony SALVIN and Henry SHAW. The Elizabethan Revival style was never as popular as its contemporary, the NEO-GOTHIC STYLE, but it survived long enough to merge with the RENAISSANCE REVIVAL STYLE in the 1860s, when that style rose to prominence in Britain.

ELLIS, HARVEY (1842–1904)

American furniture designer of the early 20th century; follower of the ARTS AND CRAFTS MOVEMENT. Ellis designed a wide range of furniture in simple, elegant designs in the Arts and Crafts tradition. These pieces were generally made of oak, with metal inlays of stylized botanical motifs similar to the decoration devised by the GLASGOW SCHOOL. Some of Ellis's pieces were manufactured at Gustav STICKLEY's United Crafts workshops.

ELM

Pale to dark brown HARDWOOD of the temperate regions of the Northern Hemisphere. Prominently figured, elm is often used as a decorative veneer and was especially popular in the 18th century. It is also the traditional material for the seat of the WINDSOR CHAIR.

ELMSLIE, GEORGE GRANT (1871–1952)

American architect and furniture designer of the PRAIRIE SCHOOL. Born in Scotland, George Elmslie came to America with his parents when he was 13. Three years later, he was apprenticed to a Chicago architect who also employed George Washington MAHER and Frank Lloyd WRIGHT. Two years later Elmslie began a 20-year employment with Louis Sullivan, before beginning his own practice. He designed oak furniture, mostly, in the spare, angular Prairie School manner, emphasizing thematic unity through the use of repeated decorative motifs. Elmslie's use of organic motif resembles Sullivan's work, understandable since much of Elmslie's furniture was intended for Sullivan's buildings. His idiom remained close to Sullivan's and much less severely geometrical than Wright's, even when he practiced on his own.

EMERY, DAVID (active since c. 1980)

AUSTRALIAN FURNITURE designer in the tradition of the modern INTERNATIONAL STYLE. Practicing the principles of FUNCTIONALISM in clean, geometrical pieces organized around such basic forms as the circle and triangle, with very little if any decoration, Emery employs fine hardwoods, sometimes in combination with glass. Much of his work is for corporate and ecclesiastical settings.

EMPIRE STYLE

French NEOCLASSICAL STYLE of early 19th century. It is associated with and was named for France's First Empire, created by Napoleon Bonaparte, who reigned as emperor in 1804–14 and for a few months in 1815. Sometimes the term is used to include the earlier CONSULATE STYLE and/or the later RESTAURATION STYLE, both of which are similar to the Empire style. The Empire mode was basically a variant of the pre-Revolutionary LOUIS XVI STYLE as it had persisted in the DIRECTOIRE STYLE and the Consulate style. Empire furniture was heavier and more consciously majestic, with strictly rectangular shapes and less subtlety of scale; pieces generally appeared massive in character, however small they were. A pedantic insistence on resemblance to ancient forms limited the range of acceptable designs. Thus, fewer forms were fashionable than before the Revolution,

Empire chair

and these tended to a degree of formality unknown since the days of Louis XIV, in the 17th century.

Like the LOUIS XIV STYLE, the Empire style was consciously developed to aggrandize a monarch. Directed by Napoleon himself, designers undertook to provide a suitably splendid setting for the new emperor; Napoleon was well aware of the propaganda value of physical grandeur, just as Louis XIV had been. He admired the work of the architect-designers Charles Percier and P.-F.-L. Fontaine (*see* PERCIER AND FONTAINE), and they were appointed court architects and became the principal developers of the new style.

A major component of the Empire style was iconography, for Napoleon hoped to associate his reign with the glory of ancient Rome. Ancient forms, known since the 18th-century excavations of Pompeii and Herculaneum, were imitated or adapted for contemporary uses. Versions of the Greek KLISMOS and the Roman SELLA CURULIS became popular chairs. The ancient tripod was adapted as a small table, and even the sarcophagus reappeared—as a wine cooler. The ornamental motifs used on Empire style furniture often referred to imperial glory, both ancient and modern, with an emphasis on martial themes; they incorporated trophies of arms and armor, crossed swords, clusters of arrows and so on. Some motifs referred expressly to Napoleon: the bee, his heraldic device; the letter *N,* often within a laurel wreath; and a profusion of grand eagles, a Roman and a Napoleonic military emblem. ÉGYPTIENNERIE motifs also became widespread after Napoleon's military expedition to Egypt in 1799 generated a great interest in that country's ancient civilization (*see* Dominique Vivant, Baron DENON). The emperor's wife, Josephine, introduced her own favorite motif, the swan, into the Empire style repertoire, and it became quite popular, especially in the Germanic countries. Other favored motifs were taken from the conventional neoclassical repertoire that had been available since the Renaissance, including various winged beasts, such as the CHIMERA; PALMETTES and other stylized foliage; and CORNUCOPIAS.

To create a uniform appearance combining simplicity and richness, furniture was usually made of only one wood, in conjunction with a relatively sparing use of gilt-bronze mounts. MAHOGANY was the material of

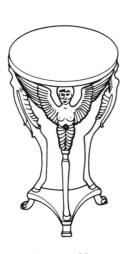

Empire table

choice for most Empire furniture, although the suspension of trade during the Napoleonic Wars kept it in short supply, and FRUITWOODS of similar color were commonly used. Bronze mounts were generally not as finely crafted as they had been in the 18th century, except possibly the work of Pierre THOMIRE. Another noted maker of furniture mounts was A.-A. RAVRIO.

Upholstery and draperies were important in the Empire style. Percier and Fontaine introduced a fashion for rooms whose walls and often ceilings were covered with loosely hung, rather than stretched, fabric, making the chamber resemble a tent and providing an attractively martial ambience. This device probably resulted from the fact that Napoleon's designers frequently had to provide him with stately quarters in farflung locales on short notice. In any case, these fabrics usually featured strong tonalities of red, green, blue, yellow and deep brown. They often bore bold, largescale embroidered motifs from the Empire repertoire.

A prominent bearer of such cloth was the LIT EN BATEAU, a massive bed that was very popular among the upper classes and was often enclosed by copious draperies that hung above it. The LIT DROIT, a less grandiose bed, was common among middle-class and provincial users. Another popular bedroom piece was the *Psyche* mirror, or CHEVAL GLASS. Typical forms of seating included the GONDOLA CHAIR and two pieces that had recently been developed—the RÉCAMIER, a daybed, and the MÉRIDIENNE, a kind of CANAPÉ. Tables were less varied than in earlier times and also tended to be heavier, often with tops of marble or porphyry; a common form was a rectangular CONSOLE TABLE whose supports took the form of a lion, eagle or chimera.

The continuity of neoclassical design from the late 18th-century Louis XVI style through Napoleon's reign and beyond is strikingly illustrated by noting the number of leading Parisian furniture makers who worked during this whole span. The most important Empire style makers included F.-J. BÉLANGER, Guillaume BENEMAN, Georges JACOB, Bernard MOLITOR and Adam WEISWEILER, all of whom had earlier worked under Louis XVI. In fact, practically the only major French Empire style maker who had not worked for the Crown was JACOB-DESMALTER, the son and close follower of Georges Jacob.

The Empire style spread beyond France, as a result of Napoleon's conquests and of the influence of his leading designers. Percier and Fontaine's work, especially as published in their 1801 PATTERN BOOK, *Recueil des décorations intérieures,* was extremely influential, both in France and elsewhere. Another important designer, Pierre de LA MÉSANGÈRE, was himself influenced by Percier and Fontaine, but his designs were intended for the bourgeoisie and thus were simpler and called for less expensive materials. La Mésangère's work was published in periodical form between 1802 and 1835 and provided another important source for many designers and furniture makers, especially in Holland (*see* Carel BREYTSPRAAK) and America (*see* C.-H. LANNUIER; Duncan PHYFE). Another important influence on the AMERICAN EMPIRE STYLE was the British REGENCY STYLE, which was itself strongly influenced by French furniture. The designs of Thomas HOPE and George SMITH and the late work of Thomas SHERATON all owe a great deal to Empire style examples.

In Spain the Consulate and Empire styles were felt even before France occupied that country in 1808–14. The FERNANDINO STYLE, as the florid Iberian version of the Empire style is known, persisted until about 1830, when REVIVAL STYLES came into fashion. In Italy the French influence was particularly strong, for Napoleon's close relatives held positions of power in Milan, Florence, Rome and Naples. They imported French craftsmen and large quantities of French furniture, and they provided patronage for Italian cabinetmakers, most notably Giovanni SOCCHI of Florence. The Empire style remained popular in Italy long after the fall of Napoleon, until about midcentury. Another country where the Empire style persisted through the 1840s was Denmark, thanks to the influence of G. F. HETSCH, who, early in his career, had studied in Paris with Percier. In Sweden, where L. W. LUNDELIUS was the style's chief exponent, the Napoleonic manner was overtaken in the 1830s by the NEO-GOTHIC STYLE and other revival styles.

In the Germanic countries, which were usually at war with France during the Napoleonic period, the French influence was important but inconsistently felt and less pervasive. J. V. RAAB of Würzburg followed French models fairly closely; he was chiefly responsible for the German popularity of Josephine's swan motif. In Austria, where Johann HAERTL was the leading furniture maker, the Empire style was principally a source of motifs and decorating ideas; it did not impose its monumentality on or change the essential informality of Viennese furniture, which anticipated the simple grace of the BIEDERMEIER STYLE. The great Munich architect Leo von KLENZE was also to be an influence on Biedermeier designers, and he, too, simplified the Empire style in informal furniture designs. The Biedermeier style, which would dominate Germanic furniture from the fall of Napoleon into the 1850s, arose as a bourgeois reaction against the grandeur of the Empire style, but it also carried on that style's simplicity of form and neoclassical inspiration.

In France, too, neoclassical furniture persisted. The Restauration style, which succeeded the Empire style, was merely a modification of it, offering continuing evidence of the impact of the Napoleonic phenomenon and of the decorative mode associated with it.

"EMPIRE" WOODS

Group of exotic foreign woods, generally from British possessions overseas, that found favor with British furniture designers in the 1930s. The unfamiliar colors and patterns of these woods were used to generate visual excitement and an aura of luxury. The woods included INDIAN LAUREL, Australian SILKY OAK and QUEENSLAND WALNUT.

EN SUITE

Designed as a matching set, referring to a group of different pieces intended for use in one room.

ENCOIGNURE

French furniture form of the 18th and 19th centuries; case piece with diagonal or curved front, intended for storage and designed to fit in a corner. Unlike the similar CORNER CUPBOARD of England and America, an *encoignure* was never intended to hang on a wall. Rather, it stood on three, sometimes four, feet. Usually a graduated series of shelves rested on the top of the piece.

ENDELL, AUGUST (1871–1925)

German ART NOUVEAU architect and designer. A member of the DEUTSCHE WERKSTÄT-

TEN movement, Endell designed furniture, textiles and jewelry. His early work is French in character—highly curvilinear and lushly decorated. Under the influence of Henri VAN DE VELDE and the geometrical character of late 19th-century German design, however, Endell's work gradually became more austere, functional and minimally decorated. He was an early designer of STEEL FURNITURE.

END JOINT

Another name for BUTT JOINT (*see under* JOINERY).

ENDIVE

Decorative motif; modern name for 17th- and 18th-century variation of the ACANTHUS leaf, composed of many small elements of foliage and thus resembling the curly leaf of the endive plant.

ENGRAILING

Another name for ROPE MOLDING (*see under* MOLDING).

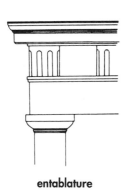

entablature

ENTABLATURE

Horizontal member or structural element borne by COLUMNS or PILASTERS in classical *orders of architecture* and in furniture decoration modeled on them. An entablature is composed of three horizontal layers. The ARCHITRAVE, generally undecorated, is on the bottom; the CORNICE, at the top, is a MOLDING or series of moldings, almost always projecting outward and upward. The FRIEZE, between them, usually carries the most decoration, bearing carved, painted or inlaid motifs, representational or otherwise.

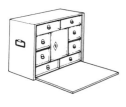

escritoire

ERCOLANI, LUCIEN (b. 1888)

Italian-British furniture designer of the mid-20th century. Ercolani is associated with a conservative taste for rustic furniture in the age of modernism. Born in Italy but a British resident since the age of three, he founded a manufacturing company, Furniture Industries Ltd., in the early 1920s. The firm still sells furniture, his own and others', under the trade name Ercol. Impressed by the WINDSOR CHAIR and by American SHAKER FURNITURE,

Ercolani created traditionally based furniture, especially versions of the basic Windsor chair design. Many of his pieces have been very popular, never going out of production.

ERGONOMIC DESIGN

Method of design, the incorporation of ergonomics—the scientific study of human efficiency in the built environment—into the conception and planning of furniture (or other objects). Highly influential in the second half of the 20th century, this discipline arose in Britain around 1950, when the term (derived from the Greek word *ergon,* "work") was coined.

In ergonomic design, furniture is made in accordance with scientific measurements of the human body and of the physical energy it expends on different tasks, such as the opening and closing of drawers and cabinets, or getting in and out of beds and seating furniture. Among the most noted practitioners of ergonomic design have been Charles EAMES, George NELSON, and Niels DIFFRIENT.

ESCABELLE

French term for low stool; more particularly, French RENAISSANCE FURNITURE form, a low, short bench.

ESCRITOIRE (also *scriptor; scritoire; scrutoire*)

Old term for DESK, especially a WRITING BOX whose sloping lid was a SLANT TOP, hinged at the bottom to open and provide a writing surface. In the 18th century the term thus came to apply to all SLANT-TOP DESKS, including the SECRETARY. Another early variety of escritoire was a small, portable CABINET with drawers and compartments and a FALL FRONT, vertical when closed, that opened to become a writing surface. In this sense, the term *escritoire* came to refer to a larger, similar piece, the WRITING CABINET.

ESCUTCHEON

Decorative metal plate surrounding a keyhole and protecting the edges of the veneer. The term also refers to a similar metal plate fitted over a keyhole and pivoting on a pin to expose or hide the hole. Third, the term may denote the shaped metal back plate of a BAIL HANDLE on a drawer. *Escutcheon* is also the term for the shield in a coat of arms, which is sometimes used as a decorative device on furniture.

ESHERICK, WHARTON (1887–1970)

Twentieth-century American furniture maker, often regarded as a key forerunner of the American HANDICRAFT REVIVAL of the 1970s. A painter and sculptor at first, Esherick made furniture in a combination shop/retreat he established near Philadelphia in 1913. He worked in a simple style that was influenced by both SHAKER FURNITURE and the geometrical branch of European ART NOUVEAU, as represented by the work of Richard RIEMER-SCHMID. With time, Esherick's style tended toward more organic, curvilinear elements, in reaction against the angularity of the INTERNATIONAL STYLE.

ESPAGNOLETTE

Ornamental device of RÉGENCE and LOUIS XV STYLE furniture; bronze decorative mount (*see* HARDWARE) in the form of a female bust. Inspired by the ethereally lovely women in the paintings of Watteau, these miniature sculptures added a dreamlike air to the elegant informality of pieces by Charles CRESSENT and others. The figures frequently were depicted wearing a stiff lace collar, a fashion associated with Spain—hence, the term.

ESTAMPILLE

Tiny maker's mark, appearing inconspicuously on much 18th-century French furniture. An *estampille* consisted of stamped intaglio lettering, identifying the name or initials of the MENUISIER or ÉBÉNISTE who was principally responsible for the piece. Between 1741 and 1791, all Parisian makers were required by law to apply their signatures in this manner to all of their output not produced for the Crown. A jury had to approve each item for sale, and this board applied its own *estampille* ("J.M.E.," for *jure des menuisiers-ébénistes*) to the piece. When the guild system was abolished by the Revolution in 1791, the *estampille* was no longer mandatory, but later craftsmen have occasionally used it voluntarily—most notably, the ART DECO master Émile-Jacques RUHLMANN.

ÉTAGÈRE

Furniture piece consisting of tiered shelves with slender supports, doors or drawers below and a back that is sometimes mirrored. Designed for the display of small objects, the étagère, also called a "whatnot," was introduced at the beginning of the 19th century but only became popular during the LOUIS XVI REVIVAL STYLE. It was prominent for the remainder of the century.

ETRUSCAN FURNITURE

Furniture of the Etruscans, the most developed of the pre-Roman peoples of central Italy, who flourished from the seventh century B.C. into Roman times. The Etruscans were greatly influenced by contemporary Greek culture and their furniture generally derived from Greek models, but they made much greater use of bronze. This material allowed them to be more daring in both decoration and shape of furniture. Thus, Etruscan furniture was usually decorated with applied bronze mounts that were quite elaborately sculpted.

The Etruscans also created several new furniture forms. The most striking was a tub-shaped chair of bronze that had a solid, curved back that continued toward the front as arms; it was mounted on a drumlike base. This form became prominent in ROMAN FURNITURE. The Etruscans elaborated on the Greek KLINE by adding ornamental head- and footrests, a development that Roman makers continued. The Etruscans also made woven basket chairs that closely resembled examples available today. However, perhaps the most characteristically Etruscan form was not adopted elsewhere. This was the CISTA, a circular or oval casket or chest that may have predated even the Etruscans, originating among the aboriginal Italic tribes.

ETRUSCAN STYLE

Type of late 18th-century NEOCLASSICAL STYLE decoration. It featured painted scenes of figures, rendered in light colors on a dark ground, often accompanied by PALMETTES and ANTHEMIONS. The black, white and terra-cotta red color scheme was derived from ancient Greco-Italian pottery, mistakenly believed to be Etruscan. Etruscan style decoration first arose in Britain in the 1760s, on ADAM STYLE furniture, and its invention is attributed to Robert ADAM. It later appeared in France in the work of F.-J. BÉLANGER and

J.-D. DUGOURC, in whose hands it became a feature of the DIRECTOIRE STYLE.

EUROPEAN REDWOOD (also *Scots pine*)
Northern European SOFTWOOD, botanically a pine. The most common construction timber in Europe, it is sometimes used in inexpensive furniture.

EVANS, EDWARD (1679–1754)
Philadelphia cabinetmaker in the WILLIAM AND MARY STYLE. Evans made the oldest dated piece of furniture produced in Philadelphia, a 1707 fall-front desk.

EXTENSION TABLE
Table whose length may be increased by inserting a LEAF or leaves. The top is divided into two halves that, along with their legs, may be separated from each other. The insertion rests on an understructure, connected to both halves, that is expandable, by means of either sliding elements or hinged, accordion-like bracing.

FALDSTOOL
Ecclesiastical furniture form; a light folding stool chiefly used by bishops for confirmations and ordinations.

FALDYN TABLE
Early term, in English TUDOR FURNITURE, for a gate-leg, or folding, table (*see* GATE-LEG TABLE).

FALL FRONT
Section of front face of cabinet, desk or drawer that is hinged at the bottom and can open by falling forward. It is supported in a horizontal, open position by chains or by sliding arms emerging from the body of the piece, LOPERS, in order to provide a writing surface. Closed, it may rest in a vertical position, as in the WRITING CABINET or SECRÉTAIRE À ABATTANT, or it may slope upward and toward the back of a piece, as in a SLANT-TOP DESK. The fall front was a development of late MEDIEVAL and RENAISSANCE FURNITURE and has been used ever since.

FALL-FRONT DESK
Desk equipped with FALL FRONT for a writing surface. In its usual American usage, the term denotes a desk with a SLANT TOP but no superstructure—that is, excluding secretaries (*see* SECRETARY). It can also refer to a desk with a fall front that is vertical when closed, such as the VARGUEÑO and the SECRÉTAIRE À ABATTANT. In the 19th century the term sometimes referred to a CYLINDER-FRONT DESK.

FAN-BACK WINDSOR CHAIR
See under WINDSOR CHAIR.

"FANCY" FURNITURE
Style of light, decorative furniture produced in America during and after the FEDERAL PERIOD. Generally based on designs by Thomas SHERATON, "fancy" furniture was light and mobile—mostly chairs with cane, rush or plank seats, including WINDSOR CHAIRS. It was ornamented with light-colored paints and often gilding; both stenciled and free-hand painting were used. Such decoration was characteristic of the NEOCLASSICAL STYLE first favored in Anglo-American furniture by Robert ADAM and later popularized by Sheraton and George HEPPLEWHITE. Lambert HITCHCOCK of Connecticut and John and Hugh FINDLAY of Baltimore were three of the best-known producers of "fancy" furniture.

FARMHOUSE WINDSOR CHAIR
See LATH-BACK WINDSOR CHAIR, *under* WINDSOR CHAIR.

FARTHINGALE CHAIR
Nineteenth-century name for an English TUDOR FURNITURE form; low, armless, upholstered chair with wide seat and low, upright back. Similar chairs were common throughout Europe. The name suggests that the form may have been designed to accommodate the farthingale, a wide structure of hoops worn beneath fashionable dresses of the day.

FAUTEUIL
French furniture form; upholstered armchair with open sides, as opposed to BERGÈRE, which has upholstered panels between arms and seat. The fauteuil arose in the late 17th century and has been made in all styles ever

farthingale chair

since. The term has come to have a broader sense, referring to any upholstered armchair, including theater seats.

FAUTEUIL À LA REINE

French furniture form of 17th and 18th centuries; a FAUTEUIL with a high, square back. Associated with the royal court, it was a formal piece intended to be set against a wall.

FAUX-BAMBOO

Wood carved and painted to resemble BAMBOO.

FEATHER BANDING

See BANDING.

FEDERAL PERIOD

First half-century in the history of the United States, following the American Revolution and the creation of a new national government—that is, from 1780s to 1830s—when furniture was characterized by the NEOCLASSICAL STYLE. Sometimes the term is applied only to the earlier half of this period, until about 1810, during which American makers were chiefly influenced by late ADAM STYLE British designers, especially George HEPPLEWHITE and Thomas SHERATON. The subsequent DIRECTORY and AMERICAN EMPIRE STYLES reflected an increasing French influence, but they were equally neoclassical, continued to demonstrate the design ethos of the new nation and are also properly classed as Federal.

AMERICAN CHIPPENDALE FURNITURE had dominated Colonial furniture prior to the American Revolution, during which little furniture of any kind was made. Following independence, furniture buyers and makers alike sought a new mode to reflect their new republican status. The neoclassical, founded on ancient Greek and Roman decoration, was iconographically suitable; it made implicit reference to the ancient Roman Republic and to the classical ideals revered by the Enlightenment thinkers whose writings provided ideological justification for the Revolution. Furthermore, neoclassical furniture was markedly austere compared to its Rococo predecessors, rectilinear in outline and restrained in ornamenta-

Federal bookcase

tion. This simplicity also harmonized with the purposeful vigor of the new nation.

American furniture makers adapted the designs published in the 1780s and 1790s by British designers, especially Hepplewhite and Sheraton, to produce light, delicate pieces, geometrical in line and ornamented with inlay and painted decoration rather than carving. This furniture was usually made of MAHOGANY, with inlay in lighter woods, especially SATINWOOD and maple (*see* BIRD'S-EYE MAPLE). Most American Federal period furniture represented an amalgam of elements from the work of both Hepplewhite and Sheraton, and it is often difficult to attribute the inspiration for a given piece to one of these designers or the other. However, speaking generally, Hepplewhite's influence prompted a greater use of curvilinear elements—especially in the hallmark SHIELD-BACK CHAIR—of square, tapered legs with spade feet (*see* SPADE FOOT, *under* FOOT), and of small-scale, sparse ornamentation, most commonly delicate, inlaid BELLFLOWER motifs and STRINGING. Sheraton's designs were more severely rectilinear, and he is particularly associated with the SQUARE-BACK CHAIR. He stimulated the use of larger elements in inlaid decoration, especially BANDING and geometrical patterns in woods of contrasting colors. Sheraton-derived table and chair legs were often rounded and decorated with REEDING. Another British designer who was notably important to American makers was Thomas SHEARER, whose furniture combined elements from the work of Hepplewhite and Sheraton. Through these British designers' PATTERN BOOKS, American makers absorbed the range of Adamesque neoclassical motifs, including URNS, HUSKS, PATERAE and foliate FESTOONS and SWAGS. To these was added the new national emblem, an eagle with spread wings, which became a widely popular, almost ubiquitous, motif of the period. In addition to inlay, painted decoration enjoyed a considerable vogue, especially in "FANCY" FURNITURE, light pieces with stenciled or freehand painted scenes and emblems.

Regional variations existed among the four major furniture-producing centers—New England, New York, Philadelphia and Baltimore. In New England the rising seaport city of Salem, Massachusetts, boasted a number of notable furniture makers, including Nehemiam ADAMS, William HOOK and the brothers Elijah and Jacob SANDERSON.

However, the most important figure in Salem furniture making was the woodcarver Samuel MᴄINTIRE, whose brilliant work decorated many pieces and made carved decoration more important here than elsewhere. In Boston, John and Thomas SEYMOUR, a father-and-son partnership, so dominated local cabinetmaking that Boston work of the time is often known as the "Seymour school." It featured extremely fine inlay, often including stringing composed of complex patterns of tiny elements in contrasting woods. The Seymours and their followers, who included John COGSWELL and Stephen BADLAM, also favored the use of TAMBOUR shutters in case furniture. The influence of Boston furniture was felt in southern New England—notably by John TOWNSEND and Holmes WEAVER, in Newport, Rhode Island, and by Aaron CHAPIN in Hartford, Connecticut.

In New York City reeding was common on chair arms and stiles, on the legs of chairs and tables, and, often, at the corners of case pieces. In the 1790s New York furniture making came to be dominated by Duncan PHYFE, a supremacy that lasted for decades. Other important makers here included Michael ALLISON, Thomas BURLING, the partnership of MILLS & DEMING and, in nearby New Brunswick, New Jersey, Matthew EGERTON Sr.

In Philadelphia ROCOCO FURNITURE continued to enjoy some popularity, and such PHILADELPHIA CHIPPENDALE FURNITURE makers as Thomas AFFLECK and Benjamin RANDOLPH prospered, though some of them, including Randolph, began to use the new neoclassical manner as well. In Philadelphia inlay was extremely simple, featuring large oval shapes of light wood set against a darker ground. Painted furniture was popular, with the color white especially favored. Among the principal Philadelphia makers of the period were John AITKEN; Joseph BARRY, who also had a shop in Baltimore; Ephraim HAINES; and Henry CONNELLY.

In Baltimore, Barry and the brothers John and Hugh FINDLAY were the leading makers. The large oval paterae of Philadelphia were also popular here, but they were accompanied by a greater amount of other MARQUETRY decoration. Favored motifs included urns with vines rising from their mouths and a bellflower variant especially associated with Baltimore, one with elongated central petals. A French decorative technique, ÉGLOMISÉ—the paint-ing of glass panels in the doors of case furniture—was adopted in Baltimore, where it became an important local speciality. *Églomisé* motifs were often figural, and such painted decoration was also popular on wood. In fact, furniture painting was another local specialty, and Baltimore was a leading center of "fancy" furniture. In nearby Annapolis, John SHAW produced fine furniture based chiefly on Hepplewhite's designs.

Beginning in about 1805 French tastes had an increasing effect on American craftsmen. Sheraton's late work and other REGENCY STYLE design were well known to American makers, and it was itself affected by French styles. Also, Americans imported increasing amounts of French furniture, and French *émigré* craftsmen, such as Charles-Honoré LANNUIER and Anthony QUERVELLE, practiced in the United States. Furthermore, the published work of Pierre de LA MÉSANGÈRE was widely circulated. The heavier furniture of the Directory style, followed by the boldly massive work of the American Empire style, was the result of this French influence. However, this furniture was less ornate than its Continental prototypes, and it continued to use characteristic Federal period decoration—notably the distinctively American eagle. The last phase of the Federal period was represented by the PILLAR AND SCROLL STYLE, a variant of the Empire mode. In it, nonclassical ornamentation began to resurface, heralding the rise of the REVIVAL STYLES.

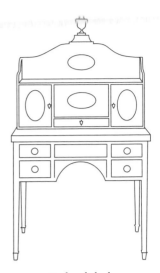

Federal desk

Federal sideboard

FENOGLIO, PIETRO (active 1890s)

Italian ART NOUVEAU architect and furniture designer. Inspired by the work of Victor HORTA, Fenoglio aspired to the Art Nouveau ideal of uniting buildings and furnishings through a single decorative theme. He employed a restrained variant of Horta's WHIPLASH CURVE as a dominant motif in furniture and metalwork designed for specific architectural contexts.

FERNANDINO STYLE

EMPIRE STYLE in Spain, popular in early 19th century, until about 1830, and named for King Ferdinand VII (reigned 1814–33). More massive and more heavily ornamented than its French models, Fernandino style furniture was usually made of MAHOGANY and adorned with carved giltwood appliqués or bronze mounts. A wide repertoire of classical motifs was used, with an emphasis on figural elements, such as swans, winged beasts and *putti* (*see* PUTTO). GONDOLA CHAIRS were especially favored, often with legs in the form of swans, dolphins or CORNUCOPIAS. Generally, the craftsmanship of this style was markedly inferior to that of French work, and, in the last decade of the period, simpler furniture came into fashion. In about 1830 the Fernandino style was eclipsed by the ISABELLINO STYLE, a revivalist mode of furniture design (*see* REVIVAL STYLES).

festoon

FESTOON

Decorative device representing either a garland of fruit and flowers or a length of cloth, tied with ribbons at each end and attached to a background so as to hang in a loop; also a horizontal chain of loops. A single festoon is sometimes imprecisely called a SWAG. The device originated in Greek and Roman architectural ornamentation, where it represented real flowers and fruit that were used to decorate temples and altars. RENAISSANCE FURNITURE makers adapted the image, and it was popular with NEOCLASSICAL STYLE designers, especially in the 18th century. It has a symbolic allusion to prosperity similar to the CORNUCOPIA's.

FEURE, GEORGES DE (1869–1928)

French ART NOUVEAU furniture designer. Samuel BING employed de Feure, who designed light, fragile pieces, mostly seating furniture of traditional 18th-century form, which were carved in the Art Nouveau style. His furniture was generally made of various light, colored or gilt woods, carved with botanical imagery, often with delicate, leafy tendrils, and upholstered in fine fabrics, usually silk. De Feure was also a graphic artist, working in a luxuriant, mildly erotic mode.

FIDDLE BACK

Chair back with single, usually unadorned, SPLAT whose curved silhouette resembles the shape of a violin. Developed in the early 18th century, the fiddle back was most common on American QUEEN ANNE STYLE chairs.

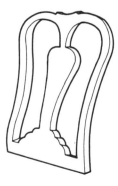

fiddle back

FIELD BED (also *tent bed*)

Small, collapsible canopied bed (*see* CANOPY) intended for travel, used from period of GOTHIC FURNITURE until mid-19th century.

FIELDED PANEL

Wood panel consisting of one or more plain rectangular areas, each bounded by a BOLECTION MOLDING (*see under* MOLDING).

FIGURING

Pattern created by exposed grain on a piece of cut wood. Some woods, cut in certain ways (*see* VENEER), have very striking figurings and are highly valued for use as decorative panels.

FILIGREE WORK

Delicate, lacelike pierced ornamentation, usually of metal. Principally a term used in jewelry making, *filigree* usually implies work on a minute scale. Wire filigree work in various precious metals has sometimes been applied to wooden furniture—especially in the KUNSTSCHRANK of northern RENAISSANCE FURNITURE—but the term is mostly used metaphorically in a furniture context to describe similarly intricate work in cruder materials, such as carved wooden FRETWORK, MUDÉJAR STYLE inlays or elements of CAST-IRON FURNITURE.

FILLET

Any narrow band or strip of material. For instance, a piece of VENEER intended for STRINGING, a surface area between two closely placed MOLDINGS and the tiny ridge between hollows in FLUTING would all be considered fillets.

FINDLAY, JOHN AND HUGH (active c. 1799–c. 1837)

Baltimore furniture manufacturers specializing in painted "FANCY" FURNITURE. Born and trained in Ireland, the Findlay brothers arrived in Baltimore in the late 1790s. There they established themselves as the leading producers of painted furniture. Generally derived stylistically from the designs of George HEPPLEWHITE and Thomas SHERATON, the Findlay's furniture featured painted decoration in a neoclassical vein. They also specialized in depicting notable Baltimore buildings on furniture. They probably made and painted the AMERICAN EMPIRE STYLE furniture that was designed by Benjamin LATROBE for the White House in 1809 and burned by British troops in 1812.

FINIAL

Decoratively turned or carved vertical ornament. It may terminate a vertical element, such as a bedpost; adorn a corner of a large piece of case furniture; or accentuate a central point, as on a pediment or at the crossing of an X-STRETCHER. Often, the ornament represents a traditional finial motif—for example, obelisks, flames, urns or acorns—but any carved image may be used.

FINISH

Decorative surface, principally of wood but also of metal, that both embellishes and protects the material. The simplest sort of finish—applied pigment, or paint—was used on ancient EGYPTIAN FURNITURE and has been used ever since (in vernacular furniture, if not always in more fashionable pieces). GOLD LEAF was also applied to furniture in ancient Egypt, and this finish was passed down through GREEK, ROMAN and BYZANTINE FURNITURE to become a feature of European furniture in the Renaissance. This and other types of GILDING have since appeared regularly as a furniture finish, both on wood and on metal, though the expense of gilding has generally limited its use to ornamentation. In medieval Europe paint continued to be the most common furniture finish. However, medieval makers began to polish wood—that is, to obtain a glossy surface by applying a liquid or semiliquid material and rubbing it into the fabric of the wood. This practice is today most closely associated with the term *finish*.

By the 16th century, polishing had largely replaced paint on European furniture. The polish was either a vegetable oil, usually linseed; walnut oil (used on walnut wood); or a mixture of beeswax and turpentine. The oil, once applied, oxidized to a rich, dark tone; the wax sealed the wood and preserved its color. Each could be rubbed until the wood was quite shiny. In the 17th century, VARNISH, an amalgam of plant resin and oil, began to replace oil

alone or wax, though neither of these earlier media died out entirely. Varnish, applied in many coats, each allowed to dry and then polished, preserved wood better and could be polished to a high gloss. In the 1670s commerce with the Orient introduced alcohol-based varnish, easier to use and glossier. LACQUER, a sort of varnish itself, was also introduced into Europe at this time; its use on CHINESE FURNITURE dates to at least the fourth century B.C., and it has also long been used in Japan. Its popularity generated the imitation-lacquer finishes known collectively as JAPANNING. A century later, varnish was the basis of an intensified procedure, FRENCH POLISHING, that yielded a truly glasslike surface.

Modern chemistry has produced a number of cellulose-based varnishes and lacquers that are easy to apply and that simply seal the wood, providing it with a new surface. On the other hand, a resurgent interest in handicraft, beginning with the ARTS AND CRAFTS MOVEMENT of the late 19th century and continuing through the HANDICRAFT REVIVAL of the 1970s, has promoted a revival of the vernacular use of oil and wax finishes in fine furniture making.

FIREHOUSE WINDSOR CHAIR
See under WINDSOR CHAIR.

FIRE SCREEN
SCREEN used to shield those seated near a fireplace from excessive heat and light. There are two basic types of fire screen. The CHEVAL SCREEN, a low panel placed directly before the fire, evolved in the Middle Ages. The POLE SCREEN was a 17th-century invention that could be adjusted to any height to shield the face of a sitting or standing person. Another minor variant was a small, usually oval panel that fitted into a slot in a chair back to protect the sitter's head. Although the development of modern central heating rendered the open fire and the fire screen superfluous, both are still appreciated for their decorative character. The 1920s and 1930s saw a revival of hand-painted ornamental fire screens.

FLAG SEAT
American term for RUSH SEAT. *Flag* is another term for the rush.

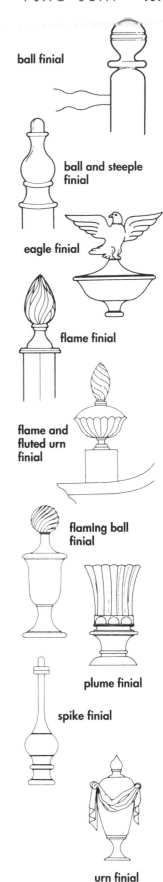

ball finial

ball and steeple finial

eagle finial

flame finial

flame and fluted urn finial

flaming ball finial

plume finial

spike finial

urn finial

FLEESON, PLUNKET (b. 1712)

Philadelphia upholsterer of the late 18th century. The leading upholsterer of his day, Fleeson was especially associated with the chairs, chaises and sofas of Benjamin RANDOLPH.

FLEMISH SCROLL FOOT
See under FOOT.

FLEMISH SCROLL LEG
See under LEG.

fleur-de-lis

FLEUR-DE-LIS (also *fleur-de-lys*)

Decorative device; stylized cluster of three flowers or petals, with central one erect and others bending outward. A heraldic device throughout Europe from late medieval times, the fleur-de-lis was used by Charles LE BRUN and other designers in the LOUIS XIV STYLE. It thus became associated with the royalty of France, where it is still a national emblem.

FLITCROFT, HENRY (1697–1769)

Eighteenth-century British PALLADIAN STYLE architect and furniture designer. Flitcroft began his career as an apprentice to a joiner. Later, as an architect, he worked with William KENT, by whom he was greatly influenced. His furniture was lavishly baroque and, like Kent's work, was organized around massive scallop shells and other large-scale motifs.

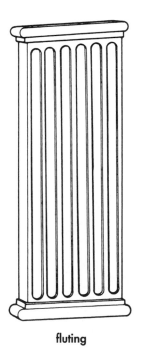

fluting

FLORENTINE MOSAIC

Another term for PIETRE DURE. This form of pictorial INLAY was used in RENAISSANCE FURNITURE, most notably in Florence.

FLORIS, CORNELIS (1514–75)

MANNERIST STYLE Flemish architect and designer. After studying in Italy, Floris returned to his native Antwerp and became an architect. He also published, beginning in 1548, many influential decorative designs, introducing the French Renaissance FRANÇOIS I STYLE into the Netherlands. This style included the use of STRAPWORK and GROTESQUE ORNAMENT, as developed by Rosso FIORENTINO and other members of the School of Fontainebleau. So impressive was his interpretation of this mode

that it became known in much of northern Europe as the "Floris style." His later work became less bizarre and more architectural in character.

FLÖTNER, PETER (c. 1485–1546)

German sculptor and RENAISSANCE FURNITURE designer. Flötner, active in Nuremberg after 1522, had traveled in Italy and was one of the first German artists to use Renaissance motifs, designing metalwork and furniture decorated with *putti* (*see* PUTTO), GROTESQUE ORNAMENT, ARABESQUES and classical architectural elements.

FLUTING

Ornamental carving consisting of shallow verticle channels or grooves, usually rounded in section, placed next to each other on the shaft of a COLUMN or PILASTER or on any other vertical surface. Sometimes a narrow, flat ridge called a FILLET separates the grooves. Originally used on columns in classical architecture (*see* ORDERS OF ARCHITECTURE), fluting was later adopted by NEOCLASSICAL STYLE cabinetmakers, from the time of RENAISSANCE FURNITURE onward. It was particularly popular in the late 18th and early 19th centuries. A variant form was STOPPED FLUTING.

FLY LEG
See under LEG.

FLY RAIL

Pivoting BRACKET attached to leg or APRON of a DROP-LEAF TABLE. When in its open position, swung away from the body of the piece, the fly rail supports the LEAF. When the fly rail is closed, the leaf hides it. A fly rail may also support a collapsible bracket shelf.

FOGGINI, GIOVANNI BATTISTA (1652–1725)

Florentine architect, sculptor and maker of BAROQUE FURNITURE. Foggini, chief designer for the Medici workshops in the early 18th century, designed and sculpted furniture with elaborate decoration in precious materials such as gold, silver, PIETRE DURE and mother-of-pearl.

FOLIATE
Term describing decoration that incorporates images of leaves or stylized leaflike forms.

FOLIOT, NICOLAS-QUINIBERT (1706–76)
French chair maker in LOUIS XVI STYLE.

FOLLOT, PAUL (1877–1941)
French ART DECO designer. Early in his career, Follot designed furniture in a Parisian variant of ART NOUVEAU, producing richly decorated pieces. As early as 1908, however, he had adopted a rectilinear style with more restrained decoration, thereby pioneering what was to become known as Art Deco. He also designed whole interiors, textiles and other household goods. Follot's work was notable for its opulent materials and fine carving, reflecting his belief that art is the "privilege of an elite." Appropriately, he was for many years director of design for the *Bon Marche* department store, serving a conservative, upper middle-class clientele.

FONDEUR-CISELEUR
French metalworker; maker of metal mounts used to ornament furniture. Under the Parisian guild system that dominated French furniture making in the 17th and 18th centuries, a furniture maker was required to have such mounts made by a member of the *fondeur-ciseleurs'* guild, who in turn could not gild them; this procedure was reserved for a DOREUR. The *fondeur-ciseleurs* were an amalgamation of two groups of specialists, casters of metal (*fondeurs*) and finishers or chasers (*ciseleurs*) of cast-metal objects. Their guild was merged with the *doreurs* in 1776, not long before the guild system was abolished by the French Revolution.

FOOT
Lower extremity of a LEG; or the lowest, usually projecting, part of a legless piece of furniture, serving as a support. There are a variety of styles of foot.

ANIMAL'S-BALL-AND-CLAW FOOT
Type of BALL-AND-CLAW FOOT (*see under* FOOT) in which the claw is that of an animal, usually a lion.

BALL-AND-CLAW BRACKET FOOT
Variety of BALL-AND-CLAW FOOT topped by and thus attached to body of a piece by brackets, arranged as in a BRACKET FOOT (*see under* FOOT).

BALL-AND-CLAW FOOT
Carved foot in the form of the claw of an animal or bird holding a ball, the ball resting on the floor. The ball-and-claw foot (also called a *claw-and-ball* foot) was fashionable in the 18th century and was most frequently used to terminate a CABRIOLE LEG (*see under* LEG). It may have originated in Europe from a Chinese decorative motif of a dragon's claw grasping a pearl.

BALL FOOT
Round, turned foot, either terminating a leg or serving independently as a support for a case piece. A ball foot may be spherical, or it may be ovoid with a vertical axis; a turned ovoid with a horizontal axis is called a BUN FOOT (*see under* FOOT). Another variant is the PEAR FOOT (*see under* FOOT).

BEAR'S-CLAW FOOT
Carved PAW FOOT (*see under* FOOT) in which the paw is a bear's.

BIRD'S-BALL-AND-CLAW FOOT
Type of BALL-AND-CLAW FOOT (*see under* FOOT) in which the claw is a bird's, usually the talon of a bird of prey.

BOOTJACK FOOT
Support at either side of a simple piece of case furniture in which the side panel extends below the bottom of the piece's body. This extension resembles a bootjack because a triangle is cut from the center of its lower edge, leaving a "foot" at front and rear. A similar arrangement is found on the medieval SLAB-ENDED STOOL, and the use of the bootjack foot on case furniture is probably at least as old.

BRACKET FOOT
Support for case furniture consisting of two BRACKETS mitered and joined below the cor-

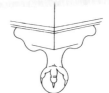
ball-and-claw bracket foot

ball-and-claw foot

ball foot

bear's-claw foot

bootjack foot

bracket foot

bun foot

cloven foot

dog's-paw foot

dolphin foot

drake foot

Dutch angular foot

Dutch foot

ners of the piece's body. The bracket foot originated in the late 17th century, probably as an adaptation of the bracket-supported leg. The brackets may take any of a variety of forms, as in the OGEE BRACKET FOOT and the FRENCH BRACKET FOOT (*see under* FOOT).

BUN FOOT
Round, turned foot flattened at top and bottom, similar to BALL FOOT (*see under* FOOT). It is sometimes called an "onion" foot. The MELON FOOT (*see under* FOOT) is a decorated variant.

CAMEL FOOT
Type of DUTCH FOOT (*see under* FOOT).

CLAW-AND-BALL FOOT
Another name for BALL-AND-CLAW FOOT (*see under* FOOT).

CLAW FOOT
Another name for PAW FOOT (*see under* FOOT).

CLOVEN FOOT
HOOF FOOT (*see under* FOOT) in which hoof is cloven. The term is especially used of 18th-century terminals of the CABRIOLE LEG (*see under* LEG), where a representation of a goat's foot was often intended.

CLUB FOOT
Type of DUTCH FOOT (*see under* FOOT).

CUSHIONED-PAD FOOT
Another name for *pad-and-disk foot,* a type of DUTCH FOOT (*see under* FOOT).

DISK FOOT
Type of DUTCH FOOT (*see under* FOOT).

DOG FOOT
Another name for DOG'S-PAW FOOT (*see under* FOOT).

DOG'S-PAW FOOT
Carved PAW FOOT (*see under* FOOT) in which paw is a dog's. Similar in appearance to the

LION'S-PAW FOOT (*see under* FOOT), though less massive, the dog's-paw foot was popular in the NEOCLASSICAL STYLE of the late 18th and early 19th centuries.

DOLPHIN FOOT
Carved foot in shape of a stylized fish, a supposed DOLPHIN. The dolphin foot was particularly popular in the British REGENCY STYLE of the early 19th century.

DRAKE FOOT
Carved foot having three, occasionally four, "toes," or prominent ribs, on its upper surface. The drake foot was most common on the legs of mid-18th-century American and British furniture.

DUTCH ANGULAR FOOT
Type of DUTCH FOOT (*see under* FOOT).

DUTCH ELONGATED FOOT
Name for either *snake foot* or *slipper foot,* two types of DUTCH FOOT (*see under* FOOT).

DUTCH FOOT
Broad term designating any of several 18th-century shaped feet used throughout Europe and America, generally to terminate a CABRIOLE LEG (*see under* LEG). Each type of Dutch foot is characterized by a flat circular or ovoid bottom, little or no carved ornamentation and a smoothly curved top with any of several profiles; the profiles distinguish the various types.

The basic shape is the *pad foot,* with a slightly rising profile. The *club foot* has a higher curve in profile, resembling the knob at the end of a wooden club. The *disk foot* is flat on top. The *pad-and-disk foot,* which represents a pad foot atop a disk, is more complex. The *Dutch angular foot* has any of these profiles and in outline is three-lobed or three-pointed rather than circular; it resembles a DRAKE FOOT but has no carving. A *Dutch elongated foot* comes to a point at its end. It is known as a *snake foot* if its profile is raised as in a pad or club foot and as a *slipper foot* if it is flat on top. A *camel foot* is a rare variation on the disk foot; its carved decoration resembles rudimentary toes. Sometimes the term *camel foot* simply denotes a disk foot, whether carved or not. The *Dutch grooved foot* is a club, pad or disk foot with carved grooves or shallow channels on its upper surface.

DUTCH GROOVED FOOT
Type of DUTCH FOOT (*see under* FOOT).

FLEMISH SCROLL FOOT
Seventeenth-century carved foot, characterized by two scrolls, one at the floor and one where foot joins leg or, in a case piece, body (*see* FLEMISH SCROLL LEG, *under* LEG). The bottom scroll turns inward, while the upper one may spiral inward or outward. The section between the two scrolls may be angular or straight in profile, and it may be decorated with grooves or other carving.

Named for Flanders, whence England received the motif in the late 17th century, the Flemish scroll foot may have originated in Spain, which then ruled the southern Netherlands. The SPANISH FOOT (*see under* FOOT) is similar to and may have been derived from this foot.

FRENCH BRACKET FOOT
Type of BRACKET FOOT (*see under* FOOT) having slender and tapering arms and a vertical profile that splays outward slightly at the bottom. (The French bracket foot is sometimes called the *French foot,* though this term more often refers to the SCROLL FOOT [*see under* FOOT].)

FRENCH FOOT
Another name for SCROLL FOOT (*see under* FOOT).

FRENCH SCROLL FOOT
Another name for SCROLL FOOT, distinguishing it from SPANISH FOOT (also known as "Spanish scroll" foot) and FLEMISH SCROLL FOOT (*see each under* FOOT).

HOOF FOOT
Carved foot in the form of an animal's hoof, either cloven (*see* CLOVEN FOOT, *under* FOOT) or solid. Dating back to ancient EGYPTIAN FURNITURE, the hoof foot reappeared in Europe in the late 17th century. A cloven foot was often used with the CABRIOLE LEG (*see under* LEG) in the 18th century.

HORSE-HOOF FOOT
Carved foot on CHINESE FURNITURE; termination for legs of square section. The foot protruded inward from the two inside faces of the leg, bulging abruptly at a point a few inches above the floor and tapering back to the original width at the bottom. The two outside faces of the leg merely tapered slightly inward at the bottom. The horse-hoof foot was popular on tables and chairs of the Ming (1368–1644) and Qing (1644–1911) dynasties.

LEAF SCROLL FOOT
Eighteenth-century SCROLL FOOT (*see under* FOOT) decorated with carved, stylized leaf forms.

LION'S-PAW FOOT
Carved PAW FOOT (*see under* FOOT) in which paw is a lion's. First appearing in ancient EGYPTIAN and MESOPOTAMIAN FURNITURE, the lion's-paw foot was a popular feature in ROMAN FURNITURE and thus in European and American NEOCLASSICAL STYLE furniture of the 18th and 19th centuries.

MELON FOOT
Decorated BUN FOOT (*see under* FOOT) with incised vertical lines spaced regularly around its circumference. It thus resembles a melon.

OGEE BRACKET FOOT
Type of BRACKET FOOT (*see under* FOOT) with a vertical profile in the form of an S-curve, convex above and concave below—that is, a *cyma reversa* curve (*see* CYMA; OGEE).

ONION FOOT
Another name for BUN FOOT (*see under* FOOT).

PAD-AND-DISK FOOT
Type of DUTCH FOOT (*see under* FOOT).

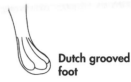
Dutch grooved foot

Flemish scroll foot

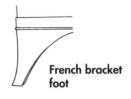
French bracket foot

hairy paw foot

hoof foot

horse-hoof foot

leaf scroll foot

lion's-paw foot

melon foot

ogee bracket foot

pad foot

rat-claw foot

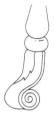

scroll foot

slipper foot

snake foot

spade foot

Spanish foot

stub foot

PAD FOOT
Type of DUTCH FOOT (*see under* FOOT).

PAINTBRUSH FOOT
American name for SPANISH FOOT (*see under* FOOT).

PAW FOOT
Carved foot taking form of an animal's paw. The paw foot has been popular since antiquity, when it figured in EGYPTIAN, MESOPOTAMIAN and ROMAN furniture. In more recent Western furniture, it was most popular in the NEOCLASSICAL STYLE furniture of the late 18th and early 19th centuries. The LION'S-PAW FOOT has been the most frequently used version; other variants are the BEAR'S-CLAW FOOT and the DOG'S-PAW FOOT (*see each under* FOOT).

PEAR FOOT
Type of BALL FOOT (*see under* FOOT), turned with a vertical profile in the form of a *cyma recta* curve, concave at top and convex at bottom (*see* CYMA). The concave upper turning thus forms a "neck" near the top of the foot.

PIED DE BICHE
French term for HOOF FOOT (*see under* FOOT).

PORTUGUESE FOOT
Another name for SPANISH FOOT (*see under* FOOT).

RAT-CLAW FOOT
Long, narrow, carved foot in form of skinny animal claw, usually grasping an ovoid ball beneath it. The rat-claw foot was popular in 18th-century Britain and America, especially on the legs of small tables.

RAT'S BALL-AND-CLAW FOOT
Another name for RAT-CLAW FOOT (*see under* FOOT).

SCROLL FOOT
Carved foot terminating a leg and taking the form of an outward and upward-turning scroll. Originating on French BAROQUE FURNITURE of the late 17th century, it achieved its greatest popularity in the ROCOCO FURNITURE of the LOUIS XV STYLE, when it was commonly used with the CABRIOLE LEG (*see under* LEG). It is also known as the "French" foot, the "French scroll" foot and the "whorl" foot.

SHELL FOOT
Carved foot in form of a seashell, a popular 18th-century motif.

SLIPPER FOOT
Type of DUTCH FOOT (*see under* FOOT).

SNAKE FOOT
Type of DUTCH FOOT (*see under* FOOT).

SPADE FOOT
Block-shaped foot, higher than wide and tapering slightly toward the bottom, thus resembling in profile the blade of a shovel or spade. The spade foot usually terminates a tapering leg, and the top of the foot is wider than the leg where they meet. This foot was most commonly used in British and American NEOCLASSICAL STYLE furniture of the late 18th century.

SPANISH FOOT
Carved foot terminating a leg and characterized by an inward-turning scroll at the bottom and vertical grooves above, creating ribs on the top surface of the scroll. Originating in the BAROQUE FURNITURE of Spain or Portugal in the 17th century, the Spanish foot may be a simpler derivative of the FLEMISH SCROLL FOOT (*see under* FOOT). It was common in England and America in the late 17th and early 18th centuries. It is also known as the "Portuguese" foot and, in America, as the "paintbrush" foot; the grooves on its upper surface suggest the bristles of a brush.

SPANISH SCROLL FOOT
Another name for SPANISH FOOT (*see under* FOOT).

STUB FOOT
Short, broad, downward-tapering foot attached to bottom of a piece of case furniture.

tern foot

TERN FOOT
Carved foot decorated with three scrolls or spiraled grooves. The tern foot was used by Thomas CHIPPENDALE and other 18th-century designers of ROCOCO FURNITURE.

THERM FOOT
Another name for SPADE FOOT (*see under* FOOT).

TRIFID FOOT
Another name for three-toed DRAKE FOOT (*see under* FOOT).

WHORL FOOT
Another name for SCROLL FOOT (*see under* FOOT).

FOOTBOARD
Part of a BED; panel enclosing and sometimes rising above the foot of the bed, where the sleeper's feet are usually placed.

FOOTSTOOL
Small platform on short legs, placed before a chair so that sitter can rest his or her feet. Made since remotest antiquity (*see* EGYPTIAN FURNITURE), the footstool has frequently been associated with the THRONE or CHAIR OF ESTATE as a symbol of high social rank. In more recent, less hierarchical European societies, the footstool has been associated with comfort, informality and gout. In its period of greatest popularity, the 19th century, it was generally upholstered. It has since grown larger; the modern footstool, sometimes called an OTTOMAN, often supports the legs as well as the feet.

FORM (1)
Medieval English term for a long bench with turned legs and stretchers. The term was also used in America.

FORM (2)
Design type in furniture, distinguished from others by basic shape, structure or purpose. A SETTEE and a SOFA, a CONSOLE TABLE and a TABLE DORMANT, a CAQUETOIRE and a CAN-TILEVERED CHAIR are all furniture forms. So, too, are TABLE, CHAIR and CUPBOARD, on a broader taxonomic scale.

FORSTER, JACOB (1764–1838)
FEDERAL PERIOD cabinetmaker of Charlestown, Massachusetts. Forster, who produced a great deal of furniture in his large shop, used both the NEOCLASSICAL STYLE and the style of BOSTON CHIPPENDALE FURNITURE, which had become old-fashioned.

FOURPOSTER
Bed with a CANOPY suspended from its four corner posts rather than from headboard, wall or ceiling. In American usage the term refers more particularly to beds with narrow, elongated posts but no canopy.

FRAMING
Basic skeleton of a piece of furniture, designed to provide shape and structural support.

FRANÇOIS I STYLE
Principal style of the first phase of French RENAISSANCE FURNITURE; the HENRI II STYLE was the later one. Named after François I (ruled 1515–47), under whose patronage it climaxed, the François I style encompassed developments from the reigns of Charles VIII (1483–98) and Louis XII (1498–1515) as well. When Charles VIII invaded Italy in 1494, he developed an enthusiasm for the new Renaissance Italian art and architecture, and he returned to France with artifacts, plans and craftsmen, intending to generate a similar revival of classicism in the applied arts of his own kingdom.

Initially, the result was an awkward mixture of Italian motifs, such as foliate scrolls and ARABESQUES, and features of GOTHIC FURNITURE like LINENFOLD paneling and the pointed arch. By the time of François's rule, Gothic elements had vanished from architecture, but furniture styles changed somewhat more slowly. Beginning in 1525, François undertook a vigorous campaign to renovate French art, primarily by undertaking a comprehensive redecoration of the royal palace at Fontainebleau, south of Paris. This project would occupy a generation of French artists and craftsmen, though François also hired many Italian artists, including, most notably, Leonardo da Vinci. Most important for the development of French furniture was the participation of the two Italian designers who headed the redecoration, Rosso FIORENTINO and Francesco PRIMATICCIO, who were to be the principal formulators of the new style.

François I style furniture differed from Gothic furniture chiefly in its Italian-influenced decoration, which emphasized such architectural elements as COLUMNS, PILASTERS and ENTABLATURES, rendered in the classical ORDERS OF ARCHITECTURE. The new and more complex ornamental motifs of the MANNERIST STYLE—including arabesques, STRAPWORK (invented by Rosso), masks and GROTESQUE ORNAMENT—also came from Italy. Furniture forms retained their Gothic characteristics, for the most part; the CHEST remained the most important case piece, and the CANOPY bed, the other predominant form, still relied on hangings. However, furniture was much more colorful, freely using GILDING and MARQUETRY, especially complex Italian INTARSIA. Carving became more intricate and bolder, especially on tables, which came to bear decoration themselves rather than merely being covered by decorative fabrics.

Following the reign of François, a self-consciously patriotic shift in French fashion replaced the Italianate conventions of the François I style. Thus, the Henri II style completed the design revolution of the French Renaissance.

FRANK, JEAN-MICHEL (1895–1941)

French ART DECO decorator and furniture designer, also associated with Surrealism. Frank's style mediated between the opulence of Art Deco and the ascetic simplicity of modern utilitarian design (see FUNCTIONALISM). His furniture is unadorned and built in basic shapes of the utmost simplicity; but it is finished with rich, sometimes exotic materials, such as lacquer, shagreen and vellum. Frank is also known for his "Surrealist" furniture, notably the famous "Mouth" settee, taken from a Dali painting of a couch in the shape of Mae West's lips. In addition, Frank produced bronze lamps and tables from designs by the sculptor Alberto Giacometti.

FRANK, JOSEF (1885–1967)

Austrian architect and designer associated with the DEUTSCHER WERKBUND and SCANDINAVIAN MODERN furniture. Educated in Vienna, Frank began designing single-family residences before the First World War, often collaborating with Oskar STRNAD. A follower of Otto WAGNER and the ideas of the Deutscher Werkbund, Frank designed furniture for his architectural commissions and also created a firm to build and sell these pieces. In the late 1920s he helped launch the Austrian counterpart to the Deutscher Werkbund. The rise of the Nazi government impelled him to leave Austria in 1934 for Sweden, where he became a well-known practitioner of the Scandinavian Modern style, combining the light simplicity of his traditional Viennese style with a concern for mass production.

FRANKL, PAUL (1878–1958)

Austrian-American furniture designer in the ART DECO and AMERICAN MODERNE styles. Trained as an architect in Vienna, Frankl came to America in 1914 and designed Art Deco furniture in the 1920s, achieving recognition for pieces he showed at the Paris Exposition of 1925. He is best known for his 1930s "Skyscraper" furniture, Art Moderne pieces in which he massed elements of various heights in desks, cupboards and bookcases, in imitation of the setbacks employed in skyscraper architecture of the day.

FREE RENAISSANCE STYLE

British variant of RENAISSANCE REVIVAL STYLE.

FREIDEBERG, PEDRO (b. 1937)

Contemporary Italian-Mexican artist and furniture maker associated with POP ART FURNITURE. Born in Italy but a resident of Mexico since early childhood, Freideberg designed, in 1963, a well-known wooden chair carved in the shape of a human hand. The palm forms the seat, and upraised fingers comprise the back.

FRENCH BRACKET FOOT

See under FOOT.

FRENCH CHIPPENDALE
American and British term for LOUIS XV STYLE in furniture.

FRENCH FOOT
See under FOOT.

FRENCH MODERN STYLE
Nineteenth-century British name for ROCOCO REVIVAL STYLE.

FRENCH POLISHING
Furniture FINISH consisting of numerous coats of transparent VARNISH, each heavily rubbed for hours to provide a highly glossy surface. French polishing was devised in France in the late 18th century and soon was in widespread use throughout Europe and America. It is susceptible to discoloring and tends to chip, but the glasslike surface it produces was nonetheless highly valued. The laborious polishing involved was later done by machine, and modern cellulose-derived LACQUER can be applied to produce much the same effect.

FRENCH PROVINCIAL FURNITURE
Furniture of French provinces, from 17th century into 20th, characterized by a belated and partial adaptation of Parisian styles, with fewer forms and much less ornamentation than in Paris, and by the use of locally available woods, especially pale, honey-colored WALNUT of France. BUFFETS, COMMODES (1) and ARMOIRES were the most important forms. Distinctive provincial styles first emerged in the 17th century, when France became so prosperous that the provincial bourgeoisie and even the wealthier peasantry could indulge in fashionable furniture. At this time, simpler versions of the highly mannered LOUIS XIII STYLE arose in various provincial centers. Most existing French Provincial furniture, though, dates from the 18th century or later. The Parisian LOUIS XV STYLE was the stimulus for most of this work; the LOUIS XVI STYLE merely provided neoclassical motifs that were applied to curving rococo forms, and the EMPIRE STYLE had even less impact in the provinces. Even in the 19th and 20th centuries, the rococo remained the basic style, though regional differences persisted. Only in

the recent past have these distinct furniture styles in France been homogenized by factory production and mass marketing.

FRENCH SCROLL FOOT
See under FOOT.

FRET
Any ornamental pattern of intersecting straight lines, but especially the ancient Greek KEY PATTERN. (The term originally meant a LATTICE; thus, it refers here to the interlacing of straight elements. *See also* FRETWORK.)

FRETSAW
Narrow-bladed, fine-toothed saw used to cut complex ornamental patterns in thin sheets of wood or metal. A fretsaw's blade is detachable from its frame and may be inserted through a small hole in the material to be sawn in order to cut OPENWORK patterns or FRETWORK. The extreme narrowness of the blade enables it to cut along the very tight curves of complicated ARABESQUES.

FRETTED PEDIMENT
See LATTICE PEDIMENT *under* PEDIMENT.

FRETWORK
Carved ornamentation consisting of intersecting lines, usually short, straight elements in geometrical patterns, often resembling a LATTICE or FRET. Fretwork may be OPENWORK or in RELIEF. Familiar to classically inspired designers through ancient Greek relief designs, especially the KEY PATTERN, fretwork became especially popular during the rococo style's (*see* ROCOCO FURNITURE) vogue for CHINOISERIE. Chinese openwork examples of similar ornamentation inspired such makers as Thomas CHIPPENDALE, who used pierced fretwork extensively. Fretwork chair backs, APRONS and galleries (*see* GALLERY) were common. Most of this work was composed in straight lines; the 19th-century development of the FRETSAW enabled openwork ARABESQUES and other complex curvilinear patterns to be cut, and such ornamentation, though no longer resembling a fret, is also called fretwork.

fretwork

FRID, TAGE (b. 1915)

Contemporary American furniture maker; participant in the 1970s HANDICRAFT REVIVAL. Simple, undecorated designs in wood—some influenced by historical models, others inventive in shape without being idiosyncratic—reflect the sensible elegance of Danish modern furniture (*see* SCANDINAVIAN MODERN), as influenced by Kaare KLINT. Frid, who came to the United States from Denmark in 1948, works in Rhode Island and makes furniture by hand, emphasizing precision workmanship and fine woods.

FRIEZE

Central section, usually decorated, of an ENTABLATURE, which is the part of a classical architectural order located above the CAPITAL. The frieze was commonly used to ornament case furniture. The horizontal section below a tabletop, which may contain the drawers and is often decorated, is also called a frieze.

FROTHINGHAM, BENJAMIN (1734–1809)

Cabinetmaker of Charlestown, Massachusetts; important maker of BOSTON CHIPPENDALE FURNITURE. Established as a furniture maker by 1756, Frothingham was also a militia officer. He produced furniture in a restrained style similar to the style of NEWPORT CHIPPENDALE FURNITURE. His elegant, sober case furniture, in both blockfront and *bombé* shapes, featured great expanses of figured veneering and very little decorative carving. He served as an artillery officer throughout the American Revolution and became a friend of George Washington. After the war he resumed furniture making, adopting the neoclassical modes (*see* NEOCLASSICAL STYLE) of the FEDERAL period.

fulcrum

FRULLINI, LUIGI (1839–97)

Italian RENAISSANCE REVIVAL STYLE furniture maker. Originally a sculptor, Frullini specialized in case furniture, frames, clocks and candelabras. These pieces were appropriate settings for his elaborate and delicate carving, which depicted motifs from the early Italian Renaissance.

FRY, EDWIN MAXWELL (1899–1987)

British INTERNATIONAL STYLE architect and furniture designer. In the 1930s, with Wells Coates and Sergius CHERMAYEFF, Fry was a British follower of such Continental pioneers as LE CORBUSIER, Walter GROPIUS and Marcel BREUER. He helped bring Gropius and Breuer to Britain when they fled Nazi Germany and practiced architecture with Gropius from 1934 to 1936. From 1951 to 1954 he collaborated with Le Corbusier on his buildings for the new provincial capital at Chandigarh, India, along with Pierre JEANNERET. Fry's furniture was austere and rectilinear in the International style manner, particularly influenced by Le Corbusier. He designed for mass production, using new materials such as molded plywood, tubular steel and latex foam.

FRY, ROGER (1866–1934)

British art critic and sometime furniture designer. Though much better known as a writer on the fine arts, Fry was also concerned with design reform, in the tradition of William MORRIS and the British ARTS AND CRAFTS MOVEMENT. In 1913 he founded the Omega Workshops, dedicated to the production of well-designed furniture and other household goods. Artists of the Bloomsbury circle—including Duncan Grant, Vanessa Bell and Fry himself—contributed designs, but their interest was chiefly in dramatic painted decorations. These featured abstract or botanical motifs in bold colors, which were applied to traditional structures and furniture types.

FULCRUM

ROMAN FURNITURE part, a headboard for the Greek KLINE. The *kline,* a couch used both for sleeping and for reclining at meals, was the basic piece of domestic furniture in the classical world. The *fulcrum,* a massive structure on which a diner reclined, was more architectural in character than the piled bedding of the *kline,* which it replaced. It was also lavishly ornamented with sculpted animal heads and busts of maenads and satyrs. This alteration in the structure of the *kline* pointed to the development of the LECTUS, the first step toward the modern couch.

FUMED OAK

OAK that has been exposed to ammonia fumes, thus receiving an artificial yellowish tint. Fumed oak furniture was popular in the late 19th and early 20th centuries.

FUNA DANSU

Traditional JAPANESE FURNITURE form; small TANSU of sturdy HARDWOOD construction and much ironwork, decorative in appearance but intended for security. The *funa-dansu,* generally called a *sea chest* or *captain's chest* in English, housed valuables aboard ship.

FUNCTIONALISM

The esthetic doctrine that equates beauty with utility and economy, in architecture and furniture design. The notion that any design using extravagant materials or having nonutilitarian elements cannot be beautiful was formulated in the late 19th and early 20th centuries, chiefly in Vienna, later at the BAUHAUS, and among Chicago architects. Though the uncompromising asceticism of the original stance has become relaxed with time, functionalism has remained an important design concept since its inception. Louis Sullivan (*see* PRAIRIE SCHOOL) gave memorable expression to the central tenet of functionalism in declaring, "Form follows function." An illustration of functionalist doctrine taken to the extreme is the title of designer Adolph LOOS's famous essay "Ornament and Crime" (1908).

While the concept of functionalism has had a major impact on architecture, it has also influenced modern furniture design, especially the works of LE CORBUSIER and Bauhaus designers, such as Ludwig MIES VAN DER ROHE and Marcel BREUER. Collectively, the architecture and furniture of these men and their followers is said to be in the INTERNATIONAL STYLE. Functionalist furniture designs focus on the importance of materials in the industrial process, often employing new, experimental materials such as metals and plastics. Also, functionalist designs generally highlight the various parts of a piece to showcase their different functions, as, for instance, chair seats versus the legs beneath them. Functionalism has affected most modern furniture design since the International style, especially SCANDINAVIAN MODERN design.

FURNESS, FRANK (1839–1912)

Philadelphia architect and furniture designer. A major architect of the period following the Civil War, Furness also designed furniture using two different styles: one an eclectic style resembling Owen JONES's work, the other a variant of Charles EASTLAKE's Modern Gothic style, with stylized decoration probably influenced by Christopher DRESSER. Furness apparently developed this variant of Modern Gothic in conjunction with his occasional collaborator, fellow Philadelphian Daniel PABST.

Louis Sullivan was one of Furness's employees during the 1870s, and Sullivan later became a leader of the PRAIRIE SCHOOL. Thus, one can partly attribute Eastlake's impact on the Prairie School to Furness.

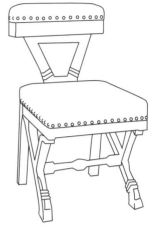

Frank Furness chair

FUROSAKI BYOBU

Japanese folding SCREEN; low, two-paneled BYOBU, consisting of two woven rush panels attached to wooden frames. The undecorated *furosaki byobu* is intended to screen the fire beneath the *furo,* a pot used to boil water for tea, and it is often rigid. Its panels form a right angle within which a small shelf to hold tea utensils may be attached.

FUSTIC (also *fustick*)

Eighteenth-century term for YELLOW-WOOD.

G

gadrooning

display case by Gallé

GABOON
Central African HARDWOOD used extensively for plywood in Europe. Also called *okoumé.*

GADROONING
Carved ornamental device; band, convex from top to bottom, of short, vertical lengths of REEDING. Each reed, or gadroon, is rounded at top and bottom. Gadrooning has been widely used as a MOLDING, as the edge of a pedestal or tabletop, or to decorate the shoulders of massive BULB TURNINGS (*see under* TURNERY). Used extensively in the 18th century as well, the reeding sometimes all curves to the left or right, creating a spiral effect.

GAILLARD, EUGÈNE (1862–1933)
French ART NOUVEAU furniture designer. Although he was from Nancy, Gaillard is better known for the design work he did for Samuel BING, in Paris. These robust pieces had heavily sculpted frames emphasizing a strong, rhythmic interplay of lines, including the WHIPLASH CURVE motif. Light, plain paneling was often contrasted with a dark, carved framework. Gaillard's interest in jewelry design led him to frequently employ elaborate metalwork details on his furniture.

GAINES, JOHN (1704–43)
Cabinetmaker of Portsmouth, New Hampshire, associated with the transition from the AMERICAN WILLIAM AND MARY STYLE to the AMERICAN QUEEN ANNE STYLE in the early 18th century. Gaines, son of an Ipswich, Massachusetts, cabinetmaker, moved to Portsmouth early in his career. He was noted for chairs

that combined established features, such as pierced carving of foliate motifs on backs, with such elements of the nascent rococo style (*see* ROCOCO FURNITURE) as vase-shaped splats and cabriole legs. His son George, later an officer in the American Revolutionary Army, was also a furniture maker.

GALLÉ, ÉMILE (1846–1904)
French ART NOUVEAU designer and glassmaker, leader of the School of Nancy (*see:* NANCY, SCHOOL OF). Principally a glassmaker, Gallé developed an interest in furniture, with a concern for new design. In 1885 he added a cabinetmaking shop to his glass and ceramic factory near Nancy. By 1889, Gallé was marketing furniture of his own design, with ornamentation characterized by swirling Art Nouveau decoration and representational marquetry depicting motifs from nature, placed on traditional RENAISSANCE REVIVAL and LOUIS XV structural forms. In creating a widely felt revival of fine marquetry, Gallé employed a great variety of woods, both local and exotic. Gallé's marquetry images ranged through all of nature, from landscapes to leaves, through birds, flowers, insects, and—influenced by oriental art—fish, including octopuses. Many of his pieces were MEUBLES PARLANT, bearing a wide range of biblical and philosophical inscriptions, including quotations from such contemporaries as Charles Baudelaire and Victor Hugo. In 1901, Gallé founded the *Ecole de Nancy, Alliance Provincial des Industies d'Art,* a workshop center modeled after the guilds of the English ARTS AND CRAFTS MOVEMENT and intended to generate a provincial renaissance in handicraft. Around this institution there formed the group of designers known as the School of

Nancy. From the '90's on, Gallé's factory produced great numbers of pieces of both glass and furniture, with outlets in Paris, London, and Frankfurt. After his death in 1904, the business continued under Victor PROUVÉ, producing work in Gallé's style until the First World War.

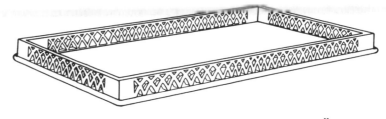

gallery

GALLÉN-KALLELA, AKSELI (1865–1931)

Finnish painter and designer; principal exponent of NATIONAL ROMANTICISM. Gallén-Kallela designed furniture for the workshop of Louis SPARRE. His design style was elegant but forthright, with some of his forms being derivative of BIEDERMEIER STYLE furniture. His pieces were modestly decorated—often with motifs adapted from Finnish folk art—and revealed an ART NOUVEAU influence.

GALLERY

Raised rim, railing or fencelike FRETWORK around the top of a table or other piece of furniture; intended to prevent small objects from falling off that surface, or used simply as decoration.

GALLOON

Trimming for UPHOLSTERY consisting of a narrow ribbon or braid of lace, fine cloth, metal thread or embroidery.

GAMING TABLE

Small table intended for playing board games. It was equipped with a specially decorated top that covered compartments for game pieces and other apparatus. One of the earliest specialized types of table, the gaming table appeared in ancient EGYPTIAN FURNITURE and has been popular ever since.

GATE-LEG TABLE

Type of DROP-LEAF TABLE characterized by, in addition to its standard legs, one or more gate-like structures. Each of these consisted of a leg attached by stretchers and hinged to a fixed vertical element beneath the tabletop; it could thus swing out, supporting a raised leaf of the table. Though the table usually had 2 gate legs, 1 gate (and leaf) was not uncommon and as many as 12 gates were known on a single piece. When closed, the tables were usually quite narrow and thus saved space. Appearing as early as the 16th century, they were most popular in England throughout the 17th century and in America, where they were introduced in about 1650, until the middle of the 18th century. They were usually produced in the baroque styles (*see* BAROQUE FURNITURE) of the 17th century—the Jacobean, Restoration (*see* JACOBEAN FURNITURE; RESTORATION FURNITURE) and WILLIAM AND MARY STYLES—which were well-suited to the contrast presented between the elaborate turnings of the legs and gates and the broad, plain surfaces of the leaves. For the most part, the gate-leg table has been supplanted in fashion by the various PEMBROKE TABLES, with their less elaborate support.

GATTI, PAOLINI & TEODORO

Italian architecture and design firm, established in Turin in 1965. This firm—headed by Piero Gatti (b. 1940), Cesare Paolini (b. 1937) and Franco Teodoro (b. 1939)—is best known for its "Sacco" chair (1969), a much-imitated design. This piece, a form completely outside the traditional concept of the chair, is simply a large leather bag filled with pebble-sized pieces of polystyrene. It can function in any position, and it is very light, portable and inexpensive.

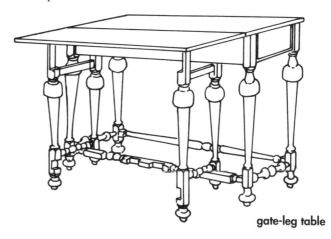

gate-leg table

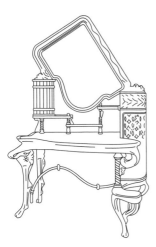

Gaudi vanity

GAUDI Y CORNET, ANTONIO (1852–1926)

Spanish architect and furniture designer associated with ART NOUVEAU. Gaudi was a Barcelona architect who also designed furniture to complement his buildings. His design style was an exuberant version of *Modernismo*, as Art Nouveau was known in Spain. His pieces are composed of extravagantly swirling scrolls of carved wood, which were sometimes combined with wrought iron.

GAUDREAU (or GAUDREAUX), ANTOINE-ROBERT (c. 1680–1751)

French furniture maker in LOUIS XV STYLE. A chief rival of Charles CRESSENT, Gaudreau was noted for sumptuous pieces decorated with elaborate bronze mounts, often made by Jacques CAFFIERI.

GEDDES, NORMAN BEL (1893–1958)

American designer associated with the AMERICAN MODERNE style. Originally a theatrical designer, Geddes established the first industrial design firm in America in 1927. He designed a great number of industrial products, ranging from soap dispensers and vending machines to whole interiors for theaters and hotels. He is perhaps best known for his ship, train and automobile designs. For these, Geddes used the principles of streamlining creating a sleek, curvilinear style that, for many, typifies the American Moderne style and is Geddes's signature. His furniture was similarly sleek and sensuous, though influenced by the relatively ascetic European INTERNATIONAL STYLE, as evidenced by its use of new materials associated with mass manufacture, mostly steel and glass, and its functionalistic emphasis on separate parts (*see* FUNCTIONALISM).

cardboard chair by Gehry

GEHRY, FRANK O. (b. 1929)

Contemporary American architect. In 1972 Gehry designed a line of laminated cardboard chairs and chaises that have become well known. Inexpensive, light, strong and versatile, the cardboard also has a pleasing, soft surface texture. Each piece is as wide as the single sheet of several-inches-thick cardboard that composes it. The cardboard is bent into a series of curves and angles to form a closed, or nearly closed, irregular geometric shape whose profile may appear to describe the seat and back of a chair. Gehry's furniture is startlingly comfortable. When the irregular shape is not completely closed, the break occurs where the seat and back meet, yielding a flexibility resembling a cantilevered chair's. In its concern with economy, utility and suitability of materials, this furniture is solidly in the modern tradition informed by the doctrines of FUNCTIONALISM and ERGONOMIC DESIGN. But in its ingenuity and wit, it is perfectly in keeping with the recent proliferation of novel, not always utilitarian, designs.

GEORGIAN PERIOD

Period of British history (1714–1830) when four kings named George reigned and when British furniture styles progressed from late baroque through rococo and neoclassical (*see* BAROQUE FURNITURE; ROCOCO FURNITURE; NEOCLASSICAL STYLE). The term *Georgian* is frequently used in British architectural history, but its application to furniture is more problematic. In 18th-century Britain the market for fine crafts expanded. Unlike France, where the taste of the royal court remained uniquely potent, Britain had a powerful and rising gentry that determined dominant tastes in the decorative arts. And also unlike France, the names of furniture styles during this period tend to commemorate their creators or popularizers rather than reigning monarchs.

At the beginning of the Georgian period, British baroque furniture continued to evolve; the QUEEN ANNE STYLE persisted throughout much of the reign of George I (1714–27), before it was superseded by the late baroque PALLADIAN STYLE. Palladian style furniture took its name from a style of architecture and its inspiration from 17th-century Italy. It was popular during most of the reign of George II (1727–60). However, in the 1750s, the impact of the French LOUIS XV STYLE spurred the development of the British rococo, a style whose leading exemplar among furniture makers was Thomas CHIPPENDALE.

The reign of George III (1760–1820) is associated stylistically with neoclassicism. British neoclassical furniture was introduced by James STUART and Robert ADAM in the 1760s. Adam's pervasive influence throughout the next two decades popularized a highly decorative neoclassical mode known as the ADAM STYLE. This manner was modified in the

1780s–1790s by George HEPPLEWHITE and Thomas SHERATON, and the furniture of those decades is sometimes said to belong to the "Hepplewhite" and "Sheraton" styles. Sheraton's work evidenced the early stirrings of the eclectic, French-influenced REGENCY STYLE, with its more literal approach to the use of ancient Greek, Roman and Egyptian forms and ornamentation, as known through archeology. At the same time, hybrid assemblages of these and other elements were generated by a fondness for new ideas that kept the neoclassical mode in flux from the turn of the 19th century through the regency (1811–20) and reign (1820–30) of George IV. The end of the Georgian period saw the development both of mass production and of the REVIVAL STYLES, whose combination marked the furniture of the early VICTORIAN PERIOD.

When discussing American Colonial furniture, nomenclature of styles is skewed by the considerable time required in the 18th century for British fashions to reach a remote province. AMERICAN QUEEN ANNE STYLE furniture was not made until well after Queen Anne's death, and it is sometimes called "George II" furniture, in honor of the king during whose reign it was dominant. Colonial rococo, or AMERICAN CHIPPENDALE FURNITURE, was mostly made during the first decades of George III's reign, but it is not normally named for him. Midway through his reign, the American Revolution occurred, and regnal names became irrelevant in the new United States.

GESSO

Material applied to furniture and decoratively carved, textured, and gilded or painted. Gesso, in use from the Middle Ages onward, is composed of a basic mixture of gypsum and sizing; other materials, such as glues or oils, are sometimes added. Similar substances also used after the 15th century were PASTIGLIA and COMPO.

GIBBONS, GRINLING (1648–1721)

English baroque sculptor who significantly influenced Restoration (see RESTORATION FURNITURE) and WILLIAM AND MARY STYLE furniture makers. Dutch-born, Gibbons pursued his career in Restoration England, carving highly embellished LIMEWOOD paneling, specializing mostly in bold arrangements of foliage, fruits and flowers carved in impeccable detail. His sweeping fluency of design affected many contemporary furniture makers.

GIBBONS, WILLIAM (active 1640–89)

Connecticut furniture maker. Gibbons, who was born and trained in London, immigrated to New Haven, where he made AMERICAN JACOBEAN FURNITURE.

GILARDI, PIERO (b. 1942)

Contemporary Italian furniture designer associated with POP ART FURNITURE. Gilardi is best known for a group of seats (1967) that were made of polyurethane foam, molded and painted to resemble rough boulders of various sizes. He has since been involved in a wide range of experimental art, and at the turn into the 21st century, he is a noted computer artist.

GILDING

Wood or metal FINISH in which thin layers of gold are applied to a surface. Gold has traditionally been applied to wood as GOLD LEAF, usually on a damp ground of GESSO, or as a powdered ingredient in a liquid medium. Walter gilding requires a gesso substratum and produces a surface that takes a very high polish. Oil gilding may be applied directly to wood and is more durable, though less lustrous, than water gilding. Until modern times, metals were treated with a solution of gold in a liquid and then fired, which burned off the medium and left a thin film of gold. The usual medium was mercury, which was used to gild the ORMOLU mounts of 18th- and early 19th-century furniture (see MERCURY GILDING). This process yielded toxic fumes and has been abandoned for the most part. Today, most gilded metal is electroplated. The metal is submerged in a chemical bath containing gold and then receives an electric charge, resulting in the chemical bonding of the gold to the metal. Wood is usually gilded with gold leaf, affixed by specially developed adhesives.

GILLINGHAM, JAMES (1736–81)

PHILADELPHIA CHIPPENDALE FURNITURE maker. Gillingham made relatively simple furniture for Philadelphia, often using the "Chippendale Gothic" mode (see Thomas CHIPPENDALE).

GILLOWS

British furniture manufacturer from 1731 to 1974. Founded in Lancaster by Robert Gillow, the company opened a branch in London in the 1760s. The main factory remained in Lancaster, and much Gillows furniture was sold to nearby Scottish buyers. The firm is best known for its late Georgian (*see* GEORGIAN PERIOD) and REGENCY STYLE furniture, though it remained one of the most important British furniture makers throughout the 19th century, using the various REVIVAL STYLES, and into the early 20th century, employing many principal designers, including Sergius Ivan CHERMAYEFF. Around the turn of the 20th century, Gillows merged with S. J. Waring & Sons and became Waring & Gillows, which closed in 1974.

GILPIN, THOMAS (1700–1766)

Philadelphia chair maker. A specialist in the manufacture of WINDSOR CHAIRS, Gilpin was originally a country craftsman; born in a small town in rural Chester County, Pennsylvania, he established himself in business there by 1721. In 1727 he moved to Philadelphia, where he made chairs until he retired in 1756.

GILTWOOD

Wood with FINISH of gold, applied by GILDING. The term usually refers to wood with carved and gilded GESSO decoration or wood coated with SILVER LEAF and a semitransparent layer of gold-colored or gold-impregnated VARNISH.

GIMP

Trimming for UPHOLSTERY consisting of one or more narrow braids of fabric, each with a stiff cord or wire running through it. These are often plaited or otherwise arranged to form an openwork pattern. Also spelled GUIMPE or *gymp*.

GIMSON, ERNEST WILLIAM (1864–1919)

Furniture designer and architect; member of the COTSWOLD SCHOOL. Ernest Gimson studied architecture under Richard Norman SHAW, became an early follower of the ARTS AND CRAFTS MOVEMENT and was influenced by the designs of Philip WEBB and George JACK. With other members of the Cotswold School, he left London in 1895 to establish a

chair by Mackintosh

workshop in the rural Cotswold Hills. Gimson's clean-lined, angular furniture designs often featured elaborate marquetry and inlay, with stylized botanical or abstract motifs.

GIOVANNI DA VERONA (c. 1457–1525)

Italian master of INTARSIA, active at about the turn of the 16th century.

GIRANDOLE

ROCOCO FURNITURE form; carved wall sconce, intended to hold a candle. Named for a type of Italian fireworks, the girandole was a prominent vehicle for exuberant rococo carving, especially in Britain.

GLASGOW SCHOOL

Four Scottish designers regarded as a branch of the ART NOUVEAU movement. The Glasgow School consisted of two sisters, Frances and Margaret Macdonald, fabric and metalwork designers, and their respective husbands, Herbert McNair and Charles Rennie MACKINTOSH, both architects and furniture designers. The four were associated with the Glasgow School of Art at the close of the 19th century. Mackintosh was the genius and dominant figure of the group, and the style associated with the Glasgow School is his, for the most part. He was influenced by the British ARTS AND CRAFTS MOVEMENT—particularly the works of C. F. A. VOYSEY and William GODWIN—and the Art Nouveau phenomenon in Europe. Mackintosh produced airy, attenuated furniture forms based on rectangles and gentle curves. Some of his decorative motifs were derived from the swirling Irish calligraphy of the early Middle Ages, revealing the influence of the Celtic revival of the time upon his work. The Glasgow School's geometrical style influenced the Art Nouveau style in Europe, particularly in Vienna (*see* SEZESSION). Also associated with the Glasgow School is the designer George WALTON.

GLASTONBURY CHAIR

TUDOR FURNITURE form; folding chair with an X-FRAME composing the front and rear leg at each side. Carved arms extended from crest rail to seat rail. The name comes from a particular piece that supposedly belonged to the last

abbot of Glastonbury, who was executed by
Henry VIII. However, the form probably did
not arise until late in the region of Elizabeth I.

GLAZING BAR

Thin wood or metal member of a glazed
panel, as in the door of a piece of case furniture. It is a strip of material, molded or cast
with a slotted edge in order to house the panes
of glass. When placed vertically, it is sometimes called a MULLION or a MUNTIN.

GNEIB, ANKI (b. 1965)

Swedish architect and furniture designer; a
contemporary producer of now-traditional
SCANDINAVIAN MODERN furniture. Gneib's
work features spare and simple forms, in boldly contrasting colors and materials, especially
fine woods.

GOBELINS

Common name for 17th-century royal French
workshops in the decorative arts. Jean-Baptiste
Colbert, Louis XIV's prime minister, engineered the royal purchase, in 1662, of the
tapestry workshops of the Gobelin family and
their conversion, in 1667, into the *Manufacture
royale des meubles de la Couronne,* intended to
produce work in all of the decorative arts.
Under the leadership of Charles LE BRUN, its
first director, the Gobelins workshops were
committed to glorifying the Sun King's reign,
and one consequence was the creation of the
LOUIS XIV STYLE in furniture. Le Brun assembled such noted cabinetmakers as the Flemish
immigrant Pierre GOLLE; the Italian Domenico
CUCCI; and Frenchmen André-Charles BOULLE,
Jean LE PAUTRE and Jean BÉRAIN. These men
produced the furnishings that helped make
Versailles the artistic capital of Europe for several generations. After Colbert's death in 1683,
Le Brun fell from royal favor, and Bérain succeeded him as Gobelin's chief. The financial crisis of 1693 resulted in the closing of the
workshops in the following year. When they
reopened in 1699, they were once again devoted solely to tapestry.

GODDARD, JOHN (1723–85)

Newport, Rhode Island, cabinetmaker; most
important exponent of NEWPORT CHIPPEN-

DALE FURNITURE. Son of a Massachusetts
builder, Goddard moved to Newport in the
early 1740s. There he was apprenticed to Job
TOWNSEND, whose daughter he soon married. With his father-in-law, Goddard is credited with the fullest development of the
BLOCKFRONT design; they also made furniture
based on the patterns of Thomas CHIPPEN-
DALE. Both the Goddards and the Townsends
were Quakers and refused to participate in the
American Revolution. The local patriots
accordingly suspected them of British sympa-
thies, their business collapsed, and Goddard
died bankrupt. The business was revived by
his son Stephen GODDARD.

GODDARD, STEPHEN (1764–1804)

Newport, Rhode Island, cabinetmaker of the
FEDERAL PERIOD. Son of John GODDARD,
Stephen Goddard, in partnership with his
brother Thomas (1765–1858), made furniture
in the NEOCLASSICAL STYLE of the day, deriving his designs from those of George
HEPPLEWHITE and Thomas SHERATON.

GODWIN, WILLIAM (1833–86)

British architect and designer; important figure
of the ART FURNITURE MOVEMENT.
Originally, Godwin was an architect in the
NEO-GOTHIC STYLE, his style being similar to
that of William BURGES, but much less extravagant. Godwin is considered one of the most
innovative designers of the 19th century. He
became familiar with Japanese art (*see*
JAPONISME) early in the 1860s and was
impressed by the emphasis in Japanese design
on the differences between elements, effected
through an architectonic juxtaposition of
solids and voids. The furniture he began
designing in 1867 expressed this interest—
light, elegant pieces, composed of machine-
made elements of ebonized wood with only
panels of Japanese paper or Japanese carved
wood as decoration. Much of his work was
made for himself or private clients (Oscar
Wilde among them), but many of his designs
were later manufactured commercially. He is
associated with the Art Furniture movement
because he addressed its goal of good, simple
design for industrially made furniture. With
Wilde and the painter James McNeill Whistler,
Godwin was a leader of the Aesthetic
Movement, which attempted to educate the

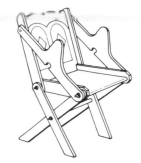

Glastonbury chair

**Anki Gneib chest
of drawers**

public to a new, lighter taste. They advocated the use of lighter colors and less ornament, and they generated enthusiasm for the exotic, including the new furniture style Godwin had created, known as Anglo-Japanese. Godwin's designs were revolutionary, and their simple, open, anti-revivalist character remained influential well into the 20th century, when their imprint can clearly be seen in the work of DE STIJL and BAUHAUS designers.

GOLD LEAF
Very thin sheets of gold used in GILDING.

GOLDFINGER, ERNO (1902–87)
British INTERNATIONAL STYLE architect and furniture designer. Goldfinger studied in Paris and settled in London in 1934. He was best known as an architect but has also designed idiosyncratic furniture. Goldfinger often used industrial design elements, such as ship's fittings, in domestic pieces. He favored such ingenious devices as pivoting shelves and drawers and stackable furniture.

Gondola chair

GOLE, CORNELIUS (BORN CORNELIS GOLLE) (active late 17th century)
Flemish BAROQUE FURNITURE maker who worked in England. Son of the noted LOUIS XIV STYLE *ébéniste* Pierre GOLLE of Paris, Cornelius Gole, as he was later known, and his brother Adriaan GOLLE were Protestants who fled France after the Edict of Nantes was revoked in 1685. Gole and his brother influenced English cabinetmakers in the WILLIAM AND MARY STYLE, providing up-to-date examples of the fashionable French manner.

GOLLE, ADRIAAN (active late 17th century)
Flemish BAROQUE FURNITURE maker who worked in France, Holland and England. Adriaan Golle, son of Pierre GOLLE, fled France after the Edict of Nantes was revoked in 1685 (*see* LOUIS XIV STYLE). He was employed in Holland by the Princess of Orange, and when she became Queen Mary II of England in 1689, he went to England with her court. He and his brother Cornelis, who had earlier gone to England, where he was known as Cornelius GOLE, influenced English

cabinetmakers in the WILLIAM AND MARY STYLE, providing up-to-date examples of the fashionable French manner.

GOLLE, CORNELIS
See GOLE, Cornelius.

GOLLE, PIERRE (d. 1684)
Flemish cabinetmaker working in France; important ÉBÉNISTE in LOUIS XIV STYLE. In Paris by 1660, Golle became a leading figure under Charles LE BRUN at the royal GOBELINS workshops. His early pieces were ebony cabinets with heavy moldings and pictorial scenes carved in low relief, influenced by the Antwerp KUNSTSCHRANK tradition. Later he specialized in floral MARQUETRY in rich materials. Prior to the mature work of André-Charles BOULLE, Golle was the leading marquetry worker in France. He created complex brass and pewter inlays, made in the manner of BOULLE MARQUETRY, which produced the effect of a gold and silver veneer. His spectacularly sumptuous furniture was an important component in the creation of an aura of magnificence around the throne, which was the major aim of the French baroque decorative arts.

GONDOLA CHAIR (also *barrel chair*)
Late 18th-century and early 19th-century NEOCLASSICAL STYLE furniture form; chair with deep, concave back whose STILES curved continuously forward and down to the SEAT RAIL. The gondola chair first appeared in France in about 1760 and remained popular throughout Europe and America for nearly a century, especially for use at a desk or writing table.

GOODISON, BENJAMIN (active 1727–67)
British PALLADIAN STYLE cabinetmaker. Goodison specialized in PARCEL GILT furniture, boldly ornamented in the manner of William KENT, with large-scale foliage and shell motifs. Until his death in 1767, he continued to make BAROQUE FURNITURE, even after its popularity began to wane.

GOSTELOWE, JONATHAN (1744–95)
A leading maker of PHILADELPHIA CHIPPENDALE FURNITURE. Gostelowe, whose name may indicate Swedish ancestry, made distin-

guished mahogany furniture in bold, sculptural forms that he devised himself, they were generally not represented in the pattern books of the day. Exceptionally rich in carved ornamentation, his work, along with Benjamin RANDOLPH's, presents the most exuberant example of the rococo style in America (*see* ROCOCO FURNITURE).

GOTHIC FURNITURE

Late MEDIEVAL FURNITURE, dominant throughout western Europe except Italy, superseding ROMANESQUE FURNITURE in the 14th century and giving way to RENAISSANCE FURNITURE in the 16th. Like earlier medieval furniture, Gothic pieces were stylistically derived from the architecture of the soaring cathedrals with which the term *Gothic* is most readily associated; the term, connoting barbaric crudity and excess, was coined as an insult to those buildings by the artist, architect and pioneer art historian Giorgio Vasari (1511–74), who was too involved in the Renaissance style to provide an impartial critique.

The Gothic architectural style is said to have begun with the construction, in 1140–44, of the abbey church of St. Denis, near Paris. It was characterized by a strong vertical emphasis in its structures and a pronounced naturalism in its decorative devices. Its most typical architectural element was the pointed arch, introduced into France from the Islamic architecture of Sicily, which was under Norman rule in the 12th century. Although Gothic architecture swept Europe rapidly, Romanesque principles and practices dominated in the applied arts until well into the 14th century, when the newer style eventually generated a greater range of furniture forms and decoration.

Europe at this time was increasingly secular. A wealthy merchant class was rising, and commercially oriented city-states, especially in northern Italy and along the shores of the North Sea, were emerging from the feudal economy. Lay patronage rivaled that of the church, and craftsmen developed a wider variety of furniture forms than had existed earlier. In bourgeois homes, rooms began to have particular uses, generating a demand for specialized furnishings. Stable and prosperous merchants, unlike the peripatetic aristocracy, did not need furniture that was designed for ease of transport. Increasingly, ornamentation and fine craft made pieces of furniture equal to jewelry and expensive fabrics as display items. One consequence of this development was the creation, in 1254, of a Parisian guild for furniture makers, presaging the elaborate specialization of labor that characterized later epochs in Europe (*see*, for instance, ÉBÉNISTE and MENUISIER).

The ornamentation of Gothic furniture was dominated by carved architectural motifs, such as ARCADING and the PILASTER. TRACERY filled the pointed arches that decorated pieces of furniture, imitating contemporary buildings, where it satisfied a practical, structural need; entirely superfluous buttresses even appeared occasionally. Ornamental carving followed the patterns developed by stonemasons who decorated cathedrals. Botanical and figural motifs long in use were more naturalistically rendered in Gothic style carving, and geometrical forms became less important. A new motif, the LINENFOLD panel, reflected the economic importance of the cloth industry.

Gothic chair

In northern Europe the timber most commonly used in making furniture was oak, while in southern France, Spain and Italy, a variety of woods, especially fruitwoods and cypress, were employed. The usual mode of construction depended mostly on MORTISE-AND-TENON JOINTS (*see under* JOINERY) reinforced with dowels or iron nails. No glue was used, except in the occasional application of a canvas or leather covering to an uncarved surface. Such a covering was then painted with ornamental or figural representations. Most furniture, whether or not so treated, was vividly painted; its appearance was far more colorful than the somber look of most surviving pieces, which usually have lost their color almost entirely.

The chest remained the most common piece of furniture, and it differed from Romanesque predecessors chiefly in decorative style; the practice of strengthening chests with wrought-iron bands in ornamental patterns continued. The TILTING CHEST, with its carved representations of knightly sport, was a decorative innovation. The BUFFET became less important as an indicator of status than it had been, and the DRESSER (1) was frankly utilitarian. The CUPBOARD, an open arrangement of shelves related to the buffet, began to evolve from the two varieties of COURT CUPBOARD into the modern enclosed form. The medieval PRESS, already enclosed, filled a number of needs, including food storage, as in the highly specialized LIVERY CUPBOARD. The LECTERN was a freestanding piece, constructed of panels on a frame; other forms of reading or writing desks were essentially boxes with sloping lids, to be placed on a tabletop.

The stool was the prevalent form of seating. It usually had three legs. In the BACK STOOL, one leg extended above the triangular seat to approximate a chair back. Late in the period, the SLAB-ENDED STOOL appeared. Benches were also common, especially for seating diners at long tables. The X-FRAME continued to be a popular type of seat, though its role as an emblem of authority was gradually assumed by the high-backed, paneled WAINSCOT CHAIR. A common version of the wainscot chair was a massive arm-chair, often fixed to its site and heavily carved with architectural ornamentation; an outstanding example is the English Coronation Chair in Westminster Abbey. Another widespread type of chair was tub-shaped, usually with a decoratively carved outer surface. The period also saw the emergence of a significant new form of seating, the SETTLE, an elaboration of the bench.

A marked development of the bed CANOPY and TESTER in Gothic times characterized the BED OF ESTATE, which became the most important furniture form in demonstrating the hierarchical status of its owner, a pervasive concern in medieval society. Even cradles of high-born babies sometimes had testers and canopies and were used for formal viewing of the infant, who slept in a less ornate version. There was great variation in these hangings, or CELURES, with HALF-TESTERS or demicelures often used. In Italy, perhaps because of the climate canopies were rare. As in earlier times, lower-status beds were generally simple, boxlike structures, and people frequently slept on benches and chests.

The TRESTLE TABLE remained common, but a number of small occasional tables appeared. These had tops of various shapes, sometimes mounted on a central pillar, anticipating the later PEDESTAL TABLE. The TABLE DORMANT gradually ceased to be made during this period.

In the Gothic era national differences of style, which had begun to be discernible earlier, became more pronounced. Most strikingly, perhaps, Italy never fully adopted the Gothic style, even in architecture; it remained under persistent classical and Romanesque influences. Italian furniture of this time featured little carving; rather, it was elaborately painted, anticipating forms such as the Renaissance CASSONE.

In France, the birthplace of the Gothic style, furniture was most insistently architectural in character. Late in the period an increasingly ornate decorative sense, which informed all northern European architecture and applied arts, was particularly strong here. Spain followed the international Gothic style that developed in France but also incorporated the influence of Islam in HISPANO-MORESQUE FURNITURE, which seemed to glitter with complicated inlay work.

In England the Gothic style did not appear until about 1200 and remained ornamentally simpler than in France. The Gothic era persisted later in England, where a strong Renaissance influence was not felt until the period of TUDOR FURNITURE, well into the 16th century. For instance, the X-frame chair retained its prestige as a symbol of social prominence far longer here than on the Continent. In Germany and Scandinavia the Gothic architectural character was reflected in massive furniture with extravagant cornices and pediments. This manner would dominate furniture of the region for several centuries.

The very factors that stimulated the rise of Gothic furniture—the rise of a secular, bourgeois market and the increasing desirability of furniture designed for particular purposes in settled domestic establishments—led to its demise, as increasingly sophisticated buyers demanded change. Beginning in Italy in the 16th century, RENAISSANCE FURNITURE appeared, using a new design vocabulary, more secular than ecclesiastical in origin, reflecting the revolution in art and thought that finally laid the long medieval era to rest.

GOTHIC SCROLL-BACK WINDSOR CHAIR
See under WINDSOR CHAIR.

GOTHIC WINDSOR CHAIR
See under WINDSOR CHAIR.

GOUJON, JEAN (d. 1567)
French MANNERIST STYLE sculptor; a leader of the HENRI II STYLE. Principally a sculptor, Goujon is also associated with a type of heavily decorated cupboard featuring figures carved in high relief. Traditionally, many such pieces

were credited to him. Now, though, it seems more likely that he made little or no furniture himself; however, his sculptures influenced those who did.

GOURDIN, MICHEL (active 1752–77)

French MENUISIER who worked in the LOUIS XV and LOUIS XVI STYLES. Gourdin, who collaborated with his brother Jean-Baptiste (active 1748–76), was noted for chairs in the TRANSITION STYLE that linked ROCOCO FURNITURE with the newer, neoclassical Louis XVI style (*See* NEOCLASSICAL STYLE).

GOUTHIÈRE, PIERRE (1732–c. 1814)

French FONDEUR-CISELEUR of LOUIS XVI STYLE. Gouthière specialized in elaborate ORMOLU mounts, making much use of MATT GILDING, which he may have invented. He provided mounts for the leading cabinetmakers of the day, including J.-H. RIESENER and Adam WEISWEILER.

GOVERNOR WINTHROP DESK

Name given in the 19th century to an 18th-century AMERICAN QUEEN ANNE STYLE or AMERICAN CHIPPENDALE furniture form, a SLANT-TOP DESK with OXBOW FRONT. The term is a misnomer, for all three of the Colonial governors named Winthrop died long before the furniture form was made.

GRAGG, SAMUEL (1772–1855)

American chair maker, noted for his early use of the BENTWOOD technique. Gragg, a New Hampshire native, had moved to Boston by 1801. There, between 1808 and 1815, he produced several models of a patented chair form (*see* PATENT FURNITURE) called the "Elastic" chair. In this chair much of the traditional joinery was eliminated by the use of a single sheet of plywood that was bent into a form that constituted the stiles, back, seat and front legs. This novel experiment foreshadowed the work of Michael THONET by a generation.

GRANDFATHER CHAIR

Nineteenth-century name for WING CHAIR.

GRASSHOPPER LEGS

Structural device sometimes used on 18th-century CARD TABLE (1). Two rear legs were attached to a hinged frame that could be pulled out to support the unfolded top.

GRAVES, MICHAEL (b. 1934)

One of the most important 20th-century American architects; also a noted furniture designer. Graves's work typifies the new eclecticism of Post-Modern architecture (*see* POST-MODERN FURNITURE). Like his architecture, the lines, colors and decoration of Graves's furniture derive from a number of sources, most notably the 19th-century neoclassical tradition (*see* NEOCLASSICAL STYLE). Since 1980 Graves has designed furniture for commercial manufacture for Memphis (*see* Ettore SOTTSASS) and other firms.

GRAY, EILEEN (1878–1976)

Irish-born French architect and furniture designer associated with ART DECO and the INTERNATIONAL STYLE. Gray attended art school in London, learned lacquer work and became a lacquer restorer before moving to Paris in 1907. There she made lacquer paintings and established a workshop (1922) to produce lacquered furniture, mainly tables and screens, of her own design. She worked in an Art Deco style with a particular emphasis on the use of the glossy surface of the lacquer itself as the chief effect. In the 1930s she designed buildings and furniture, her style revealing the influence of LE CORBUSIER and the fundamentalist canons of Modernism. Gray was a prominent member of the UNION DES ARTISTES MODERNES.

GRECIAN COUCH

Early 19th-century term for a contemporary NEOCLASSICAL STYLE furniture form; long, upholstered bench with high head-rest and half-back. (*See* COUCH.)

GREEK FURNITURE

Furniture of the ancient Greek world, made from about the ninth century B.C. and predominant in the settled portions of the Mediterranean coast from roughly the fifth century B.C. until the time of Christ. Very lit-

chair by Gragg

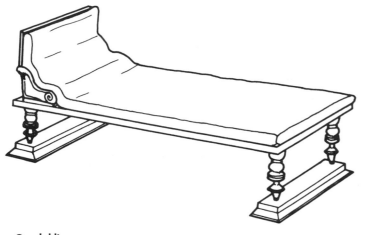

Greek kline

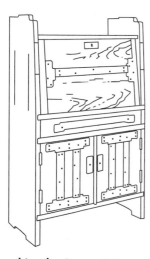

cabinet by Greene & Greene

tle Greek furniture survives, but a great many images of it do, and scholars are familiar with a wide range of forms. Greek furniture had its roots in EGYPTIAN FURNITURE, and a number of Egyptian forms survived throughout the period.

One that did not was the Egyptian bed, which changed drastically. Influenced by MESOPOTAMIAN FURNITURE, the Greeks expanded its functions to include use for reclining at meals as well as for sleeping; it thus was the most important piece of domestic furniture. It was accordingly modified in structure, becoming the characteristic Greek form, the KLINE.

Greek seating ranged from thrones to humble stools. Thrones, reserved for people of importance (and deities), tended to be heavily ornamented, often with rosettes or palmettes. Sometimes they had low backs shaped like a horse's or a lion's head; sometimes high backs terminating in volutes or heads of swans or serpents; sometimes no backs—simply monumental stools. When arms and stretchers came into use, early in the period, they, too, were ornamented with carving.

Most Greek domestic seating resembled its Egyptian models closely. Notable forms were the DIPHROS; the DIPHROS OKLADIAS; a low, undecorated stool that menial workers used; and a low seat that was essentially a small, inverted box. However, the most characteristic chair of the period, the KLISMOS, was a Greek innovation. A variety of footstools were also made. Their construction was simple, and they had varying degrees of ornamentation.

The greeks used tables much more than the Egyptians did, and they created a number of types. All were small and light, intended for use at meals and stored beneath the *kline* at other times. The most common form had an oblong or rectangular top on three legs, two at one end and one centered at the other; four-legged versions were also made. These light tables were used by one diner. In about the fifth century B.C., variations began to develop. These included a circular table on three legs terminating in deer's hooves. The Romans continued to make such forms.

The Greeks had few household goods, and many of these were hung on the walls when not in use, so the CUPBOARD was not yet needed. It first appeared in Hellenistic times (after 323 B.C.), late in the Greek period, when it may have been invented for the purpose of storing books. The CHEST continued, as in earlier epochs, to be the only important case furniture, and the Greeks used Egyptian forms, as a rule (*see* KIBOTOS).

GREEK KEY (also *meander pattern*)
Another name for KEY PATTERN.

GREENE & GREENE
American architecture and design firm created by two brothers, Charles Sumner Greene (1868–1957) and Henry Mather Greene (1870–1954), California architects and furniture designers associated with the American ARTS AND CRAFTS MOVEMENT. Originally from Cincinnati, the Greene brothers studied architecture at MIT, graduated in 1892 and moved to Pasadena, California, the next year. There they practiced architecture together and designed neo-Georgian houses until they evolved their own distinctive style. After Charles's visit to England in 1901, the brothers' work shows the progressive influence of Philip WEBB and the Arts and Crafts movement. Charles and Henry's knowledge of both Japanese and Chinese art also influenced the modern design style they developed for their architecture and furniture.

Their furniture is clean-lined, simple and rectilinear in form, and with traditional joinery, exposed or indicated, in the manner of their British predecessors and Gustav STICKLEY'S MISSION FURNITURE, which they knew and admired. However, Greene & Greene furniture was more consciously sophisticated than Stickley's, with more decoration and with such features as smoothed edges, tapered stiles and the "stepped" outlines of Chinese design. Their pieces were also more obviously costly, generally being made of walnut, mahogany or teak, having some carved ornamentation and inlays of ebony and rosewood, silver or semi-precious stones. Though rich, this decoration was modest in character and extent, and the design ideals of the Arts and Crafts tradition and Stickley were not compromised. Indeed, just as the Greenes promoted Stickley's furniture to their clients, Stickley praised Green & Greene furniture in his magazine, *The Craftsman.*

For their most important houses, the Greenes designed all the furniture, while for others only a few pieces (or none) might be made. The most important work of Greene & Greene—both architecturally and in furniture design—is encompassed in four great California houses, three of them in Pasadena and one in Berkeley, all designed between 1907 and 1909. The brothers parted after 1916, when Charles moved to Carmel, California. Though they both continued to practice architecture, neither designed more furniture.

GREGOTTI, VITTORIO (b. 1927)
Contemporary Italian architect, urban planner, furniture designer and writer on architecture and design. Gregotti has designed furniture in a mildly idiosyncratic version of the INTERNATIONAL STYLE. His best-known furniture design is a freestanding shelving and storage unit that slants toward the rear at the top, producing a ladderlike effect. He designs lighting and interiors as well.

GRENDEY, GILES (1693–1780)
Eighteenth-century British cabinet-maker. Grendey, father-in-law of John COBB, is best known for japanned furniture (*see* JAPANNING), which he exported in considerable quantity to Continental Europe. He also made mahogany furniture in a simple style.

GRIFFIN (also *griffon; gryphon*)
Decorative device representing mythological creature with eagle's head and wings and lion's body. Adapted from classical decoration by makers of RENAISSANCE FURNITURE, it was popular in all of the European NEOCLASSICAL STYLES.

GRILLE
Ornamental LATTICE of wood or metal used to protect glass doors on 18th-century secretaries (*see* SECRETARY), BOOK-CASES and CABINETS.

GRISAILLE
Decorative device; monochromatic painting in shades of grey, intended to mimic carving. Grisaille was popular on painted furniture in the late 18th and early 19th centuries.

GROHÉ, GUILLAUME (1808–85)
German-born French furniture maker of the Second Empire, noted for fine REPRODUCTION FURNITURE. Grohé, who arrived in Paris in 1827, was first an art dealer. He gradually became a maker and seller of furniture in a variety of REVIVAL STYLES. By the 1860s, he had moved into the field for which he is best known—the manufacture of reproductions of 18th-century French furniture. Renowned for the extraordinary quality of his craft, he was patronized by important collectors of furniture, including both French and British royalty.

GROPIUS, WALTER (1883–1969)
German architect, designer and teacher. Most famous as the founder and leading light of the BAUHAUS, Gropius, while principally an architect, had a great influence on modern furniture design. A believer in the beauty of practical, economic design (*see* FUNCTIONALISM), he and other Bauhaus designers stressed utilitarian style and the facilitation of manufacture by modern factory methods through improved design. He designed office furniture, interiors for railroad sleeping cars and domestic furniture, applying the functionalist esthetic of practicality in each area. He was also deeply interested in UNIT FURNITURE. Gropius did not design a great deal of furniture, but the work he did do is of considerable interest. His principal creation, the Bauhaus, had an enormous impact on modern design, particularly through the work of Marcel BREUER, Ludwig MIES VAN DER ROHE and other designers of the INTERNATIONAL STYLE. Upon the closing of the school in 1933, Gropius went first to Britain and later to the United States. After the Second World War, he established the Architect's Collaborative, an

griffin

American organization that brought together architects and designers interested in the Bauhaus design philosophy.

GROTESQUE ORNAMENT

Decorative device in RENAISSANCE, BAROQUE and ROCOCO FURNITURE, consisting of fields of small, generally bizarre, carved or painted images. Grotesque ornament was particularly important in MANNERIST STYLE design. Motifs included strangely rendered human heads; griffins and other fantastic creatures; and images from nature such as plants, birds and insects. Some of these were placed within CARTOUCHES, and the various elements were usually connected by ARABESQUE or STRAP-WORK designs. Grotesque ornament derived from ancient Roman interior decoration, which was excavated for the first time during the Renaissance.

GROULT, ANDRÉ (1884–1967)

French ART DECO furniture designer. Groult produced innovative furniture forms during the 1920s, in reaction against ART NOUVEAU. His furniture had *bombé* curves, plump upholstery and light-colored woods with decorative veneering in such rich materials as tortoise-shell or macassar ebony. He is particularly well known for pieces covered entirely in white SHAGREEN.

GRUBER, JACQUES (1870–1936)

French ART NOUVEAU glassmaker and furniture designer; member of the School of NANCY. Principally a glass-maker, Gruber also designed furniture at the Ecole de Nancy, in a

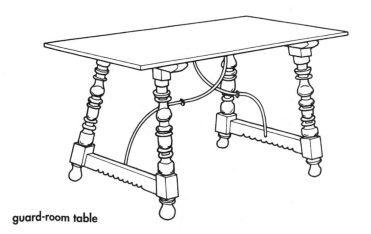

guard-room table

style similar to that of Émile GALLÉ, though heavier in proportion.

GUADAMECIL

Tooled and colored leather used as upholstery in Spanish RENAISSANCE FURNITURE. Originally a Moorish craft (the term derives from Gadames, a city in present-day Libya), *guadamecil* featured elaborate designs related to the MUDÉJAR STYLE and relying heavily on the ARABESQUE. It was exported to most of Europe for use on furniture and was especially popular in the 16th century in the Netherlands, then under Spanish rule.

GUAN MAO SHI (KUAN MAO SHIH)

CHINESE FURNITURE form made from Song (960–1279) through Qing (1644–1911) dynasties; chair whose back consisted of narrow central SPLAT topped by slender CREST RAIL, which often had EARS that jutted out slightly beyond the STILES. These ears were thought to resemble similar projections on the formal headdress worn by Mandarin scholar-officials and gave the chair its name, which means "scholar's-cap shape."

GUARD-ROOM TABLE

Modern name for a Spanish RENAISSANCE FURNITURE form. This table had two splayed legs at each end and a stretcher between them. It was strengthened by two wrought-iron rods, one joining each stretcher with the underside of the tabletop.

GUAREA

West African HARDWOOD, similar to MAHOGANY in appearance but stronger. The two varieties of guarea—one of which, scented guarea, smells like CEDAR—are used in furniture making both as solid wood and as plywood.

GUÉRIDON

Sculptural CANDLESTAND in which a candle is placed on a circular tray held by a BLACK-AMOOR figure. Originating in Italian BAROQUE FURNITURE, the *guéridon* was particularly popular in Italy, France and Britain in the 18th and early 19th centuries. The name is believed to come from that of a Moorish slave celebrated in 18th-century Provençal folk songs. The name is also applied to ordinary candlesticks, especially those that take the form of a light PEDESTAL TABLE with a small top, known in France as a *table en guéridon*.

GUGELOT, HANS (1920–64)

Swiss architect and designer associated with the post-Second World War German revival of the INTERNATIONAL STYLE. Best known for his designs for Kodak, Braun and other industrial clients, Gugelot also designed furniture, especially cabinet systems, for a number of manufacturers. He taught architecture and industrial design at the Hochschule für Gestaltung at Ulm, West Germany (*see* MAX BILL), from 1955 until his death. Gugelot, through his teaching and his work, had a great influence on German design of the period, helping to continue the spread of the functionalist ideals (*see* FUNCTIONALISM) of the BAUHAUS.

GUILFORD CHEST

Late 17th-century American furniture form; chest, usually of oak and pine, on four short legs with a drawer at the bottom. It received its name because many of the surviving pieces have come from the area around Guilford, Connecticut. The Guilford chest was similar to the HADLEY CHEST and the CONNECTICUT SUNFLOWER CHEST. Unlike them, though, it had no carved or applied ornamentation. It was painted only, in restrained curvilinear designs incorporating floral motifs from Tudor times and from Dutch sources.

GUILLOCHE

Decorative motif consisting of two bands or ribbons intertwining around a row of BOSSES. The ribbons join at each end of the figure to make a continuous band. The guilloche originated in ancient Greek architectural ornamen-

tation and was adapted by European furniture makers in all of the classically inspired traditions, beginning with RENAISSANCE FURNITURE. It was particularly popular in the British REGENCY STYLE.

GUIMARD, HECTOR (1867–1942)

French architect and furniture designer; a leader of the ART NOUVEAU movement. Guimard is best known for the entrances to the Paris Métro stations, which he designed in 1900. The style of these subway entrances typifies the sinuous, botanical French version of Art Nouveau; Guimard's work was so impressive that Art Nouveau is often called Style Métro in France. Primarily an architect and a follower of VIOLLET-LE-DUC, Guimard was also committed to the development of a new decorative style based on organic or abstract forms rather than on historical design references. His furniture was always designed to be part of an architectural context, but his pieces were strong enough to stand alone. His furniture forms had a deliberate and pronounced asymmetry and bold, curving lines including, frequently, the WHIPLASH CURVE motif—evidence of his desire to render fluidity and motion in furniture. His later work was less exuberant, but, unlike most Art Nouveau designers, Guimard continued to employ the style long after it became unfashionable.

cabinet by Guimard

GWATHMEY-SIEGEL

Contemporary American architecture and furniture design partnership associated with POST-MODERN FURNITURE. The two partners, Charles Gwathmey (b. 1938) and Robert Siegel (b. 1939), have developed a style that synthesizes elements from the European INTERNATIONAL STYLE, especially as developed by LE CORBUSIER, with the venacular architecture of New England. They have designed furniture for their own architectural commissions and for such manufacturers as Knoll International (*see* Florence Schust KNOLL).

HABERMANN, FRANZ XAVER (1721–96)

German sculptor and ROCOCO FURNITURE designer. Habermann, who worked in Augsburg, published designs for furniture, silverware and other objects. Most of his work was in a rococo manner influenced by the designs of J. M. HOPPENHAUPT. But late in his career, he produced NEOCLASSICAL STYLE work based on the French LOUIS XVI STYLE.

HADLEY CHEST

Hadley chest

Late 17th-century AMERICAN JACOBEAN FURNITURE type. The Hadley chest, usually of oak and pine, stood on four short legs with one, two or three drawers at the bottom. The front bore three recessed rectilinear panels and was decorated with shallow carving and then stained. An American variant of a standard English Jacobean style (*see* JACOBEAN FURNITURE) chest, the Hadley chest received its name because many of the known pieces have come from the Hadley, Massachusetts, area. Its decorations—simple designs of flowers, leaves and vines surrounding sets of initials—indicate that it was a piece of DOWER FURNITURE.

HAERTL, JOHANN (active c. 1810–15)

Austrian EMPIRE STYLE cabinetmaker. Haertl was the leading furniture maker in Vienna, where the French Empire style was rendered in a less formal, simpler vein that anticipated the BIEDERMEIER STYLE. Haertl specialized in ingenious designs for case furniture, such as cabinets whose fronts were shaped like lyres and a circular writing desk that resembled a classical temple.

HAINES, EPHRAIM (1755–1837)

American FEDERAL PERIOD furniture maker of Philadelphia. Haines was apprenticed to the cabinetmaker Daniel TROTTER, whose daughter he subsequently married. On his father-in-law's death, Haines inherited his business. Haines was a successful cabinetmaker, generally using the patterns published by Thomas SHERATON. Over time, however, Haines turned to the import and sale of exotic lumber to other makers and eventually became an entrepreneur rather than a craftsman.

HALF-ROUND MOLDING

Another name for SCOTIA MOLDING (*see under* MOLDING).

HALF-TESTER

In MEDIEVAL FURNITURE, bed CANOPY that did not extend all the way to the foot of the bed. The half-tester was intended for use by persons of less than the highest rank, for canopies in the Middle Ages had a hierarchical significance.

HALF-TURNING

See under TURNERY.

HALL CUPBOARD

Another name for the PRESS CUPBOARD, a 17th-century English and American furniture form. This name was more common in England and reflected the role of such a piece of furniture, which was typically placed in the entrance hall to display the solid prosperity of its owner. Sometimes the term is also applied to similarly grandiose pieces of different form, such as the COURT CUPBOARD (2) or the PRESS, when used in the same way.

HALL, JOHN (active c. 1840)
American architect and designer; author of first American PATTERN BOOK. Hall's *The Cabinet Maker's Assistant*, published in Baltimore in 1840, presented numerous designs in the PILLAR AND SCROLL STYLE.

HALL TABLE
Old name for REFECTORY TABLE.

HALLETT, WILLIAM (active 1732–70)
British ROCOCO FURNITURE maker. Although records reveal that Hallett was a fashionable and successful cabinetmaker of the day, no surviving pieces can be attributed to him.

HALVED JOINT
See CROSS-LAPPED JOINT, *under* JOINERY.

HANCOCK, WILLIAM (b. 1794, active to 1849)
Prominent Boston NEOCLASSICAL STYLE furniture maker and upholsterer of the 1820s–30s. Hancock, who is associated with the AMERICAN EMPIRE STYLE, was greatly influenced by the pattern books published in 1808 by George SMITH, the British REGENCY STYLE designer.

HANDICRAFT REVIVAL
Design trend in Britain and America in the 1970s toward finely crafted wood furniture rather than mass-produced pieces in new, synthetic materials. While looking back to pre-modern production ideals and, to some degree, styles, in reaction against FUNCTIONALISM and its effect on 20th-century design, the handicraft revivalists often develop innovative forms and types. The principal American practitioner, Wendell CASTLE, has designed furniture with swirling organic shapes somewhat reminiscent of GAUDI's work. Castle's later work has tended toward the classically inspired esthetic of POST-MODERN FURNI-

TURE. Castle's British counterpart, John MAKEPEACE, has devised a chest whose drawers, which are within no case or housing, pivot on a veneered steel column from which they are cantilevered. The influence of Makepeace has sparked a burgeoning interest in handcrafted furniture in Australia, most notably pursued by George INGHAM and Leon SADUBIN.

Unlike the followers of the British ARTS AND CRAFTS MOVEMENT of a century ago, these modern craftsmen are under no illusions about the market for which they produce. Their great emphasis on hand labor, tour-de-force designs and their frequent use of rare, exotic woods results in furniture that can only be afforded by wealthy collectors. However, these makers feel that their furniture preserves traditions threatened by industrialization, that it provides an intimate and spiritually valuable experience of the relationship between material and use and that the processes involved in handicraft generate a positive sense of involvement in production that the industrial ethos negates. The sensibility of this movement is suggested in the well-known epigram by the American craftsman Wharton ESHERICK: "A little of the hand, but the main thing is the heart and the head."

HANDKERCHIEF TABLE
American name for a type of DROP-LEAF TABLE. The handkerchief table pairs a triangular top with a triangular leaf; when the leaf is raised, the table has a square top.

HARDWARE
Metal fittings used on furniture to provide strength, protection or ornamentation. A very ancient practice, the use of hardware was known in EGYPTIAN FURNITURE, when metal hinges were first used. Iron was the most common hardware material until the 17th century. In MEDIEVAL FURNITURE elaborately shaped iron straps ornamented the CHEST, which was the chief item of furniture, while adding strength to its construction as well. Iron hardware also included protective corners, decorative hasps and lock plates. In RENAISSANCE FURNITURE, improved joinery succeeded in hiding most hinges, and door and drawer handles became the chief form of metal ornamentation, along with ESCUTCHEONS, which

hankerchief table

surrounded keyholes. Brass and bronze were used to make most metal handles, which at first were primarily DROP HANDLES. Late in the 17th century, the BAIL HANDLE became prominent, and the RING PULL followed in another hundred years. Handles and keyhole plates of this era are often collectively referred to as *brasses*. The other major type of furniture hardware that developed was the decorative mount, an applied ornamental device of brass or bronze intended both as decoration and as protection for veneers. Cast, chased and gilded, these were applied to corners, at the knees of CABRIOLE LEGS (*see under* LEG), as SABOTS on feet, along any edge or angle, and often in sweeping arrangements across veneered surfaces, incorporating any locks, handles or escutcheons. The decorative mount was especially important in French furniture of the late 17th through early 19th centuries and in French-inspired styles elsewhere. Decorative hardware has also been commonly used, especially for protective corners and lock plates, on CHINESE and JAPANESE FURNITURE.

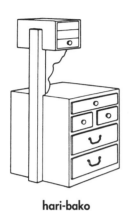

hari-bako

HARDWICK, PHILIP (1792–1870)

British architect and furniture designer. Principally an architect, Hardwick also designed NEOCLASSICAL STYLE furniture and later worked in the ROCOCO REVIVAL STYLE.

HARDWOOD

Wood from a broad-leaved tree, as opposed to SOFTWOOD, which comes from a needle-bearing tree. The term indicates the botanical origin of a wood and not its physical hardness or density. However, due to differences in the cellular makeup of the two types, there is a harder, denser range of woods among the hardwoods, However, some softwoods are physically harder than some hardwoods. Among hardwoods used in furniture, LIME-WOOD and POPLAR are quite soft; among the hardest are OAK and EBONY. Hardwoods, because of their close grain and durability, are generally valued for VENEER, for they provide greater protection.

Furniture that is to be unpainted or not otherwise covered is usually made of hardwoods. Oak, ELM, and BEECH are hardwoods traditionally important in furniture making. Notable hardwoods that began to be imported by European and American cabinetmakers in

the 18th century include MAHOGANY and ROSEWOOD.

HAREWOOD (also *silverwood*)
See SYCAMORE.

HARI-BAKO

Traditional JAPANESE FURNITURE form; tiny CHEST OF DRAWERS intended for use when sewing. A slender post rises from one side of the *hari-bako* to support a small open or lidded box containing a pincushion.

HASSOCK

Thick, firm cushion or thickly upholstered footstool with no exposed wood. An innovation of RENAISSANCE FURNITURE, the hassock is particularly associated with places of worship, where it serves as a pad to kneel on.

HATRACK

Furniture form with hooks or pegs for hanging hats or other garments. Ranging in design from a simple pole or wall plaque bearing pegs to a freestanding structure, often incorporating a bench, a mirror or an umbrealla stand, the hatrack was most elaborately developed in 19th-century Britain.

HAUPT, GEORG (1741–84)

Leading late 18th-century Swedish cabinet-maker. Haupt, born in Sweden of German parents, was apprenticed in Germany and then worked in Holland, Paris and London before returning to Stockholm in 1769. In France he was greatly influenced by the work of J.-F. OEBEN and J.-H. RIESENER, and in Sweden he worked in the French LOUIS XVI STYLE, using the full repertoire of French neoclassical motifs, especially favoring a bold VITRUVIAN SCROLL.

HAZELL, STEPHEN (active c. 1845–70)

British maker of WINDSOR CHAIRS. Hazell, who worked in Oxford, was noted for several widely imitated features in Windsor chair designs. These included OGEE-curved arms, supported at the front by turned BALUSTERS, and the addition of an OPENWORK circle around the junction of the diagonals in the back of a TABLET-BACK WINDSOR CHAIR (*see under* WINDSOR CHAIR).

HAZEL PINE

British name for American RED GUM.

HEADBOARD

Part of a BED; panel behind, and usually rising above, the pillowed end of a bed—that is, its head.

HEADREST

Furniture form; low horizontal support for head of sleeping person, intended to prevent disturbance of an elaborate hairdo. In ancient EGYPTIAN FURNITURE a headrest was often used on a bed. In AFRICAN and the PRIMITIVE FURNITURE of tribal cultures, the headrest is placed on the ground and is commonly a horizontal bar on two short feet, or it may simply be a low platform. In Japan the MAKURA, a low box, has traditionally served the same function.

HEAL, AMBROSE (1872–1959)

British entrepreneur, furniture designer and writer. Heal inherited a furniture-manufacturing company, Heal & Sons, that was associated with the progressive designs of the late 19th and early 20th centuries, particularly with the ARTS AND CRAFTS MOVEMENT and ART NOUVEAU. Heal himself designed Arts and Crafts style pieces, often with considerable inlays of metals and woods of contrasting colors. Later, in the 1920s, he adapted new materials, such as tubular steel, to traditional designs. He was also the author of a well-known book, *The London Furniture Makers from the Restoration to the Victorian Era: 1660–1840,* a scholarly compendium of registry data.

HEAL, CHRISTOPHER (b. 1911)

British furniture designer associated with the INTERNATIONAL STYLE before the Second World War and with the CONTEMPORARY STYLE afterward. A son of Ambrose HEAL, Christopher Heal studied architecture, then textile and furniture design, before joining his father's furniture manufacturing firm in 1934. By 1936 he was exhibiting his furniture with that of such International style designers as Marcel BREUER, Maxwell FRY and Raymond MCGRATH. After the war he was one of the designers encouraged by Gordon RUSSELL to develop the Contemporary style of the 1950s.

HEIN, PIET (1905–95)

Danish writer, mathematician, artist and designer. In the 1960s Hein, in collaboration with Bruno MATHSSON, designed some well-known tables and chairs. He was also a noted urban designer. Perhaps best known as an epigrammatic poet, Hein invented an idiosyncratic verse form that he calls the "grook."

HENKELS, GEORGE J. (1819–83)

Philadelphia cabinetmaker associated with the American ROCOCO REVIVAL STYLE. Active from the 1840s until 1877, Henkels used the laminating and woodbending techniques of John Henry BELTER in a milder, less exuberant variant of neo-rococo. He published a book on furniture, *Household Economy,* in 1867.

HENRI II STYLE

MANNERIST STYLE in France; second of two phases of French RENAISSANCE FURNITURE. Named after Henri II (ruled 1547–59), who instigated its development, the style continued to flourish through the reigns of François II (1559–60), Charles IX (1560–74) and Henri III (1574–89). Henri II encouraged a style in the decorative arts that was more distinctly French than that of the preceding Italianate period (*see* FRANÇOIS I STYLE). France had become a political and economic leader in Europe, and it was felt that the appurtenances of courtly life should reflect this new grandeur without relying too heavily on foreign cultural sources. In addition to the royal initiative, new designs were encouraged by a newly confident French upper middle class. This prosperous group used increasing quantities of furniture in an increasingly wide variety of ways, and they, too, wanted pieces that reflected their nationality.

Among the artists whom the king patronized were architect Philibert De L'Orme

(1510–70), sculptor Jean GOUJON and architect and designer Jacques Androuet DU CERCEAU. Du Cerceau's influence was intensified by the publication of several PATTERN BOOKS. Another important furniture designer was the Burgundian Hughes SAMBIN, who is sometimes called the first French cabinetmaker.

Though in the mainstream of international Mannerism, Henri II style decoration was remarkably sculptural, with a particular emphasis on the human figure. Other popular motifs were animals, including eagles, lions, rams and such imaginary creatures as griffins, sphinxes and chimeras. These elements were united by ARABESQUES and STRAPWORK of extraordinary complexity.

Along with this distinctive slant to decoration, more diverse forms appeared in Henri II style furniture. The CHEST remained the most prominent piece of case furniture, but various types of CUPBOARD, notably the ARMOIRE À DEUX CORPS, began to usurp its functions. The DRAW-LEAF TABLE was much admired, and its principle was applied to pieces ranging from the simple to the grandest table of the time, the TABLE À L'ITALIENNE. Tables were frequently enriched with elaborate MARQUETRY, imported PIETRE DURE work or gilded marble. Another common feature was a PENDANT FINIAL below each corner of a tabletop. Chairs, which became lighter and more movable, often had an open back with a SPLAT. Various types of armchairs proliferated, including the CAQUETOIRE, a strikingly innovative design of the time. Other common forms of seating were the PLACET and the HASSOCK, both elaborations of the STOOL. While the bed CANOPY remained in use, decoration on the bed itself assumed prominence. Headboards were heavily carved, and extravagant corner posts incorporated CARYATIDS and TERMS.

By the 1570s most of the leaders of the Henri II style had died, and later work reverted to pedantic derivations from classical architecture. The Wars of Religion (1562–98) limited the nation's capacity for cultural innovation, and the Henri II style was the last major development in French furniture before the reign of Louis XIV (*see* LOUIS XIII STYLE; LOUIS XIV STYLE).

HEPPLEWHITE, GEORGE (d. 1786)

British ADAM STYLE cabinetmaker whose posthumously published furniture designs exemplified the NEOCLASSICAL STYLE in Britain in the late 1780s and 1790s. Although records show that Hepplewhite was a practicing cabinetmaker, no furniture that can be attributed to him has survived. His fame rests on a book of about 300 of his designs, *Cabinet-Maker and Upholsterer's Guide,* published by his widow in 1788, two years after his death, and reissued in 1789 and 1794. Several of his designs also appeared in Thomas SHEARER's *Designs for Household Furniture.*

Hepplewhite modified the neoclassical furniture style of Robert ADAM, using slimmer elements in furniture that was both visually and physically lighter. He also softened the cold angularity of earlier Adam style work with gentle curves, especially by using SERPENTINE fronts and BOW FRONTS in chests of drawers and a variety of smoothly curving shapes in chair backs. A hallmark design was the SHIELD-BACK CHAIR, which he made widely popular, though he did not invent it, as is sometimes believed. He also frequently used the PRINCE OF WALES FEATHERS motif in chair backs and designed upholstered chair seats and sometimes backs. His chair and table legs were tapered and round or square in section; when square, they generally terminated in a SPADE FOOT (*see under* FOOT). He shunned elaborate and costly gilding, common in early Adam style work, but he did favor JAPANNING and MARQUETRY veneers. In keeping with the light coloring of the Adam style, Hepplewhite's preferred material was SATINWOOD.

Hepplewhite's *Guide* had so great an impact that all furniture resembling its designs is often referred to as *Hepplewhite style.* Like Thomas CHIPPENDALE's *Director,* it made its author's name a household word, both in Britain and in America, where the book strongly influenced makers of FEDERAL PERIOD furniture. Hepplewhite's influence was also felt in northern Europe, especially the Netherlands, in the last years of the 18th century.

HERBST, RENÉ (1891–1982)

French furniture designer in the INTERNATIONAL STYLE. A founding member of the UNION DES ARTISTES MODERNES and its president after the Second World War, Herbst was a leading exponent of French International style furniture design. His elegant seating furniture in tubular steel is especially notable.

American Hepplewhite

HERITAGE, ROBERT (b. 1927)
British CONTEMPORARY STYLE furniture designer. A one-time student of R. D. RUSSELL and a former staff designer for Race Furniture (see Ernest RACE), Heritage is a well-known designer of clean-lined furniture, often using innovative materials, such as cast aluminum and molded polyurethane. He has also designed cutlery, lighting and appliances.

HERMAN MILLER FURNITURE CO.
Contemporary Michigan furniture-manufacturing company associated with post-war American design, especially that of Charles EAMES. In 1931 Gilbert ROHDE, a designer employed by the company, first encouraged the firm to produce furniture from new designs. Within a few years, the firm was committed to this new direction and phased out its more traditional models. The Herman Miller Co.'s rise to its acknowledged international leadership in the marketing of progressively designed furniture began in 1946. In that year George NELSON, the company's new design director, recruited Eames, whose furniture the company has produced ever since. Nelson's ERGONOMIC DESIGN work has also been a staple product, notably including an innovative line of office systems. The firm has also manufactured noteworthy furniture designed by Verner PANTON, Isamu NOGUCHI and Don CHADWICK. With Knoll International (see Florence Schust KNOLL), the Herman Miller Furniture Co. has dominated the international furniture market over the last 30 years and has contributed to the widespread popularity of modern design today.

HERRERA STYLE
Another name for DESORNAMENTADO STYLE.

HERRINGBONE BANDING
See BANDING.

HERTER BROTHERS
New York interior decorators and furniture manufacturers of late 19th century. The brothers Christian and Gustav Herter, German immigrants, established their New York workshop in 1851. They made ordinary revivalist furniture at first, then became one of the principal American exponents of the Eastlake style (see Charles Locke EASTLAKE), producing furniture that was progressive by British standards. Later, when Japanese design (see JAPONISME) grew in popularity, they made fine, simply built furniture of ebonized wood with elaborate marquetry of Japanese motifs. One example of this work is the suite of furniture made for the railroad baron Jay Gould, which is now in the Metropolitan Museum of Art in New York.

HETSCH, GUSTAV FRIEDRICH (active 1820s–1850s)
Leading DANISH EMPIRE STYLE decorator and designer of ornamentation. Though Hetsch is best known as the director of the Copenhagen porcelain factory, he concerned himself with design of all sorts. Both through his own work and as a long-time professor at the Danish Academy, he had a great influence on all of the decorative arts in Denmark, including furniture making. As a young man, he had studied in Paris under Charles Percier (see PERCIER AND FONTAINE), and he accordingly favored a scholarly, if dramatic, NEOCLASSICAL STYLE that stressed an awareness of antique models. He furthered the survival of the Empire style in Denmark long after it had faded from fashion in France.

H-HINGE
See under HINGE.

HIBACHI
Traditional JAPANESE FURNITURE form; vessel containing burning coals, intended to heat parts of a house. *Hibachis* were made of earthenware, bronze, iron and porcelain, but the most common variety was a wooden box with an open compartment in the top, lined with sheet copper placed over a layer of clay. The paneled box often contained various drawers and compartments that were used to store tea, incense, bottles for heating sake or pipes. Used with a KOTATSU stand to provide a heated shelter over a section of floor, the *hibachi* was the winter gathering place in a traditional Japanese household.

HICKORY
HARDWOOD native to eastern United States; light reddish brown in color. Extremely strong

and durable, yet quite flexible, hickory was commonly used for the back spindles and for the arm and crest rails of American WINDSOR CHAIRS. It was also used for most ADIRON-DACK FURNITURE.

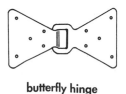

highboy

HIGHBOY

Eighteenth-century American furniture form; case piece composed of a STAND, fitted with drawers, that supported a narrower and taller CHEST OF DRAWERS. Essentially a British CHEST-ON-STAND produced in American styles of the 18th century, the highboy generally had three or more drawers in its lower element. This stand stood on four or more legs, which were usually joined by low stretchers, and was frequently reproduced separately as a matching DRESSING TABLE, the LOWBOY. The upper section contained four or more tiers of wide drawers that spanned the front of the piece. Often, highboys resembled the British TALLBOY in that the top two tiers were divided into two or three narrower drawers. Usually, the upper chest's drawers were graduated in height, with the tallest at the bottom. The term *highboy* was introduced in the late 19th century; in its own time, the piece was known as *high chest* or a *chest-on-frame*.

HIGH CHAIR

Small, long-legged dining chair intended for a child, raising him or her to a level convenient for feeding by an adult. Though not widespread until the 18th century, the high chair has been known since ancient times, when it appeared in GREEK FURNITURE.

HIGH CHEST (also *high chest of drawers*)

Eighteenth-century name for HIGHBOY.

HIGH-TECH STYLE

Furniture and interior-decoration design style made popular in the United States in the 1970s. The style is characterized by the use of industrial, utilitarian materials and equipment in domestic settings. An extreme and sometimes ironic decorative application of FUNC-TIONALISM, high-tech, also called *Industrial style,* is a phenomenon diametrically opposed to the contemporaneous HANDICRAFT REVIVAL. High-tech combines the impersonal ethos of

industrial efficiency with an enthusiasm for novelty. Notable high-tech designers include the Italian Gae AULENTI, the Americans Joseph D'URSO and David ROWLAND, and the Englishman Rodney Kinsman.

HIGH VICTORIAN STYLE

Another name for the ROCOCO REVIVAL STYLE in Britain.

HILL, OLIVER (1887–1968)

British architect and designer of the 1930s. Hill, an architect who designed furniture for his own buildings, created furniture in the INTERNATIONAL STYLE, following French and German models. His interest in experimental materials led him to design notable furniture made of glass or stone. He also designed several exhibitions promoting innovative design for furniture and other objects.

HILL, THOMAS (1829–1908)

Nineteenth-century American painter. Born in Britain, Hill is well known as a landscape painter of the American West and as a follower of Albert Bierstadt. He began his artistic career in Massachusetts as a painter of COT-TAGE FURNITURE, and his work is among the finest surviving examples of that genre.

HINGE

Device consisting of two metal plates or wings, each mounted along one edge to the same pin or post. It permits a furniture part attached to one of the plates, such as a door or a lid, to be pivoted relative to a stationary part, attached to the other plate. Hinges have been known since ancient times and have frequently been decorated. The two plates of a hinge may be in various shapes and arrangements, and a number of these configurations are distinguished by name.

BUTTERFLY HINGE

Type of wrought-iron HARDWARE developed in the Middle Ages and especially popular in AMERICAN JACOBEAN FURNITURE. Each wing of a butterfly hinge was shaped like a trapezoid. The narrow sides met at the pivot, creating, when open, a form resembling a butterfly.

butterfly hinge

COCK'S-HEAD HINGE (also *cockscomb hinge*)
Hinge in which each of the two plates is cut to resemble the silhouette of a rooster's head. Originating in the Middle Ages, the cock's-head hinge was most common in English TUDOR and JACOBEAN FURNITURE.

DEVIL-TAIL HINGE
Another name for RAT-TAIL HINGE (*see under* HINGE).

H-HINGE
Hinge with slender rectangular plates, each parallel to and much longer than the central pin. When open, the hinge resembles a letter *H,* with the short central pin as a thick crossbar.

H-L HINGE
Hinge with slender rectangular plates parallel to and much longer than the central pin, as in an H-HINGE (*see under* HINGE); however, one plate has a similarly slender, rectangular arm extending at a right angle from one end. When open, the hinge therefore resembles a combination of the letters *H* and *L.*

HORSESHOE-AND-STRAP HINGE
Hinge in which one plate is straplike and extends perpendicularly away from the central pin, while the other resembles a horseshoe and is attached to the pin by its round, or closed, end.

L-HINGE
Hinge in which one plate has two long, slender arms perpendicular to each other. One of them is parallel to the central pin, which it meets near the angle.

PIN HINGE
Hinge used on chests in early GOTHIC FURNITURE in the 12th and 13th centuries. A flange at each end of the lid overlapped the sides of the chest at the rear, and a horizontal bolt, or pin, passed through it and through the side to the back.

RAT-TAIL HINGE (also *devil-tail hinge*)
Hinge in which one plate takes the form of a thin, tapering strap and extends away from the central pin in a direction roughly parallel to the pin but describing a shallow S-curve.

STRAP HINGE
Hinge whose long, straplike plates extend perpendicularly away from the central pin to either side. The strap hinge was common on chests in MEDIEVAL FURNITURE.

HINOKI (also *Japanese cypress*)
Japanese SOFTWOOD used for framing of Japanese chests (*see* TANSU), especially the KAIDAN-DANSU, or staircase chest. Like SUGI, *hinoki* stains unevenly and is therefore traditionally coated with dark lacquer.

HIP
Another name for the KNEE of a CABRIOLE LEG (*see under* LEG).

HIP-JOINT CHAIR
In RENAISSANCE FURNITURE, the name for an X-FRAME chair, especially its Spanish version, the SILLÓN DE CADERA.

HIPPING
Carved ornamentation on the KNEE of a CABRIOLE LEG (*see under* LEG), especially when it is extended onto or above the chair's SEAT RAIL.

HISPANO-MORESQUE FURNITURE

Spanish GOTHIC FURNITURE that incorporated elaborate MUDÉJAR STYLE geometrical inlay work practiced by Moorish craftsmen living in Spain. Using small pieces of wood in complicated patterns that extended over much of a given surface, Hispano-Moresque furniture makers created an encrusted effect that remained popular in Spain into the period of RENAISSANCE FURNITURE. Though often accompanied by Christian religious images, these patterns reflected the common Islamic prohibition against the portrayal of human or animal forms.

cock's-head hinge

H-hinge

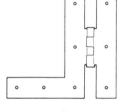

H-L hinge

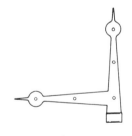

horseshoe and strap hinge

L-hinge

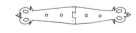

rat-tail hinge

strap hinge

Hitchcock chair

HITCHCOCK, LAMBERT (1795–1852)

Connecticut chair maker. Hitchcock produced, in 1826–44, distinctive, stencil-decorated "fancy" chairs (*see* "FANCY" FURNITURE), which are known today as "Hitchcock" chairs. Hitchcock was a cabinetmaker by training and first manufactured parts for other chair makers. Then he established his own chair factory at Barkhamstead (later Hitchcocksville, now Riverton), Connecticut, where he developed his distinctive style. A "Hitchcock" chair has turned front legs, with the rear legs extending upward to become the stiles. The turned crest rail has an enlarged center section, on which there is a decorative motif. A wide CROSS RAIL across the open back contains the main decoration. The chair usually has a rush seat, sometimes a cane or wooden one. It is generally painted black, and the back, stiles, rails and legs are always decorated in paint with stenciled, or occasionally freehand, renderings of flowers, fruit and abstract ornamentation. Apparently a poor businessman, Hitchcock lost his business and died insolvent. The factory was reopened in 1946 and produces Hitchcock reproductions.

H-L HINGE

See under HINGE.

HOENTSCHEL, GEORGES (1855–1915)

French architect, designer and potter, associated with the French ART NOUVEAU movement. Best known as a potter, Hoentschel also designed furniture for Samuel BING in a heavy Art Nouveau style involving sculptural ornamentation.

HOFFMANN, JOSEF (1870–1956)

Austrian architect and designer; a founder of the Vienna SEZESSION and major figure in the ART NOUVEAU movement. Hoffmann was influenced by the ideals of the ARTS AND CRAFTS MOVEMENT, and he traveled in Britain and became a close friend of C. R. ASHBEE. As a major figure of the Art Nouveau movement, Hoffmann sought a new design style that would not refer to styles of the past. Through the influence of Charles Rennie MACKINTOSH and the GLASGOW SCHOOL, Hoffmann and other Viennese designers developed a severe, geometrical, abstract style quite at variance with the organic, curvilinear mode of French and

cabinet by Josef Hoffmann

Belgian Art Nouveau. This style later became associated with the Viennese movement known as the Sezession, of which Hoffmann was the dominant figure. His own furniture combined rich materials and elaborate inlays with inventive rectilinear forms. He was nicknamed "Square" Hoffmann for his love of black and white squares as a decorative motif. Hoffmann also helped found, with Kolo MOSER, the WIENER WERKSTÄTTE, a workshop modeled on Ashbee's Guild of Handicrafts. In general, Hoffmann designed furniture only for his own buildings, to ensure a unified scheme of architecture and decoration, though he also designed pieces for Thonet & Sons (*see* Michael THONET). Hoffmann designed metalwork, jewelry and glassware as well, and these designs were executed by the Werkstätte. Wolfgang HOFFMANN was his son.

HOFFMANN, WOLFGANG (1900–69)

Austrian-American furniture designer. The son of Josef HOFFMANN, Wolfgang studied under his father at the WIENER WERKSTÄTTE before moving to New York in 1925 to work with Joseph URBAN. After 1934, he worked for a company in Illinois, designing a range of furniture, usually with chromium-plated steel frames.

HOGARTH CHAIR

Nineteenth-century name for 18th-century SPOON-BACK CHAIR, referring to painter William Hogarth (1697–1764), who included the form in many of his paintings.

HOLLAND, HENRY (1745–1806)

British architect and furniture designer; important early exponent of REGENCY STYLE in 1790s. Holland was principally an architect, but, seeking stylistic unity, he also designed furniture for his buildings. In the eclectic spirit of the Regency period, he incorporated elements from ancient Greek and Roman sources and from contemporary French work in the late LOUIS XVI STYLE. He financed the work of C. H. TATHAM in Rome, receiving in return many sketches of classical and ancient Egyptian ornamental details, which he used in his own designs. Among the devices Tatham reported on was the MONOPOD, which Holland then applied to Regency furniture and made popular.

Holland's furniture may have stimulated Thomas SHERATON to feature more archeologically inspired classical designs in his later books, which in any case included several of Holland's pieces. Holland also commissioned work from notable British and French cabinet-makers of the day, including John LINNELL and Adam WEISWEILER.

HOLLEIN, HANS (b. 1934)
Post-Modern Austrian architect, designer and decorator. Hollein, in reaction against FUNCTIONALISM and the dominance of the INTERNATIONAL STYLE and its successors, has used historical design elements and nonrational ornamentation, as other POST-MODERN FURNITURE designers have done. His highly idiosyncratic work recalls the Cubis, avantgarde branch of ART DECO design in its emphasis on decoration, its penchant for novelty and its richness of materials.

HOLLY
Pale HARDWOOD, greyish white and uniform in color and smooth in texture, sometimes used as veneering. Holly is seldom used in furniture due to its rarity and its irregular grain, which is difficult to work with. However, holly takes staining very well and is often used, dyed black, as a substitute for EBONY veneer. Also, in the early 18th century, undyed holly enjoyed a vogue as a vividly contrasting element in MARQUETRY, especially in the 18th-century British ADAM STYLE.

HONEYSUCKLE ORNAMENT
Another name for ANTHEMION motif.

HONG MU (HUNG MU)
Variety of PADAUK used in CHINESE FURNITURE; very heavy, dark brownish red wood.

HOOF FOOT
See under FOOT.

HOOK, WILLIAM (1777–1867)
Salem, Massachusetts, maker of NEOCLASSICAL STYLE furniture in the early 19th century. Noted for his bold inlay work, Hook was particularly influenced by British REGENCY STYLE. He made a number of massive cases for pipe organs, whose works were built by his sons George and Elias.

HOPE, THOMAS (1769–1831)
British writer, collector and furniture designer; important early leader of REGENCY STYLE. Heir to a Scottish banking fortune, Hope traveled widely in Greece and the Near East as a young man, studying classical art and architecture and collecting ancient artifacts. After settling in London in 1796, he continued collecting, adding contemporary neoclassical work to his enthusiasms. He made frequent trips to Rome and Paris, where he was acquainted with many artists and designers, including PERCIER AND FONTAINE. He designed elaborate neoclassical rooms in his London home to house his collections, and he also designed the furniture for these rooms, attempting to copy ancient furniture known from Greek vase painting. He zealously studied the engravings of the French Egyptologist Baron DENON and was prompted to design furniture in emulation of ancient Egyptian models. He is best known for these pieces, through which the taste for ÉGYPTIENNERIE became established in Britain. His house was open to interested visitors—one may have been Thomas SHERATON, who, in 1803, first published Egyptian motifs in Britain—and, in 1807, Hope published his designs for it in a book, *Household Furniture and Interior Decoration*. This work was influential throughout the Regency period, and George SMITH popularized many of its somewhat academic and stilted designs. Hope also influenced AMERICAN EMPIRE STYLE cabinet-makers, especially Duncan PHYFE.

chair by Hope

HOPKINS, GERRARD (active 1767–93)
Maker of AMERICAN CHIPPENDALE FURNITURE. The son of Samuel Hopkins, a Baltimore cabinetmaker, Gerrard Hopkins served an apprenticeship in Philadelphia and learned the elaborate design style practiced there (*see* PHILADELPHIA CHIPPENDALE FURNITURE). He then returned to Baltimore and became a prominent furniture maker.

HOPPENHAUPT, JOHANN MICHAEL (1709–c. 1755)
German designer of ROCOCO FURNITURE and interiors. Beginning in 1740, Hoppenhaupt

and his brother Johann Christian (1719–86) worked under Johann August NAHL for Frederick the Great of Prussia at Potsdam. Six years later, Johann Michael became Frederick's chief designer; he retired in 1750. His furniture is noted for contrasts of plain VENEER and complicated MARQUETRY panels. From 1751 until his death, he published many ornamental designs for furniture and other objects in a bizarre and elaborate mode based on French LOUIS XV–STYLE design. These widely known engravings influenced Franz HABERMANN and Thomas JOHNSON, among others.

HORN FURNITURE

Furniture—usually small CHAIRS, SETTEES or HATRACKS—made from the horns or antlers of deer, elk, buffalo, cattle and other animals. Horn furniture was first made in rural Europe at least as long ago as the Middle Ages. Gradually, these vernacular pieces came to the attention of makers of fashionable furniture; for instance, in the 18th century, Robert MANWARING published designs for horn chairs. In the mid-19th century, a love of novelty made horn furniture quite popular in Europe, especially in Germany and Britain. London, Hamburg and Frankfurt became the principal centers of its manufacture. In the United States the late 19th century saw the beginning of a long-lived vogue for picturesque reminders of the vanishing western frontier, and furniture was made from the horns of buffalo and Texas longhorn cattle. Shards of horn have also been used as MARQUETRY elements in fine furniture—notably by the great 17th-century French furniture maker A.-C. BOULLE.

horn chair

chair by Horta

HORRIX, MATTHIJS (1735–1809)

German-born Dutch cabinetmaker; a noted maker of French-style commodes. Horrix, born near Krefeld, Germany, was registered as a master craftsman in The Hague by 1764, and he had probably learned his craft in Paris, for he quickly became the leading Dutch maker of finely inlaid LOUIS XV–STYLE furniture. While making a range of forms, he specialized in COMMODES À ENCOIGNURES.

HORSE-HOOF FOOT

See under FOOT.

HORSE SCREEN

Another name for CHEVAL SCREEN.

HORSESHOE-AND-STRAP HINGE

See under HINGE.

HORTA, VICTOR (1861–1947)

Belgian architect and furniture designer; a major figure of the ART NOUVEAU movement. Principally an architect, Horta designed furniture for the houses he built in Brussels in the late 1800s and early 1900s. His first building, erected in 1893, was a watershed in the development of Art Nouveau. The house and furniture featured sweeping, rhythmic curves in botanical and abstract motifs. The design was so revolutionary that it was difficult for contemporaries to absorb; one critic remarked that "no detail derives from anything at all in existence," while in fact a great deal of floral imagery had been used. Horta was less rigorous than his contemporary, Henri VAN DE VELDE, in rejecting stylistic elements from the past, and Horta's furniture forms were often taken from French ROCOCO FURNITURE. His designs, however, were anything but derivative; some forms took on botanical shapes, and pieces were often made of such varied materials as cast iron, stained glass, metalwork and tile. As did all Art Nouveau designers, he sought to develop a unity of decorative theme in any given architectural context; his unifying motif was most frequently the WHIPLASH CURVE. Horta's work influenced Art Nouveau furniture makers for as long as the style was current, though he had stopped designing furniture by 1905.

HOUSED JOINT

Another name for DADO JOINT (*see under* JOINERY).

H. S. MASTER, THE (active c. 1530–1551 or later)

Name given to a 16th-century South German RENAISSANCE FURNITURE maker and designer. Known only by his initials, which he used on woodcuts and at least one piece of furniture, a chest dated 1551, this craftsman is believed to have practiced in Augsburg or Nuremberg. His woodcuts appeared in about

1330, constituting the first PATTERN BOOK of furniture designs. The H. S. Master was clearly familiar with the new Renaissance fashions from Italy. He employed motifs derived from the classical ORDERS OF ARCHITECTURE, such as columns and capitals, along with carved foliate scrolls and inlaid architectural scenes in accomplished perspective.

H-STRETCHER
See under STRETCHER.

HU CHUANG (HU CH'UANG)
Early CHINESE FURNITURE form that developed late in Han dynasty (c. 200 A.D.); any seat raised off the ground, a Western novelty probably derived from INDIAN FURNITURE. Literally meaning "barbarian seat," the term *hu chuang* persisted for several centuries, denoting a stool, chair or couch. Later, the reference to Western origins was dropped, and the term CHUANG was used. Prior to the introduction of such furniture, the Chinese sat on mats on the floor or ground, sometimes using the JI, an armrest or backrest.

HUA MU
Chinese name for BURL VENEER, literally meaning "flower wood."

HUA QI (HUA CH'I)
Painted LACQUER used on CHINESE FURNITURE during Ming (1368–1644) and Qing (1644–1911) dynasties. On a black or brown or red lacquer ground, craftsmen painted various sorts of pictorial imagery in gold or polychrome lacquers. Each stroke was painted several times, and the image was smoothed with a pumice stone after each application. In the 17th and 18th centuries, much *hua qi* lacquer was exported to Europe, where many furniture makers used sections of it as decorative paneling.

HUA ZHUO (HUA CHO)
CHINESE FURNITURE form of Ming (1368–1644) and Qing (1644–1911) dynasties; large, square table used for painting or writing.

HUANG HUA LI
Variety of ROSEWOOD used in CHINESE FURNITURE; dense, hard wood ranging in color from golden yellow to reddish orange.

HUNT, WILLIAM HOLMAN (1827–1910)
British painter and designer. Best known as a Pre-Raphaelite painter, Holman Hunt also painted and designed furniture for William MORRIS's manufacturing company. Hunt designed some furniture in the revivalist styles of the time as well, eclectically combining elements from disparate cultures.

HUNT SIDEBOARD
Late 18th- and early 19th-century furniture form of southern United States; HUNTBOARD with either drawers or cupboards. The hunt sideboard was higher than a SIDEBOARD—it stood on the long legs of a huntboard—and narrower as well.

HUNT TABLE
Another name for American HUNTBOARD or British WINE TABLE.

HUNTBOARD (also *hunting board; hunt table; hunting table*)
Late 18th and early 19th century furniture form of southern United States; long, narrow table with tall legs intended to be placed lengthwise against a wall, for serving food and drink to standing users. Its use is traditionally associated with hunters, who had spent the day on horseback and so preferred to stand. A more elaborate variant was the HUNT SIDEBOARD.

HUNZINGER, GEORGE (1835–98)
Nineteenth-century German-American chair maker; designer of PATENT FURNITURE. Hunzinger was born in Germany, where his family had been cabinetmakers since at least 1612. Hunzinger settled in Brooklyn, New York, in the 1850s and became a United States citizen in 1865. He established his own chair-manufacturing company in the following year. He eventually held more than 20 patents for furniture designs or parts. His best-known pieces were a folding chair (1866), a chair

Hunzinger chair

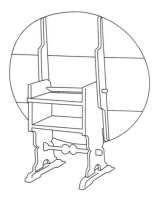

hutch table

whose seat and back were made of fabric-covered metal strips (1876) and a platform rocker (1882). The chairs were in whimsical, idiosyncratic versions of the various REVIVAL STYLES of the day and were characterized by a heavy use of novel turnery.

HUSK
Decorative motif consisting of a vertical arrangement of flowerets or catkins in diminishing sizes, with the smallest at the bottom. Derived from the image of an ear of wheat, found in ancient Greek and Roman ornamentation, the husk was popular in the NEOCLASSICAL STYLE furniture of the late 18th and early 19th centuries, especially in Britain and the United States. In American FEDERAL PERIOD furniture, there arose a distinctive variation, the BELLFLOWER motif.

HUTCH
GOTHIC FURNITURE form; originally any CHEST or COFFER, then, more specifically, a long, wide, short-legged CHEST OF DRAWERS or CABINET placed against the wall and used as side table or BUFFET. In American usage the term *hutch* refers to a chest of drawers fitted with open shelving above.

HUTCH TABLE
English and AMERICAN JACOBEAN FURNITURE form; a table consisting of a small box on legs, whose hinged lid, which is much wider than the box and is generally circular, serves as the table top when closed. Akin to the CHAIR TABLE, hutch tables descended from MEDIEVAL FURNITURE and were made in remote districts until well into the 18th century.

HVIDT, PETER (b. 1916)
Danish designer of SCANDINAVIAN MODERN furniture. Hvidt was influenced by the INTERNATIONAL STYLE from the late 1930s onward but is principally known for his experiments in pressure-molding and other industrial processes, which he conducted with Osla Mölgaard-Nielsen in the late 1940s. These experiments yielded elegant designs that exemplify the trend in Danish furniture toward mass production, a trend also illustrated in the work of Arne JACOBSEN and Poul KJAERHOLM. Hvidt and Mölgaard-Nielsen's 1950 "Ax" furniture series was particularly influential on both Scandinavian and American designs of the next decade.

IDIGBO

Nigerian HARDWOOD used in furniture as substitute for OAK, which it closely resembles.

INCE & MAYHEW (also *Mayhew & Ince*) **(extant 1759–1803)**

British furniture-making firm; partnership of William Ince (active c. 1757 1803) and John Mayhew (active from 1756, d. 1811). Ince & Mayhew's published designs emulated and resembled those of Thomas CHIPPENDALE. Popular in Britain, their engravings also had a notable influence on AMERICAN CHIPPENDALE FURNITURE makers. Ince & Mayhew later made furniture in the REGENCY STYLE.

INDIAN FURNITURE

The history of Indian furniture begins in antiquity, but it is obscure, for little furniture has survived from early periods, and the record provided by art is scanty. Furthermore, it appears that not much furniture was made, in terms of both the range of forms designed and the number of pieces built. Even today, most Indians use little or no furniture.

The earliest recorded pieces of Indian furniture, appearing in Buddhist reliefs from the second century B.C., were THRONES of stone or wood—low, flat, polygonal or lotus-shaped platforms, sometimes with flat backs. These thrones were supported on short legs carved in the form of animals' feet. Raised seating was apparently introduced to India from the West through the Hellenistic kingdom of Bactria, a remnant of the empire of Alexander the Great, centered in present-day Afghanistan. By the second century A.D., such pieces were often made of BAMBOO and CANING. Chairs were rare, however, being used only as thrones or seats of honor, until the period of European imperialism in India, which began in the 16th century.

Early Indian beds, known only from pictorial sources, seem to have been derived from ancient EGYPTIAN and MESOPOTAMIAN FURNITURE; they were low, rectangular frames on turned on carved feet. Under Moslem rule, which began in about A.D. 1000, northern India knew more massive beds, sometimes with HEADBOARDS, but the piece was never common; simple bedding placed on a floor was typical. CHESTS and a few small TABLES completed the range of Indian furniture. Into colonial times even the wealthy had little furniture. A chair, a bed, a small DRESSING TABLE fitted with compartments, perhaps a flat table for drawing and a chest or two comprised the furnishings of a sleeping chamber; other rooms were even more sparingly appointed. Instead, fabrics and carpets provided both comfort and display.

One reason why traditional Indian furniture was so rare was its expense. The materials used always had to withstand attack by insects, a very great problem in India. Wooden furniture could not last long, so stone, IVORY and metals, including SILVER, played a great role. As far as economically viable, parts were carved of stone or ivory or cast in metals. A less expensive alternative was TEAK, a relatively insect-resistant wood; even this was frequently veneered with ivory or metal, however.

European dominance, chiefly by Britain, introduced Western furniture styles and also created a considerable export market for Indian craftsmen, who applied indigenous techniques and ornamental motifs to European forms (*see* INDO-PORTUGUESE FURNITURE; BURMESE

FURNITURE). In 19th-century British India, the most prominent source of Indian-made furniture was Kashmir, in the far northwest, where a local hardwood resembling WALNUT was used to make pieces decorated with an abundance of botanical motifs; these were carved with great virtuosity.

India gave cane to Europe, and a late Indian chair design, the ROUNDABOUT CHAIR (1), was exported to Europe in the 18th century. For the most part, though, the Western influence of India was greater than India's on the West, and recent Indian furniture has generally followed British fashions.

INDIAN LAUREL

Pale to dark brown HARDWOOD with darker brown to black grain, native to India and Burma. Indian laurel, one of the "EMPIRE" WOODS, was used as veneering on British furniture in the 1930s. It is generally rare outside India, where it is used for general construction and in fine furniture.

indiscret

INDISCRET

Upholstered piece of seating furniture, comprising three armchairs radiating from a central point; the right, or left, arm of each linked to the same arm of each of the others. Each chair faced, obliquely, the back of the next; from above, the piece resembled a pinwheel. The *indiscret,* also called a "conversational sofa," originated in France during the Second Empire and was an example of the taste for elaborate furniture that arose following the development of deep-buttoned, coil-spring UPHOLSTERY, in about 1830.

INDO-PORTUGUESE FURNITURE

BAROQUE FURNITURE of 17th and 18th centuries made by Indian craftsmen in Portuguese colonial settlements of India, especially Goa. Commissioned by Portuguese merchants living on the west coast of India, Indo-Portuguese furniture boasted exceedingly luxurious materials, for Goa was one of the world's richest cities in the late 16th and early 17th centuries.

European forms were used, although details were sometimes rendered idio-syncratically, but decoration on most pieces was wholly Indian. Supports frequently took the form of carved images of humans, mermaids or fantastic vegetation. The most distinctive decoration was elaborate INLAY work, covering the whole piece, in patterns derived from the decorative arts of India. In the 17th century complicated foliate scrolls were most common, while in the 18th, intricate arrangements of overlapping circles were used. Furniture was usually made of TEAK inlaid with EBONY, Brazilian ROSEWOOD (imported from Portugal's other great colony), bone or IVORY. Teak was particularly resistant to insects, a great problem of all Indian cabinetmakers (*see also* INDIAN FURNITURE). Ivory shared this resistance; more readily available and less expensive in India than elsewhere, it was sometimes used to veneer an entire piece.

Indo-Portuguese furniture was made not only in Goa, but in Diu, Daman, Calicut and some other centers. A few Indian craftsmen went to Portugal and worked in Lisbon as well. On Ceylon (Sri Lanka), where an outpost of Portuguese India was established, a specialty in pictorial MARQUETRY arose; only boxes and chests were produced there.

INDUSTRIAL STYLE

See HIGH-TECH STYLE.

INFLATABLE FURNITURE

Collapsible furniture composed of a flexible plastic shell that is inflated with air or water. It then assumes the form of a piece of furniture, usually a chair or sofa, although the WATERBED is also an example. Popular in the 1960s–1970s, inflatable furniture is associated with POP ART FURNITURE. A well-known example was the "blow" chair (1967), designed by the Italian firm DE PAS, D'URBINO, LOMAZZI.

INGHAM, GEORGE (b. 1940)

AUSTRALIAN FURNITURE designer and maker. Born in Lahore, in what was then British India (now Pakistan), Ingham was educated and trained in Britain. He worked as an assistant to Antti NURMESNIEMI in the 1960s, and designed furniture in London before immigrating to Australia in 1982 to introduce and head the wood workshop at the Canberra Institute for the Arts, where he has remained since. He continues to design and make furniture. His finely crafted, natural wood pieces reflect his grounding in SCANDINAVIAN MOD-

FRN furniture and the INTERNATIONAL STYLE, but are also in the British HANDICRAFT REVIVAL tradition of John MAKEPEACE (at whose school Ingham once served as a visiting artist). Ingham has been highly influential on such younger Australian makers as Toby Muir WILSON and Leon SADUBIN.

INLAY
Decorative design or pattern created by embedding pieces of one material into another, usually forming a plane surface; also, as a verb, to make such a design in this way.

INTAGLIO
Carved ornamentation receding below the surrounding material; reverse of RELIEF carving.

INTARSIA (also *tarsia*)
Form of MARQUETRY used in Italian RENAISSANCE FURNITURE and wall panels. Small pieces of wood or some other material were used to make pictorial or abstract designs, often architectural representations.

INTERLACED-BOW WINDSOR CHAIR
See under WINDSOR CHAIR.

INTERNATIONAL STYLE
Modern style of architecture and furniture design that developed in Europe in the 1920s and 1930s and greatly influenced later architecture in America. The international style is characterized by clarity of structure, simplicity of line and a minimum of decoration. The term, coined by H. R. Hitchcock and Philip Johnson in 1932, is most often associated with architecture and is exemplified by the pristine glass-and-steel skyscrapers of post–Second World War America. The style was developed in Europe, however, between the world wars. It arose from a combination of design developments, including an esthetic trend toward simplicity and an interest in the problems of designing for mass manufacture. These concerns had been spreading and assuming many forms, especially in Britain and the German-speaking countries, for several generations (*see* ARTS AND CRAFTS MOVEMENT; ART FURNITURE MOVEMENT; ART NOUVEAU; DEUTSCHER WERKBUND;

DEUTSCHE WERKSTÄTTEN, WIENER WERK-STÄTTE). The International style was especially affected by one such development, the doctrine of FUNCTIONALISM, which stressed the importance of utility, of the industrial process and the materials it involves, and of the clear differentiation in a given piece between parts whose functions are different.

In the 1920s the BAUHAUS was the most important center of what was later known as the International style; Walter GROPIUS and Marcel BREUER were among its leading formulators. Ludwig MIES VAN DER ROHE, who was the most important exponent of the style through four decades, practiced independently in the 1920s but became director of the Bauhaus in 1930 until its demise in 1933. The other great center of the International style in Europe was Paris, where LE CORBUSIER, the fourth major figure of the movement, led the group associated with the UNION DES ARTISTES MODERNES, an organization founded to promote the International style.

In the 1930s the style spread to Scandinavia, where it influenced the development of SCANDINAVIAN MODERN design; to Britain (*see* Sergius Ivan CHERMAYEFF); and to America, partly through the influence of French designers and partly through the arrival of refugees from Nazi Germany, including Gropius, Breuer and Mies. After the Second World War, the important earlier furniture designs of Breuer, Mies, Le Corbusier and others were revived in America and remained influential. In Scandinavia and in Britain (*see* CONTEMPORARY STYLE), the influence of the international style remained strong through the 1960s in the work of such designers as Robin DAY and Poul KJAERHOLM, among many others. At that time in Australia, designers such as Gordon ANDREWS, George KORODY, and Clement MEADMORE responded to the International style as received from British, European, and Scandinavian sources, and currently younger designers, including Leslie John WRIGHT and Marc NEWSON, are carrying its principles into the 21st next century, in new, eclectic designs. Recently, looser, more eclectic styles have diluted the visual impact of the International style, but it remains the paradigm of modern design development, to be either furthered or reacted against. Its furniture is still very important, and many classic designs of the 1930s are still manufactured and used in great numbers.

International style chair

IONIC ORDER

Second of the three ancient Greek ORDERS OF ARCHITECTURE; developed in Ionia (Greek Asia Minor) before 500 B.C. and later adapted by the Romans. The Ionic order was characterized by a fluted COLUMN bearing a CAPITAL composed of a decorated molding, the ECHINUS, below two VOLUTES on both the front and back. On the sides of the capital was a concave surface sometimes decorated with small motifs. The column rested on a base composed of several moldings, and it supported a simple ENTABLATURE, with an undecorated FRIEZE. In the Roman Ionic order, decoration was more elaborate, especially in the frieze, and the CORNICE was generally supported by MODILLIONS.

IRIBE, PAUL (1883–1935)

French designer and illustrator associated with ART DECO. Having begun designing furniture and other household objects in the French ART NOUVEAU manner, Iribe developed a more restrained style of his own, early in this century, which influenced the development of Art Deco. He designed furniture in collaboration with Pierre LEGRAIN, was employed as a designer by Paul POIRET and was among the first to fill furniture commissions for Jacques DOUCET. He devised a conventional rose motif known as the "rose Iribe," which was adopted by others and became something of a hallmark of the emerging Art Deco style. In 1914 Iribe moved to America, where he designed sets for plays and movies, including early Cecil B. DeMille films. After returning to France in 1930, he designed jewelry, for the most part.

IRISH CHIPPENDALE FURNITURE

Modern term for 18th-century Irish ROCOCO FURNITURE modeled on published designs of Thomas CHIPPENDALE. Usually made of MAHOGANY, Irish Chippendale furniture is characterized by very broad aprons on tables, the use of the LION'S-PAW FOOT (see under FOOT) and a lion's MASK motif, and carving in low relief.

IROKO

Yellow to brown African HARDWOOD. It is similar to TEAK and used in similar ways—in outdoor furniture, for example.

IRON

Malleable, ductile metal used in various alloys as structural and decorative material since prehistoric times. Since the Roman era, wrought iron has occasionally been used by furniture makers, chiefly as ornamentation. In MEDIEVAL FURNITURE the most important piece of furniture, the CHEST, featured iron HARDWARE, including elaborate straps that both strengthened and decorated the piece. In RENAISSANCE FURNITURE brass and bronze replaced iron in furniture hardware, but the metal was still used in Spain, in braces reinforcing or replacing STRETCHERS on benches or the GUARD-ROOM TABLE, and in Italy, where iron X-FRAME stools were sometimes wrought. Iron frames for bed canopies (see CANOPY) were occasionally made in the 17th and 18th centuries, but iron furniture was uncommon until the 19th century, when technical advances made possible CAST-IRON FURNITURE, in which a range of forms was made.

IRONWOOD

Red-orange Brazilian HARDWOOD; close relative of BRAZILWOOD, used in furniture mainly as a striking decorative VENEER.

IRVING & CASSON & DAVENPORT

See DAVENPORT (2).

ISABELLINO STYLE

Spanish revival style (see REVIVAL STYLES) arising in about 1830 and popular throughout the remainder of the 19th century, named for Queen Isabella II (reigned 1833–68). Following French fashions, Isabellino style furniture combined neo-Gothic features with Rococo Revival forms derived from 18th-century French furniture. More colorful and exuberant than contemporary work elsewhere, Spanish pieces tended to be richly decorated with carved and gilt ornamentation or mother-of-pearl inlays. Rosewood with gilt-bronze mounts was a favorite combination, and brightly painted decoration was also popular.

ISHO-DANSU

JAPANESE FURNITURE form; TANSU in the form of a CHEST OF DRAWERS, intended to store clothing. An *isho-dansu* usually contains a stack of four broad drawers. The bottom drawer is narrower than the others to accommodate a small door, at the lower right, that opens to reveal two additional small drawers. The faces of the drawers have bail handles and ESCUTCHEONS, and the framing has corner plates, all of iron. Often the *isho-dansu* consists of two units placed one on top of the other. In this case, the standard arrangement of drawers is maintained; the upper chest has two drawers and the bottom one has two, plus the two additional drawers behind a door.

ISLE OF MAN STRETCHER
See under STRETCHER.

IVORY
Carved tusks of elephants and sometimes other animals, used to ornament furniture, chiefly as an element in INLAY work, in many periods and styles. Ivory has been used for decorative purposes since prehistory, and it appeared on ancient EGYPTIAN and MESOPOTAMIAN FURNITURE. The material was of particular importance in traditional INDIAN FURNITURE, where pieces were often entirely veneered with ivory, and parts, such as legs, were sometimes carved whole from it. In India ivory was relatively cheap, and it effectively withstood insect attack, a major problem for Indian cabinet-makers. For the same reasons, it also figured in INDO-PORTUGUESE FURNITURE.

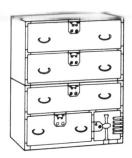

isho-dansu

J

JACK, GEORGE WASHINGTON (1855–1932)

American-born architect and designer associated with the British ARTS AND CRAFTS MOVEMENT. Jack was employed by Philip WEBB's architectural firm and was also chief designer for William MORRIS's Morris & Co. Jack was known for the high-quality craftsmanship of his pieces, which were less simple in line than Webb's and often copiously decorated with inlaid designs.

JACOB, GEORGES (1739–1814)

French furniture maker; leading chair maker in the LOUIS XVI and DIRECTOIRE STYLES and an important maker of all forms in the EMPIRE STYLE. Jacob, a Burgundian peasant, was apprenticed in Paris to the MENUISIER Louis DELANOIS, and he became a master in 1765. His early work was in the Rococo LOUIS XV STYLE, but he soon developed in the newer NEOCLASSICAL STYLE. By about 1780 he was a leading chair maker. He emphasized rectilinearity and richly carved floral and classical ornamentation; a floral motif, the MARGUERITE, became a personal hallmark. He was also a prominent figure in the trend toward greater austerity and archeological exactitude. He executed the furniture designs of the painters J.-L. DAVID and Hubert ROBERT, who were also concerned with archeological rigor, using the ETRUSCAN STYLE of decoration, a precursor of elements of the Directoire style. Furthermore, Jacob was a French pioneer in the use of MAHOGANY, and he introduced the SABER LEG (*see under* LEG) and the LYRE chair back in the late 1780s, just before the Revolution.

In 1792 Jacob was nearly ruined financially, when David arranged for him to pro-

duce Directoire style furniture, designed by PERCIER AND FONTAINE, for the Committee of Public Safety, the chief organ of government under the Reign of Terror. Jacob retired temporarily in 1796, and his workshop was operated by his sons Georges II (1768–1802) and François-Honoré-Georges (1770–1841). Jacob returned to the business in 1800, and on the death of Georges II in 1802, he entered a partnership with the other son, who took the name JACOB-DESMALTER. They produced furniture under the name Jacob-Desmalter & Cie. The Parisian guild restrictions that demanded specialization (*see* ÉBÉNISTE) had been abolished by the Revolution, and Jacob now made a wide range of furniture. He and his son worked in the grandiose Empire style, often to designs by Percier and Fontaine, and they provided much furniture for Napoleon's palaces. Jacob finally retired for good in 1813.

JACOB-DESMALTER (1770–1841)

Leading French EMPIRE STYLE furniture maker. Jacob-Desmalter was born François-Honoré-Georges Jacob, son of noted LOUIS XVI–STYLE chair maker Georges JACOB. He trained under his father, who retired in 1796 and left his business to his two sons, the other being Georges II (1768–1802). As Jacob Frères, the firm became a leading maker of furniture in the DIRECTOIRE and CONSULATE STYLES. The father returned to the business in 1800, and when Georges II died, he formed a partnership with his surviving son, who then took the name Jacob-Desmalter. (*De Desmalter* was the name of some of his Burgundian ancestors.) As Jacob-Desmalter & Cie., the new company became the most prominent of the Empire style furniture makers. It employed hundreds of workers and made most of the furniture for Napoleon's palaces, usually to designs by PERCIER AND FONTAINE, as well as large quantities of less opulent furniture for other clients. After Georges Jacob's final retirement in 1813, Jacob-Desmalter continued to make furniture in the same style and was successful despite the advent of the RESTAURATION STYLE. He also experimented with furniture in the NEO-GOTHIC STYLE. When Jacob-Desmalter retired in 1825, his son Georges-Alphonse (1799–1870) also retained the traditional Jacob manner until he sold the firm to JEANSELME in 1847.

JACOBEAN FURNITURE
English furniture of first half of 17th century. It is named for King James I, whose reign (1603–25) began the period, which continued through the reign of his son Charles I (1625–49). The Jacobean era coincided with the development on the Continent of the florid grandeur of the baroque (see BAROQUE FURNITURE), which had not yet reached England. Jacobean furniture varied little in structure and type from the TUDOR FURNITURE that preceded it. MANNERIST STYLE decoration, already known through the PATTERN BOOKS of Hans VREDEMAN DE VRIES and Wendel DIETTERLIN, became more fully developed. Italianate carving with dense fields of ARABESQUES ornamented cupboards, the chief pieces of domestic furniture. The FARTHINGALE CHAIR, the GATELEG TABLE and other light, portable pieces became increasingly popular, and the use of upholstery became more common, as a concern for comfort and convenience influenced furniture design. The period of Jacobean furniture ended with the English Civil Wars. These brought an austere 20-year interval to English design (see COMMONWEALTH FURNITURE), but afterward England came under the powerful influence of the European Baroque style. In the English Colonies of North America, AMERICAN JACOBEAN FURNITURE remained current throughout the 17th century.

JACOBSEN, ARNE (1902–71)
Danish architect and furniture designer; a major exponent of SCANDINAVIAN MODERN design. Jacobsen began his career as a successful architect in the 1920s in the Klint school

(named after the father of the furniture designer and architect Kaare KLINT). Klint school architects practiced a simple style aimed at producing rationally designed, utilitarian structures built with a strong awareness of the character of the materials employed. In the course of the 1930s, Jacobsen adopted a version of the BAUHAUS-inspired INTERNATIONAL STYLE. During the German occupation of Denmark in the Second World War, Jacobsen fled to Sweden, where he did some design work for the Finnish architect and designer Alvar AALTO. Only after the war did he begin to design furniture, his style influenced by Aalto and the work of Charles EAMES. He designed a number of molded plywood pieces supported by steel-rod substructures, including a range of stacking chairs (1952), which are still made today. During the mid-1950s, Jacobsen, with his contemporary Poul KJAERHOLM, exemplified a trend in Danish design away from handicrafts and toward mass production. Later in the 1950s Jacobsen created his most famous designs, which were further developments of the sculptural mode made possible by the new technology of molding synthetic materials. Jacobsen's "Egg" and "Swan" chairs were designs of great impact. They had plastic seats molded in sweeping, free-flowing curves, upholstered with fabric- or leather-covered foam rubber and supported by steel or cast-aluminum bases. An architect first, Jacobsen also designed cutlery, textiles, wallpaper and appliances, as well as furniture, generally designing all the furnishings for his major architectural commissions.

JAKOBSEN, HANS SANDGREN (b. 1963)
Contemporary Danish furniture designer. In his 20s, Jakobsen traveled and studied in Japan and with a Shaker community in the United States, and these two spare aesthetic traditions have helped form his style. He is best known for collaborations with several fabric designers, producing both traditional SCANDINAVIAN MODERN furniture and innovative chairs and screens for manufacturers in Europe and Japan.

JAPANESE FURNITURE
The Japanese have traditionally used very little furniture. The traditional Japanese house featured movable partitions that could be used to

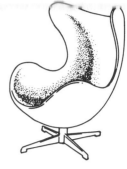

chair by Jacobsen

create any desired arrangement of interior spaces, and any furniture was necessarily small and portable. Japanese furniture has historically consisted largely of only two types: SCREENS (see BYOBU; TSUITATE) and a wide variety of storage chests, called TANSU, a word that also denotes wood cabinetry in general. Other light pieces of furniture have included small READING STANDS, the KIMONO RACK, the MAKURA (a wooden HEADREST or pillow) and the KYOSOKU, an armrest. Accustomed to sitting on the floor, the Japanese developed no seating furniture at all, and their few tables were used as writing desks. These were generally less than a foot high and supported on short legs or side panels. Sometimes they were equipped with shallow drawers. Unless lacquered (see LACQUER), they were almost undecorated, apart from brass or copper fittings at the corners and BAIL HANDLES on drawers. The only piece of furniture not made with portability in mind has been the BUTSU-DAN, or household shrine.

The Japanese have tended to make their furniture from various woods: SUGI, or cryptomeria; HINOKI, a cypress; the Japanese pine, MATSU; the chestnut, KURI; paulownia, or KIRI; and ZELKOVA. The Japanese developed several specialized sorts of lacquer decoration, including RADEN (known in the West as LAC BURGAUTÉ) and MAKI-E. In the 19th century, after the Meiji Restoration (1868) and the reopening of Japan to the West, a thriving export market to Europe and America arose (see JAPONISME). Furthermore, a number of hybrid forms developed, combining traditional elements in new arrangements and using such Western details as bracket feet (see BRACKET FOOT, under FOOT). Among these new forms was the SHODANA, intended to display and store small objects. SHIBAYAMA, an elaborate decorative cladding, was also developed at this time. Modern Japanese furniture is in transition; some work is explicitly Western in inspiration, while much is still modeled on traditional forms.

JAPANNING
Furniture FINISH of 17th and 18th centuries, consisting of GESSO, paints and varnishes applied to furniture in order to simulate the appearance of LACQUER. Lacquer became known in Europe during the Renaissance, and by the 17th century lacquer furniture and other objects were imported in great numbers from the Far East, mostly from Japan (hence, the term *japanning*). Since Europeans could not make lacquer themselves—it is based on the sap of the Asian *lac* tree, *Rhus vernicifera*—they attempted different types of japanning, with varying degrees of success. These ranged from the French VERNIS MARTIN, which was difficult to distinguish from real lacquer, except in its decoration, to pieces merely painted with CHINOISERIE motifs; an example of this latter mode was the LACCA CONTRAFATTA work of northern Italy, which strove only for a superficial resemblance to Oriental work.

The decoration of Japanese lacquer work usually consisted of pictorial scenes in gold on a black background, and European japanned pieces tended to be similarly ornamented, as in BOIS DE SPA, produced at Spa, in present-day Belgium, one of the best-known centers of the craft. However, Western Chinoiserie motifs were also employed in traditionally Western arrangements using linear perspective and often organized in the swirling compositions of Baroque painting. Images from Oriental art were presumed to accord with traditional Western genre scenes, resulting in some inaccuracies of nuance; thus, these decorations were not difficult to distinguish from their Oriental models. In addition, japanned decoration was sometimes frankly Western, especially in *vernis martin* work. Gerhard DAGLY, regarded as the greatest European japanner, devised new decorative schemes using bright primary colors on a white ground. In England the practice was especially stimulated by the publication in 1688 of STALKER & PARKER's technical manual *A Treatise of Japanning and Varnishing*. A variant of japanning peculiar to Britain was BANTAM WORK, which attempted to replicate Chinese COROMANDEL LACQUER. In 18th-century America japanning was practiced in Boston, most notably by Thomas JOHNSTON. The vogue for japanned furniture died out at the end of the 18th century, though a revival of interest in Oriental design in Britain during the VICTORIAN PERIOD generated the mass production of small japanned objects, including some furniture.

JAPONAISERIE
Another name for JAPONISME.

JAPONISME

European and American taste of the second half of the 19th century, in which elements of Japanese esthetics, as known through imported goods and works of art, were applied to Western decorative arts. The eclecticism of the VICTORIAN PERIOD promoted an interest in exotic sources of inspiration. European and American furniture designers were attracted by JAPANESE FURNITURE and art, whose clean-lined simplicity contrasted sharply with the fussy elaboration of the REVIVAL STYLES and of Victorian interior design. *Japonisme* also influenced other decorative arts, especially ceramics.

Japanese PORCELAIN and LACQUER had been well known in Europe since the 17th century, but any enthusiasm it sparked was negligible, compared to that for CHINOISERIE, until Japan was opened for trade with the West in the 1850s. Then, adherents of the British design reform movements, which had begun to develop in reaction against the mass-manufactured furniture of the day, reopened especially strongly to Japanese imports, which included some furniture. Designers of the ART FURNITURE MOVEMENT, led by William GODWIN, admired the fresh, simplifying esthetic of Japanese work. In the 1860s Godwin designed much influential furniture that, while not directly imitative of Japanese furniture, was similarly light in weight and appearance and, like its models, was based on an asymmetrical juxtaposition of solids and voids. He called his work "Anglo-Japanese" furniture. Another leading British designer who was strongly inspired by Japanese work was Thomas JECKYLL. Many others reflected the stimulus of *Japonisme*—notably T. E. COLLCUTT, Christopher DRESSER, A. H. MACKMURDO and Bruce TALBERT.

In French furniture *Japonisme* was less prominent, although in the 1880s, the revival style designer Ferdinand BARBEDIENNE created some Japanese-inspired furniture. In the 1890s French and German ART NOUVEAU designers, following Godwin and Charles Rennie MACKINTOSH, were stimulated by the simple lines and asymmetry of Japanese furniture and, especially in France, by the naturalistic motifs of Japanese art; this latter feature was later revived by French ART DECO designers, including Clément MÈRE. Through the German *Jugendstil* and Austrian SEZESSION movements, Godwin's "Anglo-Japanese" furniture also affected early modern designers of DE STIJL and the BAUHAUS.

Japonisme reached the United States from Britain in the late 1870s, and during the 1880s its influence was joined to the wildly eclectic stylistic ferment of the day. It was notable in the work of the HERTER BROTHERS and NIMURA & SATO. The latter firm specialized in BAMBOO furniture, a fad that *Japonisme* provoked, particularly in America. Shortly after the turn of the century, GREENE & GREENE, on the West Coast, and Frank Lloyd WRIGHT, in the Midwest, were also stimulated by Japanese esthetics; Wright traveled to Japan several times, beginning in 1905.

Japanese furniture has continued to influence Western tastes, and in recent years it has been strikingly represented in the work of George NAKASHIMA. However, the term *Japonisme* is generally reserved for the late 19th-century phenomenon.

Japonisme desk

JARDINIÈRE

Large ornamental stand or holder to display potted plants or cut flowers. The *jardinière* first appeared in France in the 1760s, when flower arranging became a popular way to provide visual stimulation to compensate for the increasing austerity of ornamentation and the rectilinearity of wall paneling and furniture in the LOUIS XVI STYLE.

JAZZ MODERNE

See ART DECO.

JEANNERET, CHARLES-EDOUARD

See LE CORBUSIER.

JEANNERET, PIERRE (1896–1967)

French architect and designer; best known as a collaborator with his cousin LE CORBUSIER and with Charlotte PERRIAND. Jeanneret, born and trained in Switzerland, worked in Paris for his famous cousin from 1922 to 1940 and at intervals thereafter. In the late 1920s, they and Perriand jointly created the classic modern furniture that is known as Le Corbusier's. After Perriand left the firm in 1930, she and Jeanneret lived together for seven years, and together they created a number of well-known pieces of furniture. He also continued to function as Le Corbusier's chief assistant architect.

His partnership with his cousin ended with the coming of World War II. Jeanneret fought in the French Resistance throughout the war, after which he returned to architecture. Among other things, and in addition to occasional projects with Le Corbusier, he collaborated with Jean PROUVÉ on designs for prefabricated housing. In 1951, he accepted a position as the on-site chief architect for Le Corbusier's largest project, the designed city of Chandigarh, in the foothills of the Himalayas, built to serve as the capital city of the Punjab. He stayed on in Chandigarh, serving as Chief Architect for Punjab, until his death. In accordance with his will, his ashes were strewn in the built reservoir, Sukhna Lake, a showpiece of the city.

JEANSELME

Nineteenth-century French furniture-manufacturing firm. Founded when Joseph-Pierre-François Jeanselme (d. 1860) bought the company of JACOB-DESMALTER, the Jeanselme establishment became well known during the Second Empire for furniture in a variety of the REVIVAL STYLES of the day, especially the ROCOCO REVIVAL and LOUIS XVI REVIVAL STYLES. Jeanselme left the firm to his son Charles-Joseph-Marie (b. 1827), who managed it until he retired in 1871. The business was left to other hands, who kept the name and continued to manufacture furniture until the 1930s.

JECKYLL, THOMAS (1827–81)

British furniture designer associated with the ART FURNITURE MOVEMENT and JAPONISME. Jeckyll designed Japanese-influenced metalwork and furniture for commercial manufacture and was allied with William GODWIN and the Aesthetic Movement. He is most noted for designing the furniture and woodwork for the famous Peacock Room, decorated by James McNeill Whistler. The Peacock Room is now an exhibit at the Freer Gallery in Washington, D.C., though without the movable furniture.

JELIFF, JOHN (1813–93)

New Jersey furniture maker; best known for NEO-GOTHIC STYLE furniture. Active in

Newark from about 1835 until his retirement in 1890, Jeliff was noted for well-crafted furniture with finely carved details. While much of his output was derived from Gothic elements, he also worked in other REVIVAL STYLES, notably the RENAISSANCE REVIVAL STYLE of the 1870s–1880s.

JENNY LIND STYLE

American term given in the late 19th century to SPOOL FURNITURE because the famous Swedish soprano Jenny Lind (1820–87) was said to have slept in a spool bed during her triumphal tour of America.

JENSEN, GERREIT (also *Gerrit Johnson*) (active 1680–1715)

Dutch-born English cabinetmaker in WILLIAM AND MARY STYLE. Jensen, in London by 1680, was the most highly regarded English cabinetmaker of his time. He was strongly influenced by the French LOUIS XIV STYLE, especially as represented in the work of André-Charles BOULLE. Jensen specialized in ivory and metal INLAYS in ornate arrangements of ARABESQUE and geometrical motifs, executed with the technique of BOULLE MARQUETRY. In his later work, he favored JAPANNING, probably encouraged by the publication of STALKER & PARKER's technical manual.

JEWELWORK

Decorative motif; wood carving representing cut and mounted gems.

JI (CHI)

CHINESE FURNITURE form of Han dynasty (206 B.C.–A.D. 220); backrest or armrest, consisting of small, horizontal platform on two short uprights. A *ji* was usually made of lacquered wood (*see* LACQUER). The advent of raised seating furniture in China at the end of the Han period (*see* HU CHUANG) made the *ji* obsolete.

JI CHI MU (CHI CH'I MU) (also *chicken-wing wood*)

Deep brown HARDWOOD used in CHINESE FURNITURE. The attractive markings of *ji chi mu*, in patterns resembling feathers, give it the name *chicken-wing wood*. It is relatively soft compared to other Chinese woods, and thus more vulnerable to insect attack, so it was frequently lacquered in traditional furniture. When new, it is a light greyish yellow-brown and somewhat resembles SATINWOOD, with which it has sometimes been identified in the West, although it matures to a much darker color.

JI TAI SHI AN (CHI T'AI SHIH AN) (also *altar table*)

CHINESE FURNITURE form of Ming (1368–1644) and Qing (1644–1911) dynasties; tall table with long, narrow top, intended to hold such objects as incense burners and ritual offerings and installed in a setting reserved for religious observances. The *ji tai shi an* was placed along a wall, and it was traditionally the most important and imposing piece of furniture in a Chinese home. It frequently featured upturned edges at either end of the top, in the form of attached moldings, and some varieties had one or two tiers of drawers in an apron below the top. In a modest dwelling, the *ji tai shi an* might appear in an entrance hall, but in wealthier homes, it generally stood in a separate room. The form was developed during the Yuan dynasty (1280–1367) but first became widespread during the Ming.

JIA JI (CHIA CHI)

CHINESE FURNITURE form of Ming (1368–1644) and Qing (1644–1911) dynasties; small side table, especially STOOL, or DENG, used as one.

JIA ZI CHUANG (CHIA TZU CH'UANG)

CHINESE FURNITURE form of Ming (1368–1644) and Qing (1644–1911) dynasties; TESTER bed. The *jia zi chuang* was a low platform on four legs, bordered by low walls and topped by a high tester, from which copious draperies hung, creating a warm room within a room. The walls, about a foot high, were of either solid wood or ornamental FRETWORK, and they stood on three sides of the platform and for a short distance at each end of the fourth side, leaving a space for access. The tester was supported by a sturdy post at each corner and a slighter one at either side of the

entrance. Developed early in the Ming period, the *jia zi chuang* was a more sophisticated version of the KANG, which lacked the tester and was generally walled on only three sides. Like the *kang*, the *jia zi chuang* was large enough to accommodate a small table or cupboard, even, occasionally, a stool or two on which visitors could sit.

JIAO CHUANG (CH'IAO CH'UANG) or JIAO YI (CH'IAO YI)

CHINESE FURNITURE form arising before Song dynasty (960–1279); any X-FRAME chair built with an X-frame at either side. Literally meaning "crossed seat" or "crossed chair," the term covers many styles and types of chairs constructed in this way.

JOEL, BETTY (active 1930s)

British furniture designer and decorator. Joel combined elements from the INTERNATIONAL STYLE and ART DECO in eclectic, simple yet stylish pieces. Her essentially conservative designs were often composed of "EMPIRE" WOODS, exotic materials whose unfamiliar patterns and colors added visual interest.

JOHNSON, THOMAS (1714–c. 1778)

British maker and designer of ROCOCO FURNITURE. Johnson, a carver and gilder, is best known for his engraved designs, published between 1755 and 1761, for "carver's pieces"—small tables and stands, wall sconces and other small objects that were more decorative than useful. Johnson's designs were elaborate confections in an extravagant and picturesque mode, incorporating landscape elements, carved figures and lively, asymmetrical scrollwork. They were clearly derived from the *genre pittoresque* decoration of the French LOUIS XV STYLE, but they had a distinctly British touch, being less fluid than their prototypes and including vignettes from a familiar British illustrated edition of Aesop's fables. Johnson also drew on the published work of J.-B. TURREAU and J. M. HOPPENHAUPT.

JOHNSTON, THOMAS (1708–67)

Foremost Boston japanner (*see* JAPANNING) of the late 18th century. Johnston, born in England, was active in Boston after 1732 as an

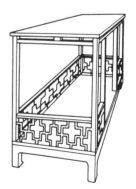

jia zi chuang

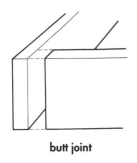

butt joint

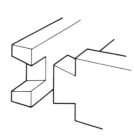

cross-lapped joint

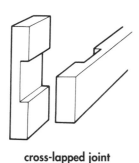

dado joint

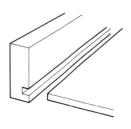

dovetail joint

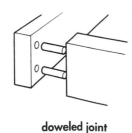

doweled joint

artist, an organ maker and a graphics designer and engraver, although his principal occupation was japanning. His style of CHINOISERIE furniture decoration exemplified the later style of Boston japanning, which was compositionally tighter and more detailed than the earlier mode, represented by the work of William RANDALL and Robert DAVIS. Johnston's sons John (active 1773–89), Thomas Jr. and Benjamin were also japanners; John was a portrait painter as well.

JOINER
Woodworker specializing in construction using techniques of JOINERY.

JOINERY
Woodworking craft in which pieces of wood are attached to each other, or joined, by being arranged in configurations known as JOINTS. Many different joints are distinguished by specific names.

BUTT JOINT (also *end joint*)
Connection of two members in which the squared end of the first is placed against a side of second, producing a right angle, or in which two pieces, each with a squared terminus, are placed end to end. Before the pieces are connected, this joint must be further secured by means of a DOWEL, as in a DOWELED JOINT; by metal plates, in a SCARF JOINT (*see each under* JOINERY); or by screws, nails and so on.

CROSS-LAPPED JOINT
Connection between two boards that cross each other, made so that their surfaces are flush where they intersect. This is done by cutting a recess, rectangular in plan and section, across the face of each board, at the point where they are to cross, and placing the recessed surfaces face to face. Each recess is as wide as the opposing board, so the two will interlock. Furthermore, their combined depths equal the thickness of the narrower of the two boards, so its uncut face will flush with the edges of the recess into which it fits. If the two boards are equally thick, the connection will be flush on both sides, in which case it may be called a *halved joint.*

DADO JOINT (also *housed joint*)
Type of RABBETED JOINT (*see under* JOINERY). A dado joint is formed by inserting the end or edge of a board into a matching groove, or rabbet, in another piece of wood.

DOVETAIL JOINT
Connection of two perpendicular boards by interlocking their shaped edges. Flaring, wedgelike projections, called *dovetails* because of their shape, are crafted at the edge of one board. They fit into a row of tailored spaces cut into the edge of the adjoining board. If these spaces do not extend all the way through the adjoining board, the joint will be invisible when seen from the uncut side; it is then called a *stopped* or *lapped* dovetail joint. The dovetail joint is commonly used where two planes intersect, as in the corners of drawers or of the carcase of a piece of case furniture. A dovetail joint may also bond two boards in the same plane. In this case, the dovetails appear on each piece, and the gaps in one board receive the dovetails of the other.

DOWELED JOINT
Any of various connections—including BUTT JOINT, SPLINED JOINT, MITER or MORTISE-AND-TENON JOINT (*see each under* JOINERY)—in which a small, usually cylindrical length of wood, or DOWEL, is fitted into aligned holes in pieces to be joined. The parts are then generally glued together. The dowel may extend completely through a joined part, with its end decoratively exposed.

END JOINT
Another name for BUTT JOINT (*see under* JOINERY).

HALVED JOINT
See CROSS-LAPPED JOINT, *under* JOINERY.

HOUSED JOINT
Another name for DADO JOINT (*see under* JOINERY).

MITER
Connection of two pieces made by beveling an edge of each piece and placing the two

angled edges face to face. They may be connected by a DOWEL, a spline, glue, screws or nails. Usually the two edges are cut at a 45-degree angle, forming a right angle when joined.

MORTISE-AND-TENON JOINT

Connection of two parts in which one has a crafted projection, or TENON, usually rectangular in shape, that is inserted into a shaped cavity or socket, or MORTISE, in the other. Often, a hole is drilled through the two joined parts, and a DOWEL is inserted, further securing the joint. The mortise may extend completely through its piece of wood, with the end of the tenon decoratively exposed.

RABBETED JOINT (also *rebated joint*)

Connection formed by inserting the edge or end of a piece of wood or of a protruding strip, or *tongue*, crafted on a piece of wood, into a matching groove, or *rabbet*, cut in another piece. The TONGUE-AND-GROOVE JOINT and DADO JOINT (*see each under* JOINERY) are common types of rabbeted joint.

REBATED JOINT

Another name for RABBETED JOINT.

SCARF JOINT

Connection between two pieces of wood held together by two metal plates. Each plate, one on either side of the joint, is attached, by screws or bolts, to both pieces of wood.

SPLINED JOINT

Connection in which a small strip or slat of wood, a *spline*, is fitted into aligned slots or grooves in the two pieces to be joined. The three parts may be glued together, or a hole may be drilled through all three and a DOWEL inserted. The spline may extend completely through either or both joined parts, with an edge or edges decoratively exposed.

TONGUE-AND-GROOVE JOINT

Type of RABBETED JOINT (*see under* JOINERY), formed by inserting a protruding strip, or *tongue*, crafted at the edge or end of a piece of wood, into a matching groove cut in another piece.

JOINT

Arrangement whereby pieces of wood are connected to each other, or *joined*. The making of various types of joints and their use in the construction of furniture and other articles constitute the craft of JOINERY.

JOINT STOOL

MEDIEVAL FURNITURE form; seat with seat rails, on four turned legs connected by stretchers, all assembled with mortise-and-tenon joints or other JOINERY. The joint stool was thus distinguished from the less sophisticated STICK STOOL.

JONES, ALLEN (b. 1937)

Contemporary British artist associated with POP ART FURNITURE. In the late 1960s Jones designed a notorious and widely publicized line of furniture, mostly chairs and glass-topped tables, featuring life-sized, erotic sculptures of scantily clad female figures.

JONES, OWEN (1809–74)

British architect, designer and writer. Jones traveled in Spain and the Middle East in 1833 and 1834 and sparked British interest in Islamic architecture and patterns of decoration through his writings on the subject. He designed furniture and many other items for Henry COLE's Summerly's Art Manufacturers. In his most important book, *The Grammar of Ornament* (1856), Jones promoted the MOORISH STYLE and stressed the importance of fine crafts and honest, quality workmanship, thereby anticipating the ideals of the ARTS AND CRAFTS MOVEMENT.

JONES, WILLIAM (active c. 1739)

British PALLADIAN STYLE and ROCOCO FURNITURE designer. In 1739 Jones published a PATTERN BOOK, *The Gentleman's or Builder's Companion,* that contained rococo designs derived from the work of Nicolas PINEAU. These were among the first examples of rococo ornamentation to be published in Britain.

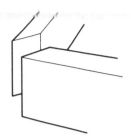

mitered joint

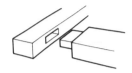

mortise-and-tenon joint

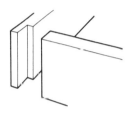

rabbeted joint

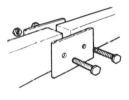

scarf joint

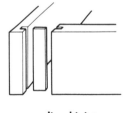

splined joint

tongue-and-groove joint

JOUBERT, GILLES (1689–1775)
French furniture maker; a leading ÉBÉNISTE in LOUIS XV STYLE. Joubert was a successful producer of well-made, conservative furniture; for instance, he favored geometrical MARQUETRY when floral patterns dominated ROCOCO FURNITURE. At the age of seventy-four, he became *ébéniste du roi* on J.-F. OEBEN's death. He retired when he was replaced in that position by J.-H. REISENER on the accession of Louis XVI in 1774.

JOURDAIN, FRANCIS (1876–1958)
French furniture designer of the 1920s and 1930s, associated with the INTERNATIONAL STYLE. Jourdain, son of the well-known ART NOUVEAU architect Frantz Jourdain, began his career as a painter but turned to the decorative arts before the First World War. He designed furniture in a simple, rectilinear style influenced by the WIENER WERKSTÄTTE and intended as inexpensive, factory-produced furniture for the masses. Jourdain also designed ceramics, textiles, and wallpaper and was a founding member of the UNION DES ARTISTES MODERNES.

JUHL, FINN (1912–89)
Danish architect and furniture designer, a major exponent of SCANDINAVIAN MODERN design. Finn Juhl's furniture first brought Danish design its international renown, in the late 1940's. Deriving from INTERNATIONAL STYLE precedents and informed by the principles of FUNCTIONALISM, Juhl's designs differ from the similarly grounded work of his contemporary Hans WEGNER in his imaginative response to the possibilities presented by the new molding processes of the time. His innovative chairs consisted of a frame seemingly separate from the seat and the back, which, attached to inconspicuous crossbars, appeared to float within the space defined by the frame. These "floating" elements were themselves molded into sculpturally intriguing, and comfortable, forms, while the frames, basically rectilinear, create abstract patterns with diagonal braces and smoothly shaped arms and legs. His tables and case furniture also demonstrate a distinct separation of their different parts, in a functionalist manner, and resemble the work of LE CORBUSIER. Juhl also designed buildings and interiors, as well as glassware, wooden ware, porcelain, carpets, and lighting fixtures.

JUVARRA, FILIPPO (1678–1736)
Italian architect and BAROQUE FURNITURE designer. The leading Italian architect of his day, Juvarra also designed furniture, in a dramatic late baroque manner perhaps influenced by his early career as a designer for the stage. His work featured large pictorial inlays and elegant figural supports rising from delicate scrollwork legs.

chair by Juhl

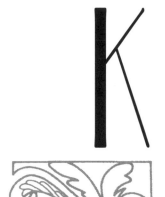

KAIDAN-DANSU (also *staircase chest*)
Nineteenth-century JAPANESE FURNITURE form; largest of the TANSU. It is a freestanding staircase, from 4 to 10 feet tall, with several drawers and compartments on one side. Developed in the late 18th century, the *kaidan-dansu* was originally intended simply to provide access to the lofts of traditional one-story Japanese buildings; the compartments evolved somewhat later. Today, antique *kaidan-dansu* are generally used decoratively; the steps serve as display shelves.

KAMBLI, JOHANN MELCHIOR (1718–83)
Swiss metalworker and cabinetmaker who made ROCOCO FURNITURE in Prussia. Kambli began to work for Frederick the Great of Prussia in 1746, making gilt-bronze mounts for pieces by J. A. NAHL and the SPINDLER brothers. He also produced furniture of his own design, specializing in MARQUETRY combining dark TORTOISESHELL with light-colored woods.

KANG (K'ANG)
CHINESE FURNITURE form. Originally, beginning in the Han dynasty (206 B.C.–A.D.), the *kang* was a low brick or clay platform built into a dwelling and often heated by pipes connected to the fireplace. Later, by the time of the Ming dynasty (1368–1644), it was a freestanding piece of wooden furniture, a large platform where two or more people could recline or sleep; it was enclosed by low walls on three sides. Though written with different ideograms, both pieces are pronounced the same, and one clearly evolved from the other. The *kang* was large enough to accommodate a

KANG JI, or table, or a KANG CUPBOARD, small pieces intended for use by the person(s) resting on the platform.

KANG CUPBOARD
CHINESE FURNITURE form of Ming (1368–1644) and Qing (1644–1911) dynasties; low CUPBOARD intended for use on a KANG or a JIA ZI CHUANG, large, platformlike pieces of furniture. In it were stored reading or writing materials, eating utensils and vessels, or other objects that might be used by those seated on the larger piece.

KANG JI (K'ANG CHI) (also *kang table*)
CHINESE FURNITURE form that developed during Han dynasty (206 B.C.–A.D. 220) but became most prominent in Ming (1368–1644) and Qing (1644–1911); short-legged table intended for use on a KANG or a JIA ZI CHUANG, large, platformlike pieces of furniture. First used on the built-in *kang* of Han times, the *kang ji* had become an elegant piece of wooden furniture by the 15th century; it was used for writing or dining by those seated on the larger piece. Though basically a simple piece with little decoration, it was often

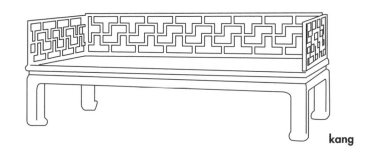

kang

adorned, beginning in the late Ming, with a frieze of relief carving between the apron and the top. In the 19th century large numbers of KANG tables were exported to Europe, where they were used as CABINET STANDS.

KANG TABLE
See KANG JI.

KARPEN BROTHERS, S., CO.
Chicago furniture manufacturers, well known in the late 19th and early 20th centuries. The S. Karpen Brothers Co. made some of the finest American ART NOUVEAU furniture, in the fluid, deeply carved French manner. The designers were inspired to produce this furniture after their senior member, Samuel Karpen, saw examples of the Art Nouveau style at the Paris Exposition of 1900.

KARTELL
Contemporary Italian furniture company. Kartell was noted for its involvement in the development of plastic furniture. The company has produced works by important Italian designers, including Joe C. COLOMBO, Anna CASTELLI FERRIERI, Marco ZANUSO and Richard SAPPER.

KAS
Alternative spelling of KAST, used especially for American variant of the form.

kast

KAST
Seventeenth-century Dutch furniture form; massive WARDROBE with four stacked components that could be disassembled for moving. It was generally heavily decorated with carved or applied Baroque style ornamentation (*see* BAROQUE FURNITURE). The feet, usually bracket or ball-turned, supported a low, rectangular case with either one wide drawer or two drawers side by side. A third component rested on this case of drawers; it enclosed shelves, later drawers, with two doors closing across the front. The fourth element was a separate, heavy, overhanging cornice that crowned the *kast*. The four components were either attached to each other with pegs or nails, or they simply rested one above the other.

Deriving from experimental forms of the late 16th century, especially those published by Hans VREDEMAN DE VRIES, the *kast* was popular throughout the 17th century and into the 18th. It was influential in the development of the CLOTHES PRESS in England, and it was the ancestral form of an American regional type. The American variant was made for more than 100 years in areas of Dutch settlement—especially in New York City, Long Island, the Hudson Valley and northern New Jersey—starting in the late 17th century. Dutch settlers imported a few *kasts* from the Low Countries, but in time they developed their own versions of the form. These more modestly decorated *kasts* were often unadorned except for painting and small applied molded ornaments. Some examples survive with elaborate pictorial painting representing huge swags of fruit, painted in *grisaille* in a *trompe l'oeil* manner intended to resemble carving. During the 18th century the *kast* changed very little; it was sometimes made with ball-and-claw or bracket feet, motifs taken from AMERICAN CHIPPENDALE FURNITURE, and sometimes incorporated in its main section a space for hanging clothes, a British modification of the wardrobe form. In general, the American *kast* reflected the conservative taste of New York and its surrounding region. *Kasts* (or *kasten*) were made into the early years of the 19th century, generally by country craftsmen but sometimes by more fashionable cabinetmakers such as the Egertons of New Brunswick, New Jersey (*see* Matthew EGERTON Sr.).

KATANA-DANSU
Traditional JAPANESE FURNITURE form; rectangular TANSU or chest for storing a sword and its fittings. Historically, a *katana-dansu* could only be owned by a Samurai, a member of Japan's aristocratic warrior caste.

KATAVOLOS-LITTELL-KELLEY
American design firm, in operation from 1949 to 1955. Formed by three designers—William Katavolos, Ross Littell and Douglas Kelley (all born in 1924)—the company designed furniture for LAVERNE ORIGINALS in the early 1950s. The designers worked in a variant of the European INTERNATIONAL STYLE, devising ingenious, elegant structures. They also produced textile and dinnerware designs.

KATSURA
Lustrous but unfigured Japanese HARDWOOD, used as plain but handsome VENEER.

KAUFFMANN, ANGELICA (1741–1807)
Swiss painter of furniture and interiors who worked in Britain. Kauffman was frequently employed by Robert ADAM to paint groups of figures in idealized pastoral and mythological settings. These works were executed on wall and ceiling panels and on a wide range of furniture, especially small chairs and large case pieces. In 1781 she married Antonio ZUCCHI, who did similar work.

KE HUI (K'O HUI)
Chinese name for COROMANDEL LACQUER.

KENT, WILLIAM (1684–1748)
British architect and furniture designer, leader of British PALLADIAN STYLE in furniture. Originally a painter, Kent become interested in architecture and went to Venice in 1710 to study the work of the Italian Renaissance architect Palladio. There, he met the British patron and architect Lord Burlington, and he returned to Britain as Burlington's assistant in 1719. The two men became the principal developers of the neo-Palladian style in architecture, which, like the work of Inigo Jones in the early 17th century, emphasized a combination of classical balance and impressive grandeur. Kent was concerned that furnishings appropriate to this new style be created, and he became the first British architect to design furniture for his buildings. Kent modeled his work on the 17th-century BAROQUE FURNITURE that he had seen in Palladio's buildings in Italy. Thus, the grandly serene facades of British neo-Palladian buildings enclosed rooms of extravagantly ornamented furniture in the sculptural tradition of Andrea BRUSTOLON. Kent was also influenced by the published engravings of Daniel MAROT and Jean Le Pautre, practitioners in the French LOUIS XIV STYLE.

Kent designed furniture as part of a given interior scheme—itself a revolutionary idea—and he favored rooms dominated by some strikingly grand feature. His massive pieces, generally designed in matching groups, focused on large-scale motifs, such as a vast scallop on the headboard of a bed, or tables supported by fiercely posing eagles. Large acanthus leaves and gilt swags abounded, amid classical masks, numerous *putti* and human figural sculpture. These pieces were sometimes so massive as to be virtually immovable. His case furniture was ponderously architectural in appearance; for instance, he designed three-door cabinets in the form of Italian Renaissance villas, topped by immense broken pediments.

Kent's floridly monumental furniture epitomized the baroque magnificence favored by the new aristocracy that adopted the Palladian style. In 1744 John VARDY published a book of Kent's designs (along with those of Inigo Jones), popularizing the style. And, until the triumph of rococo in the 1750s, Kent was the most influential designer of furniture in Britain.

KETTLE BASE
American term describing BOMBÉ case piece—that is, one that is curved or swelling in shape—especially referring to lower element in two-stage piece such as a SECRETARY or CHEST-ON-CHEST. Such pieces were a feature of BOSTON CHIPPENDALE FURNITURE.

KETTLE STAND
Eighteenth-century British furniture form; small table with marble or metal top, usually surrounded by a GALLERY, intended to support a container of hot water. Sometimes, the top was a metal-lined box. Beneath its top, a kettle stand usually had a small sliding board that could be pulled out to support a teapot.

KEY PATTERN (also *Greek key; meander pattern*)
Ornamental device; band composed of repeated small, hook-shaped forms created from a continuous line of short, straight elements joined at right angles. Originally a feature of ancient Greek architectural ornamentation, the key pattern was later adopted by NEO-CLASSICAL STYLE European furniture designers and was particularly popular in the 18th century, usually appearing as a decorative FRIEZE on case furniture.

KIBOTOS
Ancient GREEK FURNITURE form; chest for storage of linens, modeled on Egyptian chests

key pattern

(*see* EGYPTIAN FURNITURE), with short feet and a domed, hinged lid.

KIMBEL & CABUS

New York furniture-manufacturing firm, in existence from 1863 to 1882. Anthony Kimbel, formerly chief designer for Charles BAUDOUINE, and Joseph Cabus, who had designed for Alexander ROUX, began their partnership making RENAISSANCE REVIVAL STYLE pieces. In the early 1870s they became one of the chief producers of Modern Gothic, or "Eastlake style," furniture, popularized through the writings and designs of Charles Locke EASTLAKE and Bruce TALBERT.

KIMBEL, WILHELM, OF MAINZ

Early 19th-century furniture company of Mainz, Germany. Wilhelm Kimbel of Mainz was a fashionable producer of furniture in the various REVIVAL STYLES. Beginning in 1835 the firm issued a set of three pattern books in the ROCOCO REVIVAL STYLE that had wide influence in the German-speaking countries. A younger member of the family, Anthony Kimbel, left Germany and became a noted American furniture maker (*see* KIMBEL & CABUS).

chair by Kjaerholm

KIMONO RACK

JAPANESE FURNITURE form; arrangement of poles on which to hang clothes. A kimono rack consists of two vertical poles on transverse feet, connected by three horizontal poles, one between the two feet, one across the top of the poles, usually extending slightly beyond them, and one midway between top and bottom. Metal fittings, usually of bronze or copper, tightly cover each junction and the protuding ends of the top pole. For stability, the feet are made of very heavy wood.

KINGWOOD

Variety of Brazilian ROSEWOOD, especially popular among European cabinetmakers of the late 17th and early 18th centuries. Its distinctive appearance, pinkish in color and finely striped with dark brown, made it highly prized for decorative inlay work.

KINSMAN, RODNEY

See HIGH-TECH STYLE.

KIRI (also *paulownia*)

Japanese SOFTWOOD, silvery in color, used especially in chests (*see* ISHO-DANSU) intended to store silk garments. *Kiri,* in addition to being very light in weight, swells in humid weather. Thus, a chest made of this wood provides added protection against dampness.

KISS, PAUL (active 1920s)

French ART DECO metalworker. Kiss designed and built much wrought-iron furniture, especially screens and tables. His style was something of a compromise between a decorative floral mode and the new functionalistic forms of the INTERNATIONAL STYLE.

KITA, TOSHIYUKI (b. 1942)

Contemporary Japanese designer of furniture and interiors. Kita, who opened his Osaka design practice in 1964, has traveled and practiced in Italy. His bold designs combine traditional forms with novel ones and employ brilliant color.

KJAERHOLM, POUL (1929–80)

Danish furniture designer; major exponent of SCANDINAVIAN MODERN design. Though trained as a cabinetmaker, Kjaerholm designed metal furniture, usually steel, combined with a variety of other materials, such as cane, canvas, leather and wood. With Arne JACOBSEN, Kjaerholm led the trend in Danish design toward mass production. Kjaerholm's austere, functionalist style was clearly inspired by the example of the BAUHAUS and the INTERNATIONAL STYLE of the 1930s. Kjaerholm's work resembles that of MIES VAN DER ROHE, particularly in his combination of cold metal—formally and precisely deployed—and softer materials, which counter any clinical appearance. Also, like Mies, Kjaerholm preferred to use strips of flat steel rather than the more commonly employed steel tubes, and both designers demanded impeccable workmanship. Thus, Kjaerholm's pieces, although invariably factorymade, generally have a refinement of detail giving a handcrafted character.

KLENZE, LEO VON (1784–1864)

Early 19th-century German architect and furniture designer. Best known as an architect,

Klenze designed the Hermitage in Leningrad, though he mostly worked in Bavaria. He designed furniture for the royalty of the Bavarian kingdom and for other clients. Having worked briefly in his youth for PERCIER AND FONTAINE in Paris, Klenze made furniture in the EMPIRE STYLE, though he generally used lighter woods, less decoration and more figured veneering than other practitioners of the style.

KLINE

Ancient GREEK FURNITURE form; bed that was also a couch on which a user reclined while dining. Derived from the ancient Egyptian bed (*see* EGYPTIAN FURNITURE), the *kline* was a horizontal, rectangular frame on four legs. Within the frame was strung a sling of cords or leather thongs. The four supports were shaped like animal legs in earliest times but generally came to be simple rectangular or turned posts that extended above the frame. The posts at the head end were higher than those at the foot, and the bedding, usually a wool or linen mattress that rested in the sling, was lifted over these supports when the piece was used for dining, providing a soft surface against which the user could recline. Beginning in about the fourth century B.C., true headboards began to be used, anticipating the Roman FULCRUM and the later Roman form, the LECTUS.

KLINT, KAARE (1888–1954)

Danish furniture designer; important figure in SCANDINAVIAN MODERN design of the 1920s and 1930s. Klint, son of the well-known Danish architect Peter Klint, had little formal education before he joined his father's practice, though he had studied to be a painter. Characteristics of what came to be known in Denmark as the Klint school of architecture were a delight in geometry, in simplicity, and in logical solutions to design problems, with special attention given to the nature of materials used. When Kaare Klint turned his attention predominantly to furniture design, he applied these principles. Regarding furniture as "tools for living," he strove to suit the design to the purpose. He began the practice of systematic physiological research to determine the relationship between furniture and the human anatomy. He advocated the use of plain, unvarnished wood and naturally colored

textiles, and he insisted that furniture designs should be impersonal in character, without idiosyncracy or pretension. He believed in appropriating the good features of earlier traditions, discarding their particular ornamentation and incorporating the remainder into new, "timeless" designs. He was especially fond of adapting ancient Egyptian, Chinese and 18th-century neoclassical British furniture to this purpose.

In addition to maintaining his own design practice, he was appointed head of the new furniture department at the Royal Academy of Art in 1924. After 1944 he taught architecture there as well. He was for a generation the most important figure in Danish design. Thus, Klint had a major impact on the development of the Scandinavian Modern style, which attained international influence in the 1950s.

KLISMOS

Ancient GREEK FURNITURE form; a chair. A Greek innovation, the *klismos* was an especially elegant arrangement of elements. Four saber legs, slightly splayed to front and rear, supported a plaited seat. Above the seat frame, at the back, two curving stiles continued the lines of the rear legs and, with a central splat, supported a concavely curved board at shoulder height. Light, comfortable and portable, the *klismos* was popular throughout the Greek period, achieving its greatest prominence in the late fifth century B.C. In the Hellenistic era, after 323 B.C., the back board became thicker and the proportions less elegant; an even heavier version was made in Roman times.

In the late 18th century, Western NEOCLASSICAL STYLE furniture makers and designers discovered the *klismos* and revived it, generally with some variation. For example, a common American chair of the early 19th century had turned front legs in combination with the remaining features of the ancient model.

KNEE

Upper, outwardly curving bulge of CABRIOLE LEG (*see under* LEG).

KNEEHOLE CHEST OF DRAWERS

Another name for KNEEHOLE DESK.

klismos

kneehole desk

KNEEHOLE DESK
Desk with open space at center, below the top, so that sitter may sit closer to the writing surface. On either side of the kneehole are sets of drawers, called PEDESTALS, that support the top. The kneehole is usually closed at the back by a small compartment with a door.

KNEELAND, SAMUEL (1755–1828)
FEDERAL PERIOD furniture maker of Hartford, Connecticut. Kneeland is best known for the furniture he produced in partnership with Lemuel Adams between 1792 and 1795. Their firm, Kneeland & Adams, employed craftsmen from Boston and New York and produced a range of light, sophisticated furniture in the NEOCLASSICAL STYLE of the day. The firm is best known for its furniture made for the Old State House at Hartford. The building and furnishings are still extant.

KNIFE BOX
Eighteenth-century British and rare American form; small, vertical case with sloping lid that opened to reveal many slots, intended to receive carving knives and other serving tools. Knife boxes, usually in pairs, were placed on SIDEBOARD or table in a dining room. The form first appeared very late in the 17th century and continued into the 19th century. Basically rectilinear, if often had a serpentine front and, in the late 18th-century NEOCLASSICAL STYLES, was frequently made to resemble an URN.

KNOLL, FLORENCE SCHUST (b. 1917)
American furniture designer and entrepreneur. Florence Schust received her early design training at the Cranbrook Academy (*see* Eliel SAARINEN), where she associated with Charles EAMES, Eero SAARINEN and Harry BERTOIA. Later she studied architecture under Ludwig MIES VAN DER ROHE and worked briefly for Walter GROPIUS and Marcel BREUER.

Hans Knoll (1914–55), Florence's future husband, was a German immigrant who established his own furniture company in New York in 1939. She joined the firm as a designer in 1943 and married Knoll three years later. Florence Knoll assumed responsibility for the production and international distribution of much important furniture in the period following the Second World War and was also respon-

sible for commissioning new work from such young designers as Bertoia, Eero Saarinen and Isamu NOGUCHI. Her own INTERNATIONAL STYLE furniture was produced and marketed by Knoll Associates as well. In addition, the company began to manufacture the classic designs of Mies van der Rohe in the late 1940s and later produced works by Breuer.

The firm, which began to be an international concern in the early 1950s, was renamed Knoll International. It has handled the works of many progressive designers of postwar Europe, notably Poul KJAERHOLM of Denmark and Gae AULENTI, Vico MAGISTRETTI and Tobia SCARPA, all of Italy. The company has been regarded as an important arbiter of taste in postwar design, and, with its contemporary the HERMAN MILLER FURNITURE CO., has been a dominant force on the furniture market of that period. After her husband's death in 1955, Florence Knoll became president of Knoll International until her retirement 10 years later.

KNOLL ASSOCIATES
See KNOLL, Florence Schust.

KNOLL INTERNATIONAL
See KNOLL, Florence Schust.

KNORPELWERK
German term for AURICULAR STYLE. *Knorpelwerk,* meaning "cartilage work," refers, as does the English term, to the anatomical character of the motifs employed in this 17th-century mode of decoration.

KNURL
Eighteenth-century British name for SPANISH FOOT (*see under* FOOT).

KNURLING
Another name for GADROONING.

KOMAI, RAY (b. 1918)
American designer. Beginning as a graphic designer at an ad agency in the mid-1940s, Komai established himself as a multipurpose designer, with a specialty in furniture. He is

best known for an early molded plywood chair with a slit back, of 1949. He has also designed wallpapers and textiles.

KOREAN FURNITURE
Korean furniture, like Korean arts and crafts in general, has historically followed developments in CHINESE FURNITURE. Since at least the time of the Chinese Han dynasty (206 B.C.–A.D. 220), Korean furniture has resembled the work of northern China in its forms, its JOINERY and its favored materials, which have included HUA LI, the Chinese ROSEWOOD, and the Chinese nickel silver alloy PAKTONG for mounts. Recently, though, Korea has been noted in the West for case pieces resembling the TANSU of JAPANESE FURNITURE, with similar combinations of drawers and other compartments and with similarly designed mounts.

KORODY, GEORGE (active by 1930)
Hungarian-born Australian furniture designer; a pioneer of modern INTERNATIONAL STYLE design in his adopted country. An architect and designer of furniture, ceramics, and textiles, Korody fled Hungary in 1938, settling in Australia after a brief period in London. In Sydney after the Second World War, he established a studio and shop where he produced furniture to his own designs: crisp, unornamented pieces in the manner, then almost unknown in Australia, of European designs of the 1930s and 1940s. He also made copies and imitations of the work of numerous European designers, whose furniture was unavailable in Australia in the 1950s, and later imported their work, becoming, with Marion Hall BEST, one of Australia's leading importers and promoters of modern decorative arts.

KOTATSU
Traditional JAPANESE FURNITURE form; cubical frame to be placed over a fire or HIBACHI. It was intended to support a cloth cover that protected the surrounding floor from the heat of the fire. A sitter could wrap this cover around his or her legs and have a warm place to sit.

KUNSTSCHRANK
German RENAISSANCE FURNITURE form of the late 16th and early 17th centuries; early type of CABINET. The *Kunstschrank* was intended to house curios and small works of art in its numerous enclosed spaces, but it differed from earlier CHESTS and CUPBOARDS in that makers and users both regarded it as a work of art in itself—a piece of furniture whose utility was secondary. Made from only the finest woods, often exotic imports, and decorated with elaborate carving and MARQUETRY, it was frequently ornamented with precious stones and metals as well. Decorative imagery was in the MANNERIST STYLE and often included depictions of classical architecture and ruins. In Germany, Augsburg and Nuremberg were particularly noted for the *Kunstschrank,* while Antwerp, in the Low Countries, developed a local version with an emphasis on tortoiseshell inlay. Pieces were exported throughout Europe and were particularly popular in Spain.

KÜPPER, C. E. M.
See VAN DOESBURG, Theo.

KURI (also *Japanese chestnut*)
Japanese HARDWOOD used for doors and drawer fronts of high-quality chests in Japan (*see* TANSU).

KUROKAWA, KISHO (b. 1934)
Contemporary Japanese architect and designer. Kurokawa is one of a group of Japanese architects who have sought new avenues of development for Modernism. As a furniture designer, he developed an elegant variant of HIGH-TECH STYLE furniture, which combines industrial materials and finishes with forms and structures that resemble INTERNATIONAL STYLE furniture. These pieces are informed by a distinctive Japanese sensibility to the relationship between space and volume and have a gentle asymmetry.

KURUMA-DANSU
Traditional JAPANESE FURNITURE form; four-wheeled TANSU. Basically a large cupboard supported by a frame with two axles and their wheels, the *kuruma-dansu* was originally devised for the use of urban merchants evacuating their valuables on the all-too-frequent occasions of fire or earthquake. The form emerged in the

17th century and was made for 200 years. It usually featured two large sliding doors and, behind them, any of a variety of arrangements of shelves, compartments and drawers.

KUSURI-DANSU

Traditional JAPANESE FURNITURE form; pharmacist's chest. It is a variety of TANSU with any of various arrangements of many small drawers, sometimes arrayed above several larger drawers at the bottom.

kylix

KYLIX

Decorative motif used in NEOCLASSICAL STYLES of the late 18th and early 19th centuries; image of an ancient Greek pottery form, a shallow, stemmed and footed bowl intended as a drinking cup. In furniture it was used most commonly in American FEDERAL PERIOD chairs based on designs by George HEPPLEWHITE.

KYODAI

JAPANESE FURNITURE form; miniature DRESSING TABLE, about six inches high, with several tiny drawers. Before the 19th century, a *kyodai* usually had a lidded compartment in its top that held a hand mirror. More modern pieces are surmounted by a mirror hung between two uprights.

KYOSOKU

JAPANESE FURNITURE form; wooden armrest intended to be used by a person sitting on the floor, the traditional Japanese practice. Used especially at meals, the *kyosoku* resembles a small stool.

LABURNUM

European HARDWOOD used in late 17th and early 18th centuries for inlay work and as decorative veneer. It was especially popular for OYSTERSHELL VENEER.

LAC BURGAUTÉ

Decorative device in LACQUER work involving application of MOTHER-OF-PEARL, in powdered form or in tiny shards, to wet lacquer, producing a shimmering effect. Known as RADEN in Japan, where it was first developed in ancient times, *lac burgauté* has been used in the West since the 18th century in imitations of Oriental decoration (*see* JAPANNING; VERNIS MARTIN), as well as in 20th-century ART DECO furniture. The technique was also used in China, in YIN PING TUO lacquer furniture.

LACCA CONTRAFATTA

Eighteenth-century northern Italian JAPANNING technique. Clear VARNISH was applied over paper cutouts, usually depicting CHINOISERIE motifs, which were glued to painted furniture.

LACQUER

Asian VARNISH used as FINISH on CHINESE and JAPANESE FURNITURE since ancient times. Small objects can be made from solid lacquer as well. Lacquer comes from the sap of the *lac* tree, *Rhus vernicifera,* which grows in China and Japan; the sap is dissolved in rectified alcohol, or "spirits of wine." This liquid is spread in thin coats on wood. After each coat dries, it is laboriously polished. Many coats are applied, and the resulting material is very hard and can be polished to a high gloss. Coloring agents can be mixed into the liquid to produce a number of basic colors, and the finished product is commonly carved and further decorated with painting and gilding. In China, a variety of different sorts of decorative lacquer was in use by the 17th century (*see* TI HONG; DIAO TIAN; YIN PING TUO; XIANG QIAN; HUA QI; KE HUI).

Lacquer first became known to Europe through seagoing commerce in the Renaissance, and by the 17th century it was highly prized. Chinese and Japanese makers produced lacquered furniture and other objects in large numbers for export to the West. Most lacquered furniture that reached Europe in the 17th and 18th centuries was Japanese, though the Chinese decorated work known as COROMANDEL LACQUER was also imported. Unable to produce lacquer themselves, Europeans attempted to stimulate it, with varying results (*see* JAPANNING).

As the vogue for CHINOISERIE subsided in late 18th-century Europe, so did the Western demand for lacquer, though the material was still used in the Far East. In the late 19th century, Western interest revived, though, and lacquer remains a popular finish for furniture. A number of modern furniture makers have used it—most notably, perhaps, Eileen GRAY. In addition, the term applies to a modern synthetic material derived from cellulose, a glossy finish that is applied with a brush and may be clear or in any color.

LACROIX, ROGER
See VANDERCRUSE, Roger.

LADATTE (or Ladetti) FRANCESCO (1706–87)

Italian sculptor and maker of ROCOCO FURNITURE mounts. Trained in Paris, Ladatte worked under Filippo JUVARRA at the Sardinian court at Turin in the 1730s. After another stay in Paris, in 1737–43, he returned to Turin for good. His work was based on the French LOUIS XV STYLE, which he clung to long after it became unfashionable in Paris. He often made mounts for the furniture of Pietro PIFFETTI.

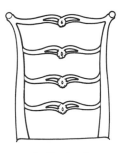

ladder back

LADDER-BACK CHAIR (also *slat-back chair*) Chair whose back resembles a ladder, being composed of three or more horizontal slats between two uprights. The ladder-back chair was first a MEDIEVAL FURNITURE form, and it has remained popular, chiefly in vernacular furniture, ever since.

LALANNE, FRANÇOIS (b. 1927)
Contemporary French artist and furniture designer associated with POP ART FURNITURE. Lalanne is best known for his whimsical furniture forms, which resemble realistic animal sculptures: a rhinoceros doubles as a desk; a flock of sheep serve as stools or hassocks. Lalanne began this line in the mid-1960s and continues to produce it.

LALIQUE, RENÉ (1860–1945)
French ART NOUVEAU designer of jewelry and glass. Once established as one of Europe's foremost jewelers, Lalique began early in the 20th century to concentrate on works in glass. Among these were screens and tables of plate-glass, etched or engraved with decorative patterns of flowers and human or animal figures.

LALONDE, RICHARD DE (active c. 1780)
French LOUIS XVI STYLE ornamental designer. Lalonde published a number of designs for furniture, wall paneling and metalwork in an austere neoclassical manner.

LAMBREQUIN
Short, deeply scalloped piece of drapery used as a VALANCE or shelf-mantel decoration; by extension, any fringelike decoration carved on furniture, especially on the APRON of a chair, table or case piece.

lambrequin

LA MÉSANGÉRE, PIERRE DE (active 1802–35)
French EMPIRE STYLE ornamental designer. La Mésangère's designs for furniture and other objects were published in periodical form between 1802 and 1835, under the title *Collection de meubles et objets de goût.* Though he was influenced by PERCIER AND FONTAINE's *Recueil des décorations intérieures* (1801), La Mésangére addressed a bourgeois rather than an imperial and aristocratic audience. His furniture was accordingly less grandiose in its ornamentation, markedly simpler in form and less opulent in materials than Percier and Fontaine's. La Mésangère's engravings were influential throughout Europe, especially in Holland, where his simple classicism was prized by furniture makers such as Carel BREYTSPRAAK.

LANGE, GERD (b. 1931)
Contemporary German furniture designer. Lange has designed furniture for Thonet Brothers (*see* Michael THONET) and other manufacturers. Lange's simple, ingenious designs are notable for their versatility and flexibility, especially his stacking chairs and modular furniture.

LANGLEY, BATTY (1696–1751)
British architect, writer and ornamental designer. Langley published many books on architecture and design, most notably *The City and Country Builder's and Workman's Treasury of Designs* (1740) and *Ancient Architecture Restored and Improved* (1742). Several furniture designs featuring rococo ornamentation appeared in the former, including material from the pattern books of J. J. SCHÜBLER and Nicolas PINEAU. In the 1742 volume Langley anticipated the fashion for CHIPPENDALE GOTHIC FURNITURE, though only with respect to the application of superficial ornamentation to simple, classically inspired shapes.

LANGLOIS, PIERRE (d. 1767)
French maker of rococo and NEOCLASSICAL STYLE furniture (*see* ROCOCO FURNITURE) who worked in London. Langlois made furniture in the French LOUIS XV and LOUIS XVI STYLES for British buyers, mostly aristocrats. His pieces were decorated with elaborate MARQUETRY and ORMOLU mounts.

LANNUIER, CHARLES-HONORÉ (1779–1819)
French-American cabinetmaker of New York City; principal practitioner of the AMERICAN

EMPIRE STYLE. Lannuier, who was born in France and trained under his brother, a Parisian *ébéniste*, moved to New York in 1803. He produced some furniture in the DIRECTORY STYLE but is best known for his American Empire style work, which is derived from the French Empire style and resembles the work of Pierre de LA MÉSANGÈRE. Although Lannuier's works are decorated with elaborate motifs, such as winged caryatids, and made of rich materials, including ormolu mounts that he imported from France, his designs are lighter and less overbearing than the French pieces they were modeled after. Lannuier and Duncan PHYFE are said to exemplify the American Empire style.

LAPPED DOVETAIL JOINT

See DOVETAIL JOINT, *under* JOINERY.

LARCH

European SOFTWOOD, light reddish brown with a prominent grain, used in 18th-century furniture as a secondary wood (*see* PRIMARY AND SECONDARY WOODS) in case furniture. Commonly used to build boats, larch has also long been used in vernacular furniture.

LARKIN, JOHN (1640–77)

Seventeenth-century maker of AMERICAN JACOBEAN FURNITURE, of Charlestown, Massachusetts. Larkin's father, a wheelwright and turner, immigrated from England in 1638 and set up shop in Massachusetts. Larkin succeeded to his father's shop and made furniture composed mainly of turned elements.

LATH

Narrow strip of wood or metal. Usually used in great number in building to support or provide backing for a wall of another material, such as plaster or stucco, laths appear as an element in light pieces of furniture such as DECK CHAIRS and LATH-BACK WINDSOR CHAIRS (*see under* WINDSOR CHAIR).

LATH-AND-BALUSTER WINDSOR CHAIR

See under WINDSOR CHAIR.

LATH-BACK WINDSOR CHAIR

See under WINDSOR CHAIR.

LATHE

Machine use in TURNERY to carve objects of wood or other material to a desired shape. The piece to be shaped is held between two points and rotated rapidly while being pressed against the cutting or abrading edge of a fixed tool. The lathe was invented in about the ninth century B.C., probably in Persia or Assyria (*see* MESOPOTAMIAN FURNITURE), though some authorities attribute it to ancient Greece or Egypt, and it has been an important tool for furniture makers ever since.

LATIMER, CLIVE (active from 1940s onward)

British CONTEMPORARY STYLE furniture designer. Latimer was a leader in the innovative design trends of the late 1940s and was one of the first designers to use cast aluminum in furniture. He collaborated with Robin DAY on the designs that won first prize at the New York Museum of Modern Art's 1948 "Low-Cost Furniture Design" competition.

LATROBE, BENJAMIN HENRY (1764–1820)

Principal American architect of the early 19th century; furniture designer in the AMERICAN EMPIRE STYLE. Latrobe is best known for his Baltimore Cathedral, but he also designed part of the United States Capitol building. Latrobe, who arrived in America from his native Britain in 1796, generally designed buildings in the NEOCLASSICAL STYLE, and his furniture, usually designed for his architectural commissions, was greatly influenced by Thomas HOPE. Latrobe designed some American Empire style furniture for the White House Oval Room in 1809 and had the pieces produced by John and Hugh FINDLAY of Baltimore. Unfortunately, these pieces, which were probably his best-known furniture designs, were burned by invading British troops in 1812.

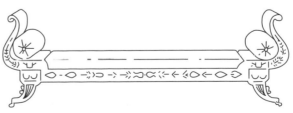

Benjamin Latrobe daybed

LATTICE

An open framework consisting of narrow strips of wood or another material, interwoven to create a repeating pattern, usually of diamond shapes.

LATTICE PEDIMENT

See under PEDIMENT.

LATTICEWORK

Another name for FRETWORK.

LAUREL LEAVES

Decorative motif representing a band or wreath of laurel leaves, symbol of triumph in ancient Greek art. The laurel motif was revived in the NEOCLASSICAL STYLE of the 18th and 19th centuries and was especially popular as decorative molding and on friezes.

LAVERNE ORIGINALS

American design firm founded in 1938. The company was established by Erwine (b. 1909) and Estelle (b. 1915) Laverne, husband and wife. Laverne Originals specialized in textiles but after the Second World War, the firm produced furniture designed by the KATAVOLOS-LITTELL-KELLEY group, as well as the Lavernes' own pieces. The Lavernes designed furniture in an INTERNATIONAL STYLE manner and are best known for their transparent plastic furniture of the late 1950s.

chair by Le Corbusier

LEAF

Hinged or removable section of tabletop, used to extend available surface. When not in use, a leaf may hang from hinges, as on a DROP-LEAF TABLE; or slide beneath a permanent top, as on a DRAW-LEAF TABLE; or simply be removed and stored elsewhere, as on an EXTENSION TABLE.

LEAF SCROLL FOOT

See under FOOT.

LEATHER LACQUER

See DIAO TIAN.

LE BRUN, CHARLES (1619–90)

French painter and designer; most important formulator of LOUIS XIV STYLE in decorative arts. A highly successful painter—a follower of Nicolas Poussin and a founding member of the French Academy—Le Brun was also a well-known interior decorator. He was chosen in 1663, by Louis XIV's prime minister, Jean-Baptiste Colbert, to head the new royal workshops at the GOBELINS factory. Colbert intended this establishment to produce costly furnishings for Versailles and the other grand royal palaces in order to create a spectacular demonstration of the wealth and grandeur of Louis's reign. Le Brun proved a brilliant and prolific designer in all of the decorative arts, and his taste set the tone for the work that would glorify the Sun King. He appreciated the vigor of the Italian baroque style but felt that true grandeur demanded classical restraint and balance, without gaudy or bizarre excess. It was this controlled drama, this air of exuberant dignity, that distinguished Louis XIV–style work from other sorts of BAROQUE FURNITURE. Le Brun was as great an administrator as he was an artist, and he organized the work and coordinated the styles of an international group of artists, including the furniture makers Pierre GOLLE, Domenico CUCCI, André-Charles BOULLE, Jean LE PAUTRE and Jean BÉRAIN. Colbert's plan succeeded, and Versailles became the artistic center of Europe. However, Le Brun's place in art history is more secure than his place at court was; when his patron Colbert died, in 1683, he was replaced by Bérain as director of the Gobelins shops.

LE CORBUSIER (1887–1965)

French architect, furniture designer, writer and painter; a leading exemplar of the INTERNATIONAL STYLE. Through his buildings and writings, Le Corbusier was a principal founder, with the BAUHAUS designers, of the International style in architecture and design. He was the most prominent member of the UNION DES ARTISTES MODERNES, the French organization that promoted the new design style. Though he designed only a few pieces of furniture—he was principally an architect—their very high quality, combined with his reputation, made them extremely influential in the subsequent development of modern furniture design.

Born Charles-Édouard Jeanneret in Switzerland, Le Corbusier studied design in Vienna and in Munich, where he studied under Peter BEHRENS, became acquainted with Walter GROPIUS and Ludwig MIES VAN DER ROHE and was influenced by the writings of Hermann MUTHESIUS. He established his architectural practice in Paris in 1922. Espousing the doctrines of FUNCTIONALISM, Le Corbusier formulated the famous dictum that a house is "a machine for living in." In his 1925 publication *L'art décoratif d'aujourd'hui,* Le Corbusier proposed that the norms of industrial production be adopted as new standards for the decorative arts. As he saw it, traditional decorative modes had failed the test of relevance to modern life. In his furniture designs, Le Corbusier focused on function, simplicity of line, and absence of decoration, always thinking of the requirements of mass manufacture.

Le Corbusier began designing furniture in 1926 in collaboration with his cousin, Pierre JEANNERET, and Charlotte PERRIAND, and their most important work was done in 1928 and 1929. These pieces are mostly of tubular steel and leather, the different materials employed so as to highlight the functions of the separate furniture parts. His "Cowboy" chair is a famous chaise-longue form. The seating element is leather stretched over a framework of intersecting strips of tubular steel. The base of this steel framework is a long, sloping curve that rests on iron legs and can be moved to adjust the angle of recline. His "Grand Confort" is an upholstered easy chair, cubical in shape, of leather cushions enclosed by a framework of thin tubular steel; thus, the upholstery does not obscure the structure (as in traditional chairs), and the function of the design has an esthetic component.

Le Corbusier stopped designing furniture after Perriand left the partnership in 1929. He is regarded as an important 20th-century designer on the strength of the few pieces that the partners produced, pieces famous for their elegance, ingenuity and comfort. Several of these were returned to production after the Second World War and remain popular today.

LE PAUTRE, JEAN (1618–82)

French furniture designer; major exponent of LOUIS XIV STYLE. Working under Charles LE BRUN at the GOBELINS workshops, Le Pautre designed carved ornamentation in a bold style featuring full-bodied nymphs, grotesques and beasts placed in luxuriant arrays of fruits, flowers and foliage. These dramatic designs supplanted the ARABESQUE-oriented two-dimensionality of late RENAISSANCE FURNITURE decoration. At the same time, Le Pautre's ebullient pictorial elements were organized in a grandly formal manner conducive to the regal calm intended by Le Brun. Le Pautre published more than 2,000 engravings of his designs and was thus one of the most important influences on BAROQUE FURNITURE makers outside France. His son Pierre LE PAUTRE was an important designer in the RÉGENCE STYLE.

LE PAUTRE, PIERRE (c. 1648–1716)

French RÉGENCE STYLE interior decorator. The son of Jean LE PAUTRE, an important LOUIS XIV STYLE designer, Pierre Le Pautre, who created interiors under the architect Jules Hardouin-Mansart, was one of the first designers to abandon the symmetry and formality that his father espoused. He thus helped to generate the transitional design of the Régence, which paved the way for the LOUIS XV STYLE.

LECTERN

Stand with sloping top, serving to support a book. The lectern was probably invented in early Christian times, when the folding book, or codex, came into use, replacing the scroll. Its first known appearance was during the Byzantine Empire, when it was very popular and was produced in great numbers, commonly in combination with a desk or writing table (*see* BYZANTINE FURNITURE). Adopted in western Europe, its use in MEDIEVAL FURNITURE was chiefly in religious settings, in churches or monastery libraries. Still used in such contexts, the lectern has also served as the prototype for the 17th-century BIBLE BOX and the modern secular READING STAND.

LECTUS

ROMAN FURNITURE form; couch or bed with sides and back. Having altered the Greek KLINE by adding the FULCRUM, Roman furniture makers went even further, in Early

cabriole leg

cupped leg

elephant-trunk leg

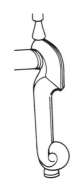

Flemish scroll leg

Christian times, by devising the *lectus,* which had boards at both ends and a back. Thus, the couch, the most important piece of domestic furniture in the classical world, began to resemble its modern successor in shape and function. The *lectus* was made in various heights, with turned legs or none. Throughout the period of the Roman Empire, a love of luxury promoted increasingly thicker mattresses, as well as the lush ornamentation characteristic of Roman furniture.

LECTUS GENIALIS
Ancient ROMAN FURNITURE form; a double-width LECTUS used as a bed and considered the "marriage bed" of a household.

LEG
Long, slender support that raises table-top, chair seat, stand or piece of case furniture an appropriate distance from the floor. A variety of styles of leg are distinguished by name.

BANDY LEG
Another name for CABRIOLE LEG (*see under* LEG).

CABRIOLE LEG
Carved, double-curved, tapering furniture leg, dominant in the 18th century. A broad upper part formed a pronounced outward curve above a tapering lower part with a long, smooth inward curve that extended down to the carved foot, which flared outward again. A properly made cabriole leg had a central, weight-bearing axis that descended from the inside of the upper part, passed through the outside of the tapering part and was anchored in the foot. First appearing in the late 17th century in England, the cabriole leg became a hallmark of 18th-century ROCOCO FURNITURE, exemplifying the smoothly flowing curves of that style. Because of the emphasis on straight lines in the NEOCLASSICAL STYLES of the later 18th century, the cabriole leg went out of fashion. Named for its resemblance to the limb of a capering animal, the cabriole leg at first generally terminated in a PAW FOOT, and then very frequently in a BALL-AND-CLAW FOOT, though other shaped feet, especially the

DUTCH FOOT, were also popular (*see each under* FOOT). The upper, outward curve, called the KNEE, usually bore carved decoration, commonly an ACANTHUS leaf or the COQUILLAGE motif.

CUPPED LEG
Turned leg with CUP TURNING (*see under* TURNERY). The cupped leg was especially popular in English RESTORATION FURNITURE.

ELEPHANT-TRUNK LEG
Support for low pieces of CHINESE FURNITURE; short, heavy leg that curved outward slightly at the top, down to a tight inward SCROLL at the bottom. The elephant-trunk leg was most popular during the Ming dynasty (1368–1644).

FLEMISH SCROLL LEG
Carved leg of 17th century, characterized by two scrolls, one at the floor and one at or close to the supported piece. The bottom scroll turned inward, while the upper one might spiral inward or outward. Occasionally, two scrolls, one spiraling in each direction, were located at the top. The section between the upper and lower scrolls was either angular or straight in profile and either plain or decoratively carved. A short Flemish scroll leg, especially one supporting a case piece, may be construed as a FLEMISH SCROLL FOOT (*see under* FOOT); it is difficult to distinguish between the two terms.

FLY LEG
Another name for a gate-leg, the movable support of a GATE-LEG TABLE.

MARLBOROUGH LEG
Straight, square leg, either undecorated or carved with simple FLUTING or STOPPED FLUTING, sometimes tapering downward, and either lacking a foot or terminating in a SPADE FOOT (*see under* FOOT). Very popular in British ROCOCO FURNITURE, the Marlborough leg was also used in NEOCLASSICAL STYLE furniture of the late 18th century, especially in America.

QUEEN ANNE LEG
Late 19th-century British name for CABRIOLE LEG (*see under* LEG). Although the cabriole leg was a feature of the 18th-century QUEEN ANNE STYLE, the term *Queen Anne leg* derives from the leg's popularity on furniture of the inaccurately named QUEEN ANNE REVIVAL STYLE.

SABER LEG (also *scimitar leg; swept leg; Waterloo leg*)
Rearward-curving front leg of chair or sofa, resembling a cavalryman's curved sword. The saber leg was usually rectangular in section, sometimes with a reeded, fluted or gently rounded front. It tapered slightly toward the bottom. Derived from the legs of the ancient Greek KLISMOS, the saber leg was popular in the late 18th and early 19th centuries, in furniture of the British REGENCY STYLE and the AMERICAN EMPIRE STYLE.

SCIMITAR LEG
Another name for SABER LEG (*see under* LEG).

SCROLL LEG
Carved leg shaped like large letter *S*. The scroll leg appeared on BAROQUE FURNITURE, especially on tables and stands, and it foreshadowed the more elegant CABRIOLE LEG (*see under* LEG).

SPIRAL LEG
Turned leg incorporating SPIRAL TURNING (*see under* TURNERY). The spiral leg was popular in many styles from the time of RENAISSANCE FURNITURE onward.

STUMP LEG
Thick, square rear leg of chair with more elaborate front legs. The stump leg was most commonly used in the QUEEN ANNE STYLE and in ROCOCO FURNITURE of the 18th century.

SWEPT LEG
Another name for SABER LEG (*see under* LEG).

SWING LEG
Table leg that is attached by horizontal member at its top to fixed member beneath the table, from which it pivots outward on a hinge to support a LEAF, as in the BUTTERFLY TABLE, or an unfolding tabletop, as in the 18th-century CARD TABLE (1). The swing leg is similar to the gate of a GATE-LEG TABLE, but it does not have a lower stretcher.

TRUMPET LEG
Turned leg incorporating TRUMPET TURNING (*see under* TURNERY). The trumpet leg was especially popular in English Restoration and WILLIAM AND MARY STYLE furniture (*see* RESTORATION FURNITURE).

WATERLOO LEG
British name for SABER LEG (*see under* LEG).

LEGRAIN, PIERRE (1889–1929)
French ART DECO furniture designer. Legrain's furniture design style is regarded as the leading example of the avant-garde wing of Art Deco, as opposed to Emile-Jacques RUHLMANN or SÜE ET MARE, who are seen as essentially traditionalist in character. Legrain worked with Paul IRIBE between 1908 and 1914 and was later chief furniture designer for Jacques DOUCET. Influenced by Cubism and African art, he produced novel pieces, during the 1920s, in bold, simple forms or futuristic shapes, employing fine, often unusual materials, such as vellum, velvet or chromium. He was particularly well known for a series of stools based on primitive African originals and for a grand piano made of glass. He was also a noted designer of book-bindings.

LEHMANN, C. F. (active c. 1755)
Danish ROCOCO FURNITURE maker. Lehmann made furniture with elaborate MARQUETRY in a heavy, opulent fashion derived from contemporary German work.

LEISTLER, CARL
See CARL LEISTLER.

LEJEUNE, LOUIS (active 1740s)
Flemish ROCOCO FURNITURE maker. Lejeune, who worked in Liège, specialized in elaborately carved furniture in the French LOUIS XV STYLE.

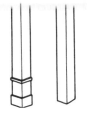

Marlborough leg

saber leg

spiral leg

trumpet leg

chair by Leonardi and Stagi

LELARGE, JEAN BAPTISTE (1743–1802)
French chair maker in LOUIS XVI and DIRECTOIRE STYLES.

LELEU, JEAN-FRANÇOIS (1729–1807)
French LOUIS XVI–STYLE furniture maker. Leleu worked for J.-F. OEBEN, and his early work was in the TRANSITION STYLE. His nature designs are generally monumental and architectural in character. He favored marquetry in geometrical patterns, also using panels of LACQUER, porcelain plaques and BOULLE MARQUETRY. He retired in 1792.

LELEU, JULES (1883–1961)
French ART DECO furniture designer. A follower of Émile-Jacques RUHLMANN, Leleu made a less elaborate, though commercially successful line of furniture, often employing *bombé* shapes veneered with such rich materials as tortoiseshell or macassar ebony.

LEMARCHAND, LOUIS-EDOUARD (1795–1872)
French RESTAURATION STYLE furniture maker. Lemarchand, son of a successful EMPIRE STYLE cabinetmaker, took over his father's business in 1817. He received many royal commissions under Charles X and Louis-Philippe, making sturdy, somewhat heavy furniture in a conservative manner reminiscent of Empire work. Perhaps his best-known piece was the coffin for Napoleon's tomb at Les Invalides in Paris. He retired in 1864.

LEMON, WILLIAM (d. 1827)
Leading FEDERAL PERIOD cabinetmaker of Salem, Massachusetts. Lemon made furniture in a NEOCLASSICAL STYLE, after the manner of George HEPPLEWHITE, but he was also an upholsterer and gilder. Lemon occasionally collaborated with the carver, Samuel MCINTIRE.

L'ENFANT, PIERRE CHARLES (1754–1825)
French architect and urban designer. L'Enfant, whose father was a court painter for Louis XVI, came to America in 1776 to join the American Revolutionary Army and served as a major of engineers. After the war he practiced architecture in America, principally in New York. He is credited with introducing the reeded leg and other NEOCLASSICAL STYLE motifs into the FEDERAL PERIOD design vocabulary, in furniture he designed for Federal Hall in New York (1789). L'Enfant is best known, however, as the designer of the basic layout of Washington, D.C.

LEONARDI, CESARE (b. 1935) and STAGI, FRANCA (b. 1937)
Contemporary Italian architects and designers; partners since 1962. Principally architects specializing in urban design, Leonardi and Stagi have also designed furniture for commercial manufacturers. Their best-known piece is the "Dondolo" rocking chair (1967). It consists of a single sheet of fiberglass, bent so that a right angle forms the seat and back and the rest of the sheet curves behind and under the seat to form the rocker and footrest. The elegance and ingenuity of this design have made it a modern classic.

LESCAZE, WILLIAM (1896–1969)
Swiss-born American architect and designer associated with the INTERNATIONAL STYLE. Lescaze came to the United States in 1920 and began practicing architecture in New York in 1923. He is best known for having designed some of the earliest skyscrapers in the International style. He also designed furniture in that style—rectilinear, austere pieces, functionalistic in character (*see* FUNCTIONALISM) and composed of such new materials as steel and glass. Lescaze often designed in tubular steel, and he followed the example of Alvar AALTO in using bent and molded plywood.

LEVASSEUR, ÉTIENNE (1721–98)
Late 18th-century French furniture maker. Levasseur was an apprentice in the workshop of the sons of André-Charles BOULLE, and he subsequently specialized in copying the furniture of that LOUIS XIV–STYLE master. He also designed new furniture in the older style, sometimes incorporating LOUIS XVI–STYLE features, such as the BREAKFRONT shape or the use of MAHOGANY.

L-HINGE
See under HINGE.

LIBERTY, ARTHUR LAZENBY (1843–1917)

British entrepreneur, associated especially with ART NOUVEAU. Liberty was a dealer in fine household goods, including furniture, from an early age. He began specializing in Middle Eastern and Oriental imports while also offering British-manufactured goods in the MOORISH STYLE and in the various European revival styles. He launched Liberty & Co. in 1875 and became involved with the ARTS AND CRAFTS MOVEMENT at about the same time. He stocked the products of Arts and Crafts designers in his store and was active in the Arts and Crafts Exhibiting Society. Liberty retailed the work of a wide range of independent furniture designers, often commissioning designs and manufacturing the furniture in the company's own shops. Such important furniture designers as C. F. A. VOYSEY and George WALTON were associated with Liberty's at this time. Perhaps the most famous item of Liberty furniture was the "Thebes" stool (1884), an ÉGYPTIENNERIE piece designed after an ancient original by the firm's chief designer, Leonard Wyburd. Arthur Liberty and William GODWIN were good friends during the 1880s, and as a result of their friendship, the firm dealt heavily in objects in the Japanese taste. Liberty's enthusiasm for British Art Nouveau design led to the production of many pieces of furniture by, among others, Walton and E. G. PUNNETT. Liberty & Co. distributed a great deal of Art Nouveau works—graphics and fabrics as well as furniture—through its Paris branch. Liberty & Co.'s impact on Art Nouveau is evidenced by the fact that in Italy, Art Nouveau is still called *Stile Liberty;* in Britain it was often known as Liberty style. Arthur Liberty was knighted in 1913. His firm is still in operation, though it is now known principally for its fabrics.

LIBERTY STYLE

See ART NOUVEAU.

LIBRARY STEPS

Eighteenth-century CONVERTIBLE FURNITURE form; set of two to four steps, designed to provide access to high bookshelves, that folded into another form, such as a chair, bench or table, when not in use. Developing in Britain in about the mid-18th century, the form evidenced the growing importance of private libraries. Library steps remained popular well into the 19th century. A nonconvertible form, also called library steps, was contemporary with the more ingenious version.

LIBRARY TABLE

Any large WRITING TABLE intended for use by two or more people. Also, in a more specific British usage, a library table has a broad rectangular top supported at each end by a set of drawers or shelves—that is, a PEDESTAL DESK, a type of case furniture.

LIGNUM VITAE

Very heavy, very hard HARDWOOD from northern South America and the Caribbean basin. Dark brown to black, with a greenish tinge, lignum vitae was a popular wood for MARQUETRY and decorative inlay in the 17th century, especially in Holland. Today, its applications are chiefly industrial.

LIMBA

Another name for AFARA.

LIMEWOOD

White to pale brown HARDWOOD of the Northern Hemisphere. Easily carved, limewood has long been used for decorative ornamentation on furniture, perhaps most notably by the 17th-century English woodcarver Grinling GIBBONS. It is also used for furniture framing and veneer, although, since the tree's primary product is its fruit, the lime, the wood is not regularly available in any quantity.

LIMING

Practice of bleaching wood furniture by coating it in a solution of lime and then cleaning it. This process lightens the color of the wood and leaves the grain quite white. Beginning in the 16th century, liming was a preliminary to painting a piece of furniture. Today it is sometimes used to produce a PICKLED FINISH.

LINENFOLD

Decorative motif appearing in carved wood on late GOTHIC FURNITURE throughout north-

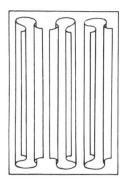

linenfold

lit en bateau

ern Europe in the 15th and 16th centuries. A conventional rendering of a piece of cloth arranged in vertical folds, linenfold carving originated in Flanders, which was a principal center of the linen industry in the 15th century. In England the motif remained in use through the 17th century, in JACOBEAN FURNITURE.

LINNELL, JOHN (d. 1796)

British GEORGIAN PERIOD furniture designer and cabinetmaker. Linnell made furniture in a wide variety of styles, ranging from PALLADIAN STYLE work through CHINESE CHIPPENDALE FURNITURE and ADAM STYLE pieces, to the plainer neoclassical mode of the REGENCY STYLE, when he was associated with architect Henry HOLLAND.

LION-CACHET, CAREL ADOLPH (1864–1945)

Dutch ART NOUVEAU furniture designer and graphic artist. Lion-Cachet worked in an elaborate, French Art Nouveau style, and he employed a great variety of luxurious materials. He also designed interiors for steamships. Lion-Cachet was an exponent of a peculiarly Dutch decorative manner derived from Indonesian batik designs.

LION'S-PAW FOOT

See under FOOT.

LIT À COLONNES

Eighteenth-century French furniture form; BED with CANOPY attached to four corner posts, which were carved to resemble classical architectural COLUMNS.

LIT À LA DUCHESSE

Eighteenth-century French furniture form; BED with CANOPY attached to the ceiling or to the wall above the bed and draping down to its foot. In Britain the *lit à la duchesse* was often called an ANGEL BED.

LIT À LA POLONAISE

Eighteenth-century French BED featuring posts at each corner that curved to form a

domelike TESTER completely draped in curtains. A form that offered even more seclusion, placed against a wall in a niche, was an ALCOVE BED, and the term *lit à la Polonaise* sometimes refers to that form, whether or not it had a tester or CANOPY.

LIT DE REPOS

French term, current since the 17th century, for a DAYBED in the general sense. The term more specifically refers to the 17th-century COUCH, with hinged arms convertible to headrests at each end.

LIT DROIT

French EMPIRE STYLE furniture form; bed with wooden headboard topped by triangular pediment. Simpler than the grandiose LIT EN BATEAU, the *lit droit,* in unadorned wood or painted with architectural decoration, was favored in the provinces and by the middle classes.

LIT EN BATEAU (also *lit en courbeille*)

French furniture form of CONSULATE and EMPIRE STYLES; bed whose headboard and footboard were shaped like the prow of a boat and sometimes terminated in an outward-scrolling curve. A massive piece, the *lit en bateau* was always carefully aligned relative to the surrounding architecture. Sometimes used as an ALCOVE BED and sometimes placed on a dais or platform, it almost always had one long side against a wall and was enclosed by draperies suspended from above. It was also called a *lit en courbeille,* or "basket-bed".

LIT EN COURBEILLE

See LIT EN BATEAU.

LIU XIAN ZHUO (LIU HSIEN CHO) (also *table of the Six Immortals*)

CHINESE FURNITURE form of Ming (1368–1644) and Qing (1644–1911) dynasties; small, square table, similar to larger BA XIAN ZHUO, or *table of the Eight Immortals*. Sometimes, though, it was fitted as a GAMING TABLE, incorporating mah-jongg tiles or other equipment. Both tables were named for figures in Taoist mythology.

LIVERY CUPBOARD

GOTHIC FURNITURE form; CUPBOARD designed to store food. Its panels were decoratively pierced to provide ventilation.

LOBATE STYLE

Another name for AURICULAR STYLE, similarly referring to the human ear. The ear's curves were associated with a principal motif in this anatomically inspired decorative mode of the 17th century.

LOCK, MATTHIAS or MATTHEW (active 1720s–1769)

British woodcarver and ROCOCO FURNITURE designer and maker. Lock was an important figure in the development of the rococo style in Britain. In 1740 he published a PATTERN BOOK of ROCAILLE ornamentation, freely interpreting French LOUIS XV–STYLE work. His designs for wall sconces and tables in 1744 and 1746 were the first British rococo designs to synthesize decoration and form in coherent pieces rather than simply applying rococo motifs to older forms. After 1752 Lock was probably employed by Thomas CHIPPENDALE, but this is uncertain. Late in his career, he produced NEOCLASSICAL STYLE designs.

LOHAN CHAIR

Another name for LUO QUAN YI, a CHINESE FURNITURE form, referring to its traditional association with monastic use. A *lohan* is the Buddhist equivalent of a saint.

LOLIONDO

See OLIVEWOOD.

LOLLING CHAIR

FEDERAL PERIOD term for the furniture form now known as the MARTHA WASHINGTON CHAIR.

LOMAZZI, PAOLO

See DE PAS, D'URBINO, LOMAZZI.

LOOP-BACK WINDSOR CHAIR

See BOW-BACK WINDSOR CHAIR, *under* WINDSOR CHAIR.

LOOS, ADOLF (1870–1933)

Austrian architect, designer and writer; early leader of modern design. Born in what is now Czechoslovakia, Loos spent three years in America, where he was influenced by Louis Sullivan (*see* PRAIRIE SCHOOL), then settled in Vienna in 1896. He designed both buildings and furniture but is best known for his writings on design. Loos stressed the importance of utility in design, asserting further that beauty is derived from form rather than ornament. His famous essay "Ornament and Crime" (1908) expressed this idea in characteristically strong terms. His furniture itself was unpretentious but rich, made of fine woods and marble in simple, foursquare designs. Though he generally practiced the asceticism he preached, he occasionally betrayed a fondness for elements drawn from CHIPPENDALE. After 1922 he lived in Paris, where he was allied with both the Dadaists and LE CORBUSIÉR.

LOPER

Sliding arm extending from the body of a cabinet or desk to support a FALL FRONT; also, such an arm used to support the leaf of a DRAW-LEAF TABLE.

LOTUS

Decorative motif representing flower of Egyptian water lily. Found in ancient Egyptian art and ornamentation, the lotus was used as an ÉGYPTIENNERIE motif on 19th-century European and American furniture.

lotus

LOUD & BROS.

Pre–Civil War piano manufacturer of Philadelphia. Noted for its elaborate ornamental work in the AMERICAN EMPIRE STYLE, the Loud & Bros. company was, after 1815, the largest, best-known piano maker in the United States.

LOUIS PHILIPPE STYLE

Another name for ROCOCO REVIVAL style, reflecting its great popularity in France during reign of King Louis Philippe (1830–48).

LOUIS SEIZE IMPÉRATRICE

See LOUIS XVI REVIVAL style.

LOUIS STYLE

Nineteenth-century name for either ROCOCO REVIVAL STYLE or LOUIS XVI REVIVAL style, more frequently the former.

LOUIS XIII STYLE

Furniture of early 17th-century France, named for king who reigned in 1610–43. The Louis XIII style was characterized by a last, gaudy, uninspired reprise of MANNERIST STYLE ornamentation in extravagant materials. In a society recovering from the exhausting Wars of Religion (1562–98), increasing prosperity brought only *arriviste* tastelessness, with very few significant advances in design. The elaborate sculptural effects and grotesque motifs of Mannerism, now almost a century old, were repeated, with an emphasis on expensive materials, including applied semiprecious stones and veneering of ebony and tortoiseshell.

Some small innovations did point toward the future, though. The elaborate CABINET, which remained the most important piece of furniture, was sometimes modified by the addition of a FALL FRONT, producing the early BUREAU. Another variant, wider than high, foreshadowed the SIDEBOARD. Also, a variety of small occasional tables, mostly oblong in shape, testified to an increasing informality in domestic usages. Two noteworthy decorative elements were introduced: the first, imported from Flanders, provided the most prominent superficial aspect of Louis XIII–style furniture—heavily molded paneling in geometrical patterns; second, the use of elaborate turnery for legs, stretchers and applied decoration increased. Both of these features—plainer work amid Mannerist excesses—anticipated the more balanced and unified style of BAROQUE FURNITURE, soon to be dominant (*see* LOUIS XIV STYLE).

LOUIS XIV STYLE

French version of Baroque style (*see* BAROQUE FURNITURE), named for the king whose reign (1643–1715) encompassed its development. Although Louis XIV–style furniture was distinctly baroque, with the dramatic manner of Italian architecture—sumptuous, symmetrical and large in scale—it was also tempered by a purposeful restraint, exemplified by the containment of decorative motifs within clear borders and by the use of dark colors, heavy

forms and severe outlines. Curves, the basic ingredient of baroque design, were modest, and the straight line was prominent. The style was intended to reflect the formal grandeur of Louis XIV's court at Versailles. This relationship was intentionally created and is at the heart of the style. Louis and his chief minister, Jean-Baptiste Colbert, formulated a strategy to glorify France through its arts. The palace at Versailles was the centerpiece of this program, and the furnishing of it and other palaces was placed in the hands of the artist Charles LE BRUN, who directed the royal workshops at the GOBELINS factory in Paris.

Le Brun assembled a group of master furniture makers. Some were foreigners, such as Pierre GOLLE of Flanders and Domenico CUCCI of Italy, but most were French, including André-Charles BOULLE, Jean LE PAUTRE and Jean BÉRAIN. They built furniture to advertise the king's wealth and power, using impressive design to flaunt expensive materials. They used a variety of exotic woods, making a staple of EBONY, with arrays of PIETRE DURE panels, imported Japanese LACQUER and INLAYS of horn, bone, ivory and precious metals. BOULLE MARQUETRY, of tortoiseshell and brass, enriched the panels of case pieces, and solid SILVER furniture was also made.

The decorative motifs of the Louis XIV style were mostly those of RENAISSANCE FURNITURE—mythological beasts, animal forms, grotesque masks, garlands of fruit and flowers—but there was a greater emphasis on bold carving. Ensembles based on robust figurative work replaced the ARABESQUE-oriented two-dimensionality of MANNERIST STYLE ornamentation. By the 1670s, the vogue for CHINOISERIE further enlivened the decorative repertoire. The FLEUR-DE-LIS, a well-known heraldic emblem, became enduringly associated with the French monarchy at this time, due to its use in Colbert and Le Brun's esthetic program.

Several new varieties of furniture evolved in the age of Louis XIV. The CHEST or COFFER was by now replaced by the COMMODE (1), a case piece, with either drawers or doors, on short legs; like other forms, the commode did not acquire its characteristic appearance until somewhat later. The CONFESSIONAL, an armchair with winglike forward extensions of the stiles, anticipated the 18th-century BERGÈRE, and the FAUTEUIL achieved the first of its various manifestations. The CANAPÉ first appeared at this time. It was a COUCH that still took the

Louis XIII chair

Louis XIV chair

simple form of an upholstered platform; it soon developed into a number of distinctive varieties. The CONSOLE TABLE was in a state of transition during the period. Massively immobile, it was established in its place against the wall and was therefore undecorated on one side. It continued to have four legs, usually, and it did not yet invariably have the CONSOLE-shaped supports that later gave it its name. These grand tables were elaborately decorated and heavily gilded, but there were also a number of small occasional tables that were made of plain wood, sometimes painted. These served a variety of purposes—to hold writing materials, light meals, toilet articles or candlesticks. Some were designed as specialized game tables.

Colbert and Le Brun's program to magnify the splendor of the Sun King's reign was highly successful. Versailles became the art capitol of Europe, and Louis's court was emulated by rulers far and wide. Two political events of his reign altered the history of the Louis XIV style. First, oddly, its influence in the rest of Europe was furthered when a number of fine Protestant craftsmen fled France—heading mostly to Holland, England and Germany—after Louis revoked the Edict of Nantes in 1685; the most notable was Daniel MAROT. Second, the financial crisis of 1693, precipitated by the king's incessant warfare, diminished the sumptuousness of the style. The silver furniture was melted down, and limitations were imposed on the use of precious metals on furniture and other objects. Magnificence was slightly marred.

In 1683 Colbert died, and his protégé Le Brun was replaced as director of the Gobelins workshops by Jean Bérain. In the next decade Bérain developed a lighter, less formal style, heralding a reaction against the grandeur of the by now less grand reign. The advent of the RÉGENCE STYLE, an early manifestation of the rococo (see ROCOCO FURNITURE), was evident in French furniture designs by Bérain, Pierre LE PAUTRE (Jean's son) and others by 1700, fifteen years before Louis's death. The Louis XIV style was exhausted, but its practitioners had nonetheless established the supremacy of France in European decorative arts; French furniture was to be a dominating influence elsewhere for more than a century.

LOUIS XV REVIVAL STYLE
Another name for ROCOCO REVIVAL STYLE.

LOUIS XV STYLE
French furniture style of about 1730–65; second phase of ROCOCO FURNITURE, following RÉGENCE STYLE. Though named for the king in whose reign it was fashionable, it was not yet fully developed when Louis XV acceded to the throne upon the death of the regent, in 1723. By 1774, when Louis died, the style was no longer fashionable, having been supplanted in the 1760s by the LOUIS XVI STYLE, a classical revival (see NEOCLASSICAL STYLE) named for his successor.

During the Régence an anticlassical precedent had been established. An artistic and social climate existed that valued informality, even idiosyncrasy, and that accepted art and ornamentation that were not based on classical architecture. Whimsical fancies of the Régence—such as the revels of SINGERIE decoration, exotic CHINOISERIE themes and ROCAILLE ornamentation based on garden rockwork—provided a vocabulary that designers in the Louis XV style could use in the 1720s. Pioneers in the style were J.-A MEISSONNIER and Nicolas PINEAU, creators of the *genre pittoresque,* a mode of pictorial decoration characterized by extravagantly swirling scrolls and whorls, casually strewn shell and flower motifs and boldly asymmetrical compositions. Another important designer of the day, Jean-Baptiste PILLEMENT, specialized in whimsical Chinoiserie scenes that delighted a society hungry for novelty.

These examples stimulated an extreme rococo style that became immediately popular and was used to decorate textiles, porcelain and silver, as well as interiors and furniture. The flower became the favored motif. Flowers in bouquets and baskets, on branches and as single blossoms, were carved on crestings and the knees of CABRIOLE LEGS (see *under* LEG) and were inlaid in elaborate MARQUETRY panels. Light, gay colors were used, including sea green, pale blue, yellow, lilac and white enriched with gold. In floral marquetry the colors of green foliage could be attained by tinting wood. The vogue for color was both stimulated and furthered by the new availability of exotic woods such as PALISANDER, KINGWOOD and PURPLEHEART. In his *Art of the Menuisier* (1769–75), furniture maker and writer A. J. ROUBO listed 50 kinds of wood commonly used in fine furniture. In addition, colorful veneers often came from Oriental LACQUER, either genuine or simulated in VER-

Louis XV chair

NIS MARTIN. PORCELAIN plaques were often incorporated into the veneer of a piece as well.

A style of interior decoration emphasizing the paneling of walls and ceiling of a room, the Louis XV style was most vigorously applied to furniture that was designed to be integrated into its architectural setting—forms such as the CONSOLE TABLE, whose scrolling supports reached heights of sculptural elaboration, great beds with fancifully ornamented headboards and corner posts, and the large CHAISE MEUBLANTE, still in use, though perhaps more as an architectural element than as seating. More functional pieces were also decorated in the rococo manner, but these stressed comfort and informality. The BERGÈRE flourished, and the smooth-lined CABRIOLE CHAIR appeared. The CANAPÉ, now an established form, diversified into several different pieces, including the CAUSEUSE, the MARQUISE, the CANAPÉ À CONFIDANTE and the VEILLEUSE. The DUCHESSE and its variants the DUCHESSE BRISÉE and the DUCHESSE EN BATEAU also catered to an ideal of relaxation.

The COMMODE (1) continued to evolve. The new COMMODE À ENCOIGNURES had display shelves at either end, but the most popular commode remained the COMMODE CRESSENT, developed during the Régence by Charles CRESSENT, who had become a leading cabinetmaker in the newer style. Another popular commode, similarly tall and light in appearance, was the COMMODE EN CONSOLE. The door-fronted COMMODE À VANTAUX appeared at this time, although it did not become truly fashionable until the subsequent Louis XVI style. The BUREAU PLAT was still the most popular sort or desk; it often had a serpentine, rather than simply rectangular, top. An adjunct to the *bureau plat*—the CARTONNIER, a file cabinet—was devised. The practicality of this piece seems related to a vogue of the 1750s and the Louis XVI period for small desks and tables, such as the SECRÉTAIRE À CAPUCIN, with built-in mechanical gadgets. A variety of other desks were popular in the Louis XV style, including the SECRÉTAIRE EN PENTE and the SECRÉTAIRE À ABATTANT. Late in the period, the ROLL-TOP DESK, known as a *bureau à cylindre,* was invented by J.-F. OEBEN. It later became a typical form of the Louis XVI style.

Besides Cressent and Oeben, the leading furniture makers in the Louis XV style included A.-R. GAUDREAU, Gilles JOUBERT,

Pierre MIGEON II and Bernard VAN RISENBURGH. Throughout the period, the former classically inspired taste never quite died away. MENUISIERS—who made chairs, tables and other carved pieces according to the guild regulations that governed specialization— were notably conservative. Some ÉBÉNISTES, too, were less than wholehearted practitioners of the *genre pittoresque.* Joubert, for instance, continued in a Régence manner throughout Louis XV's reign. Pierre ROUSSEL, practicing in any and all styles as clients required, sometimes produced pieces in the grand tradition of the 17th-century LOUIS XIV STYLE after 1750. It is thus not surprising that the full-blown rococo of the Louis XV style was short-lived; in about mid-century, a reaction set in against excessive fantasy and frivolity of design. The result was a gradual return of classical motifs, generally on curving rococo forms, in a mode called the TRANSITION STYLE. Whether this style is viewed as a late variant of the Louis XV style or as an early phase of the Louis XVI style, it was the death knell of the rococo in France.

LOUIS XVI REVIVAL STYLE

Neoclassical revival style based on the 18th-century Louis XVI style, popular mainly in France and America during the 1850s and 1860s. As a late instance of the 19th-century vogue for REVIVAL STYLES, the Louis XVI Revival marked a reacquaintance with neoclassical forms and motifs. More rectilinear and with more subdued decoration than the ROCOCO REVIVAL STYLE, its predecessor, the Louis XVI Revival style nevertheless produced furniture that was more elaborate and showy than the original Louis XVI style of the 18th century that it was based on. One striking difference was the frequent use of deep-buttoned, coil-spring upholstery in the revival pieces.

The revival was intentionally promoted at the court of Napoleon III, the new French emperor, who wished to remind his subjects of past national glories. It is therefore sometimes called the "Second Empire style." Additional support for the style came from the cult of Marie-Antoinette indulged in by the Empress Eugénie, who furnished her apartments in a particularly elaborate manner that was later called "Louis Seize Impératrice." Her furniture was produced by Paris makers Guillaume GROHÉ, L.-A.-A. BEURDELEY and Ferdinand

BARBEDIENNE. These makers also manufactured reproductions of the 18th-century Louis XVI style, a vogue for which naturally accompanied the revival.

In America the Louis XVI Revival style became popular during the late 1860s. Its principal exponents were the French *émigré* cabinetmakers Leon MARCOTTE and Alexander ROUX. The various revival styles in America tended to merge with one another to some degree. Thus, the use of ormolu and more rectilinear forms among practitioners of the RENAISSANCE REVIVAL and NEO-GREC STYLES was derived from the Louis XVI Revival style.

A further manifestation of the Louis XVI Revival lasted longer and had wider exposure than the other revival styles. With the international growth of the grand hotel from the late 19th to early 20th centuries, neoclassical furniture became widespread in a commercialized, simplified form that acquired the appellation "Louis the Hotel" style.

LOUIS XVI STYLE

French furniture style of about 1765–90. It was a NEOCLASSICAL STYLE that became popular before the reign (1774–92) of the king for whom it is named, lasted into the time of the French Revolution and then evolved into the DIRECTOIRE STYLE. The Louis XVI style was characterized by an emphasis on straight lines and geometrical shapes and by a restrained, almost pedantic, use of classically inspired decorative motifs. The furniture was nonetheless sumptuous; it was made of expensive materials and was very highly crafted by an extraordinary group of virtuoso furniture makers. The Louis XVI period has been called the "golden age of cabinetmaking," and the assemblage of skills that then served the Paris furniture market has probably never been remotely duplicated.

Among ÉBÉNISTES, the leading practitioners were German—most notably Jean-Henri RIESENER, generally held to be the finest maker of the day; Martin CARLIN; and Adam WEISWEILER. Other German makers in Paris included Ferdinand SCHWERDFEGER and Joseph STÖCKEL. Of course, there were many French *ébénistes* as well. Most highly regarded were Jean-François LELEU and Roger VANDERCRUSE; others included C.-C. SAUNIER, Charles TOPINO and Étienne LEVASSEUR. The MENUISIERS, carvers of chairs and tables, were mostly French, led by Georges JACOB, who was a dominant French furniture maker for almost 50 years. Other important chair makers included Jean-Baptiste SENÉ and J.-B. BOULARD. Elaborate metal mounts became increasingly important in a period in which other decoration was deliberately diminished. The leading makers of these ornaments were Pierre GOUTHIÈRE and Pierre THOMIRE.

Throughout the period the Louis XVI style in furniture became progressively more restrained in decoration, if no less opulent. At first, in reacting against the whimsy and frivolity of the ROCOCO FURNITURE of the LOUIS XV STYLE, designers and makers of the TRANSITION STYLE used classical motifs on pieces that retained the curves of the rococo. However, in the fully developed Louis XVI style, they rejected the curve most emphatically. The CABRIOLE LEG (*see under* LEG) was replaced by a square or cylindrical tapering leg, often fluted or spirally turned (*see* TWIST TURNING, *under* TURNERY), which became a prominent characteristic of the style. On case pieces the BOMBÉ shape was abandoned, and the SERPENTINE front was only faintly echoed in the more severe BREAKFRONT. By the 1780s even this modest bulge was ironed out. The scrolling flourishes of the rococo became neat arrangements of geometrical shapes, and the flower motif that dominated in the 1750s yielded to decorative devices derived from classical architecture. The ornamental designs of J.-F. NEUFFORGE and J.-C. DELAFOSSE did much to establish this repertoire, which encompassed building elements, such as COLUMNS and CORNICES, and decorative motifs, including the VITRUVIAN SCROLL, PALMETTE, Greek KEY PATTERN, ANTHEMION and BUCRANIUM. These devices were used in MARQUETRY designs that became increasingly plain, with fewer elements in a given space, until, after about 1780, figured wood panels became dominant. PORCELAIN plaques were also used. The wood paneling was often of MAHOGANY, a usage imported from Britain. Decoration tended to be relegated to borders and bronzes. Increasingly complex small-scale metal mounts visually complemented the expanses of plain veneer, but the thrust of the style's evolution was toward simplicity. This simplicity was felt to evoke the solemn grandeur and stoic discipline of the classical world so admired during the Enlightenment.

Louis XVI chair

Therefore, the bright colors of the rococo were toned down. Paler tones of gray and lilac became popular, as did plain white and gold.

New types of COMMODES (1) became prominent in the Louis XVI style. The door-fronted COMMODE À VANTAUX and the COMMODE À ENCOIGNURES, with open shelves at each end, became popular in the 1770s, although they had appeared earlier. A new form was the DEMILUNE commode, whose front was a semicircle; the open-shelved CONSOLE DESSERT had a similar shape. The SECRÉTAIRE À ABBATANT, architectural in character, remained popular, as did a smaller desk, the BONHEUR-DU-JOUR. The ROLL-TOP DESK, invented by the Transition style master J.-F. OEBEN, was also prominent. The wide range of small tables that had been established during the Louis XV period changed little, though a few idiosyncracies appeared, such as a three-lobed, roughly heart-shaped dressing table, perhaps also invented by Oeben, and a new sort of GUÉRIDON, composed of a round top on a columnar support, that would achieve its greatest popularity in the early 19th century. Another new form, the JARDINIÈRE, arose late in the period, as flower arranging became an important domestic art, at least in part to compensate for the increasing simplicity of furniture veneers. Chairs, while austerely rectilinear in shape, did not seem cold or severe, for they generally had upholstered seat and back panels. Also, the back could have a curved top or take the shape of a jaunty octagon or, occasionally, a shield, and the front of the seat was generally rounded.

The Louis XVI style was popular not only in France but in other countries as well. Parisian cabinetmakers sold furniture to royalty and aristocracy from Russia to Portugal and Scandinavia to Italy. Even in Britain, where the ADAM STYLE was dominant, French furniture was also prized. Neoclassical furniture was made throughout the West in various local styles, many of which were influenced by the French mode to a greater or lesser degree. The TAMBOUR, first used in Oeben's roll-top desk, found its way abroad, especially to Britain and America, where it quickly became popular. In northern Italy—especially at Turin, where G. M. BONZANIGO was the leading maker—the French style dominated. Even farther south Giuseppe MAGGIOLINI's elaborate pictorial marquetry, theatrical and colorful, adorned austerely rectilinear forms derived from French

models. In Sweden, Georg HAUPT led the fashion for furniture that frankly imitated Parisian work. A similar taste prevailed in Germany, where the simpler, later version of the Louis XVI style pointed the way to the 19th-century BIEDERMEIER STYLE. One German maker, David ROENTGEN, made Louis XVI style furniture distinguished by a traditional German fondness for such mechanical devices as secret compartments. His work was very popular in France and elsewhere, and he has been called the most successful cabinet-maker of the period.

In the 1770s and 1780s, when the excavations at Pompeii and Herculaneum became known, a trend toward archeologically correct pieces modeled on ancient GREEK and ROMAN FURNITURE produced the furniture of famed painter Jacques-Louis DAVID and similar work by the Danish painter Nikolai ABILDGAARD. These and other pieces, such as those designed by Hubert ROBERT, another painter, were decorated in what was inaccurately known as the ETRUSCAN STYLE, involving fewer and simpler ornaments and a darker color scheme than had been usual. Also, the SABER LEG (*see under* LEG) came into use on chairs at this time. These innovations were applied in the work of Georges Jacob, F.-J. BÉLANGER and J.-D. DUGOURC as the French Revolution approached.

The Revolution did not in itself end the Louis XVI style; the new, bourgeois clientele that rapidly replaced the aristocracy was content with the basic forms and types of furniture. However, opulent materials were no longer used, due to the austerities necessitated by the political and military upheavals of the early 1790s. This decreased extravagance combined with Revolutionary iconography to produce the distinctive Directoire style, named for the government that succeeded the Reign of Terror in 1794. The Directoire style was the final phase of the Louis XVI style, and it was also a preamble to the EMPIRE STYLE of the early 19th century.

LOUIS XVIII STYLE

French NEOCLASSICAL STYLE current during the reign of King Louis XVIII (1814–24); a variation of RESTAURATION STYLE. Differing very little from EMPIRE STYLE furniture, Louis XVIII style work may be contrasted with that of its successor, the CHARLES X STYLE, in being generally more massive, and with more elaborate bronzes.

LOUNGE
Nineteenth-century upholstered DAY-BED, usually with a simple headrest at one end. Also, a daybed in the general sense—any form designed for daytime reclining.

LOUNGE CHAIR
Completely upholstered, overstuffed armchair. The lounge chair arose in the mid–19th century as a particularly luxuriant application of the newly developed coil-spring UPHOLSTERY.

LOVE SEAT
Any small, upholstered SOFA intended for two people; more specifically, TÊTE-À-TÊTE (2).

LOW-BACK WINDSOR CHAIR
See under WINDSOR CHAIR.

LOWBOY
Eighteenth-century American DRESSING TABLE or low CHEST OF DRAWERS on legs. It was frequently made to match the lower section of a HIGHBOY, though it was also used independently. The arrangement of its drawers varied widely, but one or two tiers were standard, and there were often deep drawers at the sides of the lower (or lone) tier that extended below a shallower drawer in the center.

LOZENGE
Decorative device; diamond shape originally from heraldic design and used as a geometric figure, often in DIAPERING.

LEUCKENHAUSEN, HELMUT (b. 1950)
AUSTRALIAN FURNITURE designer. Lueckenhausen's highly sculptural work features bold, dramatic zoomorphic carving, with wings on the sides of case pieces and on mirrors atop chests of drawers, lip-like drawer pulls, and the like, combined with geometrically striking shapes, all emphasized with bright colors. Combining the wit of POP ART FURNITURE with the bold colors and shapes of "Memphis"

furniture (*see* SOTTSASS), but with the attention to fine woodwork associated with the HANDICRAFT REVIVAL, Lueckenhausen is a prime example of the syncretic nature of contemporary Australian design. Born in Germany, Lueckenhausen came to Australia at age 5. He is the head of the School of Design at Swinburne University.

LUNDELIUS, LORENTZ WILHELM (1787–1859)
Early 19th-century Swedish cabinetmaker in French EMPIRE STYLE. The leading craftsman in Stockholm, Lundelius followed French models closely.

LUNETTE
Decorative device, half a ROUNDEL; semi-circular shape either carved, painted or inlaid, often enclosing another motif. In GOTHIC FURNITURE lunettes were often rendered in CHIP CARVING. In the 18th century, commonly inlaid, they often depicted decorative fans.

LUO QUAN YI (LO CH'UAN YI) (also *lohan chair*)
CHINESE FURNITURE form of Ming (1368–1644) and Qing (1644–1911) dynasties; chair with a CREST RAIL that curved forward in a broad bow to form arms, each of which ended with an outward SCROLL. This rail was supported by a central SPLAT and four slender posts, one rising from each corner of the square seat. The rounded frame, while appearing to be BENTWOOD, was composed of three to five carved elements joined by sophisticated TONGUE-AND-GROOVE JOINTS (*see under* JOINERY) and reinforced by hidden DOWELS, which were uncommon in Chinese furniture. Although prominent in secular furniture, the form was traditionally associated with monastic use and was known as a *lohan chair*, a *lohan* being the Buddhist equivalent of a saint.

LUTE TABLE
See QIN ZHUO.

LUTHER CHAIR
Nineteenth-century name for the X-FRAME chair, as it appeared in German RENAISSANCE

lowboy

FURNITURE. Analogous to the Italian SAVON-AROLA CHAIR and, like it, a survival from the Middle Ages, the Luther chair was generally more elaborately decorated than its southern counterpart.

LUTYENS, EDWIN (1869–1944)

British architect and furniture designer of the late 19th and early 20th centuries. Best known as the most prominent Edwardian-period architect of British country houses, Lutyens usually designed all or part of the furniture for his architectural commissions. His most famous commission was the mammoth Viceroy's House in New Delhi, built between 1913 and 1931. Lutyens's furniture style was unoriginal, derived from historical sources ranging from 17th- and 18th-century designs to rustic British models.

LYRE

Ornamental motif found in NEOCLASSICAL STYLE furniture. It is the image—carved, inlaid or painted—of an ancient Greek musical instrument, which consisted of a frame shaped like a pair of recurved animal horns and a set of strings mounted vertically between its two hornlike arms. RENAISSANCE FURNITURE makers adopted the motif from ancient pictorial art, and it was used on neoclassical furniture throughout Europe into the 19th century. It was especially popular in the EMPIRE and AMERICAN EMPIRE STYLES.

lyre

McCOBB, PAUL (1917–69)

American furniture designer of the 1950s. McCobb specialized in low-cost, popular designs based on the simple, logical tenets of the INTERNATIONAL STYLE. He was also influenced by SCANDINAVIAN MODERN design, particularly with respect to materials—he used only natural wood, with modest foam-rubber upholstery. McCobb was the leading popular designer of his day, influencing the developing American taste for modern furniture.

MACÉ, JEAN (d. 1672)

Seventeenth-century French furniture maker. Early in his career, Macé worked in the Netherlands, where he learned the related arts of veneering (see VENEER) and MARQUETRY. He introduced these to France when he returned there in 1620 to work for Marie de' Medici. Using ebony and other exotic woods, he made furniture in a style that combined traditional RENAISSANCE FURNITURE forms with MANNERIST STYLE ornamentation, thus anticipating BAROQUE FURNITURE. Macé was also noted for fine PARQUETRY floors.

McGRATH, RAYMOND (1903–77)

Australian-born British INTERNATIONAL STYLE architect and furniture designer. Like his contemporaries Wells COATES and Serge CHERMAYEFF, McGrath responded strongly to the example of the BAUHAUS designers, producing clean-lined, rectilinear furniture with an emphasis on function (see FUNCTIONALISM). McGrath favored the exotically colored and patterned woods of Australia (see "EMPIRE" WOODS), and his use of rich materi-

als added an element of luxury to his practical furniture.

McINTIRE, SAMUEL (1757–1811)

FEDERAL PERIOD woodcarver and architect of Salem, Massachusetts. McIntire, the son of a joiner, began his career as a carver of figureheads for ships. Principally a woodcarver, he decorated furniture in the NEOCLASSICAL STYLE, influenced by Robert ADAM, George HEPPLEWHITE and Thomas SHERATON. It is known that McIntire carved decoration on pieces designed by other cabinetmakers, including Elijah and Jacob SANDERSON, but whether he designed and built furniture himself has not been conclusively established. In any case, many pieces are attributed to McIntire on the strength of his distinctive carving style, which included the frequent use of the BELLFLOWER motif, punchwork backgrounds and his particular hallmark, a basket of fruit. As an architect, he built simple, square houses distinguished chiefly by his carved wood ornamentation.

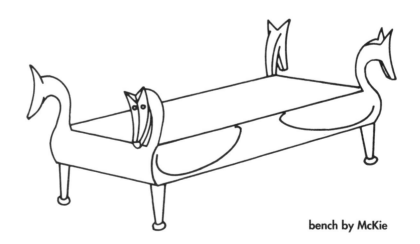

bench by McKie

McKie, Judy Kensley (b. 1944)

Contemporary American furniture maker, associated with 1970s HANDICRAFT REVIVAL. McKie's idiosyncratic furniture incorporates droll images of animals in finely crafted pieces that are both whimsical and practical.

Mackintosh, Charles Rennie (1868–1928)

Scottish architect and furniture designer; prominent ART NOUVEAU designer. As the leading member of the GLASGOW SCHOOL, Mackintosh developed a style based on the ARTS AND CRAFTS MOVEMENT, especially the work of C. F. A. VOYSEY and William GODWIN. However, he placed much less emphasis on craftsmanship and materials than Arts and Crafts purists did; he generally painted his wood, for example, and his pieces are not designed to highlight the manner of their construction. In accordance with the flowering Art Nouveau movement, his emphasis was on antirevivalist design. Through Godwin, Mackintosh was introduced to Japanese Art (see JAPONISME) and began to design light, airy furniture composed largely of open arrangements of linear elements, the forms based on straight lines and gentle curves. Chair backs were often decorated with panels of stained glass or enamel. High-backed chairs as tall as six feet and tables with slender legs were the result of Mackintosh's effort to stress his attenuated, vertical line. He adapted swirling decorative patterns from medieval Celtic art, a popular practice in the Celtic revival of the day. Mackintosh, an architect, designed a great deal of his furniture for specific placement in his buildings.

While his furniture received little recognition in Great Britain, Mackintosh was prominent in the Art Nouveau movement in other parts of Europe, and the ideas and ideals of the British Arts and Crafts movement reached German-speaking countries, in particular, through Mackintosh. The geometrical character of his work had a strong impact on Viennese Art Nouveau design and, through Josef HOFFMANN and the WIENER WERKSTÄTTE, may be said to have influenced modern furniture design as it was formulated at the BAUHAUS.

chair by Mackintosh

Mackmurdo, Arthur Heygate (1851–1942)

British designer associated with the ARTS AND CRAFTS MOVEMENT and the beginnings of ART NOUVEAU. Originally an architect, A. H. Mackmurdo, a friend and follower of both John RUSKIN and William MORRIS, founded the Century Guild in 1882. The Century Guild promoted handicraft as art and opposed the industrial manufacture of furniture and household goods. Mackmurdo's furniture, while progressive and reflective of the burgeoning Japanese influence of the day (see JAPONISME), was generally in the manner prescribed by Morris—simple and with little ornamentation. However, in one well-known early work, a chair, Mackmurdo employed the swirling asymmetry that is now considered one of the signature style elements of Art Nouveau. Aside from this chair, Mackmurdo is associated with Art Nouveau principally through his graphic work. He did little or no designing of any kind after 1904.

MACROCARPA

A SOFTWOOD of New Zealand, with dramatic orange to brown coloring. Strongly scented, macrocarpa is often used in CHESTS and CABINETS.

Maggiolini, Giuseppe (1738–1814)

Italian NEOCLASSICAL STYLE cabinetmaker famous for pictorial MARQUETRY. Maggiolini's furniture was austerely rectilinear in form, with very little carving and a restrained use of metal mounts, but it was opulently decorated. He specialized in marquetry panels depicting elaborate trophy assemblages, CHINOISERIE scenes and floral still lifes. Such pieces were further enlivened with other inlaid ornamentation in freely adapted classical architectural motifs, in the tradition of G. B. PIRANESI, which Maggiolini absorbed through the more direct influence of Giocondo ALBERTOLLI. He used many different kinds of exotic woods in a wide range of colors and disdained stains or other tinting techniques. His work has always been greatly celebrated. Italian marquetry of the period is known generically as "Maggiolini work," and pieces are often indiscriminately attributed to him.

Magistretti, Vico (b. 1920)

Contemporary Italian architect and designer. Magistretti specialized in interior design before 1960 but designed a number of storage systems in addition to his interiors. The most notable of these was a stepped shelf system (1950), designed to lean ladder-like against a wall. After 1960 he designed a great deal of well-known furniture for CASSINA and other manufacturers, including several designs for stacking chairs in molded wood or plastic. His "Maralunga" chair (1973) is a generously proportioned armchair, designed so that extra padding in the uphol-stery folds over the top of the arms and back of the chair to provide a comfortable, overstuffed seat. His "Caori" table is said to combine Italian *brio* with Japanese austerity, and this observation seems to apply to his work as a whole. Magistretti's designs show a concern for utility and material, derived from the INTERNA-TIONAL STYLE, FUNCTIONALISM and ERGO-NOMIC DESIGN, that lends a serious, though not austere, character to his furniture. He also reflects the individualism so prominent in the Italian design of the 1960s and 1970s.

MAGNOLIA
Pale, plain, American HARDWOOD used in furniture making principally for framing and interior linings.

MAHER, GEORGE WASHINGTON (1864–1926)
Chicago architect and furniture designer; member of the PRAIRIE SCHOOL. Maher was acquainted with Frank Lloyd WRIGHT and George ELMSLIE from the time of his appren-ticeship; all three designers were influenced by the architect Louis Sullivan and the British reform traditions in design. He began his own architectural practice in 1888 and acquainted himself with progressive design in Britain, France, Germany and Austria when he traveled in Europe between 1892 and 1897. On his return Maher designed furniture for a number of private residences, all of it in a simple recti-linear style. He attempted to unify all the fur-niture of a given house through the use of a theme—a decorative motif repeated on all the individual pieces. At first, Maher tended to use organic motifs, after the manner of Sullivan's architectural ornamentation. His later motifs, influenced by Wright, are more geometrical.

MAHOGANY
Pinkish to dark red-brown HARDWOOD; one of the most important woods in European and American furniture making since the 18th century. There are several varieties of mahogany. Originally, in the early 18th century, "Spanish" or "Jamaican" mahogany was imported from the Caribbean by English furniture makers and began to compete with WALNUT as the most popular material for fine cabinetry. By 1750 the Cuban variety of the same species was being shipped to Europe. "Cuban" mahogany had more pronounced figuring and was easier to work. By the 19th century, though, another species of mahogany had been found on the mainland of Central and South America; it was known variously as "Honduran," "Brazilian" or "Peruvian." It is now known as "American" mahogany, while its Caribbean relative is called Cuban mahogany, regardless of its precise source. Though plainer and paler than Cuban, Ameri-can mahogany is also stronger; it was com-monly used for the carcase beneath veneering of Cuban wood. American mahogany provides much wider planks, which were used as table-tops. Throughout most of the 18th century, mahogany was used chiefly in Britain and America. Later in the century its use spread to Continental Europe. In the early 19th centu-ry, SATINWOOD became more prestigious, but mahogany continues to be a popular furniture wood, especially in reproductions of 18th-cen-tury pieces. Today Cuban mahogany is quite rare, and American mahogany dominates the market, though its supply is supplemented by AFRICAN MAHOGANY, a more distant botani-cal cousin. The wood known as Philippine mahogany is not mahogany, but a MERANTI.

MAJORELLE, LOUIS (1859–1929)
French ART NOUVEAU furniture maker and designer; a principal member of the School of Nancy (*see* NANCY, SCHOOL OF). The son of a cabinetmaker, Majorelle studied painting in Paris under Millet. He returned to Nancy to take over the family firm, Maison Majorelle, upon his father's death in 1879. He continued in his father's specialty of ROCOCO FURNI-TURE reproductions until around 1890, when he came under the influence of Émile GALLÉ and began to produce and sell Art Nouveau furniture. Majorelle's work was always similar to Gallé's. Both used carving and marquetry and preferred organic decorative motifs, chiefly floral. Majorelle favored mahogany over the local fruitwood preferred by most

Louis Majorelle desk

School of Nancy designers, and he was fond of decorative ormolu and other metal mounts, features reminiscent of rococo design. Maison Majorelle maintained a flourishing business, with outlets in Paris and other French cities. After the First World War, Majorelle abandoned Art Nouveau for an austere classical style with geometric decoration.

MAKEPEACE, JOHN (b. 1939)

Contemporary British furniture maker; principal British exponent of the 1970s HANDICRAFT REVIVAL. Makepeace, who has made furniture by hand since the 1950s, has developed an idiosyncratic style based loosely on geometrical variants of ART NOUVEAU. He has been compared to the great French *ébénistes* of the 18th century because of his penchant for using expensive, exotic materials in complicated, impeccably executed designs. His greatest contribution, however, may be the school of crafts and furniture design he founded in Dorset in 1977. This institution, as well as Makepeace's work, have had a profound influence on the British handicraft revival.

MAKI-E

Japanese decorative device; sprinkled gold or silver dust on surface of LACQUER, also used in Chinese YIN PING TUO lacquer furniture.

Carl Malmsten

MAKORÉ

A West African HARDWOOD whose strongly striped grain and lustrous reddish-brown color make it an attractive import among European and North American furniture makers. It is also known as *cherry mahogany.*

MAKURA

Traditional JAPANESE FURNITURE form; wooden pillow, or HEADREST. A *makura* consists of a small, rectangular paneled box, on top of which a cylindrical pillow is tied with a cord attached to the box. If intended for traveling, the piece is outfitted with drawers.

MALLARD, PRUDENT (1809–79)

French-American furniture maker in the ROCOCO REVIVAL and RENAISSANCE REVIVAL STYLES. Born in France, Mallard worked in New York City from 1829 to 1838, when he moved to New Orleans. There he became well known for making large case furniture and massive beds, usually with an elaborate half-tester. He employed laminating and bending techniques similar to those of John Henry BELTER. After his predecessor, François SEIGNOURET, left New Orleans, Mallard was the principal furniture maker of the city, employing an extravagant version of the Renaissance Revival style.

MALLET-STEVENS, ROBERT (1886–1945)

French architect and furniture designer in the INTERNATIONAL STYLE. Principally an architect, Mallet-Stevens had rejected his *beaux arts* beginnings by the 1920s and adopted a modern, rectilinear style, under the influences of Charles Rennie MACKINTOSH and Joseph HOFFMANN. For the 1925 Paris Exposition (*see* ART DECO), Mallet-Stevens designed painted metal furniture in a functionalist manner (*see* FUNCTIONALISM). While he designed very little other furniture himself, he was an important exponent of the International style of architecture. Mallet-Stevens was a founding member of the UNION DES ARTISTES MODERNES.

MALMSTEN, CARL PER HENDRIK (1888–1972)

Swedish furniture designer of 1920s and 1930s. Carl Malmsten's modest furniture was designed in simple, rectilinear forms following traditional stylistic modes. His pieces were finely crafted from local woods, with occasional inlay work. However, his importance does not lie in his furniture; he was more influential as a teacher and writer. Influenced by the British ARTS AND CRAFTS MOVEMENT and the ideas of William MORRIS, he advocated simple, utilitarian handcrafted furniture. He believed that a craftsman's duty to society was to fuse beauty and utility in design. He founded three schools dedicated to handicraft in Sweden—in 1928, 1930 and 1960—and he proposed a national network of such institutions.

Though Malmsten reacted strongly against the growing influence of the INTERNATIONAL STYLE, he nonetheless had a significant impact on the development of SCANDINAVIAN MODERN furniture design, in combining a concern for function with a traditional approach to materials and construction.

MALOOF, SAM (b. 1916)

Contemporary California furniture maker; participant in the 1970s HANDICRAFT REVIVAL. Maloof, originally a graphics designer, began making furniture by hand in 1949, and he is now one of the best-known American handicrafters. His designs combine a sculptural, organic character with a pragmatic approach to function. He is noted particularly for a rocking chair in which the spindles that form the chair back have a carved, not turned, protruding section near the seat, which provides extra lower-back support.

MANGIAROTTI, ANGELO (b. 1921)

Contemporary Italian architect and designer. Mangiarotti, who taught under Ludwig MIES VAN DER ROHE in Chicago in the early 1950s, practices architecture and design in Milan, producing furniture in a fluid but architectonic version of the INTERNATIONAL STYLE. His furniture, made in a variety of materials for a number of manufacturers, including CASSINA and Knoll (see Florence Schust KNOLL), is refined and simple in form, smooth-lined and formal. He has also designed many well-known lighting fixtures, as well as metalwork, glassware and other objects.

MANNERIST STYLE

Decorative style used in the 16th and 17th centuries, especially in northern Europe, creating a transition between RENAISSANCE and BAROQUE FURNITURE. Deriving from the last phase of Renaissance art in Italy, known as Mannerism, Mannerist decoration emphasized grotesquely attenuated human figures contorted into strange postures. These were juxtaposed with other bizarre motifs, especially those of GROTESQUE ORNAMENT, in elaborate, frequently geometrical arrangements, united by ARABESQUES and STRAPWORK. This eccentric style was developed in deliberate reaction to the more rational classicism of earlier Renaissance design; it had its roots in the painted decoration that stimulated grotesque ornament rather than in classical architecture.

Mannerist ornamentation was introduced into northern Europe from Italy in the first half of the 16th century by Rosso FIORENTINO, a leader of the FRANÇOIS I STYLE in France. Mannerist furniture developed further during the subsequent HENRI II STYLE. In about mid-century the published PATTERN BOOKS of the Frenchman Jacques Androuet DU CERCEAU and the Fleming Cornelis FLORIS spread the new style throughout the Netherlands and Germany. Early German Mannerist furniture designers included Lienhart STROHMEIER and Lorenz STOER. But Hans VREDEMAN DE VRIES, another Fleming, was, with Du Cerceau, the most important of these designers. In the second half of the 16th century, he published designs that were emulated as far away as England and Scandinavia. The 1572 book of designs by the Burgundian Hughes SAMBIN also had a great influence, especially in southern Germany and Switzerland. In 1593 the German Wendel DIETTERLIN published designs that were to influence English work, although the Mannerist style in England began late and was rather subdued for the most part (see TUDOR FURNITURE; JACOBEAN FURNITURE). While Mannerist furniture is chiefly distinguished by its ornamentation, several furniture forms were particularly associated with the style. Most notable were the German KUNSTSCHRANK and the French TABLE À L'ITALIENNE.

In the 17th century, Mannerist furniture evolved toward an even greater degree of extravagance, especially in the AURICULAR STYLE, popular in Germany and Holland. Elsewhere, designs involving more figural carving and even greater complexity of decoration continued to be published, notably by Crispin DE PASSE, in 1621, and Paul VREDEMAN DE VRIES, Hans's son, in 1630. Eventually, in the second half of the 17th century, Mannerist ornamentation gave way to the no less extravagant but less eccentric and more unified baroque style (see BAROQUE FURNITURE).

MANSONIA

West African HARDWOOD somewhat resembling WALNUT and often used as VENEER. This dark, grayish-brown wood has an even texture and, usually, very little FIGURING.

MANWARING, ROBERT (active 1760s)

British maker and designer of ROCOCO FURNITURE. Manwaring published several PAT-

bed frame in Mannerist style

TERN BOOKS, mostly of chair designs. Popular in Britain, these books also influenced the development of AMERICAN CHIPPENDALE FURNITURE.

MAO GUI
See DING GUI.

MAPLE
See BIRD'S-EYE MAPLE.

MARACAIBO BOXWOOD
See under BOXWOOD.

MARBLE
Decorative stone, often boldly and irregularly colored by impurities, that has been used, especially for TABLE tops and THRONES, in ancient GREEK FURNITURE and in most Western furniture styles since, to convey an aura of grandeur and wealth. Its varied appearance—from modest, smoothly grained, nearly monochrome surfaces to brightly colored, wildly swirling patterns—makes it useful to a wide range of aesthetic intentions. In Asian furniture (*see* CHINESE, JAPANESE, and KOREAN FURNITURE), marble, though not often used, appears most frequently as an INLAY.

MARBLEIZE
To simulate marble with paint, on wood or another surface.

MARBLEWOOD
Another name for COROMANDEL WOOD.

MARCOTTE, LEON (active 1848–c. 1880)
French-American furniture maker associated with the American RENAISSANCE REVIVAL STYLE. Trained in France as an architect, Marcotte married the daughter of Auguste Émile Ringuet Le Prince, owner of a Paris decorating and furniture firm. He came to New York with his father-in-law in 1848, and they founded the firm Ringuet Le Prince & Marcotte and established themselves as the principal American exponents of the LOUIS XVI REVIVAL style. After Ringuet Le Prince's retirement in 1861, Marcotte continued to prosper, developing his own version of the Renaissance Revival style. He employed sculpted and inlaid pictorial elements and architectural devices in elaborate, geometrical arrangements.

MARGUERITE
Decorative motif; daisy or similar flower, with slender, radiating petals.

MARISCAL, JAVIER (b. 1950)
Contemporary Spanish designer. Well known in Spain as a cartoonist, poster artist and textile designer, Mariscal has created in the 1980s a number of designs for idiosyncratic furniture, produced by Memphis (*see* Ettore SOTTSASS) and other manufacturers.

MARLBOROUGH LEG
See under LEG.

MAROT, DANIEL (1663–1752)
French-born Dutch architect and BAROQUE FURNITURE designer. Son of a well known Huguenot architect, Marot was among the Protestants who fled France for Holland after the Edict of Nantes was revoked in 1685. In Holland he became chief designer for William of Orange. He designed interiors and furniture and published many of his designs, which were in an individual version of the contemporary French LOUIS XIV STYLE. Like those of Pierre LE PAUTRE, by whom he was influenced, his designs were less rigorously symmetrical than earlier work. Particularly well known for his grand beds, Marot also designed many tables and GUÉRIDONS, as well as other pieces. His furniture was gracefully exuberant, lavishly ornamented with a full repertoire of baroque decorative devices rendered in many colors and textures. William of Orange became king of England in 1689, and Marot followed him there in 1695, staying for three years. Through both his numerous commissions and his published designs, he had a great influence on designers in the WILLIAM AND MARY style. In 1698 Marot returned to Holland and concentrated on architecture.

MARQUETRY
Elaborate use of INLAY in wood veneering (*see* VENEER) to decorate furniture, often involving

pictorial designs and woods of many types and colors.

MARQUISE
Eighteenth-century French furniture form; straight-fronted CANAPÉ or upholstered SET-TEE intended for two people.

MARTHA WASHINGTON CHAIR
Armchair with upholstered seat and back; FEDERAL PERIOD form. Characterized by its tall back and slim, tapering arms and legs, this chair (known then as a "lolling chair") was made chiefly in New England, especially Massachusetts. It was an American version of a similar form that had been popular in Europe before about 1760, when it first appeared in the British colonies of America. Still a popular chair, in reproduction or imitation, the Martha Washington chair was not named after the famous first lady of the United States until the late 19th century.

MARTHA WASHINGTON TABLE
American WORKTABLE in NEOCLASSICAL STYLE, especially during FEDERAL PERIOD.

MARYLAND CHIPPENDALE CHAIR
American Chippendale chair (*see* AMERICAN CHIPPENDALE FURNITURE) made in the Chesapeake Bay area. The chair had an unusually wide pierced splat and crest rails terminating in prominent EARS. It was made in local variants of several standard Chippendale forms.

MASK
Decorative device; stylized human face used as an ornament. Derived from ancient wall paintings excavated in Rome during the early Renaissance, the mask became a prominent feature of GROTESQUE ORNAMENT and was frequently employed on RENAISSANCE FURNITURE in the MANNERIST STYLE. It remained popular throughout the next several centuries in BAROQUE and ROCOCO FURNITURE.

MASON, RALPH (1599–1679)
Boston maker of AMERICAN JACOBEAN FURNITURE. Trained as a joiner in London, Mason immigrated to Boston around 1640. Mason, Henry MESSINGER and Thomas EDSALL were the principal furniture makers of the day. Mason specialized in case furniture, especially chests.

MATHEWS, ARTHUR F. (1860–1945); LUCIA K. (1870–1955)
California designers of the early 20th century. Trained in California as an architect and painter, Arthur Mathews studied in Paris from 1885 to 1890, when he returned to the United States to direct the California School of Design. In 1894 he married Lucia Kleinhaus, a student at the school. They became close collaborators, decorating painted furniture. After the San Francisco earthquake of 1906, there was a tremendous demand for furniture to replace losses, and the Mathewses established a workshop to meet the need. Called the Furniture Shop, this enterprise employed up to 50 craftsmen who made furniture, tapestries, stained glass and other objects. Their furniture designs were based on the examples of the British ARTS AND CRAFTS MOVEMENT and MISSION FURNITURE, with elements of European ART NOUVEAU, French Symbolist painting and Oriental art incorporated into the design. Most of their pieces were painted, often with images of flowers.

Martha Washington chair

MATHSSON, KARL BRUNO (b. 1907)
Swedish furniture designer; major figure of Swedish Modern furniture (*see* SCANDINAVIAN MODERN). Bruno Mathsson was trained by his father, a master cabinetmaker. Like his contemporary Carl MALMSTEN, Mathsson has stressed the importance of fine craftsmanship, a traditional Scandinavian concern. He is best known for the chair forms he designed in the 1930s. Following Alvar AALTO's example, he experimented with laminated bentwood, and the chairs he produced had woven-leather seats stretched over a bentwood frame of elaborate curves. Though chairs were always his principal concern, he also devised a shelving unit composed of poles and shelves braced between floor and ceiling. Several of Mathsson's 1930s designs are still in production. In the 1960s Mathsson designed a number of notable tubular-steel chairs, in addition to other furniture, some in collaboration with Piet HEIN.

**Mina chair
Karl Mathsson**

MATSU (also *Japanese pine*)

Japanese SOFTWOOD used for framing of chests in that country (*see* TANSU) and, being inexpensive and common, in much vernacular furniture.

MATTA (Roberto Sebastian Antonio Matta Echaurren) (b. 1911)

Chilean-born artist and designer. Matta is best known as a Surrealist and abstract painter, an important early influence on American abstract expressionism. He trained as an architect, moved to France and worked under LE CORBUSIER in the 1930s. Matta also designed the noteworthy "Malitte" seating system (1966). The "Malitte" consists of five molded polyurethane foam pieces, covered in stretch fabric, that can be used singly as chairs (or chaises) or grouped together. Each piece has straight sides, a flat base and a curved top surface; the units can be stacked like jigsaw-puzzle pieces to form a square shape for storage.

MATT GILDING

Eighteenth-century treatment of bronze furniture mounts (*see* HARDWARE); variation of MERCURY GILDING in which portions of the cast piece have a dull, textured finish, in contrast to highly polished areas.

MATTING

Decorative device; textured surface composed of many small dots or circles punched or hammered into the material with a special light tool. Matting is usually used as a background for a carved or inlaid ornamental motif that is not textured.

MATUSCH (or Matouche) Johann (active 1701–31)

German BAROQUE FURNITURE maker. Matusch, who trained two of the leading German furniture makers of the day—Ferdinand PLITZNER and Martin SCHUMACHER—specialized in BOULLE MARQUETRY. In his pieces a late baroque manner based on the French LOUIS XIV STYLE was modified by a lighter touch that reflected the contemporary French shift toward the increased informality of rococo decoration.

MAUGHAM, SYRIE (c. 1879–1955)

British decorator and designer of the 1930s. Maugham is frequently credited with inventing the all-white room decor, though this is a matter of dispute. With Alistair MAYNARD, Maugham led a British reaction against the austerity of the INTERNATIONAL STYLE. Her furniture, while simple in form, was decorated with purposely nonutilitarian references to historical styles. She favored furniture derived from 18th-century French and Italian designs, painted white or another light color, often with a crackled finish that was something of a hallmark of her work.

MAUGUIN, PAUL (active 1850s and 1860s)

French architect and furniture designer influential in the development of the eclectic RENAISSANCE REVIVAL STYLE, which was derived from French Renaissance architecture and other sources. Mauguin designed furniture for his architectural commissions.

MAYHEW & INCE

See INCE & MAYHEW.

MAYNARD, ALISTAIR (active 1930s)

British decorator and furniture designer. With Syrie MAUGHAM, Maynard was a leader of a reaction in Britain against the austerity of the INTERNATIONAL STYLE. His furniture had bold, non-functional features, especially copiously applied decorative reeding, often covering the whole exterior of a piece.

MAZZA, SERGIO (b. 1931)

Contemporary Italian designer. Mazza, who has had a private design practice in Milan since 1950, designs interiors, furniture, lighting and ceramics. His best-known furniture design is the molded plastic "Toga" armchair (1968).

MEADMORE, CLEMENT (b. 1929)

Australian-born American sculptor; early in his career a furniture designer. Best known as a minimalist sculptor of monumental public works, Meadmore designed furniture in the 1950s and was one of Australia's first

International Style designers. In the 1960s, he immigrated to the United States, where he is now a citizen, living and working in New York.

MEANDER PATTERN
Another name for KEY PATTERN.

MEDIEVAL FURNITURE
Western European furniture of the long period following the fall of the Roman Empire, from about the fifth century to the 16th. While roughly contemporary with BYZANTINE FURNITURE, medieval furniture was much cruder in construction and design, for the complete collapse of the Roman Empire in western Europe led to both economic and cultural deprivation. The classical traditions of ROMAN FURNITURE barely survived, and regional forms could evolve only after culture had been laboriously rebuilt. Thus, though this epoch lasted more than 1,000 years, it saw only one major stylistic revolution, beginning in about the 12th century—the change from the Romanesque manner, intended to evoke the classical past, to a "modern" style, the so-called Gothic, based on a greater naturalism and emphasizing vertical structure. These trends achieved their greatest expression in architecture; related developments in the applied arts yielded first ROMANESQUE FURNITURE, then GOTHIC FURNITURE.

The gothic world was quite different from the Romanesque, in its furniture as in other ways, but certain aspects of furniture making remained constant throughout the medieval era. Only the richest and most powerful landowners possessed anything but the crudest domestic furniture, and even their furniture tended to be both simple and sparse. These nobles never lived long in one spot. They traveled constantly among various residences scattered throughout their domains, for no one tract of land could long support the immense retinues that were both a privilege and a necessary proof of a lord's power; furthermore, the lord's periodic reappearance in a given area tended to reinforce his control of it.

This way of life discouraged bulk in household goods. Status and wealth were displayed by rich fabrics, jewelry, fine plate and other light, easily transported items rather than by elaborate cabinetry. The esthetics of furniture were unimportant, for it could be usually swathed in silks or tapestries. (However, fixed UPHOLSTERY did not appear until after this period, late in the 16th century.) Furniture was designed primarily with transport in mind and usually could be disassembled, like the TRUSSING BED, for example. The French and Italian words for "furniture"—*meubles* and *mobilia,* respectively—were coined at this time and simply meant "movables"; that is, transportable objects.

Moreover, rooms in buildings did not generally have specialized uses; they were multipurpose, and even furniture associated with particular uses—such as dining tables or beds—could be, and was, set up in different rooms of a house, as circumstance or whimsy might require. This fact also promoted mobility, and the folding stool and the wheeled COUCHETTE, for instance, were thus common. The few exceptions to this tendency were either built into the fabric of the building (see AUMBRY), otherwise affixed (see TABLE DORMANT) or remarkably solid and unwieldy (see TRUNK).

The range of furniture forms was limited, and they tended to be simple and utilitarian. The CHEST was the most common item of case furniture, as had been true since remotest antiquity; only late in the period did the CUPBOARD begin to evolve into the grander forms that would become prominent in the 17th and 18th centuries. The dominant forms of seating remained the simple stool and backless bench; the latter was ordinarily used for dining. However, such forms as the BUFFET, the CHAIR OF ESTATE and the chair or bed CANOPY served as explicit emblems of status in the hierarchically oriented medieval world.

The church was a great user of furniture at this time, and style in architecture, and thus in furniture and other applied arts, was determined largely by ecclesiastical patrons. In church buildings furniture tended to be built into the architectural fabric, but in church and monastery libraries, specialized furniture forms were used, such as the LECTERN and cupboards designed for the storage of writing materials and books. Aumbrylike rooms with built-in shelving for books were common architectural features, precursors of the BOOKCASE. Decorative motifs were based on those developed by the stonemasons who adorned the façades of churches. Pieces of furniture

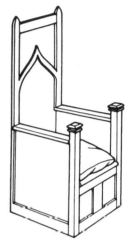

medieval chair

tended to look like miniature buildings due to the use of ARCADING, PILASTERS and so forth. Occasionally, even buttresses were applied to case furniture.

In the Gothic period the rise of secure and stable middle-class trading communities, especially in Flanders and northern Italy, generated a new way of life that led to domestic furniture of relatively fixed function and location. This phenomenon, combined with the great revolution in thought and art during the 15th and 16th centuries, made a new, more secular style of furniture inevitable, and RENAISSANCE FURNITURE evolved. However, medieval features and types persisted into the 17th century, especially in England.

MEEKS, J. & J. W.

Nineteenth-century New York furniture-manufacturing firm, best known for its revival style work. A leading firm from 1797 to 1868, J. & J. W. Meeks made furniture in a wide variety of revival styles, including the FEDERAL PERIOD and the AMERICAN EMPIRE STYLE, drawing particularly on the patterns of George SMITH. The company began to make NEO-GOTHIC STYLE pieces in the 1840s and started producing ROCOCO REVIVAL STYLE pieces, its best-known furniture, a decade later. The firm's Rococo Revival furniture was similar in technique and appearance to the work of John Henry BELTER.

MEI GUI SHI (MEI KUEI SHIH)

Seventeenth-century CHINESE FURNITURE form, during late Ming (1368–1644) and early Qing (1644–1911) dynasties; any of various chairs with a distinctively short back. It was intended to be placed before a window without disturbing the view.

MEIER, RICHARD (b. 1934)

Contemporary American architect and furniture designer. Meier, who worked for Marcel BREUER early in his career, has developed a distinctive style descended from the European INTERNATIONAL STYLE. Though he is principally an architect, Meier has designed clean-lined, functional furniture for such manufacturers as Knoll international (see Florence Schust KNOLL).

chair by Meier

MEIER-GRAEFE, JULIUS (1867–1935)

French entrepreneur associated with ART NOUVEAU. Meier-Graefe, Samuel BING's chief rival, opened his shop, *La Maison Moderne,* in 1898. He showed works by many Parisian Art Nouveau designers and maintained a workshop that employed Paul FOLLOT and Maurice DUFRÊNE, later important ART DECO furniture makers, early in their careers.

MEISSONNIER, JUSTE-AURELE (1693–1750)

French painter, architect, silversmith and designer; creator, with Nicolas PINEAU, of the *genre pittoresque,* basis of decoration used on ROCOCO FURNITURE, especially that in the LOUIS XV STYLE. Though he was accomplished in several disciplines, little of Meissonnier's work survives, other than a well-known body of 120 engravings of designs for buildings, furniture and other objects, published in the 1720s and 1730s. These designs were characterized by exaggeratedly swirling scrolls and whimsically strewn motifs of shells and flowers in boldly asymmetrical arrangements, with an animated restlessness that suggested constant movement. Meissonnier's designs for furniture were too overwrought to result in actual pieces, but their fanciful anticlassicism stimulated makers and designers in France and elsewhere for 30 years.

MEKEREN, JAN VAN (active c. 1690–1735)

Leading Dutch maker of BAROQUE FURNITURE. Mekeren specialized in big cabinets covered with large-scale floral and still-life MARQUETRY panels of various colorful woods. His designs were influenced by contemporary Dutch painting, and his work has a striking painterly quality and a degree of verisimilitude that place it among the most distinctive furniture of the time.

MELON-BULB TURNING

See under TURNERY.

MELON FOOT

See under FOOT.

MEMBER

Single structural element; any given part of the FRAMING of a piece of furniture.

MEMPHIS

See SOTTSASS, Ettore.

MENDLESHAM CHAIR

See under WINDSOR CHAIR.

MENSA LUNATA

ROMAN FURNITURE form; literally, "crescent-shaped table." This large, curved dining table appeared late in the Roman period and may perhaps have been designed for use with the SIGMA, a curved couch.

MENUISIER

French JOINER; maker of chairs, tables and other small items, as opposed to an ÉBÉNISTE, who specialized in veneered case furniture. The *menuisier's* output was considered to be minor *(menu)* relative to the grand pieces of *ébénisterie.* Under the Parisian guild system that dominated French furniture making in the 17th and 18th centuries, only a master craftsman could practice both disciplines, and this was rarely done. Furthermore, the carving that usually appeared on a piece made by a *menuisier* had to be done by another specialized artisan, a SCULPTEUR. Metal mounts for furniture, whether *ébénisterie* or *menuisierie,* were prepared by a FONDEUR-CISELEUR. Any gilding, of mounts or wood, was performed by a DOREUR, and upholstery was made by a TAPISSIER. The guild system, and with it these enforced categories of production, was abolished by the Revolutionary government in 1791.

MERANTI (also *seraya)*

Any of several Malaysian HARDWOODS, used as plywood and in furniture making. They range in color from whitish yellow to dark red-brown. The variety known as dark red meranti is exported to America as Philippine mahogany and is used for outdoor furniture.

MERCURY GILDING

Process of applying gold to metal, used on bronze ORMOLU furniture mounts (*see* HARD-WARE) in 18th and early 19th centuries. A solution of powdered gold in mercury was spread on the piece of bronze to be gilded, and the piece was then heated. The mercury vaporized, leaving a thin film of gold on the bronze. This process was repeated several times, until the gold was thick enough to be polished. The fumes from the mercury were highly toxic, and many of the artisans who used the process suffered severe brain damage. The French Revolution outlawed mercury gilding. Today it is used only occasionally, under strict safeguards.

MÈRE, CLÉMENT (1870–?)

French ART DECO furniture designer. Mère's furniture combined a simplicity of form with the use of rich materials, such as carved ivory and rare woods, in marquetry. He particularly favored tooled leather panels, tinted and textured in decorative designs reflecting a Japanese influence.

MÉRIDIENNE

French DIRECTOIRE, CONSULATE and EMPIRE STYLE furniture form; short CANAPÉ with SCROLL ARMS (2), one higher than the other.

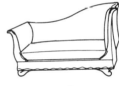

méridienne

MESOPOTAMIAN FURNITURE

Furniture from the ancient civilizations centered between the Tigris and Euphrates rivers, in present-day Iraq and Syria. The furniture of the earliest of these cultures, the Sumerian, roughly contemporary with that of ancient Egypt (*see* EGYPTIAN FURNITURE), is known from many images on stone seals found at Ur, a capital city in about 2600 B.C. Known forms include massive, thronelike stools and sideboards of lattice construction. Some of these pieces probably predate the dynastic period in Egypt. By about 2300 B.C. an X-FRAME folding stool had appeared in Sumeria; again, this probably occurred somewhat before the same development in Egypt. Slightly later, chairs with carved bull-leg supports and curving backs were made.

During the Assyrian and Babylonian empires (c. 1350–539 B.C.), Mesopotamian furniture reflected a growing taste for heavy, elaborate decoration and the use of precious materials—such as gold, ivory and ebony—for inlay work and ornaments of applied relief

chair by Mies van der Rohe

sculpture. Many decorative motifs, notably the lotus blossom, were borrowed from Egypt. Locally developed motifs came predominantly from the animal world, including eagles, lions and the characteristically Assyrian winged bull. It is believed that the lathe was invented in Mesopotamia in about the ninth century B.C. and that it found its way to Greece when the Persian Empire brought the two regions into intimate contact a few centuries later. Also, the practice of using a bed form as a dining couch, as the Greek KLINE functioned, appears to have begun in Babylonia.

MESSINGER, HENRY (active 1641–81)

Boston maker of AMERICAN JACOBEAN FURNITURE. Messinger, a joiner who emigrated from London to Boston in 1641, made chairs and case furniture in the style he had learned in England. He dominated the furniture market in Boston, along with Ralph MASON and Thomas EDSALL.

METAL FURNITURE

Furniture made of metal, while regularly recurring throughout history, is not ordinary (though furniture HARDWARE, in use since very early times, is by definition made of metal). Furniture of IRON has also been made since ancient times. Its alloy, STEEL, has been used occasionally since RENAISSANCE FURNITURE, though only in the 20th century has it been regularly employed. From the 19th century, the BRASS BED has been a popular form. To display immense wealth, solid SILVER and (very rarely) gold furniture has been made, but the precious metals have chiefly been used in INLAY work and GILDING.

METOPE

Blank space alternating with the TRIGLYPH in the decoration of a FRIEZE of the DORIC ORDER. Such decoration was often used in European furniture styles deriving from classical architecture. Sometimes metopes were decorated with PATERAE or representational imagery, though they were usually plain.

MEUBLES PARLANTS

Furniture bearing decorative inscriptions; term literally means "speaking furniture."

Meubles parlants pieces were popular in ART NOUVEAU furniture.

MIES VAN DER ROHE, LUDWIG (1886–1969)

German-American architect and furniture designer; leading exemplar of the INTERNATIONAL STYLE. A stonemason's son, Mies was trained for the building trades. He was apprenticed in 1905 to Berlin furniture maker Bruno PAUL. From 1909 to 1912 he worked in the Munich office of architect Peter BEHRENS, where he met and worked with Walter GROPIUS and LE CORBUSIER. In 1912 Mies opened his own architectural practice, and his early work, while in a neoclassical mode, reveals the influence of the Dutch architect H. P. BERLAGE. Mies began designing furniture in 1926, his first piece being a cantilevered chair of tubular steel that formed a wide, smooth curve, taking fullest advantage of the flexibility of the material. It was an advance on the earlier cantilevered designs of STAM and BREUER.

Mies once claimed that it was harder to design a good chair than a good building. His furniture designs reflect hard thought, presenting a cool elegance in which function is both highlighted and provided for with a minimum of elements, for, as he observed, "Less is more." These designs all demanded very fine craftsmanship by hand to yield their machinemade look, which is suggestive of Mies's famous remark, "God is in the details." In 1929, he designed his most famous piece, the "Barcelona" chair. At this time Mies was recognized as the leading practitioner of modern functionalist esthetics (*see* FUNCTIONALISM). In 1930 he became the director of the BAUHAUS and remained there for its last years. After the school closed, he maintained a private practice and stayed in Germany until 1938, when he moved to the United States, where he chiefly practiced architecture.

Mies's furniture and architecture were tremendously important to the development of the International style in the 1930s. When that style flowered a second time in the 1950s, Mies's furniture was again produced, chiefly by Knoll International, and exerted a renewed influence on design.

MIGEON, PIERRE, II (1701–58)

French furniture maker in LOUIS XV STYLE. Migeon specialized in small forms with ingemious fittings, such as the SECRÉTAIRE À CAPUCIN. He was an early French user of MAHOGANY.

MILLER, HERMAN
See HERMAN MILLER FURNITURE CO.

MILLER, SANDERSON (1717–80)
British NEO-GOTHIC STYLE architect and furniture designer. Miller, a noted amateur architect of the 1750s and 1760s, designed CHIPPENDALE GOTHIC furniture for his buildings and interiors in a whimsical rococo manner (*see* ROCOCO FURNITURE).

MILLS & DEMING
New York City furniture company of the FEDERAL PERIOD. William Mills and Simeon Deming, partners, produced distinguished NEOCLASSICAL STYLE furniture between 1793 and 1798. Their work was based chiefly on the designs of George HEPPLEWHITE and featured dramatic contrasting inlaid patterns.

MISERICORD
BRACKET projecting from underside of hinged seat in church choir stall, against which a standing person may lean. The misericord, whose name means roughly "a relaxation of churchly rules," was most popular in England in late medieval and Renaissance times. Usually, it was elaborately carved with representations of allegorical and mythological figures.

MISSION FURNITURE
American furniture design style of the early 20th century, especially the work of Gustav STICKLEY, J. M. YOUNG & Co., and the ROYCROFT COMMUNITY. An American offshoot of the ARTS AND CRAFTS MOVEMENT, Mission furniture was so called because it was felt by its exponents to have a mission—utility of design. Stickley, in particular, was an enthusiastic admirer of William MORRIS and his ideas. Accordingly, Stickley's furniture was manufactured at a workshop established as a quasi-socialist community. The Roycroft Community, on the other hand, was simply a manufacturing company. In both cases, the furniture adheres more closely to Arts and Crafts esthetic ideals than did most British work.

Mission furniture had a simple, rectilinear style with exposed construction techniques, unpretentious materials (usually oak, with coverings of leather, canvas or plain cloth) and little or no decoration. Through Stickley's magazine, *The Craftsman,* the Arts and Crafts gospel was spread. The Mission style was influential on the West Coast—notably in the works of GREENE & GREENE and Arthur and Lucia MATHEWS—and in the Midwest, where the PRAIRIE SCHOOL and Frank Lloyd WRIGHT absorbed and developed its tenets.

MITCHELL & RAMMELSBURG
Mid-19th-century furniture manufacturers of Cincinnati, noted for furniture in REVIVAL STYLES. Founded in 1844, Mitchell & Rammelsburg was by the 1860s one of the largest American furniture-manufacturing firms, producing work in every manner, for every market, but with a particular emphasis on the RENAISSANCE REVIVAL STYLE. Later, in the 1870s, the firm produced noteworthy examples of "Eastlake" style furniture (*see* Charles Locke EASTLAKE), generally following the examples published by Bruce TALBERT.

MITER
See under JOINERY.

MIZUYA-DANSU
JAPANESE FURNITURE form; TANSU for kitchen use. It consists of a CHEST-ON-CHEST with sliding doors, some of them composed of wire GRILLES, allowing ventilation. Usually the upper chest includes a horizontal row of small drawers below an arrangement of sliding or hinged doors. The doors that do not contain the wire grilles are composed of thin vertical slats. The lower chest is usually closed by two large slatted doors covering its entire face and revealing, when open, a variety of shelves and compartments.

MODERNE STYLE
See AMERICAN MODERNE.

MODERN GOTHIC STYLE
See EASTLAKE, Charles Locke; TALBERT, Bruce James.

Mission chair

beaded molding

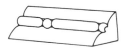

bead-and-reel molding

bevel

bolection molding

cock-bead molding

cove molding

MODILLION

Ornamental CONSOLE used in series to support a CORNICE in the CORINTHIAN, COMPOSITE or Roman IONIC ORDER of classical architecture. The modillion has been used in elaborate case furniture in various European furniture styles that derived from classical architecture.

MOGENSEN, BØRGE (1914–72)

Danish furniture designer of 1940s and 1950s. Trained as a cabinetmaker, Mogensen designed furniture for mass production from the 1940s onward, employing the principles of simplicity and rationality of Kaare KLINT, whose student and associate he had been. He designed unit furniture and other pieces with a marked concern for practicality. His pieces were usually of wood, with fabric or leather patterned in his own designs. His inexpensive furniture was very popular, and much of it is still in production.

MOLDING

Continuous band of decoration with shaped profile; used to emphasize difference in planes of surfaces or to ornament an edge of a surface, such as an APRON or tabletop, or simply to provide a linear decorative motif. A molding of any shape may or may not be further decorated with a repeating pattern. Various profiles of molding are distinguished by specific names.

ASTRAGAL MOLDING (also bead molding; roundel molding)
Decorated with small, carved semispheres that abut each other and resemble a string of pearls.

BEADED MOLDING (also *bead molding*)

BEAD MOLDING
Another name for either ASTRAGAL MOLDING or BEADED MOLDING (*see under* MOLDING).

BEAD-AND-REEL MOLDING (also *reel-and-bead molding*)

BEVEL
Undecorated, narrow, flat band set at an angle to the plane of a surface. A wide variant of this molding is called SPLAY MOLDING (*see under* MOLDING).

BOLECTION MOLDING
Any molding, but especially an OGEE MOLDING (*see under* MOLDING), forming a border between two surfaces at different levels, especially around a FIELDED PANEL or door.

CABLE MOLDING
Another name for ROPE MOLDING (*see under* MOLDING).

CAVETTO MOLDING
Concave molding, approximately quarter-circle in profile; reverse of convex OVOLO MOLDING (*see under* MOLDING).

COCK-BEAD MOLDING
ASTRAGAL MOLDING (*see under* MOLDING) applied to edges of drawer fronts in 18th-century British furniture. Cock-bead molding extended beyond the edges of the wood in order to hide the crack between the drawer and the body of the piece. It appears only on pieces made after about 1730 and is thus a useful, if rough, indicator of age.

COVE MOLDING
Large and very wide CAVETTO MOLDING (*see under* MOLDING), concave and about a quarter-circle or less in profile. It was commonly used in ROCOCO FURNITURE and interiors to link two opposed surfaces, such as a wall and SOFFIT or a wall and ceiling.

CYMA RECTA MOLDING
See OGEE MOLDING, *under* MOLDING.

CYMA REVERSA MOLDING
See OGEE MOLDING, *under* MOLDING.

EGG-AND-DART MOLDING
OVOLO MOLDING (*see under* MOLDING) decorated with EGG-AND-DART motif.

ENGRAILING
Another name for ROPE MOLDING (*see under* MOLDING).

GADROON MOLDING
Molding decorated with GADROONING, usually used to edge a furniture part, such as a tabletop.

HALF-ROUND MOLDING
Another name for SCOTIA MOLDING (*see under* MOLDING).

OGEE MOLDING
Molding with an S-shaped, or OGEE, profile. When concave above and convex below, it is sometimes called *cyma recta* molding, and when it is convex above and concave below, the terms *cyma reversa* and *reverse ogee molding* can be used.

OVOLO MOLDING (also *echinus; quarter-round molding*)
Convex molding, approximately a quarter-circle in profile; reverse of concave CAVETTO MOLDING (*see under* MOLDING). Because ovolo molding was normally used by ancient Greek architects as the *echinus* in a Doric column capital (*see* ORDERS OF ARCHITECTURE), that term is often applied to describe the molding. Since ancient times, such molding has commonly been embellished with the EGG-AND-DART motif, in which case it is sometimes called EGG-AND-DART MOLDING.

REED-AND-TIE MOLDING
Convex molding carved to resemble longitudinal REEDING crossed at intervals with straps or ribbons.

REEL-AND-BEAD MOLDING
Another name for BEAD-AND-REEL MOLDING (*see under* MOLDING).

REVERSE OGEE MOLDING
See OGEE MOLDING, *under* MOLDING.

ROLL MOLDING
Convex molding, approximately a three-quarters circle in profile.

ROPE MOLDING (also *cable molding; engrailing*)
Convex molding decorated with series of curved indentations along one edge, to resemble a length of rope.

ROUNDEL MOLDING
Another name for ASTRAGAL MOLDING (*see under* MOLDING).

SCOTIA MOLDING (also *half-round molding*)
Concave molding, roughly semicircular in profile. Scotia molding often appears with other moldings in architecture and in furniture. For instance, it is commonly arranged between two TORUS MOLDINGS (*see under* MOLDING) at the base of a column.

SPLAY MOLDING
Undecorated, very wide, flat band set at an angle to the adjacent surface; laterally enlarged BEVEL (*see under* MOLDING).

TORUS MOLDING
Large-scale convex molding, approximately semicircular in profile; enlarged ASTRAGAL MOLDING (*see under* MOLDING).

MÖLGAARD-NIELSEN, OSLA
See HVIDT, Peter.

MOLITOR, BERNARD (1755–1833)
German-born French furniture maker in DIRECTOIRE, CONSULATE and EMPIRE STYLES.

MOLLINO, CARLO (1905–73)
Italian architect, designer and writer, active after the Second World War. Mollino taught architecture and design in Turin and wrote about art, architecture and design. His designs revealed a strong Charles EAMES influence, though they were idiosyncratic as well, incorporating sculptural, organic shapes. Mollino

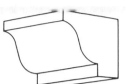

ogee molding

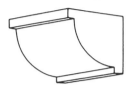

ovolo molding

reed-and-tie molding

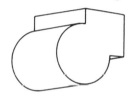

roll molding

rope molding

scotia molding

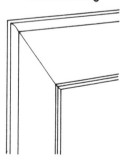

splay molding

torus molding

was an influential force on Italian design after the Second World War and spurred the development of the individualism characteristic of Italian design with his belief in the efficacy of the "fantastic," an attribute he ascribed to his eccentric, curvilinear style.

MONK'S BENCH
Another name for SETTLE-TABLE.

MONOPOD (also *monopodium;* pl. *monopodia*)
Carved NEOCLASSICAL STYLE chair or table leg in form of animal's head and torso on a single leg and foot of that animal. Based on ROMAN FURNITURE prototypes, the monopod was popular in the French EMPIRE and the British REGENCY STYLES of the early 19th century.

monopod

MOORE, JAMES (c. 1670–1726)
English BAROQUE FURNITURE maker; specialist in elaborate carved and gilded GESSO work. Moore's early decorative work, characterized by ARABESQUES and STRAPWORK motifs in low relief, represented a continuation of the influence of the elaborate French LOUIS XIV STYLE through the period of the QUEEN ANNE STYLE, when more austere ornamentation was generally favored. Later in his career, the rise of the extraordinarily exuberant PALLADIAN STYLE suited Moore's tastes, and he sometimes made furniture to the designs of William KENT. In 1714 he entered a partnership with John Gumley (active 1694–1729), a mirror maker and entrepreneur, and they succeeded Gerreit JENSEN as royal cabinetmakers in 1715, a change that indicated the triumph of gilt carving over the marquetry and veneering of earlier styles.

Morris chair

MOORISH STYLE
Popular 19th-century style of decoration, based loosely on the architectural ornament of the Middle East. The style was characterized by the use of the Moorish arch and repeated geometrical patterns and by the practice of providing chairs and sofas with many upholstered cushions. The taste for Moorish design elements is associated with the design reform movements of the day, which generally avoid-

ed historical European styles (*see* ART NOUVEAU; ART FURNITURE MOVEMENT). Owen JONES, a British designer, was an early exponent of the style, and Carlo BUGATTI continued to use the style in the early years of the 20th century.

MORRIS CHAIR
Late 19th-century British chair; woodframed armchair with adjustable reclining back and loose cushions for seat and back. Based on a rustic chair used in southern Britain, the Morris chair was created in the 1860s by ARTS AND CRAFTS MOVEMENT designer Philip WEBB for Morris & Co. He was a partner in this firm with William MORRIS, who is often but wrongly supposed to have invented the piece.

MORRIS, WILLIAM (1834–96)
British designer, painter, poet and esthetic and political theorist; leader of the ARTS AND CRAFTS MOVEMENT. Morris was probably the most influential figure in the decorative arts of the late 19th century. As a young architectural apprentice, Morris began a long association with architect Philip WEBB and painter Edward BURNE-JONES. They later founded a firm to manufacture furniture and other household goods in an effort to reform the decorative arts, which Morris described as being "in a state of complete degradation." Morris & Co., founded in 1861, was the cradle of the Arts and Crafts movement, employing such designers as Webb, George JACK and the painter William Holman HUNT to create highly crafted furniture in a simple, clean-lined style. The company shunned the elaborate ornamental decoration of the REVIVAL STYLES employed by mass manufacturers of the time. However, while applied ornament was eschewed, Morris & Co. furniture was often inlaid with stylized botanical designs or painted with representational images of idealized medieval scenes, by one or another of the Pre-Raphaelite painters, especially Burne-Jones, Hunt and sometimes Morris himself.

Following John RUSKIN's ideas, Morris perceived industrialism to be a destructive influence on the decorative arts and a return to the production methods of the Middle Ages as the counter to that influence. As a socialist, Morris further disapproved of mechanized production as being a function of the growth of modern capitalism, and he espoused an ideal of "art made by the people and for the people." Paradoxically, his uncompromising insistence on fine craftsmanship and the avoidance of mechanization resulted in products so expensive that only a wealthy minority could afford to buy them.

Though Morris never designed any furniture, he had an important influence on all early modern furniture design through the work of the Arts and Crafts designers, including Webb, A. H. MACKMURDO, H. M. BAILLIE SCOTT, C. F. A. VOYSEY, G. STICKLEY and their successors.

MORTISE

Shaped cavity drilled or chiseled in a piece of wood or other material, intended to receive a similarly shaped projection of another piece. A mortise receives a TENON in a MORTISE-AND-TENON JOINT (*see under* JOINERY). In a WINDSOR CHAIR mortises in the seat receive legs, back parts and arm supports, which are said to be "mortised into" it.

MORTISE-AND-TENON JOINT
See under JOINERY.

MOSER, KOLO (1868–1918)
Austrian ART NOUVEAU painter and designer. Principally a painter and book illustrator, Kolo Moser also designed furniture, textiles, glass and jewelry. His furniture is simple and rectilinear in form, designed in the Vienna SEZESSION style and decorated with carved or cast inlays of metal or wood. He was a member of the Sezession and, with Josef HOFFMANN, a founder of the WIENER WERKSTÄTTE.

MOTHER-OF-PEARL
Pearly lining of the shells of various mollusks, including the pearl oyster, used in decorative INLAYS. In CHINESE and JAPANESE FURNITURE, mother-of-pearl inlays have been used since ancient times, especially in LACQUER work. In RADEN, or LAC BURGAUTÉ decoration, the material is used in powdered form or in tiny shards. In the West mother-of-pearl has been used in opulet MARQUETRY since the

17th century. A particularly rich variety appeared in the MUEBLES ENCONCHADOS of SPANISH COLONIAL FURNITURE.

MOUNT
See HARDWARE.

MOURGUE, OLIVIER (b. 1939)
Contemporary French furniture designer. Mourgue is best known for his sculptural "Djinn" furniture line—polyurethane foam pieces covering tubular-steel frames and upholstered overall in brightly colored stretch fabric. These futuristic-looking chairs, ottomans, settees and chaises furnished the space station set in Stanley Kubrick's movie *2001: A Space Odyssey.* Mourgue has also designed textiles, toys and automobile interiors.

MUCHA, ALPHONSE MARIA (1860–1939)
ART NOUVEAU graphic artist and sometime furniture designer. A Czech working in Paris, Mucha was most famous for his posters and theatrical designs. In 1901 he designed some well-known furniture for the shop of the Paris jeweler Fouquet: sinuous, delicate pieces with bronze mounts depicting animals, some of the pieces upholstered in leather. He also designed some tables and chairs in the form of naturalistic tree trunks.

MUDÉJAR STYLE
Spanish-Islamic decorative manner used in the complicated geometrical inlay work that ornamented HISPANO-MORESQUE FURNITURE. The ARABESQUE developed from this style.

MUEBLES ENCONCHADOS
SPANISH COLONIAL FURNITURE, generally made in Lima, Peru, consisting of elaborately decorated case pieces in forms taken from 17th-century Spanish CHURIGUERESQUE FURNITURE. These pieces were covered entirely with MARQUETRY panels of MOTHER-OF-PEARL, in complex patterns based on decorative work of the Spanish Philippines. Early examples, from the 17th century, were Philippine-made, but local craftsmen soon adopted the style.

MULE CHEST (also *blanket chest*)
English furniture form of late 16th and 17th centuries. This chest had a single drawer, or two drawers side by side, below the principal compartment, which opened from the top. It evolved into the CHEST OF DRAWERS.

chair by Eckart Muthesius

MULLION
Vertical member separating panes of glass in a window or other glazed panel, such as a glass door on a piece of case furniture. Sometimes the term is used interchangeably with MUNTIN.

MUNINGA
East African HARDWOOD; a PADAUK. Multicolored, yellow-brown to a deep reddish brown, with irregular darker markings, *muninga* is used in furniture both as solid wood and as VENEER.

MUNTHE, GERHARD (1849–1929)
Norwegian ART NOUVEAU furniture designer. Munthe studied painting in Germany but returned to Norway to practice the decorative arts. He was a developer and the chief exponent of the Dragonesque style, an inventive local variant of Art Nouveau. Dragonesque style furniture featured rectilinear, Austrian-inspired pieces with bold colors and motifs from Viking decoration, preserved in medieval stone carvings and churches.

MUNTIN
Vertical member within, but not at either end of, a wooden panel, the framing of a chest, or a window or door. A vertical member at either end is called a *stile*. Sometimes the term *muntin* is used interchangeably with MULLION.

MURDOCH, PETER (b. 1940)
Contemporary British designer. Principally a graphic designer, Murdoch made a splash in the furniture world with a line of children's furniture made of heavy, patterned paper and folded into functional shapes (1964).

MURPHY BED
Twentieth-century American furniture form; BED that is hinged to a wall at its head, swinging up into a closet for storage and concealment. The Murphy bed is named for its inventor, William Lawrence Murphy (1876–1959).

MUTHESIUS, ECKART (1904–89)
German designer in the INTERNATIONAL STYLE. Son of a famous theorist of modern design (*see* Hermann MUTHESIUS), Eckart Muthesius is particularly associated with the Indore Palace, a design project that provided a dramatic forum for the advanced furniture design of its day. Commissioned in 1930 by the Maharaja of Indore to provide furnishings for his abode, Muthesius designed a great deal of it himself and also contracted for pieces from many leading designers of the day, including LE CORBUSIER, Eileen GRAY, Louis SOGNOT, René HERBST and Émile-Jacques RUHLMANN. The project was completed in 1933. Muthesius's own furniture was rectilinear, clean-lined and displayed a fondness for novelty, as in a pair of boxy armchairs, upholstered in a bright red synthetic material, with a reading lamp incorporated in each shoulder.

MUTHESIUS, HERMANN (1861–1927)
German architect and writer; influential figure in the development of modern design. From 1896 to 1903 Muthesius was attached to the German embassy in London to report on developments in British design and industry. He responded warmly to the ARTS AND CRAFTS MOVEMENT, especially to the work of ASHBEE and VOYSEY. Muthesius believed, however, that the movement's antipathy toward modern manufacturing processes was a serious, retrogressive flaw. He published a good deal of material in Germany on British architecture and design, both before and after his return. Muthesius became the superintendent of the Schools of Arts and Crafts for the State of Prussia in 1903. From this position, and through his role in the founding of the DEUTSCHER WERKBUND, Muthesius influenced German designers to follow the British esthetic example of simplicity and forthright construction but also to design for industrial production.

NACRE

Another name for MOTHER-OF-PEARL.

NAGAMOCHI

Traditional JAPANESE FURNITURE form; oldest and simplest of the TANSU, it is a simple, rectangular CHEST, usually about three feet high, with a hinged lid. Developed in medieval times, the *nagamochi* has generally been made with very little ornamentation, though earlier pieces frequently had elaborate iron hinges and hasps. Occasionally, the piece has had drawers or compartments with doors.

NAHL, JOHANN AUGUST (1710–85)

German woodcarver, designer and maker of ROCOCO FURNITURE. Nahl is most noted for his exceptionally free and vivacious rococo interiors at the Potsdam and Berlin palaces of Frederick the Great of Prussia. His furniture for these palaces, while also based on the French LOUIS XV STYLE, is somewhat ponderously proportioned.

NAKASHIMA, GEORGE (1905–90)

Contemporary American furniture maker. Though he used power tools and, on a small scale, mass-manufacturing techniques, Nakashima is associated with the HANDICRAFT REVIVAL, for he shared the movement's rejection of the machine age and the industrial ethos. Nakashima built furniture to his own designs and held many of the handicraft revival values: an almost spiritual attachment to wood, a naturalistic esthetic and a craftsman's concern for precision and traditional modes of construction. Structurally, his furniture was derived from such traditional forms as the WINDSOR CHAIR and SHAKER FURNITURE, but stylistically, his work was informed by an awareness of volume and space that is characteristic of Japanese art. His efforts to incorporate the natural form of the wood—the grain or the shape of a plank taken from a tree trunk or branch—into the line of a design gave his furniture a distinctive organic character, revealing the designer's philosophy of harmony between nature and art.

NAN MU

Fragrant yellowish brown HARDWOOD used in CHINESE FURNITURE.

NANCY, SCHOOL OF

Group of ART NOUVEAU designers in Nancy, France. Led by Émile GALLÉ, this group was centered around an institution he founded, called *L'Ecole de Nancy, Alliance Provincial des Industries d'Art.* The institution was devoted to establishing a renaissance of provincial handicraft, patterned after the example of the guilds associated with the British ARTS AND CRAFTS MOVEMENT but employing the new decorative style, Art Nouveau. Furniture produced by School of Nancy designers is characterized by forms often based on 18th-century ROCOCO FURNITURE designs and by a lavish use of marquetry, mainly renderings of such natural motifs as flowers, birds, fish, insects and even landscapes. The designers used local woods for the most part, especially fruitwoods, but they also used a great variety of exotic woods for marquetry. The two principal furniture designers of the group were Gallé and Louis

MAJORELLE; others were Émile Victor PROUVÉ, Eugene VALLIN and Jacques GRUBER.

NATIONAL ROMANTICISM

Finnish art and design movement of the late 19th and early 20th centuries. The movement marked the beginning of modern Finnish applied arts (*see* SCANDINAVIAN MODERN).

After Finland achieved its independence from Sweden in the early 19th century, a patriotic enthusiasm for Finland's ancient peasant culture stirred the country. Subsequently, Finnish designers were receptive to such other design influences as the BIEDERMEIER STYLE, the British ARTS AND CRAFTS MOVEMENT and *Jugendstil,* the German branch of ART NOUVEAU. The principal designers of National Romanticism, Akseli GALLÉN-KALLELA and Louis SPARRE, produced furniture similar in its simplicity and forthright craft to British and Austrian furniture of the late 19th century, with the addition of the popular Finnish folk art motifs. Later, in the 1920s, the movement was led by architect and designer Eliel SAARINEN.

NATURALISTIC STYLE

Style of decoration applied to the various REVIVAL STYLES of furniture in the early Victorian period in Britain. The style was characterized by the use of strikingly realistic representations of natural subjects, such as plants and animals.

neoclassical chair

NECESSARY CHAIR

Another name for CHAMBER CHAIR.

NECKING

Set of MOLDINGS forming a collar at the top of the shaft of a COLUMN, immediately below the CAPITAL.

NEEDLES, JOHN (1786–1878)

American furniture maker; active from 1812 to the 1850s in Baltimore. Though Needles worked in a variety of design modes, all of his designs had neoclassical elements. He was best known for his austere, architectonic AMERICAN EMPIRE STYLE furniture, characterized by figured MAPLE veneers.

NELSON, GEORGE (1907–1986)

Contemporary American architect and furniture designer an early exponent of ERGONOMIC DESIGN. Trained as an architect, Nelson began his career as a writer and editor for the architectural press. In 1936 he opened a small practice as well. An article Nelson wrote in 1945, which proposed the development of mobile storage units, now called room dividers, led the HERMAN MILLER FURNITURE CO. to offer Nelson a position with the firm. He succeeded Gilbert ROHDE as design director in 1946 and began the firm's association with Charles EAMES. Nelson's approach to design was similar to Eames's—both designers applied the doctrine of FUNCTIONALISM to newly available materials and techniques. Compared to the European INTERNATIONAL STYLE designers, however, who were their esthetic predecessors, Nelson and Eames produced more informal work, less austere and geometrical, albeit still plain and unornamented.

After 1947 Nelson returned to private architectural practice, though he maintained an association as a consultant for Herman Miller. In addition to furniture and buildings, he designed interiors, especially for offices and hospitals, most notably a series of ergonomic office systems, in association with Herman Miller. Nelson designed exhibitions, graphics and business equipment and was also a well-known writer on design, publishing several books and many essays and articles.

NEOCLASSICAL STYLE

European manner of furniture design and decoration characterized by the use of ideas, forms and motifs taken from ancient Greek and Roman art and architecture. Many European furniture styles have been classical in inspiration, beginning with RENAISSANCE FURNITURE and including late 20th-century POST-MODERN FURNITURE. However, the term is most closely associated with work of the late 18th century, which was greatly affected by the sudden expansion of classical archaeology sparked by the discovery and excavation of Pompeii and Herculaneum, beginning in the 1740s.

Renaissance furniture, made during the 15th–17th centuries, reflected that period's enthusiasm for ancient Greek and Roman culture. Two classical sources informed the work of Renaissance furniture makers: Roman architecture and the sculptural programs of ancient sarcophagi. The latter contributed such motifs as the URN, the PUTTO and mythological beasts, including the SPHINX and CHIMERA. It also stimulated a greater naturalism in carving, as opposed to the stylization of much medieval work; a by-product of this trend was the greater use of WALNUT, which was easier to carve than the traditional OAK.

The influence of classical architecture was felt particularly in the overall shape and appearance of pieces of furniture; much Renaissance case furniture resembled miniature buildings. Classical architecture also provided motifs that included various building elements—for example, COLUMNS, PILASTERS and PEDIMENTS—as well as the ornamentation of the classical ORDERS OF ARCHITECTURE, such as the VOLUTE and the ACANTHUS leaf. Renaissance designers referred not only to the ruins of ancient buildings, which were plentiful, especially in Italy, but also to the published works of Vitruvius, the Roman architect who had first classified the orders, in the first century B.C.

The Renaissance began in Italy, where the influence of ancient Rome was naturally greatest, and spread throughout Europe during the 16th century. In Spain the Italian-influenced PLATERESQUE STYLE dominated the decorative arts in the first half of that century; it was manifested in furniture chiefly in designs for elaborate MARQUETRY, continuing a well-established national tradition in that craft. The style also moved north into the German-speaking lands, and Renaissance furniture was well established there by 1550. Later, England and Scandinavia would receive Renaissance décor, as transmitted through Germany and the Netherlands. In 17th-century England Tudor style furniture (see TUDOR FURNITURE) echoed remotely the Italian ideas of two centuries earlier.

Renaissance thinking and decoration arrived in France after the French military intervention in Italy, which began in 1494. King Charles VIII and then François I brought back ideas, furniture and craftsmen and employed them in the redecoration of royal palaces and chateaux. A distinctively French style of furniture arose, the FRANÇOIS I STYLE, combining Italian ornamentation, especially architectural motifs, and GOTHIC FURNITURE forms. This mode, which emphasized the grandeur of classical architecture in

largely carved decoration, was the chief influence in Spain in the second half of the 16th century.

By then, though, the MANNERIST STYLE, a new phase in neoclassical decoration, had evolved in Italy. In furniture it would achieve its characteristic form in France. Mannerist furniture was not architectural in inspiration; it was derived from the first excavations, made in the late 15th century, of ancient Roman painted interior decoration. The main component of Mannerist decoration was GROTESQUE ORNAMENT—fields of small, generally bizarre motifs, including strange renderings of human heads, various fantastic creatures, and such images from nature as insects, plants and birds. This deliberately eccentric work developed in reaction against the more rational classicism of earlier Renaissance design, and it is not normally considered neoclassical. However, it is based on ancient Roman devices, and, more important, it transmitted neoclassical ideas in furniture design to later generations.

Mannerism in furniture reached its apogee in the French HENRI II STYLE, in which form it exerted great influence on designers in the Netherlands, the German-speaking lands, England (see JACOBEAN FURNITURE), and Scandinavia; through England, a faint reverberation of Mannerism crossed the Atlantic, in AMERICAN JACOBEAN FURNITURE. Mannerism's decadent later phases—including the LOUIS XIII STYLE and the AURICULAR STYLE—inspired a counterdevelopment, the no less extravagant but more balanced baroque.

BAROQUE FURNITURE, like Mannerist furniture, is not usually regarded as neoclassical, but it did retain an important neoclassical characteristic—the prominence of motifs derived from ancient architecture. However, these motifs were used in a highly unorthodox manner, in which columns were twisted and pediments given curving and broken silhouettes. Also, furniture ornamentation was principally sculptural, stressing figural carving, especially in Italian work. In France, which became the generally acknowledged leader of European style at this time, the LOUIS XIV STYLE was somewhat less ornate, and emphasis was placed on solemnity and grandeur, in a conscious evocation of the Roman Empire. This style was highly influential throughout Europe, especially in England and the Netherlands. The most truly neoclassical baroque fur-

eagle motif

fan inlay motif

hawk motif

lyre motif

quarter fan inlay motif

sphinx motif

swan motif

wheat shuck motif

niture was made in Germany, where a degree of austerity produced highly architectural furniture that stressed moldings and cornices.

So bold and dramatic a style as the baroque inevitably produced a powerful counterreaction. The rise of the rococo in the early 18th century marked the first time since the Middle Ages that a European decorative style was not only explicitly not classically inspired, but was even anticlassical. ROCOCO FURNITURE originated in France and then spread throughout the Western world. It remained important for a century, but it triggered a reaction in the 1760s, and that reaction was neoclassical.

The British ADAM STYLE and the French LOUIS XVI STYLE were the dominant modes of neoclassical furniture in the late 18th century, the period with which the term *neoclassical* is most closely associated. In France the TRANSITION STYLE reintroduced classical motifs and some straightening of the curvilinear shapes of rococo furniture; by 1770 neoclassical ideas dominated, and the Louis XVI style came into its own. The traditional repertoire of neoclassical motifs was revived and expanded, drawing on new sources—the excavations at Pompeii and Herculaneum; designers J.-F. NEUFFORGE and J.-C. DELAFOSSE helped to codify this material. Favored motifs included the Greek KEY PATTERN, VITRUVIAN SCROLL, PALMETTE, ANTHEMION and BUCRANIUM. The Louis XVI style was extremely influential, particularly in Germany, where David ROENTGEN was a leading maker, and in northern Italy, especially in the work of G. M. BONZANIGO.

In Britain the creator and principal exponent of 18th-century neoclassicism in furniture and interior decoration was Robert ADAM. Adam was greatly influenced by the Italian artist G. B. PIRANESI, whom he had known in Rome in the 1750s. (Piranesi's work was also important to many Italian makers, such as Giocondo ALBERTOLLI and Giuseppe MAGGIOLINI.) Adam style furniture was less solemn than its French counterpart. Though it also attempted to counter rococo frivolity, its emphasis on light-colored materials and painted decoration, especially figural panels derived from Greek vase painting, gave it an air of prettiness and gaiety. In the 1780s–1790s the Adam style was modified in the designs of George HEPPLEWHITE, Thomas SHERATON and others; this later, somewhat more austere variant was the chief influence on 18th-centu-

ry American neoclassical design during the FEDERAL PERIOD. The British style was also influential in northern Europe and as far afield as Russia.

In the last decades of the 18th century, neoclassical design became more restrained and severe. A desire to adhere closely to the simple ROMAN FURNITURE being discovered, chiefly at Pompeii and Herculaneum, led to the development of the ETRUSCAN STYLE of decoration. In addition, the coming of the French Revolution imposed austerity on French furniture makers, both as an economic necessity and as an expression of aversion to the grandeur of the *ancien régime.* The Louis XVI manner thus culminated in the simpler DIRECTOIRE STYLE.

In the early 19th century, the French EMPIRE STYLE maintained the emphasis on ancient furniture forms and limited the range of acceptable designs, stressing resemblances to such ancient pieces as the Greek KLISMOS and Roman SELLA CURULIS. Neoclassical motifs also remained prominent, as Napoleon explicitly wished the decorative arts to vaunt his reign by associating it with the glory of ancient Rome.

The Empire style was the chief influence on early 19th-century neoclassical style furniture elsewhere. The REGENCY STYLE in Britain and the DIRECTORY and AMERICAN EMPIRE STYLES in America were both very responsive to French design. In Spain the FERNANDINO STYLE was current until about 1830, reflecting the persisting cultural effects of the French military occupation of 1808–14. The important Italian designer Filippo Pelagio PALAGI worked in a personal, highly figural variant of the Empire style. His example and his influential position at the Sardinian court ensured the style's dominance in northern Italy into the 1850s. In Germany neoclassical furniture remained fashionable into the 1840s, chiefly through the influence of Leo von KLENZE. The contemporary BIEDERMEIER STYLE promoted an explicitly anti-imperial simplicity in materials and ornamentation, but it was nonetheless neoclassical in character, and its classicism had come from Napoleonic France. Scandinavia and Russia, following German examples, produced neoclassical furniture until about midcentury.

In France itself the RESTAURATION STYLE preserved neoclassical ideas for a short time after Napoleon's fall. Then, though, they were seen as stale. After the final demise of the Bourbon dynasty, in the revolution of 1830, fashions changed dramatically, and the various REVIVAL STYLES became popular.

The revival styles were well established throughout the Western world by the mid–9th century and were then generally dominant until early modern modes began to gain ascendancy in the 1880s and 1890s. Pointedly anticlassical at first, the early revival styles featured either medieval nostalgia, in the NEO-GOTHIC STYLE, or purposefully curvilinear work, in the ROCOCO REVIVAL STYLE. Soon, however, the period's penchant for rediscovering history produced the RENAISSANCE REVIVAL STYLE, which incorporated, in a wildly eclectic way, ideas and motifs from 16th- and 17th-century furniture. This furniture had been originally inspired by neoclassicism to some degree, although this more recent manifestation seemed to be part of a fashion for novelty and display. It was also allied with nationalism, especially in Italy and Germany, which were becoming unified nations; there historical references in ornamentation reflected this political process.

In France politics played a different role, as the LOUIS XVI REVIVAL STYLE was associated with the Second Empire of Napoleon III. Here rectilinearity and classical motifs derived from a nostalgia for French grandeur rather than from a concern for ancient Greek and Roman themes. ÉGYPTIENNERIE motifs, important earlier in French neoclassical furniture, were also revived in France and America at this time (see NEO-GREC STYLE), again due more to a fascination with the exotic than to a genuine antiquarian enthusiasm.

In the late 19th and early 20th centuries, the reform movements that marked the beginnings of modern design arose (see ARTS AND CRAFTS MOVEMENT; ART FURNITURE MOVEMENT; ART NOUVEAU; DEUTSCHE WERKSTÄTTEN), generally eschewing any historial references, classical or otherwise. The various subsequent modern furniture styles (see, for instance, INTERNATIONAL STYLE; SCANDINAVIAN MODERN) consistently adhered to this principle, and neoclassicism seemed a dead letter for three-quarters of a century. However, in the 1970s a reaction against the dominant International style in architecture led to a new neoclassical style, known as the Post-Modern, which has an analog in POST-MODERN FURNITURE. Relying on abstract color patterns and geometrical forms that resemble elements of classical architecture, the Post-Modern is not strictly a revival mode; it does not refer to historical styles in either intent or appearance. Rather, the classical ideals of balance and order that have repeatedly informed Western design have found new energy and a new manifestation.

NEO-GOTHIC STYLE

European manner of furniture design and decoration in 18th and 19th centuries, characterized by use of Gothic architectural ornamentation. The neo-Gothic impulse arose in Britain in the 18th century. It owed little to real GOTHIC FURNITURE, which was then largely unknown. Rather, a preromantic yearning for picturesque times gone by was combined with the period's fondness for novel, exotic decoration.

Batty LANGLEY published furniture designs incorporating medieval motifs as early as 1742, applying them to architectural, classically inspired forms. The fashion for Gothic decoration intensified in the 1750s, and CHIPPENDALE GOTHIC FURNITURE became popular. Essentially a more elaborate manifestation of the trend that Langley had initiated, and still extremely artificial, it juxtaposed such elements as pointed ARCHes and TRACERY with ROCOCO FURNITURE, sometimes even adding CHINOISERIE devices of CHINESE CHIPPENDALE FURNITURE. Besides Langley and Thomas CHIPPENDALE, from whose published designs the mode takes its name, Sanderson MILLER designed notable Chippendale Gothic furniture. The GOTHIC WINDSOR CHAIR (see under WINDSOR CHAIR) was popular at this time.

The rise of the NEOCLASSICAL STYLE in the 1760s temporarily eclipsed the Gothic revival. At the end of the 18th century, however, the REGENCY GOTHIC mode emerged amid the eclecticism of the time (see REGENCY STYLE) and reestablished a taste for "medieval" furniture, albeit in pieces that were simply neoclassical forms with Gothic ornamentation. Itself an unsuccessful style, unconvincing and rather fussy in appearance, the Regency Gothic anticipated the stronger neo-Gothic. When the neoclassical plummeted from grace and the REVIVAL STYLES surged to popularity, some time after the fall of Napoleon, the neo-Gothic quickly became dominant in Britain, chiefly because of the influence of an inspired

Neo-Gothic

designer, A. W. N. PUGIN, who created a more fully developed and historically accurate style. Other notable British furniture designers in the style included Henry SHAW, William BURGES and Richard Norman SHAW. As the design reform movements of the later 19th century arose, Bruce TALBERT and Charles Locke EASTLAKE developed a simplified version known as "Modern Gothic," and William MORRIS and the designers of the ARTS AND CRAFTS MOVEMENT were also medievalists.

The 19th century's penchant for historical revival generated the development of neo-Gothic styles in other European countries as well, although other revival styles generally predominated there. In the 1830s the French Gothic revival was variously known as *le style Troubadour* and *le style Cathédral,* and it was generally used by makers who also designed furniture in various other styles. The results were usually uninspired pastiches, but notable pieces were made by JACOB-DESMALTER and Claude Aimé CHÉNAVARD. The mode was less popular in France than the ROCOCO REVIVAL STYLE, and by midcentury it had ceased to be fashionable, although the work of VIOLLET-LE-DUC attracted some interest during the second half of the century.

In Germany in the 1830s and 1840s, many commercial manufacturers used the style in a richly romantic manner—most notably Wilhelm KIMBEL of Mainz. In Austria CARL LEISTLER, a Viennese firm, was also noted for its neo-Gothic work. Alexander Jackson DAVIS was the leading exponent of the style in America, where it had its greatest currency in 1830–70. Many other makers, among them John JELIFF and J. & J. W. MEEKS, also produced American neo-Gothic furniture. Generally, these pieces bore no resemblance to medieval models; they were simply romantic adaptations of Gothic architectural ornamentation on earlier 19th-century forms. In the 1870s–1880s, the so-called "Eastlake" style, based on the British "Modern Gothic," of Eastlake and Talbert, dominated American furniture design, preparing the way for indigenous design reformers.

With Pugin excepted, neo-Gothic style designers were generally anything but scrupulous in replicating medieval furniture. Nonetheless, the style was immensely and widely popular, expiring in many countries only with the 19th century itself, as the rapidly changing modern world began to reject historical references in design.

NEO-GREC STYLE

American design style of 1860s and 1870s; dramatic variant of RENAISSANCE REVIVAL STYLE. The neo-Grec style, despite its name, is chiefly distinguished by elaborate Egyptian decorative motifs, such as SPHINXes and lotus blossoms (*see* ÉGYPTIENNERIE), combined with the varied elements of the eclectic Renaissance Revival style, and generally applied to the neoclassical forms of the LOUIS XVI REVIVAL style. The neo-Grec style appealed to the widespread taste for novel, exotic furniture at the time. Alexander ROUX and the firm POTTIER & STYMUS were two leading exponents of the style.

NEST OF DRAWERS

Eighteenth-century term for very small CHEST OF DRAWERS.

NEST OF TABLES

Set of several small tables, graduated in size so that one can fit beneath another when not in use. When three tables are in a nest, they are sometimes called *trio tables;* when four, *quartetto tables.*

NESTFELL, JOHANN GEORG (1694–1762)

German maker of BAROQUE FURNITURE. Nestfell, who worked in Würzburg, specialized in elaborate pictorial MARQUETRY, especially representing architectural scenes.

NEUFFORGE, JEAN-FRANÇOIS (1714–91)

Flemish-born French NEOCLASSICAL STYLE furniture designer. Between 1765 and 1768 Neufforge published the first French neoclassical furniture designs of the 18th century. He used a heavy architectonic style with classical ornamentation, including an early use of ÉGYPTIENNERIE motifs. These designs had an impact on such developers of the LOUIS XVI STYLE as J.-F. BOUCHER and J.-C. DELAFOSSE and later influenced Richard de LALONDE and J.-D. DUGOURC.

NEUHOF, JOHANN (active 1660s)
German writer. After serving on a Dutch diplomatic mission to China, Neuhof published, in 1669, an illustrated account of that country, contributing to the first great wave of European enthusiasm for CHINOISERIE. The book's engravings were sometimes copied in pictorial MARQUETRY on case furniture.

NEW YORK CHIPPENDALE FURNITURE
AMERICAN CHIPPENDALE FURNITURE produced in New York City between 1755 and 1790, approximately. The furniture is characterized by restrained rococo style designs (*see* ROCOCO FURNITURE) derived largely from the pattern book of Thomas CHIPPENDALE. In New York the style was somewhat conservative in character, relative to PHILADELPHIA CHIPPENDALE FURNITURE. Very little case furniture was made, and older furniture forms, such as the corner chair, remained popular, newly equipped with pierced splats and cabriole legs. Ball-and-claw feet of a markedly squarish shape were distinctive of the New York style. Other local motifs included gadrooning on the skirts of chairs and tables and serpentine and piecrust tabletops. Carving was typically in rather shallow relief. Gilbert ASH and Samuel PRINCE were notable makers of New York Chippendale furniture.

NEWPORT CHIPPENDALE FURNITURE
AMERICAN CHIPPENDALE FURNITURE produced in Newport, Rhode Island, between about 1755 and 1790. The furniture is characterized by restrained rococo style designs (*see* ROCOCO FURNITURE) derived mostly from the pattern book of Thomas CHIPPENDALE. Newport cabinetmakers developed a distinctive local style, notably simpler and less ornamental than PHILADELPHIA CHIPPENDALE FURNITURE. In general, the cabinetmakers employed several characteristic elements: serpentine tabletops; pierced fretwork stretchers; and, on case furniture, bracket feet and the BLOCKFRONT—a form that was most fully developed in Newport. The shell motif was popular, and a subtle spiral on the bracket feet became a Newport Chippendale hallmark. The important designers of the style were all of the Goddard-Townsend family (*see* John GODDARD; Edmund TOWNSEND; Job TOWNSEND; John TOWNSEND).

NEWSON, MARC (b. 1964)
AUSTRALIAN FURNITURE designer. Marc Newson, who also designs jewelry, watches, lighting, interiors, and glassware, designs furniture in an elegant descendent of the mid-20th century INTERNATIONAL STYLE, employing smoothly shaped pieces in aluminum, fiberglass, molded plastic, BENTWOOD, and bent tubular steel frames.

One of the most successful young designers of the new century, Newson, who received his training in Sydney, lived and worked in Tokyo in the late 1980s and in Paris from 1991 to 1997. In London since 1997, Newson designs furniture and other objects (including a bicycle and an airplane interior) for manufacturers in Europe and Asia. His works are also in the collections of major museums on three continents.

New York Chippendale

NIEMEYER, OSCAR (b. 1907)
Contemporary Brazilian architect and designer associated with the INTERNATIONAL STYLE. Niemeyer is best known for the many buildings he designed in the capital city of Brasilia during the late 1950s and the 1960s. He has also designed International style furniture, influenced by LE CORBUSIER, who visited Brasil in the 1930s. Niemeyer rejected the severe, rectilinear lines of the International style in favor of the use of many curves. Accordingly, his work is light and graceful, while still recognizably functionalistic in character (*see* FUNCTIONALISM).

NIEUWENHUIS, THEODORE (1866–1951)
Leading Dutch ART NOUVEAU furniture designer. Nieuwenhuis's design style was French Art Nouveau, characterized by the use of figural motifs drawn from nature as well as curvilinear abstract lines. In addition to furniture, he designed interiors and pottery. Nieuwenhuis, Gerrit DIJSSELHOF and C. A. LION-CACHET founded Het Binnenhuis, a design workshop modeled on the guilds of the British ARTS AND CRAFTS MOVEMENT.

NIGERIAN PEARWOOD
Another name for GUAREA.

NIGHT STAND
Thomas CHIPPENDALE's term, which had wide currency in the late 18th century, for POT CUPBOARD.

NIGHT STOOL
Another name for either CLOSE STOOL or NIGHT TABLE.

NIGHT TABLE (also *close stool; commode; night stool*)
Eighteenth-century furniture form; portable toilet, successor to CLOSE STOOL. The night table appeared to be a simple cupboard above a drawer. The cupboard generally housed a washbasin and pitcher, like the contemporary POT CUPBOARD, while the "drawer" was in fact a removable close stool, with a hole in a padded seat above a chamber pot or pan. The night table was ornamented like other pieces of case furniture and came to be called, euphemistically, a "night commode" or "bedroom commode," later shortened to simply "commode." A 19th-century variant took the form of BED STEPS.

NIMURA & SATO
Japanese-American manufacturing and importing firm, located in Brooklyn, New York; leading producers of BAMBOO furniture in the 1880s and 1890s. Nimura & Sato imported bamboo and cane from Asia and constructed furniture in the United States. The enthusiasm of the day for things Japanese (*see* JAPONISME) created a market for bamboo goods but did not extend to design, generally speaking, so Nimura & Sato's furniture was strictly Western, foursquare and decorated with rows of spindles, in the manner prescribed by Charles Locke EASTLAKE.

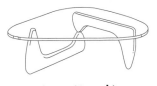

Isamu Noguchi

NOGUCHI, ISAMU (1904–88)
Contemporary American sculptor and designer. Best known as one of America's most distinguished sculptors, Noguchi also designed some memorable furniture, mostly tables, both as unique pieces and for commercial manufacture. His coffee tables with free-form sculptural legs and glass tops, designed for the HERMAN MILLER FURNITURE CO. in the 1940s, are quite well known and have been widely imitated. Noguchi also designed an extensive series of lamps as well as formal gardens and playgrounds.

NOMEN-DANSU
Traditional JAPANESE FURNITURE form; small TANSU, or chest, with square drawers intended to store masks used in Noh drama. A *nomen-dansu* was historically reserved for the aristocracy.

NONSUCH CHEST
English TUDOR FURNITURE form; chest decorated with elaborate MARQUETRY representations of classical architecture. This decoration originated in the MANNERIST STYLE ornamentation of the German KUNSTSCHRANK, and it is believed that most, perhaps all, of the makers of English Nonsuch chests were German immigrants. The term dates to the 19th century, when it was erroneously concluded that the chest's decorations were patterned on Henry VIII's palace of the same name, razed in the 17th century. The palace's name was a corruption of its designer's, the 16th-century Italian architect Toto del Nunziata.

NOSSENI, GIOVANNI MARIA (d. 1620)
Italian RENAISSANCE FURNITURE maker who worked in Dresden from 1575 until his death. Employed by the court of Saxony, Nosseni was especially noted for furniture set with semiprecious stones.

NUREMBERG CABINET
See KUNSTSCHRANK.

NURMESNIEMI, ANTTI (b. 1927)
Contemporary Finnish designer. Since the 1950s Nurmesniemi has designed prolifically in many areas, including glass, metal, wallpaper, textiles, lighting, urban design and furniture. Though he has used various materials in his furniture design, he has shown a preference for metals. Nurmesniemi's work in the late 1950s illustrates the Scandinavian revival of the INTERNATIONAL STYLE's functionalist esthetic, as does the work of his contemporary, Ilmari TAPIOVAARA.

O

OAK
Pale yellow-brown European and American HARDWOOD; one of the most important materials in furniture making since antiquity. Prior to the 18th century, the vast majority of European furniture was made of oak. In the late 17th century, more decorative woods began to be introduced, and oak fell out of favor for use in fine cabinetry. However, it has remained in use for framing and for vernacular furniture.

OBRIST, HERMANN (1863–1927)
Swiss ART NOUVEAU designer. Principally an embroidery designer, Obrist settled in Munich in 1894 and became a prominent figure in the DEUTSCHE WERKSTÄTTEN movement. He also designed some furniture in a restrained variant of the French Art Nouveau style, employing botanical decorative motifs.

OCCASIONAL TABLE
Modern term for any small, portable table intended for many uses, as circumstance demands.

OEBEN, JEAN-FRANÇOIS (1721–63)
German-born French furniture maker of LOUIS XV and TRANSITION STYLEs. Oeben arrived in Paris in the early 1740s and was first employed in the workshop of the Boulle family (see André-Charles BOULLE). He was appointed *ébéniste du roi* in 1753 and established his own business, which his wife, the sister of Roger VANDERCRUSE, took over following his early death. She subsequently married Oeben's assistant, J.-H. RIESENER, who continued to run the workshop. Oeben was a metalworker as well as a cabinetmaker, and he specialized in mechanical furniture—pieces incorporating concealed accessories and gadgetry, such as the SECRÉTAIRE À CAPUCIN. He veneered his work with elaborate MARQUETRY, using floral imagery in the Louis XV style and geometrical patterns in later work. His masterpiece, unfinished when he died and completed by Riesener, was a magnificent desk commissioned by Louis XV—the first instance of a new form that Oeben invented, the ROLL-TOP DESK.

OGEE
S-shaped curve, whether an outline of a member, as in a SCROLL PEDIMENT (see under PEDIMENT) or in an OGEE MOLDING (see under MOLDING) or as part of a two-dimensional decorative design.

OGEE BRACKET FOOT
See under FOOT.

OKOUMÉ
Another name for GABOON.

OLBRICH, JOSEPH MARIA (1867–1908)
Austrian ART NOUVEAU designer and architect. A founding member of the Vienna SEZESSION, Olbrich was also associated with the DEUTSCHE WERKSTÄTTEN movement in Munich. After 1899 he was the chief architect and designer at the artists' colony established in Darmstadt by the Grand Duke of Hesse. Olbrich designed buildings, furniture and a

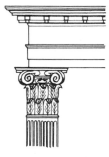

Composite order

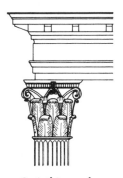

Corinthian order

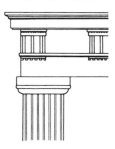

Doric order

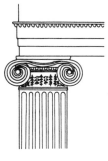

Ionic order

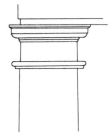

Tuscan order

wide range of other objects, including automobile bodies for Opel. He employed curvilinear abstract patterns of decoration in his restrained Art Nouveau design style.

"OLD ENGLISH" STYLE
See SHAW, Richard Norman.

OLD FRENCH STYLE
Nineteenth-century British term for the ROCOCO REVIVAL STYLE.

OLIVEWOOD
Any of several European and African HARDWOODs; woods of the fruitbearing olive tree. A handsome pale brown wood with darker markings, olivewood is most frequently seen in small figures and wares made for the tourist trade in the Mediterranean world, but it is also often used for decorative INLAY work in furniture. The European olive tree is usually short and twisted in form, so large pieces of its wood are not available, but the African trees—*East African olive* and *loliondo*—are somewhat taller and are sometimes used as flooring.

ONION FOOT
See under FOOT.

OPEN-TWIST TURNING
See under TURNERY.

OPENWORK
Decorative technique; patterned, ornamental PIERCED CARVING with openings cut completely through the material. Openwork may consist of a tight pattern with small openings, as in open FRETWORK, or it may be bolder, with more space relative to the material, as in pierced ARCADING. Openwork has been popular in furniture decoration since ancient times.

OPPENORDT, GILLES-MARIE (1672–1742)
French RÉGENCE STYLE designer of furniture and interiors. The son of a cabinetmaker, Oppenordt became the chief designer of interiors and furniture for the Palais-Royal, the Paris residence of the regent, Philippe d'Orléans. Oppenordt's interior decorations were revolutionary. He introduced decorative images that overflowed their panels, extending onto the adjacent wall. He smoothly rounded corners and junctions of wall and ceiling. As a result, the structural articulation of his rooms seemed almost unnoticeable; surface decoration was thus stressed rather than architecture, the more classical emphasis. Oppenordt also designed gracefully curvilinear pieces of furniture with extensive gilding.

ORDERS OF ARCHITECTURE
Specific styles of ancient Greek and Roman architecture, used to decorate all European furniture modeled on classical architecture, from RENAISSANCE FURNITURE through the NEOCLASSICAL STYLE to today's POST-MODERN FURNITURE. The orders consist of three Greek modes: the DORIC, IONIC and CORINTHIAN ORDERS; and five Roman ones: the TUSCAN, Doric, Ionic, Corinthian and COMPOSITE ORDERS. These types are distinguished by their differing ornamentation and relative proportions of parts in the assemblage composed of the ENTABLATURE and the COLUMNS, with bases and CAPITALS, that support it. The orders of architecture were originally classified by the ancient Roman architect Vitruvius in the first century B.C. They began to appear on furniture during the Renaissance.

ORIENTAL ROSEWOOD
Broad term used to denote any of several HARDWOODS used chiefly in CHINESE FURNITURE: HUA LI, a true ROSEWOOD; HONG MU and ZI TAN, both PADAUKs; and others.

ORMOLU
Cast bronze with FINISH of gold, applied by MERCURY GILDING, used for furniture mounts (*see* HARDWARE) in 18th and early 19th centuries, especially in France. Originally, the term *ormolu*—literally, "ground gold"—meant the prepared gold leaf or powdered gold used in any sort of GILDING. As mercury gilding of bronze became common, the term came to refer to a product of that particular process. The toxicity of mercury has resulted in the disuse of the process; today an alloy of copper, zinc and tin, resembling gold and used in decoration, is called ormolu.

OTTO, JOHANN HEINRICH (active 1780s)
Eighteenth-century German-American painter and furniture decorator of rural Pennsylvania. A number of Pennsylvania German dower chests (*see* PENNSYLVANIA GERMAN FURNITURE) bear painted decorations attributed to Otto.

OTTOMAN
Low, heavily upholstered seat or bench, usually without arms or back, for seating one or more persons. The ottoman originated in the 18th century and became most popular after the development of deep-buttoned, coil-spring UPHOLSTERY around 1830. A variety of circular and triangular versions were made in the course of the 19th century. Small ottomans have often served as footstools.

OUD, JACOBUS JOHANNES PIETER (1890–1963)
Dutch architect and designer; member of the DE STIJL group. J. J. P. Oud, principally an architect, was influenced by the writings of Hermann MUTHESIUS and H. P. BERLAGE early in his career. He then joined in the purist design reform efforts of De Stijl and designed tubular-steel furniture in the geometrical manner of the movement during the 1920s. Unlike Gerrit RIETVELD, who was more programmatic, Oud incorporated elements from the BAUHAUS designers and others into his work.

OVANGKOL
Brown West African HARDWOOD resembling WALNUT and used mainly as veneer and flooring.

OVERSTUFFED FURNITURE
See UPHOLSTERY.

OVOLO MOLDING
See under MOLDING.

OXBOW FRONT
Curved face of any 18th-century piece of case furniture that was convex at either side and concave in the middle; that is, the reverse of SERPENTINE front.

ottoman

OYSTER VENEER (also *bois de bout*)
Wood VENEER that resembles an arrangement of oyster shells. Oyster veneer is composed of a number of sheets of wood cut from a small branch, commonly of LABURNUM or WALNUT. These are sliced across the width of the branch, exposing the concentric growth rings, and then arranged as ornamentation on a surface of a piece of furniture. The small individual pieces making up the pattern are often called *oysterwood.* Oyster veneering originated in Holland in the 17th century.

OYSTERSHELL VENEER
Another name for OYSTER VENEER.

OYSTERWOOD
See OYSTER VENEER.

PABST, DANIEL (1826–1910)

Philadelphia furniture maker; exponent of EASTLAKE's and TALBERT's Modern Gothic style. Pabst, a German immigrant who came to Philadelphia in 1849, set up his own shop by 1854 and made RENAISSANCE REVIVAL STYLE furniture. These pieces were characterized by a great variety of carved surfaces, ranging from incising to high relief. Pabst's design style changed during the 1870s, however, as he was influenced by the writings of Eastlake, Talbert and Christopher DRESSER. He developed a particularly rich variant of the Modern Gothic style and continued to decorate his pieces elaborately, though he no longer carved in extremely high relief. Pabst's use of geometrically styled botanical motifs can be attributed to Dresser's influence. Pabst worked with architect and furniture designer Frank FURNESS during the 1870s and 1880s, retiring in 1896.

PAD-AND-DISK FOOT

See under FOOT.

PADAUK (also *padouk*)

Any of a number of generally reddish HARDWOODs, greatly valued in furniture making for their strength, durability, luster and vivid color. They have been used both structurally and in decorative VENEERs and INLAY work. Native to the tropics from West Africa to the East Indies, the padauks vary considerably in appearance. A variety from the Andaman Islands, a brilliant red-brown wood with dark markings, reached Europe in the early 18th century and was particularly popular in French ROCOCO FURNITURE; it was known as

"Andaman rosewood." Another padauk prominent in 18th-century furniture, especially as panels of veneer, was AMBOYNA WOOD a highly figured, yellower variety from Burma and the Moluccas. Today the most common padauks are African—notably the multicolored, less red MUNINGA, from East Africa, and a quite purplish West African variety. The woods HONG MU and ZI TAN, used in CHINESE FURNITURE, are padauks.

PAD FOOT

See under FOOT.

PAINTBRUSH FOOT

See under FOOT.

PAKTONG

Chinese nickel silver—alloy of copper, zinc and nickel—resembling pale brass. Paktong was used for HARDWARE on CHINESE FURNITURE. Although known in the West from the early 18th century onward, it was not used on furniture outside China.

PALAGI, FILIPPO PELAGIO (1775–1860)

Italian NEOCLASSICAL STYLE artist and furniture designer. Trained as a painter, sculptor and architect, Pelagio Palagi became the supervisor of the royal palaces of the Kingdom of Sardinia and the director of the royal school of design, making him the most influential Italian designer of his day. He worked in an elaborate, showy manner based on the French EMPIRE STYLE, which featured his extravagant carvings of mythological figures.

PALDAO

Decoratively colored and figured HARDWOOD from New Guinea and the Philippines, used chiefly for veneer. It is greyish brown in color with dark brown stripes.

PALISANDER

English rendering of French word for ROSE-WOOD. *Palisander* refers more particularly to the dark, purplish variety of this wood, also called "Bombay rosewood." Important as a decorative element in French furniture of the late 18th and early 19th centuries, palisander has also been popular in the 20th century, from ART DECO furniture onward.

PALLADIAN STYLE

British furniture style of early GEORGIAN PERIOD; last phase of BAROQUE FURNITURE in Britain, popular in 1720s–1740s. The style was named for contemporary neo-Palladian architecture, though the two were very different in character. Neo-Palladian buildings were grandiose in scale but serenely geometrical in appearance, stressing classical rationality and balance, while the Palladian furniture they housed was baroque in the extreme, incorporating large-scale sculptural ornamentation in massive gilded pieces that were extraordinarily florid by any standard.

This dichotomy largely resulted from the work of William KENT, a leading neo-Palladian architect and the principal developer of the furniture style as well. He was also the first British architect to make a point of designing furniture for his buildings, and his influence on the design of his day was profound. His architecture was based on that of Italian Renaissance architect Andrea Palladio (1508–80), and he and others revived the English Palladian style of Inigo Jones (1575–1652). Kent had studied Palladio's work in northern Italy for almost 10 years, and his buildings, whose symmetrical façades were based on Greek temple architecture, reflected this influence. However, when he sought to design interiors of a suitable grandeur for this architecture, he lacked classical models, for the furniture of the ancients was still largely unknown. Therefore, he adopted the style of the furnishings he had seen in Palladio's buildings in Italy—early 17th-century Italian baroque furniture in the sculptural mode of Andrea BRUSTOLON and his followers.

Palladian furniture used many architectural features, such as massive pediments and cornices, but its most obvious characteristic was a reliance on figurative sculpture, in very large-scale motifs intended to create a dramatic focus in a room. Gigantic scallop shells, eagles and acanthus leaves abounded, along with *putti,* classical masks and baroque scrolls, consoles and cartouches; these exuberant ornaments were invariably composed in symmetrical arrangements. The pieces of furniture, which were sometimes too massive and heavy to be moved, were always placed in symmetrical relation to each other as well. Though Kent was the preeminent designer of this furniture, other architects, including Henry FLITCROFT and John VARDY, followed his example. A well-known cabinetmaker in the style was Benjamin GOODISON.

The contrast between the furniture in and the façades of neo-Palladian buildings seems greater today than it did then, for both elements shared an evident grandeur, novelly expressed, at least to the British, and both pointedly rejected French models, which had dominated the decorative arts in Europe for more than a generation. These factors appealed to the new Whig aristocracy, on whom power in Britain gradually devolved during the 18th century, and to the increasingly prosperous middle class, who generally allied themselves with the Whig nobles and could now afford magnificence themselves. However, in the 1730s the first hints of a revolution in French style were felt in Britain. The invigorating rococo (*see* ROCOCO FURNITURE) offered a freedom and frivolity that seduced the fashionable world from the symmetrical rigor of the baroque, and the Palladian style in furniture was gradually displaced. By the 1750s the rococo dominated British furniture.

PALMETTE

Decorative motif; fan-shaped, stylized palm leaf. Originating in ancient Egyptian art, it was frequently used in classical Greek architecture. From this source, it was adopted by European makers of RENAISSANCE FURNITURE and other classically inspired styles, especially the NEOCLASSICAL STYLE of the late 18th and early 19th centuries.

Verner Panton chair

papier-mâché table

PANETIÈRE
FRENCH PROVINCIAL FURNITURE form; highly decorated wooden container intended to store bread.

PANGA PANGA
East African HARDWOOD, very dark brown with fine streaks of pale brown to white. Similar to its close relative WENGÉ, *panga panga* is used in European furniture as an attractive veneer and, being quite strong, as framing.

PANKOK, BERNHARD (1872–1943)
German ART NOUVEAU furniture designer. Pankok was a member of the Munich branch of the DEUTSCHE WERKSTÄTTEN movement. His furniture design style was more curvilinear and more elaborately decorated than was usual in Germany at the time. After 1902 he lived in Stuttgart, where he continued to make furniture. After 1907 he was associated with the DEUTSCHER WERKBUND.

PANTON, VERNER (b. 1926)
Danish-born Swiss furniture designer, best known for his experimental furniture in new materials. Panton was associated with Arne JACOBSEN in the early 1950s; he has followed Jacobsen's lead in making free-form, organic, sculptural furniture. Panton specialized in futuristic chairs made of one continuous element, the same bent or molded piece of material serving for seat, back, arms, and legs. His molded plastic cantilevered chair (1960) is particularly well known; it was the first molded plastic furniture design to succeed commercially. The chair was manufactured by the HERMAN MILLER FURNITURE CO. Panton has also designed lighting fixtures, textiles and carpets.

PAO ROSA
West African HARDWOOD. An attractive reddish brown, pao rosa is a dense wood that carves well and is often used in TURNERY.

PAPELEIRA
Spanish RENAISSANCE FURNITURE form. A variant of the VARGUEÑO, the *papeleira* did not have a fall front enclosing its array of small drawers. Otherwise, it resembled the related form and rested on a TAQUILLÓN or a PIE DE PUENTE.

PAPIER-MÂCHÉ FURNITURE
Furniture made from molded paper pulp. Papier-mâché originated in the ancient Orient, probably in China, and it seems to have been known in Europe as early as the 17th century, when it was used to make light objects such as mirror frames and trays. Its use for furniture began around 1820.

Papier-mâché furniture was most popular in the VICTORIAN PERIOD in Britain and, to a lesser degree, in America and elsewhere. It was principally produced in some variant of the ROCOCO REVIVAL STYLE, since the saturated paper lent itself readily to bold, curvilinear forms. The surface of a piece was generally japanned (*see* JAPANNING) or lacquered and then decorated with paint or gilt and mother-of-pearl inlay to represent naturalistic motifs such as flowers, birds, butterflies or landscapes. While papier-mâché is durable if kept dry, its fragility limited its application to very lightweight furniture, especially chairs, tables and pole screens.

PAPYRUS
Aquatic plant, the sedge *Cyperus papyrus,* used in ancient EGYPTIAN FURNITURE. Besides its much better-known role as an early form of writing material, papyrus was also used, from prehistoric times through the dynastic period, to make light stools and tables, wickerwork and woven seats of chairs and stools.

PARANA PINE
Brazilian SOFTWOOD, light yellow-brown with some reddish streaking, with a fine, even texture. Brazil's most important commercial wood, Parana pine is used as a secondary wood in furniture (*see* PRIMARY AND SECONDARY WOODS), especially for drawer parts. Not a true pine, Parana pine is closely related to the ornamental monkey puzzle tree.

PARCEL GILT
Decorated with gold (*see* GILDING) in part only, usually on ornamental details.

PARKER, RICHARD BARRY (1867–1947)

British architect and furniture designer associated with the ARTS AND CRAFTS MOVEMENT. Barry Parker's partner was Raymond Unwin, an important architect in the period before the First World War and, like Parker, a follower of the ideas of William MORRIS. Parker was primarily responsible for the interiors and furniture in their projects, which included a number of whole communities designed from scratch—notably Letchworth, famous as the first "garden city" (1903). Parker & Unwin furniture was simple and forthright, influenced by C. F. A. VOYSEY, though derived from rustic models, featuring rush-bottomed chairs and sturdy dressers and tables.

PARODI, DOMENICO (1668–1740)

Italian sculptor and BAROQUE FURNITURE maker. Like his father, Filippo PARODI, Domenico was best known as a marble sculptor. He designed CONSOLE TABLES featuring abundant sculptural motifs, such as *putti*, eagles and massed foliage.

PARODI, FILIPPO (1630–1702)

Italian sculptor and BAROQUE FURNITURE maker. Principally a sculptor in marble, Parodi had apprenticed in Rome under Bernini for six years, and the furniture he subsequently made in Genoa was highly sculptural and ornate. His son Domenico PARODI was also a sculptor and furniture maker.

PARQUETRY

Use of wood INLAY on floors. Less correctly, this term is often used to indicate MARQUETRY that is strikingly geometrical in pattern.

PARSONS TABLE

Twentieth-century furniture form; low, square occasional table of molded plastic, named for the Parsons School of Design in New York City, where the design evolved in the 1950s.

PARTNERS' DESK

British furniture form of late 18th and 19th centuries; large, squarish WRITING TABLE. The top was supported by PEDESTALS containing drawers or other compartments, so arranged that two people could work at it, facing each other.

PARTRIDGE WOOD

Brazilian HARDWOOD; dark reddish brown in color, with darker mottled streaks said to resemble a partridge's plumage. Partridge wood was very popular for INLAY work in 18th-century furniture, especially in France.

PASTIGLIA

Substance similar to GESSO, used to make molded decoration on Italian RENAISSANCE FURNITURE. *Pastiglia* consisted of either gesso or white lead combined with an egg binder. It was applied soft and then shaped by the application of wooden or metal molds carved in ARABESQUES, GROTESQUE ORNAMENT or representations of allegorical or mythological scenes. The resulting surface of relief work was then painted or gilded. *Pastiglia* was used mostly on chests, CASSONES and especially on small boxes resembling these case pieces.

PATENT FURNITURE

Ingenious furniture designs, very popular in 19th-century America, that were patented as new inventions by their developers. Patent furniture appealed to the admiration for technical progress and love of novelty that dominated popular taste at the time. It was often some kind of CONVERTIBLE FURNITURE or constructed with moving parts. PLATFORM ROCKERS and beds that converted to an astonishing number of forms, from sofas to sideboards, were some of the specialized forms that were invented in the course of this trend. Several designers and furniture makers are associated with patent furniture, including Auguste ELIAERS, Samuel GRAGG, George HUNZINGER and William Wooton, inventor of the WOOTON DESK.

PATERAE

Decorative device of ancient GREEK FURNITURE. Small, unornamented plaques, circular or ovoid, were carved or inlaid singly, as a BOSS, or arranged in a straight line.

patera

PATINA

Glossy surface and rich color produced in wood through age, repeated polishings and wear. This effect can also be created artificially.

PATTERN BOOK

Published collection of furniture designs, usually by a particular designer. Pattern books circulated from the 16th century on, transmitting stylistic developments throughout Europe and America. The first pattern book, consisting of woodcuts by the anonymous German maker the H. S. Master, was published in 1530. RENAISSANCE FURNITURE, especially in the MANNERIST STYLE, was widely spread through pattern books. Many subsequent designers and styles were perhaps most influential through such published designs. The 18th-century British designers Thomas CHIPPENDALE, GEORGE HITCHCOCK and Thomas SHERATON all published notable pattern books. Nineteenth-century NEO-CLASSICAL STYLE makers were heavily indebted to the pattern books of Thomas HOPE, PERCIER AND FONTAINE and Pierre de LA MÉSANGÈRE. NEO-GOTHIC STYLE furniture was greatly influenced by the published work of A. W. N. PUGIN.

More recently, the advent of mass manufacture has diminished the importance of pattern books. Designers submit their sketches to a corporation, not to the public; photography has tended to replace published "patterns," and the commercial distribution of more and more pieces has made published designs less necessary for styles to spread.

PAUL, BRUNO (1874–1968)

German ART NOUVEAU and ART DECO designer. Paul was a prominent member of the DEUTSCHE WERKSTÄTTEN movement. In 1906 he designed some of the first machine-made furniture, using a restrained, rectilinear Art Nouveau style. As a designer, a writer and director of the Berlin School of Arts and Crafts, he was an important influence on German design through the 1920s. His later furniture designs are in the Art Deco style.

PAULIN, PIERRE (b. 1927)

Contemporary French furniture designer. Paulin is best known for bold, sculptural furniture, composed of a steel frame covered with polyurethane foam and upholstered in stretch fabric. Paulin's daringly innovative designs yielded strikingly unusual pieces in flowing forms, such as his "Ribbon" chair (1966), in which a narrow length of foam describes a loop. The bottom of the loop, mounted above a wooden base, forms the seat, while the top of the loop, which is twisted a half-turn, forms the chair back. This and other similarly futuristic designs ally Paulin with his contemporary Olivier MOURGUE as an advocate of unconventional forms. Paulin has also designed packaging, telephones and interiors for Simca automobiles.

PAULOWNIA

Western term for Japanese wood KIRI.

PAW FOOT

See under FOOT.

PEAR FOOT

See under FOOT.

PEARWOOD

Pale, reddish brown HARDWOOD of Northern Hemisphere used for decorative inlay and MARQUETRY. While easily stained and worked, pearwood is used only decoratively in furniture, since it is generally available only in small amounts. It is also used in the manufacture of fine tools and musical instruments.

PEDESTAL

Originally the base support of a COLUMN, in classical architecture. A pedestal in furniture may have one of four definitions: (1) a central support for a tabletop or chair seat; (2) one of a pair of sets of drawers or small cupboards used to support a flat top, as in a KNEEHOLE DESK or PEDESTAL DESK; (3) a pedestal STAND, a freestanding piece of case furniture used in pairs to flank a SIDEBOARD in 18th-century Britain; (4) the base support of a column or sculpture, when appearing as ornamental detail on a piece of furniture, a common motif on architecturally inspired furniture in all styles.

PEDESTAL CHAIR

Modern seating form; chair supported by one central stem or column. Perhaps the best-known pedestal chair is Eero SAARINEN's "Tulip" chair (1957).

PEDESTAL DESK
Late 18th-century furniture form; DESK composed of flat top supported at each end by a set of drawers, or PEDESTAL.

PEDESTAL TABLE (also *tripod table*)
Table whose top is supported by one central cylinder or column. Originating in the early 18th century, the pedestal table has been popular ever since. The 18th-century version generally had a tripod base with three short legs. Usually serving as a TEA TABLE, this table generally had a fretwork GALLERY around its top.

PEDIMENT
Arched or triangular ornamental element placed atop a tall piece of case furniture, in imitation of the gable of a classical Greek or Roman temple. The pediment began to appear in European furniture during the Italian Renaissance. In the early 18th century, the commonest type became the BROKEN PEDIMENT (*see under* PEDIMENT). A variety of styles of pediments are distinguished by name.

BROKEN PEDIMENT
In 18th-century Western case furniture, arched or triangular superstructure whose sloping top lines break off before meeting at the apex, leaving a gap. It took various forms, with straight lines or curves for its top; a frequent variant was the SCROLL PEDIMENT (*see under* PEDIMENT). Originally appearing in Roman architecture, the broken pediment was revived in BAROQUE FURNITURE and became common in the early 18th century. The gap, while often simply left empty, was also used to display an elaborate FINIAL or a piece of porcelain.

BROKEN-SCROLL PEDIMENT
Another name for SCROLL PEDIMENT (*see under* PEDIMENT).

FRETTED PEDIMENT
Another name for LATTICE PEDIMENT (*see under* PEDIMENT).

LATTICE PEDIMENT
In 18th-century European case furniture; BROKEN PEDIMENT (*see under* PEDIMENT) whose front is pierced to make a LATTICE or other FRETWORK surrounded by molding. Also called a FRETTED PEDIMENT.

SCROLL PEDIMENT
Ornamental feature common atop 18th-century case furniture. The scroll pediment was a BROKEN PEDIMENT (*see under* PEDIMENT) with an arched top composed of two facing *cyma recta* curves (*see* CYMA), each terminating in a spiral. It was also known as a *scroll top*, a *broken-scroll pediment*, a *bonnet scroll* or a *swan-neck pediment*. A distinctive American variant was the BONNET TOP.

SWAN-NECK PEDIMENT
Another name for SCROLL PEDIMENT (*see under* PEDIMENT).

PEG
Another name for DOWEL, usually implying that one or both ends of it are exposed (*see* DOWELED JOINT, *under* JOINERY).

PEKING ENAMEL
See YANG CI.

PEKING LACQUER
See TI HONG.

PELLETIER, JEAN (or John) (active 1690–1710)
French-born English BAROQUE FURNITURE maker of late 17th century. A Protestant who fled France when Louis XIV revoked the Edict of Nantes in 1685, Pelletier went first to Holland and then, in the service of King William III (*see* WILLIAM AND MARY STYLE), to England. There he specialized in carved and gilt furniture, ornamented in the manner of the French LOUIS XIV STYLE.

PEMBROKE TABLE
Variant of DROP-LEAF TABLE. The Pembroke table is characterized by hinged leaves supported by brackets hinged to the frieze of the table. Popular in Britain and America from the mid-18th century, it was designed in a

pedestal table

pediment

broken pediment

lattice pediment

scroll pediment

Pembroke table

number of styles and for a variety of uses (*see* BREAKFAST TABLE; SOFA-TABLE). The origin of the name is uncertain.

PENDANT FINIAL
FINIAL that points downward, usually placed at the lower edge of an APRON or at the corners of a CORNICE.

pendant finials

PENNIMAN, JOHN RITTO (1783–1837)
Early 19th-century Boston painter; decorator of furniture. A specialist in ÉGLOMISÉ and other furniture-painting techniques, John Penniman worked for John and Thomas SEYMOUR and others.

PENNSYLVANIA GERMAN FURNITURE
Furniture of German-speaking communities of southeastern Pennsylvania in 18th and 19th centuries. This furniture was characterized by a persistence of 17th-century European features and encompassed massive, architectonic forms with ornamentation, usually carved, as well as smaller, brightly painted pieces featuring traditional German and Swiss folk motifs. German settlers, mostly Mennonites, from the Rhine Valley and elsewhere began to settle in Pennsylvania in the late 17th century, seeking religious toleration, and they established a tightly knit, tradition-bound society that is still strong today. They brought with them a furniture-making tradition that their cabinetmakers relied on exclusively.

Based on European vernacular traditions at least as old as the Middle Ages, although incorporating a few Renaissance and later features, Pennsylvania German furniture bore little relation to the work of the more fashion-conscious Atlantic seaboard. The most important forms were the SCHRANK, a massive wardrobe adapted from 17th-century German BAROQUE FURNITURE, and the painted marriage chest, a piece of DOWER FURNITURE related, through Swiss and south German models, to the CASSONE, an Italian RENAISSANCE FURNITURE form. The schrank, an architectural piece featuring heavy cornices and fielded paneling as its chief ornamentation, was built of polished HARDWOOD, usually WALNUT or CHERRY. Some schranks bore WACHSEINLEGEN, or wax inlay, decoration—renderings of geometrical and floral motifs from the German folk tradi-

tion, along with initials, names and dates, especially if the piece was associated with a marriage.

However, the chief item of dower furniture and the most characteristic and best-known Pennsylvania German form, was the painted SOFTWOOD chest. Commonly made of pine or other local timber, these chests were extremely prized, both by their makers and by subsequent generations of collectors and furniture lovers, for their intricate, brightly painted decoration. These flat and formal designs are closely related to the medieval German Fraktur style of manuscript illumination, also used on Pennsylvania German documents, such as birth and baptismal certificates, which were frequently pasted inside the lids of dower chests. The imagery was taken from the folk art traditions of Germany and Switzerland and most prominently featured the tulip and other flowers, often growing from a vase; gaily rendered birds; a heart-shaped motif that had been popular in European folk cultures since medieval times; prancing stags, unicorns and other animals; and a variety of geometrical shapes. These elements appear on the front of the chest, usually in two or three panels set against backgrounds of a bright color—most frequently blue, green, yellow or brown. Pennsylvania German dower chests have always been extremely popular, and they are still being made.

Other forms were also painted—for example, plainer chests, schranks and DESKS—but their relative unimportance is evident in their spare decoration. Sometimes they are simply of a solid color, perhaps stippled or grained. In the first quarter of the 19th century, FEDERAL PERIOD design had some impact on Pennsylvania German decorators, resulting in the appearance of painted BANDING and the American eagle motif in their work.

Characteristic Pennsylvania German furniture forms also included a TRESTLE TABLE; a SIDE CHAIR related to the Italian SGABELLO, with a polygonal seat and stick legs; a 17th-century style DAYBED; and a variety of CUPBOARDS.

PERCIER AND FONTAINE
Partnership of French architect-designers Charles Percier (1764–1838) and Pierre-François-Léonard Fontaine (1762–1853); most important EMPIRE STYLE decorators and fur-

niture designers. Close friends and collabora
tors from an early age, they studied architecture together in Paris and then Rome. They
returned to France in 1791, when the Revolutionary government commissioned them to
design furniture for the national legislature.
Their designs, in the austere mode known as
le style républicaine (*see* DIRECTOIRE STYLE),
were executed by Georges JACOB. Fontaine
went to London briefly in 1792, then
returned to France to work with Percier, who
had become chief designer for the Paris
Opera. In 1798 they received another major
furniture commission, again from the government and again executed by Jacob. In the following year they began working for Josephine
Bonaparte, Napoleon's wife, on the decoration
and furnishings for her palatial residence, the
Château de Malmaison. This body of work
established them as the leading designers of
the day and set the tone—formal and
sumptuous—for the imperial grandeur of the
Napoleonic regime.

Bonaparte understood the propaganda
value of an image of wealth and splendor, and
he appreciated what Percier and Fontaine had
achieved at Malmaison. Thus, the partners
became the principal creators of the Empire
style for Napoleon, just as Charles LE BRUN
had developed the LOUIS XIV STYLE for the
Sun King in the 17th century. Percier and
Fontaine were appointed court architects and
designed such notable structures as the Arc du
Carrousel in Paris, as well as most of the furnishings and interiors for the imperial palaces.
Their work had a unified character and purpose—to associate the reign of Napoleon with
the proud, militaristic splendor of ancient
Rome. Martial motifs such as trophies of
weapons and armor and representations of triumphal arches were used decoratively, in
conjunction with such expressly Napoleonic
elements as bees, the letter *N* and ÉGYPTIEN-
NERIE motifs. Percier and Fontaine also continued the trend of the previous several
decades (*see* LOUIS XVI STYLE, DIRECTOIRE
STYLE; CONSULATE STYLE) toward an archeologically correct use of features of ancient
GREEK and ROMAN FURNITURE. They
designed versions of the Greek KLISMOS chair;
the Roman SELLA CURULIS, or X-FRAME chair;
and the classical KLINE. They also adapted the
ancient tripod to serve as a table and even
revived the sarcophagus form as a wine cooler.
While forms and shapes were fewer and simpler than in the inventive atmosphere of the
pre-Revolutionary 18th century, Percier and
Fontaine's pieces were nonetheless grandly
theatrical, massive in scale and often used
opulent materials.

Percier and Fontaine's designs were published in an 1801 PATTERN BOOK, *Recueil des
décorations intérieures* (the first use of the phrase
interior decoration). This book, reissued in 1812,
had an extremely great influence on furniture
designers in France and throughout Europe and
America. In Britain Thomas SHERATON,
Thomas HOPE and George SMITH all reflected
its grant classicism in their work, as did designers in America who followed them, notably
Duncan PHYFE and Anthony QUERVELLE.
G. F. HETSCH, in Copenhagen, and Leo von
KLENZE, in Munich, were important exponents
of Empire style neoclassicism, both having
known Percier and Fontaine in Paris early in
their careers. Other European designers who
were particularly influenced by the *Recueil*
included Giovanni SOCCHI, J. V. RAAB and L.
W. LUNDELIUS.

After the fall of Napoleon and the
restoration of the Bourbon monarchy in
France, Percier and Fontaine continued to
receive commissions, though Percier devoted
most of his time to teaching and Fontaine
worked mostly as an architect. They remained
close and were eventually buried in the same
tomb.

PERGO, FRANZ (active c. 1605)

Swiss RENAISSANCE FURNITURE maker in the
MANNERIST STYLE, who worked in Basel.
Pergo's furniture reflected a number of diverse
influences, notably that of Hughes SAMBIN
and the cooler Mannerism of Italian paintings.

PERGOLESI, MICHAELANGELO (d. 1801)

Italian ornamental designer who worked in
Britain. Pergolesi went to London in about
1770 and worked there for Robert ADAM.
Between 1777 and 1801 he published a series
of designs that helped to popularize the ADAM
STYLE.

PERRIAND, CHARLOTTE (1903–99)

French furniture designer associated with LE
CORBUSIER. Best known as the collaborator of
Le Corbusier and Pierre Jeanneret on the

Charlotte Perriand chaise

INTERNATIONAL STYLE pieces associated with Le Corbusier's name, Perriand was already a well-known designer before her association with the famous architect began. She left the firm in 1930 but lived with Jeanneret until 1937, and together they designed a number of well-known pieces of furniture, including a notorious deck chair in the shape of a human body. Another well-known Perriand piece is a dining table with a rubber top mounted on rollers that could be stripped off after use. After leaving Jeanneret, Perriand accepted a commission in Japan and, returning, found herself stranded in Indochina for the duration of the Second World War. After the war she resumed her career, working with Jean PROUVÉ briefly and fulfilling commissions around the world. Her later work was highly influenced by Japanese design. She worked until well into her 90s, designing for, among others, the architect Renzo Piano and the fashion designer Issey Miyake.

table by Phyfe

PESCE, GAETANO (b. 1939)

Contemporary Italian architect and designer. Originally, Pesce was a conceptualist artist, working on kinetic sculptures, happenings and other nontraditional projects. He began his design practice in 1962, after studying in Venice and at the Hochschule für Gestaltung in West Germany (*see* Max BILL). Pesce's eccentric furniture, mostly in plastic, is typical of the innovative individualism of recent Italian design. His "Up" chairs (1969) were flexible polyurethane structures. Shipped compressed in a vacuum, they expanded to their proper size and density when unpacked. Pesce also produced a noteworthy series of screens, which could be folded to form shelves.

PETEL, CLEMENT (active c. 1585)

German maker of RENAISSANCE FURNITURE. Using a style that owed much to classical architecture, Petel made case furniture that resembled miniature buildings in detail.

PETIT COMMODE

Late 18th-century French CHEST OF DRAWERS; narrow COMMODE (1) on tall, slender legs, with several tiers of shallow drawers.

PHILADELPHIA CHIPPENDALE FURNITURE

AMERICAN CHIPPENDALE FURNITURE produced in Philadelphia between 1755 and 1790, approximately. The furniture is characterized by rococo style designs (*see* ROCOCO FURNITURE) derived mainly from the pattern book of Thomas CHIPPENDALE. Philadelphia Chippendale work is noted particularly for its elaborately carved detail, more extravagant than work of other Colonial cities. Chair splats were pierced in a great variety of designs, including the "Chippendale Gothic" and "Chinese Chippendale" variations. Philadelphia highboys were built with scrolled, broken pediments, often surrounding a rococo cartouche. Applied ornamentation, often pierced and always intricately carved, employed a variety of motifs. Many case pieces were given fluted colonettes at their corners. Some notable makers of Philadelphia Chippendale furniture were Thomas AFFLECK, Jonathan GOSTELOWE, Benjamin RANDOLPH, William SAVERY and Daniel TROTTER.

PHILIPPINE MAHOGANY

See MERANTI.

PHYFE, DUNCAN (1768–1854)

American furniture maker; New York's leading cabinetmaker during first half of 19th century, most important exponent of DIRECTORY STYLE and principal creator of AMERICAN EMPIRE STYLE. Born in Scotland, Duncan Fife immigrated to Albany, New York, at 16 and there served an apprenticeship to a cabinetmaker. In about 1792 he went to New York City, changed the spelling of his name and began a furniture business, becoming a leading maker in a FEDERAL PERIOD style based on the designs of Thomas SHERATON. He was at this time particularly noted for his version of a Sheraton tripod-based PEDESTAL TABLE, the first of a number of Phyfe designs that, though widely imitated, were to be associated with his name. As the 18th century ended, he began to follow the Directory style's rendering of the British REGENCY STYLE manner—again, especially as interpreted by Sheraton. Simpler than its prototypes, as was true of all of Phyfe's work, these pieces stressed figured mahogany veneers rather than carved decoration; however, the use of REEDING or STOPPED FLUTING on posts, rails and legs became something of a Phyfe hallmark, as did the frequent appearance of wood or brass paw feet (*see* PAW FOOT, *under* FOOT). Other common motifs in his work at this time were sections of twisted flutings at the tops or bottoms of legs or posts, carved foliate forms, ribbons tied in bows and patriotic American eagles. So influential and widely imitated were these pieces that the term *Duncan Phyfe style* has often been applied to all Directory style work.

After 1815 the influence of the French EMPIRE STYLE was absorbed by Phyfe and other American makers. French furniture was well known in New York, as were the PATTERN BOOKS of French designer Pierre de LA MÉSANGÈRE. Also, a number of French *émigré* cabinetmakers, most notably C.-H. LANNUIER, worked in that city. British pattern books also reflected French influence, especially Sheraton's last book, in 1805, and George SMITH's publications. The more massive, bolder forms of the new French furniture were adapted by Phyfe, but with his usual restraint. Once again, figured veneer dominated, in sparingly ornamented furniture. In this style Phyfe devised an innovative variation of the popular CURULE CHAIR, a favorite of NEOCLASSICAL STYLE designers that was derived from an ancient ROMAN FURNITURE form. Phyfe transferred the crossed legs of the piece, previously appearing at the front and back, following the ancient model, to the sides of the chair, producing a distinctively American item of furniture. In the Empire mode Phyfe particularly favored an earlier Sheraton motif, the LYRE, in chair backs, and he frequently used a lotus-leaf emblem, derived from ancient Egypt through either Sheraton, Thomas HOPE or La Mésangère. La Mésangère helped to influence Phyfe's adoption, after about 1830, of a modified version of the French RESTAURATION STYLE, known in America as the PILLAR AND SCROLL STYLE.

Toward the end of his career, Phyfe experimented with the emerging REVIVAL STYLES, but his fame rests on his long career as an interpreter of neoclassical design. He retired in 1847, having been at the peak of his profession for well over a generation.

PICKLED FINISH

Whitish patina on wood furniture. A pickled finish results when old paint and its GESSO undercoat are cleaned from a piece. Beneath these layers, the remains of the gesso and the exposed limed wood (*see* LIMING), if the original surface was so treated, present a mottled, whitish appearance. The effect may also be obtained by liming new wood.

PIE DE PUENTE

Spanish RENAISSANCE FURNITURE form; TRESTLE STAND designed to support the VANGUENO, a FALL-FRONT DESK. The *pie de puente* included two slides that could be pulled out to support the fall front of the desk.

PIE SAFE (also *food safe*)

Nineteenth-century American term denoting a CUPBOARD intended to store food. It had perforated panels of wood or tin to provide ventilation.

PIECRUST TABLE

Modern term for 18th-century circular TEA TABLE with scalloped rim, carved or molded. A piecrust table was often a TILT-TOP TABLE.

piecrust tabletop

PIED DE BICHE

See under FOOT.

PIER TABLE

Furniture form originating in 17th century; small table intended to stand against a pier, the section of wall between two tall windows. A pier table was often made *en suite* with a tall mirror, called a *pier glass*, that hung above it. This formal arrangement was popular in grand rooms until well into the 19th century.

PIERCED CARVING

Carving that cuts completely through its material, whether producing the negative spaces of three-dimensional sculpture or the patterned arrangements of OPENWORK ornamentation.

PIERCED SPLAT

Chair SPLAT ornamented with OPENWORK carving, especially FRETWORK.

PIETRE DURE

Form of INLAY used in RENAISSANCE FURNITURE, made up of pieces of marble, other very

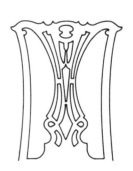

pierced splat

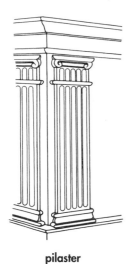

pilaster

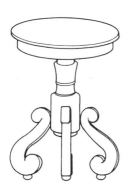

pillar-and-scroll table

pillow top

hard minerals and semiprecious stones such as agate, amethyst, chalcedony, jasper and lapis lazuli. *Pietre dure,* meaning "hard stones," evolved in Italy in the 16th century from an earlier tradition of carved vases and bowls of the same materials. The mosaics produced were typically in ARABESQUES and GROTESQUE ORNAMENT, often, especially in later work, surrounding landscapes, still lifes and architectural views. They were used as tabletops and as decorative panels on cabinets. This expensive craft was difficult and involved special tools and great expertise. Its production was principally limited to Milan, Florence and, under Florentine direction, Prague, but it was exported elsewhere from these centers to be incorporated into local furniture. The singular form *pietra dura* is sometimes used, as is the term *Florentine mosaic.*

PIFFETTI, PIETRO (c. 1700–1777)

Leading Italian ROCOCO FURNITURE maker. From 1731 Piffetti worked in Turin as cabinetmaker to Charles Emmanuel, King of Sardinia—at first under Filippo JUVARRA, whose late baroque style influenced his early work. However, the French LOUIS XV STYLE informed Pifetti's mature work, which was characterized by exceedingly intricate MARQUETRY in such opulent materials as tortoiseshell, mother-of-pearl and various rare and colorful woods. He especially favored the use of ivory, often engraved with further decoration. His case pieces were ornamented with elaborate bronze mounts, frequently made by Francesco LADATTE.

PILASTER

Longitudinal section of pillar or column set into or against a wall. Originally structural, a type of buttress, the pilaster has been a common decorative feature in European architecture and furniture since the Renaissance. It is usually ornamented in accordance with one of the classical ORDERS OF ARCHITECTURE.

PILGRIM FURNITURE

See AMERICAN JACOBEAN FURNITURE.

PILLAR-AND-CLAW TABLE

Eighteenth-century name for TRIPOD TABLE.

PILLAR-AND-SCROLL STYLE (also *American Restoration style*)

Nineteenth-century American version of French RESTAURATION STYLE. The style was briefly current after 1830 and was characterized by the use of columns or pillars as table supports and of large scrolls in other pieces. *S*-scrolls and *C*-scrolls were used as brackets or supports and as scroll arms on chairs. The pillar-and-scroll style is a late variant of the AMERICAN EMPIRE STYLE; it is simpler in form, however, and incorporates some nonclassical motifs, reflecting the rise of the REVIVAL STYLES. The Pillar and Scroll style is perhaps best exemplified in some of Duncan PHYFE's later work. It was extensively illustrated in the first American PATTERN BOOK, published by John HALL in 1840.

PILLEMENT, JEAN-BAPTISTE (1728–1808)

French rococo painter and graphic artist. Pillement published designs for MARQUETRY used on LOUIS XV STYLE furniture as well as for textile prints and ceramic painting. His work featured whimsical CHINOISERIE motifs that were to become so well known that the term *le style Pillement* was sometimes used in France to describe any rococo Chinoiserie decoration.

PILLOW TOP

Decorative device; chair CREST RAIL whose central portion is carved to resemble a cushion or pillow extending above and below the rail itself. The pillow top was a characteristic ornament of the "fancy" chairs of American FEDERAL PERIOD furniture (*see* "FANCY" FURNITURE), especially that of Lambert HITCHCOCK.

PIMM, JOHN (d. 1773)

QUEEN ANNE STYLE cabinetmaker of Boston, Massachusetts. Pimm, active between about 1740 and 1760, was a fine craftsman, although the Queen Anne style he employed was out of date. Pimm is best known for having made a piece that is more famous for another man's work—a highboy (c. 1750) elaborately japanned by Thomas JOHNSTON (*see* JAPANNING).

PIN

Another name for DOWEL, especially when it is used in MORTISE-AND-TENON JOINT (*see under* JOINERY).

PIN HINGE
See under HINGE.

PINE
Any of a number of North American SOFT-WOODS, generally light yellow-brown in color, sometimes with a reddish tinge. American pine, like its equivalents elsewhere, EUROPEAN REDWOOD and Japanese MATSU, is a traditional material for inexpensive furniture. It is also used as a *secondary wood* (*see* PRIMARY AND SECONDARY WOODS).

PINEAU, NICOLAS (1684–1754)
French ROCOCO FURNITURE and ornament designer. With J.-A. MEISSONNIER, he developed the *genre pittoresque*, basis of LOUIS XV–STYLE decoration. Using shell, flower and foliage motifs with swirling scrolls in boldly asymmetrical arrangements, Pineau's designs, with their air of restless animation, startled the 1720s. Unlike Meissonnier, Pineau produced workable furniture designs, which were widely used by contemporary makers such as Charles CRESSENT and copied by other designers, including Batty LANGLEY.

PING (P'ING)
CHINESE FURNITURE form; ornamental SCREEN. The earliest screens were used before the Han dynasty (206 B.C.–A.D. 220) as emblems of authority or honor that were placed behind designated seats. For many centuries the *ping* remained a symbol of rank, and in most periods the status of the user determined the material from which a screen could be made. Lowly scholars were entitled to BAMBOO screens, higher officials merited fabric, and paintings and precious materials were reserved for aristocrats and the imperial court. Beginning in the Tang dynasty (618–907), the *ping* frequently incorporated paintings by noted artists—a device that is still popular today.

PINKWOOD
American term for TULIPWOOD.

PIRANESI, GIOVANNI BATTISTA (1720–78)
Italian NEOCLASSICAL STYLE architect, designer and engraver, best known for his dramatic engravings of imaginatively reconstructed ancient Roman buildings. Piranesi was born in Treviso and studied architecture and stage design in Venice. He first visited Rome in 1740 and settled there five years later. His exaggerated and theatrical renderings of famous Roman sites were published over a 33-year period, beginning in 1756. They were immensely popular throughout Europe and had a wide influence on the development of 18th-century neoclassicism. Robert ADAM was especially inspired by Piranesi, whom he knew in Rome in 1754–58. Piranesi also designed furniture, though it bore little resemblance to ancient ROMAN FURNITURE. It was heavily ornamented with dramatic assemblages of Roman, Etruscan and ÉGYPTIENNERIE motifs, including PALMETTEs, winged CHIMERAs, SPHINXes, URNs, MASKs, bucrania (*see* BUCRANIUM) and CARYATIDS.

PIRETTI, GIANCARLO (b. 1940)
Contemporary Italian furniture designer. Piretti's furniture is simple, refined and functionalistic (*see* FUNCTIONALISM); mass-produced; and made of prefabricated elements. His "Plia" chair (1969) is a simple, chrome metal folding chair with a molded seat made of transparent or colored plastic. It is an inexpensive, easily manufactured piece that has become a modern design classic. Piretti has recently collaborated with architect Emilio Ambasz on several lines of furniture, designed in accordance with ergonomic research and experimentation.

PITCH PINE
American SOFTWOOD. One of the hardest and strongest softwoods, pitch pine was commonly used in the 19th century for institutional furniture, such as schoolroom desks and church pews.

PITMAN, MARK (1779–1829)
FEDERAL PERIOD cabinetmaker of Salem, Massachusettes.

PLACET
Furniture form common throughout Europe in the 17th century; very low four-legged stool covered with fabric. The placet permitted the user to sit very close to the floor.

placet

PLANE WOOD
Wood of the European plane tree; pale brown HARDWOOD with a distinctively flecked appearance when cut as veneer. It is used in panels or in inlay work. The similar and related American plane is known as SYCAMORE.

PLANK SEAT
Seat of solid wood, especially in a WINDSOR CHAIR.

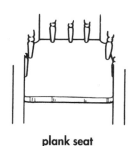

plank seat

PLASTIC FURNITURE
Furniture made of plastic, a family of synthetic materials. Plastic, which has been used to make furniture since the Second World War, is an extremely versatile material. It can be molded into virtually any shape and can be made into fiber, cloth, veneer and foam padding, as well as a whole furniture piece. It is easy to work with, since plastic is soft and malleable when heated, yet durable when cooled, and it can also be colored a wide range of hues. Moreover, plastic furniture is much less expensive to produce than metal or wood furniture, in terms of both labor and materials.

Although the first plastic was made in 1862, the numerous synthetic materials available today were not developed until the 1930s. Designers Eero SAARINEN and Charles EAMES were the first to utilize plastic in furniture design. Other furniture designers who have worked with plastics include Robin DAY, Verner PANTON, Arne JACOBSEN, Eero AARNIO and Joe C. COLOMBO, to name a few (*see also* POP ART FURNITURE; WATERBED).

platform rocker

PLATERESQUE STYLE
Decorative style of Spanish RENAISSANCE FURNITURE and architecture in first half of 16th century. Originally used by silversmiths (hence the name—*plata* is Spanish for "silver"), the plateresque style in furniture generally appeared in MARQUETRY. It was characterized by the use of such Italian Renaissance motifs as masks, urns, *putti,* wreath-enclosed heads and GROTESQUE ORNAMENT. Nevertheless, in its rich complexity and its tendency toward geometrical designs, plateresque marquetry resembled its immediate antecedent, the medieval MUDÉJAR STYLE. Furniture decorated in the plateresque style was simple in shape, allowing much flat surface for inlay work. In the second half of the century, plateresque decoration was replaced by a simpler Italianate mode that relied more on classical architectural motifs and used more carving and less marquetry.

PLATFORM ROCKER
Type of ROCKING CHAIR in which the chair rocks on springs mounted on an immobile base, or platform. Also called a spring rocker, this form was part of the popular body of work known as PATENT FURNITURE. A number of platform rockers had been patented and were in production by the 1860s, and the form was popular into the early 20th century. In its day it replaced the standard rocking chair, which tended to make noise, creep across the floor while in use and trip up the unwary with its extended rockers. George HUNZINGER and John JELIFF were two well-known furniture makers who produced platform rockers.

PLATNER, WARREN (b. 1919)
Contemporary American architect and furniture designer. Platner worked for Eero SAARINEN early in his career but designed his best-known furniture, wire chairs, for Florence KNOLL, between 1953 and 1967. These chairs were elaborately modeled configurations requiring up to 1,400 welds per piece. They resembled, in their smooth, curvilinear shapes, the work of Saarinen and Charles EAMES. Since establishing a private practice in 1967, Platner has received many major architectural commissions. He has also designed furniture, especially office systems, for Knoll and other manufacturers, as well as interiors and lighting fixtures.

PLIANT
Eighteenth-century French X-FRAME folding STOOL. Like the TABOURET, the *pliant* was a staple at court, where chairs were reserved for royalty on formal occasions.

PLINTH
Projecting or recessed base of a piece of CASE FURNITURE. In traditional furniture, plinths were always projecting and lent an air of architectural massiveness to a chest or cabinet. (The term itself is originally architectural,

referring to the square, slightly projecting, lowest element of an ancient Greek column.)

The recessed plinth, essentially a low box supporting the piece above it, is a modern development, providing toe room for the user, an especially appropriate feature on tall cabinets such as WARDROBES, or in cramped quarters. A recessed plinth is also less subject to damage than a projecting plinth.

PLISHKE, ERNST ANTON (1903–92)

Viennese furniture designer of the INTERNATIONAL STYLE. In his youth Plishke studied with Peter BEHRENS, then later become a teacher himself. In his furniture and as a teacher, Plishke came to exemplify a formal, ascetic style derived from the BAUHAUS esthetic and the study of Japanese design. He left Nazi Austria for New Zealand in the mid-1930s but sometime after the Second World War returned to Vienna, where he was particularly influential as a teacher.

PLITZNER, FERDINAND (1678–1724)

German interior designer and BAROQUE FURNITURE maker. Plitzner, who trained under Johann MATUSCH, made furniture in a close imitation of the French LOUIS XIV STYLE. He especially favored BOULLE MARQUETRY and ivory INLAYS.

PLUM

European HARDWOOD, yellow-brown in color; tree most important for its fruit. It was used occasionally in MARQUETRY in the 17th and 18th centuries, when it was often dyed, for it takes stain well. From medieval times until the 17th century, it was used, where available, in vernacular furniture.

PLYWOOD

Industrially produced material comprising several sheets, or plies, of wood glued together face to face. The grain of one ply lies perpendicular to that of an adjacent one. Wood is weakest across its grain; in plywood, one ply counteracts its neighbor's weakness. Similarly, each ply's tendency to expand or contract with temperature and humidity is balanced by that of its neighbor. Thus, plywood is much stronger than solid wood, and it is more flexible.

Plywood was first used in a limited fashion in the 18th century. Early 19th-century experimenters with BENTWOOD, such as John Henry BELTER, made good use of its flexibility and strength, but deficiencies in glue restricted its use until later in the century. Since the Second World War, methods of molding plywood, developed by Charles EAMES and others, have resulted in revolutionary furniture designs.

POILLERAT, GILBERT (1902–88)

French ART DECO furniture designer. Poillerat created distinctive furniture employing elaborate ironwork decoration with handsome hardwoods. Like Emilio TERRY, he worked into the late 1940s and 1950s, when Art Deco was long out of fashion. His furniture was rediscovered and regained popularity in the 1990s.

POIRET, PAUL (1879–1944)

French couturier, interior decorator and manufacturer of ART DECO furniture. Famous as a couturier, Poiret toured Germany and Austria around 1909 and was impressed by the work of the WIENER WERKSTÄTTE and the DEUTSCHE WERKBUND. In Paris he established a workshop to manufacture and sell furniture and other household objects. He commissioned designers, including Paul IRIBE, to work in the new Art Deco style, which developed in reaction to ART NOUVEAU. Poiret is credited with having triggered a French revival in painted furniture with his "Martine" line (1910).

POLE SCREEN

Specialized FIRE SCREEN. It consists of a small panel and an upright pole, usually on a tripod or pedestal foot, to which the panel is attached by a sliding mechanism. The panel may be raised and lowered along the pole and fixed at any point in order to shield the face, but not the body, of a nearby person from heat and light. The pole screen was developed in Europe in the 17th century.

POLLARD, JOHN (1740–87)

Eighteenth-century Philadelphia woodcarver. Pollard, an emigrant from London, was

pole screen

employed in 1765 by Benjamin RANDOLPH, a leading maker of PHILADELPHIA CHIPPENDALE FURNITURE. With Hercules COURTENAY, Pollard was responsible for much of Randolph's elaborate carved decoration. Pollard later worked for himself, specializing in "Chinese Chippendale" decoration (*see* Thomas CHIPPENDALE).

PONTI, GIO (1891–1979)

Italian architect, designer, teacher and writer. Ponti, one of Italy's most renowned architects, also designed much furniture for CASSINA and other manufacturers. Before the Second World War, he designed INTERNATIONAL STYLE furniture for a worldwide market. He is especially noted for a group of 1950s chair designs—light, refined, modern variants of the CHIAVARI CHAIR. Beginning in the 1920's, Ponti was a principal promoter of modern design in Italy. In 1928, he founded the architecture and design magazine *Domus,* still an important publication, and was its editor, except for a short period, until his death. He also founded and headed another magazine, *Stile,* in the 1940s. A well-known professor of architecture in Milan, Ponti wrote nine books and hundreds of articles. He also designed ceramics, enamels, mosaics and textiles as well as stage sets for La Scala.

POP ART FURNITURE

Stylistic trend of the 1960s inspired by the Pop Art movement in painting and sculpture. In both furniture and the fine arts, Pop Art was a reaction against the prevailing tastes of the 1950s. Pop Art furniture thus defied the smooth, sensible "good taste" of the INTERNATIONAL STYLE, SCANDINAVIAN MODERN, the CONTEMPORARY STYLE and the work of Charles EAMES, Eero SAARINEN and their followers. Instead, Pop Art furniture used the vivid colors, commonplace motifs and often purposefully vulgar imagery of popular, consumerist culture. Unlike the high seriousness of the design reform movements that preceded it, Pop Art is often deliberately humorous—as in the baseball-glove-shaped "Joe" chair by DE PAS, D'URBINO, LOMAZZI or Jon WEALLANS's settee in the form of false teeth. Sometimes it is grotesque and disquieting as well, as in Allen JONES's pornographic pieces. Such disturbing motifs exemplify the style's tone of amusement, oddity and satire as well as its underlying sense of ambiguity and alienation and reflect the social and political upheaval of the 1960s.

POPLAR

Any of a number of whitish European and American hardwoods, traditionally used for vernacular furniture. Not very strong, poplar has never been used for commercially made furniture, though it enjoyed some popularity in inlay work during the 16th and 17th centuries. In America aspen and cottonwood are well-known poplars.

PORCELAIN

Hard, translucent ceramic, made from mixture of kaolin, a clay, and other materials and fired at high temperature. Porcelain is usually glazed, and it may be decorated with painted patterns or images either beneath or over the glaze. It was first made in China in about the eighth century, but it played no role in furniture until the Ming dynasty (1368–1644), when the DUN, a barrel-shaped stool, was frequently made of porcelain for outdoor use. Porcelain plaques were occasionally set into the backs of chairs then as well.

In Europe the porcelain-making process was unknown until 1709, when it was discovered at Meissen, in Saxony. The Saxon government attempted to keep this technique secret, but it soon spread throughout Europe. In furniture porcelain plaques—sometimes decorated with CHINOISERIE motifs, but just as often with floral imagery or rustic scenes—began to be applied to French ROCOCO FURNITURE in about 1750. In the subsequent LOUIS XVI STYLE, the practice was particularly popular, and plaques made at the factory at Sèvres, France, appeared on much furniture by Martin CARLIN, Adam WEISWEILLER and others. Many other European countries followed the French lead, and porcelain plaques appeared on NEOCLASSICAL STYLE furniture of the late 18th and early 19th centuries. In the second half of the 19th century, porcelain plaques were often featured in the eclectic ornamentation of the RENAISSANCE REVIVAL STYLE, especially in America.

PORTUGUESE FOOT

See under FOOT.

PÖSSENBACHER

Late 19th-century German furniture manufacturing firm. Pössenbacher based in Munich, produced notable furniture in several manners, especially the RENAISSANCE REVIVAL STYLE. However it is probably best known for a group of ROCOCO REVIVAL STYLE pieces made for Neuschwanstein, the famous palace of King Ludwig II of Bavaria.

POST-MODERN FURNITURE

Furniture associated with Post-Modern architecture, a style that arose in the late 1970s. Post-Modern furniture reflects the dissatisfaction of many architects and designers with FUNCTIONALISM and the European INTERNATIONAL STYLE. Rejection of these dominant ideas is expressed in decoration that obscures underlying structure (in opposition to functionalized doctrine) and in forms, shapes and decoration drawn from historical styles, especially the NEO-CLASSICAL STYLE. Most notable designers of Post-Modern furniture are also architects, including Gae AULENTI, Michael GRAVES and the GWATHMEY-SIEGEL partnership.

POT CUPBOARD (also *commode; night stand*)

Furniture form of 18th and 19th centuries; small case piece intended to house a chamber pot. A washbasin and pitcher were generally kept on the potcupboard's single shelf, while the chamber pot sat on the floor of the piece. In the early 19th century, an EMPIRE STYLE pot cupboard was called a POT TABLE (pronounced "poe").

POT TABLE (pronounced "poe")

Early 19th-century furniture form; type of POT CUPBOARD, small case piece intended to house a chamber pot (*see* CLOSESTOOL). A French design in the EMPIRE STYLE, the pot table was cylindrical. It was frequently decorated with broad FLUTING to resemble a PEDESTAL in the form of a classical column; the door was usually camouflaged. Within, there was one shelf, on which a washbasin and pitcher were ordinarily kept. The chamber pot sat on the floor of the piece.

POTTIER & STYMUS

New York furniture-manufacturing firm; principal exponent of the NEO-GREC STYLE in the 1870s and 1880s. Founded in 1859 by cabinetmaker Auguste Pottier and upholsterer William Pierre Stymus, the company became one of New York's most fashionable furniture makers and produced pieces using ornamentation derived from antiquity through earlier 19th-century REVIVAL STYLES.

POUDREUSE

Eighteenth-century French furniture form; small DRESSING TABLE whose top unfolded. The central section of the top was hinged at the back and had a mirror on its underside, exposed when it was unfolded. The two side elements of the tabletop, hinged at the outside, folded over 180 degrees to provide extra horizontal surfaces. Beneath the top were compartments for brushes, bottles and so on. Most fashionable in the LOUIS XV STYLE, the *poudreuse* was made throughout the 18th century. In the 19th century the term *poudreuse* was also used to refer to any sort of dressing table.

POUF (also *pouffe*)

Upholstered stool or backless seat, usually round. Associated with the REVIVAL STYLES, the pouf was introduced in France after the development, in about 1830, of deep-buttoned, coil-spring UPHOLSTERY, and it was a prominent form in European and American furniture throughout the 19th century. It generally had carved wooden legs, though the supports were sometimes hidden in later versions.

PRAIRIE SCHOOL

Group of architects and designers centered around Chicago from the 1880s through the turn of the century. The most important members of the group, in terms of furniture design, were Louis H. Sullivan (1856–1924), Frank Lloyd WRIGHT, George Grant ELMSLIE and George Washington MAHER. The Prairie School was named for the midwestern land in which they worked. Its designers developed an approach to furniture design derived from the British design reform movements (*see* ARTS AND CRAFTS MOVEMENT; ART FURNITURE MOVEMENT), as disseminated in America in the writings of EASTLAKE and TALBERT. The school's second great influence was the teaching and example of Sullivan, the elder master of the

pot table

pouf

group. Though Sullivan did not design furniture, his use of pronounced, stylized decoration on each of his buildings influenced the furniture design of the younger members of the group, as they developed their own increasingly abstract, decorative idiom. Another influential practice of Sullivan's was to impose a unity of theme on his buildings and ornamentation, which connected the major lines of a building with all the minor motifs of decoration and furnishings. Unity of theme became a concern of the furniture designers of the group, who designed their pieces for specific placement in specific buildings. Each of the furniture designers of the Prairie School developed his own decorative repertoire: Wright, who was also involved with Japanese design, evolved toward a geometrical abstraction; Elmslie and Maher remained closer to Sullivan's organic style. All Prairie School furniture, however, tends to be simple and rectilinear in form, with an emphasis on the vertical. Decoration is typically bold, though simple and well integrated into the form of the piece, and is consistently employed in all the pieces in any group, thereby imposing a thematic unity.

PREMIÈRE-PARTIE
See BOULLE MARQUETRY.

PRESS
Originally, a simple, massive CUPBOARD popular in medieval Europe. The press was generally made of oak and had shelves to store clothing or linens. The term later came to refer to the 17th-century form also known as the PRESS

press cupboard

CUPBOARD. By then the medieval press was being succeeded by its more specialized descendants—the CLOTHES PRESS, the ARMOIRE, the KAST, the SCHRANK and the WARDROBE.

PRESS BED
Type of CONVERTIBLE FURNITURE of 17th and 18th centuries; bed that unfolded or was lowered from a large cupboard or PRESS. The doors were usually hinged at the top; when open, they were supported by posts and formed a TESTER.

PRESS CUPBOARD
Seventeenth-century English and American furniture form; two-tiered oak CUPBOARD with hinged doors. The lower tier was the taller, and both were fully enclosed, with hinged doors. The lower section had shelves as well. The upper tier, more recessed than the lower, left a narrow shelf in front and was usually divided into three compartments, the outside two of which were often angled backward slightly, widening the shelf at its sides. The shelf bore at its front corners two turned or carved columns that supported a projecting cornice. In the 17th century these columns, at first quite bulbous and heavy, evolved in design to become mere pendant knobs, hanging decoratively from the top corners of the piece. The HALL CUPBOARD, as this piece was often called, was generally carved and ornamented elaborately, being intended for both display and storage. A Welsh variant was the TRIDARN.

"PRETZEL-BACK" CHAIR
Variant of the LADDER-BACK CHAIR; popular in the 18th century. The centers of the back rails were carved in openwork renderings of pretzel-shaped figures. The chair was illustrated in Thomas CHIPPENDALE's *Director* and was often built by other makers.

PRIE-DIEU
Eighteenth-century furniture form; low chair whose back was padded on top. The prie-dieu was intended for prayer, and the user would kneel on the seat. Developing in the late 17th century, the form remained popular until well into the 19th. An earlier form of the same name, known in medieval times, was a small

LECTERN or DESK with a low, projecting shelf on which to kneel.

PRIMARY AND SECONDARY WOODS

A distinction may be made between those materials that can be seen on the outside of a piece of wooden furniture and those that cannot. The former are called PRIMARY WOODS, whether solid wood parts, such as a LEG or APRON, or surface VENEERS. The material of the hidden parts—interior fittings or structural elements beneath the veneer—are called *secondary woods*. In general, more decorative, often imported and usually more expensive woods have been used as primary woods, while local, less expensive and more readily available woods have served as secondary woods. The geographical origin of a piece of furniture may sometimes be determined by the origin of its secondary woods, while its primary woods will more likely indicate its place in style history.

PRIMATICCIO, FRANCESCO (1504–70)

Italian painter, architect, sculptor and designer; important influence on French RENAISSANCE FURNITURE. Primaticcio, who studied in Rome under Raphael's leading follower, Giulio Romano, came to France in 1532 at the invitation of King François I. He and Rosso FIORENTINO became the leaders of the School of Fontainebleau and of the FRANÇOIS STYLE.

PRIMITIVE FURNITURE

Furniture of those tribal cultures that have never been part of the urban, technological civilizations that originated in Europe and Asia. These cultures have traditionally, if imprecisely, been referred to as primitive but have ranged in sophistication from truly primitive Stone Age hunting and gathering groups to the culturally complex empires of precolonial West Africa, pre-Columbian America and precolonial West Africa. In this book AFRICAN FURNITURE, better known and more widely collected in the West, is dealt with separately in some detail. Few artifacts of these cultures exist from periods prior to their contact with Westerners, but it seems likely that they have used very little furniture, in the conventional Western sense of the term.

In such societies storage containers are made of basketry and ceramics; beds and chairs are hammocks, woven mats or stretched animal skins. Except for the largest pottery vessels, all of these items are extremely light and portable, well suited to the seminomadic life-style of many of these groups. In places where large populations have lived in fixed abodes, as in the cities of West Africa and Mesoamerica, sleeping and sitting platforms have generally been built into the architecture, with little other furniture made.

In the Eastern Hemisphere, tribal culture is concentrated in Africa and in the Pacific islands. In both areas there are two principal furniture forms—the STOOL and the HEADREST. Sometimes these stools consist of a seat with legs, but more frequently they are carved from a single block of wood, in figural or abstract motifs that vary widely from tribe to tribe. The final result is frequently a pedestal-like form. Often the pierced carving of such a stool leaves sculptural elements resembling legs between base and seat. A headrest is a low, horizontal bar on which the user places his or her head to raise the head or to protect an elaborate hairdo while sleeping. The headrest may be supported by legs a few inches high, or it may be several inches high itself, resting on the ground, its lower portion heavily pierced with carving. Both stools and headrests are usually elaborately ornamented, with carving, painting, inlaid shells and other decoration.

In the Western Hemisphere the Mayan, Incan and other civilizations were economically advanced enough to have architecture with built-in sleeping and sitting platforms and, sometimes, tablelike altars. But aside from a few carved wooden stools known to have been made in the Caribbean, similar in form to those of Africa and the Pacific, there was little other pre-Columbian furniture. No North American Indians used wooden furniture, except for the tribes of the Pacific Northwest, who made storage chests and, influenced by Europeans, seating furniture. These pieces were mostly of cedar. Long, thin planks a foot or two wide, made with adzes, were steamed and bent into a rectangular configuration to form all four walls of a chest from one piece. At one corner, the ends of the plank were joined with pegs, and the whole was pegged to a bottom plank. Another adze-hewn plank formed the top. These chests were elaborately carved with the zoomorphic motifs peculiar to the region. From about the mid-19th century, settles and chairs modeled on European forms were made and were similarly carved.

PRINCE, SAMUEL (d. 1778)

American cabinetmaker; exponent of NEW YORK CHIPPENDALE FURNITURE. A conservative follower of Chippendale, Prince used many elements of the earlier PALLADIAN STYLE and favored expanses of figured veneering instead of elaborate ornamentation. Thomas BURLING apprenticed under him.

PRINCE OF WALES FEATHERS

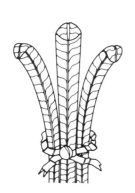

Prince of Wales feathers

Decorative motif representing three ostrich feathers tied together at their shafts and held vertically; heraldic blazon for the Prince of Wales. This device was popular in late 18th-century British NEOCLASSICAL STYLE furniture, appearing especially frequently in the designs of Thomas SHERATON and George HEPPLEWHITE.

PROUVÉ, ÉMILE VICTOR (1858–1943)

French ART NOUVEAU designer; member of the School of Nancy (*see* NANCY, SCHOOL OF). Born in Nancy, Victor Prouvé studied drawing and painting in Paris, then returned to Nancy to work under Émile GALLÉ. He designed glass, jewelry and furniture, all in a style similar to Gallé's, as well as representational marquetry panels for both Gallé and Louis MAJORELLE. After Gallé's death in 1904, Prouvé ran the Gallé workshops and designed much of their later output. He traveled to Munich to study the work of the DEUTSCHE WERKSTÄTTEN movement in 1905 and organized a congress at Nancy on modern German design in 1908 and 1909. His son Jean PROUVÉ, born in 1901, became a prominent modern architect and furniture designer.

PROUVÉ, JEAN (b. 1901–84)

French INTERNATIONAL STYLE architect and furniture designer. Son of Émile Victor PROUVÉ, Jean Prouvé was trained as a metalworker and exhibited sheetsteel furniture as early as 1925. He was primarily a designer of architectural elements and is credited with the invention of prefabricated structures. He continued to design furniture through the 1940s,

in association with the UNION DES ARTISTES MODERNES, and specialized in the employment of new materials, especially aluminum and plastics.

PSYCHE

Nineteenth-century French term for a CHEVAL GLASS in the EMPIRE STYLE.

PUGIN, AUGUSTUS CHARLES (1762–1832)

French-born British designer and writer, an exponent of the REGENCY GOTHIC style; probably best known as the father of A. W. N. PUGIN. A. C. Pugin arrived in London by 1792 and worked there as an architectural draftsman. He also published writings and designs for Gothic-inspired buildings and furniture. One noteworthy book, *Gothic Furniture* (1827), was completed in collaboration with his soon-to-be-famous son.

PUGIN, AUGUSTUS WELBY NORTHMORE (1812–52)

British architect and designer; most important exponent of NEO-GOTHIC STYLE. Son of Augustus Charles PUGIN, A. W. N. Pugin began his career designing furniture in the REGENCY GOTHIC style that his father espoused. However, he rapidly developed a simpler but more archeologically correct style that became vastly influential in both architecture and furniture design. A converted Catholic, Pugin brought religious zeal to his work, much of it ecclesiastical. His belief in the use of medieval forms and decoration, the originals having been devised in a morally sounder world, was propounded in his numerous books, which included *Gothic Furniture in the Style of the 15th Century* (1835), *The True Principle of Pointed or Christian Architecture* (1841) and *Foliated Ornament* (1849)

Pugin's furniture was based on actual medieval models, and he accordingly favored foursquare, boldly massive forms, revealed construction and discreet ornamentation, commonly including wrought-iron hinges and linenfold paneling. His later work used more elaborate decoration, such as crockets and tracery carving. He designed a huge amount of furniture, mostly for his ecclesiastical and domestic architectural commissions. Pugin produced more than 1,200 pieces for his largest commission alone, the furnishing of Charles BARRY's Houses of Parliament in London, a project with which Pugin was involved from about 1840 until his death.

Due to his great output and zeal and his solid, sensible buildings and furniture, Pugin influenced all subsequent Gothic revival design, from his contemporaries through the ARTS AND CRAFTS MOVEMENT and other design reformers of the latter half of the 19th century in Britain and abroad, from Germany to America. He also designed stained glass, tiles, wallpaper, textiles, jewelry and metalwork.

PULVINATED FRIEZE
Another name for CUSHION FRIEZE.

PUNNETT, E. G. (active 1890s–1900s)
British ART NOUVEAU furniture designer. Punnett was a principal designer for Liberty & Co. (see Arthur Lazenby LIBERTY). He designed for William Birch after 1901, using a geometrical style influenced by Charles Rennie MACKINTOSH.

PURPLE SANDALWOOD
See ZI TAN.

PURPLEHEART (also *amaranth*)
Vivid purple to red South American HARD-WOOD used chiefly for MARQUETRY and other decorative veneering.

PUTTO (pl. *putti,* or *amorini*)
Winged infant, or cupid, used as a carved decorative motif in European furniture styles from RENAISSANCE FURNITURE through 19th-century REVIVAL STYLES.

QIN ZHUO (CH'IN CHO) (also *lute table*)

CHINESE FURNITURE form of Ming (1368–1644) and Qing (1644–1911) dynasties; any of several small, low tables, long and narrow in shape. The *qin zhuo* was thus suitable for holding a Chinese lute, or *qin*, though it did not necessarily serve this purpose.

QUADRANT

BRACKET shaped like a quarter-circle, sometimes used in late 18th- and early 19th-century Britain and America to support the FALL FRONT of a desk.

QUARTETTO TABLES

See NEST OF TABLES.

QUARTI, EUGENIO (1867–1931)

Italian ART NOUVEAU furniture designer. Quarti's furniture had austere shapes derived from the geometrical style of Austrian Art Nouveau but were richly decorated with marquetry, inlays of silver or mother-of-pearl, and carved wood or cast-bronze ornamentation, often in an organic Parisian style.

QUATREFOIL

Ornamental motif in GOTHIC FURNITURE; radially symmetrical, formalized, fourlobed leaf form, usually enclosed in a circle. Commonly used in Gothic TRACERY, both in architecture and furniture, the quatrefoil was also popular in the NEO-GOTHIC STYLE of the 18th and 19th centuries.

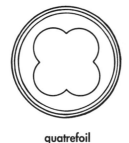

quatrefoil

QUEEN ANNE LEG

See under LEG.

QUEEN ANNE REVIVAL STYLE

British furniture style of second half of 19th century, characterized by use of late 18th-century NEOCLASSICAL STYLE elements. Like the contemporary LOUIS XVI REVIVAL STYLE in France and America, the Queen Anne Revival style marked a return to the neoclassicism against which the REVIVAL STYLES had earlier reacted. In fact, the QUEEN ANNE STYLE of the early 18th century was not neoclassical in inspiration; the revival style actually takes its name from an architectural trend led by country-house architects such as Richard Norman SHAW, who emulated the Renaissance neoclassicism of 17th-century England, which was ruled by Queen Anne's Stuart predecessors. Her name was erroneously applied to this 19th-century architectural style and thus to the furniture used in its buildings.

Queen Anne Revival style furniture was made principally by commercial manufacturers such as COLLINSON & LOCK. It relied largely on elements taken from the ADAM STYLE work of Robert ADAM, George HEPPLEWHITE and Thomas SHERATON. But it also drew on its rival, the ROCOCO REVIVAL STYLE, in its use of curvilinear features. In fact, the popularity of the CABRIOLE LEG (*see under* LEG) at this time led to its being termed the *Queen Anne leg*.

QUEEN ANNE STYLE

Style of British BAROQUE FURNITURE in early 18th century. Named for Queen Anne (1702–14), in whose reign it arose, the style persisted through the first quarter of the century, before being supplanted by the PALLADIAN STYLE of the early GEORGIAN PERIOD. When Anne acceded to the throne, English design had been dominated for several generations by an influx of ideas and craftsmen from the Continent (*see* RESTORATION FURNITURE; WILLIAM AND MARY STYLE). A thorough assimilation of these influences, combined with a patriotic reaction against all things French—stirred by the War of the Spanish Succession (1701–14)—yielded a distinctively English national style in the decorative arts under the new queen. Though its love for unified ensembles of repeated curves was wholly baroque, this new mode eschewed the ornate and pursued a subtly dramatic simplicity. The two principal elements in furniture design were a reliance on figured WALNUT veneering (in place of ornamental inlays and carving) and an emphasis on the harmonious arrangement of a variety of flowing curves.

These sophisticated compositions were organized around the newly perfected CABRIOLE LEG (*see under* LEG), whose bold double curve was skillfully echoed in the smooth shaping of YOKEBACK CHAIRS, SERPENTINE arms, fiddleback splats (*see* FIDDLE BACK; SPLAT) and rounded seat frames. The CHAIR-BACK SETTEE, an innovation of the period, multiplied the opportunities for designers to take advantage of such relationships. Carved ornamentation was minimized. It appeared mostly as single motifs on the KNEE of a leg or in the center of a seat rail or table apron—the ACANTHUS leaf and the COQUILLAGE, or scallop shell, were most often used—and in the BALL-AND-CLAW FOOT (*see under* FOOT). Improved joinery techniques, notably the CORNER BLOCK, allowed stretchers to be abandoned, and chairs, tables and other legged pieces now rose delicately aloft above a set of sturdy curves.

Case furniture likewise bore little carving, other than bracket feet and perhaps fluted pilasters on the front or a simple architectural pediment above. The TALLBOY was newly prominent at this time, and a variety of secretaries (*see* SECRETARY) and other DESKS catered to the 18th-century craze for letter writing, a function of dramatically improving communications throughout the country. The CHINA CABINET reflected another contemporary enthusiasm—the collecting of Oriental porcelains. These cabinets, whose internal structure was generally of DEAL or OAK, were elegantly veneered in boldly figured WALNUT; BURL walnut was especially in demand. Fancy MARQUETRY and JAPANNING went out of fashion in British work, although elaborately inlaid Dutch cabinets continued to be imported throughout the period.

Furniture forms reflected the nation's growing prosperity and the increasing degree of leisure and luxury that the expanding middle class enjoyed. The WING CHAIR, introduced late in the 17th century, became very popular, and homemade needlework was favored for its upholstery. The SPOON-BACK CHAIR, whose back was shaped to fit the human spine, was a conscious attempt to make the sitter more comfortable and was perhaps based on Chinese models (*see* CHINESE FURNITURE), known through expanding commerce with the Orient. The CARD TABLE (1) arose, as a gambling mania swept society, and numerous small TEA TABLES and STANDS appeared, furnishing households where food, drink and entertainment commanded much attention.

The Queen Anne style in furniture persisted for a time after the death of that monarch, but by 1725 the increasing popularity of MAHOGANY, a very workable and handsome wood, led to a return to elaborate carving in the PALLADIAN STYLE, the last phase of the baroque in Britain. In British North America, however, the Queen Anne style was only beginning to be important, and it remained influential there for decades (*see* AMERICAN QUEEN ANNE STYLE).

QUEENSLAND MAPLE
Pale reddish brown HARDWOOD of tropical Australia. Queensland maple resembles MAHOGANY in appearance, though it is paler and lighter in weight. Quite strong, it is regarded in Australia as an ideal material for fine cabinetry and is used there as solid wood, veneering and plywood. Elsewhere, it is chiefly used as a decorative veneer.

QUEENSLAND WALNUT
Grey to brown HARDWOOD with darker grain, native to Australia. Though not a true walnut, it resembles that wood closely. It is used in flooring and cabinetry in Australia, where it is common. Elsewhere, its use is limited to decorative veneering. It was popular in Britain in the 1930s as one of the "EMPIRE" WOODS.

QUERVELLE, ANTHONY (1789–1856)
French-born Philadelphia cabinetmaker, associated with the AMERICAN EMPIRE STYLE.

Christened Antoine-Gabriel, Quervelle arrived in Philadelphia in 1817. There he became the principal developer of a local version of the American Empire style. Drawing on both French EMPIRE STYLE examples and the published designs of George SMITH, Quervelle made elegant furniture whose, ponderous mass was offset by the use of precisely carved architectural features, foliate forms and other devices—sometimes including marble or mirrored panels in case furniture.

QUIRK
Very narrow longitudinal groove in a MOLDING or between moldings.

RAAB, JOHANN PHILIPP (1736–1802)

German BAROQUE FURNITURE maker. In the 1760s Raab, who worked in Mainz, made furniture in a late baroque manner, using geometrical MARQUETRY.

RAAB, JOHANN VALENTIN (active c. 1808–12)

German EMPIRE STYLE furniture maker. Working in Würzburg, Raab followed French models to some degree, but he made furniture that was less formal and featured more carved decoration. He especially favored the swan motif (taken from PERCIER AND FONTAINE's designs for Malmaison); as a result, it became extremely popular throughout the German-speaking countries.

RAACKE, PETER (b. 1928)

Contemporary German designer. He is principally known for his designs in metal and glass for kitchenware and tableware. In 1967 Raacke also created a popular line of furniture made of cardboard and designed in a functionalist style (*see* FUNCTIONALISM).

RABBET (also *rebate*)

Groove or channel, usually rectangular in section, cut in surface of piece of wood in order to accommodate the edge of another piece of wood or a protruding strip, or TONGUE, crafted on that piece of wood. The two pieces are thereby connected by a RABBETED JOINT (*see under* JOINERY). A rabbet may also be cut in the edge of a cabinet door, matching a protrusion or edge of another door or of a STILE, to keep dust out of the cabinet when closed.

RACE, ERNEST (1913–63)

British CONTEMPORARY STYLE designer. He trained as an architect, then studied weaving in India in the late 1930s and began designing furniture after the Second World War. Race was one of a group of young designers—including Robin DAY, Clive LATIMER and Dennis YOUNG—who were influenced by Gordon RUSSELL and would develop the Contemporary style of the 1950s. Race had worked in the British aircraft industry during the war and he was aware of the commercial possibilities of surplus war matériel. His "BA" chair (1945) pioneered the use of cast aluminum in furniture, an innovation that became popular in Britain throughout the next several decades. Race continued to develop designs that used new materials in original ways, notably in his well-known "Antelope" chair (1950), though he also had a taste for upholstered pieces that recalled more traditional furniture. Since his death, his company, Race Furniture, which employed designers such as Robert HERITAGE, has continued to specialize in the use of new materials.

RACKING

Damage present in some old wooden furniture; state of being warped, sometimes to the point where the fabric of the wood is actually broken.

RADEN

Japanese decorative technique for LACQUER furniture. It involves the placement of many tiny shards of MOTHER-OF-PEARL in wet lacquer, yielding a shimmering effect when dry and polished. Developed in very early times in

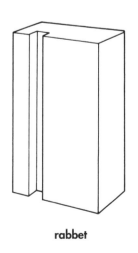

rabbet

Japan, *raden* was also used in China, in YIN PING TUO lacquer furniture. It is known in the West as LAC BURGAUTÉ.

RAIL

Horizontal bar supported by and joining vertical posts. Examples include the CREST RAIL of a chair and the simple STRETCHER between two legs of a chair or table. The term also refers to a horizontal member of the framing of a wooden panel that fits into each STILE.

RAKE

Inclination from the vertical of a normally upright member of a piece of furniture, such as a slanted chair back or a splayed table leg.

RAMIN

Pale Indonesian HARDWOOD first used in furniture in about 1950. Almost white, *ramin* can be stained to resemble more expensive woods, especially when used as veneer. It is also very light and strong and thus serves well for drawer parts, doweling and other miscellaneous uses.

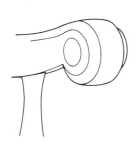

ram's-horn arm

RAMS, DIETER (b. 1932)

Contemporary German industrial designer. Principally known as chief designer for Braun, Rams had a great influence on the development of that company's distinctively functionalist look (*see* FUNCTIONALISM). He has also designed furniture, especially storage units and seating, in a personal variant of the INTERNATIONAL STYLE that stresses modularity and flexibility of use.

RAM'S-HORN ARM

Chair arm terminating at its forward end in a deeply carved, downturned spiral; popular in BAROQUE FURNITURE, especially in the LOUIS XIV STYLE.

Ralph Rapson rocker

RANDALL, WILLIAM (active 1715–39)

Boston cabinetmaker and japanner (*see* JAPANNING). One of the earliest Boston japanners, Randall used loosely composed arrangements of CHINOISERIE motifs, each fairly large in scale. These typified the early Boston style (a later mode was represented by the tighter work of Thomas JOHNSTON). Randall retired in 1739 (to open a tavern) and transferred his business to his partner and future son-in-law, Robert DAVIS.

RANDOLPH, BENJAMIN (1721–91)

Leading maker of PHILADELPHIA CHIPPENDALE FURNITURE. Randolph made elaborately ornamented mahogany furniture that, along with the work of fellow-Philadelphian Jonathan GOSTELOWE, most lavishly represented ROCOCO FURNITURE in America. By 1762 Randolph had a large shop that employed many craftsmen, including carvers hired from London (*see* Hercules COURTENAY; John POLLARD). His richly elegant furniture made Randolph a very successful man, but when the American Revolution broke out, he closed his business and moved to southern New Jersey, where he manufactured pig iron for the Revolutionary Army. After the war he resumed furniture making on a smaller scale, and some of his work foreshadowed the coming NEOCLASSICAL STYLE of the FEDERAL PERIOD.

RANDOM JOINTS

Seams or JOINTS in furniture paneling, floors or walls made of boards, in which boards are of varying dimensions or where grains of adjoining boards do not match.

RANGE TABLES

Set of several identical tables intended to be placed side by side to make one large table.

RAPSON, RALPH (b. 1914)

American architect and furniture designer. Best known as an architect, Ralph Rapson was associated in the 1940s and 1950s with Charles EAMES and Eero SAARINEN, among others, as one of the leading American producers of modern INTERNATIONAL STYLE furniture. He also marketed and promoted SCANDINAVIAN MODERN furniture by Bruno MATHSSON, Arne JACOBSEN, and others.

RAT-CLAW FOOT

See under FOOT.

RATEAU, ARMAND-ALBERT (1882–1938)
French ART DECO interior decorator and furniture designer. Rateau first designed in a Parisian ART NOUVEAU style but progressed with the times to the elegant sumptuousness of Art Deco. He specialized in the design of whole interiors, including furniture. Rateau is noted for bronze pieces modeled closely on bronze furniture from Pompeii and other classical sites.

RAT'S-BALL-AND-CLAW FOOT
See under FOOT.

RAT-TAIL HINGE
See under HINGE.

RATTAN
Type of climbing or trailing vinelike palm native to southern Asia, Malaysia and China. Its outer bark is used for CANING, and its inner, reedlike section is used to weave WICKER furniture. Introduced to the West in the early 19th century, rattan has become the standard material for caning, and its strength and manipulability have made it the most popular of the many materials used in wickerwork.

RAVESTEYN, SYBOLD VAN (b. 1889–1983)
Dutch DE STIJL furniture designer. Influenced deeply by Cubism, Ravesteyn manipulated horizontal and vertical elements in ingenious ways to create unusual and elegant furniture pieces.

RAVRIO, ANTOINE-ANDRÉ (1759–1814)
French EMPIRE STYLE bronze worker. Trained by his father, also a bronze founder, Ravrio was an established craftsman by the 1780s, but his greatest success came during the Empire, when he was frequently employed by Napoleon's court. His furniture mounts were used by Georges JACOB, Guillaume BENEMAN and others. Ravrio employed many workers and became a wealthy man.

READING STAND
Small table with adjustable sloping top designed to hold a book. Descended from the LECTERN, the reading stand evolved late in the period of RENAISSANCE FURNITURE and reached a peak of popularity in 18th-century Britain. Similar pieces appear in JAPANESE FURNITURE.

REBATE
Another name for RABBET.

REBATED JOINT
Another name for RABBETED JOINT (see under JOINERY).

RÉCAMIER
French DIRECTOIRE, CONSULATE and EMPIRE STYLE furniture form; DAYBED with back or headboard scrolled at top and symmetrically curving footboard, usually shorter. It was named for a prominent figure in Paris society, the famous and beautiful salon hostess, Mme. Juliette Récamier (1777–1849).

RECESSED CARVING
Decorative technique, used in 17th-century England, in which a design or pattern on a wood surface was emphasized or set off by shallowly carving away the background and texturing it with a punch.

RECESSED STRETCHER
See under STRETCHER.

RÉCHAMPI
French term denoting ornamental details that are gilded or painted in contrast to a ground of another color. In ROCOCO FURNITURE réchampi ornamentation was frequently gold against a white or green ground.

RED GUM
American HARDWOOD, pink to reddish brown in color, sometimes with dark brown markings. Finely textured and smooth in appearance, red gum is used in furniture both as a solid and as plywood. It was popular in 18th- and 19th-century furniture of the Hudson River valley, especially in case pieces. Now limited to the American market, red

reading stand

gum was a popular imported wood in Britain in the first half of the 20th century. It was known there as *satin walnut* or *hazel pine*.

REDWOOD (also *sequoia*)

American SOFTWOOD, native to coastal regions of northern California, pink to reddish brown in color. Light in weight and very resistant to decay, redwood is frequently used for outdoor furniture. Also, the wood from the very large BURLS of redwood is often cut and polished for used as tabletops or decorative VENEER. Botanically a cousin of the giant sequoia, American redwood is not related to EUROPEAN REDWOOD, which is a member of the pine family.

REED-AND-TIE MOLDING

See under MOLDING.

reeding

REEDING

Ornamental carving consisting of narrow ridges, rounded in section, abutting each other and usually covering a vertical surface. Except in being convex rather than concave, reeding resembles FLUTING and was derived from it by NEOCLASSICAL STYLE furniture designers of the late 18th century, who frequently used it to adorn chair and table legs. In more modern times it has been used by such 20th-century designers as Émile-Jacques RUHLMANN and Alistair MAYNARD, who thereby indicated their interest, in historical styles in the face of Modernism.

REEL-AND-BEAD MOLDING

See BEAD-AND-REEL MOLDING, *under* MOLDING.

REEL-AND-BEAD TURNING

See under TURNERY.

REFECTORY TABLE

Modern name for a MEDIEVAL FURNITURE form; long table, often with six or eight legs joined by stretchers just above the floor. Associated with the refectory, or dining room, of a monastery, this piece was also common in secular domestic furniture. It was placed in the hall, or principal room, of a medieval dwelling and was thus once known as a *hall table*. Refectory tables were made into the 17th century.

RÉGENCE STYLE

French furniture style of early 18th century; first phase of ROCOCO FURNITURE, transitional between LOUIS XIV and LOUIS XV STYLES. After the death of Louis XIV in 1715, a regency was established because the late king's grandson, Louis XV, was only five years old. The regent, Philippe, duc d'Orléans, ruled until his own death in 1723, but the style named for his government both arose earlier and lasted longer; it is generally dated from about 1700 to 1730. The Régence was a period of reaction against the rigorous formality of the Sun King's reign, which ended with economic troubles and social unrest brought on by years of warfare. Even before Louis's death, the aristocracy began to desert his court at Versailles, where the king continued to enforce a stultifying, hierarchical formality. Instead, a new social world emerged in Paris, where the nobility refurbished old houses and built new ones in which to entertain and be entertained in an informal, even frivolous ambience. After 1715 the architectural centerpiece of this new society was the regent's residence, the Palais-Royal. Here Gilles-Marie OPPENORDT supervised a massive redecoration and introduced a revolutionary new style in wall paneling, in which overflowing ornamentation and smoothly curved corners broke down the rigid symmetry that dominated earlier rooms.

Changes in the decorative arts were under way much earlier. Even before 1700 Jean BÉRAIN, successor to Charles LE BRUN as Louis XIV's chief designer, had introduced an element of idiosyncratic fantasy in his decorative images, incorporating absurd vignettes of monkeys and whimsical CARYATIDS. His lightness of spirit was exercised within the formal restraints of the Louis XIV style, but it anticipated later work by Pierre LE PAUTRE and Oppenordt.

In furniture formality was similarly abandoned by the use of sensuous, relaxed curves, in preference to the generally straight lines of Louis XIV pieces. The CABRIOLE LEG (*see under* LEG) came into its own and became the most characteristic element of rococo furniture. The stretchers between these legs became correspondingly sinuous, before disappearing altogether. The COMMODE (1) took on new shapes. The COMMODE À LA RÉGENCE, a heavy, three-drawered piece, echoed the new curvilinearity with a scrolling apron below a SERPENTINE front. The leading cabinetmaker of the period, Charles CRESSENT, devised a lighter piece raised high on cabriole legs, the COMMODE CRESSENT. Another famous maker of commodes was André-Charles BOULLE, who, though principally associated with the Louis XIV style, adapted to changing tastes and became a leader in the use of lighter-colored woods, such as KINGWOOD and TULIP-WOOD, in preference to ebony and walnut in marquetry. Marquetry was generally quite plain, with expanses of figured wood or arrangements of simple geometrical shapes, especially LOZENGES. In contrast with this plainer wood, ORMOLU mounts were used more expansively, ranging across the veneering. Cressent in particular was noted for his vigorous bronzes. The classical masks and stylized flowers of the earlier style gave way to foliate scrolling, ACANTHUS leaves and the ESPAGNO-LETTE, a naturalistic rendering of a female head, an image made popular in the paintings of Watteau. In fact, the fine arts, in which anti-classicism informed a marked change in iconography, had a considerable influence on the period. The world of the Olympian gods was replaced by the Arcadia of shepherds and shepherdesses, whose themes were those of lovemaking, hunting and play. And details of naturalistic outdoor scenes in paintings by Watteau and others became decorative motifs. Waves and reeds, plants and shells in natural settings, supplanted the formal scrolls and festoons of the baroque. This development was furthered by the continuing enthusiasm for CHINOISERIE, begun in the previous century, because similar motifs and themes were found in Chinese and Japanese painting and decoration. This manner of decorating with natural elements was called *rock and shell* work—in French, *rocaille et coquille.* The term ROCAILLE, meaning "rockwork" of a garden, is the root of the word *rococo,* and it came to apply loosely to any ornamentation in that style. A COQUIL-LAGE is a scallop-shell motif, a device that was used in baroque decoration but became far more popular in the 18th century.

Chairs at first tended to retain 17th-century ornamentation, being made by MENUISIERS, who were a conservative group. But by 1720 an important alteration in structure precipitated a general change in appearance. The new fashion for hoop skirts required that chair arms be shortened and arm supports be placed at least a quarter of the way back on the seat rail. At the same time, chair backs were lowered to avoid interference with the elaborate coiffures of the day. The BERGÈRE, a comfortable upholstered armchair, was fully developed from earlier beginnings and became a staple item. Upholstery became more important than ever before, leading to a vogue for different suites of upholstered furniture for the different seasons of the year. The inconvenience and expense of this fashion led in turn to the development of SLIPCOVERS. Tables, too, were less formal. The BUREAU PLAT replaced the BUREAU MAZARIN as the desk of choice, and the CONSOLE TABLE took on the lighter, more decorative form that gives it its name, coming to be supported only on its scrolled front legs.

The Régence was a transitional period in which the decorative arts evolved sufficiently far from classical grandeur to make possible the *genre pittoresque* of J.-A. MEISSONNIER and Nicholas PINEAU—the stimulus for the later, more extreme rococo manner, the Louis XV style.

REGENCY GOTHIC
Late 18th- and early 19th-century British NEO-GOTHIC STYLE of furniture and interior decoration, characterized by unsystematic application of Gothic decorative details, taken from ecclesiastical architecture, to contemporary furniture forms. The principal exponent of Regency Gothic work was A. C. PUGIN. Unconvincing, rather fussy in appearance and not fully worked out, the style merely anticipated the more vigorous and historically accurate manner developed by Pugin's famous son, A. W. N. PUGIN.

REGENCY STYLE
Late NEOCLASSICAL STYLE of British furniture, prominent during first four decades of 19th century. The Regency style was characterized by a pronounced eclecticism, using forms and decoration derived from ancient GREEK, ROMAN and EGYPTIAN FURNITURE, as known through archeology, along with vari-

Régence chest of drawers

Regency chair

ous elements taken from contemporary French furniture and other sources, including CHINESE FURNITURE. Ornamentation was consciously restrained; it took the form of sculptural supports, inlaid or painted decoration elsewhere and sparingly used bronze mounts, often setting off simple figured veneering. Forms were generally rectilinear in shape, usually symmetrical, and conspicuously balanced, in open configurations such as PEDESTAL TABLES or chairs composed of slender elements. Though named for the period (1811–20) when Britain was formally ruled by the Prince of Wales as regent for his insane father, King George III, the style arose much earlier, in the last years of the 18th century, and persisted beyond the regent's own reign as George IV (1820–30) into the 1840s, when neoclassicism gave way to the newly popular REVIVAL STYLES, in the early VICTORIAN PERIOD.

The earliest stirrings of the Regency manner were evident in the late ADAM STYLE designs of Thomas SHERATON; these were influenced by the strict linearity and relative austerity of late LOUIS XVI–STYLE work. In both France and Britain, an increasing enthusiasm for classical archeology inspired furniture designers to produce faithful copies of ancient Greek and Roman furniture, particularly as it was known from Greek vase painting. In Britain these craftsmen included Henry HOLLAND, C. H. TATHAM and, most prominent, Thomas HOPE. The X-FRAME stool was a popular form, as it had been in ancient times. The Greek KLISMOS chair was the most characteristic form to develop. With its SABER LEG (see under LEG) and broad, tablet-shaped CREST RAIL bearing ETRUSCAN STYLE decoration, often figural painting, this simple but elegant piece exemplified the idea of rational beauty known in the ancient world and revived in an enlightened age. It was often made as an armchair, with arms that curved forward and down to the seat rail in a smooth, open scroll whose airy grace is still regarded as typical of the Regency style at its best.

Early in the 19th century, the influence of the French DIRECTOIRE and CONSULATE STYLES was felt in Britain. Heavier, more monumental forms appeared, as did more carved decoration, especially in the form of heavy paw feet (see PAW FOOT, under FOOT) and animal's-head MASKS. Darker colors became fashionable, and such woods as MAHOGANY and ROSEWOOD regained popularity. EBONIZED wood was frequently used. The trend to massiveness produced the SOFA-TABLE, a more elaborate form than earlier PEMBROKE TABLES; it often had a sculptural central support. New classical motifs were introduced, including the GUILLOCHE; the DOLPHIN, long popular in France; and the ACANTHUS leaf. The leading cabinetmaker of the day was Thomas CHIPPENDALE Jr., who had followed French tastes since the 1770s. The French Egyptologist Baron DENON was widely read in Britain, and ÉGYPTIENNERIE motifs began to proliferate in furniture decoration; Hope designed pieces based on Denon's engravings of Egyptian originals. Sheraton's later PATTERN BOOKS, published in 1803 and 1805, also reflected this new French influence, along with that of classical archeology in general. Sheraton's designs were the principal means by which the Regency manner reached America, where it stimulated the development of the DIRECTORY STYLE.

Hope's work, whether classical or Egyptian in inspiration, tended to be pedantic. It was cold, academic and uncomfortable to use. But George SMITH published popularized versions of Hope's work that spread his ideas widely, in more generally acceptable furniture designs. Smith's book of 1808 was especially influential in America, where it contributed to the rise of the AMERICAN EMPIRE STYLE. Smith, the most important Regency designer after Hope, was also a cabinetmaker, and his work, both crafted and published, illustrates the eclectic nature of the period. He produced furniture ranging from the manner of Hope, through varying French modes—including, especially in the 1820s, the EMPIRE and RESTAURATION STYLES—to NEO-GOTHIC STYLE pieces and even, briefly, CHINOISERIE furniture, which had been popular 40 years earlier as CHINESE CHIPPENDALE FURNITURE.

The increasing diversity of Regency design through the early 19th century attested to a continuing diffusion of the commitment to the ideal of archeological purity that had informed the work of Hope and others in the late 1790s. This development was a manifestation of great changes in British society at large, brought about by the stresses of the Napoleonic Wars and the influence of the French Revolution. As society changed, so did fashion, and in the 1830s the revival styles rose to prominence as a vast new middle-class furniture-buying public rejected the neo-classical taste associated with the elites of the 18th century in favor of furniture forms that were designed for creature comfort rather than for their resemblance to ancient models. Thus, the eclecticism of the Regency era culminated in the welter of stylistic tendencies that, combined with the new techniques of mass production, characterized the early Victorian period.

RELIEF

Carved ornamentation projecting from surrounding material; the opposite of INTAGLIO work.

RÉMOND, FELIX (active c. 1800–33)

French furniture maker in EMPIRE and RESTAURATION STYLES. Rémond was an established craftsman as early as 1806 but had his greatest success under the restored Bourbon monarchy, receiving many royal and aristocratic commissions.

RENAISSANCE FURNITURE

European furniture of 15th through 17th centuries, which reflected the period's interest in the classical world and its cultural and esthetic themes. This revival of classical concerns gave the Renaissance its name, literally meaning "rebirth," and in the arts it was manifested by the adaptation of ancient architectural and decorative principles and devices. The Renaissance began in about the late 14th and early 15th centuries in Italy, where the Gothic style of northern Europe (*see* GOTHIC FURNITURE) had never wholly taken hold and classical ideas had never been entirely supplanted.

Initially, the Renaissance revolution in style was chiefly ornamental; Renaissance furniture forms carried on the unspecialized tradition of the Middle Ages (*see* MEDIEVAL FURNITURE). The principal manifestation of the new style was the use of ancient Roman decorative motifs, especially those of the classical ORDERS OF ARCHITECTURE and from the sculptural motifs of ancient sarcophagi; these included the PUTTO, the URN and depictions of such mythological beasts as the SPHINX and the CHIMERA. Human features were also popular, especially in the roundels

known as ROMAYNE WORK. A greater emphasis on naturalism in carving replaced the stylization of medieval work. Walnut, a handsome wood that was easier to carve than the traditional oak, was increasingly used, and elaborate INLAY techniques, including INTARSIA and PIETRE DURE, were developed.

At first, the only new furniture form to arise was the CASSONE, which was basically a traditional CHEST decorated in a new way—with paintings, as well as with ornamentation of carved or molded GESSO or PASTIGLIA. However, throughout Europe over the next several centuries, particular pieces of furniture began to be associated with specific uses and with specific rooms reserved for those uses, and a wider array of furniture types emerged. By the 16th century, the *cassone* had evolved, with the addition of arms and a back, into the CASSAPANCA. A light, portable SIDE CHAIR, the SGABELLO, came into use. The contemporary CREDENZA, a sideboard, also arose in Italy and became a standard piece. The MULE CHEST, and then the CHEST OF DRAWERS, became familiar in the 16th century. The CUPBOARD evolved into many types of storage furniture, including the WARDROBE, the ARMOIRE and the elaborate CABINET, which exemplified the new importance of furniture as an emblem of wealth and status that deserved the finest application of the decorative arts. Another such piece was the monumental table known in France, where it was most popular, as a TABLE À L'ITALIENNE.

A distinctively French amalgam of Italian decorative motifs and Gothic furniture forms, the FRANÇOIS I STYLE, flourished in the first half of the 16th century. France had invaded Italy in 1494, and French royalty subsequently acquired a taste for the arts of the Italian

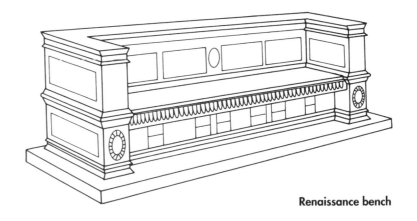

Renaissance bench

Renaissance. Consequently, several French kings hired a number of Italian decorators and designers, culminating in the elaborate program of King François I at Fontainebleau Palace, intended to inculcate classicism into the French decorative arts. ROSSO FIORENTINO and Francesco PRIMATICCIO were most notable among the Italian artists whose example generated a new Gallic idiom. These designers practiced in a newer, more complex Renaissance mode, the MANNERIST STYLE. Mannerist furniture was still rooted in an enthusiasm for the classical, but it was inspired by the first excavations of ancient Roman painted interior decoration rather than by classical architecture. Therefore, it was wildly organic and extravagantly bizzare in appearance, being heavily carved and decorated over much of its surface with the strange and complicated motifs of GROTESQUE ORNAMENT.

In France, Mannerism continued to dominate furniture decoration in the second half of the 16th century. In the HENRI II STYLE, it was a more sculptural mode favoring images of the human figure. Its chief practitioners were J. A. DU CERCEAU, Jean GOUJON and Hughes SAMBIN. New furniture forms that developed at this time included the CAQUETOIRE, a light chair; the PLACET, a stool; and the armoire. The continuing evolution of lighter chairs produced the open back and the SPLAT. Increased concern for comfort meant a greater use of upholstery. In the early 17th century, French Renaissance furniture reached a decadent anticlimax in the LOUIS XIII STYLE.

The Renaissance reached Spain directly from Italy at first, then from France and from the Low Countries, which Spain ruled at the time. In the early 16th Century, Italian motifs merged with the powerful medieval MUDÉJAR STYLE, with its abstract ARABESQUE patterns, to produce the PLATERESQUE STYLE, which featured elaborate MARQUETRY. Later, more architecturally inspired decoration was more severe. Exotic materials, such as GUADAMECIL leather and pierced metalwork over velvet, were used in surface decoration. Repeated sumptuary legislation could not eliminate the extravagant use of silver ornamentation on furniture. A distinctly Spanish form arose at this time, the VARGUEÑO, a fallfront desk supported by the PIE DE PUENTE or the TAQUILLÓN. A new chair, the SILLÓN DE FRAILEROS, derived from Flemish models.

In the Low Countries and the rest of Europe, Mannerism spread from France and dominated the furniture of the late 16th and early 17th centuries. A chief agent in this transmission was the published PATTERN BOOK, which provided craftsmen with advanced designs. Especially important were the pattern books of Du Cerceau and Flemish designers Cornelis FLORIS and Hans VREDEMAN DE VRIES.

In Germany the influence of Italian art was strong early in the 16th century, and by 1550 a number of German designers were well versed in classical decoration—most notably, Heinrich ALDEGREVER, Peter FLÖTNER and the anonymous H. S. MASTER. The KUNSTSCHRANK, a complex cabinet in architectural form, was the most prominent German contribution to Renaissance furniture. In the late 16th and early 17th centuries, the Mannerist Wendel DIETERLIN was highly influential, especially in England, where TUDOR FURNITURE remotely echoed Italian decorative ideas.

The Renaissance was an adventurous period of discovery and ferment; it eventually gave way to a time of consolidation. The increasingly bizarre character of Mannerist decoration reached an extreme in the AURICULAR STYLE of northern Europe, and a reaction set in. The baroque style (*see* BAROQUE FURNITURE), grand and extravagant but less eccentric and more balanced and unified, replaced Mannerist exuberance in the decorative and fine arts.

RENAISSANCE REVIVAL style

European and American furniture style of second half of 19th century. It was characterized by rectilinear and massive forms, especially in highly architectonic case furniture, and by elaborate ornamentation, which featured colorful contrasts of materials, a variety of techniques and the eclectic use of decorative motifs taken from RENAISSANCE and BAROQUE FURNITURE and architecture of the 16th and 17th centuries, respectively. Arising in about the mid-19th century, Renaissance Revival style furniture was most popular in the 1860s and 1870s, but it remained fashionable into the 20th century in some locales.

The Renaissance Revival style succeeded the ROCOCO REVIVAL and NEO-GOTHIC STYLES as the leading mode in furniture design. Along with the QUEEN ANNE REVIVAL STYLE and the LOUIS XVI REVIVAL STYLE, contemporary and somewhat overlap-

American Renaissance Revival

ping developments, it marked a return of interest in neoclassicism (*see* NEOCLASSICAL STYLE) on the part of designers in the REVIVAL STYLES. However, classical ideals were no longer a main concern. Rather, a love of exoticism and opulence in ornamentation and the patriotic fervor that pervaded Europe at the time were key motivations behind the style. The former was expressed in crowded juxtapositions of carved, turned and inlaid motifs of all sorts, rendered in a variety of woods, often painted or EBONIZED, with added richness provided by the frequent use of GILDING, PORCELAIN plaques and ORMOLU mounts. Nationalism was evident in the distinctive variations typical of the style. The forms and decorative schemes most prominent in the Renaissance furniture of a given country— such as the Italian CASSONE, the German KUNSTSCHRANK or the MANNERIST STYLE sculptural ornamentation in French and English ROMAYNE work—tended to be featured in the revival furniture of that country.

National variation was most pronounced in Italy and Germany, where unified states were being created from the remains of the feudal world. In Italy, Renaissance-inspired designs were published as early as 1840 by Giuseppe CIMA, and in the 1870s the Florentine makers Andrea BACCETTI and Luigi FRULLINI received particular acclaim. In Germany a number of established furniture-making firms were associated with the style, including Wilhelm KIMBEL of Mainz and PÖSSENBACHER in Munich. In Vienna, German motifs were also popular and were used by such firms as those of Anton BEMBÉ and Carl LEISTLER. In France, Guillaume GROHÉ and Claude Aimé CHÉNAVARD made notable furniture based on the HENRI II and LOUIS XIII STYLES, but the Louis XVI revival tended to dominate in that country, as it was favored at the court of Napoleon III.

In the English-speaking countries, national fervor was less evident in Renaissance Revival style furniture. In Britain the style was known as *Free Renaissance*, a name indicative of its extraordinary eclecticism. However, one influence there was the avowedly British ELIZABETHAN REVIVAL STYLE, which contributed an emphasis on elaborate TURNERY. The NATURALISTIC STYLE of decoration added images from nature. Among the most important British designers of Renaissance Revival style furniture were Charles BARRY,

Robert EDIS and T. E. COLLCUTT. In America, Renaissance Revival work was even less related to genuine historical furniture. A fashionable exoticism found expression in the NEO-GREC STYLE, in which ÉGYPTIENNERIE motifs played a prominent part in busy decorative schemes. Effects of magnificence were striven for through combinations of rich materials and multiplied motifs, moderated only by a preference for flat ornamentation, in incised designs or low relief. By the 1880s this American fashion had been absorbed by the more restrained "Eastlake" style (*see* Charles Locke EASTLAKE). Among the leading makers of Renaissance Revival style furniture in America were Thomas BROOKS, John JELIFF, Alexander ROUX and Leon MARCOTTE.

The ponderous proportions, extremely elaborate ornamentation and indiscriminate historical references of Renaissance Revival style furniture made it a target of the design reform movements that emerged in the late 19th century (*see* ARTS AND CRAFTS MOVEMENT; ART FURNITURE MOVEMENT; ART NOUVEAU; DEUTSCHE WERKSTÄTTEN). However, it remained popular among much of the furniture-buying public and was still made, especially in Germany and Italy, until the First World War.

RENT TABLE

British NEOCLASSICAL STYLE furniture form of late 18th century; DRUM TABLE whose drawers bore the names of the days of the week or other numbers or letters, evidently to classify accounts or records. Some rent tables also contained a hidden compartment below a panel in the center of the top. The rent table is traditionally supposed to have been used by landlords to store collected rents.

rent table

REPRODUCTION FURNITURE

Furniture made in imitation of ANTIQUES, by replicating old furniture exactly, using antique construction techniques and finishes, or by simply creating pieces with the same external appearance without regard to material or technique. Reproduction furniture differs from purposeful forgeries of antiques in being explicitly new, marketed as such, with no intent to defraud. Although copies of earlier furniture had been made occasionally since the mid-18th century, usually to replace lost or damaged pieces, the commercial manufacture of reproduction furniture began only in the second half of the 19th century, with the growth of antique collecting. Many prominent furniture makers who worked in the various REVIVAL STYLES of the day were known for their fine reproductions, notably Guillaume GROHÉ, WASSMUS FRÈRES and GILLOWS. Reproduction furniture has become more popular throughout the 20th century, and today reproduction making is a vast industry. Consumers can even buy pieces in kit form and assemble preshaped components themselves, and pattern books for the home craftsman also abound. This furniture varies greatly in its fidelity to the originals, but it often offers close copies of genuine pieces.

RESERVE
Area in a scheme of decoration left in the natural state or color of the material being decorated; serves as background to the motif.

REST BED
Another name for DAYBED in that term's general sense—that is, any furniture form designed for daytime reclining.

Restauration chair

RESTAURATION STYLE
French NEOCLASSICAL STYLE of the period that lasted from the fall of Napoleon, in 1814, until about 1830 and was named for the restoration of the Bourbon monarchy after the era of Revolution and Empire. Restauration style furniture differed very little from that of the preceding EMPIRE STYLE. Furniture continued to be in the same simple forms adapted from ancient Greek and Roman prototypes, and it remained massive in appearance, for monumentality was found to aggrandize the restored monarchy no less than it had the Empire. The only other important change was in tonality; mahogany was no longer in fashion, being replaced by light-colored woods, called BOIS CLAIR, which were often inlaid with darker woods. As in the Empire style, furniture was designed with an emphasis on figured veneering contrasted with dramatic but sparingly used bronze mounts. These mounts continued to present the classically inspired Empire repertoire of motifs, although specifically Napoleonic imagery was of course

discarded. Favored motifs were the swan, the LYRE and the ACANTHUS leaf. Many designers and craftsmen of the earlier period continued to be successful under the restoration, including P.-F.-L. Fontaine (see PERCIER AND FONTAINE), Pierre de LA MÉSANGÈRE, JACOB-DESMALTER, Felix RÉMOND and P.-A. BELLANGÉ. Another important furniture maker of the period was L.-E. LEMARCHAND. In its close resemblances to its predecessor, the Restauration style provided a final testimony to the power of the Empire style, which, though shortlived, had exerted an influence that was hard to displace. However, after the final fall of the Bourbons in the revolution of 1830, France seemed irrevocably changed, and the REVIVAL STYLES, along with the NEO-GOTHIC STYLE, rose to prominence.

RESTORATION CHAIR
Another name for CHARLES II CHAIR.

RESTORATION FURNITURE
English furniture of the reign of Charles II (1660–89), restored to the throne after the revolutionary rule of the Commonwealth. The first English BAROQUE FURNITURE, Restoration furniture is characterized by an exuberance of line, as opposed to the static foursquare quality of the JACOBEAN and COMMONWEALTH FURNITURE that preceded it. Spiral turnings, frequent use of scrolls and deep carving were the principal ingredients of its flamboyant decorative style. When Charles II was restored, he brought with him a taste for luxury and grandeur that reflected the decorative arts of the LOUIS XIV STYLE, for he had lived at the king's court; he had been further exposed to the European baroque in Holland. During his reign a number of Dutch, Flemish and French craftsmen worked in England—including, most notably, Grinling GIBBONS. These craftsmen brought with them a taste for WALNUT rather than OAK, for carved and gilded GESSO decoration and for elaborate MARQUETRY veneers, especially in floral motifs. Also, knowledge of exotic materials and techniques from the Orient became available in England through Dutch commercial connections. JAPANNING with CHINOISERIE decoration was developed in imitation of Oriental LACQUER, and CANING was used in a new, light furniture form, the CHARLES II CHAIR.

The great fire of London in 1666 destroyed much of the city, creating a market for many new buildings, and furniture to fill them, just as this new taste was emerging.

New forms appeared in English furniture, including the CHEST OF DRAWERS, developing from the MULE CHEST and similar Dutch pieces. An early CHEST-ON-STAND, a chest of drawers on a low, tablelike stand, came into use. A growing demand for comfort and convenience was answered by the WING CHAIR and the DAYBED. Similarly, small, portable occasional tables proliferated, and the GATELEG TABLE remained popular. French examples spurred the evolution of the BUREAU from a WRITING BOX on a stand into a piece of case furniture, a SLANT-TOP DESK, with drawers and compartments. A variant was the ESCRITOIRE, predecessor of the SECRETARY and the WRITING CABINET. As French standards of splendid living required, canopy beds became very tall and were hung with extremely copious and expensive draperies. King Charles himself was responsible for the most extravagant Restoration furniture: he commissioned chairs, tables and small case pieces veneered in worked sheets of silver, in emulation of the cast-SILVER furniture at Louis XIV's court. Once established in England, baroque furniture continued to develop, but a natural reaction against its excesses produced milder versions in the subsequent WILLIAM AND MARY and QUEEN ANNE STYLES.

REVIVAL STYLES

Group of dominant 19th-century European and American furniture styles, arising in about 1830 in reaction against the NEOCLASSICAL STYLE and thus characterized by references to earlier decorative modes. The neoclassical taste of the late 18th and early 19th centuries survived only a short time after the fall of Napoleon. By the 1830s the market for architecture, furniture and interior design was increasingly dominated by the rising bourgeoisie, and this factor is reflected in the proliferation of styles that then arose. The buyers in this new market neither desired nor could afford the magnificence of the EMPIRE STYLE and its 18th-century predecessors. Yet while desiring new styles, this newly prosperous class also sought the reassurance that familiarity can generate. Looking back past the recent neoclassical styles, buyers and designers turned to earlier periods for inspiration.

The two periods that first attracted this public were the medieval (*see* NEO-GOTHIC STYLE) and the early 18th century, or rococo (*see* ROCOCO REVIVAL style). While both revivals found adherents throughout Europe and America, their popularity varied, in that nationalistic age, in different countries and regions. The Gothic tended to be more popular and more rigorously applied in the English-speaking countries, while the rococo, reflecting French taste, was more prominent on the Continent. Beginning in about the mid-19th century, a third strain of revivalism took hold in the Western world, the RENAISSANCE REVIVAL style, based on Renaissance models. Even more than the earlier revivals, this one had patriotic overtones. In Britain it was foreshadowed and influenced by the ELIZABETHAN REVIVAL style. In France it drew upon the French Renaissance, in Italy on the Italian Renaissance and so on. Moreover, it became associated with the unification process that both Italy and Germany were undergoing in the 1860s and 1870s.

Some neoclassical elements were present in Renaissance Revival decoration, for RENAISSANCE FURNITURE had itself been classical in inspiration, so the revival styles eventually began to reabsorb 18th-century neoclassical forms and motifs. In Britain the ADAM STYLE reemerged in the 1860s, in a trend that is inaccurately termed the QUEEN ANNE REVIVAL STYLE. For the rest of the century, elements from the designs of Robert ADAM, George HEPPLEWHITE and Thomas SHERATON appeared in British and American furniture, along with the first widespread appearance of a vogue for collecting ANTIQUES and REPRODUCTION FURNITURE.

This phenomenon also accompanied the French LOUIS XVI REVIVAL style, as freely curvilinear Rococo Revival style furniture gave way to more rectilinear, neoclassically informed pieces. This mode was purposefully promoted at the court of Emperor Napoleon III (reigned 1852–70), who wished to remind his subjects of France's past glories. In America a Louis XVI revival arose in the 1860s and merged into the American Renaissance Revival style. Late in the century designers in the revival styles turned to a sometimes spectacular eclecticism, perhaps most strikingly manifested in a taste for the ÉGYPTIENNERIE motifs that had been associated with neoclassicism in Napoleonic times (*see* NEO-GREC STYLE).

**Henry Hobson Richardson
seat**

While many leading 19th-century designers created excellent furniture in one or more of the revival styles, there was also a less pleasing aspect to the period. Factories supplied the immense and growing furniture market of the day with great quantities of revival-style furniture that was mediocre, if not inferior, in design and manufacture. A reaction among artists and designers ensued. As early as mid-century, beginning in Britain, design reform movements began to cause European furniture makers to reject the revival styles (*see* ARTS AND CRAFTS MOVEMENT; ART FURNITURE MOVEMENT; ART NOUVEAU). Furthermore, the rapidly changing modern world generated new styles from designers who sought to reflect social and technological advances in their work. The revival styles were moribund at the beginning of the 20th century and disappeared altogether with the First World War.

REVOLVING CHAIR (also *swivel chair*)
Chair whose seat is attached to central pivot so that it can swivel in any direction. Known since medieval times, the revolving chair has been used widely since the 18th century. The 19th-century craze for mechanical designs produced a tremendous variety of revolving chairs, mostly for commercial use. The form is still chiefly manufactured for business purposes, especially as desk chairs in offices, but it also remains in domestic use.

RIART, CARLOS (b. 1944)
Contemporary Spanish designer of POST-MODERN FURNITURE. Also a designer of interiors and exhibitions, Riart uses elements abstracted from both recent and more remote design history in his furniture.

RIBBAND-BACK CHAIR (or *ribbon-back*)
Eighteenth-century British furniture form; chair designed by and especially associated with Thomas CHIPPENDALE. It was distinguished by an elaborately pierced SPLAT in the form of a carved ribbon, tied in a bow at the top and criss-crossing downward in wide loops, between slender C-scrolls. The form was named by Chippendale in his book the *Director* (1754), in which several versions of it appeared. He wrote of these chairs, "If I may speak without vanity, they are the best I have ever seen."

RICHARDSON, HENRY HOBSON (1838–86)
American architect and designer; most important American architect of the post–Civil War era. Most of Richardson's furniture is built into the woodwork of his public buildings, but he did design movable furniture as well. Richardson's early furniture shows the influence of EASTLAKE and TALBERT, particularly his chairs and benches with exposed joinery and rows of spindles intended as ornamentation. In addition to developing his neo-Romanesque style of architecture, Richardson produced some massive furniture designs with elaborate, carved ornamentation, spiral-turned legs and chair backs of spiral-turned spindles. He specialized in designing dining chairs with high, curved spindle backs and heavy dining tables on spiral-turned pedestals.

RIEMERSCHMID, RICHARD (1868–1957)
German architect and furniture designer associated with ART NOUVEAU and early modern design. Riemerschmid was influenced by the British design reform movements of the late 19th century (*see* ARTS AND CRAFTS MOVEMENT; ART FURNITURE MOVEMENT); he was also an important member of both the DEUTSCHE WERKSTÄTTEN movement and the DEUTSCHER WERKBUND. He designed furniture and other objects in a simple, geometrical version of Art Nouveau, influenced particularly by Henri VAN DE VELDE. Riemerschmid designed some of the first machine-made furniture, which was produced in 1906 by a Werkstätten shop.

RIESENER, JEAN-HENRI (1734–1806)
German-born French ÉBÉNISTE, generally regarded as the leading cabinetmaker of the LOUIS XVI STYLE. Riesener, who was born near Essen, arrived in Paris and entered the workshop of J.-F. OEBEN in about 1754. His early work was ROCOCO FURNITURE similar to Oeben's, using a combination of floral MARQUETRY and geometrical motifs on TRANSITION STYLE forms. On Oeben's death in 1763, Riesener took over the business at the request of the master's widow, whom he married five years later. In the meantime, he completed a number of projects that Oeben had begun, including the famous *bureau du roi*, the first ROLL-TOP DESK, which the king had

commissioned in 1769. Riesener's style gradually changed as the neoclassical taste flowered, but his work changed most when he was appointed royal cabinetmaker on the accession of Louis XVI, in 1774, succeeding Gilles JOUBERT. This was Riesener's period of greatest accomplishment. His furniture became simpler, almost austere. His forms were heavier and more rigorously rectilinear, although he did continue to use the BREAKFRONT shape after it had become generally unfashionable. He replaced marquetry veneering with plain mahogany, and his gilt-bronze mounts were increasingly less elaborate. Riesener used only the finest materials, the level of his craftsmanship was second to none, and his furniture was correspondingly expensive. In 1784 he was replaced as *ébéniste du roi* by a less expensive maker, Guillaume BENEMAN, as part of a budget trimming, but he continued to receive many royal and aristocratic commissions. After the Revolution, Riesener found very little work, and he retired in 1801.

RIETVELD, GERRIT THOMAS (1888–1964)

Dutch architect and furniture maker; important member of DE STIJL school. Gerrit Rietveld abandoned his formal education at the age of 11 to work for his father, a cabinetmaker, and was independently established by 1911. Rietveld made simple furniture in a style influenced by the work of Frank Lloyd WRIGHT and the writings of H. P. BERLAGE. He designed his famous "Red-Blue" chair—a landmark object in 20th-century design—in 1918, about the same year that he became associated with the De Stijl group. Composed of modular elements assembled without joinery, the "Red-Blue" chair was theoretically inexpensive and easy to manufacture, though no one chose to do so. It presented a paradigm of rebellion against revivalist styles and against the elitism implicit in fine (and expensive) craftsmanship. The chair was also a realization of the De Stijl concept of "spiritual" purity of design: it was composed of right angles, which were perceived as the basic relationship in design, and it was painted in primary colors to separate the different elements of the piece from each other visually. The fact that the chair was both uncomfortable and unstable did not disturb Rietveld, for he sought to distill a doctrine in sculptural form, not to fulfill a function. This approach produced characteristically impractical results in most of his designs and distinguishes him from esthetically sympathetic contemporaries, mostly associated with the BAUHAUS, who accepted the precepts of FUNCTIONALISM. However, these designers, who were also in search of a radical new design theory, knew Rietveld's furniture well and valued it highly. The early work of Marcel BREUER, in particular, is indebted to his example. In general, Rietveld's influence on modern furniture was as a model of rigorous purity rather than as a maker of exemplary furniture. After the early 1920s he worked principally as an architect. He did occasionally design furniture into the 1940s, but none of his designs was commercially manufactured.

RIJSWIJK, DIRK VAN (active 1640s)

Dutch BAROQUE FURNITURE maker. Van Rijswijk developed a striking MARQUETRY technique, setting shaped pieces of mother-of-pearl in black marble, generally in floral designs.

RINALDI, GASTONE (b. 1920)

Contemporary Italian furniture designer. Since 1948 Rinaldi has specialized in metal furniture and is best known for modular, collapsible and stackable pieces.

RINCEAU

Eighteenth-century French decorative motif consisting of connected series of carved, inlaid or painted spiraling stems of foliage, often with ACANTHUS leaves.

RING HANDLE

Another name for RING PULL.

RING PULL (also *ring handle*)

Type of furniture HARDWARE; door or drawer handle composed of circular loop of metal, usually brass, suspended from the center of a back plate that is sometimes oval or circular, sometimes in the form of a lion's head or other ornament. Introduced in RENAISSANCE FURNITURE, the ring pull was especially popular in NEOCLASSICAL STYLE furniture of the late 18th and early 19th centuries.

"Red-Blue" chair by Rietveld

ring pull

RING TURNING
See under TURNERY.

RINGUET LE PRINCE, AUGUSTE ÉMILE
See MARCOTTE, Leon.

RISAMBURGH, BERNARD VAN
See VAN RISENBURGH, Bernard.

RIVEN TIMBER
Planks of wood of great strength produced by a technique developed in medieval architecture and shipbuilding and used in furniture since Romanesque times (*see* ROMANESQUE FURNITURE). A tree trunk is split along its medullary rays—that is, from its bark along radii to its center.

ROBERT, HUBERT (1733–1808)
French painter. Best known as a painter of preromantic rococo landscape fantasies, Robert also designed a small amount of furniture in 1787—chairs for Marie-Antoinette's mock dairy at Rambouillet. These pieces, executed by Georges JACOB, were in a variant of the ETRUSCAN STYLE, featuring PALMETTES and other classical motifs.

ROBINSON, GERRARD (1834–91)
British furniture maker in the ROCOCO REVIVAL STYLE. A woodcarver, Robinson worked in Newcastle-upon-Tyne, specializing in massive sideboards with extremely elaborate carved decoration that depicted many figures, often taken from romantic scenes in literature.

**rococo console table
by Bernard Van Risenburgh**

ROCAILLE
French term meaning "rockwork" used in gardens. Originally referring to the rockwork in the artificial grottoes of Versailles, the term came to be applied to any ROCOCO FURNITURE ornamentation resembling a shell or the irregular shapes of garden rocks. It became common in the early 18th century in the phrase *rocaille et coquille,* or "rock and shell," which described the naturalistic ornamentation of the RÉGENCE STYLE. In the 1790s, at a height of enthusiasm for the NEOCLASSICAL STYLE, *rocaille* was derisively altered to *rococo,* thus coining that term, which has since denoted all styles that use *rocaille* ornamentation.

ROCKING CHAIR
Chair mounted on curved slats, called *rockers,* that permit it to be tipped forward and backward. Probably derived from the rocker-mounted CRADLE, the rocking chair first appeared in the United States in the mid–18th century. The most common early rocker, as the chair itself is familiarly called, was an appropriately mounted WINDSOR CHAIR. A number of specific forms later evolved, such as the BOSTON ROCKER. Although the rocking chair has generally been much less popular in the Old World than in the New, one European design has been strikingly successful, the BENTWOOD rocker manufactured by Thonet Brothers (*see* Michael THONET). In the 19th century the rocking chair, itself an ingenious form, lent itself to the age's enthusiasm for mechanical devices and was frequently represented in PATENT FURNITURE; the PLATFORM ROCKER was the most successful variation of the period. Still very popular today, the rocking chair is widely made, both as REPRODUCTION FURNITURE and from new designs.

ROCOCO FURNITURE
Eighteenth-century European furniture characterized by elaborate asymmetrical scrollwork, naturalistic and picturesque decorative motifs and curvilinear forms designed with informality and comfort in mind. This style evolved in reaction against the formal, classically oriented grandeur of the baroque (*see* BAROQUE FURNITURE) and then provoked, in the second half of the century, a return to a NEOCLASSICAL STYLE.

Rococo furniture originated and matured in France before spreading to other European countries. As early as the 1690s, the rigid symmetries of the LOUIS XIV STYLE began to be modified, especially in the work of designer Jean BÉRAIN. The resulting RÉGENCE STYLE was the first phase of the French rococo, led by interior designers Jean LE PAUTRE and Gilles-Marie OPPENORDT and cabinetmaker Charles CRESSENT. Furniture became less formal and more comfortable, and its decoration began to rely on such naturalistic images as shells and flowers rather than classical architectural motifs. The curve dominated furniture forms, and SERPENTINE fronts and arms joined the CABRIOLE LEG (*see under* LEG) as staple elements. A continuing fondness for a 17th-century development, CHINOISERIE decoration, which evoked the landscapes and colorful materials of the Orient, further encouraged an enthusiasm for picturesque and lighthearted decoration. SINGERIE themes, depicting frolicking monkeys, often in human dress, became popular. LACQUER and japanned veneers (*see* JAPANNING) added color to case furniture.

The evolution of the Régence style led to the more extreme *genre pittoresque,* created by J.-A. MEISSONNIER and Nicolas PINEAU in the 1720s. Characterized by bold asymmetry, exaggeratedly swirling scrolls and capriciously strewn motifs, this restless and animated work was the basis for ornamentation in the climactic phase of French rococo design, the LOUIS XV STYLE. New colors, materials and forms contributed to the liveliness of furniture in this extravagant mode. Chinoiserie ornamentation reached new heights of whimsicality in the designs of J.-B. PILLEMENT. Cressent continued to be a leading furniture maker, and A.-R. GAUDREAU, Bernard VAN RISENBURGH, J.-F. OEBEN and others rose to prominence.

Beginning in about 1730, designers and makers in other countries began to adopt the Louis XV style, known chiefly through the published designs of Meissonnier and Pineau. In Spain, French taste was followed closely, if belatedly, but ancient Moorish features (*see* HISPANO-MORESQUE FURNITURE) persisted in complex marquetry applied to rococo forms. In the Catholic centers of Austria, southern Germany and Italy, where the Counter-Reformation had most encouraged baroque grandeur, curvilinear French rococo forms were exaggerated even further, and makers favored exceptionally expensive materials. For example, the leading Italian cabinetmaker at this time, Pietro PIFFETTI, specialized in complex marquetry using such materials as ivory, tortoiseshell, mother-of-pearl and rare imported woods. Elaborate giltbronze mounts were much favored; the leading Italian maker of them, Francesco LADATTE, had trained in Paris.

In southern Germany a long-standing tradition of fine decorative carving was stimulated by the new repertoire of motifs coming from Paris. The great Bavarian architect François CUVILLIÉS designed furniture with much carved decoration in a sparkling manner

even more delicate than that of his French models. Johann van der AUVERA, a sculptor, was noted for console tables that were extremely ornately carved. In northern Germany, French notions of comfort and informality did not always prevail, and rococo decoration was often used simply to embellish older, more stately baroque forms. Again, richness of materials was a priority. In Prussia designer J. M. HOPPENHAUPT, furniture makers J. A. NAHL and the SPINDLER brothers, and metalworker J. M. KAMBLI worked for Frederick the Great, furnishing his palaces at Berlin and Potsdam. The grandly superficial German manner tended to spread northward to Scandinavia (*see* C. F. LEHMANN). In the Low Countries, French influence dominated both carvers, such as Louis LEJEUNE of Liège, and specialists in marquetry, including Andries BONGEN of Amsterdam. However, some Continental furniture makers, notably Abraham ROENTGEN, followed British fashion in adopting a more restrained version of the rococo.

In Britain the French example spurred a rejection of late baroque PALLADIAN STYLE furniture, but the British rococo was milder and less extravagant than the Louis XV style. Palladian architectonic forms, even the suave symmetries of QUEEN ANNE STYLE curves, persisted to some degree. Still, the lighthearted fantasy and animated asymmetry of Meissonnier and Pineau informed British ornamentation, which included ROCAILLE and COQUILLAGE motifs, and serpentine curves were used with enthusiasm. Thomas JOHNSON was the only British designer to approach the extreme restlessness of the *genre pittoresque,* though other makers emulated the decorative opulence of French work, notably Vile & Cobb (*see* William VILE; John COBB), John CHANNON and especially Pierre LANGLOIS, a Frenchman working in England.

PATTERN BOOKS abounded in Britain, ensuring a broad awareness of the new style. An Italian designer, Gaetano BRUNETTI, and a Frenchman named DE LA COUR published rococo designs early in the period, as did Englishman William JONES. Matthias LOCK, Henry COPLAND and Matthias DARLY published books in the 1740s and early 1750s. Darly especially helped to spread a taste for Chinoiserie motifs. In 1754 Thomas CHIPPENDALE published the most influential British pattern book, *The Gentleman and Cabinetmaker's Director,* which dominated rococo fur-

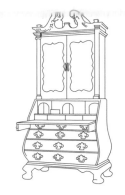

American rococo secretary George Bright

rococo chair

niture design thereafter in both Britain and America (*see* AMERICAN CHIPPENDALE FURNITURE). The success of the *Director* spurred several other designers to issue similar books in the next few years, including Johnson, INCE & MAYHEW and Robert MANWARING.

Chippendale helped to popularize two uniquely British types of rococo furniture, and his book was so prominent that they have been named for him. CHINESE CHIPPENDALE FURNITURE grew out of the period's taste for the exotic, of which Chinoiserie was an example, and it lapsed from fashion when the rococo did, in the 1760s. However, CHIPPENDALE GOTHIC FURNITURE was more than an addition to the picturesque repertoire of rococo devices; it was also a herald of the NEOGOTHIC STYLE, which was to become prominent in the 19th century. Other notable designers who participated in the vogue for Gothic furniture in the 1750s included Batty LANGLEY and Sanderson MILLER.

In France in the 1760s, a reaction against the animation and whimsicality of the rococo began to grow, giving rise to the TRANSITION STYLE, which in turn paved the way for the neoclassical LOUIS XVI STYLE. At about the same time, a similar impulse resulted in the sweeping popularity in Britain of the ADAM STYLE. From the 1770s onward, a neoclassical style was dominant in both countries, and the rococo was doomed. By the time of the French Revolution, beginning in 1789, when the austere new mode was identified with republican virtue, the rococo had been gone for nearly a generation in France and Britain, and elsewhere it was moribund. It lasted into the 1790s only in Venice, Iberia and parts of Germany.

ROCOCO REVIVAL STYLE
Nineteenth-century European and American furniture style, characterized by emphasis on curves, in rounded profiles, CABRIOLE LEGS (*see under* LEG) and scroll feet (*see* SCROLL FOOT, *under* FOOT); by elaborately carved, frequently gilded ornamentation consisting of S- and C-scrolls (*see* SCROLL) and naturalistic motifs; and by use of luxuriant UPHOLSTERY on seating. After the fall of Napoleon in 1815 and the end of the long period of turmoil sparked by the French Revolution, the decorative arts of Europe changed dramatically, and the REVIVAL STYLES came into fashion. The

rising bourgeoisie, rather than royal or aristocratic patrons, became the chief furniture buyers, and they rejected the NEOCLASSICAL STYLE of the previous half-century, looking instead to earlier periods for inspiration. Rococo Revival style furniture followed the 18th-century French LOUIS XV STYLE, but it also bore some resemblance to the earlier BAROQUE FURNITURE of the LOUIS XIV STYLE: it was usually symmetrical, BOULLE MARQUETRY enjoyed a revival, and both C- and S-scrolls were highlighted elements in the ornamental repertoire. Coil-spring upholstery, which was developed at this time, suited the curvilinear character of the Rococo Revival style particularly well, and a number of a new seating forms arose, especially in France. These included the POUF, the BORNE, the CRAPAUD and the INDISCRET. The deeper SEAT RAILS necessitated by the use of coil springs provided a prominent venue for the carved decoration—typically featuring naturalistic fruits, flowers and foliage—that was an important feature of the style.

The Rococo Revival style arose in Britain, where, despite the Napoleonic Wars, French tastes had long been prized. The eclecticism of the REGENCY STYLE promoted experimentation, and as early as 1826, in his PATTERN BOOK of that year, George SMITH published a number of rococo designs; another early designer in this style was Benjamin Dean WYATT. In general, the NEO-GOTHIC STYLE was more popular than the Rococo Revival mode in the British design world of this period, but the more curvilinear furniture enjoyed great commercial popularity and was made through the rest of the century by such well-known firms as GILLOWS.

In France the style became extremely popular during the reign of King Louis Philippe (1830–48), for whom it is sometimes named. It remained fashionable alongside the LOUIS XVI REVIVAL STYLE under the Second Empire and was made in France until the First World War. Among the notable French makers in the style were Claude Aimé CHÉNAVARD, Guillaume GROHÉ, L.-E. LEMARCHAND and the JEANSELME firm.

Italy retained a taste for the neoclassical EMPIRE STYLE until about the mid-19th century, so the Rococo Revival manner, when it arose, quickly tended to incorporate elements of the nationalistic RENAISSANCE REVIVAL STYLE, associated with the unification of the

Italian state, which was completed in 1870. Giuseppe CIMA had published Rococo Revival designs in his *L'Addobatore Moderna* of 1840, and a number of makers produced furniture in the style, especially in the 1850s, but on the whole it was not successful south of the Alps.

The German-speaking countries, influenced by France, were more receptive. In Vienna, the center of Austrian fashion, the Rococo Revival style was quite popular by the 1840s. Among the leading makers there were Heinrich DUBELL and the firm of CARL LEISTLER. Michael THONET also made rococo-inspired furniture before he began his epochal experiments with BENTWOOD, and the curvilinearity of his later work betrays a marked affinity with the revival style. The center for furniture production in Germany itself was Mainz, in Hesse, where Anton BEMBÉ and the firm of Wilhelm KIMBEL of Mainz had introduced the Rococo Revival style as early as the late 1830s. However, in the important states of Bavaria and Prussia, the neoclassical style remained strong, due chiefly to the influence of Leo von KLENZE and Karl Friedrich SCHINKEL, and the rococo-derived manner did not have much success before the 1850s. In Germany, as in Italy, the Renaissance Revival style had largely superseded the Rococo Revival by 1870, although King Ludwig II of Bavaria commissioned much Rococo Revival style furniture, for his fairy-tale castle at Neuschwanstein and for other projects, from such firms as PÖSSENBACHER of Munich. His influence kept the style alive in his kingdom until late in the century.

In America the Rococo Revival style dominated furniture fashion in the 1840s–1870s, when the Renaissance Revival style succeeded it. American Rococo Revival style furniture was spectacularly sculptural, and it is generally held to have been the most successful of the 19th-century rococo schools. Pieces overflowed with naturalistic carving of fruits, flowers and even birds. The leading maker in the style was a German immigrant in New York, John Henry BELTER, who introduced two technical refinements that made possible the virtuosity of this furniture. First, he devised a way to laminate and bend woods, producing forms that were curved in more than one direction and that were strong enough to permit intricate OPENWORK carving. Second, he invented a mechanical saw that could carve complicated figures. His ROSEWOOD furniture was widely imitated, and the term *Belter fur-*

niture came to be applied to all American Rococo Revival pieces. Other important makers in America included Charles BAUDOUINE, J. & J. W. MEEKS and Alexander ROUX, all of New York; George HENCKELS of Philadelphia; François SEIGNOURET of New Orleans; and MITCHELL & RAMMELSBURG, a Cincinnati firm.

ROENTGEN, ABRAHAM (1711–93)

German ROCOCO FURNITURE maker. Roentgen worked in Britain from 1731 to 1738 and followed British styles thereafter, establishing his own workshop at Neuweid, on the Rhine above Bonn, in 1750. He specialized in fine pictorial MARQUETRY on pieces whose other ornamentation was restrained, sometimes influenced by the published designs of Thomas CHIPPENDALE. He also favored mechanical devices such as hidden drawers, complex locks and musical boxes. He retired in 1772, leaving the business to his son David ROENTGEN, soon to be among the foremost cabinetmakers in Europe.

ROENTGEN, DAVID (1743–1807)

German NEOCLASSICAL STYLE cabinetmaker. Roentgen was an apprentice at the workshop of his father, Abraham ROENTGEN, at Neuweid, on the Rhine near Bonn. David took over the company when his father retired in 1772. He increased the volume of production and expanded the range of the market for his work, becoming the most successful furniture maker of his time. He pioneered the construction of furniture by what amounted to assembly methods, with hundreds of craftsmen all working under one roof, at the workshop's height. In 1779 Roentgen established a warehouse and sales office in Paris, and he immediately received more royal patronage than any of the Parisian makers. The Paris guild insisted that he become a member, which he did in 1789, although he never worked in France. He traveled widely, selling much furniture to Catherine the Great of Russia in 1783 and establishing outlets in Vienna and Naples. In 1791 he became court furnisher of Prussia.

However, the French Revolution ruined Roentgen. His Paris stock was confiscated by the Revolutionary government, and not long afterward, in 1794, his Neuweid workshop was sacked by the French army. Roentgen fled to Berlin and did not return to Neuweid before 1802. He was unable to reestablish his business before he died at Wiesbaden in 1807.

At first, Roentgen's furniture followed the British-influenced rococo mode of his father, but gradually it came to conform to the rising neoclassical taste. Curves disappeared, though Roentgen's solid, rectilinear forms tended to be more massive than most Parisian LOUIS XVI–STYLE work. Naturalistic ornamentation gave way to columns, cornices and other elements of classical architecture. Before 1780 Roentgen favored elaborate pictorial marquetry, often taken from the work of French graphic artist J.-B. PILLEMENT, French rococo painter François Boucher (1703–70) and German painter Januarius Zick (1730–97). After 1780, though, he emphasized plain wood veneering, usually of figured MAHOGANY. He also specialized in furniture with intricate mechanical devices, such as concealed drawers and elaborate locks. Furthermore, many of his pieces could be disassembled for transport, an ingenious innovation.

roll-top desk

ROHDE, GILBERT (1894–1944)
American furniture designer of the 1930s associated with the INTERNATIONAL STYLE. Rohde, the son of a cabinetmaker, was principally a furniture designer. With Raymond Loewy and others, however, Rohde is associated with the advent of modern industrial design in America. He was an important promoter of the avant-garde European styles of the day and designed furniture in the International style. Rohde was particularly influenced by the work of Ludwig MIES VAN DER ROHE, designing furniture that was austere, simple and geometrical in form, with lines expressive of a piece's function. Like his European contemporaries, he considered it important to address the problems of mass manufacture, in terms of form and materials. He responded to the example of the Finnish designer Alvar AALTO and began to use bentwood and laminated plywood in his furniture. Rohde's influence in spreading the functionalist ideas of the International style (*see* FUNCTIONALISM) was furthered by his association with the HERMAN MILLER FURNITURE CO., for which he began designing in 1931. Rohde subsequently became the firm's design director

and remained with the firm until his death, when he was succeeded by George NELSON.

ROHLFS, CHARLES (1853–1936)
American furniture designer associated with ART NOUVEAU and ARTS AND CRAFTS MOVEMENT. Rohlfs was both an actor and a designer of cast-iron stoves before turning to furniture design. He established a workshop in Buffalo, New York, and manufactured individually crafted pieces to order. Rohlfs worked in the Arts and Crafts tradition, employing simple rectilinear designs with exposed joinery. Later he was well known for his decorative carving and marquetry, which resembled European Art Nouveau styles. It has also been said that some of his ornamentation may have derived from the work of American architect Louis Sullivan (*see* PRAIRIE SCHOOL). Sullivan's Guaranty Building, built in Buffalo in 1894, is noted for its organic decorative detail. Rohlfs's later work was very popular in Europe, where he was regarded as the principal American examplar of Art Nouveau.

ROLL MOLDING
See under MOLDING.

ROLL-TOP DESK
Desk with convex TAMBOUR shutter that slides over the working surface, creating a horizontal quarter-cylinder. Invented by the French *ébéniste* Jean-François OEBEN in about 1760, the roll-top desk has remained popular ever since.

ROLLWORK
Another term for STRAPWORK.

ROMANESQUE FURNITURE
Early MEDIEVAL FURNITURE. It emerged as part of a distinctive cultural style after the fall of the Roman Empire and prevailed until the ascendancy of GOTHIC FURNITURE in the 14th century. Almost no furniture has survived from the centuries of chaos in western Europe after Rome's fall, though occasional illustrations and subsequent practices in vernacular furniture suggest that it was extremely crude for the most part—simple forms com-

posed of roughly hewn logs and branches. However, a few remnants from the time of the Carolingian dynasty in France (751–987)—most notably the so-called Throne of Dagobert, an elaborate X-FRAME chair of bronze—reveal that forms and ideas survived from ROMAN FURNITURE.

By about the year 1000, a distinctive and fully developed culture had evolved. Its principal artistic expression produced great masonry cathedrals, and Romanesque furniture took its inspiration from religious architecture. Medieval furniture forms tended to look like miniature buildings, with applied PILASTERS and various types of ARCADING. The Romanesque period takes its name from the semicircular, or rounded, arch, associated with ancient Roman buildings, that predominated among these architectural motifs. Other motifs included simple geometric arrangements, such as bands of alternating diamonds and circles, either incised or painted. Painted decoration was in brilliant, vivid hues on gilded or colored grounds. Another popular method of ornamentation, CHIP CARVING, also derived from masonry work. Most furniture of the period was made of oak, generally of RIVEN TIMBER.

Only wealthy landowners, a small minority of people in the Romanesque world, could afford or appreciate furniture of any pretensions to excellence. One function of medieval furniture was to display its owner's position in the social hierarchy of an extremely status-conscious world. The forms that chiefly fulfilled this purpose were the BUFFET and the elaborate CHAIR OF ESTATE. This latter piece often preserved the curving X-frame legs of the Roman SELLA CURULIS. At the end of the period, the CANOPY over a chair or bed appeared, apparently from BYZANTINE FURNITURE, and also assumed the same socially symbolic role. Another aspect of Romanesque furniture that reflected the elite position of its users was an emphasis on portability, for the powerful lords of the time led itinerant lives, constantly moving from one residence to another (see MEDIEVAL FURNITURE).

CHESTS remained the most common furniture form, and a distinctive Romanesque decorative mode emerged in connection with them—the iron bands used to strengthen these pieces were made in whorls and other geometrical shapes. Such ironwork also appeared on the simple CUPBOARDS and PRESSES that were used at this time. Crude joinery, chiefly built to withstand hard travel, was concealed somewhat by vivid polychrome decoration. An exception to the insistence on portability were a few truly massive standing presses that remained in the nearly bare residence in its owner's absence.

Another such exception was the large TABLE DORMANT. Most tables, though, were smaller and made in various shapes. A semicircular form, intended for use against a wall, may have recalled the CONSOLE TABLE of late Roman times, and it certainly presages the later reemergence of that form. Tables were ordinarily undecorated and made of crude joinery, for they were invariably covered with TABLECLOTHS when in use. Writing tables, equipped with small cupboards for storing materials, and the LECTERN, often combined with such a table, appeared in Romanesque furniture, having first been developed in the Byzantine Empire.

Common stools and benches were the most prominent types of seating. These were simple assemblages of elements, with turned or rectangular members, usually painted in brilliant colors; benches sometimes doubled as tables. The X-frame stool still bore the stamp of official dignity associated with its classical original, and it was a lesser relative of the chair of estate. This stool is probably the furniture form most frequently illustrated in Romanesque manuscript painting. Chairs were rare, apart from the chair of estate, and were generally accompanied by a footstool.

Two sorts of bed were made. One was based on chest construction, with low, wall-like sides. A gap in the middle of one side enabled the user to get in and out more easily. More stately beds had complexly turned members joined in a frame. The TRUSSING BED was also common, and the wheeled COUCHETTE was one of several variant forms that could be used as a DAYBED. The bed canopy, when it appeared late in the period, was a separate structure surrounding the bed.

While the Romanesque was truly an international style in furniture, the beginnings of national distinctions can be inferred, despite the generally scanty evidence. In Italy, where the influence of the Byzantine Empire was stronger than elsewhere in western Europe, the emphasis on architectural references in furniture was most pronounced. The subsequent Gothic style was not popular in Italy, and Romanesque furniture continued to be made there until the Renaissance. French Romanesque furniture was noted particularly for extensive arcading. England followed the French example, receiving the style late, after the Norman Conquest in 1066. In Germany and Scandinavia a penchant for turnings yielded rows of spindles between framing elements, and split BALUSTERS were used decoratively as APPLIQUÉS, placed edge to edge in geometrical patterns on vertical surfaces. By the late 12th century, the Gothic style in architecture had spread throughout northern Europe, though Romanesque features dominated the applied arts into the 14th century.

ROMAN FURNITURE

Furniture of ancient Roman Republic and Empire, used wherever Rome was dominant, from about the third century B.C. until the beginning of the Middle Ages. Drawing largely on GREEK FURNITURE—and therefore retaining ideas and forms that dated all the way back to EGYPTIAN FURNITURE—the Romans developed their own characteristic style, marked by a love of lush ornamentation and a penchant for practicality.

Both of these traits were present in the FULCRUM, an addition to the Greek KLINE, the COUCH that was the most important piece of furniture in the classical world. This alteration of the *kline* led, in the first century A.D., to the development of the LECTUS, a form with a back and sides that has ever since been associated with the term *couch*. Late in the Roman period, a specialized couch designed for use by a group of reclining diners, the SIGMA, appeared.

As was true throughout the ancient world, the stool was the most common form of seating, and the Romans adopted all the standard Greek forms, including the DIPHROS and the DIPHROS OKLADIAS. The latter, a folding stool, inspired the Roman SELLA CURULIS, which served as a symbol of political authority. A Greek chair, the KLISMOS, was also used by the Romans, though in a heavy version lacking the grace and easy portability that had originally characterized the form. A distinctive tub-shaped chair originated by the Etruscans (*see* ETRUSCAN FURNITURE) was adopted more successfully. It appeared in wickerwork, and the back often extended into a hood above the user. This chair was very popular throughout the Roman Empire and was manufactured in far-flung territories such as England.

Roman tables were derived from Greek models but also included some new forms. The small, round, three-legged tables devised in Greece continued to be used by individual diners and were popular throughout Roman times, though late in the era, a larger dining table, the MENSA LUNATA, appeared. Similar to the smaller tables were light, collapsible frames with three or four legs connected by crossbars that could move up and down the legs on slides. These frames, which were also sometimes made as rigid stands, supported trays or bowls.

The Romans introduced the use of side tables in the dining room, including the first examples of the CONSOLE TABLE, built against the wall, which would reappear in later European furniture. And under the Empire a large table with a rectangular wood or marble top supported at either end by an elaborately carved upright marble slab was devised. This form was to be appropriated enthusiastically by Italian Renaissance furniture makers (*see* RENAISSANCE FURNITURE). In addition, the Romans pioneered the use of four-legged tables with stretchers, often low enough to function as seats but also used as worktables in kitchens or workshops.

The CUPBOARD came into its own in the Roman era, being used more widely than it had been in Hellenistic times, when it was new. Otherwise, case furniture remained limited to chests, which generally were quite substantial carcases, on low feet, decorated with sculptural bronze mounts.

The Roman love of opulent decoration was reflected in intricate inlay work in wood (citrus woods and maple were prized rarities), ivory and precious metals, as well as in elaborate carving and applied ornamentation.

Roman furniture was the most highly developed and sophisticated in ancient Europe, in terms of both complexity of ornamentation and range of forms. It made a later contribution to furniture history when, following the relatively desolate centuries between antiquity and the Renaissance (*see* MEDIEVAL FURNITURE), European thinkers, artists and designers began to rediscover the ideas and designs of the classical world, which have continued to exert an influence to the present day (*see* NEOCLASSICAL STYLE).

ROMAN SPINDLE WINDSOR CHAIR
See SPINDLE-BACK WINDSOR CHAIR, *under* WINDSOR CHAIR.

ROMAYNE WORK
Decorative motif on RENAISSANCE FURNITURE of northern Europe, especially England, consisting of a human head carved in high relief and set in a ROUNDEL. Inspired by an awareness of the Italian Renaissance, Romayne—that is, "Roman"—work was intended as a classical motif, but it was commonly applied on pieces otherwise uninformed by classicism, and it is regarded as an indication of the unsophisticated character of early TUDOR FURNITURE.

ROOT FURNITURE
CHINESE FURNITURE genre, in which stools, chairs and tables were made from tree roots, chosen for their knotty, twisted appearance and minimally pruned and worked. These odd-looking pieces are depicted in paintings of the Song dynasty (960–1279) and may have been produced even earlier. However, they are particularly associated with the Ming dynasty (1368–1644) and were made through the Qing (1644–1911). Their rustic simplicity was combined with ingenious JOINERY that made the furniture sturdy while interfering as little as possible with the organic growth pattern of the material.

Artificial ornamentation or carving was never used on root furniture. Like Chinese sculpture consisting of oddly shaped stones, it was associated with an attitude toward nature, of seeing natural forms and details as important sources of philosophical and artistic stimulation, that Taoism and certain Buddhist sects shared. Root furniture was often found in the rural retreats of scholar-artists, but its combination of simplicity and sophistication had a wide appeal, and it was also used by urban officials, aristocrats and even some emperors. In the 19th century root furniture was sometimes made in the West, in emulation of the Chinese mode.

ROPE MOLDING
See under MOLDING.

ROPE TURNING
See under TURNERY.

ROSELLI, ALBERTO (1921–76)
Italian architect and industrial designer. Son-in-law and partner of Gio PONTI, Roselli also had his own industrial practice, for which he developed a wide range of product designs. In the 1970s he designed molded plastic furniture in a style clearly influenced by the work of Charles EAMES and Eero SAARINEN.

ROSETTE
Decorative device; circular shape carved, inlaid or painted as a stylized flower. The rosette has been used as ornamentation in all styles since ancient GREEK FURNITURE.

ROSEWOOD
Any of a number of HARDWOODS found from Southeast Asia and India to Central and South America. The rosewoods are highly decorative in appearance, ranging in color from dark purple-brown to pink, often with pronounced figuring. The name refers to the wood's scent when fresh. There are several important varieties of rosewood. Bombay rosewood, from India, is quite purple and often very dark. Rio rosewood, from Brazil, is browner, and it is more boldly figured, as the Western Hemisphere species are in general. Another Brazilian variety, KINGWOOD, is quite pink. While it is difficult to work, its appearance has made rosewood popular with European and American cabinetmakers, who have used it, especially for veneering and decorative inlay work, since the 17th century. It was particularly prominent in 18th-century Britain.

ROSSO FIORENTINO (1495–1540) (born *Giovanni Batista Rosso*)
Florentine painter, decorator and stuccoist; leading practitioner of the MANNERIST STYLE and an important influence on French RENAISSANCE FURNITURE. He was brought to France by King François I in 1532 and was, with Francesco PRIMATICCIO, a leader of the School of Fontainebleau and the FRANÇOIS I STYLE. Generally credited with the invention of the decorative device STRAPWORK, Rosso was also an important designer of silver plate.

ROUBO, ANDRÉ JACOB (1739–91)
Eighteenth-century French furniture maker and designer. Roubo, a MENUISIER who worked

Romayne work

rosette

in both the LOUIS XV and LOUIS XVI STYLES, issued a series of engravings between 1769 and 1775 that encompassed both ROCOCO FURNITURE and some of the earliest published designs in the NEOCLASSICAL STYLE.

ROUNDABOUT CHAIR (1)

Chair made in India and the East Indies in the 18th century. It had six legs that supported a circular seat, with a semicircular back that was canted to the rear. It was sometimes made as a REVOLVING CHAIR. The roundabout chair was often produced for export to Europe, and makers frequently used such distinctly European features as the CABRIOLE LEG (*see under* LEG). From the East Indies this chair was exported to Holland, where it was known as a *burgomaster chair.*

ROUNDABOUT CHAIR (2)

Another name for CORNER CHAIR, INDISCRET and COMPANION CHAIR.

ROUNDEL

Decorative device; small, circular ornament, often containing a representation or motif. A roundel may be used singly, sometimes as a BOSS, or in a linear series. The roundel, a very ancient device, has been used in all styles of ornamentation.

ROUNDEL MOLDING

Another name for ASTRAGAL MOLDING (*see under* MOLDING).

ROUSSEAU, CLÉMENT (1872–1950)

French ART DECO furniture maker. Rousseau is noted for his simple, elegant designs, which combined exotic materials with nontraditional forms. He was one of the furniture makers commissioned by Jacques DOUCET in the 1920s.

ROUSSEL, PIERRE (1723–82)

French furniture maker in both LOUIS XV and LOUIS XVI STYLES. Roussel specialized in MARQUETRY of all sorts, from plain veneering through geometrical patterns and floral motifs to complex pictorial representation.

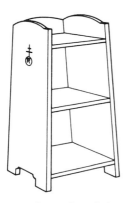

Roycroft standing shelves

ROUX, ALEXANDER (active 1837–81)

New York furniture maker in several of the REVIVAL STYLES. Roux, a French immigrant, exemplified the eclecticism of 19th-century American furniture. He produced fine work in virtually all of the revival modes, from the NEO-GOTHIC STYLE of the 1840s to the NEO-GREC STYLE of the 1860s and 1870s, and he used decorations that included wood carving, ormolu mounts, porcelain plaques and *faux*-bamboo turnery. Roux also imported and sold furniture made by his brother, a Parisian cabinetmaker.

ROWAN

See WHITEBEAM.

ROWLAND, DAVID (b. 1924)

Contemporary American furniture designer; a leading maker of furniture in the HIGH-TECH STYLE. Before the Second World War, Rowland studied in California with the Hungarian artist László Moholy-Nagy; afterward he attended the Cranbrook Academy in Michigan (*see* Eliel SAARINEN). In the early 1950s he went to work for Norman Bel GEDDES in New York. Rowland then established his own design practice in 1955, and soon began his experiments in the use of steel and plastics in furniture. He was intent on accomplishing, in his own words, "the most with the least." Rowland is particularly noted for two designs, the "40-in-4" stacking chair (1964) and the "Sof-Tech" chair (1979). The "40-in-4" is named because it is so delicate and finely engineered that 40 chairs will form a stack only four feet high. The "Sof-Tech" chair, manufactured by Thonet Brothers (*see* Michael THONET), is an ingenious application of industrial materials. Its resilient seat and back are sections of steel-wire upholstery springs coated with the plastic PVC and attached to a tubular-steel frame.

ROYCROFT COMMUNITY

Community of manufacturing workshops in East Aurora, New York; producers of Arts and Crafts style furniture (*see* ARTS AND CRAFTS MOVEMENT). Elbert Hubbard, a wealthy businessman, established the Roycrofters in 1895. He had met William MORRIS the year before and been impressed by him, so the first product of a Roycroft shop was a book (*The Song of Songs*) modeled on the output of Morris's Kelmscott Press. Hubbard declined to adopt Morris's political ideals, however. The Roycroft Community was not a socialist, profit-sharing enterprise like Gustav STICKLEY's United Crafts; Hubbard was a capitalist who paid his craftsmen a salary and pocketed the profits. Leather-bound books and other leather goods were the community's principal output—Roycrofter furniture was only one of many product lines. The furniture was modeled on British Arts and Crafts pieces. Accordingly, it was rectilinear, simple and unadorned, though generally heavier and less elegant than its British counterparts. Hubbard once described it as "severe and rarely beautiful." Like Stickley's work, Roycrofter furniture became known as MISSION FURNITURE. A design feature that became a Roycroft hallmark was a tapering leg ending in a distinctive, cushion-shaped foot. All pieces bore the Roycroft logo, an *R* within a circle, topped with a double-armed cross. Hubbard was well known as a writer, especially for the book *A Message to Garcia*. The workshop continued to operate until 1938, more than a generation after Hubbard's death on the *Lusitania* in 1915.

RUCKER, THOMAS (c. 1532–1606)

German metalworker and maker of RENAISSANCE FURNITURE. A noted crafter of sword hilts and scientific apparatus, Rucker also made furniture, including a notable chair of steel that the city of Augsburg presented to the Holy Roman Emperor in 1574. Rucker chiseled its decoration, an elaborate sculptural program of figures and reliefs depicting scenes from classical history.

RUHLMANN, ÉMILE-JACQUES (1879–1933)

Leading French ART DECO furniture maker. Born in Paris, Ruhlmann began his career as a painter but turned to furniture design in 1901, first exhibiting his work in 1910. After the First World War, he established a workshop to manufacture furniture in his distinctive style. Favoring a balance between massive and delicate elements, Ruhlmann was partial to heavy pieces with finely tapered legs ending in ivory or metal sabots, decorated with exquisite ivory or wood inlays of floral motifs. He used only

cabinet by Ruhlmann

the most costly, precious materials, exemplifying the frank opulence so characteristic of Art Deco. Ruhlmann's work also typifies the traditionalist aspect of Art Deco: his designs were often based on traditional forms, and scroll-work and reeding were prominent in his decorative repertoire. He also used the ESTAMPILLE, an 18th-century method of signing pieces. On the other hand, Ruhlmann could be quite innovative in the design of decorative elements. For instance, he devised a leg, tapered at both the top and bottom, that seemed to emerge organically from the carcase of the piece rather than be attached to it. This became his hallmark, along with exemplary proportions and craftsmanship, which has often been classed with the work of the great *ébénistes* of the 18th century. Ruhlmann remained an important practitioner of the style of his day. In his last years he moved toward the sleeker, undecorated INTERNATIONAL STYLE and contributed pieces to the Indore Palace (*see* Eckart MUTHESIUS).

RUMPP, JOHANNES (active c. 1740)

German BAROQUE FURNITURE designer. In about 1740 he published a PATTERN BOOK of late baroque designs for case furniture with particularly florid ornamentation.

RUNNER FEET

Another name for SLEDGE FEET.

RUNNING DOG

Another name for VITRUVIAN SCROLL.

rush seat

RUSH SEAT
Woven seat for stool or chair, made from cylindrical stems of one of the aquatic family of rush plants. Woven rushes, used to make baskets in ancient cultures, were first used to make seating in medieval times.

RUSKIN, JOHN (1819–1900)
British writer and art historian. Ruskin wrote on all aspects of society and culture. Though he was never a designer, he influenced furniture design greatly through his writings and, indirectly, through the work of his follower William MORRIS. Preaching that the true and proper integration of art and society had existed in the days of the medieval craft guilds and that the Industrial Revolution had damaged this ideal world, Ruskin advocated a conscious rejection of industrialization and a return to the exclusive use of handmade goods. This reactionary posture sparked a renewed interest in craftsmanship among designers, especially Morris, whose work stimulated many pre-modernist design movements, such as the British ARTS AND CRAFTS MOVEMENT and the various German movements (*see* DEUTSCHER WERKBUND; DEUTSCHE WERKSTÄTTEN; WIENER WERKSTÄTTE.)

RUSSELL, GORDON (1892–1980)
Twentieth-century British furniture designer associated with the INTERNATIONAL STYLE and UTILITY FURNITURE. Gordon Russell joined his father's furniture-making company in rural Worcestershire after the First World War. At first, he designed furniture after the manner of the ARTS AND CRAFTS MOVEMENT, especially the work of Ernest GIMSON. In the course of the 1920s, however, he gradually absorbed modernist design developments; by the 1930s he was producing distinctly austere machinemade furniture in the International style. Russell expanded the family firm with an outlet in London, through which he sold Thonet chairs (*see* Michael THONET) and furniture by Alvar AALTO as well as his own work. During the Second World War, Russell was responsible for overseeing the designs employed in Britain's Utility Furniture program. After the war he was the first director of the Council on Industrial Design, a government-sponsored enterprise intended to improve British Industrial design and ultimately bolster Britain's export trade. From his position as director, Russell influenced a new generation of British furniture designers, including Robin DAY and Ernest RACE.

RUSSELL, RICHARD DREW (1903–1981)
British architect and CONTEMPORARY STYLE furniture designer. Trained as an architect, R. D. Russell, brother of Gordon RUSSELL, entered the family furniture-manufacturing firm in 1929 and soon became its design director. After the Second World War, in private practice, Russell designed furniture in the emerging Contemporary style. His work was particularly influential because he was also a popular professor of furniture design at the Royal College of Art. He participated in the well-known redesign of the Greek galleries of the British Museum in the late 1960s.

Saarinen, Eero (1910–61)

American architect and furniture designer. Son of Eliel SAARINEN, Eero Saarinen was educated at his father's Cranbrook Academy, and then in Paris, where he studied sculpture, and at the architecture school of Yale University. Principally an architect—one of the most original and important of his generation—Saarinen also produced several important furniture designs. In 1940 he collaborated with Charles EAMES in designing storage units and molded plywood chairs. Their designs won prizes at the Museum of Modern Art's influential "Organic Design in Home Furnishings" competition. These chairs were the first in which multidirectional curves were used in the molding process; they thus represented an advance beyond earlier work by such designers as Alvar AALTO and Marcel BREUER. A single sheet of plywood—manipulated to form the chair's seat, back and arms—was mounted atop slender legs. This sculptural form anticipated later work in plastics and sparked a revolution in the use of new materials and techniques.

In 1946 Saarinen designed the "Womb" chair for Knoll Associates (*see* Florence Schust KNOLL). This chair was a sculpted fiberglass shell clearly derived from his 1940 designs with Eames, but it was much deeper and wider than those earlier models. Its proportions were very generous, and it had foam-rubber cushions and upholstery; it hung by the arms from a substructure of steel rods. This extremely comfortable piece has become a modern classic, as has Saarinen's "Tulip" chair (1957), also for Knoll. The "Tulip" chair—manufactured in a range that includes stools, side chairs and armchairs—was also made of fiberglass. Its shell was less elaborately

molded than the "Womb" chair's and was mounted on a cast-aluminum pedestal stem with a flaring circular base. The whole constitutes a fluid, organic arrangement of curves. Matching tables on pedestal feet were made in various sizes and with wood or marble tops.

Their unornamented simplicity and their reliance on new materials and processes make these chairs true descendants of European INTERNATIONAL STYLE furniture. However, Saarinen's work also represents the tendency of postwar American design to move away from the earlier, BAUHAUS-inspired geometrical angularity toward a freer, more sculptural style. This shift marked the beginning of a new epoch in the history of 20th-century furniture.

Saarinen, Eliel (1873–1950)

Finnish-American architect, designer and educator. As a young architect, Eliel Saarinen designed furniture for his commissions, which included the Finnish pavilion at the Paris Exposition of 1900. His furniture designs represented a restrained variant of ART NOUVEAU, synthesizing the influences of the WIENER WERKSTÄTTE and the DEUTSCHE WERKSTÄTTEN movements with the NATIONAL ROMANTICISM of Finland. But Saarinen was principally an architect and in 1922 he was awarded second prize in the architectural competition to design the Chicago Tribune Tower, prompting him to immigrate to America. There he became involved with the Cranbrook Academy, an arts-oriented secondary school near Ann Arbor, Michigan, first as architect and later as director and teacher. Cranbrook was to be Saarinen's home until his death. He designed all of its buildings and much of its furniture. The furniture was executed in a clean, modern

Saarinen chair

style, owing much to contemporary ART DECO designs, subdued in character but rich in fine woods. Saarinen appointed Charles EAMES to a post at Cranbrook in the late 1930s, and the academy produced a number of subsequently important American furniture designers, including Florence Schust KNOLL, Harry BERTOIA and Saarinen's son, Eero SAARINEN.

SABER LEG
See under LEG.

SABOT
Metal fitting for bottom of a furniture leg, used especially in French furniture beginning in the very late 17th century. *Sabot* means "hoof"—and, by extension, "wooden clog" or "shoe"—and its purpose was to protect the veneer of a piece of furniture at the feet, where it was particularly likely to be chipped.

sabot

SACK-BACK WINDSOR CHAIR
See BOW-BACK WINDSOR CHAIR, *under* WINDSOR CHAIR.

SADDLE SEAT
Carved chair seat resembling a saddle, in that the seating surface has a modestly depressed central area, with a slight central ridge running back from the front edge. The saddle seat is best known as a feature of the WINDSOR CHAIR.

SADUBIN, LEON (b. c. 1945)
AUSTRALIAN FURNITURE designer and maker. Sadubin, who has traveled to Scandinavia to study, has been a leading Australian exponent of the simple, clean-lined wood furniture popularized throughout the world by SCANDINAVIAN MODERN makers. His work of the 1990s, however, has involved more sculptural forms and the use of additional materials, such as slate.

armoire by Sambin

SALEM ROCKER
See BOSTON ROCKER.

SALEM SECRETARY
FEDERAL PERIOD case-furniture form; glass-doored bookcase mounted on a FALL-FRONT DESK. This secretary was developed and made in Salem, Massachusetts, in the late 18th century.

SALTIRE STRETCHER
See under STRETCHER.

SALVIN, ANTHONY (1799–1881)
British architect and furniture designer in the ELIZABETHAN REVIVAL STYLE. In his day Salvin was regarded as a principal authority on the architecture and furniture of the Elizabethan period, though when designing furniture for his architectural commissions—country houses, for the most part—he largely used 17th-century elements, as did other practitioners of the so-called Elizabethan style.

SAMBIN, HUGHES (c. 1515–1600)
French designer and woodcarver, associated with RENAISSANCE FURNITURE. Sambin is often cited as the earliest French cabinetmaker, although no piece of furniture can be attributed to him with certainty. His reputation rests on a number of engravings published in 1572 as a PATTERN BOOK, *Oeuvres de la diversité des termes,* a collection of designs for decorative TERMS and CARYATIDS. Much furniture of the time was clearly influenced by these designs and by those of J. A. DU CERCEAU, and this body of work constitutes the first distinctively French furniture, deliberately different from that of the Italian Renaissance, in the spirit of the HENRI II STYLE. Sambin's designs are in the MANNERIST STYLE of the day, using elaborate carving to render extremely fanciful imagery.

SAN CAI TU HUI (SAN TS'AI T'U HUI)
CHINESE FURNITURE form popular from Song dynasty (960–1279) into Ming (1368–1644); folding chair with X-FRAME at each side, back with headrest and long arms reaching well forward. The legs were joined at the feet by front and rear STRETCHERS, the front one bearing a broad footrest. The back of the *san cai tu hui* sloped to the rear, permitting the user to recline. Its name translates as "chair of the old man who has been drinking," and this piece resembled a later chair with a similar name, the ZUI WENG YI, or "drunken lord's chair."

SANDALWOOD

Aromatic HARDWOOD from India, valued chiefly for its oil, a perfume ingredient. Sandalwood, which is very easily carved, is also used in India to make furniture and small decorative objects.

SANDERSON, ELIJAH (1751–1825)

FEDERAL PERIOD furniture maker of Salem, Massachusetts. With his brother Jacob (1757–1810), Sanderson made much well-crafted furniture for export to the American South and to Latin America. Samuel MCINTIRE carved the ornamentation on some of the Sandersons' pieces.

SAPELE

West African HARDWOOD resembling MAHOGANY and often used in modern furniture of Europe and America. It is also used to make plywood.

SAPPER, RICHARD (b. 1932)

Contemporary German-Italian industrial designer. Born in Germany and trained there in engineering and economics, Sapper was a designer for Daimler-Benz before moving to Italy in 1958. There he worked for Gio PONTI and, until 1977, often collaborated with Marco ZANUSO. Sapper and Zanuso produced notable functionalist furniture (see FUNCTIONALISM) that revealed an emphasis on the use of new materials. However, Sapper is primarily known as a designer of electronic goods. Since 1980 he has been a principal product-design consultant for IBM.

SATIN WALNUT

British name for RED GUM.

SATINWOOD

Two satinwoods, from related trees on opposite sides of the globe, have been used by European and American cabinetmakers. Both hardwoods are a warm yellow in color. WEST INDIAN SATINWOOD was prominent in the 18th century and is associated with the NEOCLASSICAL STYLE; since the early 19th century, though, CEYLON SATINWOOD has been more commonly used. The term is sometimes applied, inaccurately, to JI CHI MU, a wood used in CHINESE FURNITURE.

SAUNIER, CLAUDE-CHARLES (1735–1807)

French LOUIS XVI STYLE cabinetmaker. The son and grandson of ÉBÉNISTES, Saunier succeeded his father in the family business in 1765. He specialized in small, graceful ROLL-TOP DESKS and CONSOLES DESSERTS, usually veneered in a light-colored wood inlaid with ebony or another dark wood. He also used Oriental LACQUER and VERNIS MARTIN.

SAUSAGE TURNING

See under TURNERY.

SAVERY, WILLIAM (1721–88)

Maker of PHILADELPHIA CHIPPENDALE FURNITURE. With Thomas AFFLECK, Savery represented the more restrained Philadelphia furniture makers. A Quaker, he favored relatively plain designs, ranging from quite simple, undecorated chairs to soberly elegant Chippendale highboys. In addition to examples provided by Chippendale, Savery also drew on the patterns of Batty LANGLEY, another British designer.

SAVONAROLA CHAIR

Nineteenth-century name for an Italian MEDIEVAL and RENAISSANCE FURNITURE form: X-FRAME chair with six or more frames, arranged from front to back. Its structure resembled that of its ultimate ancestor, the ancient Roman SELLA CURULIS. The Savonarola chair was decorated with classical motifs, generally inlaid or carved in low relief. While it had some of the character of the Medieval CHAIR OF ESTATE, it was not so explicitly a symbol of rank, and many were made. Much later, VICTORIAN PERIOD designers associated the chair with Girolamo Savonarola (1452–98), the Tuscan religious and political reformer whose execution for heresy was a key event of the Italian Renaissance.

Savonarola chair

SCAGLIOLA

Mixture of plaster and various sorts of powdered stone, used to imitate marble. Known since Roman times, when it was used for interior architectural ornamentation, scagliola first appeared in furniture in 16th-century Italy. It was employed to make tops for tables and commodes, throughout Europe, especially in the 17th and 18th centuries. It could also be used to simulate PIETRE DURE work.

**Scandinavian Modern
Finn Juhl**

SCANDINAVIAN MODERN

Style of furniture designed and made in Scandinavia—especially in Finland, Sweden and Denmark—in the 20th century. In general, Scandinavian Modern designers have stressed excellent craftsmanship and traditional materials and techniques while also responding to modern influences and producing innovative furniture in a variety of styles, all of them functional in character.

The Scandinavian Modern style is grounded in the late 19th and early 20th centuries, when modern design styles began to affect traditional Scandinavian cabinetmaking. Most important, German publications dealing with ART NOUVEAU and visits to Britain by Scandinavian craftsmen, such as Louis SPARRE (*see* NATIONAL ROMANTICISM), brought the British ARTS AND CRAFTS MOVEMENT to Scandinavia.

Following the First World War, Finnish architect and designer Alvar AALTO studied and was impressed by early 20th-century Viennese furniture, and his interest led to a continuing interest in industrial design in his country. Aalto's work was influential in Sweden during the 1930s, and his example was reinforced by the presence in that country of Austrian expatriate Josef FRANK, who had been associated with the DEUTSCHE WERKSTÄTTEN movement. A well-known designer of furniture and textiles, Frank shared the growing concern for designing effectively for mass manufacture. All these influences helped spur the first truly distinctive new Scandinavian mode in furniture design—a style known throughout Europe and America as "Swedish Modern." Such designers as Gunnar ASPLUND, Karl Bruno MATHSSON and Carl MALMSTEN produced pointedly utilitarian furniture in a style derived from traditional design.

During the 1930s leadership in Scandinavian design shifted to Denmark. The most important Danish designer before the Second World War was Kaare KLINT. By virtue of his long teaching career and the example of his own designs, Klint was able to preserve a tradition of fine wood handicraft in the face of the burgeoning influence of the INTERNATIONAL STYLE and the BAUHAUS designers. However, he also advocated a homegrown doctrine of beauty-in-utility that paralleled the FUNCTIONALISM of modern design theory. Klint's influence led to an emphasis on craft that distinguished Danish furniture from the more machined Finnish work, even when Danish designs were later mass-produced.

Since the Second World War, Scandinavian furniture has had an international audience and influence. Beginning in the late 1940s, Danish work, along with Aalto's, became phenomenally popular abroad, especially in the United States. The most important figures in this flowering were the Danes Arne JACOBSEN, Poul KJAERHOLM, Finn JUHL and Hans WEGNER. A trend toward mass production and experimentation with new materials and industrial processes was begun by Peter HVIDT and others and made popular by Jacobsen and Kjaerholm. Juhl designed in a free-form sculptural style that Jacobsen, Verner PANTON and Finnish designer Eero AARNIO carried further. Jacobsen was famous for his extraordinary designs in molded plastic, and Panton was also an important innovator in this medium. Kjaerholm followed the German International style leader Ludwig MIES VAN DER ROHE and adopted an austere rectangular style; Magnus STEPHENSEN also pursued a functionalist esthetic, though with less impact. A later follower of this tradition is Jørn UTZON. The two most important postwar Finnish designers, Antti NURMESNIEMI and Ilmari TAPIOVAARA, also practice a revived International style, influenced by Mies and LE CORBUSIER.

The success of Scandinavian furniture design in this century is attributable in part to social and political forces. Scandinavian governments have long promoted the manufacture of well-made, well-designed furniture, through both grants and supportive export policies. Moreover, the Scandinavian countries are small and historically not highly industrialized, facilitating a close cooperation among designers, craftsmen and manufacturers not always seen elsewhere. As a result, Scandinavian furniture displays a degree of excellence that has naturally contributed a great deal to its international popularity.

SCARF JOINT

See under JOINERY.

SCARPA, CARLO (1906–78)

Italian architect and furniture designer, best known for his museum interiors. Scarpa's architecture and furniture designs were greatly affected by the early work of Frank Lloyd WRIGHT. He produced furniture that was severely rectilinear but light in feeling, reflecting Wright's Japanese-influenced treatment of volume. Scarpa also designed cutlery and other metalware. His son Tobia is a noted contemporary furniture designer (*see* Tobia and Afra SCARPA).

SCARPA, TOBIA (b. 1935), and AFRA (b. 1937)

Contemporary Italian furniture designers. Tobia Scarpa, son of architect Carlo SCARPA and originally a designer of glass objects, has designed furniture and lighting fixtures in collaboration with his wife, Afra, since 1960. They have designed, for CASSINA and others, luxury furniture in a strikingly monumental mode. Their pieces are made of steel or wood in geometrical shapes, are sometimes inlaid with rare woods or other materials and are often upholstered in leather.

SCHENKSCHIEVE

German RENAISSANCE FURNITURE form; four-doored CUPBOARD or SIDEBOARD. This adaptation of the Italian CREDENZA was usually ornamented with bold horizontal and vertical bands of carved garlands and other botanical motifs. Sometimes the *Schenkschieve* was also decorated with panels of colored or tooled leather, often GUADAMECIL imported from Spain.

SCHINDLER, RUDOLF M. (1887–1953)

Austrian-American architect and designer of the 1930s. Schindler was born in Vienna and studied there under Otto WAGNER. He immigrated to Chicago in 1914, where he worked for Frank Lloyd WRIGHT. In the 1930s he created furniture for a number of houses he had designed in California. These extremely simple pieces were inexpensively made and evidently influenced by the doctrines and work of the DE STIJL group, as well as by Wright, especially in their thematic unity with the buildings for which they were designed.

SCHINKEL, KARL FRIEDRICH (1781–1841)

German architect and furniture designer of early 19th century. The most important German architect of his time, Schinkel also produced much furniture that showed a concern for unity of design in any given context—an interest that foreshadows modern concerns (*see* ART NOUVEAU; BAUHAUS). He initially worked in the NEOCLASSICAL STYLE, tempered by an interest in the new NEO-GOTHIC STYLE. But he evolved an uncomplicated personal style that relied on basically classical forms with ornamentation derived primarily from architectonic motifs of no particular historical design vocabulary. The clean lines and simple character of his work influenced the development of the BIEDERMEIER STYLE, and his designs exerted a powerful influence throughout the 19th century, affecting such pioneer modernists as Peter BEHRENS.

SCHLEGEL, FRITZ (1896–1965)

Danish designer of the 1930s. Schlegel designed unit furniture and bentwood pieces for commercial production in Copenhagen. His austere style was influenced by Franz SCHUSTER and the BAUHAUS school.

SCHMIDT, KARL (1873–1948)

German designer and maker of furniture. Schmidt, a Dresden cabinetmaker, was influenced by the British ARTS AND CRAFTS MOVEMENT and was an important participant in the similar DEUTSCHE WERKSTÄTTEN movement. In 1906 he designed some of the first machinemade furniture. His own factory, in Dresden, produced architect-designed furniture by Bruno PAUL and others.

SCHRAGENTISCH

German RENAISSANCE FURNITURE form. This table was a variant of the WANGENTISCH that featured turned or carved cylindrical legs.

SCHRANK

Massive WARDROVE form; originally of 17th-century Germany and later, in a modified form, of American PENNSYLVANIA GERMAN FURNITURE of the 18th century. The schrank,

R. M. Schindler seat

schrank

resembling the Dutch KAST, was made in sections that could be taken apart. Unlike the *kast,* though, the schrank's feet were permanently joined to its lower section—a case with one wider drawer, or two drawers side by side, surrounded by heavy molding. The main section, above this, was an upright box with shelves or drawers fronted by two doors. A heavy, overhanging architectural cornice topped the piece. The most typical form of BAROQUE FURNITURE in Germany, the schrank varied a good deal regionally. In Austria, for instance, the cornice was always rather modest; there were often no drawers, and decoration was frequently derived from the Italian MANNERIST STYLE, especially as promoted in the pattern book of Friedrich UNTEUTSCH. In northern Germany, where the influences of Hans VREDEMAN DE VRIES and the *kast* were felt, the schrank came to be decorated in an increasingly simple manner through the century, yielding such variations as the WELLENSCHRANK and the STOLLEN-SCHRANK.

The schrank was brought to America by German Palatine immigrants, who settled in Pennsylvania and other colonies beginning in 1683. In America the schrank became even less ornamented, relying considerably on paint and on an old German wax inlay technique, WACHSEINLEGEN, a linear mode. The motifs used were those of the medieval Swiss and German dower chest (*see* DOWER FURNITURE)—names and initials surrounded by hearts, tulips, birds and flowers. The schrank, sometimes known as the *shonk* in America, remained a popular form in German-speaking areas of the United States until the end of the 18th century.

SCHÜBLER, JOHANN JAKOB (1689–1741)
German designer of BAROQUE FURNITURE. In 1720 and 1730 Schübler published popular PATTERN BOOKS. They featured ingenious designs for novel furniture forms—such as a collapsible bed and a dining table incorporating a DUMB-WAITER with a water supply—all in a lush version of the French LOUIS XIV STYLE.

SCHULTZ, RICHARD (b. 1926)
Contemporary American furniture designer. Long associated with the Knoll firm (*see* Florence Schust KNOLL), which he joined in 1951, Schultz has come to specialize in outdoor furniture.

SCHUMACHER, MARTIN (1695–1781)
German ROCOCO FURNITURE maker. Schumacher specialized in elaborate BOULLE MARQUETRY, which he learned under Johann MATUSCH.

SCHUSTER, FRANZ (1892–1976)
Austrian architect and designer; developer of UNIT FURNITURE. Schuster was an adviser to the German Home Furnishing Association, a governmental body concerned with the housing shortage, following the First World War. The association asked Schuster, in 1927, to design affordable furniture that would be inexpensive to manufacture and economical of space. His response, a version of unit furniture, became well known and influenced later design developments, particularly in Scandinavia.

SCHWERDFEGER, FERDINAND (active c. 1760–89)
German-born French LOUIS XVI STYLE furniture maker. Though Schwerdfeger generally favored simple designs featuring figured MAHOGANY veneers, he is also noted for a heavily ornamented cabinet—boasting elaborate mounts by P.-P. THOMIRE, applied plaques of bronze and porcelain, and mother-of-pearl inlay—that the city of Paris presented to Queen Marie-Antoinette in 1787.

SCIMITAR LEG
See under LEG.

SCOTIA MOLDING
See under MOLDING.

SCOTS PINE
British name for EUROPEAN REDWOOD.

SCOTT, ISAAC (1845–1920)
Chicago furniture maker of 1870s and 1880s.
Scott was an apprentice carver in Philadelphia
before he moved to Chicago in 1873. There
he designed and built some of the best furniture of the "Eastlake" style (*see* Charles Locke
EASTLAKE).

SCREEN
Ornamental furniture form; portable arrangement of panels or of frames covered with
leather, wood, glass, paper or textiles. A screen
is intended to provide privacy, to protect
against drafts of cold air or the heat of an
open fire or to divide a room into distinct
areas. It may consist of a single panel or of several panels attached by hinges. In Europe,
screens were first made in medieval times.
They were usually single panels mounted on
flat transverse feet and were meant to shelter
small areas of large, drafty rooms or to shield
fireplaces (*see* CHEVAL SCREEN; FIRE SCREEN.)
In the 17th century the POLE SCREEN developed, and large folding screens came into use,
possibly through the influence of Oriental
examples. These more elaborate pieces were
generally covered with expensive materials,
such as velvets, tapestries and GUADAMECIL or
other decorated leathers. Since the 18th century, Europe and America have imported many
Oriental screens. These have led to lighter
frames and exotic decoration in Western
designs, especially reflected in CHINOISERIE
and, later, JAPONISME. Many modern furniture designers have produced screens—
notably Eileen GRAY and Charles EAMES.

In CHINESE FURNITURE the screen, or
PING, has been in use for more than 2,000
years. Made from many materials including
glass and mica, they featured wood frames
often decorated with inlaid jade or precious
metals. Chinese screens may consist of as
many as 40 panels, each bearing its own decorative scheme. The openness of the traditional
Japanese house has made the screen common
in JAPANESE FURNITURE. The Japanese folding screen, the BYOBU, generally depicts one
painted scene that stretches across all of its
panels, usually six in number. Another
Japanese piece, the TSUITATE, is similar to the
European cheval screen.

SCREEN DRESSING-GLASS
Nineteenth-century name for CHEVAL GLASS.

SCREW TURNING
See under TURNERY.

SCRIBE
To mark or score wood, metal or other material with a pointed instrument, a scriber, in
order to indicate the course of desired cutting
or shaping.

SCRIPTOR
Another name for ESCRITOIRE.

SCRITOIRE
Another name for ESCRITOIRE.

SCROLL
Decorative device in form of a scroll. A scroll
may be a two-dimensional spiraling line or a
three-dimensional shape for a furniture part, a
plane or strip of material in a spiraling configuration resembling a rolled-up piece of paper.
The scroll first appeared as the VOLUTE of a
classical column CAPITAL and this was prominent in classically inspired European furniture
from the Renaissance onward, both in decorative columns and, most notably, as a terminal
of arms, legs and other components (*see*
SCROLL ARM [1]; SCROLL FOOT, FLEMISH
SCROLL FOOT, SPANISH FOOT [*see each under*
FOOT]; and SCROLL PEDIMENT, *under* PEDI-
MENT). The scroll form has also been used as
the model for whole members, as in the
SCROLL LEG (*see under* LEG) and SCROLL ARM
(2). The term also refers to a two-dimensional
spiral, as in the OPENWORK arrangement of spiraling curves known as SCROLLWORK. Doubly
curved S-SCROLLS were of great importance in
BAROQUE FURNITURE decoration, and ROCO-
CO FURNITURE featured the C-SCROLL. The
VITRUVIAN SCROLL, an arrangement of repeat-

ed curves, was popular on 18th-century NEO-CLASSICAL STYLE furniture.

scroll arm

SCROLL ARM (1)
Carved wooden chair or sofa arm whose front terminates in a downward-curving spiral.

SCROLL ARM (2)
Upholstered chair or sofa arm whose top forms a cylinder, offset to the outside. Thus, its rounded upper surface seems to roll over on itself and in cross section is like a spiral, or scroll.

SCROLL-BACK WINDSOR CHAIR
See under WINDSOR CHAIR.

SCROLL FOOT
See under FOOT.

SCROLL LEG
See under LEG.

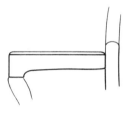

seat rail

SCROLL PEDIMENT
See under PEDIMENT.

SCROLL TOP
Eighteenth-century American term for SCROLL PEDIMENT (*see under* PEDIMENT).

SCROLLWORK
Decorative device involving use of repeated spiral curves, or SCROLLS, for embellishment, especially as OPENWORK.

SCRUTOIRE
Another name for ESCRITOIRE.

SCULPTEUR
French woodcarver specializing in decoration on unvarnished furniture made by a MENUISI-ER. Under the guild system that dominated French furniture making in the 17th and 18th centuries, a *menuisier* could not decorate his pieces in his own shop but had to employ an independent *sculpteur*. Similarly, any gilding of

the carved ornamentation had to be done by a DOREUR.

SEARLE, WILLIAM (1634–67)
Maker of AMERICAN JACOBEAN FURNITURE. Born in Devonshire, England, the son of a joiner, Searle made furniture in Ipswich, Massachusetts. His pieces were simple in form and heavily carved with Jacobean style ornamentation (*see* JACOBEAN FURNITURE).

SEAT
Any of various furniture forms intended for sitting, such as CHAIR, STOOL, BENCH, SOFA and so on. Also, the horizontal part of any of these forms on which the user sits.

SEAT BLOCK
Another name for CORNER BLOCK.

SEAT RAIL
On CHAIR or other type of seating, member of horizontal frame that supports the SEAT. A square frame has four seat rails; a circular bentwood frame is itself a seat rail.

SEAWEED MARQUETRY
English decorative device of late 17th and early 18th centuries; delicate interlacing pattern of INLAY work resembling sprays of marine plant life.

SECESSION
See SEZESSION.

SECONDARY WOOD
See PRIMARY AND SECONDARY WOODS.

SECOND EMPIRE STYLE
Another name for LOUIS XVI REVIVAL STYLE of 1850s–1860s, especially as used at the court of Emperor Napoleon III of France.

SECRÉTAIRE
French term for any of a number of 17th- and 18th-century DESKS, all of them case pieces

with FALL FRONTS (though not limited to SLANT-TOP DESKS, as is the analogous English term SECRETARY). Like the secretary, the *secrétaire* has its roots in the medieval ESCRITOIRE, a portable WRITING BOX. In the 17th century two sorts of case pieces arose. The earlier of these, the SECRÉTAIRE EN PENTE, was a slant-top desk; the second was the SECRÉTAIRE À ABATTANT, whose fall front closed to a vertical position. The *secrétaire en pente* came to be frequently equipped with a bookcase superstructure, but it did not predominate among large 18th-century desks, as the secretary did in Britain. However, the *secrétaire à abattant*, also related to the German KUNSTSCHRANK and possibly the Spanish VARGUEÑO, did rise to prominence, along with the flat-topped BUREAU PLAT, another type of French desk.

SECRÉTAIRE À ABATTANT
French DESK of 18th and 19th centuries. It was an upright case piece whose FALL FRONT formed a vertical front surface, as opposed to the SECRÉTAIRE EN PENTE, a SLANT-TOP DESK. When open, the fall front was supported by chains or rested on retractable LOPERS and provided a writing surface. When closed, it covered numerous small drawers and compartments. Below, the piece took the form of a CUPBOARD or of a CHEST OF DRAWERS. It first appeared in the 17th century, became prominent in the LOUIS XV STYLE and was especially popular in the NEOCLASSICAL STYLES of the late 18th and early 19th centuries.

SECRÉTAIRE (also *table; bureau*) À CAPUCIN (also *à la Bourgogne*)
Eighteenth-century furniture form; table convertible to a desk. Half of the top covered a rectilinear structure containing drawers that could be raised by a ratchet, while the other half was a leaf that unfolded toward the user, providing a writing surface.

SECRÉTAIRE EN ARMOIRE
Another name for SECRÉTAIRE À ABATTANT, referring to its resemblance to an ARMOIRE when its FALL FRONT is closed.

SECRÉTAIRE EN DOS D'ÂNE
French furniture form of 17th and 18th centuries; DESK for two people. It was made in the form of two SLANT-TOP DESKS, or SECRÉTAIRES EN PENTE, back to back. Thus, the two users faced each other.

SECRÉTAIRE EN PENTE
French furniture form developed in 17th century; small SLANT-TOP DESK without superstructure, the earliest SECRÉTAIRE. A piece incorporating two *secrétaire en pente* back to back was called a SECRÉTAIRE EN DOS D'ÂNE.

SECRÉTAIRE EN TOMBEAU
Another name for secrétaire à abattant, referring to its resemblance to an upright sarcophagus when its FALL FRONT is closed.

SECRETARY
English and American furniture form developed in 17th and 18th centuries; SLANT-TOP DESK above CHEST OF DRAWERS with superstructure consisting of BOOK-CASE with doors. The term does not cover similar desks with FALL FRONTS that are vertical when closed, such as the WRITING CABINET, and thus is narrower in meaning than the analogous French term, SECRÉTAIRE. The secretary evolved from the ESCRITOIRE in the 17th century and reached its peak of popularity in the 18th. English and American designers used large-scale architectural motifs, such as pediments and arches, on secretaries in all styles, from the WILLIAM AND MARY STYLE onward. The secretary is still popular today, whether as a reproduction or a newly designed piece.

secretary

SECRETARY DRAWER
Drawer with a FALL FRONT that, when down, creates a writing surface.

SEDDON, GEORGE (1727–1801)
British NEOCLASSICAL STYLE furniture maker. Seddon, from Lancashire, established a furniture workshop in London by 1760 and soon became an important maker, employing up to 400 craftsmen in the 1780s. After his death, his sons and other relatives continued to operate the business until the late 1860s.

SEIGNOURET, FRANÇOIS (1768–?)
New Orleans furniture maker of second quarter of 19th century, associated with the

ROCOCO REVIVAL STYLE. Born and trained in France, Seignouret arrived in New Orleans in 1815 and established his own shop in 1822. He became the acknowledged leader of New Orleans's cabinetmakers, working in a massive, heavily carved version of the Rococo Revival style. A piece known as the "Seignouret" chair, which he developed, was a gondola chair with a carved splat. In the 1840s he used laminating and wood-bending techniques similar to those of John Henry BELTER. Seignouret returned to France in 1853, and preeminence in New Orleans fell to Prudent MALLARD.

SELLA CURULIS
ROMAN FURNITURE form; X-FRAME folding stool with curved legs that served as emblem of office. Adapted from a GREEK FURNITURE form, the DIPHROS OKLADIAS, the *sella curulis* (literally meaning "seat of office") consisted of up to six X-frames, and each leg was an S-curve. The legs were joined by a bolt through their crossing points and by a flexible leather seat. It was employed by local magistrates and carried behind them by slaves, to be unfolded and used when situations demanding official attention were observed. The curved and crossed legs of the *sella curulis* remained a symbol of state in MEDIEVAL FURNITURE, when THRONES and CHAIRS OF ESTATE sometimes displayed them. As the CURULE CHAIR, the form was adapted by NEOCLASSICAL STYLE furniture makers, from the time of RENAISSANCE FURNITURE onward.

SEMAINIER
Eighteenth-century French furniture form; CHEST OF DRAWERS, often a CHIFFONNIÈRE, with seven drawers. Named from the French word *semaine,* meaning "week," the *semainier* could contain a separate supply of linen, shirts and so on for each day of the week.

SEN
Whitish Japanese HARDWOOD with dark grain, used in Japanese furniture, especially as decorative VENEER.

SENÉ, CLAUDE, I (1724–92)
French chair maker in LOUIS XV and LOUIS XVI STYLES, chiefly the former. His son, Jean-Baptiste-Claude SENÉ, a leading chair maker late in the 18th century, was better known.

SENÉ, JEAN-BAPTISTE-CLAUDE (1748–1803)
French LOUIS XVI–STYLE chair maker. Son of Claude SENÉ I, an important maker in the LOUIS XV STYLE, Jean-Baptiste-Claude Sené formally became a master MENUISIER in 1769. In the 1780s he was a major supplier of furniture to the royal family. His chairs were characterized by delicate spiral fluting on the legs, fluted columns with carved capitals on either side of an upholstered back and conventional neoclassical motifs. He also made chairs with a LYRE back. After the Revolution, Sené made large quantities of office furniture, including desks, for the new government.

SEQUOIA
British term for American REDWOOD.

SERPENTINE
Undulating, repeatedly curving. More specifically, composed of a convex curve flanked by two concave curves. A *serpentine front* on a case piece was concave at either side and convex in the center. The top of a *serpentine table* was so shaped on each of its four sides. Both of these designs were common in ROCOCO FURNITURE. More loosely, a SERPENTINE STRETCHER (*see under* STRETCHER) or a *serpentine arm* were simply formed of curves, in no particular configuration.

SERPENTINE STRETCHER
See under STRETCHER.

SERPENTINE X-STRETCHER
See under STRETCHER.

SERRURIER-BOVY, GUSTAVE (1858–1910)
Belgian ART NOUVEAU furniture designer. Originally influenced by the British ARTS AND CRAFTS MOVEMENT, Serrurier-Bovy developed his own designs in the Art Nouveau style. His furniture employed patterns of abstract, curvilinear, sculptural elements and resembles the work of his contemporary

Victor HORTA. Serrurier-Bovy established a factory in Liège in 1899 and became a principal commercial manufacturer of furniture in the Art Nouveau style.

SETTEE

ARMCHAIR extended laterally to accommodate two or more people. The settee came into use in the 17th century as a more comfortable replacement for the SETTLE. It was often upholstered with leather or fabric, thus anticipating the SOFA, which replaced it in the 18th century.

SETTLE

GOTHIC FURNITURE form; BENCH with back panel and arms or side panels, intended to accommodate two or more sitters. A more elaborate, less portable form than the medieval bench, the settle was evidence of the increasingly stable household that accompanied the rise of the middle class in the late Middle Ages. In the 17th century, it gave way to the somewhat more comfortable SETTLE. In AMERICAN JACOBEAN furniture, makers commonly enclosed the supports of a settle and hinged the seat to create a storage space, producing a form similar to the Italian CASSAPANCA.

SETTLE-TABLE (also *monk's bench*)

GOTHIC FURNITURE form; SETTLE with large, hinged back that folded down onto the arms to form a table, in the manner of a CHAIR-TABLE.

SEWING TABLE

Another name for WORKTABLE.

SEYMOUR, JOHN (c. 1738–1818) and THOMAS (1771–1848)

Leading Boston furniture makers of the FEDERAL period; partnership of father and son. John Seymour, born in Glasgow and trained in Britain, immigrated to Maine in 1784 and 10 years later moved to Boston. He and Thomas produced furniture in a large workshop that employed joiners, carvers, inlay workers, finishers, painters and gilders and used imported materials and factory methods

settee

to produce a wide range of furniture in considerable quantity. Their pieces were made in a variant of the NEOCLASSICAL STYLE of the day, deriving largely from the designs of Thomas SHERATON and Geroge HEPPLEWHITE. The Seymours were famed for distinctively delicate satinwood banding, in which strips of complex inlaid patterns bordered expanses of figured mahogany veneer. The Seymours also popularized the TAMBOUR desk. They so dominated Boston cabinetmaking in the late 18th and early 19th centuries that Boston work of the time is sometimes said to belong to the "Seymour school."

SEZESSION

Group of Austrian artists who seceded from the Viennese Academy in 1897; also, the severe, geometrical ART NOUVEAU style practiced in Austria. Led by the painter Gustav Klimt and the designers Josef HOFFMANN, Kolo MOSER and J. M. OLBRICH, the Sezession was principally concerned with architecture, sculpture and painting, but the group also addressed

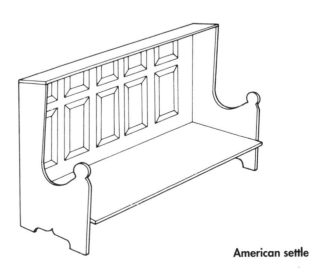

American settle

issues in the decorative arts. In exhibiting furniture and other objects by Charles Rennie MACKINTOSH and the GLASGOW SCHOOL, among others, the Sezession provided a stimulus to, and a name for, the impulse toward new design in Vienna. The Sezession style corresponds to the Art Nouveau styles developed elsewhere in Europe but is a more austere, angular variant of the style.

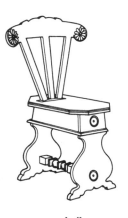

sgabello

SGABELLO

Italian for "stool" or "bench"; more particularly, an Italian RENAISSANCE FURNITURE form. This light, portable wooden chair consisted of a quite elaborately carved, often pierced, back above a plank seat supported not by legs but by carved vertical slabs of wood at front and back. The *sgabello* appeared in the 16th century and influenced the design of many subsequent types of BACK STOOL throughout Europe.

SHAGREEN

Hide of shark or ray, dried, polished and stretched on panels for use as furniture VENEER. This whitish, granular material is often dyed a bolder color. It was introduced in the 18th century for use on small boxes and items of furniture such as tea caddies and KNIFE BOXes, and it has occasionally been popular since—most recently in ART DECO furniture. Before the 18th century the term referred to a type of untanned leather with a granular surface artificially produced by pressing small seeds into the soft, flexible material before drying. It was used in much the same way as sharkskin shagreen, and it, too, was often dyed, usually blue or green.

Shaker rocker

SHAKER FURNITURE

Furniture designed and built beginning in the 19th century by the Shakers, an American religious community. An ascetic communitarian sect that was founded in Britain and came to the United States at the time of the Revolution, the Shakers pursued self-sufficiency as a group. They manufactured furniture for sale, having developed their designs by making their own pieces. The Shakers anticipated the modern doctrine of FUNCTIONALISM, for they held the belief that laboring to make impractical things was sinful and that, accordingly, "beauty rests on utility." This

design concept, combined with industrial methods of production, yielded inexpensive furniture that was simple and unornamented, with clean, elegant lines. Best known of their pieces are the varieties of "Shaker" chair, a ladder-back design derived from British country furniture but slimmer and taller, often with a thin bar across the top of the back from which a cushion was suspended. In terms of manufacture and design theory, the Shakers may be seen as heralds of modernity. Indeed, Shaker furniture, which first came into fashion in the 1860s, has remained popular to the present time.

SHARKSKIN
See SHAGREEN.

SHAW, HENRY (1800–1873)
British architect and furniture designer in the ELIZABETHAN REVIVAL STYLE. Shaw published a highly influential pattern book, *Specimens of Ancient Furniture* (1836), which contained not only examples of genuine Tudor furniture but also a number of medieval pieces, thereby helping to foster the NEO-GOTHIC STYLE.

SHAW, JOHN (1745–1829)
Annapolis, Maryland, cabinetmaker of the FEDERAL PERIOD. A Scot by birth, Shaw was one of the most skillful craftsmen of his day, specializing in fine marquetry decoration. Stylistically, his furniture was derived from the designs of George HEPPLEWHITE and Thomas SHERATON.

SHAW, RICHARD NORMAN (1831–1912)
British architect and designer associated with NEO-GOTHIC STYLE furniture and QUEEN ANNE REVIVAL STYLE architecture. In his early furniture work, Norman Shaw followed the leading neo-Gothic designer, William BURGES; in the 1860s he developed his own lighter, Gothic-influenced style known as "Old English." This later work is characterized by plain paneling, exposed joinery, elaborate iron hardware and sturdy, functional forms. As a country-house architect, his principal career, Shaw was the most important developer of what became known as the Queen Anne

Revival style, though he designed little furniture in that manner.

SHAWL-BACK WINDSOR CHAIR
See under WINDSOR CHAIR.

SHEAF-BACK CHAIR
French furniture form of late 18th and early 19th centuries; small chair whose back was composed of thin, vertical rods joined to each other by a thinner horizontal bar. The rods fanned out above the bar to the CREST RAIL and below it to a CROSS RAIL just above the seat. They appeared to be gathered together like a sheaf of grain.

SHEARER, THOMAS (active 1788)
British NEOCLASSICAL STYLE furniture designer known only from his PATTERN BOOK of 1788, *The Cabinet-Maker's London Book of Prices.* This book, later reissued as *Designs for Household Furniture,* with a few additional plates by George HEPPLEWHITE, presented a conservative, unpretentious variant of the ADAM STYLE. His pieces featured a number of ingenious mechanical devices, such as hidden drawers in desks. Shearer's book had a particular influence on American FEDERAL PERIOD makers.

SHELL FOOT
See under FOOT.

SHERATON, THOMAS (1751–1806)
British NEOCLASSICAL STYLE furniture designer, important in evolution of both ADAM and REGENCY STYLES. Sheraton was trained in the north of England as a journeyman cabinetmaker, but no furniture made by him is known. When he was about 40, he moved to London, where he made a living as a draftsman, teacher and compiler of PATTERN BOOKS of furniture designs, on which his fame rests. The first of these, *The Cabinet-Maker and Upholsterer's Drawing Book,* was published in segments between 1791 and 1794. In it Sheraton offered an anthology of furniture designs interpreting the Adam style, as George HEPPLEWHITE had also done, in a less heavily ornamented, more practical and more popular version than Robert ADAM had

established in the 1760s. More severe and rectilinear than Hepplewhite's pieces, Sheraton's were nonetheless simple, light and delicate. He favored flat inlaid or painted decoration, especially BANDING and geometrical patterns of contrasting VENEERS, though he also used occasional ARABESQUES and even figural scenes drawn from ancient Greek vase painting. In addition, he used images from Adam's repertoire, including URNS, LYREs and SWAGs, especially in the openwork splats of his SQUARE-BACK CHAIRS, a hallmark design. This final phase of the Adam style had so great an impact that it is often called *Sheraton style,* both in Britain and in America, where, in combination with Hepplewhite's designs, it was tremendously important to FEDERAL PERIOD cabinetmakers. However, Sheraton's designs also evidenced a French influence, anticipating the Regency style. They featured certain elements of the LOUIS XVI STYLE, such as spirally turned feet and an insistence on linear components, in both shape and ornamentation, and they also illustrated such French forms as the BONHEUR DU JOUR.

In 1803 Sheraton issued a less successful pattern book, *Cabinet Dictionary,* in which, perhaps influenced by Thomas HOPE, he presented the first ÉGYPTIENNERIE motifs to be published in Britain. The importance of French design increased in his later work, and his furniture took on the eclectic character of the Regency period. He planned a massive volume, entitled *The Cabinet-Maker, Upholsterer, and General Artist's Encyclopedia,* but Sheraton, apparently somewhat deranged throughout his life, fell victim to insanity before he could complete it. However, the unfinished work was published in 1805. It reflected strongly the influence of the French DIRECTOIRE and CONSULATE STYLES, which had become known in Britain during the Peace of Amiens (1802–3), a brief hiatus in the Napoleonic Wars. Heavier, more monumental forms appeared, and they bore much more carved decoration, especially in the form of lion's MASKS, animal heads atop uprights, monopodia supports (*see* MONOPOD) and heavy paw feet (*see* PAW FOOT, *under* FOOT). Sheraton's later work was especially popular and influential in America, among AMERICAN EMPIRE STYLE furniture makers. Sheraton was an ordained Baptist minister, and he wrote several religious tracts, including *The Character of God As Love* (1805), his last work. After his

sheaf-back chair

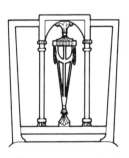
Sheraton square-back

death a volume of his selected designs was published as *Designs for Household Furniture.*

SHIBAYAMA

Decorative device of 19th-century JAPANESE FURNITURE; ivory cladding or applied plaque, itself inlaid with mother-of-pearl and semi-precious stones. This gaudy technique was mostly used on furniture intended for export to the West.

SHIELD-BACK CHAIR

British and American chair of 1780s and 1790s; chair with an open, framed back shaped like a shield. Shield-back chairs are generally associated with George HEPPLEWHITE, whose *Cabinet-Maker and Upholsterer's Guide* contained several designs for them.

shield-back

SHODANA

Nineteenth-century JAPANESE FURNITURE form; display CABINET with many shelves, compartments and drawers in an asymmetrical arrangement, with both solid and FRETWORK paneling. Often decorated with LACQUER and SHIBAYAMA, the *shodana* was made for the Western export market.

SHOEMAKER, JONATHAN (1726–93)

A maker of PHILADELPHIA CHIPPENDALE FURNITURE. Shoemaker worked in a conservative manner that was transitional from the QUEEN ANNE STYLE. He published a pattern book in 1766.

SHONK

Term sometimes used in America for SCHRANK, a German furniture form that appeared in PENNSYLVANIA GERMAN FURNITURE.

SHU GUI (SHU KUEI)

CHINESE FURNITURE form of Ming (1368–1644) and Qing (1644–1911) dynasties; tall CUPBOARD on short legs, wider at base than at top. Its two doors met at a central upright, where they were secured by fittings of brass or BAI TONG. Inside, it had both shelves and drawers. The interior was generally lacquered in a solid color, while the exterior was of polished HARDWOOD.

SIAMOISE

Another name for TÊTE-À-TÊTE, a 19th-century sofa for two people. The term derived from the original Siamese twins (1811–74), prominent in the media of the day.

SIDEBOARD

British and American NEOCLASSICAL STYLE furniture form of 18th and 19th centuries; table with wide, shallow central drawer flanked by deeper drawers or cupboards, intended to be placed against a dining-room wall for use in serving food and drink. The earliest pieces called sideboards were designed by Robert ADAM in the 1760s, although these did not have drawers or other compartments. An Adam sideboard was distinguished from similar side tables by its appearance *en suite* with flanking PEDESTALS and KNIFE BOXes; sometimes a matching CELLARETTE was also placed beneath the sideboard. During the late 18th century, designers developed the standard form, and the functions of the flanking pedestals were absorbed by drawers and compartments, one of which was frequently a built-in cellarette.

In the early 19th-century British REGENCY STYLE and its transatlantic counterparts, the DIRECTORY and AMERICAN EMPIRE STYLES, another sideboard design evolved. The same tabletop with shallow drawer was supported on a pedestal compartment at each end. Behind the top rose a vertical board, frequently in the form of a triangular PEDIMENT, giving the piece a ponderous, architectural character. But the lighter 18th-century form still continued to be made, and a variant of it, the taller and narrower HUNT SIDEBOARD, developed in the southern United States.

SIDE CHAIR

Small chair without arms, intended to be placed against a wall when not in use.

SIÈGE COURANT

Another name for CHAISE COURANTE.

SIÈGE MEUBLANT

Another name for CHAISE MEUBLANTE.

SIGMA
ROMAN FURNITURE form; large semicircular couch. Devised late in the empire, the *sigma* was intended to accommodate six or more reclining diners, in conjunction with a circular table or the MENSA LUNATA.

SILKY OAK (also *Australian silky oak*)
Pale reddish brown mottled HARDWOOD native to Australia. The silky oak tree is not an oak, though the wood resembles true oak. Used chiefly as a decorative veneer, silky oak enjoyed a vogue in British furniture of the 1930s as one of the "empire" woods.

SILLÓN DE CADERA
Spanish RENAISSANCE FURNITURE form; variant of the X-FRAME chair, introduced from Italy in the 16th century. The *sillón de cadera* was usually decorated with elaborate geometrical ivory inlays in the MUDÉJAR STYLE.

SILLÓN DE FRAILEROS
Spanish RENAISSANCE FURNITURE form; simple, rectilinear chair upholstered with leather or fabric. This chair's front stretcher was a wide plank heavily carved, frequently with coats of arms. Stretchers at the sides and back were of normal dimensions. The chair often rested on SLEDGE FEET. The upholstery was either leather, frequently GUADAMECIL, fixed with decorative nails, or rich fabric, usually fringed. The *sillón de fraileros,* or "monk's chair," named for its simplicity of design, descended from Flemish models. It appeared in Spanish furniture in the mid-16th century, after Spain began to rule the Netherlands.

SILVER
Shiny, whitish, ductile and malleable precious metal, used in furniture chiefly as ornamentation, due to its expense. Silver has appeared in decorative INLAY work since ancient EGYPTIAN FURNITURE. In CHINESE FURNITURE it has been set in LACQUER since at least the Tang dynasty (618–907). In European work it has commonly appeared as SILVER LEAF, adorning MOUNTS (*see* HARDWARE) and other sculptural ornamentation. It has been used in many styles and periods, including the present.

From time to time, silver has also been used to a greater degree. In 16th- and 17th-century Europe, the great flow of bullion from Spain's American colonies led to the use of precious metals in crafts, including the production of luxury furniture. In Spain sumptuary legislation forbade the manufacture of silver furniture, referring chiefly to pieces veneered with sheets of the metal but also mentioning solid silver work. These statutes attested to the furniture's popularity, but the work itself rarely escaped the melting pot.

In 17th-century France several famous suites of cast-silver furniture were made for Louis XIV's palace at Versailles. A particularly dramatic ensemble boasted a throne with an 8-foot-high back, flanked by 15-foot CARYATIDs bearing a CANOPY. Within a decade, however, this extravagant furniture had all been reconverted to bullion to help pay for Louis's catastrophic wars. Nevertheless, Versailles had many imitators. Charles II of England, for example, commissioned both solid silver furniture and wooden pieces veneered with the metal. Other courts also followed Louis's lead, to whatever degree their finances permitted, but nearly all of this work has subsequently been melted down.

In India, the opulence of silver furniture can be associated with a practical rationale. Since protection against insects was always an important consideration for makers of traditional INDIAN FURNITURE, cast-silver legs, and occasionally whole pieces, were one response to this problem.

SILVER-GRAY WOOD
Variety of the Indian wood CHUGLAM, popular in 19th-century British furniture as veneering and in MARQUETRY.

SILVER LEAF
Very thin sheets of silver, applied as FINISH to wood or metal.

SILVERWOOD
Another name for *harewood,* dyed variety of SYCAMORE.

SINGERIE
Eighteenth-century decorative motif representing a gathering of monkeys, generally

sillón de fraileros

skirt

slab-ended stool

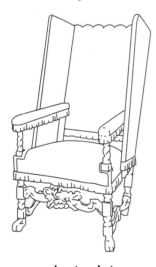

sledge feet

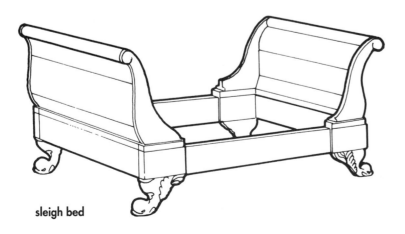

sleeping chair

dressed as humans and busily engaging in such activities as card playing, hunting or acting in the commedia dell'arte. *Singerie* first appeared in the work of Jean BÉRAIN in the late 17th century and was especially popular in the 18th. *Singerie* was often used in conjunction with CHINOISERIE motifs.

SINGLE BOW-BACK WINDSOR CHAIR

Another name for LOOP-BACK WINDSOR CHAIR (*see* BOW-BACK WINDSOR CHAIR, *under* WINDSOR CHAIR).

SIX-BOARD CHEST

Another name for BOARD CHEST.

SIX IMMORTALS, TABLE OF THE

See LIU XIAN ZHUO.

SKIRT

Another name for APRON.

SLAB-ENDED STOOL

Common form of seat in GOTHIC FURNITURE. Invented in the 15th century, the slab-ended stool consisted of a plank top supported on two opposite sides by vertical planks. These sides were connected by seat rails and, sometimes, stretchers between them. In imitation of Gothic architecture, the supporting slabs were often shaped at the shoulder to resemble building buttresses, and each slab typically had a cusped, ogival or trefoil Gothic arch cut through its bottom. Slab-ended benches were made similarly.

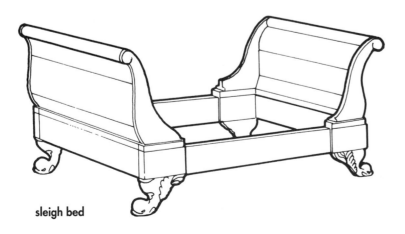

sleigh bed

SLANT TOP

Lid for compartment in a DESK. It slopes inward and upward from the front of the piece, providing a surface on which to write or place a book. Usually hinged at the bottom, it falls forward and presents another writing surface. When open, it is usually supported by extendable arms, or LOPERS, or by chains. Sometimes, especially on the medieval WRITING BOX, a slant top was hinged at the top.

SLANT-TOP DESK

American equivalent of British BUREAU—that is, a desk with a SLANT TOP and compartments, with or without the superstructural cupboard of the SECRETARY.

SLAT-BACK CHAIR

Another name for LADDER-BACK CHAIR.

SLEDGE FEET (also *runner feet*)

Structural device for chairs and tables in Spanish RENAISSANCE FURNITURE. It consisted of two rails, one running beneath a front and a rear leg on each side of the piece, usually with a forward projection along the floor. Sledge feet were often used on the GUARD-ROOM TABLE and the SILLÓN DE FRAILEROS.

SLEEPING CHAIR

BAROQUE FURNITURE form; a tall-backed upholstered chair, the back set at a rearward slant for reclining, with rectangular wings on either side of the back, extending below the seat. The wings are meant to both capture the heat of a fireplace and protect against drafts.

SLEIGH BED

AMERICAN EMPIRE STYLE furniture form, popular in America during first half of 19th century; bed with a high headboard and a footboard, usually slightly lower, each of which had a scrolled top. It thus resembled a horse-drawn sleigh. Like the contemporary French LIT EN BATEAU, from which the form was derived, the sleigh bed was usually placed lengthwise against a wall and was therefore undecorated on one long side.

SLIP SEAT (also *drop-in seat*)

Removable chair seat; upholstered or caned framework designed to fit within the frame of the chair and rest on CORNER BLOCKS. Intended to facilitate the cleaning, repair and replacement of the upholstery or caning, the slip seat has been widely used since it was developed in the early 18th century.

SLIPCOVER
Loose, fitted, removable cloth cover for furniture UPHOLSTERY, permitting variation of texture and pattern, usually to suit the season of the year. The use of slipcovers arose in early 18th-century France, amid the exuberant frivolity of the RÉGENCE STYLE, in which decorative furniture upholstery took on great importance. The fashion of having different upholstery in different seasons arose and first created a demand for multiple suites of furniture, each suitably covered. The extravagance of this practice soon prompted a more sensible approach, and the slipcover was born.

SLIPPER CHAIR
American furniture form of 18th and 19th centuries; short-legged, high-backed chair, usually upholstered, intended for use in a bedroom.

SLIPPER FOOT
See under FOOT.

SLODTZ, ANTOINE-SEBASTIEN (c. 1695–1754) and PAUL-AMBOISE (1702–58)
French designers of LOUIS XV STYLE furniture. Principally set designers for court festivities and the theater, the Slodtz brothers also designed furniture that others, notably A.-R. GAUDREAU, built.

SMITH, GEORGE (active 1804–28)
Leading British REGENCY STYLE cabinetmaker and furniture designer. Smith made furniture in a wide, eclectic range of tastes, based generally on the late NEOCLASSICAL STYLE of Thomas HOPE but also including NEO-GOTHIC STYLE work and CHINOISERIE. He is best known, however, for several PATTERN BOOKS that were important to a genera-

tion of British and American cabinetmakers. The first of these, *A Collection of Designs for Household Furniture and Interior Decoration,* appeared in 1804 and, in a more fully developed edition, in 1808. In it Smith chiefly strove to provide popular, practical designs based on Hope's work, which was more related to archeology than to ordinary comfort. Smith's *The Cabinet-Maker's and Upholsterer's Guide* (1826) was far more eclectic, reflecting the French EMPIRE and RESTAURATION STYLES and also including neo-Gothic and Chinoiserie designs. Smith's influence, both in Britain and in America (*see* AMERICAN EMPIRE STYLE), was very great and lasted well into the VICTORIAN period.

SMOKER'S BOW WINDSOR CHAIR
See under WINDSOR CHAIR.

SNAKE FOOT
See under FOOT.

SNAP TABLE
British term for TILT-TOP TABLE.

SOCCHI (or *Socci*), GIOVANNI (active 1805–15)
Italian EMPIRE STYLE cabinetmaker. Socchi worked at the Florentine court of Napoleon's sister, whom her brother named grand duchess of Tuscany. Socchi followed the French taste, but in a distinctly idiosyncratic manner. He is best known for a series of ingenious convertible writing desks. When closed, each of these appeared to be an oval-topped, six-legged table, set on a low plinth and equipped with deep compartments below the top. One "compartment," with the adjacent legs and a section of the plinth, pulled out from the body of the piece to reveal an upholstered chair. Furthermore, the top was in two halves that slid to each side to expose a writing surface. This surface could be drawn toward the chair, and, by a mechanical contrivance, a container for writing materials rose up at the back. Socchi also designed for the Pitti Palace a number of cylindrical tables decorated to resemble drums, supported on low feet in the form of pine cones.

SOCIABLE

Double REVOLVING CHAIR of the VICTORIAN PERIOD. Two upholstered seats were mounted at either end of a long base, also upholstered, and supported by short legs. The form was an ingenious application of coil-spring, deep-buttoned UPHOLSTERY, which was developed in about 1830. The sociable reflects the fondness for both comfort and technological novelty among the expanding middle class of the 19th century.

SOFA

Bench with upholstered seat, back and arms, for seating two or more people. A less formal piece of furniture than the SETTEE, the sofa is designed for comfort. Developed in the mid-18th century, the sofa became immensely popular following the emergence, in about 1830, of deep-buttoned, coil-spring UPHOLSTERY. By the end of the 19th century, it had replaced the settee.

SOFA-BED

Convertible sofa (*see* CONVERTIBLE FURNITURE) whose seat, usually on a spring-mounted frame, unfolds to form a bed.

SOFA TABLE

A form of PEMBROKE TABLE popular in the late 18th and early 19th centuries in England and America. The table is characterized by a variety of elaborate leg designs, several drawers, and, frequently, a range of uses that incorporate such devices as game boards and rising platforms for reading or writing. Thomas SHERATON, who published early designs of the sofa table, declared its function, "to take a useful place before the sofa." It is the heaviest, most elaborate sort of Pembroke table, as opposed to the BREAKFAST TABLE.

SOFFIT

Underside of a horizontally projecting member of a piece of furniture, such as a cornice or a shelflike molding. Taken from architecture, the term can be used in discussing furniture in the various Western styles, from RENAISSANCE FURNITURE through the NEOCLASSICAL STYLE to present-day POST-MODERN FURNITURE, that have been derived from the classical architecture of the ancient world.

SOFTWOOD

Wood from a needle-bearing tree, as opposed to a HARDWOOD, from a broad-leaved tree. The term indicates the botanical origin of a wood and not its physical softness or porosity. However, due to their cellular makeup, the wood of the needle-bearing trees tends to be softer and less dense than that of the broad-leaved trees. However, some hardwoods are physically softer than some softwoods. Among the hardest softwoods used in furniture are PITCH PINE and especially YEW, which is almost as hard as OAK, one of the harder hardwoods. Softwoods are generally less expensive than hardwoods and are thus common in vernacular furniture. They are often used as secondary wood (*see* PRIMARY AND SECONDARY WOODS) in pieces where they are covered with hardwood VENEER. Softwoods take stain easily and are therefore used in MARQUETRY. PINE, CEDAR and SPRUCE are softwoods that have traditionally been important in furniture making.

SOGNOT, LOUIS (active 1920s and 1930s)

French furniture designer associated with the INTERNATIONAL STYLE. Originally an ART DECO designer, Sognot adopted the International style in the course of the 1920s and was a prominent member of the UNION DES ARTISTES MODERNES for many years. His designs in collaboration with Charlotte Alix were employed in the Indore Palace (*see* Eckart MUTHESIUS). Sognot was noted for elegant designs that incorporated such experimental materials as aluminum and glass.

SOMMER, JOHANN DANIEL (1643–?)

German BAROQUE FURNITURE maker; specialist in BOULLE MARQUETRY in the 1680s. His work demonstrates the immediate and widespread influence of the French LOUIS XIV STYLE.

SOTTSASS, ETTORE (b. 1917)

Contemporary Italian furniture designer. Sottsass designs highly idiosyncratic furniture, imaginative and extravagant in form and detail. He is also known for industrial designs, especially for Olivetti office equipment, that are cleanly functional and in the mainstream of modern design. The son of an Austrian architect, Sottsass studied architecture before

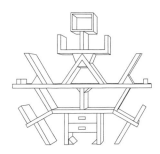

Ettore Sottsass

the Second World War and opened an office in Milan in 1947. In 1956 he spent a year in the United States, working for George NELSON. In the 1970s Sottsass made his first mark in furniture design with large freestanding cabinets painted in bright colors and bold patterns, equivalents in furniture of the hard-edged, "post-painterly" abstraction then current in the fine arts. In 1980 he organized Memphis, a commercial design group dedicated to challenging conventional esthetics with colorful, eccentric, generally startling designs for furniture and other objects. Recent Sottsass designs have included sideboards and room dividers with bold shapes, often incorporating diagonal shelves (useful for bottle storage) and other unexpected arrangements of elements, veneered in plastic laminates, with various colors and patterns in each piece. He also designs lighting fixtures, metalware and ceramics.

SOUPIÈRE
French term for URN motif.

SOUTHERN CYPRESS (also *swamp cypress*)
American SOFTWOOD, not a true CYPRESS, varying in color from very light brown to a deep, almost black, chocolate tone. Notably durable and decay-resistant, it is a prominent construction timber. It was often used as a secondary wood (*see* PRIMARY AND SECONDARY WOODS) in furniture made in 18th-century Charleston, South Carolina (*see* AMERICAN CHIPPENDALE FURNITURE).

SPADE FOOT
See under FOOT.

SPANISH COLONIAL FURNITURE
Furniture made in Spain's American colonies from 17th century into 19th. After the Spanish conquests of native civilizations in Mexico (1519) and Peru (1534), the colonial rulers rapidly became rich, due to mineral wealth, and Spaniards in America soon began to expect fine furniture. At first, this demand was met by imports from Spain, but a local craft tradition quickly developed. Early work followed the Spanish MUDÉJAR and PLATERESQUE STYLES, but by the mid-17th century, distinct colonial styles had evolved.

The chief centers of furniture design, production and use were Lima, Peru, and Mexico City; secondary but nevertheless notable centers were Quito, Ecuador, and Bogota, Colombia. Spanish Colonial furniture was generally European in structure and form, but decoration was influenced by indigenous traditions. In Mexico elements of Mayan pictorial art were featured as carved decoration; in what is now the southwestern United States, simple geometrical ornaments of the local Indian tribes were borrowed; and Incan motifs were used in South America. SILVER, much more readily available than in Europe, was used extensively in decoration, even as veneer for case furniture, especially in Peru.

In 17th-century Mexico the influence of the austere Spanish DESORNAMENTADO STYLE was strong, and it lasted, especially in remote regions, throughout the colonial period. In Peru, on the other hand, baroque CHURRIGUERESQUE FURNITURE was dominant. A particularly rich body of work, MUEBLES ENCONCHADOS, was made in Lima: case furniture was entirely veneered with panels of complex mother-of-pearl MARQUETRY, secured with bands of silver or IVORY.

In the 18th century local motifs and schemes became increasingly frequent, although the Spanish baroque remained the major influence. However, there were significant regional variations. In Mexico the simpler *desornamentado* mode was not entirely superseded, and its heavy moldings and fielded panels persisted even in fashionable work. In Peru, baroque ornamentation only became heavier and more elaborate. Toward the end of the 18th century, British ROCOCO FURNITURE became somewhat influential in Lima, but in general, Spanish Colonial furniture kept its baroque character. Even with the appearance of NEOCLASSICAL STYLE forms, beginning in about 1810, decoration continued to be baroque, with native elements as well.

SPANISH FOOT
See under FOOT.

SPANISH SCROLL FOOT
See under FOOT.

SPARRE, LOUIS (1863–1964)

Swedish-born Finnish designer; principal exponent of NATIONAL ROMANTICISM. Sparre, a close friend of Finnish painter Akseli GALLÉN-KALLELA, traveled widely in Europe and studied the design reform movements of the day before settling in Finland in 1897. He established a workshop there dedicated to the production of furniture and other household goods in the tradition of the British ARTS AND CRAFTS MOVEMENT and the ideas of William MORRIS, of whom Sparre was a follower. Sparre began designing furniture in 1894, in the style of National Romanticism—a strong, simple variant of ART NOUVEAU—and his work shows the influence of Charles Rennie MACKINTOSH and various Austrian designers, whose work he had seen at Liberty & Co. in London (*see* Arthur Lazenby LIBERTY).

sphinx supports

SPARVER

Originally, in MEDIEVAL FURNITURE, a conical CANOPY hung from the ceiling above a throne or CHAIR OF ESTATE. After the 15th century, in RENAISSANCE FURNITURE, the term denoted a bed canopy hung from the ceiling rather than from a TESTER. By extension, the term, which passed out of use after the 17th century, sometimes referred to a bed with such a tent-shaped canopy.

SPHINX

Decorative motif, the representation, of a fabulous creature, a lion, sometimes winged, with human female torso and head. Originating in ancient Egyptian art, the sphinx was a popular device in RENAISSANCE FURNITURE and in 19th-century NEOCLASSICAL STYLE furniture, especially in the EMPIRE, AMERICAN EMPIRE and NEO-GREC STYLES.

spindle

SPIDER-LEG TABLE

Eighteenth-century British and AMERICAN CHIPPENDALE FURNITURE form; small GATE-LEG TABLE with extremely slender turned legs and stretchers.

SPINDLE

Slender piece of turned wood. It is used in series in chair backs, as in the WINDSOR CHAIR, and as a decorative element—often as an

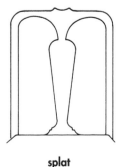

splat

applied ornament, a *split spindle*—most notably in RENAISSANCE FURNITURE, JACOBEAN FURNITURE and the 19th-century EASTLAKE style. A turned spindle is not actually cut in two to make split spindles. Rather, two pieces of wood of the appropriate size are glued together temporarily and turned together on a lathe (*see* TURNERY). When separated, they form two split spindles.

SPINDLE-BACK CHAIR

Chair with a back composed of slender uprights, usually of turned wood.

SPINDLE-BACK WINDSOR CHAIR

See under WINDSOR CHAIR.

SPINDLER, JOHANN FRIEDRICH AND HEINRICH WILHELM (active 1750–99)

German ROCOCO FURNITURE makers. The Spindler brothers made furniture for the palaces of Frederick the Great of Prussia at Potsdam and Berlin. They specialized in floral MARQUETRY based on French LOUIS XV–STYLE design, executed in opulent materials such as mother-of-pearl, silver and ivory. Their work was further ornamented with extravagant bronze mounts by J. M. KAMBLI.

SPIRAL LEG

See under LEG.

SPIRAL TURNING

See under TURNERY.

SPLAT (also *back splat*)

Flat, upright, central support of a chair back. A splat is generally shaped, pierced or otherwise decorated and is an important ornamental element. A chair back usually has a single, central splat, if any, but two or more may appear, especially in a CORNER CHAIR or in larger forms of seating furniture.

SPLAY MOLDING

See under MOLDING.

SPLINE

Small strip of wood inserted in SPLINED JOINT (*see under* JOINERY).

SPLINT SEAT

Woven chair seat made of thin, flexible wooden strips; widely used in country furniture since the 18th century.

SPLIT BALUSTER

See under BALUSTER.

SPLIT SPINDLE

See under SPINDLE.

SPOOL FURNITURE

Mass-produced American furniture of mid- to late 19th century, composed of lengths of SPOOL or BOBBIN TURNING (*see under* TURNERY), which had been developed for commercial production of spools for thread. Instead of being cut up into many small spools, these ribbed lengths of wood served as legs, bedposts and crossbars. The furniture became so popular that spool factories intended to supply the thread industry could sell their entire stock to furniture makers instead. Spool beds were the commonest forms made.

SPOOL TURNING

See under TURNERY.

SPOON-BACK CHAIR

American name for chair whose back curves to fit the human spine. The spoon-back chair was developed in the early 18th century, and the term often refers specifically to such a chair in the QUEEN ANNE STYLE. A similarly curved chair back was often favored in the traditional CHINESE FURNITURE.

SPRING ROCKER

See PLATFORM ROCKER.

SPRUCE (also *whitewood*)

American and European SOFTWOOD; pale but lustrous, almost white in color. Strong and easily worked, spruce is an important wood for interior fittings in case furniture. It is also commonly used for painted furniture.

SPUR STRETCHER

See under STRETCHER.

SQUAB

Eighteenth-century term for removable stuffed seat cushion.

SQUARE-BACK CHAIR

NEOCLASSICAL STYLE chair associated with Thomas SHERATON, popular in 1790s, in late ADAM STYLE British furniture and FEDERAL PERIOD American furniture. Square-back chairs featured a back composed of a square or rectangular frame with a rectilinear openwork splat featuring such neoclassical motifs as the LYRE, the KYLIX or PRINCE OF WALES FEATHERS.

SQUIRREL-CAGE SUPPORT

Another name for BIRDCAGE SUPPORT.

S-SCROLL

Decorative device, taking form of letter *S*, with a spiral at each end. An S-scroll was often a carved member of a piece of furniture, such as a leg or an ARM STUMP, and was often used on BAROQUE and ROCOCO FURNITURE as well as on furniture in the ROCOCO REVIVAL STYLE.

STAIRCASE CHEST

English name for Japanese KAIDAN-DANSU.

STALKER & PARKER (active c. 1688)

John Stalker and George Parker, authors of *A Treatise of Japanning and Varnishing* (published at Oxford, England, in 1688), a technical manual describing various sorts of JAPANNING—imitations of Oriental LACQUER work. The book also contained engravings of CHINOISERIE designs and was the first PATTERN BOOK with Asian designs published in England.

STAM, MART (1899–1986)

Dutch architect and designer associated with the DE STIJL group; inventor of the CAN-

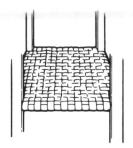

splint seat

spoon-back chair

square-back chair
American Sheraton

TILEVERED CHAIR. In 1924 Stam proved that tubular steel had the strength to cantilever a chair from its two front legs. Comfort, through the resiliency of the steel and its very light weight, was thus combined with the extreme simplicity of design and construction valued by early Modernism. Stam's idea was also employed by other designers, notably Marcel BREUER, with whom it is popularly identified.

STAND

Any small drawerless table intended to support or display something. Some stands, such as the CANDLESTAND, were designed for particular purposes, while others, resembling OCCASIONAL TABLES in appearance and function, were available for any need. Larger stands were built to display large pieces of porcelain (*see* CHINA STAND) or important pieces of case furniture (*see* CABINET STAND).

STANDARD

Medieval term for a common ROMANESQUE and GOTHIC FURNITURE form. The standard was a large CHEST designed not for transport or even mobility, as the COFFER or ARK were, but rather for placement in a fixed spot. Standards were frequently heavily ornamented with architectural motifs—such as arcading, columns and pilasters—and with a variety of decorative moldings.

STANDING TRAY

Eighteenth-century name for OCCASIONAL TABLE, DUMBWAITER or BUTLER'S TABLE.

STAY (also *stay rail*)

Another name for CROSS RAIL.

STAY-BACK WINDSOR CHAIR

Another name for SCROLL-BACK WINDSOR CHAIR (*see under* WINDSOR CHAIR).

STEEL FURNITURE

Steel—a very hard but malleable alloy of iron, carbon and often other metals—has been used to make cutting tools and weapons since prehistoric times, but it has only been used in furniture since the Renaissance and, until the 20th century, only occasionally. German RENAISSANCE FURNITURE makers, especially in Augsburg and Nuremberg, made steel furniture that was ornamented with chiseled decoration; the best-known maker was Thomas RUCKER. The only other notable premodern maker of steel furniture was the TULA IRONWORKS, in Russia, where in the 18th century a furniture-manufacturing operation arose as a by-product of the local small arms industry.

The accelerating Industrial Revolution of the 19th century spurred experimentation in furniture manufacture, as in other fields, and steel was used now and then, especially in Britain, usually as a supporting framework for other materials. Late in the 1890s the Munich designer August ENDELL produced some of the first modern furniture made entirely of steel. The development of tubular steel—thin, hollow rods of the material—presented new opportunities. Such designers as Mart STAM, Marcel BREUER, Ludwig MIES VAN DER ROHE, Serge CHERMAYEFF and LE CORBUSIER designed furniture using both tubes and strips of steel. The CANTILEVERED CHAIR was a particularly successful form. Since the Second World War, steel has remained popular among furniture manufacturers and designers; it is favored for both its structural capacities and its sleek appearance. Most notable contemporary designers have used the material.

STENCILING

Decorative technique in which a standardized design is transferred to a surface by applying paint through a sheet of cut-out metal or paper. Sometimes used on individual pieces of GOTHIC FURNITURE, stenciling later represented an important early use of mass-production methods in factorymade American furniture of the early 19th century, notably that of Lambert HITCHCOCK.

STEPHENSEN, MAGNUS (b. 1903)

Danish SCANDINAVIAN MODERN designer of the 1950s. Better known for his ceramic and metalware designs, Stephensen also designed prize-winning furniture in the early 1950s. His pieces are in a conservative Scandinavian Modern mode, combining forms influenced by the INTERNATIONAL STYLE tradition with the simple, honest materials at the heart of Danish design (*see* Kaare KLINT).

STICKLEY, GUSTAV (1857–1942)

American furniture designer; most important maker of MISSION FURNITURE and leading American follower of the ARTS AND CRAFTS MOVEMENT. Stickley, born in Wisconsin and trained as a stonemason, began his career with an uncle in Pennsylvania, making ordinary, revival style furniture. In 1898 he traveled through Europe and met C. F. A. VOYSEY and other designers of the Arts and Crafts movement. Stickley returned as a convert to the ideas of William MORRIS and established his own firm, the Gustav Stickley Co., in Eastwood, New York, that same year. Stickley began making furniture in simple, rectilinear designs, with exposed joinery and unpretentious traditional materials. He made plain tables, settles and chairs, including a version of the MORRIS CHAIR. His intention, as he described it, was to have each piece be "simple, durable, comfortable, and fitted for the place it was to occupy and the work it had to do." In 1901 his firm was reorganized as United Crafts, a profit-sharing cooperative of craftsmen, organized in accordance with Morris's ideas.

Stickley showed at exhibitions, distributed catalogs, opened a New York showroom and altogether expended a great deal of energy in promoting his furniture, which he sold under the brand name *Craftsman*. Craftsman furniture became very popular and is considered to be among the finest examples of Mission furniture. The popularity of Stickley's style, however, generated many imitators, including his brothers, who left his employ in 1901 to form their own company, known as L. & J. G. Stickley capitalizing on the Stickley name and manufacturing very similar furniture. Stickley was not a very good businessman, apparently, for the United Crafts Co. went bankrupt in 1915.

In 1901 Stickley founded a periodical, *The Craftsman*, to propagate the tenets of the Arts and Craft movement. The first two issues were devoted to the doctrines of Morris and John RUSKIN. Following Stickley's bankruptcy, *The Craftsman* folded, but Stickley's work and ideas did gain a wide American following through the magazine. Moreover, his brothers, their friendly rivals J. M. Young & Co., and other

sideboard by Stickley

manufacturers, continued to make Mission furniture for decades. Stickley's influence can be seen in the work of such West Coast designers as GREENE & GREENE and Arthur and Lucia MATHEWS, as well as in that of the Chicago designers associated with the PRAIRIE SCHOOL, most notably Frank Lloyd Wright.

STICK STOOL

MEDIEVAL FURNITURE form; seat with legs that were placed through holes in the seat and held in position by wedges driven into their exposed tops. The same crude technique was used to make tables. These pieces are distinguished from those assembled by more sophisticated JOINERY (*see* JOINT STOOL).

STILE

Vertical member of the framing of a chest, wood panel, window sash or door. By extension, the term also designates one of the two vertical rear supports of a chair; each comprises, in one piece of wood, rear leg and side support of the back and extends from FOOT to CREST RAIL. Stiles are ordinarily mortised to receive the tenons of rails or other horizontal members (*see* MORTISE-AND-TENON JOINT, *under* JOINERY).

STILE LIBERTY

See ART NOUVEAU.

STÖCKEL, JOSEPH (1743–1800)

German-born French LOUIS XVI–STYLE cabinetmaker. Stöckel, who arrived in Paris in 1769 and formally became a master ÉBÉNISTE

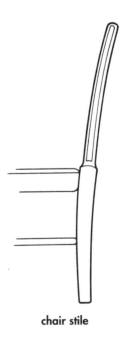

chair stile

in 1775, worked in a heavy, simple style featuring plain VENEERS of figured MAHOGANY.

STOER, LORENZ (active mid-16th century)

German designer of MARQUETRY in RENAISSANCE FURNITURE. In 1567 Stoer published a PATTERN BOOK that contained elaborate MANNERIST STYLE images of classical architecture. His inlays were used on the most important German furniture form of the time, the KUNSTSCHRANK.

STOLLENSCHRANK

Seventeenth-century German WARDROBE form; SCHRANK on a stand rather than with a case of drawers. The *Stollenschrank,* like the WELLENSCHRANK, was decorated exclusively with concentric moldings. Made in northern Germany, it usually stood on a stand with turned legs connected by X-stretchers.

STONE

Material used chiefly for TABLE tops and outdoor furniture, since ancient times. Though not comfortable or easily worked, stone is both durable and has an air of grandeur. In ancient EGYPTIAN FURNITURE, some ceremonial tables were carved from alabaster, and carved THRONEs of MARBLE and granite appear in both GREEK and ROMAN FURNITURE. The Greeks also introduced outdoor furniture using stone. Marble table tops have graced the grand rooms of Europe and America since RENAISSANCE FURNITURE. Artificial stone, most notably in the form of SCAGLIOLA and CONCRETE, has also been used in furniture making.

STOOL

The most basic seating form; seat for one person, composed only of a horizontal surface with legs. The stool is a very ancient form. It appeared in both EGYPTIAN and MESOPOTAMIAN FURNITURE in its two fundamental configurations—either with four straight legs or with crossed legs, the X-FRAME stool. In classical GREEK FURNITURE the stool was prominent as the four-legged DIPHROS and the X-frame DIPHROS OKLADIAS. The latter evolved into the SELLA CURULIS, a ROMAN FURNITURE form that was a symbol of high political office.

In MEDIEVAL FURNITURE variants appeared—for example, three-legged pieces, such as the STROZZI STOOL, and the SLAB-ENDED STOOL, in which a plank top is supported by a vertical plank at each end rather than by legs. At the end of the Middle Ages, more sophisticated carpentry replaced the STICK STOOL with the JOINT STOOL, but stools have not changed in their basic patterns since, although many different appearances and functions have evolved and been given distinctive names (*see* BACK STOOL; FOOTSTOOL; HASSOCK; PLACET; POUF; TABOURET.)

STOPPED DOVETAIL JOINT

See DOVETAIL JOINT, *under* JOINERY.

STOPPED FLUTING

Ornamental device; a type of FLUTING in which lower portion of each concave channel or groove, usually about the bottom third, features a rounded convex strip resembling REEDING. Stopped fluting was popular in NEOCLASSICAL STYLE furniture of the late 18th and early 19th centuries, especially in America.

STRAP HINGE

See under HINGE.

STRAPWORK

Ornamental device used in MANNERIST STYLE of RENAISSANCE FURNITURE. It consisted of carved or painted bands that resembled leather straps and were interlaced in geometrical patterns or ARABESQUEs. Strapwork first appeared in the stucco work done in 1535 by Rosso FIORENTINO at the palace of Fontainebleau, in France, and it quickly spread throughout northern Europe, thanks especially to the published PATTERN BOOKS of Jacques Androuet DU CERCEAU, Cornelis FLORIS, Hans VREDEMAN DE VRIES and Wendel DIETTERLIN.

STRAWBERRY HILL WINDSOR CHAIR

See under WINDSOR CHAIR.

STRETCHER

Crossbar connecting, and thus strengthening, two legs of a piece of furniture; also, an arrangement of such crossbars that joins all four legs. A variety of styles of stretchers are distinguished by name.

ARCHED STRETCHER

STRETCHER, commonly X-STRETCHER (*see under* STRETCHER), that bows upward decoratively, adding interest to the horizontal line.

BOX STRETCHER

Four crossbars used to connect furniture legs around a square perimeter, without crossing the space within that perimeter, unlike an H- or X-STRETCHER (*see each under* STRETCHER). The elements of a box stretcher, each a simple stretcher itself, need not be at the same height from the floor.

COW-HORN STRETCHER

Type of STRETCHER, or crossbar connecting the legs of, usually, a WINDSOR CHAIR; also called a *crinoline, spur* or *crescent stretcher*. A bowlike rod, curved beneath the seat, connects the two front legs. From it, two short rods, or spurs, extend rearward, one to each back leg. The rarer *double cow-horn stretcher* combines two of these elements, back to back, one connecting the front legs, the other the back legs; it is also known as a *serpentine X-stretcher*.

CRESCENT STRETCHER

Another name for COW-HORN STRETCHER (*see under* STRETCHER).

CRINOLINE STRETCHER

Another name for COW-HORN STRETCHER (*see under* STRETCHER).

CROSS-STRETCHER

Another name for X-STRETCHER (*see under* STRETCHER).

DOUBLE COW-HORN STRETCHER

See COW-HORN STRETCHER, *under* STRETCHER.

DOUBLE H-STRETCHER

See H-STRETCHER, *under* STRETCHER.

DOUBLE-LYRE STRETCHER

Early 18th-century table STRETCHER in which two LYRE-shaped segments connect the legs. The open end of each lyre faces an end of the table, with each arm of the lyre attached to one leg. The two lyres are joined at their curved sections.

H-STRETCHER

STRETCHER in which two crossbars—one joining the front and back legs of a piece of furniture on each side—are themselves connected in the middle by a third crossbar; their arrangement resembles a letter *H*. A *double H-stretcher* has two bars connecting those at the sides. Another variant of the H-stretcher is the COW-HORN STRETCHER (*see under* STRETCHER).

ISLE OF MAN STRETCHER

Nineteenth-century British STRETCHER used on three-legged furniture, chiefly stools. Each leg is joined by a horizontal member to another such member extending from an adjacent leg. Thus, each of the three stretcher elements connects a leg and another stretcher rather than two legs. The three stretcher members form a triangular configuration beneath the seat.

RECESSED STRETCHER

Crossbar of H-STRETCHER (*see under* STRETCHER), set back from front legs of a table or chair.

SALTIRE STRETCHER

Another name for X-STRETCHER (*see under* STRETCHER).

SERPENTINE STRETCHER

Any STRETCHER whose members curve more than once between one leg and another. The simplest example is the double cow horn stretcher (*see* COW-HORN STRETCHER, *under* STRETCHER), which forms an S-curve between each front leg and its opposite rear leg.

arched stretcher

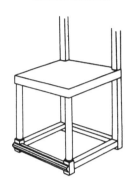

box stretcher

cow-horn stretcher

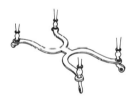

double-lyre stretcher

H-stretcher

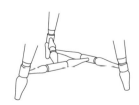

Isle of Man stretcher

serpentine stretcher

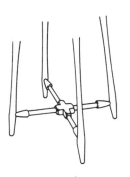

X-stretcher

SERPENTINE X-STRETCHER
Another name for *double cow-horn stretcher* (*see* COW-HORN STRETCHER, *under* STRETCHER).

SPUR STRETCHER
Another name for COW-HORN STRETCHER (*see under* STRETCHER).

X-STRETCHER
Also called a *cross-stretcher* or *saltire stretcher;* STRETCHER in which two crossbars, each joining one front leg of a piece of furniture to the rear leg on the opposite side, are connected to each other in the middle. Their arrangement resembles a letter *X*.

STRINGING
Decorative device; very thin strip of inlaid wood contrasting in color with surrounding VENEER. Stringing is similar to BANDING but it is much finer.

STRIPPING
Process of removing applied finish, especially paint, from wooden furniture. This may be done by applying chemicals or by scraping, usually with sandpaper.

STRNAD, OSKAR (1879–1935)
Austrian architect and furniture designer of 1920s. A follower of Otto WAGNER and Josef HOFFMANN, Strnad pursued the design reform ideals of the WIENER WERKSTÄTTE after they had become unfashionable, due to the rise of ART DECO, with its emphasis on costly materials and decoration. He continued to teach and practice at the Werkstätte and produced simple, well-proportioned furniture, stressing fine craftsmanship and a sparing use of ornamentation.

STROHMEIER, LIENHART (active mid-16th century)
German RENAISSANCE FURNITURE maker. An Augsburg master, Strohmeier worked in the extravagant MANNERIST STYLE of the day.

STROZZI STOOL
Italian MEDIEVAL FURNITURE form; three-legged STOOL with circular or polygonal seat.

STUART, JAMES (1713–88)
British NEOCLASSICAL STYLE architect and designer. Stuart is best known for conducting the first detailed survey of ancient Greek buildings, which spurred the Greek Revival style in architecture and contributed to the rise in popularity of neoclassicism in the decorative arts, including the ADAM STYLE. His book *The Antiquities of Athens* (1762) earned him the name "Athenian" Stuart, by which he was well known. A minor architect, he designed mostly ornamental buildings, such as monuments and garden follies. In 1757 he also designed what would have been the first room in Britain entirely in the neoclassical style, including the furniture, but it was apparently never built.

STUB FOOT
See under FOOT.

STUMP
See ARM STUMP.

STUMP LEG
See under LEG.

STYLE ANTIQUE, LE
French term of very late 18th and early 19th centuries for the archeologically inspired NEOCLASSICAL STYLE of decoration adapted from Greco-Roman and Egyptian sources in furniture of DIRECTOIRE and EMPIRE STYLES.

STYLE MÉTRO
Popular name in France for ART NOUVEAU. The term was inspired by Hector GUIMARD's designs (1900) for the station entrances of the Métro. These exuberant, sinuous designs typified the Art Nouveau style for many people.

STYLE RÉPUBLICAINE, LE
French term of 1790s for austere contemporary style of furniture made during the French revolution. This mode was subsequently named the DIRECTOIRE STYLE, after the government of 1794–99.

SUBES, RAYMOND (1893–1972)
French ART DECO metalworker. Subes designed and built furniture and furnishings—including tables, screens, lamps and radiator cases—in wrought iron and other metals.

SÜE ET MARE
Name referring to *Compagnie des Arts Français,* commercial manufacturer of ART DECO furniture and other household goods. The company was founded in 1919 by Louis Süe (1875–1968) and André Mare (1885–1932), both one-time painters who had turned to interior decoration and furniture design. The firm produced furniture in a conservative Art Deco mode, opulent in materials but simple in design.

SUGAR CHEST
Nineteenth-century American furniture form, especially popular in southern United States; legged CHEST with hinged top that covered two compartments, one for white and one for brown sugar.

SUGI (also *cryptomeria*)
Japanese SOFTWOOD; most common material for framing of chests (*see* TANSU), as it is widely available and very light in weight. Though pale brown, *sugi* is traditionally coated with dark lacquer when used in furniture, due to its tendency to take stain unevenly.

SULTANE (1)
Eighteenth-century French furniture form in LOUIS XV STYLE; CANAPÉ or upholstered SETTEE with SCROLL ARMS (2) as high as the back at each end. The *sultane*'s name reflected the period's enthusiasm for the exotic and encouraged the belief, apparently created by merchandisers, that the design was Turkish. In addition to upholstery, the *sultane* usually had seat cushions and bolsters.

SULTANE (2)
French name for 19th-century OTTOMAN.

SUMMERS, GERALD (b. 1902)
British INTERNATIONAL STYLE furniture designer. Summers is noted for the designs in bent plywood he devised during the 1930s. Influenced by the example of Alvar AALTO and the BAUHAUS designers, Summers designed chairs made from a single sheet of plywood, as well as other pieces, for a London company named Simple Furniture.

SUNBURST
Decorative device composed of stylized rays of light radiating from a circular center.

SUNFLOWER CHEST
See CONNECTICUT SUNFLOWER CHEST.

SUZURI-BAKO
Traditional JAPANESE FURNITURE form; small TANSU, or chest, with several drawers intended to store writing materials (including the *suzuri,* or inkstone) and an abacus. The *suzuri-bako* was a standard feature in Japanese shops.

SWAG
Decorative motif; image of a garland of fruit and flowers or of a length of cloth, tied with ribbons and attached to a background. If tied at both ends and suspended from them in a loop, a swag is generally called a FESTOON; sometimes the term *swag* refers only to a festoon of cloth, not to fruit and flowers.

SWAMP CYPRESS
Another name for SOUTHERN CYPRESS.

SWAN-NECK HANDLE
See BAIL HANDLE.

SWAN-NECK PEDIMENT
See under PEDIMENT.

SWEPT LEG
See under LEG.

SWING LEG
See under LEG.

SWISS WINDSOR CHAIR
See under WINDSOR CHAIR.

swag

SWIVEL CHAIR
Another name for REVOLVING CHAIR.

SYCAMORE
American PLANE WOOD, a HARDWOOD similar to its close relative the European plane. Pale brown, with a distinctively flecked appearance, sycamore is used in furniture as a veneer, in panels or in inlay work. In Britain the term *sycamore* refers to a species of maple whose wood is traditionally used to make violins and was occasionally used for marquetry in 18th-century furniture, often dyed a greyish brown hue, when it was called *harewood.*

TA CHUANG (T'A CH'UANG)

CHINESE FURNITURE form of Ming (1368–1644) and Qing (1644–1911) dynasties; wide SETTEE, deep enough to permit users to sit cross-legged or to lounge. Lighter and smaller than the similar KANG, the *ta chuang* generally had a caned seat, whose frame rested directly on the four-footed base. The base curved inward at the top, forming a pronounced groove where it met the seat. This groove became decoratively wider and deeper and was sometimes the site of an applied frieze of relief work. The *ta chuang* was usually backed by a low wall, which extended some distance forward on the two sides as well.

TABAKO-BON

JAPANESE FURNITURE form of 16th–19th centuries; miniature HIBACHI used by pipe smokers. The *tabako-bon*—literally, "tobacco box"—was developed after the Portuguese introduced tobacco to Japan in the 16th century. It had various forms, though it was most commonly rectangular, and it sometimes included various tiny drawers and compartments. It invariably incorporated a circular, copper-lined receptacle in the top, to hold ashes containing coals used to light a pipe, and a small piece of jointed bamboo that served as an ashtray and cuspidor.

TABLE

Furniture form in which one or more vertical LEGS support raised horizontal surface, on which objects may be placed. Often DRAWERS or other compartments are placed below the tabletop. Tables have been made since prehistoric times; the earliest known pieces were examples of ancient EGYPTIAN FURNITURE, in which specialized GAMING TABLES, some including small drawers, had already been invented. Tables have been built by craftsmen in most cultures, in many styles and for many purposes. Many varieties of table have been given specific names. (*See* ALTAR TABLE; BA XIAN ZHUO; BREAKFAST TABLE; BUFFET; BUREAU PLAT; BUTLER'S TABLE; BUTTERFLY TABLE; CABINET STAND; CANDLESTAND; CANTERBURY (2); CARD TABLE (1; 2); CARLTON HOUSE TABLE; CAST-IRON FURNITURE; CHAIR TABLE; CHIFFONIER (2); CHINA STAND; COFFEE TABLE; CONSOLE TABLE; COUNTER-TABLE; CREDENCE; CREDENZA; DRAW-LEAF TABLE; DRESSING TABLE; DROP-LEAF TABLE; DRUM TABLE; DUMBWAITER; EXTENSION TABLE; FALDYN TABLE; GATE LEG TABLE; GUARD-ROOM TABLE; HANDKERCHIEF TABLE; HUA ZHUO; HUNTBOARD; HUNT SIDEBOARD; JI TAI SHI AN; KANG JI; KETTLE STAND; LIBRARY TABLE; LIU XIAN ZHUO; MARTHA WASHINGTON TABLE; MENSA LUNATA; NEST OF TABLES; PARSONS TABLE; PEDESTAL TABLE;

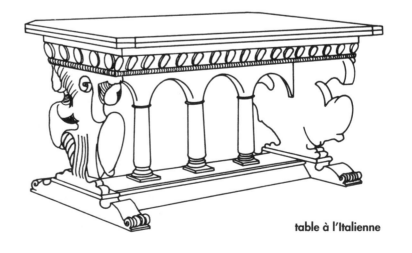

table à l'Italienne

PEMBROKE TABLE; PIE DE PUENTE; PIECRUST TABLE; PIER TABLE; QIN ZHUO; RANGE TABLES; REFECTORY TABLE; RENT TABLE; ROOT FURNITURE; SCHRAGENTISCH; SETTLE-TABLE; SIDEBOARD; SOFA TABLE; SPIDER-LEG TABLE; STAND; TABLE À ÉCRIRE; TABLE À L'ITALIENNE; TABLE DORMANT; TABLE EN CHIFFONNIÈRE; TANG HUA AN; TEAPOY; TEA TABLE; TILT-TOP TABLE; TURRET-TOP TABLE; WANGENTISCH; WINDSOR TABLE; WINE TABLE; WORKTABLE; WRITING TABLE; YAN JI.)

TABLE À ÉCRIRE
French furniture form; small BUREAU PLAT or WRITING TABLE.

TABLE À L'ITALIENNE
French RENAISSANCE FURNITURE form. This monumental table featured a rectangular wood or marble top, supported at either end by a massive slab of wood carved in a rich MANNERIST STYLE to represent human figures or bizarre mythological creatures. The two slabs were joined by a broad, low central STRETCHER. Between stretcher and tabletop ran a wood curtain of carved decoration, often architectural in character. The *table à l'Italienne* was a French adaptation of an Italian formulation of an ancient ROMAN FURNITURE form. It was placed in the center of a room or some other prominent position and was a prized symbol of wealth and status.

TABLE AMBULANTE
Eighteenth-century French term for OCCASIONAL TABLE.

TABLE-CHAIR
Another name for CHAIR-TABLE.

TABLE DORMANT
Medieval term for a ROMANESQUE and GOTHIC FURNITURE form; large table not intended to be moved and therefore attached to the floor. *Tables dormant* were generally crudely made because they were covered by rich fabrics when their owner was in residence. The term sometimes referred to tables that could be moved from one room to another but whose tops were permanently attached to their supports, as opposed to the more usual arrangement of boards set on trestles (*see* TRESTLE TABLE), designed for ease of transport.

TABLE EN CHIFFONNIÈRE
Eighteenth-century French furniture form intended for sewing. It was a small table with a GALLERY around its top and, usually, a drawer in the frieze and a shelf between its legs. In the 19th century, this piece tended to be called a CHIFFONIÈRE and to be used as an all-purpose OCCASIONAL TABLE, thus inspiring the British CHIFFONIER (2).

TABLECLOTH
Piece of fabric used to cover a table. Originally, in MEDIEVAL FURNITURE, rich fabrics and tapestries, being lighter and easier to transport than fine cabinetry, were used far more than furniture to display wealth and status. Accordingly, most pieces of furniture, and especially tables, were covered with cloth when in use and disassembled when not in use. Gradually, these roles have reversed, and a tablecloth, however decorative, serves primarily to protect the finish of a table and is generally used only during meals.

TABLET-ARM CHAIR
Chair with writing surface attached to one arm, ubiquitous in schoolrooms. Perhaps the most striking example of a tablet-arm chair is the 18th-century WRITING-ARM WINDSOR CHAIR (*see under* WINDSOR CHAIR), the first to be developed and the antecedent of all others.

TABLET-BACK **WINDSOR** CHAIR
See under WINDSOR CHAIR.

TABOURET (also *taboret*)
French furniture form of 17th and 18th centuries; low, rectangular STOOL on four short legs. Originally drum-shaped (the term means "little drum"), the tabouret was a well-known piece of furniture at the courts of the Bourbon kings, where rigorous canons of etiquette determined who could use it.

TAILPIECE
Another name for BOBTAIL (*see under* WINDSOR CHAIR).

TALBERT, BRUCE JAMES (1838–81)

British designer and writer. Trained as an architect, Bruce Talbert became instead a prolific furniture designer, designing for many commercial manufacturers. Stimulated by the NEO-GOTHIC STYLE of A. W. N. PUGIN and William BURGES, Talbert and Charles EASTLAKE developed a less elaborate mode called Modern Gothic. Talbert and Eastlake stressed simple, rectilinear design forms, constructed on traditional frameworks with mortise-and-tenon joinery. They disdained curves and elaborate ornamentation, though Talbert had a taste for more applied decoration than Eastlake did. In 1867 Talbert published a book of his designs, *Gothic Forms Applied to Furniture, Metalwork and Decoration for Domestic Purposes,* which influenced commercial design for several decades, particularly in America, where it had a significant impact on the "Eastlake" design style. Following the ideas of Henry COLE, the ART FURNITURE MOVEMENT—including Talbert, Eastlake and such other designers as Burges and T. E. COLLCUTT—advocated the use of fine design for everyday objects. With Burges and William GODWIN, Talbert was one of the first British designers to appreciate Japanese art and design (*see* JAPONISME), and he occasionally employed Japanese motifs in his work. In his later, less celebrated work, Talbert adopted the ELIZABETHAN REVIVAL STYLE. He also designed metalwork and wallpaper.

TALLBOY

Eighteenth-century British furniture form; case piece composed of one CHEST OF DRAWERS on top of another, slightly wider one. The lower chest was shorter than the upper one. Essentially a 17th-century CHEST-ON-CHEST made in 18th-century styles, the tallboy only received its name late in the 18th century. In 18th-century styles it was a plain piece, generally made of WALNUT. It usually bore very little ornamentation, apart from a molding at the top of the lower section and a cornice or pediment above.

TALLON, ROGER (b. 1929)

Contemporary French designer; best known as an industrial designer specializing in cameras, typewriters, small appliances and lighting fixtures. In the 1960s Tallon also produced some noteworthy furniture in an idiosyncratic variant of the INTERNATIONAL STYLE. It featured

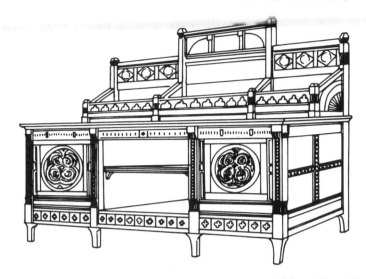

sideboard by Talbert

molded polyester foam upholstery with deeply modeled textures on its exposed surfaces.

TAMBOUR

Flexible door or cover used in case furniture. The tambour consists of narrow strips of flat or molded wood glued side by side on a backing, usually of canvas duck. This stiffened cloth, each of whose edges is set in grooves in the body of the piece, extends, when in use, to enclose a space and wraps around a concealed cylinder when the space is open. The best-known use of the tambour has been in the ROLL-TOP DESK, where the slats of wood are set horizontally, but it has also been used on vertical doors in some forms of case furniture. Developed in 18th-century France, the tambour has been made ever since.

TANG HUA AN (T'ANG HUA AN)

CHINESE FURNITURE form of Ming (1368–1644) and Qing (1644–1911) dynasties; tall, quite long table. Like the JI TAI SHI AN, or *altar table,* but wider, the *tang hua an* was a domestic showpiece. It was typically placed against a wall, beneath a prized painting, and choice art objects were displayed on it. This ensemble, completed by a BA XIAN ZHUO, or *table of the Eight Immortals,* which stood in front of the *tang hua an,* was a basic component of a respectable Chinese home.

TANG XIANG (T'ANG HSIANG)

CHINESE FURNITURE form of Ming (1368–1644) and Qing (1644–1911) dynasties; long, narrow CHEST designed to store heavy, fur-lined garments. These were folded lengthwise, to prevent damage, and thus did not fit on the shelves of wardrobes.

TANSU

Any of a wide variety of Japanese storage chests; *tansu* is also the Japanese word for wood cabinetry in general. Collectively, the chests (*tansu* is also the plural form) make up by far the largest part of the sparse body of traditional JAPANESE FURNITURE. While a few *tansu* are known to have existed in early medieval times, it was not until early in the Edo period (1615–1868), when a prosperous merchant class emerged, that the many specialized varieties of *tansu* developed. In the late 19th and early 20th centuries, sometimes regarded as the golden age of *tansu,* the range of types was at its widest, and most extant pieces were made at that time.

Larger *tansu* fall into a number of categories (the term is altered to -*dansu* in compound words): the ISHO-DANSU was a clothing chest, and the MIZUYA-DANSU was used in the kitchen. A pharmacist's chest, the KUSURI-DANSU, and the CHO-DANSU, a merchant's chest, were used in shops. The FUNA-DANSU was a traditional sea chest. Other large *tansu* included the spectacular KAIDAN-DANSU, a freestanding staircase with built-in compartments; the NAGA-MOCHI, a linen chest; and the KURUMA-DANSU, a wheeled form.

In addition, a number of smaller chests are classed as *tansu,* such as the HIBACHI, a brazier; the HARI-BAKO, a sewing kit; the TABAKO-BON, or tobacco box; and several other specialized boxes—the ZENI-DANSU, the DOGU-BAKO, THE HAN-BAKO and the SUZURI-BAKO.

TANZANIAN WALNUT

Erroneous name for ANINGERIA.

TAPE SEAT

Chair seat composed of interwoven strips of cotton fabric. The tape seat has long been part of the vernacular furniture of western Europe.

tape seat

TAPIOVAARA, ILMARI (b. 1914)

Finnish SCANDINAVIAN MODERN designer. While a student in Helsinki, Tapiovaara worked for Alvar AALTO and later, in Paris, for LE CORBUSIER. Then, after he had begun his own practice in Helsinki in 1950, he spent two years in Chicago working for Ludwig MIES VAN DER ROHE. Accordingly, Tapiovaara was well grounded in FUNCTIONALISM and the INTERNATIONAL STYLE. His furniture is designed for industrial production and is generally made of metal and molded plastic, in elegant but austere pieces whose elements are clearly separated from one another, in the functionalist manner. He and Antti NURMES-NIEMI are particularly associated with the revival of the International style in Scandinavia in the late 1950s. Before 1960 he was principally occupied with interior and furniture design; since then he has also painted, sculpted and designed cutlery, stereo equipment and other industrial products.

TAPISSIER

French craftsman who specialized in making furniture UPHOLSTERY, along with curtains and other draperies. Under the guild system that dominated French furniture making in the 17th and 18th centuries, a MENUISIER who made a chair could not upholster it in his own shop but had to employ a *tapissier.*

TAQUILLÓN

Spanish RENAISSANCE FURNITURE form. This chest or CHEST OF DRAWERS was designed to support the VARGUEÑO, a FALL-FRONT DESK. Below its top, the *taquillón* had two slides that could be pulled out to support the FALL FRONT of the desk.

TARSIA

Another name for INTARSIA.

TASSEL

Piece of ornamental upholstery appearing on SEAT RAILS or bed canopies (*see* CANOPY). It is a pendant cluster of short lengths of cord, usually silk, gathered around a wooden sphere covered with cloth. Tassels may dangle singly, especially at the corners of canopies, or be placed in a line to form a fringe. Tassels were especially popular on furniture in Britain during the Victorian period.

TATHAM, CHARLES HEATHCOTE (1772–1842)

British architect and designer; important early exponent of REGENCY STYLE. As Henry HOLLAND's assistant, Tatham studied classical architectural ornamentation in Rome, providing many designs that helped his influential employer to introduce archeologically inspired late NEOCLASSICAL STYLE furniture to Britain. He later published books of classical designs (1799 and 1806) intended for metal-workers and architects. His brother Thomas TATHAM was a notable furniture maker of the day.

TATHAM, THOMAS (1763–1817)

British REGENCY STYLE furniture maker. Brother of C. H. TATHAM, Thomas Tatham made furniture both in a NEOCLASSICAL STYLE that was inspired by ancient Greek architecture and furniture and in the "Chinese" taste of the day (*see* CHINOISERIE).

TATLIN, VLADIMIR (1885–1953)

Russian Constructivist painter, sculptor and designer. Tatlin is perhaps best known for an architectural sculpture that was never built, the *Monument to the Third International.* He was a leader of the group of Russian artists who fervently believed that the Russian Revolution of 1917 seemed to offer the opportunity for a modern design culture for the people. This group also included Alexander Rodchenko and Lyubov Popova. Until the Soviet regime instituted politically and artistically repressive policies in the late 1920s, these artists produced a wide range of designs, for furniture and many other products. In 1927 Tatlin created the best-known Russian furniture design of this period, a cantilevered chair of tubular steel that resembled the contemporary products of Marcel BREUER and Mart STAM, although it required two separate steel tubes, one for the seat and another for back and arms. Its curvilinearity recalled ART NOUVEAU. Not accepted in Russia, the chair has subsequently been produced in Italy.

TAVERN TABLE

Modern American term for a furniture form popular in America and Britain from the late 17th to the early 19th centuries. The tavern table was a simple, low, rectangular, and sometimes rounded, table with turned legs and stretchers or, sometimes, carved supports at each end connected by a STRETCHER. This sturdy, strong piece was widely used domestically, not only in taverns.

TCHITOLA

African HARDWOOD, yellow to brown with darker grain, often attractively figured. Resembling WALNUT, *tchitola* is a popular furniture veneer in Europe.

TEA TABLE

Small table introduced in 18th century, intended for serving light meals and usually equipped with a GALLERY around its top to prevent spillage.

TEAK

Golden brown to dark brown HARDWOOD, sometimes figured; an important material in contemporary furniture making. Native to Burma (*see* BURMESE FURNITURE), though grown commercially elsewhere, teak is exceptionally durable and strong. It is thus an important ship-building timber. It was particularly popular in SCANDINAVIAN MODERN furniture of the mid-20th century, and it remains fashionable, especially as veneer.

TEAPOY

Eighteenth-century British furniture form; small PEDESTAL TABLE with three short legs and most typically equipped with a small box that served as tea caddy. Although the association of this form with tea is now well established in England usage, and although teapoys were often used as TEA TABLES, the term did not originally derive from any connection with the beverage. Such tables were often made in 18th-century British India, though to European designs, and *teapoy* was an Indo-Persian word meaning "three-footed."

TENON

Shaped projection crafted on a piece of wood or other material, intended for insertion in a similarly shaped cavity, or MORTISE, in another piece, thereby forming a MORTISE-AND-TENON JOINT (*see under* JOINERY).

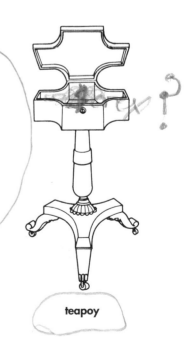

teapoy

TENT BED
Nineteenth-century name for FIELD BED.

TERM
Decorative device; sculpted pedestal tapering toward the bottom and topped by a bust of a human, animal or mythical creature. Derived from ancient Greek religious statuary, the term was popular in RENAISSANCE, BAROQUE and ROCOCO FURNITURE, most often as a support for a table or cabinet stand.

TERN FOOT
See under FOOT.

TERRAGNI, GIUSEPPE (1904–42)
Italian architect and designer associated with the INTERNATIONAL STYLE. With Gio PONTI, Terragni was one of the few practitioners of modern esthetics in Italy under Mussolini, whose regime favored a heavy, ornate revival style employing references to the Italian Renaissance. His furniture, rectilinear and functional, was clearly influenced by both the BAUHAUS designers and LE CORBUSIER. Terragni died in the Second World War.

TERY, EMILIO (1890–1969)
French ART DECO furniture designer. Terry created Art Deco furniture well into the post-Second World War era, when the mode was decidedly out of fashion. In defiance of FUNCTIONALISM, he drew on the 18th-century LOUIS XVI and DIRECTOIRE STYLES, while using lighter woods and a more discreet employment of decoration (though in such opulent materials as ivory and gold-leaf). Terry liked to describe his work as being in the "Louis XVII style," naming Louis XVI's son, who never reigned because of the French Revolution.

TESSENOW, HEINRICH (1876–1950)
Austrian architect and furniture designer associated with the DEUTSCHE WERKSTÄTTEN movement. In 1909, with Richard RIEMER-SCHMID and others, Tessenow helped design a Dresden housing project that pioneered the use of simple, modern furniture designs intended for mass production and use. Tessenow also

taught design in Vienna, where Franz SCHUSTER was one of his students.

TESTER
In MEDIEVAL FURNITURE and later, framework from which fabrics constituting the CANOPY over a bed were suspended. The term has also come to refer to the canopy itself or to the framework and canopy together. Early testers were suspended from the ceiling above a bed; later they became fixed to a vertical board above the head of the bed, the CELURE, or were supported by the bedposts. In CHINESE FURNITURE a tester bed was also made, the JIA ZI CHUANG.

TÊTE-À-TÊTE (1)
Another name for CAUSEUSE.

TÊTE-À-TÊTE (2) (also *confidante; love seat; siamoise; vis-ê-vis*)
Nineteenth-century furniture form; upholstered sofa or double armchair whose seats faced in opposite directions. Their rounded backs, when seen from above, form an S-curve.

THERM FOOT
See under FOOT.

THEYNS
Ancient GREEK FURNITURE form; a footstool used for access to a high piece of furniture such as a KLINE or a THRONE.

THOMIRE, PIERRE (or *P.-P.*) (1751–1843)
Leading French LOUIS XVI and EMPIRE STYLE bronze worker. An assistant to Pierre GOUTHIÈRE in the 1770s, Thomire established his own business in 1777. His mounts were used by Guillaume BENEMAN, Adam WEISWEILER and others. During the Revolution, Thomire manufactured arms and ammunition for the new French government. Under Napoleon he returned to the decorative arts and became the leading maker of furniture mounts and other objects in the Empire style. He was no longer a craftsman by this time but rather the director of a factory, where he employed nearly 1,000 workers.

After Napoleon's fall, Thomire continued to prosper under the restored monarchy (*see* RESTAURATION STYLE). He retired in 1823.

THONET, MICHAEL (1796–1871)

German furniture maker and designer; developer of BENTWOOD furniture. Thonet was born in the kingdom of Prussia. He established a cabinetry business that specialized in parquetry floors and in ROCOCO REVIVAL and BIEDERMEIER STYLE furniture. He began to experiment with methods of bending wood around 1830. His experiments began with bundles of strips of veneering, and he eventually devised a means of bending solid rods of copper beechwood. He used the bentwood principally to make chair frames, for which he and his company soon became famous.

The bentwood rods were used for the legs, arms and often the entire chair backs; the seats and sometimes the backs were usually made of cane. Thus, the opportunity for carved ornamentation greatly diminished due to the chair-making process. This simplification of design was a continuation of Biedermeier design reaction against the elaborate character of the EMPIRE STYLE and was also a precursor of the modern taste for unembellished design. It is also true, however, that the curvilinearity of Thonet's chairs was acceptable to the neo-rococo taste of the 1840s and after. Michael Thonet was, though, as much a businessman as a designer, and his famous chairs must be seen as an instance of design being influenced by new methods of manufacture. Thonet established a factory system of mass production as modern as anything in his century, and the elegant simplicity of the best-known Thonet designs only arrived with this development.

Thonet moved to Vienna in 1842, under the aegis of Prince Metternich, the leading statesman of the Austro-Hungarian Empire. He was granted a monopoly on the wood-bending process until 1869 (after which rivals entered the field, producing very similar furniture). Thonet Brothers (named after Michael's sons) continued to dominate, however; just before the First World War, it employed more than 6,000 workers and marketed 2 million pieces of furniture annually throughout the world.

No new designs were created by Michael Thonet's sons after his death, but the company continued to innovate. The firm was among the first manufacturers to commission and produce architect-designed furniture. Beginning early in this century, Thonet Brothers commissioned work by Adolf LOOS, Josef HOFFMANN, Otto WAGNER and others. From the 1920s to the present, the firm (now merged with several of its old rivals) has produced furniture designed by Marcel BREUER, Ludwig MIES VAN DER ROHE and LE CORBUSIER.

Michael Thonet was ahead of his time in terms of both designs and manufacturing methods. The rudimentary beginnings of modern mass-production methods were present in his bentwood factory, and the simple, lightweight designs, made possible by the new processes, still have a clean-lined, contemporary look. Thonet chairs are the earliest modern classics, and several of his designs have never gone out of production, through more than a century of changing tastes.

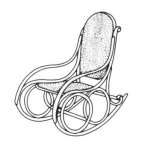

bentwood rocker by Thonet

THORN-PRIKKER, JOHANN (1968–1932)

Dutch Symbolist painter associated with ART NOUVEAU furniture design. Primarily a painter, Thorn-Prikker designed upholstery for a number of chairs by Henri VAN DE VELDE, using an austere, curvilinear style and abstract motifs influenced by Javanese batiks. He also designed a few chairs himself, in a straightforward, rectilinear mode.

THREE-BACK WINDSOR CHAIR

See under WINDSOR CHAIR.

THRONE

Seat occupied by a sovereign or other exalted person on ceremonial occasions. In ancient times thrones were generally fixed to their sites and could be either STOOLS or CHAIRS, with or without arms. At least since the time of MEDIEVAL FURNITURE, thrones have taken the form of highly ornamented ARMCHAIRS, usually dignified further by an attached FOOTSTOOL or by placement on a dais or under a CANOPY.

THROWN CHAIR

Another name for TURNED CHAIR.

THUYA WOOD

African SOFTWOOD, reddish brown in color with handsome dark mottling, used in furniture for decorative veneering and inlay work.

TI HONG (T'I HUNG) (also *Peking lacquer*)
Carved red LACQUER used on CHINESE FURNITURE of Ming (1368–1644) and Qing (1644–1911) dynasties. Although known in the West as *Peking lacquer, ti hong* pieces were made in many well-known workshops throughout China. Up to 36 layers of red lacquer—occasionally interspersed with a layer of yellow, green or black—were built up on a wooden core and then delicately carved in relief, in intricate patterns covering the whole surface of the piece. Floral motifs were most common, followed by birds and dragons; sometimes landscapes appeared. In certain small areas and lines, the carving reached a differently colored layer, producing a striking variation. Very little if any *ti hong* furniture was exported, and it was not known in the West until the late 19th century. It was, however, widespread in China and was used on a broad range of furniture forms.

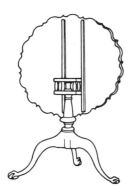

tilt-top table

TIFFANY, LOUIS COMFORT (1848–1933)

American ART NOUVEAU designer. Though Tiffany is best known for his designs in stained glass, especially for the lamps that bear his name, he also influenced American furniture design of the late 19th and early 20th centuries. With painters John La Farge, Lookwood DE FOREST and others, Tiffany founded a decorating firm, Louis C. Tiffany and Associated Artists, in 1879. Following William MORRIS's ideals, the company aspired to the revival of the decorative arts and the education of the public as to fine design. However, unlike Morris, Tiffany had a taste for the exotic and for the sinuous curves and organic motifs of European Art Nouveau. This firm was short-lived, but it had several successors through which Tiffany continued to promote new design (None of these experimental enterprises had any connection with Tiffany & Co., the famous fine metalwork and jewelry firm, which Louis Tiffany inherited upon the death of his father, Charles, in 1902.)

Tiffany's small firms produced many kinds of furniture and objects. Some of these pieces were frankly exotic, such as HORN FURNITURE, and some of them revived design elements from Greek and Roman antiquity (*see* NEOCLASSICAL STYLE). Much of their work employed the surface decoration and functional design associated with the British ART FURNITURE MOVEMENT, though Islamic abstract decorative motifs were also an influence. The Art Nouveau style

Tiffany made his own in his glass designs was not much in evidence in this furniture. A great deal of Tiffany furniture was distinguished by a hallmark—a foot consisting of a glass ball clasped by a brass claw.

TILLIARD, JEAN-BAPTISTE, I (1685–1766)

Leading French chair maker in LOUIS XV STYLE. Tilliard, whose work was richly carved and gilt, was influential in the MENUISIERS' adoption of the rococo style. On his retirement in 1764, he was succeeded in the family business by his son Jean-Baptiste Tilliard II (active 1752–97), who worked in the LOUIS XVI STYLE.

TILT-TOP TABLE (also *snap table*)
Eighteenth-century TRIPOD TABLE with hinged top that could be tilted to a vertical position when not in use, to save space. This could be accomplished by a BIRDCAGE SUPPORT or a more conventional hinge.

TILTER
Ball-and-socket device used on back legs of chairs in 19th-century SHAKER FURNITURE. It enabled the chair to be tipped backward by the sitter while its feet remained flat on the floor, enhancing stability and preventing wear on rugs or floor. Each leg terminated in a socket that housed a wooden hemisphere, flat on the bottom. A short rawhide thong was attached to its domed top, passed through the chair leg and pinned, thus securing the ball in its socket. These wooden devices tended to split with use, and a metal "tilting boot" was later developed on the same principle and patented.

TILTING CHEST
In GOTHIC FURNITURE, a chest with ornamentation depicting, in carved relief, two knights jousting. Prompted by the widespread pictorial stone carving on buildings at this time, tilting chests were very popular with aristocrats throughout northern Europe in the 14th and 15th centuries.

TISCH, CHARLES (active 1870–90)

VICTORIAN PERIOD New York furniture maker, associated with the "Eastlake" style (*see*

Charles Locke EASTLAKE). Influenced by the British ART FURNITURE MOVEMENT, Tisch produced elaborate pieces with the flat decoration prescribed by Eastlake and Bruce TALBERT. The bold asymmetry of his work may indicate an awareness of Oriental art.

TOBEY FURNITURE CO.

Chicago furniture manufacturers, founded in 1875 by the brothers Charles and Frank Tobey. From 1888 the Tobey Furniture Co. began to manufacture furniture to architects' specifications as well as for general sale. The firm made fine furniture in a number of popular styles of the day, including the RENAISSANCE REVIVAL STYLE, ART NOUVEAU and, especially, the Mission style (*see* MISSION FURNITURE). Some of the company's anonymous designs seem to have been influenced by the stylized, botanical ornamentation of Chicago architect Louis Sullivan (*see* PRAIRIE SCHOOL).

TOILETTE (also *table de toilette*)

French name for DRESSING TABLE.

TOILETTE EN PAPILLON

Eighteenth-century French DRESSING TABLE shaped like a butterfly or stylized heart. It had two rounded lobes projecting forward on either side of the user, each containing a set of drawers.

TONGUE

Protruding strip along edge or end of a board, intended for insertion into matching groove, or RABBET, cut in another piece of wood. The two pieces are thereby connected in a TONGUE-AND-GROOVE JOINT (*see under* JOINERY).

TOPINO, CHARLES (c. 1725–89)

French ÉBÉNISTE of the Louis XV and TRANSITION STYLES. Born in Arras, Topino went to Paris in 1745. He specialized in small tables and BONHEURS DU JOUR. Throughout his career, he used features of ROCOCO FURNITURE, especially the CABRIOLE LEG (*see under* LEG), even when the neoclassical LOUIS XVI STYLE was in vogue. Topino's distinctive style of pictorial MARQUETRY featured domestic still lifes, including images of flower vases, Oriental ceramics and inkstands with quill pens.

TORCHÈRE

French name for CANDLESTAND.

TORO, JEAN-BERNARD

See TURREAU, JEAN-BERNARD.

TORTOISESHELL

Ornamental material; mottled, semi-transparent shell of certain tortoises, used on European furniture in sumptuous inlay work, especially BOULLE MARQUETRY, since the 17th century. The rich appearance of tortoiseshell is often made more striking by mounting it over a sheet of colored metal foil whose tint, most often red, can be seen through the shell.

TORUS MOLDING

See under MOLDING.

TOWNSEND, EDMUND (1736–1811)

Newport, Rhode Island, cabinetmaker; maker of NEWPORT CHIPPENDALE FURNITURE. Son of Job TOWNSEND, Edmund Townsend was particularly noted for his fine carving. His taste was conservative, preserving elements of the QUEEN ANNE STYLE in furniture that, like all the Newport work of the day, derived largely from the rococo patterns (*see* ROCOCO FURNITURE) of Thomas CHIPPENDALE.

TOWNSEND, JOB (1699–1765)

Newport, Rhode Island, furniture maker; a developer of NEWPORT CHIPPENDALE FURNITURE. A Quaker, Job Townsend was established as a craftsman by about 1720, when he made furniture with his brother Christopher in a conservative version of the QUEEN ANNE STYLE. He later applied the patterns of Thomas CHIPPENDALE in a restrained manner that, as developed by Townsend and his son-in-law John GODDARD, became associated with Newport. With Goddard, Townsend is credited with full development of the BLOCK-FRONT. After his death, his business was inherited by his son Edmund TOWNSEND.

TOWNSEND, JOHN (1732–1809)

Newport, Rhode Island, furniture maker, associated with NEWPORT CHIPPENDALE FURNITURE. Son of Job TOWNSEND's brother

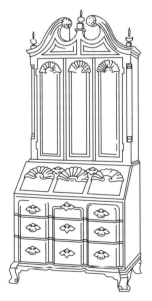

Townsend

Christopher, John Townsend worked in the Newport manner based on the patterns of Thomas CHIPPENDALE. Late in his career, though, his work began to reflect the influences of George HEPPLEWHITE and Thomas SHERATON.

TRACERY

Decorative motif in GOTHIC FURNITURE; delicate, latticelike arrangement of bars or lines creating ornamental patterns, usually of foliate or abstract forms, especially the TREFOIL and the QUATREFOIL. Like much ornamentation on MEDIEVAL FURNITURE, tracery derived from the masonry architecture of the period—following, in this case, the decorative framework placed within a window to support the pieces of glass, which at that time could be made only in small sections. On furniture, tracery took the form of pierced, inlaid, incised or painted decoration. Much later, it was popular in furniture in the NEO-GOTHIC STYLE.

TRACY, EBENEZER (1744–1803)

New England furniture maker, noted especially for WINDSOR CHAIRS. Tracy, in his large shop in Lisbon, Connecticut, made great quantities of Windsor chairs and other furniture, using an early approximation of factory methods, with many workers assembling pieces from ready-made parts.

TRAFALGAR FURNITURE

British REGENCY STYLE fashion; furniture decorated with nautical motifs, especially with TWIST TURNING (*see under* turnery), which resembled ropes of ship's rigging. This furniture commemorated Admiral Horatio Nelson, who died heroically at the Battle of Trafalgar in 1805, in which Britain was victorious. Such furniture, including the popular NELSON WINDSOR CHAIR (*see under* WINDSOR CHAIR), was made into the 1840s.

TRAFALGAR WINDSOR CHAIR

Another name for NELSON WINDSOR CHAIR (*see under* WINDSOR CHAIR).

TRANSITION STYLE

Style of French furniture of the 1760s that amalgamated features of the preceding LOUIS XV STYLE and the coming LOUIS XVI STYLE. In Transition furniture NEOCLASSICAL STYLE motifs appeared on the curving ROCOCO FURNITURE of the day. Curves were generally toned down—almost completely, for instance, in the case of the BREAKFRONT commode, a characteristic piece of the period—and the swelling SERPENTINE front of earlier forms was echoed in a more severe shape. Jean-François OEBEN was the leading cabinetmaker of the period, along with his brother-in-law Roger VANDERCRUSE. Some of the leading makers of the Louis XVI period, including J.-H. RIESENER and J.-F. LELEU, began their careers in the Transition style.

TRAY CORNER

Another name for DISHED CORNER.

TREFOIL

Ornamental motif in GOTHIC FURNITURE; radially symmetrical, three-lobed, formalized leaf form, usually enclosed by a circle. Commonly used in TRACERY, both in architecture and in furniture, the trefoil could appear singly or in a repeated pattern. It was also popular in the NEO-GOTHIC STYLE of the 18th and 19th centuries.

TRESTLE

Portable support consisting of horizontal beam and arrangement of legs. In the common sawhorse (a trestle), two pairs of diverging legs are attached, one at each end of the beam. In a more decorative version, which is more common in furniture, the beam rests atop a column or columns rising from a foot that is also a horizontal beam, parallel to the top. The trestle has been used since medieval times as a support for furniture that can be disassembled, most notably the TRESTLE TABLE.

TRESTLE BED

Furniture form used mostly in hospitals. It consists of a movable bed frame supported, when in use, by TRESTLES.

TRESTLE STAND

Small stand resembling an arrangement of TRESTLES, often used as support for a CHEST.

trefoil

A trestle stand consists of three elements. Two of them, identical, are trestlelike, each comprising a column or columns rising from a low, beamlike foot to support a horizontal top beam. Joining these is a short stretcher or stretchers, sometimes taking the form of a FRIEZE like carved panel. A tabletop or chest rests on the two horizontal top beams.

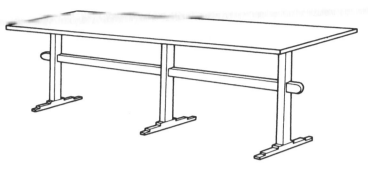

trestle table

TRESTLE TABLE
Table made of a board or boards supported by TRESTLES. Originally a MEDIEVAL FURNITURE form, the trestle table was a prime example of the emphasis on mobility and ease of transport that characterized furniture design in the Middle Ages. The form remained popular through the 17th century; it was eventually replaced by the various DROP-LEAF TABLES. It has been revived in recent years, however, especially in pieces with glass tops.

TRIDARN
Type of PRESS CUPBOARD developed in Wales in the 17th century. The tridarn was distinctive because it was divided into three sections, one above the other. A cupboard enclosed with two doors occupied the bottom level. Above it ran a row of three low spaces, each also enclosed. This row was set back, leaving a narrow ledge in front for the display of small objects. The top level was an open shelf, also for display.

TRIFID FOOT
See under FOOT.

TRIGLYPH
One of a series of projecting blocks, each decorated with three vertical grooves, alternating with METOPES in a FRIEZE of the DORIC ORDER. Such decoration was often used in European furniture styles deriving from classical architecture.

TRIO TABLES
See NEST OF TABLES.

TRIPOD TABLE
Another name for 18th-century PEDESTAL TABLE.

TROTTER, DANIEL (1747–1800)
Maker of PHILADELPHIA CHIPPENDALE FURNITURE. Known particularly for his Chippendale "PRETZEL-BACK" CHAIRS, Trotter adopted a NEOCLASSICAL STYLE in the FEDERAL PERIOD. His apprentice, son-in-law and successor was Ephraim HAINES.

TROUBADOUR, LE STYLE
Nineteenth-century French term for NEO-GOTHIC STYLE.

TRUCKLE BED
Sixteenth-century term for TRUNDLE BED.

TRUMBLE, FRANCIS (c. 1716–98)
Philadelphia chair maker of second half of 18th century. Trumble is best known for having made 114 WINDSOR CHAIRS for the Continental Congress in 1778.

TRUMPET LEG
See under LEG.

TRUMPET TURNING
See under TURNERY.

TRUNDLE BED
RENAISSANCE FURNITURE form; low bed on wheels, designed to roll under a larger bed when not in use. The trundle bed evolved in the 15th century and remained popular in Europe and America into the 19th century.

TRUNK
Early MEDIEVAL FURNITURE form; crude CHEST made of a hollowed-out length of tree

trunk, often girdled with bands of iron to provide additional strength and guard against splitting. At first, a lengthwise slice from a side of the tree trunk was used as a lid, though planked lids later followed. The trunk's bulk made it difficult to transport, and its round shape made it awkward to use it as a seat, table or bed, as other chest forms commonly were. The trunk was thus not very popular, but it was sufficiently economical that it continued to be made into the 17th century. Subsequently, the term has come to refer, by extension, to any large BOX, crate or chest that is purely utilitarian, undecorative and used for storage or transport.

TRUSSING BED
MEDIEVAL and RENAISSANCE FURNITURE form; bed that could be folded or dismantled and then wrapped, or trussed, for transport.

TSUITATE
JAPANESE FURNITURE form; wide, low, single-panel SCREEN of solid wood, used to separate the vestibule of a house from the room beyond it and to protect against drafts. The *tsuitate* has a heavy wood frame and is supported by low, transverse feet. A variant form consists of a stand with four short uprights arranged in pairs opposite each other and a screen panel that remains vertical by being placed between them.

TUDOR FURNITURE
English RENAISSANCE FURNITURE of late 16th and early 17th centuries. Tudor furniture, named after the dynasty that ruled England from 1485 until 1603, reflected the influence of the northern European MANNERIST STYLE and the close cultural ties between England and the Protestants of the Netherlands and Germany. Dutch and German craftsmen and pieces of furniture traveled to England during this period. Most important, though, were the published PATTERN BOOKS of well-known designers, especially those of Wendel DIETTERLIN and Hans VREDEMAN DE VRIES. In general, the Tudor style was an unsophisticated, provincial rendering of Renaissance ideas, mixing simple new motifs—for example, ROMAYNE WORK—with such medieval ones as CUSPING or LINENFOLD

paneling. Some significant new developments occurred, however. The new decorative style found distinctively English expression in the NONSUCH CHEST. And, as elsewhere, lighter chairs evolved; a notable English version was the FARTHINGALE CHAIR. The DRAW-LEAF TABLE was a common form by about 1550. Furthermore, new woods such as EBONY and HOLLY were gradually integrated with the traditional local timbers—OAK, ASH and ELM.

TUFFT, THOMAS (c. 1738–88)
Maker of PHILADELPHIA CHIPPENDALE FURNITURE. A master of carved detail, Tufft, who used some of the "Chippendale Gothic" patterns (*see* Thomas CHIPPENDALE), made pieces that were simpler than those of his Philadelphia contemporaries.

TUFTING
See UPHOLSTERY.

TULA IRONWORKS
Eighteenth-century Russian manufacturer of STEEL FURNITURE. Principally a small arms factory, the Tula Ironworks, at Tula, south of Moscow, also made furniture, chiefly small pieces, from about 1725 until the early 19th century. Most Tula furniture was of cut steel, with sometimes as many as a thousand small, shaped elements in a single piece. In style, the factory's output ranged from traditional Russian pieces, with OPENWORK panels of ARABESQUEs, to designs reminiscent of British ADAM STYLE work, probably influenced by Matthew Boulton (1728–1809), a British metalworker whose work was well known in Russia.

TULIP POPLAR (also *yellow poplar; American whitewood*)
Wood of tulip tree of eastern United States; pale, white to light brown HARDWOOD, often with characteristic green streaks; not a true poplar. Tulip poplar's most frequent use in furniture is for interior fittings, especially drawer parts. It is also used for WINDSOR CHAIR seats. It stains well and is often dyed to resemble walnut or maple when used as a primary wood (*see* PRIMARY AND SECONDARY WOODS). It is sometimes inaccurately called TULIPWOOD.

TULIPWOOD

Brazilian HARDWOOD; close relative of ROSE-WOOD, used in decorative MARQUETRY and inlays. It was especially popular in 18th-century French furniture. Tulipwood is yellow in color with reddish stripes. Like rosewood, it is difficult to work, but its appearance is highly prized. In France it is called *bois de rose;* in America, *pinkwood.* Also, in America the term *tulipwood* is sometimes used for TULIP POPLAR wood.

TUPELO

Yellow to pale brown HARDWOOD of southeastern United States, used in furniture for framing. It is also a common component of plywood.

TURKEY-BREAST CUPBOARD

Form of CORNER CUPBOARD with four sides, two against the wall of the room and two with doors projecting forward at a sharp angle. It was produced only by 18th-century craftsmen on the Delmarva Peninsula, on the eastern shore of Chesapeake Bay. The angular piece was named for its resemblance to the sharp keel bone of a turkey. Its design, usually produced in simplified variants of the British PALLADIAN STYLE, enabled the corner cupboard to hold more without requiring that it occupy more wall space.

TURKEY SOFA

Eighteenth-century name for OTTOMAN.

TURKEY WORK

Type of embroidery popular on furniture UPHOLSTERY in England in the 17th century. Turkey work was frankly imitative of Oriental carpets, especially those from Persia, which came to England via Turkey and were thus misnamed.

TURNED CHAIR

MEDIEVAL FURNITURE form; type of BACK STOOL whose arms, legs and back are constructed of turned members (*see* TURNERY).

TURNER

Woodworker specializing in TURNERY—the making of furniture parts such as LEGS, STRETCHERs, BALUSTERs and SPINDLEs with a LATHE.

TURNERY

Process of shaping wood, metal or another material by spinning it against cutting or abrading tools on a LATHE. The shaped objects so made, symmetrical around the axis on which they have been spun, are also known as turnery. Turnery has been an important process in furniture making since ancient times, yielding long members (such as LEGS STRETCHERs, BALUSTERs and SPINDLEs) and rounded ones (such as FINIALs, ball feet and bun feet [*see* BALL FOOT *and* BUN FOOT, *under* FOOT]). A woodworker who specializes in turnery is called a TURNER; the finished shapes of turned lengths of wood are called *turnings.* By arranging the cutting blades of a lathe in different configurations, and by moving them during the turning process, various complex turnings can be made. A number of turnings are distinguished by name. Frequently, though, a turned member is composed of more than one such turning and/or is carved after being turned.

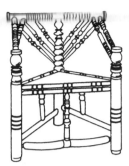
turned chair

BALL TURNING

Turned member composed of a series of spherical shapes. This turning was especially popular in northern European and American furniture of the late 17th century.

BALL-AND-RING TURNING

Turned member composed of alternating series of spherical shapes and narrow rings.

ball turning

BALUSTER TURNING

Turned member incorporating section shaped like a large, widemouthed vase. This section is usually carved after turning, often with GADROONING along its long axis, giving it an undulating shape. The term BALUSTER also denotes a stout turned member of any shape.

BAMBOO TURNING

Turned member carved with narrow rings to resemble length of BAMBOO.

baluster turning

BARLEY-SUGAR TURNING

Another name for TWIST TURNING (*see under* TURNERY), referring to its resemblance to a traditional candy.

bamboo turning

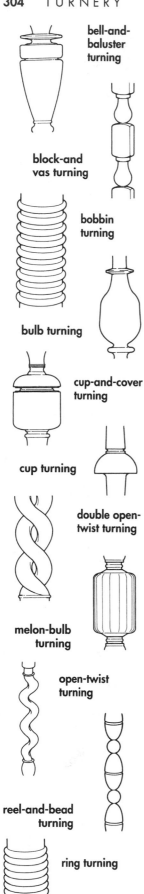

bell-and-baluster turning

block-and-vas turning

bobbin turning

bulb turning

cup-and-cover turning

cup turning

double open-twist turning

melon-bulb turning

open-twist turning

reel-and-bead turning

ring turning

BELL-AND-BALUSTER TURNING
Turned member incorporating wide-mouthed vase shape of BALUSTER TURNING below inverted cup shape of CUP TURNING (*see each under* TURNERY); the two elements are separated by a gap.

BLOCK-AND-VASE TURNING
Turned member composed of square or rectangular shapes alternating with short, vase-like shapes (*see* VASE TURNING, *under* TURNERY).

BOBBIN TURNING
Turned member composed of a series of narrow, raised rings separated by gaps of approximately their own width. Together, two rings plus the gap between them resemble a bobbin, a short spool for thread.

BULB TURNING
Turned member incorporating large, swollen oblong section. Bulb turnings were frequently carved after turning (*see* MELON-BULB TURNING, *under* TURNERY) and were most common in massive table legs and bedposts of RENAISSANCE FURNITURE.

CUP TURNING
Turned member incorporating profile of inverted cup.

CUP-AND-COVER TURNING
Turned member shaped like a chalice with domed lid. Cup-and-cover turning was used especially for legs in TUDOR and JACOBEAN FURNITURE.

DOUBLE OPEN-TWIST TURNING
Turned member formed as two separate but intertwining spirals. The double open twist is produced by PIERCED CARVING after turning.

HALF-TURNING
Decorative APPLIQUÉ produced on a lathe; split SPINDLE or split BALUSTER.

MELON-BULB TURNING
BULB TURNING (*see under* TURNERY) carved with vertical grooves or other indentations, thus resembling a melon. The melon-bulb turning was most commonly used in TUDOR and JACOBEAN FURNITURE.

OPEN-TWIST TURNING
Turned member formed as a spiral of wood, resembling a corkscrew. This type of turning was popular in RENAISSANCE FURNITURE.

REEL-AND-BEAD TURNING
Turned member composed of alternating spherical and ovoid shapes. The ovoids are much longer than the spheres and are usually grooved with rings around their central, widest parts. This type of turning was used in MEDIEVAL FURNITURE.

RING TURNING
Turned member banded by series of parallel grooves.

ROPE TURNING
Another name for TWIST TURNING (*see under* TURNERY).

SAUSAGE TURNING
Turned member composed of series of abutting ovoid swellings, resembling linked sausages.

SCREW TURNING
Another name for TWIST TURNING (*see under* TURNERY).

SPIRAL TURNING
Another name for TWIST TURNING (*see under* TURNERY).

SPOOL TURNING
Prior to 19th century, synonym for BOBBIN TURNING (*see under* TURNERY); more specifically, an element in 19th-century American SPOOL FURNITURE—length of turned wood intended to provide spools for thread, composed of a series of separated narrow rings.

TRUMPET TURNING
Turned member incorporating profile of upturned trumpet, generally topped by a dome. Trumpet turning was often used on legs in RESTORATION FURNITURE as well as furniture in the WILLIAM AND MARY STYLE.

TWIST TURNING (also *barley-sugar turning; spiral turning; rope turning; screw turning*)
Turned member resembling a rope, with groove or shallow depression spiraling along its length. The twist turning was often used for legs and stretchers in late 17th-century furniture.

VASE TURNING
Turned member incorporating profile of a stylized vase with swelling base and tapering neck.

VASE-AND-BALL TURNING
Turned member composed of alternating vase-like (*see* VASE TURNING, *under* TURNERY) and spherical shapes.

TURN-UP TABLE
Eighteenth-century term for TILT-TOP TABLE.

TURREAU (or Toro), JEAN-BERNARD (1672–1731)
French sculptor and designer of ornamentation. Turreau, from the Mediterranean port of Toulon, was originally a carver of ships' figureheads. In Paris, between 1716 and 1719, he published three PATTERN BOOKS of designs, both elegant and grotesque, that influenced ROCOCO FURNITURE designers in France and Britain.

TURRET-TOP TABLE
Modern name for type of TEA TABLE made in Boston in 18th century. It was characterized by a shaped top with semicircular projections arrayed around the edges. Each of these semicircles was designed to hold a cup and saucer; the whole DISHED TOP was surrounded by molding.

TUSCAN BED
Italian RENAISSANCE FURNITURE form. This bed had an elaborate carved and gilded headboard and, at each corner, a spiral-turned column (*see* SPIRAL TURNING, *under* TURNERY) topped with an urn-shaped finial. It was a particularly popular form in Tuscany in the mid-16th century.

TUSCAN ORDER
One of the ancient Roman ORDERS OF ARCHITECTURE, perhaps of Etruscan ancestry—hence, the name. The Tuscan order was characterized by a smooth, tapering COLUMN on a circular base. A NECKING of MOLDINGS decorated the shaft below a CAPITAL similar to that of the DORIC ORDER. The Tuscan order initially had only a CORNICE above the columns, but it later developed a simple ENTABLATURE based on that of the IONIC ORDER.

TWIN BED
One of a pair of identical beds used in the same bedroom. Twin beds were first introduced in the early 19th century by Thomas SHERATON, who placed them both under a single canopy, observing that their use would help sleepers keep cool during hot weather. They first achieved notable popularity in about 1840 and have remained in use ever since.

TWIST TURNING
See under TURNERY.

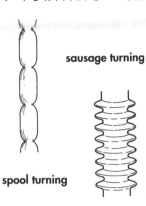
sausage turning
spool turning
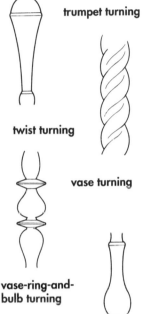
trumpet turning
twist turning
vase turning
vase-ring-and-bulb turning

vase-and-ball turning

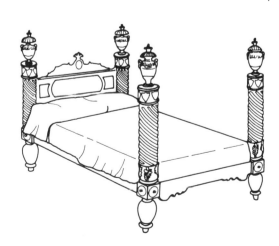
Tuscan bed

U

ÜBERBAUSCHRANK

German RENAISSANCE FURNITURE form; two-tiered CUPBOARD. The recessed upper stage featured a prominent CORNICE supported at the corners by short columns, often CARYATIDS, resting on the top of the lower element. The whole was elaborately ornamented with carving and rich MARQUETRY. Closely resembling the English PRESS CUPBOARD, the *Überbauschrank* evolved in the Rhineland from a French GOTHIC FURNITURE form, the DRESSER (1).

UMBRELLA-BACK CHAIR

Another name for WHEEL-BACK CHAIR.

UNION DES ARTISTES MODERNES

Organization of French architects and designers founded in 1930. The group was established to further the development of the modern INTERNATIONAL STYLE. The institute became the most prominent locus of modern functionalist design outside Germany (*see* BAUHAUS; FUNCTIONALISM). The U.A.M., as it was known, was founded by a group including René HERBST, Francis JOURDAIN and Robert MALLET-STEVENS. Prominent among the furniture designers who were members were LE CORBUSIER, Pierre CHAREAU, Eileen GRAY and Charlotte PERRIAND.

UNIT FURNITURE

Modular furniture developed in Germany in the 1920s. Influenced by the ideas of the DEUTSCHER WERKBUND and the need, following the First World War, for furniture that was both inexpensive to make and economical of space (in view of the pervasive housing shortage of the period), BAUHAUS and other designers, especially Franz SCHUSTER, devised the modular unit furniture system. These ranges of furniture consisted of similar modular elements, each usable in a number of different ways—as, for instance, chest/table or shelf/cabinet/chest of drawers combinations. The modules could be acquired in different combinations, according to the owner's finances or available space, and added to or rearranged at will. Since they were similar or identical in basic design, the modules could be manufactured easily and inexpensively. The idea spread rapidly and remains evident in contemporary furniture.

UNTEUTSCH, FRIEDRICH (active c. 1650)

German AURICULAR STYLE cabinetmaker and furniture designer. Unteutsch, from Frankfurt am Main, published a PATTERN BOOK (c. 1650) whose designs influenced much Dutch and German work of the late 17th century, in the last phase of MANNERIST STYLE furniture.

UPHOLSTERY

Cloth, leather or other material attached, usually along with stuffing or padding, to seat and back of chairs and other seating forms to increase comfort and decorativeness. In its most basic sense—simply stretching material across a rigid frame—upholstering has been practiced in Western furniture making since ancient times (*see* EGYPTIAN FURNITURE). Later, loose cushions were used along with such upholstery or on solid wooden furniture. Eventually, in the late 16th century, the padding and the cushion were covered together by the material, which was tacked to the frame, and upholstery in its modern sense was born. French furniture makers pioneered these early advances, and they led in the development of upholstery until the 20th century, when American technology began to produce most of the innovative materials that are used in much contemporary furniture.

In the 17th century the basic structural arrangements of upholstery were perfected. Narrow strips of fabric or leather webbing were interlaced across a seat frame, and a piece of linen was tacked above it. On this base, a quantity of horsehair was placed, and a second piece of linen was fastened over it to keep it in place. An exterior covering of heavier fabric or leather was placed over all of these layers and nailed to the chair frame. Backs, and later arms, were treated the same way. The most common form to develop with upholstery was the FARTHINGALE CHAIR. In the 17th century, and at various times thereafter, the nailheads securing the upholstery were regarded as decorative and were arranged in ornamental clusters or other patterns.

At first, no effort had been made to shape the horsehair stuffing, giving much 17th-century seating a domed appearance. Then, in a new procedure, 18th-century makers gathered the hairs and held them down to the lower layer of fabric with long basting stitches. This work could be kept invisible, but it became fashionable to draw these stitches through the outer layer at several points, tying them and decorating the knots with tufts of silk. These tufted knots were arranged in decorative patterns on the seat or back. This practice, called *tufting*, was the forerunner of *buttoning*, which was very important in the 19th century.

In about 1750 another improvement was made—strengthening the front edge of the seat, the site of greatest wear, by adding a tightly sewn roll of extra stuffing to form a firm edge. Also, the SLIP SEAT was developed, enabling the upholstering to be done on a separate seat frame that was then dropped into place. A number of new forms arose in 18th-century France, taking advantage of this more sophisticated upholstery. These included the BERGÈRE and the CANAPÉ, or SOFA. In the 1780s the four-square rigor of NEOCLASSICAL STYLE forms stimulated the development of *square-stuffing*, in which the horsehair stuffing was built up and tightly stitched at all four edges so that top and sides met at stiff right angles.

In the 18th century, crude upholstery springs consisting of flexible metal strips, analogous to those used in carriage suspensions, had been experimented with, but it took the invention of coil springs to produce modern upholstery. The 1822 invention of the helical metal spring is generally attributed to one Georg Junigl, of Vienna. By the 1830s its use in furniture was widespread throughout Europe and America. In this new upholstery the same interlaced webbing was still used, but it now supported a group of coil springs instead of horsehair. Each spring was sewn to the webbing and all of them were tied down to a certain height and to each other so as to resist lateral pressure. A piece of canvas covered them, and a thin layer of horsehair on top cushioned the sitter from the springs themselves. As before, the exterior material covered all and was attached to the furniture frame.

Coil-spring upholstery necessitated a great change in the appearance of a chair or sofa, for the seat now had to be much deeper. In about 1820 the loose tassels of silk used in tufting disappeared in favor of buttons, finished in the same fabric as the seat or back. By about midcentury this feature was combined with coil-springing in the technique known as *deep-buttoning*: the springs were placed between the buttons, which were drawn downward, creating a series of indentations. Excess fabric was gathered into pleats at the buttons. Deep-buttoning helped to hold the coils in place and to maintain the shape of the seat.

These developments suited the increasing desire for comfort and luxury in furniture on the part of the expanding new bourgeois market generated by the Industrial Revolution and the collapse of the *anciens régimes* in Europe. The VICTORIAN PERIOD witnessed the most pronounced manifestation of this trend in *overstuffed furniture*. Rounded corners, replacing square-stuffing, were combined with coil-springing and deep-buttoning in forms that were both massive and opulent in appearance. Often, all of the wooden framework of a piece was covered by upholstery. Novel forms proliferated, notably the BORNE, DIVAN, LOUNGE CHAIR and various sorts of OTTOMAN.

During the second half of the 19th century, a movement advocating design reform arose (*see* ARTS AND CRAFTS MOVEMENT; ART FURNITURE MOVEMENT). It favored a greater asceticism and prompted a decreased role for upholstery in fashionable furniture. Nevertheless, heavily upholstered furniture continued to be made commercially in great quantities, and the techniques developed earlier remained in use. Beginning in the second quarter of the 20th century, new synthetic materials were devised (*see* PLASTIC FURNITURE), and a new sort of upholstery resulted; it has since been used alongside traditional coil-springing. Fine wiremesh springing and latex tapes and cords can now serve as supports for foam rubber or polyurethane stuffings, covered in synthetic, often elasticized, fabrics. Molded plastic furniture covered in stretch fabric is upholstered to the same degree as was a plush Victorian sofa whose wood was invisible, but the new material makes possible the slim, streamlined look that is more prized today. Among modern furniture designers who have taken advantage of synthetic upholstery are Eero AARNIO, Don CHADWICK, MATTA, Olivier MOURGUE and Eero SAARINEN.

Utility chair

UPJOHN, RICHARD (1802–78)

British-American architect and furniture designer. In the 1840s and 1850s, Upjohn was the principal American church architect in the NEO-GOTHIC STYLE. He also designed furniture, in a somewhat more eclectic, if sober, vein; his simple, four-square Gothic pieces were modestly ornamented with architectural motifs from the RENAISSANCE REVIVAL STYLE.

URBAN, JOSEPH (1872–1933)

Austrian-American SEZESSION style designer. In 1911, after an association as an architect and designer with the Sezession movement and the WIENER WERKSTÄTTE in Vienna, Urban emigrated to the United States. There, he began a career as an interior and theatrical designer. From 1918 to 1933 he was the chief designer of the Metropolitan Opera in New York; in addition, during this period, he directed 20 films and several Broadway shows. He also designed interiors for houses, hotels and theaters, and he designed much furniture for these projects as well. He remained close to the style of pre-First World War Vienna (in 1922 he opened a branch of the Wiener Werkstätte in New York). His furniture was strongly rectilinear and compact, with geometric ornamentation and a strong penchant for black and white, often in the form of silver or ivory inlays in blackstained wood. He also designed some simple bentwood furniture for Thonet Brothers (*see* Michael THONET).

URN

Decorative motif; tall, usually footed, vaselike vessel. Originally made in ancient Greece to contain the ashes of the dead, the urn was adopted as a motif by makers of RENAISSANCE FURNITURE from the carved decoration of Roman sarcophagi. It was popular in all NEO-CLASSICAL STYLE furniture thereafter, especially in the 18th century.

UTILITY FURNITURE

Works produced under Britain's Utility Furniture program, instituted by the national government during the Second World War and discontinued in 1952. In the interest of controlling the use of materials and minimizing labor costs, the British government dictated furniture design to the industry, providing manufacturing firms with the only furniture designs that could legally be produced. Gordon RUSSELL, a well-known INTERNATIONAL STYLE designer, was appointed design consultant to the program and was responsible for the character of the Utility Furniture designs. Utility Furniture was simple and rectilinear, modestly proportioned and with little or no ornamentation. A taste for more ornately decorated furniture emerged after the war, but public recognition of the high quality of Utility Furniture, combined with a sales tax exemption for those who purchased it, helped to ensure the continued popularity of Utility Furniture until the program was disbanded. The example of practical FUNCTIONALISM offered by the Utility program was very widely felt throughout the British furniture industry and greatly influenced practices and designs in British furniture in the 1940s and 1950s (*see* CONTEMPORARY STYLE).

UTZON, JØRN (b. 1918)

Danish architect and designer of the 1960s. Once a student of Alvar AALTO and Frank Lloyd WRIGHT, Utzon is best known as the architect of the Opera House in Sydney, Australia. He also designed furniture in a variant of the INTERNATIONAL STYLE—strictly functionalistic pieces in metal and molded plastic or plywood, with foam-rubber upholstered in fabric or leather (*see* FUNCTIONALISM).

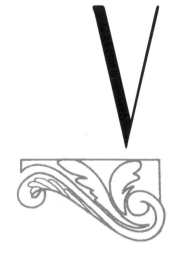

VAISSELIER

Eighteenth-century French DRESSER (1). Often very wide, the *vaisselier,* sometimes called a *buffet-vaisselier,* held as many as five cupboards side by side below its tablelike surface and an arrangement of shelves above it.

VALANCE

Horizontal band of drapery created by hanging gathered or pleated fabric from the TESTER or CANOPY of a bed; similarly, a short curtain of fabric hanging from the frame of a bed or chair to the floor to conceal the space underneath. Also, a stylized drapery carved on the lower edge of an APRON or other horizontal element of a piece of furniture.

VALLIN, EUGÈNE (1856–1922)

French ART NOUVEAU furniture designer; member of the School of Nancy (*see* NANCY, SCHOOL OF). Vallin's early work was in the neo-Gothic and neo-ROCOCO REVIVAL STYLES, but he had begun to respond to Émile GALLÉ's style by 1895. Subsequently, he produced Art Nouveau pieces similar to Gallé's, though plainer and less ambitious. Vallin's later work, in the 1920s, was greatly simplified and bore some resemblance to modern functionalist designs.

VAN DE VELDE, HENRI (1863–1957)

Belgian architect and designer; prominent ART NOUVEAU figure and important early modernist. Originally a painter, Van de Velde began working in architecture and the decorative arts in the 1890s, influenced by the ideas of William MORRIS and the British ARTS AND CRAFTS MOVEMENT. He designed and built a

house for himself between 1894 and 1895. In order to unify its design, he designed all of the furniture, fixtures, silver and kitchenware as well. The concept of the unity of design was one element of the design reform movements of the time; Van de Velde and others also wished to develop a new style that would not refer to or revive historical styles. Van de Velde's house exemplified these ideals in a style based on the dynamic play of abstract lines. It became famous, or notorious, as an instance of revolutionary design.

Samuel BING hired Van de Velde to design furniture and rooms for his Paris shop, *L'Art Nouveau.* From then on, Van de Velde's influence was widely felt among designers. He also

valance

vaisselier

chair by Van de Velde

designed the façade and the fixtures for the shop of Bing's principal rival. He established his own manufacturing firm near Brussels, making furniture and metalworks, and filled many design commissions in Germany. Van de Velde's work advanced the new direction in design in several countries. His furniture style—influenced by Charles Rennie MACKINTOSH, in particular—was in the abstract geometrical, more Germanic wing of the Art Nouveau movement. After 1899 Van de Veldc lived in Berlin and was principally active in Germany. His work at this time reflects his effort to design fine furniture for mass production; he retained the basic, curvilinear Art Nouveau shapes but began to use simpler materials and a more austere style. Thus, Van de Velde is a figure of consequence in the evolution of modern functionalist furniture design

In 1901 he began working for the German duchy of Weimar, providing designs and overseeing production for state-sponsored cottage industry. He designed for potters, toymakers and basketweavers, as well as for furniture makers (including pieces made of wicker, then an experimental material). These furniture designs departed altogether from Art Nouveau and were very simple and rectilinear, in the Arts and Crafts tradition. In 1904 he became director of Weimar's Arts School & School of Arts and Crafts, the immediate predecessor of the BAUHAUS. In fact, Van de Velde was responsible for the appointment of Walter GROPIUS as his successor. In the 1920s Van de Velde left Germany, returning first to Holland and then to his home, Brussels, where he directed a decorative arts school. Subsequently, he designed very little furniture, using a severe modern style. He retired and lived in Switzerland after 1947.

VAN DER VINNE, LEONARDO (active 1660s–1690s)

Dutch or Flemish cabinetmaker who worked in Italy. Van der Vinne introduced floral MARQUETRY to Florence, where he was employed by the Medici ducal workshop and rose to become its chief cabinetmaker. He specialized in pieces with elaborate marquetry, usually using a great deal of ivory.

VAN DOESBURG, THEO (1883–1931)

Dutch painter, writer and designer; leader of the DE STIJL group. His real name was C. E.

M. Küpper. Principally a painter, Van Doesburg designed tubular-steel furniture in the 1920s, following the examples of Mart STAM and Marcel BREUER. Though he held the same ideals as Gerrit RIETVELD—a fellow De Stijl leader—Van Doesburg approached furniture design in a more practical, less programmatic manner and produced pieces that are less striking but more useful. He lectured at the BAUHAUS school and elsewhere and was a principal publicist of modernist ideas. Van Doesburg also practiced some architecture, in collaboration with J. J. P. OUD and others.

VANDERCRUSE, ROGER (also Roger Vandercruse Lacroix) (1728–99)

French ÉBÉNISTE who worked in the LOUIS XV, TRANSITION and LOUIS XVI STYLES. Vandercruse, who took the name *Lacroix* and is known by both, worked for Pierre MIGÉEON II early in his career. Like Migéon, Vandercruse specialized in small pieces. He made GUÉRIDONs and BONHEURs DU JOUR with delicate floral MARQUETRY or VERNIS MARTIN panels. He also used decorative porcelain plaques. He was a brother-in-law of J.-F. OEBEN.

VAN KEPPEL-GREEN

Los Angeles furniture company, extant 1938–72. After the Second World War, the partnership of Hendrick Van Keppel and Taylor Green (both born in 1914) became well known for outdoor furniture in a simple and inexpensive but elegant variant of the INTERNATIONAL STYLE. They marketed their own designs and also designed for other manufacturers.

VAN LEYDEN, LUCAS (1494–1533)

Dutch painter and designer of ornamentation for RENAISSANCE FURNITURE. Best known as a painter, van Leydon was an early exponent of Italian Renaissance ideas and techniques in Holland. He published engravings of Renaissance ornamental motifs that influenced Dutch craftsmen in the 1520s and 1530s.

VAN RISENBURGH (or Van Risamburgh), BERNARD (c. 1700–1765)

French ÉBÉNISTE who worked in LOUIS XV STYLE. Van Risenburgh, born in Flanders, specialized in VERNIS MARTIN, a type of simulated lacquer veneer; he sometimes incorporated panels of genuine Oriental LACQUER into his work. He was also the first cabinetmaker to use applied porcelain plaques as decoration. Until his identity was discovered in 1957, Van Risenburgh was known only by the initials *B.V.R.B.,* which he used as a maker's mark.

VANITY
Modern name for DRESSING TABLE.

VARDY, JOHN (d. 1765)
British PALLADIAN STYLE architect and furniture maker. Vardy's early furniture designs were strongly influenced by those of William KENT, though he subsequently produced ROCOCO FURNITURE as well. In 1744 he published an influential book of architecture and furniture designs, *Some Designs of Mr. Inigo Jones and Mr. William Kent,* that did much to popularize the Palladian taste.

VARGUEÑO
Spanish RENAISSANCE FURNITURE form; desk with a FALL FRONT exposing, when open, an array of small drawers richly decorated with elaborate INLAY. The outside of the fall front, visible when it was closed, was usually much more plainly decorated. A sturdy but decorative iron loop was mounted on each end panel so that the piece could be carried. The *vargueño* rested on either a TAQUILLÓN, an early type of chest of drawers, or a trestle table, the PIE DE PUENTE. Early *vargueños,* from the late 15th century, were decorated in the MUDÉJAR STYLE of HISPANO-MORESQUE FURNITURE. Then, in the first half of the 16th century, the PLATERESQUE STYLE introduced such Italian Renaissance motifs as classical urns and GROTESQUE ORNAMENT, but the Moorish influence was still plainly evident. Later in the century, a simpler, Italianate decorative style evolved, more reliant on architectural imagery. The 17th-century *vargueño* was influenced by the contemporary German KUNSTSCHRANK and featured very elaborate ornamentation, including complex representational MARQUETRY in numerous rich materials. The form remained popular into the early 18th century.

VARNISH
Coating for wood; transparent FINISH consisting of resinous material in a medium, applied as a liquid and drying to a thin film capable of taking a glossy shine. Varnish was used on ancient EGYPTIAN FURNITURE, but the technique of varnishing was lost in Europe until the 17th century, when oil-based varnishes were used. Chinese and Japanese woodworkers have employed varnishes continuously since antiquity. They used as resin the sap of the *lac* tree, the basic ingredient of LACQUER. Oriental varnish employed a base of rectified alcohol, or "spirits of wine." Alcohol-based varnish, both glossier and easier to use, superseded the oil-based variety once it became known in the West, in about 1670. Western resins were produced from linseed or from shellac made from insect secretions imported from India. Modern oil-based varnish, invented in the 19th century, is a paint, usually made from cellulose.

VASE TURNING
See under TURNERY.

VASE-AND-BALL TURNING
See under TURNERY.

VEDEL, KRISTIAN (b. 1923)
Contemporary Danish furniture designer. Trained under Kaare KLINT, Vedel has independently designed furniture and other household goods since 1955. He is known for simple, geometrical furniture in the Klint tradition.

VEILLEUSE
Eighteenth-century French furniture form; short SOFA in LOUIS XV STYLE. Its back was higher at one end than at the other, and there were a serpentine crest rail and thick cushions, intended for lounging. *Veilleuses* were generally made in pairs and placed to face each other, often on opposite sides of a fireplace.

VELLUM
Finely textured parchment made from skin of lambs, calves or young goats, sometimes used on panels as furniture VENEER. As an expen-

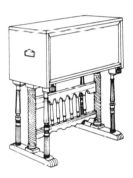

vargueño

sive novelty, vellum was attractive to several early modern furniture designers—notably Carlo BUGATTI and Pierre LEGRAIN—who were intent on purposeful extravagance.

VENEER

Thin sheet of fine wood or other material, attached to underlying layer of less expensive material for decorative effect; as a verb, to make such an attachment or to provide a piece of furniture with such a layer of surface material. In addition to its ornamental character, veneering gives extra strength to the piece, particularly if the grain—in the case of wood, the most common veneer—is placed at right angles to that of the substratum. When making sheets of wood veneer from a log, different methods of cutting will produce different sorts of FIGURING. Slicing horizontally across a tree trunk exposes the concentric growth rings. A longitudinal slice, parallel to the long axis, yields a striped grain. By rotary peeling, in which a log is rotated on a lathe against a long blade to produce a continuous sheet of veneer, a boldly variegated pattern is obtained. Also, depending on the part of the tree they come from, different sheets of wood will bear other distinctive figures, such as those in CURL VENEER, OYSTER VENEER and BURL VENEER. Furthermore, successive sheets from the same piece of wood bear the same figuring, and such matching sheets may be halved or quartered and the pieces placed in striking configurations.

The use of veneer goes back as far as ancient EGYPTIAN FURNITURE. However, after some use in ROMAN FURNITURE, veneering disappeared in Europe until the 16th century. Then, in RENAISSANCE FURNITURE, the use of INTARSIA and other INLAY work created veneers composed of many small pieces. The development of finer saws made possible the use of sheets of wood over whole surfaces, and veneer has been widely used in European and American furniture since the second half of the 17th century. In the Far East (see CHINESE FURNITURE; JAPANESE FURNITURE; KOREAN FURNITURE), traditional furniture bears little or no veneering, but in INDIAN FURNITURE ivory veneer was frequently applied to wood; ivory was relatively common in India, and it protected wood against insects, a serious problem for Indian cabinetmakers. In modern times veneers of new materials, especially plastics such as Formica, are common everywhere, though traditional wood veneering is still popular.

VERDIGRIS

Decorative device; paint on wood simulating blue-green patina found on ancient bronze. Verdigris is lighter in tone than ANTIQUE VERT, which it resembles.

VERNIS MARTIN

Eighteenth-century French JAPANNING technique, requiring many coats of varnish, that produced a rich and brilliant surface capable of being carved in low relief. Almost indistinguishable from fine Oriental LACQUER, it was named after the Martin brothers, who perfected the technique in about 1730.

VICTORIAN PERIOD

Reign of the British monarch Queen Victoria (1837–1901); period of complex stylistic evolution in Britain and America. Though the REGENCY STYLE was still prominent early in this period, the development of the REVIVAL STYLES produced the elaborate decoration and eclecticism most characteristic of Victorian furniture. Simultaneously, the Industrial Revolution made possible the production of vast amounts of furniture for an increasingly large furniture-buying public. The inferior design accompanying this commercialism spurred the development of such design reforms as the ARTS AND CRAFTS MOVEMENT and the ART FURNITURE MOVEMENT, which called for both simplification and the rejection of historical styles. These movements invoked the clean and simple example of Oriental art (see JAPONISME) and would strongly influence ART NOUVEAU and the emergence of modern design. Thus, furniture design in the Victorian period echoed the two conflicting cultural themes of this time—a nostalgic antiquarianism on the one hand and, on the other, a progressive impulse toward accommodation with a rapidly changing world.

VIENNA SECESSION

See SEZESSION.

VIENNESE CHAIR

Northern European (especially Scandinavian) term for BENTWOOD chair. The usage refers to the production of bentwood furniture (mostly chairs) by the 19th-century Viennese firm of Michael THONET and its successors.

Vitruvian scroll

VIKING REVIVAL STYLE

Another name for the Dragonesque style of late 19th- and early 20th-century Scandinavia, represented most notably by Gerhard MUNTHE.

VILE, WILLIAM (c. 1700–1767)

British PALLADIAN STYLE and ROCOCO FURNITURE maker, best known for furniture produced in partnership with John COBB in 1755–65. Vile's earlier work was in a late baroque manner influenced by William KENT, but his partnership with Cobb produced massive mahogany pieces with carved rococo ornamentation. The firm Vile and Cobb was extremely successful. It enjoyed royal patronage and sold large quantities of the highest-priced furniture of the day. Vile retired in 1765.

VIOLET WOOD

Another term for KINGWOOD.

VIOLLET-LE-DUC, EUGÈNE-EMMANUEL (1814–79)

French architect and writer; promoter of the NEO-GOTHIC STYLE. Principally a restorer of medieval structures—Notre Dame in Paris and the walls of Carcassonne, among others—Viollet-le-Duc also wrote on architecture and design, advocating design reform based on what he perceived to be the "rationalism" of 13th-century architecture. His book *Dictionnaire raisonée du mobilier français* (1858), which included drawings of medieval furniture, exerted a greater influence on design than the very small amount of furniture he himself produced.

VIROLA

South American HARDWOOD, very light and therefore used in furniture for interior elements, especially drawer parts. It is used mainly in America.

VIS-À-VIS

Another name for TÊTE-À-TÊTE (2).

VITRUVIAN SCROLL (also *wave scroll; running dog*)

NEOCLASSICAL STYLE decorative motif; continuous series of VOLUTEs in a horizontal row, usually used in a FRIEZE below a tabletop or CORNICE. The Vitruvian scroll—named after Vitruvius, the ancient Roman architectural authority—was derived from classical architecture. It was especially favored by William KENT and other PALLADIAN STYLE furniture designers in early 18th-century Britain.

VIVANT, DOMINIQUE

See DENON, Dominique Vivant, Baron.

VOLTAIRE CHAIR

Nineteenth-century term for American PILLAR AND SCROLL STYLE furniture form of 1830s—low-seated, upholstered armchair with tall, scroll-topped back. The term is a misnomer, for the French philosopher died decades before the chair was developed; it probably refers to the French origins of the form, adapted by American makers—most notably Duncan PHYFE—from similar pieces in the RESTAURATION STYLE. The form was also seen in Britain and Germany.

VOLUTE

Simple spiral SCROLL ornamenting a column CAPITAL in IONIC, CORINTHIAN and COMPOSITE ORDERS of classical architecture. The volute appeared in classically inspired European architecture and furniture from the Renaissance on, both in capitals and in other sorts of decoration, notably as terminals of arms, legs or other members of a piece of furniture. The term is also used to denote other types of scroll, such as the foliate spiral of Gothic architecture.

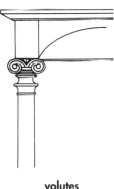

volutes

VON RHEYDT, MELCHIOR (active after 1600)

German RENAISSANCE FURNITURE maker. Von Rheydt worked in Cologne and specialized in case furniture with elaborate MARQUETRY and carving in the extravagant MANNERIST STYLE.

VOYEUSE (also *conversation chair*)

Eighteenth-century French furniture form; BERGÈRE or upholstered armchair with upholstered pad atop the back. Intended for an observer of a card game, the *voyeuse* permitted the user to straddle the chair and rest his arms on the pad; it was also used as an ordinary armchair. A version with a lower seat, the *voyeuse à genoux,* could be knelt on and was intended for women; their skirts—and the mores of the time—inhibited their sitting astride the seat.

Arts and Crafts chair by Voysey

VOYSEY, CHARLES FRANCIS ANNESLEY (1857–1941)

British architect and furniture designer; major figure of the ARTS AND CRAFTS MOVEMENT. Principally an architect, C. F. A. Voysey was also well known for fabric, wallpaper and furniture designs. He studied with A. H. MACKMURDO and, through him, was introduced to the ideas of William MORRIS. In furniture design Voysey developed a distinctive style of great elegance and charm, featuring pierced copper appliqués and heart-shaped motifs in furniture with strong vertical elements. Voysey continued the practices of the Arts and Crafts movement in his furniture design, using traditional materials (especially OAK) and simple, unpretentious lines, reminiscent of British country furniture.

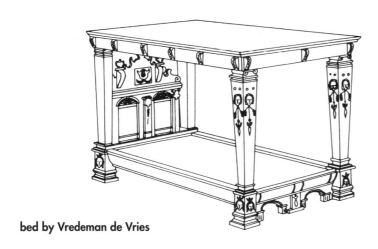

bed by Vredeman de Vries

The more urbane charm of his decorative effects anticipates ART NOUVEAU.

VREDEMAN DE VRIES, HANS (1527–1604)

Flemish painter, architect, designer and engraver. Though a minor figure in painting and architecture, Vredeman de Vries's designs and engravings made him the most important influence on northern European furniture in the last quarter of the 16th and the first half of the 17th centuries. His furniture designs were published in a number of PATTERN BOOKS between 1560 and 1588; the most significant was the last one, *Differents pourtraicts de menuiserie.* Vredeman de Vries designed in the MANNERIST STYLE of the day, promoting the FRANÇOIS I STYLE as expressed by Cornelis FLORIS. He applied intricate carved ornamentation to architecturally inspired forms, using STRAP-WORK, bizarre masks, CARYATIDS and other GROTESQUE ORNAMENT motifs. He lived and worked in a number of cities—including Antwerp, Hamburg and Amsterdam—and his style was imitated throughout the Netherlands, Germany, England and Sweden until well into the second half of the 17th century. His influence was continued in the published designs of his son Paul VREDEMAN DE VRIES.

VREDEMAN DE VRIES, PAUL (1567–?)

Flemish designer and engraver of MANNERIST STYLE furniture. The son of Hans VREDEMAN DE VRIES, Paul is best known for a PATTERN BOOK of 1630, known as *Verscheyden Schrynwerck* or *Plusiers Menuiseries.* In this collection he reproduced many of his father's designs and also included work of his own, which was very similar but ever richer, with a great emphasis on figural carving.

WACHSEINLEGEN

German decorative technique of 17th century. The process involves making incised patterns, which are then filled in with a pale yellow mixture of sulfur and wax or putty. This mode of linear decoration was commonly used in PENNSYLVANIA GERMAN FURNITURE, especially on the panels of the SCHRANK.

WAGNER, OTTO (1841–1918)

Austrian architect and designer; pioneer of modern design. Principally an architect, Wagner designed furniture chiefly for his own buildings and for the manufacturers Thonet & Sons (see Michael THONET). In architecture and furniture design, he began by employing elements from the RENAISSANCE REVIVAL STYLE but later adopted a functionalistic style (see FUNCTIONALISM), which emphasized simplicity, horizontal lines and sparseness of decoration. He believed that the designer's "expressive power" derived from the relationship between construction and materials. A member of both the Vienna SEZESSION and the DEUTSCHER WERKBUND, Wagner had a great influence on the new Viennese designers of the day, especially Josef HOFFMANN, J. M. OLBRICH and Adolf LOOS.

WAINSCOT CHAIR

French, English and American armchair of 16th and 17th centuries, originally a development of GOTHIC FURNITURE. The word *wainscot* derived from a Dutch term for an excellent grade of oak used for fine interior work. The form apparently evolved from a fixed arrangement of a seat to a paneled wall. It was characterized by carved panels joined to a simple, foursquare frame. Sometimes all four sides were paneled down to the floor, and, at another extreme, sometimes only the back and seat were paneled and were attached to turned posts and stretchers. The carving on the panels was generally in very low relief, using the elaborate motifs associated with various types of Mannerism (see MANNERIST STYLE), notably the Jacobean style (see JACOBEAN FURNITURE) in England and America, where the wainscot chair was very popular. In America the form was a prominent element in AMERICAN JACOBEAN FURNITURE and continued to be made well into the 18th century.

WALNUT

European and North American HARDWOOD, of considerable importance in the history of Western furniture. European walnut is a variable greyish brown in color with very dark streaks. It came into use with the rise of RENAISSANCE FURNITURE in Europe; its fine grain facilitated the elaborate carving characteristic of the period, and its dark, lustrous surface gave a handsome, monumental appearance to the finished piece. American black walnut, used in the British colonies and in England beginning in the late 17th century, is a more uniform dark purple-brown. Walnut was the most popular wood for European furniture until well into the 18th century, when MAHOGANY superseded it.

WALTON, GEORGE (1867–1903)

Scottish designer associated with the GLASGOW SCHOOL. Walton established a business as a decorator and furniture designer in Glasgow in 1888 and was able to open a branch of the

chair by Wagner

wainscot chair

business in London 10 years later. He designed furniture with Charles Rennie MACKINTOSH for some of Mackintosh's architectural projects and also designed glassware. His furniture, some of which was manufactured and sold by Liberty & Co. (*see* Arthur Lazenby LIBERTY) was of simple design, in the tradition of the ARTS AND CRAFTS MOVEMENT, but influenced by Mackintosh's geometrical, attenuated style.

WANGENTISCH
German RENAISSANCE FURNITURE form of about 1500; sturdy table with splayed legs joined by a low BOX STRETCHER (*see under* STRETCHER). A variant form, the SCHRAGENTISCH, had cylindrical legs, either turned or carved.

WANSCHAFF, KARL GEORGE (1775–1848)
Berlin cabinetmaker in EMPIRE and BIEDERMEIER STYLES. After 1725 Wanschaff was employed by the Prussian royal court. He practiced in the clean-lined, simple manner of the architect and designer K. F. SCHINKEL.

WARDROBE
CASE FURNITURE form designed to store clothing; a tall CUPBOARD or cupboard with a CHEST OF DRAWERS. The form derived from the medieval PRESS. As it developed in 16th- and 17th-century Europe, it came to include drawers below a cupboard with shelves, and it produced the English CLOTHES PRESS, the Dutch KAST and the German SCHRANK. The term *wardrobe* (which, in the Middle Ages, denoted a room for storing clothes and linens rather than a piece of furniture) received its present meaning in the 18th century, when the piece was first equipped with a tall section or sections with hangers sliding on metal rods. In this form, to which a mirror was often fitted on the inside or outside of the door, the wardrobe was very popular throughout the VICTORIAN PERIOD. In the 20th century the wardrobe has largely been replaced by its built-in equivalent, the closet.

WASH-HAND STAND (also *wash-hand table*)
Nineteenth-century term for WASHSTAND.

WASHING STAND
Another name for WASHSTAND.

WASHSTAND (also *basin stand; wash-hand stand; washing stand*)
Furniture form of 18th and 19th centuries; small stand or table with a basin in the top and shelves or compartments below it to store a ewer and toilet accessories. In the VICTORIAN PERIOD the washstand was often very elaborate, including a hinged mirror and/or a CHEST OF DRAWERS.

WASSMUS FRÈRES
Well-known Parisian furniture manufacturer of mid-19th century, especially noted for reproductions (*see* REPRODUCTION FURNITURE) of pieces by André-Charles BOULLE and other 18th-century makers.

WATER LEAF
Decorative motif; elongated, undulating leaf with a central rib, based on the lanceolate laurel leaf (*see* LAUREL LEAVES). The water leaf was popular in 18th- and early 19th-century NEOCLASSICAL STYLE furniture in France, Britain and America, especially in the work of AMERICAN EMPIRE STYLE makers.

WATERBED
Bed consisting of large, flexible plastic cushion filled with water, contained in a low box or frame of wood or some other material. The user reclines or sleeps on the top surface of the cushion, gently rocked by the motion he or she imparts to the water within. A heater is generally necessary to keep the water from chilling the user. A popular novelty in the 1960s, the waterbed has since been improved by the development of leakproof liners and of interior baffles to control the motion of the water. Its share of the bed market—in America, at least—has been increasing slowly over the past two decades.

WATERHOUSE, ALFRED (1830–1905)
British architect and designer. Waterhouse, principally an architect, designed a great deal of furniture as well. In his early work he was a follower of A. W. N. PUGIN, but most of his

output is in the "Old English" style developed by Richard Norman SHAW. He was versatile enough to employ elements of the lighter Art Furniture style or even the Anglo-Japanese style in his work when appropriate (*see* ART FURNITURE MOVEMENT; William GODWIN). Waterhouse was particularly noted for his use of decorative tile, in both architecture and furniture.

WATERLOO LEG
See under LEG.

WATSON, CRAIG (active from c. 1975)
AUSTRALIAN FURNITURE designer and architect. Craig Watson studied the craft of furniture-making with Leon SADUBIN, who took much from SCANDINAVIAN MODERN design, but his own work owes little or nothing to that style. It is quintessentially POST-MODERN FURNITURE, reflecting his interest in classical and neoclassical architecture, the architectural qualities of BIEDERMEIER STYLE furniture, and the spatial manipulations of DE STIJL. In his eclecticism, Watson reflects the main current of late 20th-century Australian design.

WAVE SCROLL
Another name for VITRUVIAN SCROLL.

WEALLANS, JON (active 1960s)
Contemporary British designer, associated with POP ART FURNITURE. In the 1960s Weallans produced furniture designs ranging from relatively sedate pieces, such as brightly painted stool-tables shaped like the suit symbols of a deck of cards, to more flamboyant pieces—notably, a settee in the form of a giant set of teeth.

WEAVER, HOLMES (1769–1848)
Newport, Rhode Island, cabinetmaker of the FEDERAL PERIOD. Weaver made well-crafted furniture in a style derived from the work of George HEPPLEWHITE and Thomas SHERATON.

WEBB, PHILIP SPEAKMAN (1831–1915)
British architect and designer; close associate of William MORRIS and an important figure

table by Webb

in the ARTS AND CRAFTS MOVEMENT. Webb, one of the leading late-Victorian architects, was also the most important furniture designer for Morris's manufacturing firm. He designed simple, massive oak pieces with heavy cornices and large flat surfaces, which often bore representational paintings by Edward BURNE-JONES or another of the Pre-Raphaelite painters. Webb also designed the MORRIS CHAIR, a simple reclining chair based on a rustic model from southern England. After 1875 he focused more on built-in furniture for his own buildings, but his austere style continued to influence the designers associated with the Arts and Crafts movement.

WEBER, KEM (1889–1963)
German-born American ART DECO furniture designer. Born Karl Emmanuel Martin Weber, Kem Weber studied in Berlin under Bruno PAUL. Commissioned to design the German pavilion at a 1914 exposition in San Francisco, Weber was unable to return to Germany when World War I began. He remained in America, establishing himself in Los Angeles, where he designed furniture for a number of American manufacturers.

WEGNER, HANS (b. 1914)
Danish furniture designer; leading exponent of SCANDINAVIAN MODERN design. Apprenticed to a cabinetmaker in his youth, Wegner retained the techniques and materials of Scandinavian woodworking tradition when he began designing his own furniture in 1940. His two most famous designs are the "Peacock" chair (1947) and "The Chair," as it

chair by Wegner

is known (1949). The first was a spindle-back piece resembling the old WINDSOR CHAIR design, though the arms were separated from any element of the back and diagonal braces run through the seat from stretcher to arms. "The Chair," was an equally simple piece in which arms and back rail were one sculptural form, a sweeping line in the horizontal plane set atop the four legs. The framed cane or cord seat of "The Chair" looked molded rather than carved, curving slightly up on one axis, slightly down on the other. The two designs illustrate the blend of traditional craftsmanship and modern design that characterized Wegner's work. His innovative, functionalistic, simple design style shows the impact of modern design trends (*see* FUNCTIONALISM) upon his work, while his traditional concern with fine handicraft and materials such as wood and cane is reflective of his early training in cabinetmaking. In this duality Wegner is perhaps the perfect paradigm of Scandinavian Modern design—a central figure between the rigorously anonymous traditionalism of Kaare KLINT on the one hand and the industrial, idiosyncratic enthusiasm of Arne JACOBSEN and Verner PANTON on the other. Wegner has experimented with tubular steel in recent years, but it is his elegant wooden furniture, much of it never yet out of production, that continues to influence modern furniture design.

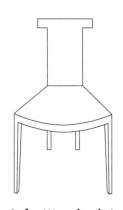

Stefan Wewerka chair

WEISWEILER, ADAM (c. 1750–1810)

German-born French ÉBÉNISTE; a leading maker in LOUIS XVI STYLE. Weisweiler was an assistant to David ROENTGEN in Neuweid, Germany, before going to Paris in 1778. There he specialized in small, delicate pieces. Despite his training with Roentgen, a notable user of pictorial marquetry, Weisweiler favored plain veneering of MAHOGANY or LACQUER, sometimes inset with porcelain plaques or PIETRE DURE panels taken from late 17th-century LOUIS XIV STYLE furniture. A hallmark of his pieces was his use of stretchers in the form of interlaced bands resembling STRAPWORK. Weisweiler survived the French Revolution and became a prominent furniture maker in the EMPIRE STYLE, often collaborating with mount maker P.-P. THOMIRE.

WELLENSCHRANK

German furniture form of late 17th century; a type of SCHRANK. Its distinguishing feature was its ornamentation, a series of rectangular moldings set within one another on each door, creating an effect of waves (*wellen*). The *Wellenschrank* was particularly associated with the city of Frankfurt, though it was also made elsewhere.

WENGÉ

Very dark brown West African HARDWOOD with distinctive fine streaks of pale brown to white. Closely related to the similar PANGA PANGA, *wengé* is increasingly popular in European furniture, both as an attractive veneer and, being quite strong, as framing.

WEST INDIAN SATINWOOD

Caribbean HARDWOOD; finely textured, creamy yellow wood with distinctive satinlike gloss. A beautiful wood, it was extensively used by European and American cabinetmakers of the 18th century, especially in the NEO-CLASSICAL STYLE. Today it is not widely available and has generally been replaced by the similar CEYLON SATINWOOD.

WEWERKA, STEFAN (b. 1928)

German architect, artist, and designer. Stefan Wewerka became an architect following the Second World War, working on the development of housing. He continues to practice architecture, while adding other arts and disciplines with remarkable virtuosity. In the 1960s, he turned to art, making paintings and prints, films, and sculptures. He was associated with Fluxus, a Belgian group of surrealistic artists. His sculptures, for which he is best known as an artist, often featured distorted or damaged pieces of furniture and other domestic objects, intended to agitate our images of familiar things. In the late 1970s, he added to his concerns the design of actual furniture, which is made by several European manufacturers. His designs are generally derived from the INTERNATIONAL STYLE repertoire. His popular tables and chairs, while quite sensible and ergonomically sound (*see* ERGONOMIC DESIGN), often take unusual shapes, which lend visual interest without affecting comfort or utility.

WHATNOT

Another name for the ÉTAGÈRE.

WHEEL-BACK CHAIR (also *umbrella back chair*)
Eighteenth-century British chair whose back was composed of slender spokes radiating from a medallion at the center.

WHEEL-BACK WINDSOR CHAIR
See under WINDSOR CHAIR.

WHIPLASH CURVE
Decorative motif associated with ART NOUVEAU. It consisted of a long, sweeping, sinuous curve that terminated in one or more short reverse curves. Its resemblance to the tendrils of a vine made it especially popular with French Art Nouveau designers, who were noted for their use of botanical decorative motifs. However, the whiplash curve first appeared as an abstract element in the work of the Belgian architect and designer Victor HORTA.

WHITE WALNUT
Another name for BUTTERNUT.

WHITEBEAM
European HARDWOOD, white to pale reddish brown in color, with fine, uniform texture, resembling PEARWOOD. Whitebeam, like its near relative *rowan*, is used as veneer in INLAY work.

WHITEWOOD
Another name for European SPRUCE. *American whitewood* is the British name for TULIP POPLAR.

WHORL FOOT
See under FOOT.

WICKER
Furniture or other objects woven in any of a variety of materials, most commonly RATTAN. Generally associated with Victorian tastes, wicker furniture is in fact very ancient. Its production derived from basket weaving, and wicker baskets and furniture were made in ancient Egypt, Greece and Rome. Wicker furniture was common in American and European households of the 17th- and 18th-centuries. The most common pre-Victorian furniture form in wicker was the so-called BASKET CHAIR. In the 19th and 20th centuries, the range of forms expanded to include all types except some case furniture.

Before the 19th century, willow twigs were ordinarily used in wickerwork; the term wicker is sometimes used to refer to this material. Then rattan was introduced to the Western world when the British colonized Malaya and other parts of Southeast Asia. This strong, easy-to-manipulate and inexpensive material became popular among 19th-century furniture designers. Not only could it be formed to produce the extravagant curves and shapes demanded by many of the REVIVAL STYLES, but it also made for light, versatile pieces that appealed to the period's love of the exotic and that were useful indoors or out. In the 20th century simpler styles have generally prevailed. Most wicker furniture is now woven in Asia and the finished pieces imported to Europe and America. Some new materials, such as prairie grass, a marsh plant of the American West, have been experimented with in wickerwork, with varying degrees of success.

WIENER SEZESSION
See SEZESSION.

WIENER WERKSTÄTTE
Viennese workshop, in operation from 1903 to 1932, that promoted design reform and manufactured furniture and other objects. Influenced by C. R. ASHBEE's Guild of Handicrafts and the ideals of the British ARTS AND CRAFTS MOVEMENT, Josef HOFFMANN and Kolo MOSER (both members of the Vienna SEZESSION) founded the Wiener Werkstätte. Besides manufacturing goods, the Werkstätte exhibited the work of such foreign designers as Ashbee, Charles Rennie MACKINTOSH, Henri VAN DE VELDE and Parisian ART NOUVEAU designers. Up to the First World War, the Werkstätte's leather goods, metalwork, textiles, furniture and other products were in the style of the Vienna Sezession—a geometrical variant of Art Nouveau. After the war, until its closing in 1932, the Werkstätte design style was a variant of ART DECO. In the 1920s the Werkstätte was represented in the United

whiplash curve

wicker chair

Wiener Werkstätten chair

States by a New York branch established by Joseph URBAN. The traditions of the Werkstätte were also influential in the development of SCANDINAVIAN MODERN design, especially in Finland.

WILHELM KIMBEL OF MAINZ
See KIMBEL, Wilhelm, of Mainz.

WILLIAM AND MARY STYLE
Style of late 17th-century BAROQUE FURNITURE made in England (*see also* AMERICAN WILLIAM AND MARY STYLE). Named for the joint reign of King William III (1689–1702) and Queen Mary II (1689–94), the William and Mary style represented a sobering of the exuberance of RESTORATION FURNITURE and a transition to the first great style of 18th-century Britain, the QUEEN ANNE STYLE. King William was the stadtholder of Holland when he was invited by the English Parliament to assume the English throne jointly with his wife, the daughter of Kings James II, in the change of government known as the Glorious Revolution of 1689. He brought with him a retinue of designers and craftsmen who extended the Dutch influence on English decorative arts that had begun during the Restoration. However, the underlying stimulation remained that of the French LOUIS XIV STYLE, all the more so since Louis's revocation of the Edict of Nantes, in 1685, had caused Protestant craftsmen who had worked under Charles LE BRUN at the GOBELINS workshops to flee to more sympathetic countries in northern Europe; in England, Daniel MAROT was the most important of these refugees. Not only did this fresh infusion of Continental furniture makers influence the style of the time but it contributed to an improvement in native craftsmanship.

William and Mary furniture was largely made of WALNUT, but the increasing elaborate MARQUETRY that characterized the period also used HOLLY, EBONY, SATINWOOD and PURPLEHEART, sometimes along with engraved ivory plaques. Floral marquetry, a Dutch export, was prominent in patterns of floral and foliate motifs and, especially popular in England, as images of flowers in a vase. Also from Holland came SEAWEED MARQUETRY and OYSTER VENEER. French BOULLE MARQUETRY was made, most notably by Gerreit JENSEN, a Dutch-born cabinetmaker. Such workmanship expressed a concern with surface decoration that was further evidenced by the development of new finishes such as VARNISH and JAPANNING.

The reign of William and Mary witnessed increasing prosperity in England, and this greater wealth and leisure stimulated the development of new forms of furniture. The SECRETARY, a FALL-FRONT DESK surmounted by a bookcase, was the most important of these. Also, numerous specialized OCCASIONAL TABLES appeared, including the TEA TABLE and the CARD TABLE (1). These would not reach their fullest development until the 18th century, however. Lighter, often upholstered, armchairs became common in middle-class homes. Twist-turning characteristic of furniture supports during the Restoration, persisted, especially on tables, but turned BALUSTERs and carved SCROLL supports also became popular. The carved SPANISH FOOT was as widespread as the turned BALL FOOT and BUN FOOT (*see each under* FOOT), especially on chair legs. Most important, the DUTCH FOOT (*see under* FOOT) was combined with a scrolling leg in a rudimentary predecessor of the CABRIOLE LEG (*see under* LEG).

The William and Mary style incorporated the last great wave of foreign influences on English furniture design. The subsequent Queen Anne style was to represent the emergence of a truly distinctive national style.

WILLOW
Very pale, unfigured HARDWOOD. Not used in furniture itself, its thin young shoots were the traditional material for WICKER work before the introduction of RATTAN.

WILSON, TOBY MUIR (b. c. 1950)
AUSTRALIAN FURNITURE designer and maker; a follower of John MAKEPEACE and George INGHAM in producing finely crafted handmade furniture in the tradition of the HANDICRAFT REVIVAL movement, but also informed by the INTERNATIONAL STYLE. Living and working in a remote region of Tasmania, Wilson has access to exotic hardwoods with which he makes simple, clean-lined furniture with occasional opulent touches such as leather UPHOLSTERY and INLAY work with MOTHER-OF-PEARL.

WINDOW SEAT

Bench with arms or raised ends, but no back, designed to be placed beneath a recessed window, just filling the available space. The window seat was particularly popular in NEOCLASSICAL STYLE furniture of the late 18th and early 19th centuries.

WINDOW-SPLAT **WINDSOR CHAIR**

See under WINDSOR CHAIR.

WINDSOR CHAIR

British and American furniture form; wooden chair whose legs are separated from back and arms by a SADDLE SEAT, into which legs, back parts and arm supports, if any, are mortised (*see* MORTISE). The Windsor chair developed in England in the late 17th century, was made in America by about 1725 and has been popular in both countries ever since, appearing in many styles. The origin of the term is obscure, for the chair has always been made in many parts of Britain other than the town of Windsor, to which the name is often thought to refer.

Different varieties of Windsor chair, distinguished by the design of their backs, have been made and are denoted by specific names; they are described individually. In general, the backs have had either a horizontal top, as in the COMB BACK and SCROLL-BACK types (*see each under* WINDSOR CHAIR), or a BENTWOOD curved outline, as in the BOW-BACK WINDSOR CHAIR (*see under* WINDSOR CHAIR). BRACING STICKS (*see under* WINDSOR CHAIR) have sometimes been used to provide extra support for the backs. Windsor armchairs frequently incorporate an ARM BOW (*see under* WINDSOR CHAIR), a roughly semicircular length of bentwood comprising both arms and a connecting rail across the back. The legs of Windsor chairs have generally been turned (*see* TURNERY), but early versions, made before 1740, sometimes had simple stavelike legs, and in about 1725–1810, carved CABRIOLE LEGS (*see under* LEG) were also used. Whatever their form, the legs of Windsor chairs are typically connected by STRETCHERs, most frequently the H-STRETCHER or COW-HORN STRETCHER (*see each under* STRETCHER).

While a few mid-18th-century examples were made entirely of MAHOGANY, most Windsor chairs have been constructed of several woods, due to the different demands placed on the various parts: the bent parts and spindles, the most common components of Windsor backs, require strength with flexibility; the saddle seat must be easily shaped; and legs and arm supports generally have to lend themselves to turning. In British ASH, YEW and various FRUITWOODS are thus used for bent elements; ELM, for seats; and BEECH, for turned parts. In America HICKORY, CHESTNUT, OAK and ash fill the first role; TULIP POPLAR and PINE, the second; and maple (*see* BIRD'S-EYE MAPLE), chestnut, hickory, or oak, the third. Because of the resulting variegated appearance, Windsor chairs have almost always been painted, usually a single, dark color. The traditionally favored hues have been dark green and black, but many others have also been used. In early 19th-century America, Windsor chairs sometimes figured as "FANCY" FURNITURE and were gaily painted in a medley of colors.

American Windsor chairs have differed somewhat from British ones. In 18th-century America backs composed entirely of spindles were the norm, while those with SPLATS were in great vogue in Britain. Also, at this time American backs were usually higher than British ones, sometimes featuring a second, smaller bow or comb atop the main back. Cabriole legs were uncommon on American examples, and seats were often considerably thicker and the carved "saddle" accordingly deeper. Legs tended to be set at a rakish slant and were attached to the seat at points slightly toward the middle rather than at the corners, as was done in Britain. Some variations, such as the ARROW-BACK WINDSOR CHAIR (*see under* WINDSOR CHAIR), simply did not exist in Britain. An 18th-century American development, the various LOW-BACK WINDSOR CHAIRS, including the famed CAPTAIN'S CHAIR (*see each under* WINDSOR CHAIR) did not reach Britain until the 1840s.

The Windsor chair remains widely popular, and it is made in large numbers in both traditional and new styles. The modern British designer Lucien ERCOLANI is particularly noted for his Windsor chair designs.

ARM BOW

Structural device featured in many Windsor armchairs; length of roughly semicircular BENTWOOD that comprises both arms and a

arm bow

arrow-back Windsor chair

balloon-back Windsor chair

bergere-bow Windsor chair

bobtail

bow-back Windsor chair

connecting rail across the back between them. SPINDLES in the back usually run through holes in the arm bow and are set in MORTISES at top and bottom. At the sides spindles mortised beneath the arms run to the seat. A central SPLAT, if present, is set against the front of the arm bow, while any secondary splats, and sometimes the spindles, are applied in two parts, one above and one below the arm bow; both are mortised into it. The arm bow first appeared in Windsor armchairs in about 1720, and it has been used ever since.

ARROW-BACK WINDSOR CHAIR
Any late 18th- or early 19th-century American NEOCLASSICAL STYLE Windsor chair whose back incorporated a row of flattened spindles carved to resemble downward-pointing arrowheads or spearheads.

BACK BOW
See BOW-BACK WINDSOR CHAIR, *under* WINDSOR CHAIR.

BALLOON-BACK WINDSOR CHAIR
Rare variant of 18th-century COMB-BACK WINDSOR CHAIR (*see under* WINDSOR CHAIR) in which the comb was narrower than the seat or the comb was replaced by a half-disk, into which the back's SPINDLES were mortised (*see* MORTISE). In either case, the spindles bent inward, creating an impression of ballooning below, in contrast with the flaring FAN-BACK WINDSOR CHAIR (*see under* WINDSOR CHAIR). The balloon-back Windsor chair usually lacked a central SPLAT.

BERGÈRE-BOW WINDSOR CHAIR
Late 19th-century British LOW-BACK WINDSOR CHAIR (*see under* WINDSOR CHAIR), in which a curving ARM BOW (*see under* WINDSOR CHAIR), supported by turned SPINDLES or a carved SPLAT, swept high in back and terminated at the arms in pronounced downward SCROLLs. This striking form was common in British public buildings in the second half of the 19th century, beginning in the 1860s.

BOBTAIL (also *tailpiece*)
Structural device on some Windsor chairs; carved, lobelike rearward projection from back

of seat, with two MORTISES, in which BRACING STICKS (*see under* WINDSOR CHAIR), used to give extra support to the chair's back, are set.

BOW-BACK WINDSOR CHAIR
Either of two varieties of Windsor chair in which top of back is formed by a *back bow,* a broadly curving BENTWOOD member. In the SACK-BACK WINDSOR CHAIR (*see under* WINDSOR CHAIR), the back bow is roughly semicircular and is mortised (*see* MORTISE) into the top of the ARM BOW (*see under* WINDSOR CHAIR), which crosses the back at the level of the arms. The back SPINDLES, if any, are mortised into the underside of the back bow and extend through holes drilled in the arm bow down to mortises in the top of the seat. A central SPLAT, if present, is set into the front of the arm bow, while secondary splats, and sometimes spindles, are applied in two parts, one set between back bow and arm bow, the other between arm bow and seat.

In the LOOP-BACK WINDSOR CHAIR (*see under* WINDSOR CHAIR), the back bow is horseshoe-shaped and mortised into the top of the seat at each rear corner. In this case, it frames the entire back, whose spindles or splats are set between bow and seat. With no arm bow the arms of a loop-back armchair are mortised into the back bow's two verticals.

Early instances of bow-back Windsor chairs had only spindles in their backs, but in Britain a central splat framed by spindles soon became much more popular, as did multiple splats. In America though, splats have never been favored. The sack-back chair was the earlier form to arise; it evolved from the use of the bentwood arm bow in COMB-BACK WINDSOR CHAIRS (*see under* WINDSOR CHAIR). By 1750 the loop-back chair had been developed, and both forms have been in production ever since.

BRACING STICKS
Structural device appearing behind backs of some 18th-century COMB-BACK or BOW-BACK WINDSOR CHAIRS (*see each under* WINDSOR CHAIR). It consisted of a pair of spindlelike wooden rods, each extending diagonally downward toward the center from a MORTISE near one end of the COMB (*see under* WINDSOR CHAIR) or back bow to a lobelike

rearward extension of the seat, called a BOB-TAIL (*see under* WINDSOR CHAIR). There they were set in two adjacent mortises. Bracing sticks helped to solve the distinctive structural problem of a Windsor chair—the weakness at the junction of seat and back.

BUCKLE-BACK WINDSOR CHAIR

SCROLL-BACK WINDSOR CHAIR (*see under* WINDSOR CHAIR) whose CROSS RAIL consisted of a panel of PIERCED CARVING, featuring botanical or abstract motifs that sometimes resembled elaborate contemporary belt buckles. The buckle-back chair was popular in Britain in the second half of the 19th century.

CAPTAIN'S CHAIR

Nineteenth-century LOW-BACK WINDSOR CHAIR (*see under* WINDSOR CHAIR), in which the ARM BOW (*see under* WINDSOR CHAIR), supported by turned SPINDLES, curved abruptly downward in front to be mortised (*see* MORTISE) into the seat at the front corners. Its legs were connected by a BOX STRETCHER (*see under* STRETCHER). Originally used in the pilot houses of Mississippi River steamboats, the chair was popular in Britain as well as America by the 1860s and remained so into the 1890s.

COMB

CREST RAIL of comb-back WINDSOR CHAIR (*see under* WINDSOR CHAIR).

COMB-BACK WINDSOR CHAIR

Eighteenth-century Windsor chair with a horizontal CREST RAIL surmounting SPINDLES, splat or both, which were mortised (*see* MORTISE) into its underside. The basic form, with a simple back composed of spindles and crest rail, resembled a hay rake or large comb—hence, the name. The top of the comb, as the crest rail was called, had a carved profile that varied with current styles, and it frequently terminated in shaped lobes, or EARs, on either side. Most comb-back armchairs featured an ARM BOW (*see under* WINDSOR CHAIR), but the arms may also have been mortised into the STILES. Many variants of the comb-back were made, including the BALLOON-BACK, FAN-

BACK and SHAWL-BACK WINDSOR CHAIRS (*see each under* WINDSOR CHAIR).

CONTINUOUS-ARM WINDSOR CHAIR

Eighteenth-century American version of LOOP-BACK WINDSOR CHAIR (*see under* WINDSOR CHAIR), in which the arms, each supported at the front by a turned BALUSTER, were made from a single piece of BENTWOOD that rose at the rear to function as a back bow (*see* BOW-BACK WINDSOR CHAIR, *under* WINDSOR CHAIR). Thus, the back bow was not mortised into the seat, as in a loop-back chair, but was supported by its numerous spindles, the front balusters and usually a pair of BRACING STICKS (*see under* WINDSOR CHAIR).

DOUBLE WINDSOR CHAIR

Another name for WINDSOR SETTEE.

FAN-BACK WINDSOR CHAIR

Variant of 18th-century COMB-BACK WINDSOR CHAIR (*see under* WINDSOR CHAIR), in which the comb was wider than the rest of the chair, causing the back's SPINDLES to fan out. It was often made with a central SPLAT.

FARMHOUSE WINDSOR CHAIR

See LATH-BACK WINDSOR CHAIR, *under* WINDSOR CHAIR.

FIREHOUSE WINDSOR CHAIR

Nineteenth-century LOW-BACK WINDSOR CHAIR (*see under* WINDSOR CHAIR), in which the ARM BOW (*see under* WINDSOR CHAIR) and its cresting, supported on simply turned SPINDLEs, were plain and practical, without the scrollings of its antecedent, the SMOKER'S BOW WINDSOR CHAIR (*see under* WINDSOR CHAIR). Its legs were connected by a BOX STRETCHER (*see under* STRETCHER). Developed in the United States in about midcentury, it was immediately popular in both Britain and America and remained so into the 1890s. It was frequently used by the volunteer fire departments that proliferated at that time—hence, its name.

bracing sticks

buckle-back Windsor chair

captain's chair

comb-back Windsor chair

continuous arm Windsor chair

fan-back Windsor chair

firehouse Windsor chair

**Gothic scroll-back
Windsor chair**

Gothic Windsor chair

**interlaced-bow Windsor
chair**

GOTHIC SCROLL-BACK WINDSOR CHAIR
Nineteenth-century British variant of SCROLL-BACK WINDSOR CHAIR (*see under* WINDSOR CHAIR) in which an arched profile was carved at the bottom edge of the top rail and the top edge of the CROSS RAIL. The two parts were linked by small turned BALUSTERs, and the whole resembled medieval ARCADING. This example of NEO-GOTHIC STYLE furniture was most popular in about 1840–70.

GOTHIC WINDSOR CHAIR (also *Strawberry Hill Windsor chair; window-splat Windsor chair*) Eighteenth-century British variant of either COMB-BACK or BOW-BACK WINDSOR CHAIR (*see each under* WINDSOR CHAIR), in which back consisted of three pierced SPLATs, carved in imitation of Gothic window TRACERY, without SPINDLEs. Often, smaller, matching splats also appeared, one below each arm. Occasionally, the bow-back Gothic chair featured a back bow (*see* BOW-BACK WINDSOR CHAIR, *under* WINDSOR CHAIR) formed as a pointed arch. The Gothic Windsor chair was popular for about 20 years in the mid-18th century—an example of the Gothic Revival taste in British ROCOCO FURNITURE (*see* NEO-GOTHIC STYLE; CHIPPENDALE GOTHIC FURNITURE)—and since the Second World War, it has enjoyed a modest revival. It is distinct from the 19th-century GOTHIC SCROLL-BACK WINDSOR CHAIR (*see under* WINDSOR CHAIR).

INTERLACED-BOW WINDSOR CHAIR
Nineteenth-century variant of LOOP-BACK WINDSOR CHAIR (*see under* WINDSOR CHAIR), in which back's SPINDLEs or SPLATs were replaced by a bold OPENWORK arrangement of smoothly curving bands of plain wood, representing any of several images, mostly neo-Gothic in taste (*see* NEO-GOTHIC STYLE), including interlaced arches and elements of TRACERY. The interlaced-bow chair was popular in about 1810–70.

LATH-AND-BALUSTER WINDSOR CHAIR
Nineteenth-century British variant of LATH-BACK WINDSOR CHAIR (*see under* WINDSOR CHAIR) with decorative central SPLAT flanked by LATHs. In the 1850s the use of an ornamental splat began to be revived from 18th-

century Windsor chairs, and the feature remained popular for the rest of the century.

LATH-BACK WINDSOR CHAIR
Variant of 19th-century British WYCOMBE-STYLE WINDSOR CHAIR (*see under* WINDSOR CHAIR), in which the back was composed of STILEs, CREST RAIL and flattened LATHs. The laths and stiles were curved to follow the profile of the human spine, swelling forward in their bottom third to support the small of the sitter's back. This approach to comfort evolved from the shaped SPINDLEs of the somewhat earlier SPINDLE-BACK WINDSOR CHAIR (*see under* WINDSOR CHAIR). The use of curved laths had a great influence on later DECK CHAIR design.

The lath-back Windsor chair was developed in the 1850s and remained popular into the 1920s, especially in the simplest, sturdiest models, which were known as *farmhouse Windsor chairs*. A more elaborate version was the LATH-AND-BALUSTER WINDSOR CHAIR (*see under* WINDSOR CHAIR).

LOOP-BACK WINDSOR CHAIR
One of two varieties of BOW-BACK WINDSOR CHAIR (*see under* WINDSOR CHAIR).

LOW-BACK WINDSOR CHAIR
Any of several Windsor chair designs popular in Britain and America in 19th century, all having low backs composed of ARM BOW (*see under* WINDSOR CHAIR) topped by shaped cresting no more than six inches high and supported on decoratively turned SPINDLEs. The low-back chairs were developed in America from 18th-century SACK-BACK and COMB-BACK WINDSOR CHAIRs (*see each under* WINDSOR CHAIR), in which increasingly lower COMBs (*see under* WINDSOR CHAIR) and back bows (*see* BOW-BACK WINDSOR CHAIR, *under* WINDSOR CHAIR) gave greater importance to arm bows. The three best-known varieties of low-back Windsor chair were of American origin but were popular on both sides of the Atlantic. These were the SMOKER'S BOW and FIREHOUSE WINDSOR CHAIRs and the CAPTAIN'S CHAIR (*see each under* WINDSOR CHAIR). A fourth variety, the BERGERE-BOW WINDSOR CHAIR (*see under* WINDSOR CHAIR), was chiefly British.

ended horizontal panel, was mounted on two STILEs and the SPINDLEs or LATHs between them. The name refers to a district that was a major center of production of these and other Windsor chairs. Two basic varieties of Wycombe style chair were made, beginning in about 1840: the SPINDLE-BACK and LATH-BACK WINDSOR CHAIRs (*see each under* WINDSOR CHAIR). The latter proved more successful and was made in large quantities into the 1920s.

WINDSOR SETTEE

Eighteenth-century British and American furniture form; SETTEE constructed like a Windsor chair—that is, arm supports and back were mortised (*see* MORTISE) into the top of the seat, and legs were mortised into the bottom of it. The backs of Windsor settees were either composed of linked sets of two or three chair backs, designed in one of the Windsor chair styles, or of SPINDLEs below a continuous back bow (*see* BOW-BACK WINDSOR CHAIR, *under* WINDSOR CHAIR) or COMB (*see under* WINDSOR CHAIR).

WINDSOR TABLE

Eighteenth-century American furniture form; small three- or four-legged table constructed similarly to a WINDSOR CHAIR, usually by makers who specialized in the chair. Its turned legs were mortised (*see* MORTISE) to the underside of a frequently round tabletop. They were connected to each other by turned STRETCHERs mortised, in turn, into them. Never made in great numbers, Windsor tables are rarely seen today.

WINE TABLE (also *hunt table*)

Late 18th-century British furniture form; horse-shoe-shaped table intended for serving wine. Wine tables sometimes featured metal poles, from which horizontal arms bearing trays pivoted to bring bottles to any side conveniently.

WING CHAIR (also *grandfather chair; club chair*)

British and American furniture form; high-backed EASY CHAIR with upholstered panels, or "wings." These project forward from the sides of the back and curve down to meet the upholstered arms, which scroll outward.

Designed to protect a sitter from drafts, the wing chair first appeared in the RESTORATION FURNITURE of the late 17th century. It was highly fashionable in Britain through the mid-18th century and somewhat later in America. Ever since a very popular form, the wing chair is still made today.

WIRE FURNITURE

Furniture made of metal wire, usually iron or steel. The development of wiremaking machinery in the mid-19th century sparked the use of metal wire, and manufacturers began to produce small, delicate pieces of furniture, principally for outdoor use. The airy lightness of this furniture has made it a favorite ever since. In recent times advances in metal plating have made wire furniture attractive for indoor use as well, and some designers—most notably Harry BERTOIA—have created popular indoor furniture of steel wire.

WOOD, EDGAR (1860–1935)

British architect and furniture designer in the ARTS AND CRAFTS MOVEMENT tradition. At about the turn of the century, Wood designed furniture for his architectural commissions; he preferred built-in furniture to movable pieces. Working in a traditional Arts and Crafts mode, he produced sturdy, rectilinear pieces with much painted decoration, both geometrical and representational. By 1922 he had retired to Italy, where he concentrated on painting and designing furniture decoration in an increasingly elaborate geometrical style that recalled Islamic motifs.

WOODRUFF, GEORGE (active 1808–16)

New York cabinetmaker in the REGENCY STYLE. Woodruff was a follower of Duncan PHYFE, and his pieces are difficult to distinguish from those of the better-known master. He produced furniture in a restrained manner, emphasizing reeding as a decorative device.

WOOTON DESK

Ingenious piece of PATENT FURNITURE, widely popular in 1870s–1880s. In 1870 William S. Wooton established a furniture company in Indianapolis, Indiana, that specialized in church, school and office furniture. In 1874 he

three-back Windsor chair

wheel-back Windsor

writing-arm Windsor chair

invented and patented a desk that featured two cabinetlike doors containing dozens of slots, shelves and pigeonholes. Manufactured in four models and in various price ranges, the Wooton desk was immediately popular throughout America and, following its display at the 1876 Centennial Exhibition in Philadelphia, in Europe as well. Custom models were owned by John D. Rockefeller, Jay Gould, Ulysses S. Grant and other notables. Its extraordinary popularity continued for two decades until, in the 1880s and 1890s, the development of typewriters and other office equipment generated a volume of paperwork too great for even this gem to hold. The filing cabinet was conceived, and desk users reverted to simpler designs.

WORKTABLE (also *sewing table*)

Late 18th- and early 19th-century furniture form; small table intended for use when sewing. A worktable was equipped with a drawer or drawers containing fitted compartments for bobbins and other tools. It usually also had a cloth bag or pouch, suspended below, to hold work in progress.

WORMLEY, EDWARD (b. 1907–95)

Contemporary American furniture designer. After studying at the Chicago Art Institute in the late 1920s, Wormley designed modest modern furniture through the 1930s for the Dunbar Furniture Corp. of Berne, Indiana, and became the firm's design director. In the 1950s, in private practice but still designing for Dunbar, Wormley became well known for handsome furniture that reflected the influence of the more organic, less machined look of postwar SCANDINAVIAN MODERN design on the mainstream INTERNATIONAL STYLE.

WRIGHT, FRANK LLOYD (1867–1959)

American architect and designer; leading member of the PRAIRIE SCHOOL. Wright, born in Wisconsin, was apprenticed in his youth to an architect in Chicago, where he met George Grant ELMSLIE and George Washington MAHER, later fellow members of the Prairie School. Wright was introduced to the British ARTS AND CRAFTS MOVEMENT and the Modern Gothic style of EASTLAKE and TALBERT through Louis Sullivan; Wright's pursuit of simplicity and use of oak in most of his early furniture reveal the influence of these

design movements on his work. Unlike proponents of the Arts and Crafts movement, however, Wright came to be enthusiastic about machinemade furniture, with its sharp, straight lines.

Wright began making furniture for himself in 1895, and he immediately developed a fondness for an exaggerated vertical line, expressed in long, narrow slats, that characterized all his work. In accordance with a central tenet of the Prairie School, his furniture designs were elements of his larger architectural scheme, each piece designed for a specific architectural context and intended to reflect and emphasize the lines of the building. In 1904 Wright designed the Larkin Administration Building in Buffalo, New York, complete with all its metal furniture—the first time office furniture had been designed for the particular purposes and locations it was to occupy. The well-known wooden chair resembling a cube that he also designed in 1904 exemplifies the strict, geometrical style of his mature work, much of which was built directly into the fabric of the building it was designed for. From early on, his work was strikingly informed by his acquaintance with Japanese design, furthered by several trips to Japan, beginning in 1905 (*see also* JAPONISME).

After the series of great "prairie houses" of 1900–1915, Wright's furniture designs became less notable, being chiefly variations on principles he had already developed. Wright's design principles, however, were to have a tremendous impact on modern design, particularly through Gerrit RIETVELD and the BAUHAUS. Wright's furniture, however, although tremendously important in terms of the development of the modern esthetic, has generally been decried as uncomfortable. Some have observed that furniture designed with a house plan in mind does not necessarily relate well to the human body. Wright himself wrote, "Somehow I always had black and blue spots my whole life long from all too close contact with my own furniture."

WRIGHT, LESLIE JOHN (b. 1951)

AUSTRALIAN FURNITURE designer. After his initial training in crafts, Leslie John Wright traveled to Scandinavia, Britain, the United States, and Italy (where he was especially struck by the work of Tobia and Afra SCARPA), observing the best examples of the major modern furniture traditions. Returning to Australia, he studied design and began to make his signature

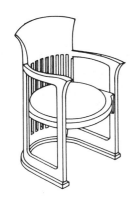

chair by Frank Lloyd Wright

rearward extension of the seat, called a BOB-TAIL (*see under* WINDSOR CHAIR). There they were set in two adjacent mortises. Bracing sticks helped to solve the distinctive structural problem of a Windsor chair—the weakness at the junction of seat and back.

bracing sticks

BUCKLE-BACK WINDSOR CHAIR

SCROLL-BACK WINDSOR CHAIR (*see under* WINDSOR CHAIR) whose CROSS RAIL consisted of a panel of PIERCED CARVING, featuring botanical or abstract motifs that sometimes resembled elaborate contemporary belt buckles. The buckle-back chair was popular in Britain in the second half of the 19th century.

CAPTAIN'S CHAIR

Nineteenth-century LOW-BACK WINDSOR CHAIR (*see under* WINDSOR CHAIR), in which the ARM BOW (*see under* WINDSOR CHAIR), supported by turned SPINDLES, curved abruptly downward in front to be mortised (*see* MORTISE) into the seat at the front corners. Its legs were connected by a BOX STRETCHER (*see under* STRETCHER). Originally used in the pilot houses of Mississippi River steamboats, the chair was popular in Britain as well as America by the 1860s and remained so into the 1890s.

COMB

CREST RAIL OF COMB-BACK WINDSOR CHAIR (*see under* WINDSOR CHAIR).

COMB-BACK WINDSOR CHAIR

Eighteenth-century Windsor chair with a horizontal CREST RAIL surmounting SPINDLES, splat or both, which were mortised (*see* MORTISE) into its underside. The basic form, with a simple back composed of spindles and crest rail, resembled a hay rake or large comb—hence, the name. The top of the comb, as the crest rail was called, had a carved profile that varied with current styles, and it frequently terminated in shaped lobes, or EARs, on either side. Most comb-back armchairs featured an ARM BOW (*see under* WINDSOR CHAIR), but the arms may also have been mortised into the STILES. Many variants of the comb-back were made, including the BALLOON-BACK, FAN-

BACK and SHAWL-BACK WINDSOR CHAIRS (*see each under* WINDSOR CHAIR).

CONTINUOUS-ARM WINDSOR CHAIR

Eighteenth-century American version of LOOP-BACK WINDSOR CHAIR (*see under* WINDSOR CHAIR), in which the arms, each supported at the front by a turned BALUSTER, were made from a single piece of BENTWOOD that rose at the rear to function as a back bow (*see* BOW-BACK WINDSOR CHAIR, *under* WINDSOR CHAIR). Thus, the back bow was not mortised into the seat, as in a loop-back chair, but was supported by its numerous spindles, the front balusters and usually a pair of BRACING STICKS (*see under* WINDSOR CHAIR).

buckle-back Windsor chair

DOUBLE WINDSOR CHAIR

Another name for WINDSOR SETTEE.

FAN-BACK WINDSOR CHAIR

Variant of 18th-century COMB-BACK WINDSOR CHAIR (*see under* WINDSOR CHAIR), in which the comb was wider than the rest of the chair, causing the back's SPINDLES to fan out. It was often made with a central SPLAT.

FARMHOUSE WINDSOR CHAIR

See LATH-BACK WINDSOR CHAIR, *under* WINDSOR CHAIR.

captain's chair

FIREHOUSE WINDSOR CHAIR

Nineteenth-century LOW-BACK WINDSOR CHAIR (*see under* WINDSOR CHAIR), in which the ARM BOW (*see under* WINDSOR CHAIR) and its cresting, supported on simply turned SPINDLEs, were plain and practical, without the scrollings of its antecedent, the SMOKER'S BOW WINDSOR CHAIR (*see under* WINDSOR CHAIR). Its legs were connected by a BOX STRETCHER (*see under* STRETCHER). Developed in the United States in about midcentury, it was immediately popular in both Britain and America and remained so into the 1890s. It was frequently used by the volunteer fire departments that proliferated at that time—hence, its name.

comb-back Windsor chair

continuous arm Windsor chair

fan-back Windsor chair

firehouse Windsor chair

Gothic scroll-back Windsor chair

Gothic Windsor chair

interlaced-bow Windsor chair

GOTHIC SCROLL-BACK WINDSOR CHAIR
Nineteenth-century British variant of SCROLL-BACK WINDSOR CHAIR (*see under* WINDSOR CHAIR) in which an arched profile was carved at the bottom edge of the top rail and the top edge of the CROSS RAIL. The two parts were linked by small turned BALUSTERs, and the whole resembled medieval ARCADING. This example of NEO-GOTHIC STYLE furniture was most popular in about 1840–70.

GOTHIC WINDSOR CHAIR (also *Strawberry Hill Windsor chair; window-splat Windsor chair*) Eighteenth-century British variant of either COMB-BACK or BOW-BACK WINDSOR CHAIR (*see each under* WINDSOR CHAIR), in which back consisted of three pierced SPLATs, carved in imitation of Gothic window TRACERY, without SPINDLEs. Often, smaller, matching splats also appeared, one below each arm. Occasionally, the bow-back Gothic chair featured a back bow (*see* BOW-BACK WINDSOR CHAIR, *under* WINDSOR CHAIR) formed as a pointed arch. The Gothic Windsor chair was popular for about 20 years in the mid-18th century—an example of the Gothic Revival taste in British ROCOCO FURNITURE (*see* NEO-GOTHIC STYLE; CHIPPENDALE GOTHIC FURNITURE)—and since the Second World War, it has enjoyed a modest revival. It is distinct from the 19th-century GOTHIC SCROLL-BACK WINDSOR CHAIR (*see under* WINDSOR CHAIR).

INTERLACED-BOW WINDSOR CHAIR
Nineteenth-century variant of LOOP-BACK WINDSOR CHAIR (*see under* WINDSOR CHAIR), in which back's SPINDLEs or SPLATs were replaced by a bold OPENWORK arrangement of smoothly curving bands of plain wood, representing any of several images, mostly neo-Gothic in taste (*see* NEO-GOTHIC STYLE), including interlaced arches and elements of TRACERY. The interlaced-bow chair was popular in about 1810–70.

LATH-AND-BALUSTER WINDSOR CHAIR
Nineteenth-century British variant of LATH-BACK WINDSOR CHAIR (*see under* WINDSOR CHAIR) with decorative central SPLAT flanked by LATHs. In the 1850s the use of an ornamental splat began to be revived from 18th-century Windsor chairs, and the feature remained popular for the rest of the century.

LATH-BACK WINDSOR CHAIR
Variant of 19th-century British WYCOMBE-STYLE WINDSOR CHAIR (*see under* WINDSOR CHAIR), in which the back was composed of STILEs, CREST RAIL and flattened LATHs. The laths and stiles were curved to follow the profile of the human spine, swelling forward in their bottom third to support the small of the sitter's back. This approach to comfort evolved from the shaped SPINDLEs of the somewhat earlier SPINDLE-BACK WINDSOR CHAIR (*see under* WINDSOR CHAIR). The use of curved laths had a great influence on later DECK CHAIR design.

The lath-back Windsor chair was developed in the 1850s and remained popular into the 1920s, especially in the simplest, sturdiest models, which were known as *farmhouse Windsor chairs*. A more elaborate version was the LATH-AND-BALUSTER WINDSOR CHAIR (*see under* WINDSOR CHAIR).

LOOP-BACK WINDSOR CHAIR
One of two varieties of BOW-BACK WINDSOR CHAIR (*see under* WINDSOR CHAIR).

LOW-BACK WINDSOR CHAIR
Any of several Windsor chair designs popular in Britain and America in 19th century, all having low backs composed of ARM BOW (*see under* WINDSOR CHAIR) topped by shaped cresting no more than six inches high and supported on decoratively turned SPINDLEs. The low-back chairs were developed in America from 18th-century SACK-BACK and COMB-BACK WINDSOR CHAIRs (*see each under* WINDSOR CHAIR), in which increasingly lower COMBs (*see under* WINDSOR CHAIR) and back bows (*see* BOW-BACK WINDSOR CHAIR, *under* WINDSOR CHAIR) gave greater importance to arm bows. The three best-known varieties of low-back Windsor chair were of American origin but were popular on both sides of the Atlantic. These were the SMOKER'S BOW and FIREHOUSE WINDSOR CHAIRs and the CAPTAIN'S CHAIR (*see each under* WINDSOR CHAIR). A fourth variety, the BERGERE-BOW WINDSOR CHAIR (*see under* WINDSOR CHAIR), was chiefly British.

curvilinear BENTWOOD furniture. Using native woods, usually in light colors, often with glass and stone, his pieces combine the clean geometry and luxuriant sensuousness of form of the INTERNATIONAL STYLE with a simple rusticity that reflects his chosen location on the austere desert coast of Western Australia.

WRIGHT, RUSSELL (1904–76)

American designer in the AMERICAN MODERNE style. Originally a theatrical designer, Wright turned to designing products for mass manufacture in the late 1920s, influenced at least in part by his friend Norman Bel GEDDES. He designed very successful dinnerware, for which he is still best known. Wright also designed several lines of furniture dating from the mid-1930s to the early 1950s. His American Moderne furniture combined the austere FUNCTIONALISM of the European INTERNATIONAL STYLE with the more sensuous, luxurious character of French ART DECO furniture. The pieces were composed of basic, rectilinear forms made of inexpensive materials suitable for mass production, employing contrasts of color and texture together with rounded, soft details. He also designed fabrics, appliances, packaging, and domestic and commercial interiors.

WRITING-ARM WINDSOR CHAIR

See under WINDSOR CHAIR.

WRITING BOX

Medieval furniture form; small, portable DESK—paneled box with sloping top. The writing box provided a storage space for papers and writing materials as well as a slanted writing surface. Originally, its lid was hinged at the top. In Renaissance times, though, the hinge was placed at the bottom, and thus, the writing surface appeared when the lid was open. This form, known as an ESCRITOIRE, evolved into the SLANT-TOP DESK on the one hand and, on the other, the WRITING CABINET, with a FALL FRONT that closed vertically. The original medieval form survived through the 18th century.

WRITING CABINET

British DESK of 18th and 19th centuries; upright case piece with FALL FRONT forming a vertical front surface, unlike in a SLANT-TOP DESK. When open, the fall front was supported by chains or rested on retractable LOPERs and provided a writing surface. When closed, it concealed numerous small compartments and drawers. The lower part of the piece took the form of a CHEST OF DRAWERS. Like its French equivalent, the SECRÉTAIRE À ABATTANT, the writing cabinet evolved from a portable WRITING BOX with a vertical front.

WRITING CHAIR

British name for CORNER CHAIR.

WRITING TABLE

Flat-topped DESK; table with drawers or compartments below the tabletop for storage of writing materials. The BUREAU PLAT and the LIBRARY TABLE are writing tables. The PEDESTAL DESK, flat but not a table, is not; nor is the CARLTON HOUSE table, which has a superstructure.

WRITING TABLE AND BOOKCASE

Eighteenth-century name for SECRETARY.

WU MU

Chinese term for EBONY, occasionally used in CHINESE FURNITURE. Small pieces such as the JI and the KANG JI were sometimes made of *wu mu,* through the Tang dynasty (618–907). In more recent times, though, the wood has been used more in particularly elaborate INLAY work.

WYATT, BENJAMIN DEAN (1775–1850)

British architect and furniture designer. A member of a famed family of architects, Wyatt was primarily an architect himself, best known for London's Drury Lane Theater. But he designed furniture, mostly in the NEOCLASSICAL STYLE, for his architectural commissions as well. He was also one of the earliest exponents of the ROCOCO REVIVAL STYLE.

WYBURD, LEONARD

See LIBERTY, Arthur Lasenby.

WYCOMBE-STYLE WINDSOR CHAIR

See under WINDSOR CHAIR.

X-frame chair

X-FRAME

Furniture element, usually in seating, in which two supports are arranged to resemble a letter *X*. Two or more sets of these legs are then joined by the seat (or tabletop) and/or by STRETCHERs or a bolt through all of the crossing points. A very ancient concept, appearing in EGYPTIAN FURNITURE as early as 2000 B.C., the X-frame stool was used in ROMAN FURNITURE as an emblem of political authority, the SELLA CURULIS. In MEDIEVAL FURNITURE X-frame seating remained an indicator of rank, or at least of precedence in the medieval social hierarchy—in the CHAIR OF ESTATE, for example. In RENAISSANCE FURNITURE the SAVONAROLA CHAIR had a similar, if less formal, connotation. The X-frame has survived to the present, in both chairs and tables; it was particularly popular in NEOCLASSICAL STYLE furniture of the 18th and 19th centuries.

X-STRETCHER

See under STRETCHER.

XIANG QIAN (HSIANG CH'IEN)

Technique of applying INLAYs of MOTHER-OF-PEARL and other materials in LACQUER; used on CHINESE FURNITURE of Ming (1368–1644) and Qing (1644–1911) dynasties. *Xiang qian* was a dry technique, as opposed to the more common YIN PING TUO procedure. A recess to fit the inlaid motif was cut into the dry lacquer. The cutout motif was then glued into place with a lacquer-based putty. In addition to mother-of-pearl, other precious materials—including gold, SILVER, jade, lapis lazuli and IVORY—were also used.

XIANG SHA MU (HSIANG SHA MU)

Aromatic variant of PINE; one of few SOFTWOODs used in CHINESE FURNITURE. Used exclusively as a secondary wood (*see* PRIMARY AND SECONDARY WOODS), *xiang sha mu* was invariably lacquered (*see* LACQUER) to protect against insects.

XIU DUN (HSIU TUN)

CHINESE FURNITURE form of Ming (1368–1644) and Qing (1644–1911) dynasties; barrel-shaped STOOL, or DUN, with OPENWORK sides. The motifs formed by the pierced carving were CARTOUCHES and floral motifs similar to those in brocaded fabrics—hence, the piece's name, which means "embroidered stool."

YAN JI (YEN CHI)

CHINESE FURNITURE form of Ming (1368–1644) and Qing (1644–1911) dynasties; DRAW-LEAF TABLE. Used at receptions and parties, the *yan ji*—literally, "swallow table"—was named for the bird, a conventional symbol of frivolous pleasures.

YANAGI, SORI (b. 1915)

Contemporary Japanese furniture and industrial designer. A leading modern industrial designer who works with Western technology and ideas, Yanagi is also grounded in the heritage of Japanese craft and uses traditional materials and forms whenever suitable. He was trained in Tokyo as a painter and architect and in the 1940s worked for French designer Charlotte PERRIAND, who worked in Japan as a design consultant for a time. Yanagi's molded wooden furniture reflects both Western and Eastern influences, utilizing a modern technical process to produce in fine woods pieces that, while functional and modern, also illustrate the character of traditional Japanese architecture.

YANG CI (YANG TZ'U) (also *Canton enamel; Peking enamel*)

Decorative technique used in CHINESE FURNITURE; enamel painting on plaques of gold or, more commonly, copper, which are applied to small TABLEs and caskets. *Yang ci*—literally, "foreign porcelain"—was learned from Western artists in the early 18th century, at the insistence of Emperor Kangxi. It was used on furniture featuring both Chinese and Western motifs, much of it for export. In the West it is known as *Canton enamel*, after the port from which it was exported. Work believed to have been made in the imperial workshops is sometimes called *Peking enamel.*

YELLOW POPLAR

Another name for TULIP POPLAR.

YELLOWWOOD

Central American SOFTWOOD; pale yellow aging to brown. Easily worked and with an even texture, yellowwood was used for INLAY work in 18th-century British furniture. It was then known as *fustic.* Today it is rarely exported.

YEW

European SOFTWOOD; red darkening to brown with age. Famous as the wood of English longbows, yew is also the traditional material for the BENTWOOD parts of WINDSOR CHAIRs. It is often used in fine handcrafted furniture, as it works easily and polishes well.

YIN PING TUO (YIN P'ING T'O)

Technique of placing INLAYs of MOTHER-OF-PEARL and other precious materials in LACQUER, used in CHINESE FURNITURE of Ming (1368–1644) and Qing (1644–1911) dynasties. A moist technique, as opposed to the dry XIANG QIAN procedure, the first step in *yin ping tuo* work was an application of a lacquer-based putty into which were pressed cutout motifs of mother-of-pearl, gold, SILVER, jade, lapis lazuli and IVORY. The piece of furniture was then covered with a layer of lacquer that was later burnished down to reveal the inlaid material.

YOKE-BACK CHAIR

Early 18th-century chair whose CREST RAIL consisted of a downward curve in the center and two upward curves at the sides; the whole formed a smooth line flowing from the stiles. The yoke back exemplified the sophisticated curves used in the QUEEN ANNE STYLE.

YOKE RAIL

Another name for CROSS RAIL.

YOUNG, DENNIS (active 1940s–50s)

British CONTEMPORARY STYLE furniture designer. Young was one of the group of young British designers—also including Robin DAY, Clive LATIMER and Ernest RACE—who developed the Contemporary style after the Second World War. Young responded strongly to the work of American designer Charles EAMES, especially Eames's use, in seating furniture, of a plastic shell mounted atop a substructure of steel rods. Young also employed anthropometric data in his furniture designs.

YOUNG, J. M. & CO.

American furniture manufacturer of MISSION STYLE furniture, competitor of—and, later, collaborator with—the L. & J.G. Stickley Co., successors to Gustav STICKLEY. The firm was founded near Syracuse, New York, in 1872, by J. M. Young, a Scottish immigrant woodcarver, and was owned and run by his descendents until 1973. It specialized in heavily carved VICTORIAN PERIOD furniture before turning, around 1902, to the Mission style, doubtless under the influence of the nearby Stickley operation, though Young is known to have visited London in the 1890s and may well have gained an appreciation of the English ARTS AND CRAFTS MOVEMENT at around the same time Gustav Stickley did.

J.M. Young & Co. made other sorts of furniture as well, but their most successful lines were Mission style. Friendly relations with L. & J.G. Stickley led to cooperative manufacturing and designing, with the Stickleys subcontracting some of their own business to the Youngs, whose manufacturing plant was both larger and more modern, and the Youngs sharing in the Stickleys' stock of finishes, construction techniques, and design ideas. By 1920, the two firms shared sales representatives, and J.M. Young regularly manufactured parts for L. & J.G. Stickley's furniture. When the Stickley firm dropped their own Mission line in the mid-1920s, they approved its continuing production and sale by the Youngs, who made "Stickley" furniture until the late 1940s. Only after the Second World War, with the popularity of more modern, INTERNATIONAL STYLE furniture, did J.M. Young & Co. gradually phase out the Mission furniture for which they are best known. The firm continued to operate until 1979.

ZANUSO, MARCO (b. 1916)

One of the leaders of Italian design since the Second World War. As a designer and architect, as a teacher and as the influential editor of the magazine *Casabella,* Zanuso has been a principal exponent of modern, functionalist ideas (*see* FUNCTIONALISM) in Italy. He trained as an architect before the war and established an architecture and design practice in Milan in 1945. Zanuso has designed a wide variety of industrial products, ranging from factory buildings to small objects and furniture. Between 1958 and 1977 he collaborated with Richard SAPPER on many projects, including television sets and other electronic products, as well as some furniture. Zanuso's experimentation with materials has yielded a variety of pieces of furniture—for example, chairs with a foam-rubber upholstery, sheet-metal furniture and, with Sapper, a children's stacking chair that represented an early use of polyethylene in furniture. All of Zanuso's furniture is executed in a clean-lined modern style descended from the INTERNATIONAL STYLE and influenced by SCANDINAVIAN MODERN furniture and postwar American design.

ZANZIBAR CHAIR

American chair type of PILLAR AND SCROLL STYLE; BERGÈRE with SCROLL ARMS(1) and a caned back and seat in place of upholstery. Made in the seaports of Boston and Salem, Massachusetts, the Zanzibar chair was probably named for a now-unknown caned prototype from the island off the east coast of Africa, then a British colonial outpost.

ZAPF, OTTO (b. 1931)

Contemporary German designer. Zapf is a noted designer of furniture, especially office systems, for Knoll (*see* Florence Schust KNOLL.) He has also produced a number of well-known lighting designs.

ZEBRAWOOD (also *zebrano*)

Colorful African HARDWOOD used chiefly for MARQUETRY. Zebrawood is yellow or light brown, with many narrow stripes in different shades of darker brown.

ZELKOVA (also *keyaki*)

Japanese HARDWOOD; dark brown and richly figured. In Japan it is the most highly valued wood for the doors and drawer fronts of high-quality chests (*see* TANSU).

ZENI-DANSU

Traditional JAPANESE FURNITURE form; small TANSU, or chest. It was a thick-walled wooden box intended for storing money and other valuables. Named for the *zeni,* a coin of the Edo period (1615–1868), the *zeni-dansu* usually had a hinged top, often with a slot, that could be locked by a hasp at the front edge of the box. There were often small drawers below the main compartment, and secret drawers and compartments were also common.

ZHANG MU (CHANG MU)

Chinese name for CAMPHORWOOD.

ZHUAN LUN JING CHANG (CHUAN LUN CHING CH'ANG)

CHINESE FURNITURE form of the Tang dynasty (618–907 A.D.); large revolving bookcase, intended to house the sacred texts in Buddhist temple libraries. The *zhuan lun jing chang* was usually octagonal in shape, with two doors on each side. Behind the doors were many pigeonholes, for scrolls, and some shelves, for books, which were rarer. The form rotated on a central shaft and sometimes had a brake.

ZI TAN (TZU T'AN) (also *purple sandalwood; blackwood*)

Type of PADAUK used in CHINESE FURNITURE; hard, heavy, dense wood, dark purplish brown in color, with a very smooth surface. In the West it has sometimes been called *blackwood* because of its very dark color. *Zi tan*—literally, though inaccurately, "purple sandalwood"—was used in fine Chinese pieces since the Tang dynasty (618–907), although it always had to be imported from Southeast Asia. It was frequently decorated in a distinctive manner. Some *zi tan* was sanded, yielding orange sawdust, which was then sprinkled on the *wood* and covered with a thin coat of clear LACQUER. The resulting variegated surface was called *jin si zi tan*, or "golden-threaded purple sandalwood."

Zoarite chair

ZOARITE FURNITURE

Nineteenth-century American furniture made by a utopian community in Zoar, Ohio. The Zoarite craftsmen, who came from the German state of Württenburg and settled in Ohio in 1817, made simple furniture with carved decoration, related to German models. These ranged from the vernacular *brettstuhl*, or BOARD CHAIR, to pieces in the contemporary BIEDERMEIER STYLE.

ZUCCHI, ANTONIO (1726–95)

Italian painter of furniture and interiors who worked in Britain. Zucchi, a Venetian, met Robert ADAM while the British architect was living in Italy, and he subsequently went to Britain, where he fulfilled many commissions for Adam, painting idealized mythological scenes on furniture and wall panels. In 1781 he married Angelica KAUFFMANN, who did similar work.

ZUI WENG YI (TSUI WÊNG YI)

CHINESE FURNITURE form of Qing dynasty (1644–1911); BAMBOO chair that could be converted into a DAYBED by drawing forward a footrest from beneath the seat. The *zui weng yi*—literally, a "drunken lord's chair"—also had a caned back (see CANING) set at a rearward slant and topped by a bolsterlike headrest, thus resembling the earlier SAN CAI TU HUI, or "chair of the old man who has been drinking."

A Guide to Buying Furniture

"Buying furniture" can mean several different things. Considering fine antiques, browsing at a flea market, or shopping the discount malls for utilitarian unfinished furniture are certainly different sorts of pursuit. Yet they are all activities that yield the most satisfaction if one makes a plan and follows it. Or, as I was long ago instructed by a U.S. Army motor pool sergeant, "Prior Planning Prevents Poor Performance."

This may seem silly—furniture is furniture, after all. Can't one just find stuff one likes and then buy it? But there are potential pitfalls and petty (or not so petty) aggravations that can be avoided. Shopper's remorse is not a pleasant sensation. Decisions made while actively shopping are likely to be hasty, or influenced by the seller, or by your own too-enthusiastic first impressions. So, most importantly, make your basic decisions before you shop!

Make sure you know exactly what sort of furniture you want to buy. A full-size couch or a love seat? A futon or a conventional sofa bed? Armchair or side chair? Should the dining table have several extra leaves? Should the chest of drawers be tall or short? Do you want to hang a picture above it? Don't find yourself deciding these sorts of things in the store; do it at home where you can visualize carefully how your rooms will appear with the new furniture in them.

Related to such considerations is the advice to measure the space you intend to fill with your new piece of furniture. A new couch that is merely one foot too wide may make your side tables interfere with the curtain pulls for the windows on either side. A dining table must not be so grand it leaves too little room around it for dining chairs. If your new bed blocks the bedroom door, you'll have little choice but to return the piece, expending unnecessary money and energy. And apartment dwellers, don't forget to measure the elevators in your building, as well.

Do you want to emphasize comfort or appearance? Of course, you will usually want to strike a balance here. At or near the extremes, the room you're furnishing may be intended for entertaining guests and the furniture meant to be especially striking, functioning as virtual works of art; or you may be planning a comfy den or bedroom and your eye will be for particularly comfortable pieces of furniture, without respect to style or the integration of the new piece with other pieces. If the latter, don't let a fine antique prove irresistible and eat up your budget; if the former, don't let a bargain become a flat spot in your otherwise splendid assembly. Shop only with your plan in mind.

***

Antiques are potentially the most rewarding sort of furniture to shop for, but of course, they are also the most treacherous. The prices can be quite high (though they aren't necessarily so), and the potential for misjudgment is great. Many pieces of furniture in the antiques market are not what they seem to be. Although fraudulently contrived pseudo-antiques exist and are bought and sold, most erroneous descriptions result from a dealer's error or ignorance rather than fraud (though it must be conceded that misjudgment might just possibly be influenced by anticipation of profits). Centennial period reproductions may be bought as Federal or Chippendale pieces, or later reproductions mistaken as Centennial in date. Revival-style furniture may be thought to be in the original style of centuries earlier. A piece composed of parts of several old pieces may not be detected for what it is. And a piece excellent in itself, and genuinely of its period, may be misattributed to a very famous or very rarely encountered maker and accordingly valued much too highly.

To avoid such pitfalls, there are two all-important things to remember:

- Shop at reputable antique dealers! This also applies to auction houses. You may find "a steal" at a garage sale, but you will probably be the victim. Remember, if it looks too good to be true, it almost surely *isn't* true. The higher prices you can expect to pay by seeking only accredited sellers may be considered as insurance costs—or as tuition, for you will be learning about antiques when you talk with good dealers, who know their trade. Which brings us to the second important point:

- Study, study, study! The more you know, the more comfortable you will be while hunting for antiques, less plagued by worry about "mistakes." The time spent will be rewarded, not just in more assurance in the marketplace, but in the greater likelihood of finding a splendid antique and in enhanced appreciation of its virtues once you have found it—in short, the pleasures of the hunt.

Antique dealers can be found through their advertising in publications devoted to antiques, or at antique shows (themselves usually advertised in the same places, as well as in local newspapers), or simply by walking into their shops. Reputable dealers usually will be members of such organizations as The National Antique and Art Dealers Association and The Art and Antique Dealers League of America and as such will have committed themselves to warranting the authenticity of every item they sell. The dealers at vetted antique shows—where all items on sale have been checked for authenticity by committees of experts—are thereby doubly reliable. However, such shows tend to be high-end, in terms of prices, and many other dealers are also fully committed to the authenticity of their stock. Good antique dealers are prepared to write a descriptive statement of authenticity on the receipt for a sold piece, guaranteeing it to be "genuine, as represented."

If you know your area of interest, speak about it to any dealer whom you like, or whose inventory seems attractive, and ask for helpful hints. You can learn a lot from such conversations. And don't be afraid to ask questions; a good dealer is delighted to answer, not only out of the pleasure he or she takes in the material, but also because a new customer can be made of any inquirer. If you are seeking a particular sort of piece, say so (include some sort of price range), and most dealers will be delighted to keep an eye out for you in the wider marketplace. You are absolutely *not* obligated to buy, and no dealer will suppose that you are. Even if they have bought the piece in order to sell it to you, they can and will sell it to someone else. If a dealer tries to pressure you on this point, you should demur politely and shop elsewhere!

While studying antiques will make you able to converse sensibly with dealers, don't expect to learn as much as they know, unless you give your working life to it, as they do. But study hard, nevertheless. The more you know, the more fun the hunt will be, not only because you will have more confidence in your judgment, but also because you will become aware of so much more that is interesting and beautiful. There are many, many books on furniture at all levels of specialization, available in libraries and bookstores (in large cities one can often find bookstores dedicated entirely to art and antiques). Read all you can. If you are a real beginner, start by learning to distinguish the basic style ranges of Western furniture since the Renaissance: baroque, rococo, neoclassical, modern. You will soon progress to differences in national versions of these styles, and then to local or chronological variants, such as Newport versus Philadelphia Chippendale, or Empire versus Louis XVIII. Nineteenth-century furniture often combines several styles in a single piece, and in time you will be able to sort them out. The various modes of modern furniture are no less fascinating. Eventually, you will learn the construction techniques and materials employed at different times and places and on which, in addition to stylistic criteria, experts base their datings and attributions.

As your eye for these things improves, you will understand more and more fully the distinctions between similar pieces that experts consider when judging one piece of furniture superior to another (you may, of course, disagree with them, once you know what they are talking about). Viewing fine furniture, even imitations of it, becomes as delightful as any other aesthetic experience. Soon, every room you enter will offer the pleasure of assessing the stylistic characteristics of the furniture, for even the crummiest office suite has been designed by someone, and that someone has drawn on some tradition or other, even if unknowingly. Spotting this sort of thing is something like bird-watching, except that by going to a museum or an antique show, you can be sure of seeing beauties and rarities every time. And these pleasures will not likely be diminished by time. There is virtually no end to the things that can be learned about antique furniture! Any dealer or curator or other expert will tell you that they are always learning new things, from books, from conversations with their colleagues and knowledgeable collectors, and from each significant piece they examine.

And—an important tip on the actual shopping process—decide ahead of time what your budget is. It is a good idea to adopt as an upper limit to what you are willing to pay, for either a single piece or a whole assemblage, an amount that is somewhat below what you know you can afford. Then, should lightning strike (and consider carefully whether that has really happened, or if that was merely a 1,000-watt light bulb that flashed) and the greatest piece of furniture you ever dreamed of owning turns up at just a little over budget, you can buy it. But shop for that lower figure and don't violate the second one! Bear in mind that lightning can deliver a bad shock.

Of course, the worst shock a buyer of antique furniture can receive is to learn that a piece he has bought is not authentic. That is, it is not by the maker, perhaps not even of the period, one had believed it was, and had paid for. Following the advice above to deal only with reputable dealers insures against this. If you can present reasonable evidence to doubt the authenticity of a piece you have bought from a good dealer, such as the opinion of a museum curator, or perhaps even a convincing exposé by another dealer, your seller will be willing to buy the piece back, at the price you paid for it. In fact, while they don't usually want to do it, many dealers can be prevailed upon to buy back a major piece if you've merely decided you don't like it—unless, of course, the market for antiques has declined in the meantime. If the status quo ante can be achieved, then they will simply sell it again, having had the interest-free use of your money in the meantime.

However, if you buy at flea markets, garage sales, from want ads, and so on, you had better be able to avoid at least the garden-variety sorts of fraudulent antiques. The fraud, of course, may very well have been perpetrated upon whoever sells it to you and not by them, but you'll be the one left holding the bag. The most common mode of antique "manufacture" is the assembling of genuinely old parts into a new piece of furniture. For instance, an old settee is worth far more than several chairs, so unscrupulous people have been known to disassemble a few armchairs and put them back together as a settee. Similarly, spinning wheel spindles are sometimes recycled as the legs of "country" (and thus "funny-looking") candlestands or tea tables. The entire pedestal and legs of a clock reel (a device for winding yarn) may go to the same purpose. But clock reels were rather shorter than the tables of their day; this gives the game away, but only to those who know, while at the same time it makes the new table an ideal height for modern, lower seating furniture. Such combinations are called "assembled pieces."

So-called "married pieces" are multipart items—such as a chest-on-chest, or a secretary desk, or a kas with dismountable cornice and feet—whose parts are originally from separate pieces, none of which have survived whole. Moldings can hide slight differences in dimension, but they will look "wrong" to the experienced viewer. The dovetail joints in the two parts may be differently cut or proportioned. Also, differences in style or in wood type are often apparent. The presence of finished wood in unexpected places, as on the top of a desk now—as part of a secretary—surmounted by a bookcase, is a giveaway. If it had been beneath the bookcase originally, that wood would have been left unfinished. Sometimes a piece will survive without legs, and new ones will have been added to it. Check underneath for new wood and/or modern screws. (There were *no* screws until about 1680, and they were handmade—with very little taper, very shallow threads, and an off-center slot—until 1850. And until the last decades of the 18th century, nails were also handmade—and look it.)

Also, as fashions change, antiques are sometimes altered to suit. For instance, a chest of drawers can be made narrower by removing wood; the piece remains entirely old, and all of its parts are original, but its value is diminished. Here, you must hope your study will have brought you a good enough "eye" to detect that *something* isn't right, even if you can't put a finger on it. Likewise for genuinely old pieces that have been jazzed up with new inlay work or carving. You must know, again, what good originals look like—even the most skilled modern carvers can only produce near-replicas, because the same tools are often unavailable (the number of tools an 18th-century workman used routinely is far greater than the modern repertoire; for some carved effects on, say, Philadelphia Chippendale pieces, the tools used are only uncertainly identifiable); they were not trained from youth in their use; they often don't understand the rationale behind the motifs (and so carve the wrong species of vine, for instance); in short, they were not brought up in the same tradition. This shows, but you have to have looked at a lot of carving to recognize it with confidence.

Reproductions—pieces made in an old style, perhaps exact copies of particular old pieces—usually present less difficult problems. Most reproductions are made without deceit in mind, and the makers simply use the modern tools at hand—power saws and planers, finely machined screws and bolts, machines that cut joints, and so on. The marks made with these tools are quite evident. Most strikingly, saws leave slight ridges; rotary saws make concentric arcs, and handsaws leave parallel straight lines. Also, modern factory-made finishes are almost always detectable, especially if an effort has been made to "antique" the piece with false wormholes and the like. Reproduction makers, intending only to sell new furniture, often use a wood that was popular and economical when it was made, like stained birch in a "mahogany" dining table, though it would not have been used in the period of the original. Similarly, especially early in the 20th century during the days of Colonial Revival furniture, when the enthusiasm for collecting antique furniture was just arising and before detailed knowledge of antiques was widespread, reproduction makers would sometimes inadvertently mix styles or modes, combining features used in two different places or times, in a single piece. Even when a reproduction has been made with an understanding of style, using antique tools, and with an effort to replicate the old construction process, something will be amiss, and the educated eye will see it.

In all of these instances of potentially regrettable purchases, the original lessons are seen to be most valuable: (1) know that your seller is a knowledgeable professional; (2) educate yourself. Knowledge of and familiarity with genuine antiques, seen in museums and at antique shows and auctions and galleries, are one's best protection against error, fraud, or mistaken enthusiasm.

***

If your concern is not with antiques but rather with buying contemporary furniture from a retailer or a factory outlet, much of the same advice pertains, of course. Know what it is you are looking for. Know what size you need. Know how much you are willing to pay. And it bears repeating: shop with your plan in mind.

There are some further considerations you can make when shopping for newly made furniture. Check for certain characteristics of fine furniture that some manufacturers will omit for reasons of cost. Such omissions and shortcuts may be entirely acceptable to you, for the savings they bring, but know what you are paying for. For instance, the back of a case piece should not be nailed to the edges of the sides and top, but rather set within them and nailed or screwed to a rabbet cut in those edges. This way, the edges of the back will contribute to maintaining the stability of the whole piece. Similarly, the backs and sides of drawers should be joined with dovetail joints, for maximum stability. Drawers should be equipped with drawer stops, small blocks of wood that keep the closing drawer from hitting the back of the piece, and should open and close smoothly, without binding. Dust panels between the drawers, if present, should be of wood, not cardboard or some similar product.

In upholstered seating furniture, the hidden framework of the piece is often made of softwood, which is both cheaper and easier to work with. But where the frame actually supports the upholstery, as on the curved top of a couch, it should be of hardwood, which is more durable and will not lose shape through wear. Check whatever hardware is used on a piece to see that it is made of substantial metal that will not easily dent or bend. Door hinges on cupboards, in particular, must be sturdy enough to bear the weight of the door without difficulty. Similarly, glass shelves in display cabinets should be *at least* 3/8" thick, and glass table tops should be *at least* 1/2" thick. Check chairs and tables for wiggle, to see that the legs are securely attached and properly designed. And check the slides on extendible dining room tables to ensure that they operate smoothly.

Here, as with antiques, it is best to know your seller. Dealers who are helpful and are interested in customer satisfaction as a matter of ordinary business practice will answer your questions and let you poke around until you are satisfied. Just make sure, for your part, that you are prepared—with a plan, a budget, a measuring tape, and some knowledge—and you will emerge not only with furniture you can enjoy owning, but with memories of the acquisition process that you can enjoy as well.

Places to Visit

This list encompasses some of the most notable public collections throughout the United States and elsewhere whose holdings in furniture, whether inclusive or locally oriented, are of great interest and beauty.

ALABAMA

Birmingham

Birmingham Museum of Art
2000 Eighth Avenue North
Birmingham, AL 35203
(205) 254-2566
A notable collection of Chinese furniture and a substantial 18th-century French one.

CALIFORNIA

Los Angeles

Los Angeles County Museum of Art
5905 Wilshire Boulevard
Los Angeles, CA 90036
(323) 857-6000
Comprehensive art museum containing collections of European and American furniture, with an emphasis on the Arts and Crafts Movement.

The J. Paul Getty Museum
1200 Getty Center Drive
Los Angeles, CA 90049
(310) 440-7300
Art museum, housing a collection of European decorative arts from the Renaissance through the 19th century, with an emphasis on the major works of French *ébénistes* during the Louis XIV, Louis XV, and Louis XVI periods.

San Francisco

Asian Art Museum of San Francisco
Golden Gate Park
San Francisco, CA 94118
(415) 379-8800
America's greatest museum of Asian art houses much fine furniture, especially Chinese.

CONNECTICUT

Hartford

Wadsworth Atheneum
600 Main Street
Hartford, CT 06103
(203) 278-2670
Art museum with a strong emphasis on European and American decorative arts, especially 17th- and 18th-century American furniture.

New Haven

Yale University Art Gallery
1111 Chapel Street
P.O. Box 208271
New Haven, CT 06520-8271
(203) 432-0600
Art museum, including the famed Mabel Brady Garvan collection of American antiques.

Woodstock

Bowen House, 1846
Route 169
Woodstock, CT 06281
(860) 928-4074
Neo-Gothic house museum, complete with original furnishings.

DELAWARE

Winterthur Museum, Garden & Library
Winterthur, DE 19735
(800) 448-3883
The major American decorative arts collection, with 175 period rooms and a museum wing, featuring furniture ranging in date from 1640 to 1860. Plus, 25 miles away, ten house museums, in Odessa, Delaware.

DISTRICT OF COLUMBIA

The Diplomatic Reception Rooms of the Department of State
2201 C Street NW
Washington, DC 20520
(202) 647-3241
These grand rooms, furnished with museum-quality American antiques dating from 1750 to 1825, are used for official functions but are open on weekdays for prearranged tours at no charge. Reservations are required and should be made approximately four weeks in advance, due to the large volume of requests.

Arthur M. Sackler Gallery
1050 Independence Avenue SW
Washington, DC 20560
(202) 357-4880
This branch of the Smithsonian Institution has a range of Asian art including a collection of Chinese hardwood and lacquer furniture.

GEORGIA

Atlanta

The High Museum of Art
1280 Peachtree Street NE
Atlanta, Georgia 30309
(404) 733-4400
Art museum with a fine American antique furniture collection.

HAWAII

Honolulu

Honolulu Academy of Arts
900 South Beretannia
Honolulu, HI 96814-1495
(808) 532-8701; (808) 532-8700.
Excellent collection of Chinese hardwood furniture.

ILLINOIS

Chicago

The Chicago Art Institute
111 South Michigan Avenue
Chicago, IL 60603
(312) 443-3600
Superior art museum with much European and American furniture of all periods from about 1600 to the present, as well as a small collection of Chinese furniture.

KENTUCKY

Bowling Green

The Kentucky Museum
Western Kentucky University
One Big Red Way
Bowling Green, KY 42101-3576
(270) 745-2592
Sizable American furniture collection, not all Kentuckian.

MAINE

Ellsworth

Colonel Black Mansion, "Woodlawn" (1827)
West Main Street, Route 172
Ellsworth, ME 04605
(207) 667-8671
House museum, with restored garden and carriage house.

Portland

Portland Museum of Art
7 Congress Square
Portland, ME 04101
(207) 775-6148
Art museum with decorative arts collection focused on Federal and Empire periods.

Saco

The York Institute Museum
371 Main Street
Saco, ME 04072
(207) 282-3031

York Harbor

Sayward-Wheeler House, c. 1718
79 Barrell Lane Extension
York Harbor, ME 03911
(603) 436-3205
House museum with original 18th- early 19th-century furnishings.

MARYLAND

Baltimore

Baltimore Museum of Art
Art Museum Drive
Baltimore, MD 21218-3898
(410) 396-7100
A varied art museum with a wing of period rooms featuring antiques from Maryland and elsewhere.

Maryland Historical Society
201 West Monument Street
Baltimore, MD 21201-4674
(410) 685-3750
Museum collection including much fine furniture of all periods made in Maryland.

MASSACHUSETTS

Andover

Addison Gallery of American Art
Phillips Academy
180 Main Street
Andover, MA 01810
(978) 749-4027
Small but select collections of American art and furniture.

Boston

Museum of Fine Arts
465 Huntington Avenue
Boston, MA 02115
(617) 267-9300
Comprehensive art museum, with impressive furniture holdings in a range of areas.

Harrison Gray Otis House, 1796
141 Cambridge Street
Boston, MA 02114
(617) 227-3956
House museum, headquarters of the Society for the Preservation of New England Antiquities (owners of several other house museums in this listing), this Bulfinch-designed urban residence has been meticulously restored and houses many pieces of fine, high-style Federal period furniture.

Deerfield

Historic Deerfield
Box 321
Deerfield, MA 01342-0321
(413) 774-5581
Famed treasure trove, a 1,000-acre "campus" with 14 house museums and more.

Lincoln

Gropius House, 1938
68 Baker Bridge Road
Lincoln, MA 01773
(781) 259-8098
House museum designed by Walter Gropius for himself, includes original furniture designed by Marcel Breuer and made at the Bauhaus.

Newbury

Coffin House, c. 1654
14 High Road, Route 1A
Newbury, MA 01951
(978) 462-2634
House museum with extensions built in 1700 and 1785, exhibiting furniture of three centuries.

Plymouth

Pilgrim Hall Museum
75 Court Street
Plymouth, MA 02360
(508) 746-1620
A small but choice collection of Pilgrim Furniture.

Salem

Peabody Essex Museum
East India Square, Salem, MA 01970

(978) 745-9500; (800) 745-4054
A marine and ethnological museum with a fine collection of New England decorative arts; twenty-three period buildings, some furnished, and America's only Chinese period building, an 18th-century merchant's house.

MICHIGAN

Detroit

The Detroit Institute of Arts
5200 Woodward Avenue
Detroit, Michigan 48202
Art museum with collections of 18th- and 19th-century American and European furniture.

MINNESOTA

Minneapolis

Minneapolis Institute of Arts
2400 Third Avenue South
Minneapolis, MN 55404
(612) 870-3131; (888) 642-2787
Comprehensive art museum with one of the best Chinese furniture collections outside China or Japan. Also good European and American pieces of all periods.

MISSOURI

Kansas City

The Nelson-Atkins Museum of Art
4525 Oak Street
Kansas City, Missouri 64111-1873
(816) 751-1278
Comprehensive art museum, with impressive holdings of French, American, and other furniture, mostly displayed in period rooms. Also, an especially fine Chinese furniture collection.

NEW HAMPSHIRE

Keene

Horatio Colony House
199 Main Street
Keene, NH 03431
(603) 352-0460
Federal period house museum.

Manchester

The Currier Gallery of Art
201 Myrtle Way
Manchester, NH 03104
(603) 669-6144
Art museum with a small but good collection of American furniture that emphasizes New England and New Hampshire. (Frank Lloyd Wright's Zimmerman House can be reached by a van from the museum. Reservations are required; call [603] 669-6144.)

Portsmouth

The "Portsmouth Trail" presents six of the city's historic houses. A 32-page brochure with a map of the trail is available at any of the houses. Hours and admission to each house vary; call for more info.

• Governor John Langdon House, 143 Pleasant Street, (603) 436-3205
• John Paul Jones House, Middle & State Streets, (603) 436-8420
• Moffatt-Ladd House, 154 Market Street, (603) 436-8221
• Rundlet-May House, 364 Middle Street, (603) 436-3205
• Warner House, Daniel & Chapel Streets, (603) 436-5909
• Wentworth-Gardner House, Mechanic & Gardner Streets, (603) 436-4406

Strawbery Banke Museum
Bounded by Marcy, State, Washington and Hancock Streets
(603) 433-1100
Historic waterfront neighborhood featuring more than 40 buildings, dating from colonial times (1695) to the early 1900s, including the Chase House (1762), the Drisco House (1790), the Capt. Keyran Walsh House (1796), the Governor Goodwin Mansion (1860), and the Thomas Bailey Aldrich House (1870).

NEW JERSEY

Freehold

Monmouth County Historical Association
70 Court Street
Freehold, NJ 07733
(732) 462-1466
Offering a museum and four local historical houses.

NEW YORK

Garrison

Boscobel (1804–08)
Route 9D
Garrison, NY 10524
(914) 265-3638
House museum, with a fine collection of New York Federal and Empire furniture.

New York City

Brooklyn Museum of Art
200 Eastern Parkway
Brooklyn, NY 11238
(718) 638-5000
Comprehensive art museum, including many good American period rooms, and a small collection of Chinese furniture.

Cooper-Hewitt, National Design Museum
2 East 91st Street
New York, NY 11128
(212) 849-8400
General design museum, including a comprehensive collection of chairs.

The Frick Collection
1 East 70th Street
New York, NY 10021-4967
(212) 288-0700
Fine French furniture, displayed as if in a domestic setting, amid a great painting collection.

Metropolitan Museum of Art
1000 Fifth Avenue
New York, NY 10028-0198
(212) 535-7710
One of the great art museums of the world, with many period rooms and displays of furniture from an amazing range of times and cultures.

Museum of American Folk Art
61 West 62nd Street
New York, NY 10019
(212) 977-7170
Folk art of all sorts, including American country and idiosyncratic furniture.

Museum of Modern Art
11 West 53rd Street
New York, NY 10019
(212) 708-9400
The original modern art museum, with a comprehensive design department featuring virtually all styles of modern furniture.

Tarrytown

Historic Hudson Valley
150 White Plains Road
Tarrytown, NY 10591
(914) 631-8200
Headquarters for six historic landmarks, including:

- Philipsburg Manor, in Tarrytown, an early 18th-century farm restored to working status, whose manor house is furnished with period furniture and decorative arts.
- Montgomery Place, in Annandale-on-Hudson, an early 19th-century mansion furnished with period antiques, some original to the house.

- Van Cortlandt Manor, an 18th-century stone house in Croton-on-Hudson, with a collection of period furniture, most of which is original to the house, plus a restored 18th-century tavern nearby.
- Sunnyside, in Sleepy Hollow, restored home of the author Washington Irving, a 17th-century Dutch colonist's cottage remodeled by Irving in 1835.
- Kykuit, the Rockefeller country retreat in Pocantico Hills, furnished with Nelson Rockefeller's collections of fine furniture, ceramics, and sculpture.
- Union Church of Pocantico Hills, with stained glass windows by Chagall and Matisse.

NORTH CAROLINA

Winston-Salem

MESDA (Museum of Early Southern Decorative Arts)
P.O. Box 10310
Winston-Salem, NC 27108-0310

Old Salem Visitors Center
Academy Street
Winston-Salem, NC 27101
(336) 721-7360.
Premier southern museum of decorative arts.

PENNSYLVANIA

Philadelphia

Philadelphia Museum of Art
26th Street and the Benjamin Franklin Parkway
Philadelphia, PA 19130
(215) 763-8100
A major art museum, including Japanese, Chinese, medieval, and 18th-century French period rooms, and important Philadelphia and Pennsylvania-German furniture and decorative arts collections.

Pittsburgh

Carnegie Museum of Art
4400 Forbes Avenue
Pittsburgh, PA 15213-4080
(412) 622-3131
Art museum with a chronological installation of European and American decorative art from the 17th century to the present.

RHODE ISLAND

Newport

Preservation Society of Newport County
424 Bellevue Avenue
Newport, RI 02840

(401) 847-1000
Caretaker of many of the 19th-century Newport mansions, including The Breakers, Rosecliff, and The Elms, which feature opulent examples of the interior design of America's wealthy industrialists.

Providence

Rhode Island School of Design Museum
224 Benefit Street
Providence, RI 02903
(401) 454-6100
Art museum with furniture from medieval to Post-Modern, with particular strengths in American, and especially Newport, work of the 18th and 19th centuries.

SOUTH CAROLINA

Charleston

The Charleston Museum
360 Meeting Street
Charleston, SC 29403
(843) 722-2996
Owner of two house museums:
- The Joseph Manigault House (1803), 350 Meeting Street, Charleston, a grand neoclassical town house furnished with a collection of American, English, and French furniture of the period.
- The Heyward-Washington House, 87 Church Street, a town house furnished with a fine collection of Charleston furniture, plus a rare separate kitchen building that is open to the public.

Historic Charleston Foundation
P.O. Box 1120
Charleston, SC 29402
(843) 723-1623
Owners of several historical buildings, including:
- Nathaniel Russell House (1808), 51 Meeting Street, Charleston, one of America's best neoclassical house museums.
- Aiken-Rhett House (1818–58), 48 Elizabeth Street, Charleston, a house museum, a fine example of an "urban plantation."

TEXAS

Dallas

Dallas Museum of Art
1717 North Harwood
Dallas, TX 75201
(214) 922-1200
Art museum with a substantial collection of 18th- and 19th-century American furniture.

Houston

Museum of Fine Arts
1001 Bissonnet (at Main)
Houston, TX 77005
Comprehensive art museum, including good 20th-century furniture

Bayou Bend
One Westcott Street
Houston, TX 77007
House museum with the remarkable Miss Ima Hogg's American decorative arts collection, including a wealth of furniture.

VERMONT

Bennington

The Bennington Museum
West Main Street
Bennington, VT 05201
(802) 447-1571
Local history museum with a small but excellent collection of Vermont-made furniture.

VIRGINIA

Williamsburg

Colonial Williamsburg
Williamsburg, VA 23187
(757) 220-7286
The famed "outdoor museum," consisting of 88 restored buildings in the historical center of the town, numerous museum and gallery buildings, and, eight miles distant, Carter's Grove (1737), a house museum.

WISCONSIN

Milwaukee

The Chipstone Foundation
7820 North Club Circle
Milwaukee, WI 53217
(414) 223-3035
A splendid collection of American antique furniture of all periods, though the small size of its display space means much of it is on loan throughout the country.

The Milwaukee Art Museum
750 North Lincoln Memorial Drive
Milwaukee, WI 53202
(414) 224-3200
Art museum with expanding collection of American furniture, from the 18th through the 20th centuries.

CANADA

Toronto

Royal Ontario Museum
100 Queen's Park
Toronto, Ontario M5S2C6
CANADA
(416) 586-5549

ENGLAND

Leeds

Temple Newsam House (16th and 17th centuries)
Temple Newsam Road (off Selby Road)
Leeds LS15 0AE
Palatial house museum.

Harewood House
Harewood, Leeds, West Yorkshire LS17 9LQ
Palatial house museum.

London (and vicinity)

Ham house (1610–70s)
Ham Street
Richmond upon Thames, Surrey TW10 7RS
House museum with original furniture and art, plus a textile collection.

Kenwood (remodeled in 1760, by Robert Adam)
Hampstead Lane
London NW3 7JR
Museum of the 18th century, with much furniture, some of it original to the house.

Strawberry Hill (1753–76)
St. Mary's College
Waldergrave Road
Strawberry Hill TW1 4SX
House museum, Horace Walpole's famous neo-Gothic creation.

The Victoria and Albert Museum
Cromwell Road
South Kensington, London SW7 2RL
World's largest, and possibly best, museum of decorative arts.

The Wallace Collection
Hertford House
Manchester Square, London SW7 2RL
Art museum whose French furniture collection is said to be the best outside France.

FRANCE

Paris

Château de Bagatelle
Bois de Boulogne
Decorative arts collections in an 18th-century folly designed by François-Joseph Belanger, built by a French nobleman to pay off a bet with Queen Marie-Antoinette.

Le Musée des Arts Décoratifs
Palais du Louvre
107, rue de Rivoli
The decorative arts wing of the Palais du Louvre, with its magnificent collection of medieval and Renaissance furnishings.

Musée national des Arts Asiatiques
Guimet 6, place d'Iéna
19, avenue d'Iéna, 75116 Paris
Fine collection of Chinese furniture.

GERMANY

Weil am Rhein

Vitra Design Museum
Charles-Eames-Strasse 1
Though maintained by a commercial furniture manufacturer, this collection "dedicated to history and current trends in industrial furniture design" is well worth seeing.

ITALY

Florence

Museo dell' Opificio delle Pietre Dure
Via degli Alfani, 78
The great collection of Italian pietra dure work, including furniture.

NETHERLANDS

Amsterdam

Rijksmuseum
Stadhouderskade 42, Amsterdam
A great art museum, with lots of great furniture as well.

PEOPLE'S REPUBLIC OF CHINA

Beijing

Central Academy of Arts and Design
Department of Environmental Art Design

No. 34 Dong San Huan Bei Lu
Beijing, People's Republic of China 100020

People's Palace
Beijing, People's Republic of China
Some of the remains of the Imperial Chinese household furnishings.

Hong Kong

Hong Kong Museum of Art
10 Salisbury Road
Tsim Sha Tsui, Kowloon, Hong Kong
Small collection of *huang hua li* furniture on display.

The Tsui Museum of Art
4, Henley Building
5 Queens Road Central, Hong Kong
Chinese hardwood furniture in period rooms.

Shanghai

Shanghai Museum
Renmin Dadao 0201
People's Square
Shanghai, People's Republic of China
Home of the famed Wang Shixiang Collection of Chinese furniture, plus a good collection of other furniture. This site also houses the remarkable miniature wood furniture recently excavated from a Ming dynasty tomb.

REPUBLIC OF CHINA (TAIWAN)

Taipei

National Palace Museum
Taipei
Collection of Qing dynasty *zitan* furniture.

SINGAPORE

Singapore

The Asian Civilizations Museum
39 Armenian Street
Singapore 179939
Late Ming and early Qing hardwood furniture.

BIBLIOGRAPHY

This is not intended to be a definitive bibliography of furniture—such a compilation would make a book in itself—but is rather a list of books I've found most useful in writing this one, along with others I think may be of general interest or usefulness.

Adamson, Jeremy Elwell. *American Wicker: Woven Furniture from 1850 to 1930.* New York: Rizzoli, 1993.

Albrecht, Donald, ed. *The Work of Charles and Ray Eames: A Legacy of Invention.* New York: Abrams, 1997.

Algoud, H., et al. *Authentic French Provincial Furniture from Provence, Normandy and Brittany.* Mineola, N.Y.: Dover Publications, 1993.

Andres, Edward Deming, and Faith Andrews. *Shaker Furniture: The Craftsmanship of an American Communal Sect.* Mineola, N.Y.: Dover Publications, 1964.

————. *Religion in Wood: A Book of Shaker Furniture.* Bloomington: Indiana University Press, 1966.

Andrews, John. *British Antique Furniture: Price Guide and Reasons for Values.* Wappingers Falls, N.Y.: Antique Collectors Club, 1990.

Andrews, John, and Joan Andrews. *Victorian and Edwardian Furniture: Price Guide and Reasons for Values.* Wappingers Falls, N.Y.: Antique Collectors Club, 1993.

————. *Antique Furniture (Starting to Collect Series).* Wappingers Falls, N.Y.: Antique Collectors Club, 1998.

Antonelli, Paola, ed. *Sitting on the Edge: Modernist Design from the Collection of Michael & Gabrielle Boyd.* New York: Rizzoli, 1999.

Asensio, Francisco. *The Home Furniture Design of the New Century.* Duluth, Minn.: Atrium Publishing Group, 2000.

Auslander, Leora. *Taste and Power: Furnishing Modern France.* Berkeley: University of California Press, 1998.

Bachmann, Konstanze, ed. *Conservation Concerns: A Guide for Collectors and Curators.* Washington, D.C.: Smithsonian Institution Press, 1962.

Bates, Elizabeth Bidwell, and Jonathan Fairbanks. *American Furniture: 1620 to the Present.* New York: Richard Marek Publishers, 1981.

Bayer, Patricia, ed. *The Fine Art of the Furniture Maker: Conversations with Wendell Castle, Artist, and Penelope Hunter-Stiebel, Curator, about Selected Works from the Metropolitan Museum of Art.* Rochester, N.Y.: Memorial Art Gallery at the University of Rochester, 1981.

Beard, Geoffrey. *Upholsterers and Interior Furnishing in England 1530–1840.* New Haven, Conn.: Yale University Press, 1997.

Beckerdite, Luke, ed. *American Furniture 1994.* Hanover, N.H.: Chipstone Foundation, 1994.

———. *American Furniture 1995.* Hanover, N.H.: Chipstone Foundation, 1995.

———. *American Furniture 1996.* Hanover, N.H.: Chipstone Foundation, 1996.

———. *American Furniture 1997.* Hanover, N.H.: Chipstone Foundation, 1997.

———. *American Furniture 1998.* Hanover, N.H.: Chipstone Foundation, 1998.

———. *American Furniture (American Furniture 1999).* Hanover, N.H.: Chipstone Foundation, 2000.

Becksvoort, Christian. *The Shaker Legacy: Perspectives on an Enduring Furniture Style.* Newtown, Conn.: Taunton Press, 1998.

Berliner, Nancy, et al. *Beyond the Screen: Chinese Furniture of the 16th & 17th Centuries.* Wappingers Falls, N.Y.: Antique Collectors Club, 1996.

Berliner, Nancy, and Sarah Handler. *Friends of the House: Furniture from China's Towns & Villages.* Salem, Mass.: Peabody Essex Museum, 1996.

Beurdelay, Michel. *Chinese Furniture.* New York: Kodansha International, 1979.

Bishop, Robert. *American Furniture, 1620–1720.* Dearborn, Mich.: The Edison Institute, 1975.

———. *Centuries and Styles of the American Chair, 1640–1870.* New York: Dutton, 1972.

———. *How to Know American Furniture.* New York: Dutton, 1973.

Bishop, Robert, and Patricia Coblentz. *Furniture 1: Prehistoric through Rococo (Smithsonian Illustrated Library of Antiques).* Washington, D.C.: Smithsonian Institution, 1981.

Bjerkoe, Ethel Hall. *The Cabinetmakers of America.* Atglen, Penn.: Schiffer Publishing, 1978.

Blakemore, Robbie G. *History of Interior Design and Furniture: From Ancient Egypt to Nineteenth-Century Europe.* New York: John Wiley & Sons, 1997.

Boas, George, and James D. Breckenridge. *The Age of Elegance: The Rococo and Its Effect.* Baltimore, Md.: Baltimore Museum of Art, 1959.

Bogle, Michael, and Peta Landman. *Modern Australian Furniture.* Carlsbad, Calif.: Craftsman House, 1989.

Bridenbaugh, Carl. *The Colonial Craftsman.* New York: NYU Press, 1950.

Bruce, Grace Wu. *Chinese Classical Furniture.* New York: Oxford University Press, 1996.

Brunhammer, Yvonne, et al. *Art Nouveau Belgium/France.* Houston, Tex.: Rice University Press, 1976.

Brunt, Andrew. *Phaidon Guide to Furniture.* Englewood Cliffs, N.J.: Prentice-Hall, 1983.

Burks, Jean M., and Timothy D. Rieman. *The Complete Book of Shaker Furniture.* New York: Abrams, 1993.

Burton, E. Milby. *Charleston Furniture 1700–1825.* Columbia: University of South Carolina Press, 1997.

Butler, Joseph T. *American Antiques, 1800–1900.* New York: Odyssey Press, 1965.

————. *Field Guide to American Antique Furniture: a Unique Visual System for Identifying the Style of Virtually Any Piece of American Antique Furniture.* New York: Henry Holt, 1987.

Byars, Mel. *50 Tables: Innovations in Design and Materials.* New York: Whitney Library of Design, 1998.

Camard, Florence (translated by David Macey). *Ruhlmann: Master of Art Deco.* New York: Abrams, 1993.

Cathers, David M. *Furniture of the American Arts and Crafts Movement: Furniture Made by Gustav Stickley, L. & J. G. Stickley, and the Roycroft Shop.* Philmont, N.Y.: Turn of the Century Editions, 1996.

Cescinsky, Herbert. *English Furniture: From Gothic to Sheraton.* Mineola, N.Y.: Dover Publications, 1968.

Chinnery, Victor. *Oak Furniture, the British Tradition.* Wappingers Falls, N.Y.: Antique Collectors Club, 1986.

Clark, Michael E., et al. *J. M. Young Arts and Crafts Furniture.* Mineola, N.Y.: Dover Publications, 1994.

Clark, Robert Judson, ed. *The Arts and Crafts Movement in America, 1876–1916.* Princeton, N.J.: Princeton University Press, 1972.

Clarke, Rosy. *Japanese Antique Furniture: A Guide to Evaluating and Restoring.* New York: Weatherhill, 1983.

Clunas, Craig. *Chinese Furniture.* Chicago: Art Media Resources, 1990.

Collard, Frances. *Regency Furniture.* Wappingers Falls, N.Y.: Antique Collectors Club, 1985.

Colombo, Sarah. *The Chair: An Appreciation.* London: Aurum, 1998.

Comstock, Helen. *American Furniture: Seventeenth, Eighteenth, and Nineteenth Century Styles.* Atglen, Penn.: Schiffer Publishing, 1997.

Cooper, Wendy. *In Praise of America: American Decorative Arts, 1650–1830.* New York: Alfred A. Knopf, 1980.

Cotton, Bernard D. *The English Regional Chair.* Wappingers Falls, N.Y.: Antiques Collectors Club, 1990.

Cranz, Galen. *Chair: Rethinking Culture, Body, and Design.* New York: W.W. Norton, 2000.

Crossman, Carl L. *The China Trade; Export Paintings, Furniture, Silver and Other Objects.* Princeton, N.J.: Pyne Press, 1972.

Cummings, Abbott Lowell, ed. *Rural Household Inventories: Establishing the Names, Uses and Furnishings of Rooms in the Colonial New England Home, 1675–1775.* Boston, Mass.: Society for the Preservation of New England Antiquities, 1964.

D'Ambrosio, Anna Tobin. *Masterpieces of American Furniture from the Munson-Williams-Proctor Institute.* Utica, N.Y.: Munson-Williams-Proctor Institute, 1999.

Davidson, Marshall. *Bantam Illustrated Guide to Early American Furniture.* New York: Bantam Books, 1980.

Day, David, and Albert Jackson. *Care and Repair of Furniture.* Newtown, Conn.: Taunton Press, 1994.

De Dampierre, Florence. *The Best of Painted Furniture.* New York: Rizzoli, 1987.

Domergue, Denise. *Artists Design Furniture.* New York: Abrams, 1984.

Drexler, Arthur. *Charles Eames: Furniture from the Design Collection.* New York: Museum of Modern Art, 1973.

Dubrow, Eileen, and Richard Dubrow. *American Furniture of the Nineteenth Century: 1840–1880.* Atglen, Penn.: Schiffer Publishing, 1983.

Duncan, Alastair. *Paris Salons; Furniture 1895–1914.* Wappingers Falls, N.Y.: Antique Collectors Club, 1996.

———. *Art Deco Furniture: The French Designers.* New York: Thames & Hudson, 1997.

———. *Modernism: Modernist Design 1880–1940.* Wappingers Falls, N.Y.: Antique Collectors Club, 1998.

———. *American Art Deco.* New York: Thames & Hudson, 1999.

———. *Art Nouveau Furniture.* New York: C.N. Potter, 1982.

———. *Louis Majorelle: Master of Art Nouveau Design.* New York: Thames & Hudson, 1991.

Duncan, Alastair, and Bruce M. Newman, eds. *Fantasy Furniture*. New York: Rizzoli, 1989.

Eames, Ray, and John and Marilyn Neuhart. *Eames Design: The Work of the Office of Charles and Ray Eames*. New York: Abrams, 1989.

Earl, Polly Anne, and Ian M. G. Quimby, eds. *Technological Innovation and the Decorative Arts*. Charlottesville, Va.: University Press of Virginia, 1974.

Ecke, Gustav. *Chinese Domestic Furniture*. Hong Kong: Hong Kong University Press, 1968.

Ecke, Gustave, ed. *Chinese Domestic Furniture in Photographs and Measured Drawings*. Mineola, N.Y.: Dover Publications, 1986.

Edwards, Clive D. *Twentieth-Century Furniture: Materials, Manufacture and Markets (Studies in Design and Material Culture)*. Manchester, U.K.: Manchester University Press, 1994.

———. *Victorian Furniture: Technology and Design (Studies in Design and Material Culture)*. Manchester, U.K.: Manchester University Press, 1994.

———. *Eighteenth Century Furniture (Studies in Design and Material Culture)*. Manchester, U.K.: Manchester University Press, 1996.

Elder, William Voss. *Baltimore Painted Furniture, 1800–1840*. Baltimore, Md.: Baltimore Museum of Art, 1972.

———. *John Shaw, Cabinetmaker of Annapolis*. Baltimore, Md.: Baltimore Museum of Art, 1983.

Ellsworth, Robert Hatfield. *Chinese Furniture (Hardwood Examples of the Ming and Early Ch'ing Dynasty)*. 1970. Reprint, New York: Robert H. Ellsworth, 1998.

Emery, Marc. *Furniture by Architects*. New York: Abrams, 1983.

Evans, Nancy Goyne. *American Windsor Chairs*. New York: Hudson Hills Press, 1993.

———. *American Windsor Furniture: Specialized Forms*. New York: Hudson Hills Press, 1998.

Evans, Nancy Goyne, et al. *New England Furniture at Winterthur: Queen Anne and Chippendale Periods*. Winterthur, Del.: Winterthur Museum, 1997.

Fabian, Monroe H. *The Pennsylvania-German Decorated Chest*. New York: Universe Books, 1978.

Failey, Dean F., et al. *Long Island Is My Nation: The Decorative Arts & Craftsmen, 1640–1830*. Setauket, N.Y.: Society for the Preservation of Long Island Antiquities, 1976.

Fales, Dean A., Jr. *The Furniture of Historic Deerfield*. New York: Dutton, 1976.

———. *American Painted Furniture 1660–1880*. New York: Dutton, 1979.

Fielden, James, ed. *The Antiques Clinic: A Guide to Damage, Care, and Restoration*. Hauppauge, N.Y.: Barrons Educational Series, 1998.

Fiell, Charlotte, and Peter Fiell. *1,000 Chairs*. New York: Taschen, 1998.

Fleming, John, and Hugh Honour. *Dictionary of the Decorative Arts*. New York: Harper & Row, 1976.

Forrest, Tim. *The Bulfinch Anatomy of Antique Furniture: An Illustrated Guide to Identifying Period, Detail, and Design*. Boston, Mass.: Bulfinch Press, 1996.

Freund, Thatcher. *Objects of Desire: The Lives of Antiques and Those Who Pursue Them*. New York: Penguin USA, 1995.

Giedion, Sigfried. *Mechanization Takes Command: A Contribution to Anonymous History*. New York: Oxford University Press, 1948.

Gilbert, Christopher. *English Vernacular Furniture, 1750–1900*. New Haven, Conn.: Yale University Press, 1991.

Gilborn, Craig A. *American Furniture, 1660–1725*. London: Hamlyn Publishing, 1970.

———. *Adirondack Furniture and the Rustic Tradition*. New York: Abrams, 1987.

Gilliam, Jan Kirsten. *Furnishing Williamsburg's Historic Buildings*. Williamsburg, Va.: Colonial Williamsburg Foundation, 1992.

Giusti, Anna Maria. *Pietre Dure: Hardstone in Furniture and Decorations*. London: Philip Wilson, 1992.

Gloag, John. *A Social History of Furniture Design from B.C. 1300 to A.D. 1960*. New York: Crown Publishers, 1966.

Gray, Stephen. *Roycroft Furniture*. New York: Turn of the Century Editions, 1981.

Greenberg, Cara. *Mid-Century Modern: Furniture of the 1950s*. New York: Harmony Books, 1995.

———. *Op to Pop: Furniture of the 1960s*. Boston, Mass.: Bulfinch Press, 1999.

Greene, Jeffrey P. *American Furniture of the 18th Century*. Newtown, Conn.: Taunton Press, 1996.

Habegger, Jerryll, and Joseph H. Osman. *Sourcebook of Modern Furniture*. New York: W.W. Norton, 1996.

Hanks, David A. *The Decorative Designs of Frank Lloyd Wright*. New York: Dutton, 1979.

———. *Innovative Furniture in America: From 1800 to the Present*. New York: Horizon Press, 1981.

Harling, Robert, ed. *Studio Dictionary of Design & Decoration*. New York: Viking Press, 1973.

Harwood, Barry Robert. *The Furniture of George Hunzinger: Invention and Innovation in Nineteenth-Century America*. Brooklyn, N.Y.: Brooklyn Museum Bookshop, 1997.

Hayward, Helena, ed. *World Furniture: An Illustrated History from Earliest Times.* London: Hamlyn Publishing, 1965.

Heckscher, Morrison H. *American Furniture in the Metropolitan Museum of Art: The Queen Anne and Chippendale Styles.* New York: Metropolitan Museum of Art, 1964.

Hillier, Bevis. *The World of Art Deco.* New York: Dutton, 1971.

Himmelheber, Georg. *Biedermeier Furniture.* London: Faber and Faber, 1974.

———. *Cast-Iron Furniture and All Other Forms of Iron Furniture.* London: Philip Wilson, 1996.

Honour, Hugh. *Cabinet Makers and Furniture Designers.* New York: Putnam, 1969.

Hornor, William Macpherson, Jr. *The Blue Book of Philadelphia Furniture, William Penn to George Washington.* Washington, D.C.: Highland House, 1977.

Howe, Katherine S., ed. *Herter Brothers: Furniture and Interiors for a Gilded Age.* New York: Abrams, 1994.

Hurst, Ronald L., and Jonathan Prown. *Southern Furniture 1680–1830: The Colonial Williamsburg Collection.* New York: Abrams, 1997.

Hyde, Bryden B. *Bermuda's Antique Furniture and Silver.* Baltimore, Md.: Maryland Historical Society, 1971.

Jacobson, Dawn. *Chinoiserie.* London: Phaidon Press, 1999.

Jervis, Simon. *Victorian Furniture.* Sydney, Australia: Wardlock, 1968.

Jobe, Brock W., and Myrna Kaye. *New England Furniture: The Colonial Era: Selections from the Society for the Preservation of New England Antiquities.* Boston, Mass.: Houghton Mifflin, 1984.

Jobe, Brock W., and Myrna Kaye. et al. *American Furniture with Related Decorative Arts, 1660–1830: The Milwaukee Art Museum and the Layton Art Collection.* New York: Hudson Hills Press, 1992.

———. *Portsmouth Furniture: Masterworks from the New Hampshire Seacoast.* Hanover, N.H.: University Press of New England, 1993.

Johnson, Hugh, et al. *The International Book of Wood.* London: Artists House, 1982.

Joyce, Ernest. *Encyclopedia of Furniture Making.* New York: Sterling Publications, 1989.

Kane, Patricia E., and Charles F. Montgomery, eds. *American Art: 1750–1800, Towards Independence.* New York: New York Graphic Society, 1976.

———. *300 Years of American Seating Furniture: Chairs and Beds from the Mabel Brady Garvan and Other Collections at Yale University.* New York: New York Graphic Society, 1976.

Kassay, John. *The Book of Shaker Furniture.* Amherst: University of Massachusetts Press, 1980.

————. *The Book of American Windsor Furniture: Styles and Technologies.* Amherst: University of Massachusetts Press, 1998.

Kates, G. *Chinese Household Furniture.* Mineola, N.Y.: Dover Publications, 1962.

Kaye, Myrna and Jobe, Brock W. *Fake, Fraud, or Genuine?: Identifying Authentic American Antique Furniture.* Boston, Mass.: Bulfinch Press, 1990.

Kenny, Peter M., et al. *American Kasten: The Dutch-Style Cupboards of New York and New Jersey, 1650–1800.* New York: Metropolitan Museum of Art, 1991.

————. *Honoré Lannuier, Cabinet Maker from Paris: The Life and Work of a French Ebéniste in Federal New York.* New York: Abrams, 1998.

Ketchum, William C., Jr. *Furniture 2: Neoclassic to the Present (Smithsonian Illustrated Library of Antiques).* Washington, D.C.: Smithsonian Institution, 1981.

————. *The Knopf Collectors' Guides to American Furniture: Volume 2—Chests, Cupboards, Desks & Other Pieces.* New York: Alfred A. Knopf, 1982.

————. *American Cabinetmakers: Marked American Furniture, 1640–1940.* New York: Crown, 1995.

Killen, G. *Ancient Egyptian Furniture.* Warminster, England: Aris & Phillips, 1980.

————. *Egyptian Woodworking and Furniture.* Princes Risborough, U.K.: Shire, 1994.

Kinmonth, Claudia. *Irish Country Furniture, 1700–1950.* New Haven, Conn.: Yale University Press, 1995.

Kirk, John T. *Early American Furniture: How to Recognize, Evaluate, Buy & Care for the Most Beautiful Pieces—High Style, Country, Primitive & Rustic.* New York: Alfred A. Knopf, 1970.

————. *American Furniture & the British Tradition to 1830.* New York: Alfred A. Knopf, 1982.

Kirkham, Pat. *Charles and Ray Eames: Designers of the Twentieth Century.* Cambridge, Mass.: MIT Press, 1998.

Koizumi, Kazuko (translated by Alfred T. Birnbaum). *Traditional Japanese Furniture: A Definitive Guide.* New York: Kodansha International, 1995.

Lever, Jill. *Architects' Designs for Furniture.* New York: Rizzoli, 1982.

Levison, Deanne, and Albert Sack. *The New Fine Points of Furniture: Early American, Good, Better, Best, Superior, Masterpiece.* New York: Crown Publishing, 1993.

Lewin, Leonard Bruce. *Shopping for Furniture: A Consumer's Guide.* New York: Linden Publishing, 1988.

Linley, David. *Classical Furniture.* New York: Abrams, 1993.

————. *Extraordinary Furniture.* New York: Abrams, 1996.

Little, Nina. *Little by Little: Six Decades of Collecting American Decorative Arts.* New York: Dutton, 1984.

Lo, Kai-Yin. *Classical and Vernacular Chinese Furniture in the Living Environment.* Chicago, Ill.: Art Media Resources, 1998.

Lucie-Smith, Edward. *Furniture: A Concise History.* New York: Thames & Hudson, 1985.

Macquoid, Percy. *A History of English Furniture: In Four Volumes.* Mineola, N.Y.: Dover Publications, 1972.

Madigan, Mary Jean, et al. *Nineteenth Century Furniture: Innovation, Revival and Reform.* New York: Billboard Publications, 1982.

————. *Early American Furniture: From Settlement to City.* New York: Billboard Publications, 1983.

Makepeace, John. *The Art of Making Furniture.* Edison, N.J.: Chartwell Books, 1988.

Mang, Karl. *History of Modern Furniture.* New York: Abrams, 1979.

Margon, Lester. *Construction of American Furniture Treasures: Measured Drawings of Selected Museum Pieces with Complete Information on Their Construction and Reproduction.* Mineola, N.Y.: Dover Publications, 1975.

Martin, Ann Smart. *Makers and Users: American Decorative Arts, 1630–1820, from the Chipstone Collection.* Wappingers Falls, N.Y.: Elvehjem Art Center, 1999.

Meadmore, Clement. *The Modern Chair: Classic Designs by Thonet, Breuer, Le Corbusier, Eames and Others.* Mineola, N.Y.: Dover Publications, 1997.

Metropolitan Museum of Art. *American Furniture in the Metropolitan Museum of Art.* New York: Metropolitan Museum of Art, 1964.

Montgomery, Charles F. *American Furniture: The Federal Period, in the Henry Francis du Pont Winterthur Museum.* New York: Viking Press, 1966.

Morley, John. *The History of Furniture: Twenty-Five Centuries of Style and Design in the Western Tradition.* Boston, Mass.: Bulfinch Press, 1999.

Muller, Charles R. *The Shaker Chair.* Amherst: University of Massachusetts, 1992.

Myerson, Jeremy. *Makepeace: A Spirit of Adventure in Craft & Design.* New York: Cross River Press, 1995.

Naeve, Milo M. *Identifying American Furniture: A Pictorial Guide to Styles and Terms, Colonial to Contemporary.* Walnut Creek, Ca.: Altamira, 1998.

Nutting, Wallace. *Furniture Treasury (2 Volumes in 1).* New York: IDG Books Worldwide, 1954.

Oates, Phyllis Bennett. *The Story of Western Furniture.* Franklin, N.Y.: New Amsterdam Books, 1999.

Obbard, John. *Early American Furniture: A Practical Guide for Collectors.* Paducah, Ky.: Collector Books, 1999.

Osborne, Harold. *The Oxford Companion to the Decorative Arts.* New York: Oxford University Press, 1985.

Ostergard, Derek E. *Mackintosh to Mollino: Fifty Years of Chair Design.* New York: Barry Friedman, Ltd., 1984.

Parissien, Steven. *Regency Style.* London: Phaidon Press, 1996.

Parsons, Charles S. *The Dunlaps and Their Furniture.* Manchester, N.H.: Currier Gallery of Art, 1970.

Payne, Christopher. *Nineteenth Century European Furniture* Wappingers Falls, N.Y.: Antique Collectors Club, 1988.

Payne, Christopher, ed. *Sotheby's Concise Encyclopedia of Furniture.* Wappingers Falls, N.Y.: Antique Collectors Club, 1995.

Payne, Christopher, et al. *Miller's Collecting Furniture: The Facts at Your Fingertips.* London: Octopus Publishing Group, 1996.

Pevsner, Nikolaus. *The Sources of Modern Architecture and Design.* New York: Thames & Hudson, 1985.

Pile, John. *Dictionary of 20th Century Design.* New York: Facts On File, 1990.

———. *Furniture: Modern and Postmodern.* New York: John Wiley & Sons, 1990.

Pina, Leslie A. *Fifties Furniture.* Atglen, Pa.: Schiffer Publishing, 1996.

———. *Classic Herman Miller.* Atglen, Pa.: Schiffer Publishing, 1998.

———. *Furniture 2000: Modern Classics and New Designs in Production.* Atglen, Pa.: Schiffer Publishing, 1998.

Quimby, Ian M. G., ed. *Material Culture and the Study of American Life.* New York: W.W. Norton, 1978.

Randall, Richard H., Jr. *American Furniture in the Museum of Fine Arts, Boston.* Boston, Mass.: Museum of Fine Arts, 1965.

Rheims, Maurice. *The Flowering of Art Nouveau.* New York: Abrams, 1966.

Riley, Noel, ed. *World Furniture.* London: Octopus Books, 1980.

Riley, Noel, and Tom Rowland, *A–Z Guide to Cleaning, Conserving and Repairing Antiques.* North Ponfret, N.H.: Trafalgar Square, 1998.

Roque, Oswaldo Rodriguez. *American Furniture at Chipstone.* Madison: University of Wisconsin Press, 1984.

Royka, Paul A. *Mission Furniture: Furniture of the American Arts and Crafts Movement.* Atglen, Pa.: Schiffer Publishing, 1997.

Ruddy, Robin. *French Provincial Furniture.* Atglen, Pa.: Schiffer Publishing, 1998.

Santore, Charles. *The Windsor Style in America: The Definitive Pictorial Study of the History and Regional Characteristics of the Most Popular Furniture Form of 18th-Century America, 1730–1840.* Philadelphia, Pa.: Courage Books, 1997.

Saunders, Richard. *Collecting and Restoring Wicker Furniture.* New York: Crown Publishers, 1976.

Schaffner, Cynthia V. A., and Susan Klein, *American Painted Furniture: 1790–1880.* New York: Clarkson Potter, 1998.

Schiffer, Nancy. *America's Oak Furniture: With Price Guide.* Atglen, Pa.: Schiffer Publishing, 1998.

Schwartz, Marvin D. *American Interiors, 1675–1885: A Guide to the American Period Rooms in the Brooklyn Museum.* Brooklyn, N.Y.: Brooklyn Museum, 1968.

———. *The Knopf Collectors' Guides to American Furniture: Volume 1—Chairs, Tables, Sofas & Beds.* New York: Alfred A. Knopf, 1982.

Seale, William. *The Tasteful Interlude: American Interiors Through the Camera's Eye, 1860–1917 (American Association for State and Local History Book Series).* Walnut Creek, Ca.: Altamira Press, 1985.

Selz, Peter, ed. *Art Nouveau and Design at the Turn of the Century.* New York: Museum of Modern Art, 1959.

Sembach, Klaus-Jurgen, ed. *Modern Furniture Designs 1950–1980s: An International Review of Modern Furniture.* Atglen, Pa.: Schiffer Publishing, 1997.

Sieber, Roy. *African Furniture and Household Objects.* Bloomington: Indiana University Press, 1980.

Soros, Susan Weber. *E. W. Godwin: Aesthetic Movement Architect and Designer.* New Haven, Conn.: Yale University Press, 1999.

———. *The Secular Furniture of E. W. Godwin.* New Haven, Conn.: Yale University Press, 2000.

Spencer, Robin, et al. *The Aesthetic Movement and the Cult of Japan.* London: Fine Arts Society, 1972.

Sprigg, June. *By Shaker Hands: The Art and the World of the Shakers—The Furniture and Artifacts, and the Spirit and Precepts Embodied in Their Simplicity, Beauty and Functional Practicality.* New York: Alfred A. Knopf, 1975.

Stickley, Gustav, et al. *Collected Works of Gustav Stickley.* New York: Turn of the Century Editions, 1989.

Stimpson, Miriam. *Modern Furniture Classics.* New York: Whitney Library of Design, 1997.

Svarth, Dan. *Egyptian Furniture-Making in the Age of the Pharaohs.* Aarhus, Denmark: Aarhus University Press, 1998.

Swedberg, Robert W., and Harriet Swedberg, *Furniture of the Depression Era: Furniture and Accessories of the 1920s, 1930s and 1940s.* Paducah, Ky.: Collector Books, 1990.

Taragin, Davira S. *Furniture by Wendell Castle.* New York: Hudson Hills Press, 1996.

Thornton, Peter. *Seventeenth-Century Interior Decoration in England, France & Holland.* New Haven, Conn.: Yale University Press, 1978.

Tracy, Charles. *English Medieval Furniture and Woodwork.* Wappingers Falls, N.Y.: Antique Collectors Club, 1989.

Von Vegesack, Alexander, et al. *Thonet: Classic Furniture in Bent Wood and Tubular Steel.* London: Hazar, 1996.

Walker, Aidan, ed. *The Encyclopedia of Wood: A Tree-by-Tree Guide to the World's Most Versatile Resource.* New York: Facts On File, 1989.

Walkling, Gillian. *Upholstery Styles: A Design Sourcebook.* New York: Van Nostrand Reinhold, 1989.

———. *Antique Bamboo Furniture.* London: Bell & Hyman, 1979.

Wang, Shixiang. *Connoisseurship of Chinese Furniture: Ming and Early Qing Dynasties.* Chicago, Ill.: Art Media Resources, 1990.

———. *Classic Chinese Furniture: Ming and Early Qing Dynasties.* Chicago, Ill.: Art Media Resources, 1991.

Ward, Gerald W. R., ed. *The Eye of the Beholder: Fakes, Replicas, and Alterations in American Art.* New Haven, Conn.: Yale University Press, 1970.

———. *American Case Furniture in the Mabel Brady Garvan and Other Collections at Yale University.* New Haven, Conn.: Yale University Press, 1988.

Warren, David B. *Bayou Bend: American Furniture, Paintings, and Silver from the Bayou Bend Collection.* Princeton, N.J.: Princeton University Press, 1998.

Watson, Sir Francis, et al. *The History of Furniture.* London: Orbis Publishing, 1976.

Wharton, Edith, and Ogden Codman, Jr. 1902. *The Decoration of Houses.* Reprint, New York: W.W. Norton, 1978.

Wilson, Richard Guy, et al. *The American Renaissance, 1876–1917.* Brooklyn, N.Y.: Brooklyn Museum, 1979.

Winterthur Museum. *Neoclassicism in the Decorative Arts: France, England and America.* Winterthur, Del.: Winterthur Museum, 1971.

Zea, Philip. *The Dunlap Cabinetmakers: A Tradition in Craftsmanship.* Mechanicsburg, Pa.: Stackpole Books, 1994.

INDEX

INDEX **Boldface** page numbers denote main entries. All articles on wood types are listed under *wood*.

A

Aalto, Hugo Alvar Henrik **1**, 176, 266
Aarnio, Eero **1**, 266, 308
abacus **1**
Abildgaard, Nikolai Abraham **2**, 184
acanthus **2**
acroter **2**
Adam, Robert **2**, 122, 249, 334
  sideboard 276
Adam style **2–3**, 208, 249. *See also*
  Hepplewhite, George; Sheraton,
  Thomas
    square-back chair 283
    wood types 143
Adams, Nathaniel **3**
Adams, Nehemiam **3**, 106
Adirondack furniture **3–4**
Adnet, Jacques **4**
aegricanes **4**
Aesthetic Movement 125–26
Affleck, Thomas **4**, 107, 224
African furniture **4–6**
  akonkromfi chair 6, 7
  caryatid stool 50
Aitken, John **7**, 107
akonkromfi chair 6, 7
Albers, Josef **7**
Albertolli, Giocondo **7**
Albini, Franco **7**
Albrizzi, Alexander **7**
Aldegrever, Heinrich **7**, 246
Alden, John **7**
Alix, Charlotte. *See* Sognot, Louis
Allison, Michael **8**, 107
Alma-Tadema, Lawrence **8**
altar table **8**, 157
aluminum **8**
Ambasz, Emilio. *See* Piretti, Giancarlo
ambry. *See* aumbry
American Chippendale furniture **8–9**,
  123, 192
    bonnet top 35
    Boston Chippendale 36–37, 163
    country Chippendale 74–75
    Maryland Chippendale chair 193
    New York Chippendale 211
    Newport Chippendale 211
    Philadelphia Chippendale 224
    spider-leg table 282
American Empire style 9, **9**
  Michael Allison 8
  decorative motifs 316
  Charles-Honoré Lannuier 170–71

Duncan Phyfe 224–25
Anthony Quervelle 237–38
  saber leg 175
  sleigh bed 278
American Jacobean furniture **9–10**, 207
  Bible box 32
  Brewster chair 40
  butterfly hinge 140
  Carver chair 50
  Connecticut sunflower chest 70
  Thomas Dennis 84
  Nicholas Disbrowe 87
  Thomas Edsall 96
  Guilford chest 133
  hadley chest 134
  hutch table 146
  Ralph Mason 193, 198
  Henry Messinger 193, 198
  William Searle 270
  settle 273
  wainscot chair 10, 315
American Moderne **10**
  Donald Deskey 84
  Paul Frankl 116
  Norman Bel Geddes 122
  William Lescaze 176
  Gilbert Rohde 256
  Russell Wright 329
American Queen Anne style **10–11**,
  123
American Regency style. *See* Directory
  style
American Restoration style. *See* pillar-
  and-scroll style
American William and Mary style
  11–12
amorini. *See* putto
Andrews, Gordon **12**, 149
angel bed **12**, 178
Anglo-Japanese style 125–26
animal's-ball-and-claw foot 111
antefix **12**
anthemion **12**
anthemion-back chair **12**
Antique, Le Style. *See* Style Antique, Le
antique vert **13**
antiques **12–13**
  reproduction furniture 247–48
Antwerp cabinet 167
appliqué **13**
apron (skirt) **13**
arabesque **13–14**
Arbus, André **14**

arcading **14**
arch **14**
arched stretcher 287
architecture and design firms
  De Pas, D'Urbino, Lomazzi 82
  Gatti, Paolini & Teodoro 121
  Greene & Greene 130–31
  Gwathmey-Siegel 133
architrave **14**
Archizoom **14**
  Paolo Deganello 83
ark **14**
arm bow 321–22
arm stump **14**
armadio **14–15**
armoire **15**
armoire à deux corps **15**
Arndt, Alfred **15**
arrow-back Windsor chair 322
art cabinet **15**
Art Deco **15–16**
  Émile-Jacques Ruhlmann 93, 96,
    103, 204, 261
  Süe et Mare 289
Art Furniture movement **16**, 293
  Collinson & Lock 67, 236
  Charles Locke Eastlake 95, 210,
    293
  William Godwin 125–26, 155
Art Moderne. *See* Art Deco
Art Nouveau **16–18**
  decorative motifs 319
  Glasgow School 124
  Hector Guimard 133
  Josef Hoffmann 142
  Victor Horta 144
  Arthur Lazenby Liberty 177
  Charles Rennie Mackintosh 188,
    274, 316, 319
  Nancy, School of 205–6
  Theodore Nieuwenhuis 211
  Henri Van de Velde 309–10
articulate **18**
Arts and Crafts movement **18–19**
  Charles Robert Ashbee 19
  Mackay Hugh Baillie Scott 23
  Edward Burne-Jones 43
  Cotswold School 73
  Greene & Greene 130–31
  Mission furniture 199
  William Morris 202–3, 210, 317
  John Ruskin 262
  Gustav Stickley 199, 285

Charles Francis Annesley Voysey
  314
  Philip Speakman Webb 317
Ash, Gilbert **19**
Ash, Thomas **19**
Ashbee, Charles Robert **19**, 319
Asplund, Gunnar **19**, 266
astragal (glazing bar) **19**, 125
astragal molding 200
Athénienne **19–20**, 96
Atlas **20**
auger flame **20**
Augsburg cabinet. *See* Kunstschrank
Aulenti, Gae **20**, 231
aumbry (armby) **20**
auricular style **20**, 207, 246
  Friedrich Unteutsch 306
Australian furniture **20–21**
  Gordon Andrews 12, 149
  Marion Hall Best 32
  George Korody 149, 167
  Helmut Lueckenhausen 185
  Clement Meadmore 149, 194–95
  Marc Newson 149, 211
  Leon Sadubin 264
  Craig Watson 317
  Toby Muir Wilson 320
  Leslie John Wright 328–29
Auvera, Johann Wolfgang Van der **21**,
  253

B

B.V.R.B. *See* Van Risenburgh, Bernard
ba xian zhuo (pa hsien cho) **22**
Baccetti, Andrea **22**, 247
bachelor's chest **22**
back post **22**
back splat 282
back stay **22**
Badlam, Stephen **22**
bahut **22–23**
bai yan (pai yen) **23**
bail handle **23**
Baillie Scott, Mackay Hugh **23**
ball foot 111
ball turning 303
ball-and-claw foot 111
ball-and-ring turning 303
balloon-back chair **23–24**
balloon-back Windsor chair 322
baluster **24**
baluster turning 303
bamboo **24**, 212, 334

bamboo turning 303
banding **24**
bandy leg 174
banister. *See* baluster
banister-back chair **24**
banker **24**
Bantam work **24–25**
Barbedienne, Ferdinand **25**, 183
barley-sugar turning 303
Barnsley, Ernest and Sidney 73
baroque furniture **25–26**, 207
    American William and Mary 11–12
    Andrea Brustolon 40–41
    decorative devices 132, 283, 296
    decorative motifs 50
    Indo-Portugese furniture 148
    Filippo Juvarra 160
    Jan van Mekeren 196
    Palladian 217
    Queen Anne 236–37
    Restoration 248–49
    schrank 267–68
    sleeping chair 278
    William and Mary 320
barrel chair **26**, 126
Barry, Charles **26**, 235, 247
Barry, Joseph B. **26**, 107
bas armoire **26**
Basile, Ernesto **26–27**
basin stand **27**, 316
basket chair **27**, 319
bast seat **27**
Baudoine, Charles A. **27**, 255
Bauhaus **27**
    Josef Albers 7
    Alfred Arndt 15
    Marcel Lajos Breuer 39–40
    Walter Gropius 85, 131–32, 149,
        198, 310
    International style and 149
    Ludwig Mies van der Rohe 149,
        198, 284
    unit furniture 306
bead molding. *See* astragal molding
bead-and-butt **27–28**
bead-and-reel molding 200
bead-and-reel motif **28**
beaded drawer **28**
bear's-claw foot 111
Beau Brummel **28**
Becchi, Allessandro **28**
bed **28**. *See also* daybed; *lit* listings
    African furniture 4–5
    alcove 7, 178
    angel 12, 178
    brass 39
    Byzantine furniture 45
    canopy 48, 134
    cast-iron 52
    chair-bed 54
    couchette 74
    cradle 76
    crib 77
    cupboard-bed (closet-bed) 78
    Egyptian furniture 97–98
    field (tent) 108
    footboard 115
    fourposter 115
    Gothic furniture 128
    headboard 137
    headrest 137
    Indian furniture 147
    jia zi chuang 157
    kline 118, 165
    lectus 173–74
    Murphy 204
    patent furniture 219
    press 232

Romanesque furniture 257
sleigh 278
sofa-bed 280
trestle 300
trundle 301
trussing 302
Tuscan 305
twin 305
waterbed 316
bed of estate **28–29**
bed steps **29**
bedstead **29**
beeldenkast **29**
Behrens, Peter **29**
Bel Geddes, Norman. *See* Geddes,
    Norman Bel
Bélanger, François-Joseph **29**, 87, 100,
    184
bell-and-baluster turning 304
Bellangé, Alexandre-Louis **29**288
Bellangé, Pierre-Antoine **29**
bellflower **29**
Bellini, Mario **30**
Belter, John Henry **30**, 229, 255
Bembé, Anton **30**, 247, 255
bended-back chair **30**
Beneman, Guillaume **30**, 87, 100, 251
Bennett, Ward **30**
bentwood **30–31**, 229
    bow-back Windsor chair 322
    continuous-arm Windsor chair 323
    Samuel Gragg 129
    Michael Thonet 31, 297
    Viennese chair 312
    Leslie John Wright 328–29
    yew 331
Bérain, Jean **31**, 172, 180, 242, 278
bergère **31**
bergère-bow Windsor chair 322
Berlage, Hendrikus Petrus **31**
Bermuda furniture **31**
Bertoia, Harry **31–32**, 327
Best, Marion Hall **32**
Beurdeley, Louis-Auguste-Alfred **32**, 182
bevel 200
Bible box **32**
Biedermeier style **32–33**
    Josef Danhauser 80
    Michael Thonet 297
Biennais, Martin-Guillaume **33**
Bill, Max **33**
Bing, Samuel **33**, 309, 310
birdcage support **33**
bird's-ball-and-claw foot 111
blackamoor **34**
blanket chest **34**
Blau, Luigi **34**
Blin, Peter **34**
block-and-vase turning 304
blockfront **34**, 299
bo **34**
board chair **34**
board chest (boarded chest) **34**
bobbin turning 304
bobtail (tailpiece) 322
Bohlin, Jonas **35**
bois clair **35**
bois de bout 215
bois de spa **35**
bolection molding 200
bolster top **35**
bombé **35**
Bonetto, Rodolfo **35**
Bongen, Andries **35**, 253
bonheur du jour **35**
bonnet scroll. *See* scroll pediment
bonnet top **35**
bonnetière **35**

Bonzanigo, Giuseppe Maria **36**, 184
bookcase **36**
bootjack foot 111
borne **36**
boss **36**
Boston chair **36**
Boston Chippendale furniture **36–37**,
    163
    John Cogswell 66–67
    Benjamin Frothingham 118
Boston rocker **37**
Boucher, Juste-François **37**
Boulard, Jean-Baptiste **37**, 183
Boulle, André-Charles **37**, 172, 180, 243
Boulle marquetry **37–38**
    Gerreit Jensen 156, 320
    Johann Daniel Sommer 280
    Martin Schumacher 268
    tortoiseshell 299
Bouvier, Michael **38**
bow-back Windsor chair 322
bowfront **38**
box stretcher 287
box-bed. *See* cupboard-bed
bracing sticks 322–23
bracket **38**
    console 71
bracket foot 111–12
Bradley, Will H. **38**
Brandt, Edgar 16, **38**
Brangwyn, Frank **38–39**
brass **39**
brass bed **39**
brasses **39**
brattishing **39**
Brauwers, Joseph **39**
breakfast table **39**
breakfront **39**
Breuer, Marcel Lajos **39–40**, 149, 284
    cantilevered chair 48
Brewster chair **39**
Breytspraak, Carel **40**
Bridgen, Robert **40**
Bright, George **40**
broken pediment 221
bronze **40**
Brooks, Thomas **40**, 247
Brunetti, Gaetano **40**, 253
Brustolon, Andrea **40–41**
Bruyère, André **41**
buckle-back Windsor chair 323
bucranium **41**
buffet **41**
Bugatti, Carlo **41**, 202, 312
buhl **41**
bulb turning 304
bun foot 112
bureau **41–42**
bureau à cylindre **42**
bureau à gradin **42**
bureau bookcase **42**
bureau dressing table **42**
bureau en pente **42**
bureau Mazarin **42**
bureau plat **42**
bureau-table **42**
Burgat, Claude-Louis **42**
Burges, William **42–43**, 210, 293
burgomaster chair **43**, 260
burl (burr) **43**
burl veneer **43**
Burling, Thomas **43**, 107
Burmese furniture **43**
Burne-Jones, Edward **43**, 202, 317
Burnham, Benjamin **43**
Burton, Scott **43–44**
butler's table (butler's tray) **44**

butsudan **44**
butt joint (end joint) 158
butterfly hinge 140
butterly table **44**
buttoning 307
buying guide 335–39
byobu **44**
    furosaki byobu 119
Byzantine furniture **44–45**
    decorative devices 77

C

cabinet **46**
    art cabinet 15
    china cabinet 60
    corner 73
cabinet stand (casket stand) **46**
cabinetmaker **46**
cable fluting **46**
cable molding 201
cabochon **46**
cabriole chair or sofa **46–47**
cabriole leg 111, 112, 113, 114, 165,
    174, 242–43
Caffieri, Jacques **47**
cambriole chair or sofa **46–47**
camel foot. *See* Dutch foot
camel-back sofa **47**
campaign furniture **47**
canapé **47**
    sultane 289
    canapé à confidante (confidante) **47**
    canapé de l'amitié (confidante) **47**
candlestand (*torchère*) **47**
    guéridon 132–33
canephorus **48**
caning **48**, 241, 248
cannellated **48**
canopy bed **48**, 134, 305
canterbury (rack) **48**
canterbury (serving stand) **48**
cantilevered chair **48**, 283–84
Canton enamel (*yang ci*) 331
capital **49**
captain's chair 323
*Capucin, secrétaire à. See secrétaire à
    Capucin*
*Capucine, chaise à la. See chaise à la
    Capucine*
caquetoire **49**
Carabin, François-Rupert **49**
carcase **49**
card table **49**
Carl Leistler **49**, 210, 247, 255
Carlin, Martin **49**, 183
Carlton House table **50**
Carolean chair **50**
Carolean furniture **50**
Carrier-Belleuse, Albert-Ernst **50**
cartonnier **50**
Carton-Pierre **50**
cartouche **50**
Carver chair **50**
caryatid **50**
caryatid stool 5, **50**
case furniture **50**
    plinth 228–29
    Salem secretary 264
    wardrobe 316
casket stand **50**
cassapanca **51**
Cassina **51**
    Mario Bellini 30
    Vico Magistretti 188–89
    Tobia and Afra Scarpa 267
cassone **51**
    cassone nuziale **51**
Castelli Ferrieri, Anna **51**

Castiglioni, Achille **51**
cast-iron bed **52**
cast-iron furniture **51–52**
Castle, Wendell **52**, 135
castor **52**
Cathédrale, Le Style **52**, 210
causeuse **52**, 70, 296
Cauvet, Gilles-Paul **52**
cavetto molding 200
cellarette **53**
celure (*celour*) **53**
Centennial period reproduction furniture **53**
certosina work **53**
César **53**
Chadwick, Don **54**, 72, 308
chair **54**. *See also* rocking chair; stool
    Adirondack furniture 3–4
    African furniture 6
    akonkromfi 6, 7
    anthemion-back 12
    back stool 22
    balloon-back 23–24
    banister-back 24
    barrel 26, 126
    basket 27, 319
    bended-back 30
    bentwood 30–31
    bergère 31
    board 34
    borne 36
    Boston 36
    Brewster 40
    burgomaster 43, 260
    cabriole 46–47
    cantilevered 48, 283–84
    caquetoire 49
    Carver 50
    cast-iron 51
    chair of estate 55
    chair-bed 54
    chair-table 55
    chaises 55
    chamber 56
    Charles II 57
    chauffeuse 57
    chiavari 59
    Chinese furniture 61
    chuang (*ch'uang*) 64
    coiffeuse (1) 67
    companion 70, 73, 260
    confessional 70
    corner 73, 260
    crapaud 76
    Cromwellian 77
    curule 78
    Dante (Dantesca) 80
    De Pas, D'Urbinio, Lomazzi 82
    deck 83
    deng gua shi yi 84
    director's 87
    easy chair 95
    elbow chair 98
    farthingale 105
    fauteuil 105–6
    fiddle back 108
    Glastonbury 124–25
    gondola 26, 126
    Gothic furniture 128
    guan mao shi 132
    high chair 140
    hip-joint 141
    Hogarth 142
    jiao chuang 157
    klismos 165
    ladder-back (slat-back) 170
    lohan 179
    lolling 179

lounge 185
luo quan yi 179, 185
Luther 185–86
Martha Washington 193
Maryland Chippendale 193
mei guishi 196
Morris 202, 317
pedestal 220
"pretzel-back" 232
prie-dieu 232–33
revolving (swivel) 250
ribband-back (ribbon-back) 250
root furniture 259
roundabout 73, 260
san cai tu hui 264
Savonarola 265
settee 273
sheaf-back 275
shield-back 276
side 276
sillón de cadera 277
sleeping 278
slipper 279
sociable 280
spindle-back 282
spoon-back 283
square-back 283
tablet-arm 292
Thonet 31, 297
turned 303
Viennese 312
Voltaire 313
voyeuse (conversation) 313–14
wainscot 10, **315**
wheel-back (umbrella-back) 319
Windsor 321–27
wing (grandfather; club) 327
yoke-back 332
Zanzibar 333
zui weng yi 334
chair of estate **55**
chair-back settee **54**
chair-bed **54**
chaise à la Capucine **55**
chaise à l'officier **55**
chaise à Reine **55**
chaise courante **55**
chaise d'affaires **55**
chaise en cabriolet 46–47
chaise lounge **55**
    daybed 81 82
    duchesse 91, 92
    chaise meublante 55
    chaise percée 55
    chaise volante 55
chamber box **56**
chamber chair **56**
chamber horse **56**
Chambers, William **56**
Chambert, Erik **56**
chamfer (*champfer*) **56**
Channon, John **56**, 253
Chapin, Aaron **56**
Chapin, Eliphalet **56**
Chareau, Pierre **56–57**, 306
Charles II chair **57**
Charles X style **57**
Charpentier, Alexandre **57**
chasing **57**
chatol **57**
chauffeuse **57**
cheesebox seat **57**
Chénavard, Claude Aimé **57**, 210, 247, 254
Chermayeff, Sergius Ivan **57**, 284
chest **58**
    ark 14

bachelor's 22
blanket 34
board 34
cassone 51
cedar 52–53
cellarette 53
coffer 66
coffret 66
Connecticut sunflower 10, 70
    Guilford 10, 133
    Hadley 134
Romanesque furniture 257
standard 284
sugar 289
tang xiang (*t'ang hsiang*) 293–94
tansu 294
tilting 298
trunk 301–2
chest of drawers **58**, 249
    bachelor's chest 22
    chest-on-chest 58
    chest-on-stand 58
    chiffonier (1) 59
    chiffonnière 59
    commode (1) 68–69
    demilune commode 83
    dresser (2) 90
    hari-bako 136
    hutch 146
    lowboy 185
    nest of drawers 210
    petit commode 224
    semainier 272
    tallboy 293
    taquillón 294
chesterfield **58–59**
chest-on-chest **58**
chest-on-stand **58**
cheval glass (horse dressing-glass) **59**
cheval screen **59**
chevron **59**
chiavari chair **59**
chiffonier (chest of drawers) **59**
chiffonier (side table) **59**, 292
chiffonnière **59**
chimera **59–60**
china cabinet (china closet) **60**
china stand **60**
china table **60**
Chinese Chippendale furniture **60**, 254
Chinese furniture **60–62**
    bai yan 23
    bamboo 24
    chuang 64
    decorative technique 331
    deng 83–84
    deng gua shi yi 84
    ding gui shi 84
    dun 92–93
    elephant-trunk leg 174
    guan mao shi 132
    hu chuang 145
    hua zhuo 145
    ji 156
    ji tai shi an 157
    jiao chuang 157
    kang 161
    kang cupboard 161
    kang ji 161–62
    lacquer inlay 330, 331
    lacquers 85, 145, 169, 298
    luo quan yi 179, 185
    mei gui shi 196
    Oriental rosewood 214
    ping 227
    qin zhuo 236
    root furniture 259
    san cai tu hui 264

    shu gui 276
    ta chuang 291
    tang hua an 293
    tang xiang 293–94
    woods 96, 156–57, 214, 216, 330
    xiu dun 330
    yan ji 331
    zhuan lun jing chang 334
    zui weng yi 334
Chinoiserie **62–63**, 248
chip carving **63**
Chippendale, Thomas 8, 60, **63**, 72, 81, 209, 220, 244, 250, 253–54
Chippendale, Thomas, Jr. **63**
Chippendale Gothic furniture **63**, 209, 254
    Batty Langley 170
    Sanderson Miller 199
Chippendale style. *See* rococo furniture
cho-dansu **64**
Christian VIII style. *See* Danish Empire style
Christiansen, Hans **64**
chuang (*ch'uang*) **64**
Churchill, Lemuel **64**
Churrigueresque furniture **64–65**, 281
Cima, Giuseppe **65**, 247, 255
cinquefoil **65**
cista **65**
claw foot 114
claw table **65**
claw-and-ball foot 111
Clawson, John **65**
close stool (night stool) **65**
close stool 212
close stool chair 56
closet-bed 78
clothes press **65–66**
cloven foot 112
club chair **66**, 327
club foot 112–13
coal furniture **66**
Coard, Marcel 16, **66**
Coates, Wells **66**
Cobb, John **66**, 253
cock-bead molding 200
cock's-head hinge 141
coffee table **66**
coffer **66**
coffret **66**
Cogswell, John **66–67**
coiffeuse (dressing table) **67**
coiffeuse (open chair) **67**
coil-spring upholstery 307
Coit, Job, Jr. **67**
Cole, Henry **67**
Collcutt, Thomas Edward **67**, 155, 247, 293
Collinson & Lock **67**, 236
Colombo, Joe Cesare **67–68**, 228
colonette **68**
colonial furniture. *See* campaign furniture
Colonial Revival furniture **68**
Colonna, Edward **68**
column **68**
comb-back Windsor chair 323
Cometti, Giacomo **68**
commode (chest of drawers) **68–69**
commode à encoignures **69**
commode à la Régence **69**
commode à vantaux **69**
commode (bedroom pot cupboard) **69**
commode chair. *See* chamber chair
commode Cressent **69**
commode en console **69**
commode-tombeau **69**
Commonwealth furniture **69–70**
    Cromwellian chair 77

companion chair **70**, 73, 260
compass seat **70**
compo (composition) **70**
Composite order **70**, 214
concrete **70**
confessional **70**
confidante 47, 52, **70**, 296
confortable **70**
Connecticut sunflower chest **70**
    Peter Blin 34
    Nicholas Disbrowe 87
Connelly, Henry **70–71**, 107
Conran, Terence **71**
console **71**
console dessert **71**
console table **71**
Consulate style **71**
    Jacob-Desmalter 152–53
    lit en bateau 178
    Récamier 241
Contemporary style **71–72**
    Richard Drew Russell 262
    Utility Furniture 308
    Dennis Young 332
continuous-arm Windsor chair 323
contre-partie. *See* Boulle marquetry
conversation chair 313–14
conversational sofa. *See indiscret*
convertible furniture **72**
    library steps 177
    press bed 232
    sofa-bed 280
Copland, Henry **72**, 253
coquillage **72**
Coray, Hans **72**
Corbusier, Le. *See* Le Corbusier
Corinthian order 2, **72**, 214
corner block **72–73**
corner cabinet **73**
corner chair **73**, 260
corner cupboard **73**
cornice **73**
cornucopia **73**
Coromandel lacquer (*ke hui*) **73**, 169
Cotswold School **73**
    Ernest William Gimson 124
cottage furniture **73**
couch **74**
    daybed 81–82
    divan 88
    Grecian 129
couchette **74**
counter-table **74**
country Chippendale furniture **74–75**
    Eliphalet Chapin 56
    Dunlap family 93
Cour, de la **75**, 253
court cupboard (1 and 2) **75**
Courtenay, Hercules **75**
cove molding 200
cow-horn stretcher 287
Cowperthwaite, John **76**
cradle **76**
Craftsman furniture 285
Craftsman magazine 3, 199, 285
Cranbrook Academy 94, 263–64
crapaud **76**
credence **76**
credenza **76**
    Schenkschieve 267
crescent stretcher 287
Cressent, Charles **76**, 182, 243, 252
Cresson, Louis **76**
crest rail (cresting rail) **76**
Criaerd, Mathieu **77**
crib **77**
crinoline stretcher 287
crocket **77**

croft **77**
Cromwellian chair **77**
Cromwellian furniture **69–70**, 77
cross banding 24
cross rail **77**
cross-lapped joint 158
cross-stretcher 288
crotch veneer **78**
crown chair **77**
crow's nest **77**
C-scroll **77–78**
Cucci, Domenico **78**, 172, 180
cup turning 304
cup-and-cover turning 304
cupboard **78**
    armoire 15
    beeldenkast 29
    Byzantine furniture 45
    court (2) 75
    livery 179
    press 232
    Schenkschieve 267
    Überbauschrank 306
cupboard-bed (closet-bed) **78**
cupped leg 174
curl veneer (crotch veneer) **78**
curule chair **78**
cushion capital **78**
cushion frieze **78–79**
cushioned-pad foot 112–13
cusping **79**
cutwork **79**
Cuvilliés, François **79**
cylinder-front desk **79**
cyma **79**
cyma molding 79, 201
cyma recta **79**
cyma reversa **79**
cypher splat **79**

D
dado joint (housed joint) 158
Dagly, Gerhard **80**
Danhauser, Josef **80**
Danish Empire style **80**
    chatol 57
    Gustav Friedrich Hetsch 139
Danko, Peter **80**
Dante chair (*Dantesca* chair) **80**
Darly, Matthias (Matthew) **81**, 253
davenport (desk) **81**
davenport (sofa) **81**
David, Jacques-Louis **81**, 184
Davis, Alexander Jackson **81**, 210
Davis, Robert **81**
Day, Robin **81**, 149, 228, 262, 332
Day, Thomas **81**
daybed **81–82**
    chaise lounge 55
    couch 74
    lit de repos 178
    lounge 185
    Récamier 241
    rest bed 248
    zui weng yi 334
De Forest, Lockwood **82**
De Pas, D'Urbino, Lomazzi **82**, 148, 230
De Passe, Crispin **82**, 191
De Stijl **82–83**
    J. J. P. Oud 215, 310
    Gerrit Thomas Rietveld 251
    Mart Stam 283–84
    Theo Van Doesburg 310
deal **83**
deck chair **83**
deep-buttoning. *See* upholstery
Deganello, Paolo **83**

Archizoom 14
Delafosse, Jean-Charles **83**, 183
Delanois, Louis **83**
demicelure (demicelour). *See celure*
demilune **83**
demilune commode **83**
deng (teng) **83**
deng gua shi yi (teng kua shih yi) **84**
Dennis, Thomas 10, **84**
Denon, Dominique Vivant, Baron **84**, 98, 244
denticulation **84**
De Pas, Jonathan **82**
desk **84**
    bureau à cylindre 42
    bureau table 42
    cylinder-front 79
    davenport 81
    drop-front 90
        escritoire 102
    fall-front 105
    Governor Winthrop 129
    kneehole 166
    pedestal 221
    roll-top 256
        secrétaire 270–71
    secretary 271
    slant-top 278
        vargueño 311
    Wooton 327–28
    See also writing table
Deskey, Donald 10, **84**
desk-on-frame **84**
desornamentado style **84–85**, 281
Deutsche Werkstätten 27, **85**
    August Endell 101–2
    Hermann Obrist 213
    Joseph Maria Olbrich 213–14
    Bernhard Pankok 218
    Bruno Paul 220
    Richard Riemerschmid 250
    Karl Schmidt 267
    Heinrich Tessenow 296
Deutscher Werkbund 27, **85**
    Hermann Muthesius 204
    Bernhard Pankok 218
    Richard Riemerschmid 250
    Otto Wagner 315
devil-tail hinge 141
diao tian (tiao t'tien) **85**
diapering **85–86**
Dietterlin, Wendel **86**, 191, 246, 286
Diffrient, Niels **86**
Dijsselhof, Gerrit **86**, 211
ding gui (ting kuei; mao gui) **86**
diphros **86**
diphros okladias **86**
Directoire style **86–87**, 288
    decorative devices 50
    Georges Jacob 152
    Jacob-Desmalter 152–53
    Récamier 241
director's chair **87**
Directory style (American Regency style) **87**
    Duncan Phyfe 9, 107, 224–25, 313
Disbrowe, Nicholas 10, **87**
dished corner (tray corner) **87**
dished seat **87**
dished top **87**, 305
disk foot 112–13
distressing **87**
Ditzel, Hanna **87–88**
divan **88**
document drawer **88**
dog's-paw foot 112
dogu-bako **88**
dolphin **88**

dolphin foot 112
Dominique 16, **88**
"Dondolo" rocking chair 176
doreur **88**
Doric order **88**, 214, 301
dorser (dosser) **88**
double open-twist turning 304
double-lyre stretcher 287
Doucet, Jacques **89**
dovetail **89**, 158
dowel **89**
doweled joint 158
dower furniture **89**
Dragonesque style. *See* Munthe, Gerhard
drake foot 112
drawer **89–90**
drawer stop **90**
draw-leaf table **89**
dresser (buffet) **90**
dresser (chest of drawers) **90**
Dresser, Christopher **90**, 155
dressing table **90**
    Beau Brummel 28
    kyodai 168
    lowboy 185
    poudreuse 231
    toilette en papillon 299
dressoir **90**
drop **90**
drop handle **91**
drop-front desk **90**
drop-in seat **91**
drop-leaf table **91**
drum table **91**
Du Cerceau, Jacques Androuet, the Elder **91**, 138, 191, 246, 286
Dubell, Heinrich **91**, 255
Dubois, Jacques **91**
Dubois, René **91**
duchesse **91**
duchesse brisée **92**
duchesse en bateau **92**
Dufrêne, Maurice **92**
Dugourc, Jean-Démostène 87, **92**, 184
dumbwaiter **92**
dun (tun) **92–93**
Dunand, Jean 16, **93**
Dunlap family **93**
Dunlap, John **93**
Dunlap, Samuel **93**
D'Urbino, Donato. *See* De Pas, D'Urbino, Lomazzi
D'Urso, Joseph Paul **93**
dustboard **93**
Dutch foot 112–13

E
Eames, Charles **94–95**, 139, 206, 228, 229, 263, 264
ear **95**
Eastlake, Charles Locke 16, **95**, 210, 293
Eastlake style 210
easy chair **95**
ébéniste **95–96**
    Martin Carlin 49, 183
    Pierre Golle 126, 172, 180
    Gilles Joubert 160, 182, 251
    Jean-Henri Riesener 183, 213, 250–51, 300
    Joseph Stöckel 183, 285–86
    Charles Topino 183, 299
    Bernard Van Risenburgh (Van Risamburgh) 182, 253, 310–11
    Roger Vandercruse (Roger Vandercruse Lacroix) 183, 300, 310
    Adam Weisweiler 100, 183, 318

Eberts, J.-H. **96**
ebonized **96**
echinus **96**
Eckmann, Otto **96**
Edis, Robert William **96**, 247
Edsall, Thomas **96**, 193, 198
Egerton, Matthew, Sr. **96**, 107
egg-and-dart **96**
egg-and-dart molding 96, 201
églomisé **97**
Egyptian furniture **97–98**
    papyrus used in 218
    wood types 96
Égyptiennerie (Egyptian Revival style)
    98
Eight Immortals, table of the 22
elbow chair **98**
    John Gaines 120
elephant-trunk leg 174
Elfe, Thomas **98**
Eliaers, Auguste **98–99**, 219
Elizabethan Revival style **99**, 249
    Anthony Salvin 264
    Henry Shaw 274
Ellis, Harvey **99**
Elmslie, George Grant **99**, 231, 232
Emery, David **99**
Empire style **99–101**, 208
    bas armoire 26
    chaise à l'officier 55
    decorative devices 50
    Fernandino style 107–8
    Johann Haertl 134
    Georges Jacob 152
    Jacob-Desmalter 152–53
    lit droit 178
    lit en bateau 178
    Lorentz Wilhelm Lundelius 185
    Percier and Fontaine 222–23
    Récamier 241
    Pierre Thomire 183, 296–97, 318
"Empire" woods **101**
    Indian laurel 148
    Queensland walnut 237
    silky oak 277
en suite **101**
encoignure **101**
Endell, August **101–2**, 284
endive **102**
engrailing 201
entablature 14, **102**
Ercolani, Lucien **102**, 321
ergonomic design
    Mario Bellini 30
    Niels Diffrient 86
    Charles Eames 94–95
    George Nelson 206
escabelle **102**
escritoire **102**
escutcheon **102–3**
Esherick, Wharton **103**
espagnolette **103**
estampille **103**
étagère **103**
Etruscan furniture **103**
    cista 65
Etruscan style **103–4**
    François-Joseph Bélanger 29, 87,
      92
    Jean-Démostène Dugourc 87, 92
Evans, Edward **104**
extension table **104**

F

faldstool **105**
faldyn table **105**
fall front **105**
fall-front desk **105**

fan-back Windsor chair 323
"fancy" furniture **105**
    decorative motifs 73
    John and Hugh Findlay 107,
      108–9
    Lambert Hitchcock 142
    Windsor chair 321
farmhouse Windsor chair 324
farthingdale chair **105**, 307
fauteuil **105–6**
fauteuil à la Reine **106**
faux-bamboo **106**
feather banding 24
Federal period **106–7**
    decorative motifs 29
    Matthew Egerton, Sr. 96
    William Lemon 176
    Salem secretary 264
    John and Thomas Seymour 273
    John Shaw 274
    square-back chair 283
Fenoglio, Pietro **107**
Fernandino style **107–8**
Feure, Georges de **108**
festoon **108**
fiddle back **108**
field bed (tent bed) **108**
fielded panel **108**
figuring **108**
filigree work **108**
fillet **108**
Findlay, John and Hugh 107, **108–9**
finial **109**
    auger flame 20
    pendant 222
finish **109**
    French polishing 117
    gilding 123
    giltwood 124
    japanning 154
    varnish 311
fire screen **109**
    cheval screen 59
    pole screen 229
firehouse Windsor chair 323
flag seat **109**
Fleeson, Plunket **110**
Flemish scroll foot 113
Flemish scroll leg 113, 174
fleur-de-lis (fleur-de-lys) **110**
Flitcroft, Henry **110**, 217
Florentine mosaic **110**
Floris, Cornelis **110**, 191, 246, 286
Flötner, Peter **110**, 246
fluting **110**
fly leg 174
fly rail **110**
Foggini, Giovanni Battista **110**
foliate **110**
Foliot, Nicolas-Quinibert **111**
Follot, Paul 15, 16, **111**
fondeur-ciseleur **111**
Fontaine, Pierre-François-Léonard
    222–23, 248
foot **111–15**
footboard **115**
footstool **115**
    Byzantine furniture 45
    hassock 136
form (bench) **115**
form (design type) **115**
Forster, Jacob **115**
fourposter **115**
framing **115**
François I style **115–16**, 245–46
    Francesco Primaticcio 233, 246
    Rosso Fiorentino 233, 246, **259**
Frank, Jean-Michel 16, **116**

Frank, Josef **116**, 266
Frankl, Paul 10, **116**
Free Renaissance style **116**
Freideberg, Pedro **116**
French Chippendale **117**
French foot 114
French modern style **117**
French polishing 109, **117**
French Provincial furniture **117**
    bonnetière 35
    panetière 218
French scroll foot 114
fret **117**
fretsaw 117
fretted pediment 221
fretwork **117**
Frid, Tage **118**
frieze **118**
    cushion frieze 78–79
Frothingham, Benjamin **118**
Frullini, Luigi **118**, 247
Fry, Edwin Maxwell **118**
Fry, Roger **118**
fulcrum **118**
fumed oak **118**
funa-dansu **119**
functionalism **119**
    Utility Furniture 308
Furness, Frank **119**
furniture design firms
    Katavolos-Littell-Kelley 162, 172
    Laverne Originals 172
    Percier and Fontaine 222–23
furniture manufacturers
    Carl Leistler 49, 210, 247, 255
    Cassina 30, 51, 188–89, 267
    Collinson & Lock 67, 236
    Dominique 16, 88
    Gillows 124, 254
    Herman Miller Furniture Co. 54,
      94, 139, 206, 212, 218, 256
    Herter Brothers 139, 155
    Ince & Mayhew 147, 254
    Jeanselme 156, 254
    Karpen Brothers, S., Co. 162
    Kartell 162
    Kimbel & Cabus 164, 247
    Wilhelm Kimbel of Mainz 164,
      210, 247, 255
    Liberty & Co. 177, 235, 316
    J. & J. W. Meeks 196, 255
    Mills & Deming 107, 199
    Mitchell & Rammelsburg 199, 255
    Nimura & Sato 24, 155, 212
    Pössenbacher 231, 247
    Pottier & Stymus 210, 231
    Süe et Mare 289
    Thonet & Sons 315
    Tobey Furniture Co. 299
    Tula Ironworks 302
    Van Keppel-Green 310
    Wassmus Frères 316
    Young, J. M. & Co. 332
    furosaki byobu 119

G

gadroon molding 201
gadrooning **120**, 201
Gaillard, Eugène **120**
Gaines, John **120**
Gallé, Émile **120–21**, 205
Gallén-Kallela, Akseli **121**
gallery **121**
galloon **121**
gaming table **121**
gate-leg table **121**
Gatti, Paolini & Teodoro **121**

Gaudi y Cornet, Antonio **122**
Gaudreau (Gaudreaux), Antoine-Robert
    122, 182, 253
Geddes, Norman Bel 10, **122**
Gehry, Frank O. **122**
genre pittoresque 196, 227, 243, 253
Georgian period **122–23**
gesso **123**
Gibbons, Grinling **123**, 177, 248
Gibbons, William **123**
Gilardi, Piero **123**
gilding 109, **123**, 126
Gillingham, James **123**
Gillows **124**, 248, 254
Gilpin, Thomas **124**
giltwood **124**
gimp **124**
Gimson, Ernest William **124**, 262
Giovanni da Verona **124**
girandole **124**
Glasgow School **124**, 274
    Charles Rennie Mackintosh 188,
      316, 319
    George Walton 315–16
Glastonbury chair **124–25**
glazing bar 19, **125**
Gneib, Anki **125**
Gobelins **125**, 180, 181
    Pierre Golle 126, 172
    Charles Le Brun 172
Goddard, John **125**, 299
Goddard, Stephen **125**
Godwin, William 16, **125–26**, 155
gold leaf 109, **126**
Goldfinger, Erno **126**
Gole, Cornelius **126**
Gole, Adriaan **126**
Golle, Cornelis. *See* Gole, Cornelis
Golle, Pierre **126**, 172, 180
gondola chair 26, **126**
Goodison, Benjamin **126**, 217
Gostelowe, Jonathan **126–27**, 224, 240
Gothic furniture **127–28**
    decorative devices 77, 79, 284
    decorative motifs 177–78, 300
    dresser (1) 90
    Hispano-Moresque furniture 141
    hutch 146
    livery cupboard 179
    ornamental motifs 65, 236
    pin hinge 141
    settle 273
    settle-table (monk's bench) 273
    slab-ended stool 278
    standard 284
    table dormant 292
    tilting chest 298
    wainscot chair 315
Gothic scroll-back Windsor chair 324
Gothic Windsor chair 324, 326
Goujon, Jean **128–29**, 138, 246
Gourdin, Michel **129**
Gouthière, Pierre **129**, 183
Governor Winthrop desk **129**
Gragg, Samuel **129**, 219
grandfather chair 327
grasshopper legs **129**
Graves, Michael **129**, 231
Gray, Eileen 16, **129**, 204, 306
Grecian couch 327
Greek furniture **129–30**
    decorative devices 219
    diphros 86
    diphros okladias 86
    kibotos 163–64
    kline 118, 165
    klismos 165
    theyns 296

Greek key pattern 163
Greene & Greene **130–31**, 199, 285
Gregotti, Vittorio **131**
Grendey, Giles **131**
griffin (griffon; gryphon) **131**
grille **131**
grisaille **131**
Grohé, Guillaume **131**, 182, 247, 248, 254
Gropius, Walter 27, 85, **131–32**, 149, 198, 310
grotesque ornament **132**, 193, 207
Groult, André 16, **132**
Gruber, Jacques **132**, 206
guadamecil **132**
guan mao shi (kuan mao shih) **132**
guard-room table **132**
guéridon **132–33**
Gugelot, Hans **133**
Guilford chest 10, **133**
guilloche **133**
Guimard, Hector **133**, 288
Gwathmey-Siegel **133**, 231

H

Habermann, Franz Xaver **134**
hadley chest **134**
Haertl, Johann **134**
Haines, Ephraim 107, **134**
half-round molding 201
half-tester **134**
half-turning 304
Hall, John **135**
   first American pattern book 226
hall cupboard **134–35**
hall table. *See* refectory table
Hallett, William **135**
halved joint 158
Hancock, William **135**
handicraft revival **135**
   Wendell Castle 52
   John Makepeace 190
handkerchief table **135**
hardware **135–36**
   bail handle 23
   brass 39
   brasses 39
   bronze 40
   drop handle 91
   ring pull 251
Hardwick, Philip **136**
hardwood **136**
hari-bako **136**
hassock **136**
hatrack **136**
Haupt, Georg **136**, 184
Hazell, Stephen **136–37**
headboard **137**
headrest **137**
   African furniture 4–5, 6
   primitive furniture 233
Heal, Ambrose **137**
Heal, Christopher **137**
Hein, Piet **137**
Henkels, George J. **137**, 255
Henri II style **137–38**, 207, 246
   Jacques Androuet Du Cerceau, the Elder 91, 138, 191, 246, 286
   Jean Goujon 128–29
Hepplewhite, George 3, 123, **138**, 234, 249, 275, 276
Herbst, René **138**, 204, 306
Heritage, Robert **139**
Herman Miller Furniture Co. 54, 94, **139**, 212, 218
   George Nelson 206
   Gilbert Rohde 256
Herrera style 84–85, 281

herringbone banding 24
Herter Brothers **139**, 155
Hetsch, Gustav Friedrich 80, **139**
H-hinge 141
hibachi **139**
high chair **140**
High Victorian style **140**
highboy **140**
high-tech style **140**
   Gae Aulenti 20
   Joseph Paul D'Urso 93
   David Rowland 260
Hill, Oliver **140**
Hill, Thomas **140**
hinge **140–41**
hip **141**
hip-joint chair **141**
hipping **141**
Hispano-Moresque furniture **141**
Hitchcock, Lambert **142**, 226, 284
H-L hinge 141
Hoentschel, Georges **142**
Hoffmann, Josef 85, **142**, 203, 319
Hoffmann, Wolfgang **142**
Hogarth chair **142**
Holland, Henry **142–43**, 244
Hollein, Hans **143**
honeysuckle ornament 12
hoof foot 113
Hook, William 106, **143**
Hope, Thomas **143**, 220, 244
Hopkins, Gerrard **143**
Hoppenhaupt, Johann Michael **143–44**, 253
horn furniture **144**
Horrix, Matthijs **144**
horse dressing-glass 59
horse screen 59
horse-hoof foot 113
horseshoe-and-strap hinge 141
Horta, Victor **144**, 319
housed joint 158
H. S. Master, The **144–45**, 246
H-stretcher 287
hu chuang (hu ch'uang) **145**
hua mu **145**
hua qi (hua ch'i) **145**
hua zhuo (hua cho) **145**
Hubbard, Elbert 260–61
Hunt, William Holman **145**
hunt sideboard **145**
hunt table **145**
huntboard **145**
Hunzinger, George **145–46**, 219, 228
husk **146**
hutch **146**
hutch table **146**
Hvidt, Peter **146**, 266

I

Ince & Mayhew **147**, 254
Indian furniture **147–48**
   bamboo 24
   caning 48
   ivory 151
   veneer 312
indiscret **148**
Indo-Portuguese furniture **148**
Indore Palace 204, 261, 280
Industrial style. *See* high-tech style
inflatable furniture **148**
Ingham, George **148–49**
inlay **149**
   Boulle marquetry 37–38
   Florentine mosaic 110
   ivory 151
   lacquer techniques 330, 331
   marquetry 192–93

mother-of-pearl 203
   parquetry 219
   pietre dure 225–26
   seaweed marquetry 270
intaglio **149**
intarsia (tarsia) **149**
   certosina work 53
   Giovanni da Verona 124
interlaced-bow Windsor chair 324
International style **149**
   Hans Coray 72
   George Korody 167
   Le Corbusier 172–73
   William Lescaze 176
   Ludwig Mies van der Rohe 198, 284
   Gio Ponti 230
   Ralph Rapson 240
   Gordon Russell 262, 308
   Union des Artistes Modernes 306
Ionic order **150**, 214
Iribe, Paul **150**
Irish Chippendale furniture **150**
iron **150**
Irving & Casson & Davenport 81
Isabellino style **150**
isho-dansu **150–51**
Isle of Man stretcher 287
ivory **151**

J

Jack, George Washington **152**
Jacob, Georges 87, 100, **152**, 183, 184, 223
Jacob-Desmalter **152–53**, 156, 210, 248
Jacobean furniture **153**
   cock's-head hinge 141
   spindle 282
   turning used in 304
Jacobsen, Arne **153**, 228, 266
Jakobsen, Hans Sandgren **153**
Japanese furniture **153–54**
   bo 34
   butsudan 44
   byobu 44
   cho-dansu 64
   decorative devices 190, 276
   dogu-bako 88
   funa-dansu 119
   furosaki byobu **119**
   hari-bako 136
   hibachi 139
   isho-dansu 150–51
   kaidan-dansu 161
   katana-dansu 162
   kimono rack 164
   kotatsu 167
   kuruma-dansu 167–68
   kusuri-dansu 168
   kyodai 168
   kyosoku 168
   lacquer 169
   makura 190
   mizuya-dansu 199
   nagamochi 205
   nomen-dansu 212
   screen 269
   shodana 276
   suzuri-bako 289
   tabako-bon 290
   tansu 294
   tsuitate 302
   zeni-dansu 333
japanning 109, **154**, 169, 248, 312
   Bantam work 24–25
   bois de spa 35
   Gerhard Dagly 80
   Robert Davis 81

Thomas Johnston 157–58
   lacca contrafatta 169
   William Randall 240
   vernis Martin 312
Japonisme (Japonaiserie) **155**
jardinière **155**
Jazz Moderne. *See* Art Deco
Jeanneret, Charles-Edouard. *See* Le Corbusier
Jeanneret, Pierre **155–56**, 173, 223–24
Jeanselme **156**, 254
Jeckyll, Thomas **156**
Jeliff, John **156**, 228, 247
Jenny Lind style **156**
Jensen, Gerreit **156**, 320
jewelwork **156**
ji (chi) **156**
ji tai shi an (chi t'ai shih an) 8, **157**
jia zi chuang (chia tzu ch'uang) **157**
jiao chuang (ch'iao ch'uang); jiao yi (ch'iao yi) **157**
Joel, Betty **157**
Johnson, Gerrit. *See* Jensen, Gerreit
Johnson, Thomas **157**, 253
Johnston, Thomas 8, 154, **157–58**, 226
joiner **158**
joinery **158–59**
joint **159**
joint stool **159**
Jones, Allen **159**, 230
Jones, Owen **159**, 262
Jones, William **159**, 253
Joubert, Gilles **160**, 182, 251
Jourdain, Francis **160**, 306
Juhl, Finn **160**, 266
Juvarra, Filippo **160**

K

kaidan-dansu (staircase chest) **161**
Kambli, Johann Melchior **161**, 253, 282
kang (k'ang) **161**
kang cupboard **161**
kang ji (k'ang chi; kang table) **161–62**
Karpen Brothers, S., Co. **162**
Kartell **162**
kas **162**
kast **162**
katana-dansu **162**
Katavolos-Littell-Kelley **162**, 172
Kauffmann, Angelica **163**, 334
ke hui (k'o hui) 73, 169
Kent, William **163**, 217, 313
kettle base **163**
kettle stand **163**
key pattern (Greek key) 163
kibotos **163–64**
Kimbel, Wilhelm, of Mainz **164**, 210, 247, 255
Kimbel & Cabus **164**
kimono rack **164**
Kinsman, Rodney 140
Kiss, Paul 16, **164**
Kita, Toshiyuki **164**
Kjaerholm, Poul 149, **164**, 266
Klenze, Leo von **164–65**, 208, 255
Klimt, Gustav 273
kline 118, **165**
Klint, Kaare **165**, 266
klismos **165**
knee **165**
kneehole desk **166**
Kneeland, Samuel **166**
knife box **166**
Knoll, Florence Schust **166**
Knoll Associates **166**, 263, 268, 333
knorpelwerk **166**
knurl 114, **166**
knurling. *See* gadrooning

Komai, Ray **166–67**
Korean furniture **167**
Korody, George 149, **167**
kotatsu **167**
Kunstschrank **167**, 212
Küpper, C. E. M. *See* Van Doesburg, Theo
Kurokawa, Kisho **167**
kuruma-dansu **167–68**
kusuri-dansu **168**
kylix **168**
kyodai **168**
kyosoku **168**

L
La Mésangère, Pierre de 101, **170**, 220, 225, 248
lac burgauté **169**, 240
lacca contrafatta **169**
lacquer 109, **169**
    Coromandel lacquer 73
    decorative devices 169
    diao tian (leather) 85
    hua qi 145
    ti hong (Peking) 298
Lacroix, Roger. *See* Vandercruse, Roger
Ladatte (Ladetti) Francesco **169–70**
ladder-back chair (slat-back) **170**
Lalanne, François **170**
Laliquc, René **170**
Lalonde, Richard de **170**
lambrequin **170**
Lange, Gerd **170**
Langley, Batty 8, **170**, 209, 254
Langlois, Pierre **170**, 253
Lannuier, Charles-Honoré 9, **170–71**
Larkin, John **171**
lath **171**
lath-and-baluster Windsor chair 324
lath-back Windsor chair 324
lathe **171**
Latimer, Clive **171**, 332
Latrobe, Benjamin Henry **171**
lattice **171**
lattice pediment 221
latticework. *See* fretwork
laurel leaves **172**
Laverne Originials **172**
Le Brun, Charles **172**, 180, 181
Le Corbusier 149, 155–56, **172–73**, 198, 223–24, 284
    Indore Palace furnishings 204
    Union des Artistes Modernes 306
Le Pautre, Jean 172, **173**, 180, 252
Le Pautre, Pierre **173**
leaf **172**
leaf scroll foot 113
leather lacquer 85
lectern **173**
    Byzantine furniture 45
lectus **173–74**
lectus genialis **174**
leg **174**
Legrain, Pierre 16, **175**, 312
Lehmann, C. F. **175**
Leistler, Carl. *See* Carl Leistler
Lejeune, Louis **175**, 253
Lelarge, Jean Baptiste **176**
Leleu, Jean-François **176**, 183, 300
Leleu, Jules 16, **176**
Lemarchand, Louis-Edouard **176**, 248, 254
Lemon, William **176**
L'Enfant, Pierre Charles **176**
Leonardi, Cesare and Stagi, Franca **176**
Lescaze, William 10, **176**
Levasseur, Étienne **176**, 183
L-hinge 141

Liberty, Arthur Lazenby **177**
Liberty & Co. **177**, 235, 316
Liberty style. *See* Art Nouveau
library steps **177**
library table **177**
liming **177**
linenfold **177–78**
Linnell, John **178**
Lion-Cachet, Carel Adolph **178**, 211
lion's-paw foot 113
lit à colonnes **178**
lit à la duchesse 12, **178**
lit à la Polonaise 7, **178**
lit droit **178**
lit en bateau (lit en courbeille) **178**
liu xian zhuo (liu hsien cho; table of the Six Immortals) **178**
lobate style **179**
Lock, Matthias (Matthew) 72, **179**, 253
lohan chair **179**, 185
lolling chair **179**
Lomazzi, Paolo. *See* De Pas, D'Urbino, Lomazzi
loop-back Windsor chair 322
Loos, Adolf **179**
loper **179**
lotus **179**
Loud & Bros. **179**
Louis Philippe style **179**
Louis Seize Impératrice. *See* Louis XVI Revival style
Louis style **180**
Louis XIII style **180**, 207, 246
Louis XIV style **180–81**, 207
    André-Charles Boulle 37
    Domenico Cucci 78
    decorative devices 110
    Pierre Golle 126, 172, 180
    Charles Le Brun 172
    Jean Le Pautre 173
    ram's-horn arm 240
    Johann Daniel Sommer 280
Louis XV Revival style. *See* Rococo Revival style
Louis XV style 122, **181–82**
    genre pittoresque 196, 227, 243, 253
    Gilles Joubert 160, 251
    Juste-Aurele Meissonnier 196
    ornamental devices 103
    Nicolas Pineau 227
    sultane (1) 289
    Jean-Baptiste Tilliard I 298
    Charles Topino 299
    Bernard Van Risenburgh 253, 310–11
    veilleuse 311
Louis XVI Revival style **182–83**, 249
    Leon Marcotte 192
Louis XVI style **183–84**, 208
    Jean Bérain 31
    Martin Carlin 49
    Georges Jacob 152
    Jean-Henri Riesener 213, 250–51, 300
    Claude-Charles Saunier 265
    Jean-Baptiste-Claude Sené 272
    Joseph Stöckel 285–86
    Pierre Thomire 296–97, 318
    Adam Weisweiler 318
Louis XVIII style **184–85**
lounge **185**
    daybed 81–82
lounge chair **185**
love seat **185**
low-back Windsor chair 324
lowboy **185**
lozenge **185**

Lueckenhausen, Helmut **185**
Lundelius, Lorentz Wilhelm 101, **185**
lunette **185**
luo quan yi (lo ch'uan yi; lohan chair) 179, **185**
lute table 236
Luther chair **185–86**
Lutyens, Edwin **186**
lyre **186**, 207

M
Macé, Jean **187**
Mackintosh, Charles Rennie **188**, 274, 316, 319
Mackmurdo, Arthur Heygate 155, **188**
Maggiolini, Giuseppe 184, **188**
Magistretti, Vico **188–89**
Maher, George Washington **189**, 231, 232
Majorelle, Louis **189–90**, 205–6
Makepeace, John 135, **190**
maki-e **190**
makura **190**
Mallard, Prudent **190**
Mallet-Stevens, Robert **190**, 306
Malmsten, Carl Per Hendrik **190–91**, 266
Maloof, Sam **191**
Mangiarotti, Angelo **191**
Mannerist style **191**, 207, 220, 246
    grotesque ornament 132
    Henri II style 137–38
    ornamentation 212, 286, 292
    Rosso Fiorentino 233, 246, 259, 286
Manwaring, Robert 8, 72, **191–92**, 254
mao gui 86
maple. *See* wood, bird's-eye maple
Maracaibo boxwood. *See* wood, boxwood
marble 192
marbleize **192**
marblewood. *See* wood, Coromandel
Marcotte, Leon 183, **192**, 247
Mare, André. *See* Süe et Mare
marguerite **192**
Mariscal, Javier **192**
Marlborough leg 174
Marot, Daniel **192**, 320
marquetry **192–93**
    André-Charles Boulle 37, 172, 180, 243
    certosina work 53
    intarsia (tarsia) 149
    Giuseppe Maggiolini 184, 188
    Johann Georg Nestfell 210
    Nonsuch chest 212
    Dirk van Rijswijk 251
    Abraham Roentgen 255
    Pierre Roussel 260
    seaweed marquetry 270
    softwood 280
    Johann Friedrich and Heinrich Wilhelm Spindler 282
    Lorenz Stoer 286
    Leonardo Van der Vinne 310
    zebrawood 333
marquise **193**
Martha Washington chair **193**
Martha Washington table **193**
Maryland Chippendale chair **193**
mask **193**
Mason, Ralph **193**, 198
Mathews, Arthur F. **193**, 199, 285
Mathews, Lucia K. **193**, 199, 285
Mathsson, Karl Bruno **193**, 266
matt gilding **194**
Matta (Roberto Sebastian Antonio Matta Echaurren) **194**, 308

matting **194**
Matusch (Matouche), Johann **194**
Maugham, Syrie **194**
Mauguin, Paul **194**
Mayhew & Ince. *See* Ince & Mayhew
Maynard, Alistair **194**
Mazza, Sergio **194**
McCobb, Paul **187**
McGrath, Raymond **187**
McIntire, Samuel 107, **187**
McKie, Judy Kensley **188**
Meadmore, Clement 149, **194–95**
meander pattern 163
medieval furniture **195–96**
    ark 14
    back stool 22
    bahut 22–23
    bed of estate 28–29
    chair of estate 55
    chair-table 55
    chip carving 63
    coffer 66
    coffret 66
    couchette 74
    court cupboard (1) 75
    Dante chair (Dantesca chair) 80
    daybed 82
    decorative motifs 14
    diapering 85–86
    dorser (dosser) 88
    fall front 105
    Gothic furniture 127–28
    half-tester 134
    joint stool 159
    ladder-back chair 170
    refectory table 242
    Romanesque furniture 256–57
    Savonarola chair 265
    stick stool 285
    strap hinge 141
    strozzi stool 288
    tester 296
    trestle table 301
    trunk 301–2
    trussing 302
    trussing bed 302
    turned chair 303
    turning used in 304
    writing box 329
Meeks, J. & J. W. **196**, 255
mei gui shi (mei kuei shih) **196**
Meier, Richard **196**
Meier-Graefe, Julius **196**
Meissonnier, Juste-Aurele **196**, 227
    genre pittoresque 196, 227, 243, 253
Mekeren, Jan van **196**
melon foot 113
melon-bulb turning 304
member **197**
Memphis. *See* Sottsass, Ettore
Mendlesham chair 325
mensa lunata **197**
menuisier **197**
    Louis Cresson 76
    Louis Delanois 83
    Louis XVI style 183
    André Jacob Roubo 181, 259–60
    Jean-Baptiste-Claude Sené 272
mercury gilding **197**
Mère, Clément 16, **197**
Méridienne **197**
Mesopotamian furniture **197–98**
    wood types 96
Messinger, Henry 193, **198**
metal furniture **198**
metope **198**
meubles parlants **198**

Mies van der Rohe, Ludwig 149, **198**, 284
Migeon, Pierre, II 182, **198–99**
Miller, Herman. *See* Herman Miller Furniture Co.
Miller, Sanderson 199, 209, 254
Mills & Deming 107, **199**
mirrors
    cheval glass 59
    pier table 225
misericord **199**
Mission furniture **199**
    Roycroft Community 260–61
    Gustav Stickley 285
    J. M. Young & Co. 332
Mitchell & Rammelsburg 199, 255
miter 158–59
mizuya-dansu **199**
Modern Gothic style 95, 210, 293
Moderne style. *See* American Moderne
modillion **200**
Mogensen, Børge **200**
molding **200–201**
Mölgaard-Nielsen, Osla 146
Molitor, Bernard 87, 100, **201**
Mollino, Carlo **201–2**
monk's bench 273
monopod **202**
Moore, James **202**
Moorish style **202**
    Owen Jones 159
Morris, William **202–3**, 210, 285, 317
Morris & Co. 43, 202
Morris chair **202**, 285, 317
mortise **203**
mortise-and-tenon joint 159
Moser, Kolo **203**, 319
mother-of-pearl **203**, 239
mount. *See* hardware
Mourgue, Olivier **203**, 308
Mucha, Alphonse Maria **203**
Mudéjar style **203**, 246
muebles enconchados **203**, 281
mule chest (blanket chest) **204**
mullion **204**
Munthe, Gerhard **204**, 313
muntin **204**
Murdoch, Peter **204**
Murphy bed **204**
Muthesius, Eckart **204**
Muthesius, Hermann **204**

N
nacre. *See* mother-of-pearl
nagamochi **205**
Nahl, Johann August **205**, 253
Nakashima, George **205**
Nancy, School of **205–6**
    Emile Gallé 120–21
    Louis Majorelle 189–90
    Émile Victor Prouvé 234
    Eugène Vallin 309
Napoleon Bonaparte 71, 84, 86, 87, 98, 99, 100, 153, 176, 208, 223, 241
Napoleon III 182, 209, 247, 249
National Romanticism **206**
    Akseli Gallén-Kallela 121
    Eliel Saarinen 263–64
    Louis Sparre 282
Naturalistic style **206**
necessary chair 56
necking **206**
Needles, John **206**
Nelson, George **206**
Nelson Windsor chair 325
neoclassical style **206–9**
    Adam style 2–3
    arrow-back Windsor chair 322

Charles X style 57
curule chair 78
decoration 41, 84, 108, 131, 146, 168, 172, 186, 207–8, 217, 234, 308, 313, 316
drum table 91
Etruscan style 103–4
gondola chair (barrel chair) 126
Grecian couch 129
George Hepplewhite 123, 138
Louis XVI style 183–84
Louis XVIII style 184–85
Marlborough leg 174
Filippo Pelagio Palagi 216
Regency style 243–45
rent table 247
Restauration style 248
ring pull (ring handle) 251
David Roentgen 255–56
George Seddon 271
sideboard 276
square-back chair 283
West Indian satinwood 318
neo-Gothic style **209–10**
    Alexander Jackson Davis 81
    Augustus Welby Northmore Pugin 220, 234–35
    Regency Gothic 209, 234, 243
neo-Grec style **210**
    Pottier & Stymus 231
    Alexander Roux 183, 260
nest of drawers **210**
nest of tables **210**
Nestfell, Johann Georg **210**
Neufforge, Jean-François 183, **210**
Neuhof, Johann **211**
New York Chippendale furniture **211**
    Gilbert Ash 19
    Samuel Prince 234
Newport Chippendale furniture **211**
    John Goddard 125
    Edmund Townsend 299
    Job Townsend 299
    John Townsend 299–300
Newson, Marc 149, **211**
Niemeyer, Oscar **211**
Nieuwenhuis, Theodore **211**
Nigerian pearwood. *See* wood, guarea
night stand 69, **212**
night table (night stool) **212**
Nimura & Sato 24, 155, **212**
Noguchi, Isamu **212**
nomen-dansu **212**
Nonsuch chest **212**
Nosseni, Giovanni Maria **212**
Nuremberg cabinet 167
Nurmesniemi, Antti **212**, 266, 294

O
Obrist, Hermann **213**
occasional table **213**, 292
Oeben, Jean-François 182, 184, **213**, 250, 253, 256, 300, 310
ogee **213**
ogee bracket foot 113
ogee molding 79, 201
Olbrich, Joseph Maria **213–14**
"Old English" style 274–75
Old French style. *See* Rococo Revival style
onion foot 112
open-twist turning 304
openwork **214**
Oppendordt, Gilles-Marie **214**, 242, 252
orders of architecture **214**
    abacus 1
    Composite 70
    Corinthian 2, 72

Doric 88, 214, 310
entablature 14, 102
Ionic 150
Tuscan 305
ormolu **214**
Otto, Johann Heinrich **215**
ottoman **215**
    sultane 289
Oud, Jacobus Johannes Pieter **215**, 310
overstuffed furniture. *See* upholstery
ovolo molding 96, 201
oxbow front **215**
oyster veneer (*bois de bout*) **215**

P
Pabst, Daniel **216**
pad foot. *See* Dutch foot
pad-and-disk foot. *See* Dutch foot
paintbrush foot. *See* Spanish foot
paktong **216**
Palagi, Filippo Pelagio 208, **216**
Palladian style 122, **217**
    decorative motifs 313
    William Kent 163, 313
palmette **217**
panetière **218**
Pankok, Bernhard 85, **218**
Panton, Verner **218**, 228, 266
papeleira **218**
papier-mâché furniture **218**
papyrus **218**
parcel gilt **218**
Parker, Richard Barry **219**
Parodi, Domenico **219**
Parodi, Filippo **219**
parquetry **219**
Parsons table **219**
partners' desk **219**
pastiglia **219**
patent furniture 72, **219**
    George Hunzinger 145–46, 228
    platform rocker 228
    Wooton desk 327–28
paterae **219**
patina **219**
pattern book **220**
    Thomas Chippendale 8, 60, 63
    Matthias (Matthew) Darly 81
    Crispin De Pas 82
    Wendel Dietterlin 86
    Jacques Androuet Du Cerceau 91, 138, 191, 246, 286
    first American 145, 226
    John Hall 135, 226
    Thomas Johnson 8
    William Jones 159
    Kimbel & Cabus 164
    Pierre de La Mésangère 225
    Batty Langley 8
    Matthias (Matthew) Lock 179
    Mannerist style 191, 220, 246
    Robert Manwaring 8, 191–92, 254
    Percier and Fontaine 101, 223
    rococo furniture 253–54
    Johannes Rumpp 261
    Hughes Sambin 264
    Johann Jakob Schübler 268
    Henry Shaw 274
    Thomas Shearer 3, 275
    Thomas Sheraton 3, 244, 275
    George Smith 254, 279
    Stalker & Parker 154, 283
    Lorenz Stoer 286
    strapwork 286
    Jean-Bernard Turreau (Toro) 305
    Friedrich Unteutsch 306
    Hans Vredeman de Vries 246, 286, 314

Paul Vredeman de Vries 314
Paul, Bruno 85, **220**
Paulin, Pierre **220**
paw foot 114
pear foot 114
pedestal **220**
pedestal chair **220**
pedestal desk **221**
pedestal table (tripod table) **221**
pediment **221**
peg **221**
Peking enamel 331
Peking lacquer 298
Pelletier, Jean (John) **221**
Pembroke table 39, **221–22**, 280
pendant finial **222**
Penniman, John Ritto **222**
Pennsylvania German furniture **222**
    Wachseinlegen 315
Percier, Charles **222–23**
Percier and Fontaine 101, 152, 153, 220, **222–23**
Pergo, Franz **223**
Pergolesi, Michaelangelo **223**
Perriand, Charlotte **223–24**, 306
    Pierre Jeanneret and 155–56
    Le Corbusier and 173
Pesce, Gaetano **224**
Petel, Clement **224**
petit commode **224**
Philadelphia Chippendale furniture **224**
    Thomas Affleck 4
    James Gillingham 123
    Jonathan Gostelowe 126–27, 240
    Benjamin Randolph 107, 230, 240
    William Savery 265
    Daniel Trotter 301
    Thomas Tufft 302
Philippine Mahogany. *See* wood, meranti
Phyfe, Duncan 9, 107, **224–25**, 313
pickled finish **225**
pie de puente **225**
pie safe (food safe) **225**
piecrust table **225**
pied de biche 113
pier table **225**
pierced carving **225**
pierced splat **225**
pietre dure **225–26**
Piffetti, Pietro **226**
pilaster **226**
Pilgrim furniture. *See* American Jacobean furniture
pillar-and-scroll style (American Restauration style) **226**
    Duncan Phyfe 224–25
    Voltaire chair 313
pillar-and-claw table 221
Pillement, Jean-Baptiste **226**, 253
pillow top **226**
Pimm, John **226**
pin **226**
pin hinge 141
Pineau, Nicolas **227**
    genre pittoresque 196, 243, 253
    ping (p'ing) **227**
pinkwood. *See* wood, tulipwood
Piranesi, Giovanni Battista **227**
Piretti, Giancarlo **227**
Pitman, Mark **227**
placet **227**
plank seat **228**
plastic furniture **228**
    Kartell 162
    upholstery 308
    See also Pop Art furniture
plateresque style **228**
platform rocker **228**

Platner, Warren **228**
pliant **228**
plinth **228–29**
Plishke, Ernst Anton **229**
Plitzner, Ferdinand **229**
plywood **229**
Poillerat, Gilbert **229**
Poiret, Paul **229**
pole screen **229**
Pollard, John **229–30**
Ponti, Gio **230**, 259, 296
Pop Art furniture **230**
    De Pas, D'Urbino, Lomazzi 82
    inflatable furniture 148
    Jon Weallans 317
porcelain **230**
Portugese foot 114
Pössenbacher **231**, 247, 255
Post-Modern furniture **231**
    Gae Aulenti 20
    Michael Graves 129
    Gwathmey-Siegel 133
pot cupboard 69, **231**
pot table **231**
Pottier, Auguste **231**
Pottier & Stymus 210, **231**
poudreuse **231**
pouf (pouffe) **231**
Prairie School 119, 199, **231–32**
    George Grant Elmslie 99
    George Washington Maher 189
    Stickley influence 285
    Frank Lloyd Wright 199, 328
première-partie. *See* Boulle marquetry
press **232**
press bed **232**
press cupboard **232**
    tridarn 301
"pretzel-back" chair **232**
prie-dieu **232–33**
primary and secondary woods **233**
Primaticcio, Francesco **233**, 246
primitive furniture **233–34**
Prince, Samuel **234**
Prince of Wales feathers **234**
Prouvé, Émile Victor 206, **234**
Prouvé, Jean 156, 224, **234**
Psyche **234**
Pugin, Augustus Charles **234**, 243
Pugin, Augustus Welby Northmore 210, 220, **234–35**
pulvinated frieze. *See* cushion frieze
Punnett, E. G. **235**
putto (amorini) **235**

Q

qin zhuo (ch'in cho; lute table) **236**
quadrant **236**
Quarti, Eugenio **236**
quatrefoil **236**
Queen Anne leg 175
Queen Anne Revival style **236**, 249
    Queen Anne leg 175
    Richard Norman Shaw 274–75
Queen Anne style 122, **236–37**
    spoon-back chair 283
    stump leg 175
    yoke-back chair 332
Quervelle, Anthony 9, **237–38**
quirk **238**

R

Raab, Johann Philipp **239**
Raab, Johann Valentin **239**
Raacke, Peter **239**
rabbet (rebate) **239**
rabbeted joint (rebated joint) 159

Race, Ernest **239**, 262, 332
racking **239**
raden 169, **239–40**
rail **240**
rake **240**
Rams, Dieter **240**
ram's-horn arm **240**
Randall, William **240**
Randolph, Benjamin 107, 224, 230, **240**
random joints **240**
range tables **240**
Rapson, Ralph **240**
rat-claw foot 114
Rateau, Armand-Albert **241**
rat-tail hinge (devil-tail hinge) 141
rattan 48, **241**, 319
Ravesteyn, Sybold Van **241**
Ravrio, Antoine-André **241**
reading stand **241**
rebate. *See* rabbet
Récamier **241**
recessed carving **241**
recessed stretcher 287
réchampi **241**
reed-and-tie molding 201
reeding **242**
reel-and-bead molding 200
reel-and-bead turning 304
refectory table **242**
Régence style **242**, 252
    decorative devices 50
    ornamental devices 103
Regency Gothic 209, **243**
    Augustus Charles Pugin 234
Regency style **243–45**
    decorative motifs 88, 133
    Henry Holland 142–43
    Thomas Hope 143
    Mendlesham chair 325
    Augustus Welby Northmore Pugin 210, 220, **234–35**
    saber leg 175
    Thomas Sheraton 275
    George Smith 279
    Charles Heathcote Tatham 295
    Thomas Tatham 295
    Trafalgar furniture 300
relief **245**
Rémond, Félix **245**
Renaissance furniture **245–46**
    armadio 14–15
    armoire à deux corps 15
    bed of estate 28–29
    bog oak used in 34
    caquetoire 49
    cassapanca 51
    cassone 51
    close stool (night stool) 65
    court cupboard (1) 75
    credenza 76
    Dante chair (Dantesca chair) 80
    decorative detail 39, 50, 59–60, 88, 108, 132, 217, 259, 286, 296, 308
    escabelle 102
    fall front 105
    Florentine mosaic 110
    François I style 115–16
    guadamecil 132
    guard-room table 132
    hassock 136
    Henri II style 137–38
    hip-joint chair 141
    intarsia (tarsia) 149
    Kunstschrank 167
    papeleira 218
    pastiglia 219

pattern books 220
pie de puente 225
plateresque style 228
    Anthony Salvin 264
    Hughes Sambin 264
    Savonarola chair 265
    Schenkschieve 267
    Schragentisch 267
    sgabello 274
    sillón de cadera 277
    sillón de fraileros 277
    sledge feet (runner feet) 278
    spindle 282
    steel furniture 284
    table à l'Italienne 292
    taquillón 294
    trundle bed 301
    trussing 302
    trussing bed 302
    Tudor furniture 302
    turning used in 304
    Tuscan bed 305
    Überbauschrank 306
    vargueño 311
    walnut 315
    Wangentisch 316
Renaissance Revival style **246–47**, 249
rent table **247**
reproduction furniture **247–48**
reserve **248**
rest bed **248**
Restauration style **248**
Restoration furniture **248–49**
    Charles II chair 57
    cupped leg 174
    turning used in 305
reverse ogee molding. *See* ogee molding
revival styles 123, 209, **249–50**
    Anton Bembé 30
    Elizabethan Revival style 99
    Isabellino style 150
    Louis XVI Revival style 182–83
    Naturalistic style 206
    pouf (pouffe) 231
    Queen Anne Revival style 236
    Renaissance Revival style 246–47
    Rococo Revival style 254–55
    Alexander Roux 260
    Viking Revival style 313
revolving chair (swivel chair) **250**
Riart, Carlos **250**
ribband-back chair (ribbon-back) **250**
Richardson, Henry Hobson **250**
Riemerschmid, Richard 85, **250**, 296
Riesener, Jean-Henri 183, 213, **250–51**, 300
Rietveld, Gerrit Thomas **251**
Rijswijk, Dirk van **251**
Rinaldi, Gastone **251**
rinceau **251**
ring pull (ring handle) **251**
ring turning 304
Ringuet Le Prince, Auguste Émile. *See* Marcotte, Leon
Risamburgh, Bernard Van. *See* Van Risenburg, Bernard
riven timber **252**
Robert, Hubert 184, **252**
Robinson, Gerrard **252**
rocaille **252**
rocking chair **252**
    Boston rocker 37
    "Dondolo" 176
    platform 228
rococo furniture **252–54**
    American Chippendale 8–9
    cabriole leg 111, 112, 113, 114, 165, 174

Chinese Chippendale 60
Thomas Chippendale 63
coiffeuse (1) 67
commode (1) 68–69
Henry Copland 72
François Cuvilliés 79
decoration 50, 72, 77–78, 132, 283, 296
genre pittoresque 196, 227, 243, 253
girandole 124
Franz Xaver Habermann 134
Matthias (Matthew) Lock 179
Louis XV style 181–82
Marlborough leg 174
molding 200
Pietro Piffetti 226
Régence style 242–43
rocaille 252
serpentine design 272
stump leg 175
Rococo Revival style **254–55**
    John Henry Belter 30
    Anton Bembé 30
    decorative devices 283
    Michael Thonet 297
    Benjamin Dean Wyatt 329
Roentgen, Abraham **255**
Roentgen, David 184, **255–56**, 318
Rohde, Gilbert 10, 206, **256**
Rohlfs, Charles **256**
roll molding 201
roll-top desk **256**
rollwork. *See* strapwork
Roman furniture **258**
    Etruscan furniture 103
    fulcrum 118
    lectus 173–74
    lectus genialis 174
    mensa lunata 197
    sella curulis 272
    sigma 277
Roman spindle Windsor chair 325–26
Romanesque furniture **256–58**
    cushion capital 78
    standard 284
    table dormant 292
Romayne work **259**
root furniture **259**
rope molding 201
rope turning 305
Roselli, Alberto **259**
rosette **259**
Rosso Fiorentino (Giovanni Batista Rosso) 233, 246, **259**, 286
Roubo, André Jacob 181, **259–60**
roundabout chair 73, **260**
roundel **260**
roundel molding. *See* astragal molding
Rousseau, Clément 16, **260**
Roussel, Pierre **260**
Roux, Alexander 183, 247, 255, **260**
Rowland, David **260**
Roycroft Community **260–61**
Rucker, Thomas **261**, 284
Ruhlmann, Émile-Jacques 16, 93, 96, 103, 204, **261**
Rumpp, Johannes **261**
runner feet 278
running dog 313
rush seat **262**
Ruskin, John **262**, 285
Russell, Gordon 72, **262**, 308
Russell, Richard Drew **262**

S

Saarinen, Eero 228, **263**, 308
Saarinen, Eliel **263–64**

saber leg 175
sabot **264**
sack-back Windsor chair 322
saddle seat **264**
Sadubin, Leon **264**
Salem rocker. *See* Boston rocker
Salem secretary **264**
saltire stretcher. *See* X-stretcher
Salvin, Anthony **264**
Sambin, Hughes 138, 191, 246, **264**
san cai tu hui (san ts'ai t'u hui) **264**
Sanderson, Elijah 106, **265**
Sapper, Richard **265**, 333
satin walnut. *See* wood, red gum
Saunier, Claude-Charles 183, **265**
sausage turning 304
Savery, William 224, **265**
Savonarola chair **265**
scagliola **265–66**
Scandinavian Modern **266**
    Hugo Alvar Henrik Aalto 1
    Gunnar Asplund 19
    functionalism 119
    Arne Jacobsen 153
    Finn Juhl 160
    Poul Kjaerholm 149, 164
    Kaare Klint 165
    Karl Bruno Mathsson 193
    teak 295
    Hans Wegner 317–18
scarf joint 159
Scarpa, Carlo **267**
Scarpa, Tobia and Afra **267**
Schenkschieve **267**
Schindler, Rudolf M. **267**
Schinkel, Karl Friedrich 255, **267**
Schlegel, Fritz **267**
Schmidt, Karl **267**
schragentisch **267**
schrank **267–68**
    Stollenschrank 286
    Wellenschrank 318
Schübler, Johann Jakob **268**
Schultz, Richard **268**
Schumacher, Martin **268**
Schuster, Franz **268**, 306
Schwerdfeger, Ferdinand 183, **268**
scimitar leg 175
scotia molding (half-round) 201
Scots pine. *See* wood, European redwood
Scott, Isaac **269**
screen **269**
    byobu 44
    cheval 59
    fire 109
    furosaki byobu 119
    ping (p'ing) 227
    pole 229
    tsuitate 302
screen dressing-glass. *See* cheval glass
screw turning 304
scribe **269**
scriptor 102
scritoire 102
scroll **269–70**
scroll arm (upholstered) **270**
scroll arm (wooden) **270**
scroll foot 114
scroll leg 175
scroll pediment 221
scroll-back Windsor chair 325
scrollwork **270**
scrutoire 102
sculpteur **270**
Searle, William 10, **270**
seat **270**
seat block. *See* corner block
seat rail **270**

seaweed marquetry **270**
Secession. *See* Sezession
Second Empire style **270**
secrétaire **270–71**
secrétaire à abattant **271**
secrétaire à Capucin **271**
secrétaire en armoire **271**
secrétaire en dos d'âne **271**
secrétaire en pente **271**
secrétaire en tombeau **271**
secretary **271**
secretary drawer **271**
Seddon, George **271**
Seignouret, François 255, **271–72**
sella curulis **272**
semainier **272**
Sené, Claude, I **272**
Sené, Jean-Baptiste-Claude 183, **272**
sequoia. *See* wood, redwood
serpentine **272**
serpentine stretcher **287**
serpentine X-stretcher. *See* cow-horn
    stretcher
Serrurier-Bovy, Gustave **272–73**
settee **273**
    canapé 47
    causeuse 52
    chair-back 54
    sultane 289
settle **273**
settle-table (monk's bench) **273**
sewing table 328
Seymour, John 107, **273**
Seymour, Thomas 107, **273**
Sezession **273–74**
    Josef Hoffmann 85, 142, 203, 319
    Kolo Moser 203, 319
    Joseph Maria Olbrich 213–14
    Joseph Urban 308
    Otto Wagner 315
    sgabello **274**
shagreen **274**
Shaker furniture **274**
    tilter 298
sharkskin. *See* shagreen
Shaw, Henry 210, **274**
Shaw, John 107, **274**
Shaw, Richard Norman 210, **274–75**
shawl-back Windsor chair 325
sheaf-back chair **275**
Shearer, Thomas 3, **275**
shell foot 114
Sheraton, Thomas 123, 220, 234, 249,
   275–76, 283
    pattern books 3, 244, 275
    sofa table 280
    twin bed 305
    shibayama **276**
shield-back chair **276**
shodana **276**
Shoemaker, Jonathan **276**
shonk **276**
shu gui (shu kuei) **276**
Siamoise **276**
side chair **276**
sideboard **276**
siège courant. See chaise courante
siège meublante. See chaise meublante
sigma **277**
sillón de cadera **277**
silver **277**
silver leaf **277**
silverwood. *See* wood, sycamore
singerie **277–78**
single bow-back Windsor chair 322
Six Immortals, table of the 178
six-board chest 34
skirt. *See* apron

slab-ended stool **278**
slant top **278**
slant-top desk **278**
slat-back chair 170
sledge feet (runner feet) **278**
sleeping chair **278**
sleigh bed **278**
slip seat (drop-in seat) **278–79**
slipcover **279**
slipper chair **279**
slipper foot. *See* Dutch foot
Slodtz, Antoine-Sebastien **279**
Slodtz, Paul-Amboise **279**
Smith, George 244, 254, **279**
smoker's bow Windsor chair 325
snake foot. *See* Dutch foot
snap table 298
Socchi (Socci), Giovanni 101, **279**
sociable **280**
sofa **280**
    cabriole 46–47
    camel-back 47
    canapé 47
    causeuse 52
    chesterfield 58–59
    couch vs. 74
    davenport 81
    love seat 185
    settee 273
    upholstery 280, 307, 308
    veilleuse 311
sofa table **280**
sofa-bed 72, **280**
soffit **280**
softwood **280**
Sognot, Louis 204, **280**
Sommer, Johann Daniel **280**
Sottsass, Ettore **280–81**
soupière 281
spade foot 114
Spanish Colonial furniture **281**
    muebles enconchados 203
Spanish foot (scroll foot) 114
Sparre, Louis **282**
sparver **282**
sphinx 207, **282**
spider-leg table **282**
spindle **282**
spindle-back chair **282**
spindle-back Windsor chair 325–26
Spindler, Heinrich Wilhelm 253, **282**
Spindler, Johann Friedrich 253, **282**
spiral leg 175
spiral turning 304, 305
splat (back splat) **282**
splay molding 201
spline **283**
spline seat **283**
splined joint 159
split baluster 24
split spindle 282
spool furniture **283**
    Jenny Lind style 156
spool turning 304
spoon-back chair **283**
spring rocker 228
spur stretcher **287**
squab **283**
square-back chair **283**
squirrel-cage support 33
S-scroll **283**
Stagi, Franca 176
staircase chest 161
Stalker & Parker 154, **283**
Stam, Mart **283–84**
    cantilevered chair 48
stand **284**
    candlestand 47

china stand 60
dumbwaiter 92
washstand 316
standard **284**
standing tray **284**
stay (stay rail). *See* cross rail
stay-back Windsor chair 325
steel furniture **284**
    Tula Ironworks 302
stenciling **284**
Stephensen, Magnus 266, **284–85**
stick stool **285**
Stickley, Gustav 3, 199, **285**
Stickley, L. & J. G., Co. 285, 332
stile **285**
Stile Liberty. *See* Art Nouveau
Stöckel, Joseph 183, **285–86**
Stoer, Lorenz **286**
Stollenschrank **286**
stone **286**
stool **286**
    African furniture 5–6
    back stool 22
    Byzantine furniture 45
    caryatid 5, 50
    Chinese furniture 61–62
    close (night) 65
    deng (teng) 83
    diphros 86
    diphros okladias 86
    dun (tun) 92–93
    Egyptian furniture 97
    escabelle 102
    faldstool 105
    footstool 115
    Gothic furniture 128
    joint stool 159
    placet 227
    pliant 228
    pouf (pouffe) 231
    primitive furniture 233
    Romanesque furniture 257
    sella curulis 272
    slab-ended 278
    stick 285
    strozzi 288
    tabouret (taboret) 292
    xiu dun (hsiu tun) 330
stopped dovetail joint 158
stopped fluting **286**
straight banding 24
strap hinge 141
strapwork **286**
Strawberry Hill Windsor chair 324, 326
stretcher **287–88**
stringing **288**
stripping **288**
Strnad, Oskar **288**
Strohmeier, Lienhart **288**
strozzi stool **288**
Stuart, James 122, **288**
stub foot 114
stump 14
stump leg 175
Style Antique, Le **288**
Style Métro **288**
Style Républicaine, Le **288**. *See also*
    Directoire style
Stymus, William Pierre 231
Subes, Raymond 16, **289**
Süe et Mare 16, **289**
sugar chest **289**
Sullivan, Louis H. 231–32
sultane (ottoman) **289**
sultane (settee) **289**
Summers, Gerald **289**
sunburst **289**
sunflower chest 70

suzuri-bako **289**
swag **289**
swamp cypress. *See* wood, southern cypress
swan-neck handle. *See* bail handle
swan-neck pediment. *See* scroll pediment
swept leg 175
swing leg 175
Swiss Windsor chair 326
swivel chair 250

T

ta chuang (t'a ch'uang) **291**
tabako-bon **290**
table **290–91**
   altar 8, 157
   ba xian zhuo 22
   breakfast 39
   butler's (butler's tray) 44
   butterfly 44
   Byzantine furniture 45
   cabinet stand (casket stand) 46
   candlestand (torchère) 47
   canterbury 48
   card 49
   Carlton House 50
   chair-table 55
   chiffonier 59, 292
   china stand 60
   coal furniture 66
   coffee 66
   console 71
   console dessert 71
   counter-table 74
   credence 76
   draw-leaf 89
   dressing 90
   drop-leaf 91
   drum 91
   dumbwaiter 92
   extension 104
   faldyn 105
   gaming 121
   gate-leg 121
   guard-room 132
   handkerchief 135
   hua zhuo (hua cho) 145
   hunt 145
   hutch 146
   ji tui shi an 8, 157
   kang ji 161–62
   kettle stand 163
   library 177
   liu xian zhuo 178
   Martha Washington 193
   mensa lunata 197
   nest of tables 210
   occasional 213, 292
   Parsons 219
   pedestal (tripod) 221
   Pembroke 221–22
   piecrust 225
   pier 225
   qin zhuo 236
   range 240
   refectory 242
   rent 247
   Roman furniture 258
   root furniture 259
   schragentisch 267
   secrétaire à Capucin 271
   settle-table 273
   sewing 328
   sofa 280
   spider-leg 282
   stand 284
   table à l'Italienne 292
   table dormant 292

tang hua an 293
tavern 295
tea 295
teapoy 295
tilt-top (snap) 298
trestle 301
turret-top 305
Wangentisch 316
washstand 316
Windsor 327
wine (hunt) 327
worktable 328
writing 42, 292, 329
yan ji (yen chi) 331
table à écrire 292
table à l'Italienne 292
table ambulante 292
table dormant 292
table en chiffonnière 292
table-chair 55, 72
tablecloth 292
tablet-arm chair 292
   writing-arm Windsor chair 326
tablet-back Windsor chair 326
tabouret (taboret) 292
tailpiece 322
Talbert, Bruce James 155, 210, **293**
tallboy 293
Tallon, Roger **293**
tambour 293
tang hua an (t'ang hua an) 293
tang xiang (t'ang hsiang) **293–94**
tansu **294**
   cho-dansu 64
   dogu-bako 88
   funa-dansu 119
   hari-bako 136
   isho-dansu 150–51
   kaidan-dansu 161
   katana-dansu 162
   kuruma-dansu 167–68
   kusuri-dansu 168
   mizuya-dansu 199
   nagamochi 205
   suzuri-bako 289
   tabako-bon 290
   zeni-dansu 333
Tanzanian walnut. *See* wood, aningeria
tape seat **294**
Tapiovaara, Ilmari 266, **294**
tapissier **294**
taquillón **294**
tarsia. *See* intarsia
tassel **294**
Tatham, Charles Heathcote 244, **295**
Tatham, Thomas **295**
Tatlin, Vladimir **295**
tavern table **295**
tea table 295, 305
teapoy **295**
tenon **295**
tent bed 108
term **296**
tern foot 115
Terragni, Giuseppe **296**
Tery, Emilio **296**
Tessenow, Heinrich **296**
tester **296**
tête-à-tête 52, 70, **296**
therm foot. *See* spade foot
theyns **296**
Thomire, Pierre (or P.-P.) 183, **296–97**, 318
Thonet, Michael 31, 255, **297**, 312, 315
Thorn-Prikker, Johann **297**
three-back Windsor chair 326
throne **297**
   chair of estate 55

thrown chair. *See* turned chair
ti hong (t'i hung; Peking lacquer) **298**
Tiffany, Louis Comfort **298**
Tilliard, Jean-Baptiste, I **298**
tilter **298**
tilting chest **298**
tilt-top table (snap table) **298**
Tisch, Charles **298–99**
Tobey Furniture Co. **299**
toilette (table de toilette) 90
toilette en papillon **299**
tongue **299**
tongue-and-groove joint 159
Topino, Charles 183, **299**
torchère (candlestand) 47
Toro, Jean-Bernard. *See* Turreau, Jean-Bernard
tortoiseshell **299**
torus molding 201
Townsend, Edmund **299**
Townsend, Job **299**
Townsend, John **299–300**
tracery **300**
Tracy, Ebenezer **300**
Trafalgar furniture **300**
   Nelson Windsor chair 325
Transition style **300**
   Charles Topino 299
tray corner 87
trefoil **300**
trestle **300**
trestle bed **300**
trestle stand **300–301**
trestle table **301**
tridarn **301**
trifid foot 115
triglyph **301**
trio tables 210
tripod table 221
Trotter, Daniel 224, **301**
truckle bed **301**
Trumble, Francis **301**
trumpet leg 175
trumpet turning **305**
trundle bed **301**
trunk **301–2**
trussing bed **302**
tsuitate **302**
Tudor furniture **302**
   cock's-head hinge 141
   farthingale chair 105
   Glastonbury chair 124–25
   Nonsuch chest 212
   turning used in 304
Tufft, Thomas **302**
tufting 307
Tula Ironworks 284, **302**
Turkey sofa 215, 289
Turkey work **303**
turkey-breast cupboard **303**
turned chair **303**
turner **303**
turnery **303–5**
turn-up table 298, **305**
Turreau (Toro), Jean-Bernard **305**
turret-top table **305**
Tuscan order 214, **305**
twist turning **305**

U

Überbauschrank **306**
umbrella-back chair 319
Union des Artistes Modernes 149, **306**
   Eileen Gray 16, 129, 204
   René Herbst 138
   Francis Jourdain 160
   Le Corbusier 149, 172–73
   Robert Mallet-Stevens 190

Jean Prouvé 234
   Louis Sognot 280
unit furniture **306**
   Franz Schuster 268
Unteutsch, Friedrich **306**
upholstery **306–8**
   slipcover 279
   tapissier 294
   trimming 121, 124
   Turkey work 303
Upjohn, Richard **308**
Urban, Joseph **308**, 320
urn **308**
Utility Furniture 262, **308**
Utzon, Jorn 266, **308**

V

vaisselier **309**
valance **309**
Vallin, Eugène 206, **309**
Van de Velde, Henri 27, 85, **309–10**, 319
Van der Vinne, Leonardo **310**
Van Doesburg, Theo **310**
Van Keppel-Green **310**
van Leyden, Lucas **310**
Van Risenburgh (Van Risamburgh), Bernard 182, 253, **310–11**
Vandercruse, Roger (Roger Vandercruse Lacroix) 183, 300, **310**
vanity. *See* dressing table
Vardy, John 217, **311**
vargueño **311**
varnish 109, **311**
vase turning 305
vase-and-ball turning 305
Vedel, Kristian **311**
veilleuse **311**
vellum **311–12**
veneer **312**
   burl 43
   curl (crotch) 78
   hua mu 145
   katsura 163
   oyster (*bois de bout*) 215
   shagreen 274
   wood types 64
verdigris **312**
vernis Martin 311, **312**
Victorian period 123, **312**
   art cabinet 15
   papier-mâché furniture 218
   upholstery 307
Vienna Secession. *See* Sezession
Viennese chair **312**
Viking Revival style **313**
   Gerhard Munthe 204
Vile, William 253, **313**
violet wood. *See* wood, kingwood
Viollet-le-Duc, Eugène-Emmanuel **313**
vis-à-vis 52, 70, 296
Vitruvian scroll (wave scroll; running dog) **313**
Vivant, Dominique. *See* Denon, Dominique Vivant, Baron
Voltaire chair **313**
volute **313**
Von Rheydt, Melchior **313**
voyeuse (conversation chair) **313–14**
Voysey, Charles Francis Annesley 285, **314**
Vredeman de Vries, Hans 191, 246, 286, **314**
Vredeman de Vries, Paul 191, **314**

W

Wachseinlegen **315**
Wagner, Otto 85, **315**

wainscot chair **315**
Walton, George **315–16**
Wangentisch **316**
Wanschaff, Karl George **316**
wardrobe **316**
    armoire **15**
    schrank 267–68
    Stollenschrank 286
wash-hand stand 19–20, **316**
washing stand 19–20, **316**
Washington, George 7
washstand 19–20, **316**
Wassmus Frères 248, **316**
water leaf **316**
waterbed **316**
Waterhouse, Alfred **316–17**
Waterloo leg 175
Watson, Craig **317**
wave scroll 313
Weallans, Jon 230, **317**
Weaver, Holmes **317**
Webb, Philip Speakman 202, **317**
Weber, Kem **317**
Wegner, Hans 266, **317–18**
Weisweiler, Adam 100, 183, **318**
wellenschrank **318**
Wewerka, Stefan **318**
whatnot 103
wheel-back chair **319**
wheel-back Windsor chair 326
whiplash curve **319**
white walnut. *See* wood, butternut
whitewood. *See* wood, spruce
whorl foot **114**
wicker **319**
Wiener Sezession. *See* Sezession
Wiener Werkstätte **319–20**
    Josef Hoffmann 85, 142, 203
    Kolo Moser 203
    Joseph Urban 308
Wilhelm Kimbel of Mainz. *See* Kimbel,
    Wilhelm, of Mainz
William and Mary style **320**
    trumpet leg 175
    turning 305
Wilson, Toby Muir **320**
window seat **321**
window-splat Windsor chair 326
Windsor chair **321–27**
    Thomas Gilpin 124
    Stephen Hazell 136–37
    saddle seat 264
    spindle 282
    Ebenezer Tracy 300
    Francis Trumble 301
Windsor settee **327**
Windsor table **327**
wine table (hunt table) **327**
wing chair 66, **327**
wire furniture **327**

wood
    abura **2**
    acacia **2**
    afara (limba) **4**
    African mahogany **6**, 189
    African walnut **6**
    afrormosia **6**
    afzelia **7**
    alder **8**
    Amboyna wood (Amboina) **8**, 216
    Andaman rosewood **12**
    aningeria *(anegré)* **12**
    ash **19**
    Austrialian blackwood **20**
    baywood **27**
    beech **29**
    birch **33**
    bird's-eye maple **33**
    black bean **34**
    bog oak **34**
    bois clair **35**
    boxwood **38**
    brazilwood **39**
    bubinga **41**
    butternut (white walnut) **44**
    camphorwood *(zhang mu)* **47**
    cedar **52–53**
    Ceylon satinwood **53–54**
    cherry **57–58**
    chestnut **59**
    chuglam **64**
    cinnamon **65**
    Coromandel (marblewood) **73**
    cypress **79**
    deal **83**
    ebony **96**, 329
    elm **99**
    "Empire" woods **101**, 148, 237,
        277
    European redwood (Scots pine)
        104
    gaboon **120**
    guarea **132**
    hardwood **136**
    hickory **139–40**
    hinoki (Japanese cypress) **141**
    holly **143**
    hong mu (hung mu) **143**
    huang hua li **145**
    idigbo **147**
    Indian laurel **101**, **148**
    iroko **150**
    ironwood **150**
    ji chi mu (chi ch'i mu) **156–57**
    katsura **163**
    kingwood **164**
    kiri (paulownia) **164**
    kuri (Japanese chestnut) **167**
    laburnum **169**
    larch **171**

    lignum vitae **177**
    limewood **177**
    macrocarpa **188**
    magnolia **189**
    mahogany **189**
    makoré **190**
    mansonia **191**
    matsu (Japanese pine) **194**
    meranti (seraya) **197**
    muninga **204**
    nan mu **205**
    oak **213**
    olivewood **214**
    Oriental rosewood **214**
    ovangkol **215**
    padauk (padouk) **216**
    paldao **217**
    palisander **217**
    panga panga **218**
    pao rosa **218**
    Parana pine **218**
    partridge **219**
    pearwood **220**
    pine **227**
    pitch pine **227**
    plane wood **228**
    plum **229**
    poplar **230**
    primary and secondary **233**
    purpleheart (amaranth) **235**
    Queensland maple **237**
    Queensland walnut **101**, **237**
    ramin **240**
    red gum **241–42**
    redwood (sequoia) **242**
    rosewood **259**
    sandalwood **265**
    sapele **265**
    satinwood **265**
    sen **272**
    silky oak (Australian) **101**, **277**
    silver-gray wood **64**, **277**
    softwood **280**
    southern cypress (swamp cypress)
        281
    spruce (whitewood) **283**
    sugi (cryptomeria) **289**
    sycamore **290**
    tchitola **295**
    teak **295**
    thuya **297**
    tulip poplar **302**
    tulipwood **303**
    tupelo **303**
    virola **313**
    walnut **315**
    wengé **318**
    West Indian satinwood **318**
    whitebeam **319**
    willow **320**

xiang sha mu (hsiang sha mu) **330**
yellowwood **331**
yew **331**
zebrawood (zebrano) **333**
zelkova (keyaki) **333**
zi tan (tzu t'an) **334**
Wood, Edgar **327**
Woodruff, George **327**
Wooton desk **327–28**
worktable (sewing table) **328**
Wormley, Edward **328**
Wright, Frank Lloyd 199, 231, 232,
    328
Wright, Leslie John 149, **328–29**
Wright, Russell 10, **329**
writing box **329**
writing cabinet **329**
writing chair 73, 260
writing table **329**
    bureau plat **42**
    Carlton House **50**
    partners' desk **219**
    table à écrire **292**
    See also desk
writing-arm Windsor chair 292, 326
wu mu **329**
Wyatt, Benjamin Dean 254, **329**
Wyburd, Leonard. *See* Liberty, Arthur
    Lasenby
Wycombe style Windsor chair 326–27

X
X-frame **330**
xiang qian (hsiang ch'ien) **330**
xiu dun (hsiu tun) **330**
X-stretcher 288

Y
yan ji (yen chi) **331**
Yanagi, Sori **331**
yang ci (yang tz'u) **331**
yellow poplar. *See* wood, tulip poplar
yin ping tuo (yin p'ing t'o) **331–32**
yoke rail 77
yoke-back chair **332**
Young, Dennis 285, **332**
Young, J. M. & Co. 199, **332**

Z
Zanuso, Marco 265, **333**
Zanzibar chair **333**
Zapf, Otto **333**
zeni-dansu **333**
zhang mu (chang mu). See wood, cam-
    phorwood
*zhuan lun jing chang (chuan lun ching
    ch'ang)* **334**
Zoarite furniture **334**
Zucchi, Antonio **334**
zui weng yi (tsui wêng yi) **334**